Courtyard with ritual fountain, Grand Mosque, Dakar, Senegal. Built in 1964, the mosque, with its tiles and pointed horseshoe arches, faithfully follows the Moorish architectural style. Björn Bölstad-Peter Arnold, Inc.

Funk & Wagnalls New Encyclopedia

VOLUME 21

PIERO DI COSIMO to PYTHON

LEON L. BRAM
Vice-President and Editorial Director

NORMA H. DICKEY
Editor-in-Chief

Funk & Wagnalls Corporation

Publishers since 1876

Volumes are published subsequent
to copyright dates to contain
the latest updated information

ISBN 0-8343-0094-x
Library of Congress Catalog
Card Number 72–170933

MANUFACTURED IN THE UNITED STATES OF AMERICA
PRINTED AND BOUND BY R.R. DONNELLEY & SONS COMPANY

aie 10 9 8 7 6 5 4 3 2

Funk & Wagnalls New Encyclopedia is liberally provided with **finding devices** that aid in the search for information. The brief descriptions and suggestions that follow are intended to encourage the proper use of these devices so that full use is made of the information resources within these pages.

The **index** in volume 29 should be the starting point in a search for information. If a search is made *without* the use of the index, the following suggestions should be kept in mind:

- If the search is *unsuccessful*, the index should be used to search again. The topic may be discussed in an article that was overlooked. Only after use of the index can a search be considered thorough or completed.

- If the search is initially *successful*, the index should be used to find additional information. A topic may be discussed in several articles; the index can locate the less-obvious ones.

The use and structure of the index is explained in the Guide to the Index, volume 29, pages 6–8.

Cross-references of several types are used frequently within most articles in Funk & Wagnalls New Encyclopedia. Each cross-reference directs the search for information to other articles that contain additional or related information. The types of cross-references and their specific uses are explained in the Guide to Funk & Wagnalls New Encyclopedia, volume 1, pages 60–63, under the subhead, Cross-references.

Bibliography cross-references follow all the major articles in Funk & Wagnalls New Encyclopedia. They direct the search for further information from the articles to appropriate **reading lists** of books and periodicals in the **bibliography** in volume 28. The reading lists may also be used for independent study. A full description of bibliography cross-references and reading lists is found in the Preface and Guide to the Bibliography, volume 28, pages 186–87.

SELECTED ABBREVIATIONS USED IN TEXT*

AC alternating current
AD *anno Domini* (Lat., "in the year of the Lord")
alt. altitude
AM *ante meridiem* (Lat., "before noon")
AM amplitude modulation
amu atomic mass unit(s)
Arab. Arabic
Arm. Armenian
A.S. Anglo-Saxon
ASSR Autonomous Soviet Socialist Republic
atm. atmosphere
at.no. atomic number
at.wt. atomic weight
b. born
BC before Christ
b.p. boiling point
Btu British Thermal Unit
bu bushel(s)
Bulg. Bulgarian
C Celsius
c. *circa* (Lat., "about")
cent. century
Chin. Chinese
cm centimeter(s)
Co. Company, County
cu cubic
d. died
Dan. Danish
DC direct current
Du. Dutch
E east; eastern
ed. edited, edition, editors
e.g. *exempli gratia* (Lat., "for example")
Egypt. Egyptian
Eng. English
est. established; estimated
et al. *et alii* (Lat., "and others")
EV electron volt(s)
F Fahrenheit
Finn. Finnish
fl. flourished
FM frequency modulation
Fr. French
ft foot, feet
g gram(s)
gal gallon(s)
Ger. German
GeV billion electron volts
Gr. Greek
ha hectare(s)
Heb. Hebrew
hp horsepower
hr hour
Hung. Hungarian
Hz hertz or cycle(s) per second
Icel. Icelandic
i.e. *id est* (Lat., "that is")
in inch(es)
inc. incorporated
Ital. Italian
Jap. Japanese
K Kelvin
kg kilogram(s)
km kilometer(s)
kw kilowatt(s)
kwh kilowatt hour(s)
Lat. Latin
lat latitude
lb pound(s)
long longitude
m meter(s)
mass no. mass number
MeV million electron volts
mg milligram(s)
mi mile(s)
min minute(s)
ml milliliter(s)
mm millimeter(s)
m.p. melting point
mph miles per hour
Mt(s). Mount, Mountain(s)
N north; northern
Nor. Norwegian
O.E. Old English
O.Fr. Old French
O.H.G. Old High German
O.N. Old Norse
Op. *Opus* (Lat., "work")
oz ounce(s)
Pers. Persian
PM *post meridiem* (Lat., "after noon")
Pol. Polish
pop. population
Port. Portuguese
q.v. *quod vide* (Lat., "which see")
r. reigned
R. River
repr. reprinted
rev. revised
Rom. Romanian
Rus. Russian
S south; southern
sec. second(s); secant
SFSR Soviet Federated Socialist Republic
Skt. Sanskrit
Span. Spanish
sp.gr. specific gravity
sq square
sq km square kilometer(s)
sq mi square mile(s)
SSR Soviet Socialist Republic
St. Saint, Street
Sum. Sumerian
Swed. Swedish
trans. translated, translation, translator(s)
Turk. Turkish
Ukr. Ukrainian
UN United Nations
U.S. United States
USSR Union of Soviet Socialist Republics
v. versus; verse
Ved. Vedic
vol. Volume(s)
W west; western
yd yard(s)

*For a more extensive listing, see ABBREVIATIONS AND ACRONYMS. Charts of pertinent abbreviations also accompany the articles DEGREE, ACADEMIC; ELEMENTS, CHEMICAL; MATHEMATICAL SYMBOLS; and WEIGHTS AND MEASURES.

FUNK & WAGNALLS NEW ENCYCLOPEDIA

PIERO DI COSIMO, real name PIERO DI LORENZO (1462–1521), Italian painter of religious works and imaginative mythological scenes. He was born in Florence, where he studied with the painter Cosimo Rosselli (1439–1507). In 1482 he accompanied Rosselli to Rome and assisted him in painting frescoes in the Sistine Chapel of the Vatican. Subsequently Piero returned to Florence and gained a reputation as one of the most original painters of the Renaissance. Although Piero was influenced by the work of Leonardo, Botticelli, and other great painters of his day, he never was imitative. His panels, especially those depicting classical themes, are characterized by imaginative and bizarre representations of human figures and animals, set against skillfully executed landscape backgrounds. Among the most remarkable of his paintings are *The Visitation* (c. 1500, National Gallery of Art, Washington, D.C.), *Venus and Mars* (former State Museums, Berlin), and *Death of Procris* (c. 1510, National Gallery, London).

PIERRE, city, capital of South Dakota and seat of Hughes Co., on the east bank of the Missouri R., near the geographical center of the state; inc. 1883. It is the administrative center of South Dakota and a distribution point for the surrounding agricultural region, in which cattle and grain are raised. Points of interest include the South Dakota Cultural Heritage Museum, with displays of historical, military, and Indian artifacts; the State Capitol (completed 1910); and the governor's mansion (1936). A school for Indian children is here. Oahe Dam and Lake Oahe, components of an important irrigation, power, and flood-control project on the Missouri R., and Farm Island State Recreation Area are located nearby. The community was established on the site of the fortified capital of the Arikara Indians. Fort Pierre, across the river, developed as a fur-trading post during the first half of the 19th century. After 1880, when Pierre became a railroad terminus, it experienced a period of rapid growth. In 1889, when South Dakota entered the Union, the city became the state capital. Pop. (1980) 11,973; (1990) 12,906.

PIERREFONDS, city, Île-de-Montréal Co., S Québec Province, on the Rivière (River)-des-Prairies, opposite Île Bizard; inc. 1963. Pierrefonds is primarily a residential suburb of Montréal. The community was established as Ste-Geneviève Parish in 1845 and was given its present name in

Death of Procris *(c. 1510) by Piero di Cosimo.*
National Gallery, London

1958, when it was incorporated as a town. Pop. (1986) 39,605; (1991) 48,735.

PIETERMARITZBURG, city, E South Africa, capital of Natal Province, near the Umsunduzi R. and Durban. The city is one of the world centers of the wattle industry; wattle-tree bark yields tannin extract, which is used in leather processing. Pietermaritzburg is a commercial center and is also noted for the manufacture of footwear, furniture, and metal, rubber, and canvas products. It is the site of the University of Natal (1910) and a teachers college. Dutch immigrants founded the city in 1838 and named it after two of their leaders, Pieter Retief (1780?–1838) and Gerrit Maritz (1798–1839). Pop. (1985, greater city) 192,417.

PIETISM, originally, a German Lutheran reform movement of the 17th and 18th centuries. The movement emphasized individual conversion, "living faith," and the fruits of faith in daily life. The name Pietism is derived from the *collegia pietatis* (informal devotional meetings) organized by Philipp Jakob Spener while he was a pastor in Frankfurt. First held in Spener's home on Sunday afternoons, these meetings soon became popular across Germany. Participants did not separate from the established church and its worship but tried to change the church from within. They held prayer meetings, studied the Bible individually and in small groups, and led a disciplined Christian life. Claiming that faith is not the acceptance of correct theological propositions but trust in Christ, they insisted that pastors should have such faith in addition to their theological learning. Convinced that the world could be won for Christ through the conversion and Christian training of individuals, Pietists stressed the importance of education.

August Hermann Francke (1663–1727), whom Spener recruited, was a brilliant organizer and teacher who made the newly founded University of Halle the intellectual center of Pietism. The university and other institutions organized by Francke in Halle sent out lay and clerical leaders to influence the ruling class of Protestant Germany and the younger generation of pastors. They also prepared missionaries for service around the world. Many of the Lutheran pastors in colonial America were Pietists educated at Halle, and so were most of the early Protestant missionaries in Africa and Asia. One of the most renowned students at Halle was Nikolaus Ludwig Graf von Zinzendorf, who eventually became bishop of the Renewed Church of the Unity of the Brethren (Moravian Church).

Pietism was influenced by English Puritanism (q.v.) through German translations of the works of Richard Baxter, Lewis Bayly (1565?–1631), and John Bunyan, and in turn it affected religious development in England and America, especially through its influence on John and Charles Wesley and Methodism (q.v.). In the Scandinavian countries, Pietism, with the support of the nobility and the monarchy, revitalized the church. Eclipsed for a time by the Enlightenment, Pietism reappeared in the 19th century and became important in the Christian church. Modern Pietists place emphasis on an ecumenical spirit, the "kingdom of God" and its realization in history, ethics, and personal Christian experience. G.W.F.

PIETRO DA CORTONA (1596–1669), Italian painter and architect, one of the leaders of the 17th-century high baroque style in Rome. Born in Cortona on Nov. 1, 1596, his original name was Pietro Berrettini. Cortona studied painting in Florence and in 1613 settled in Rome, where he lived for the rest of his life.

Cortona's most important works were his illusionistic frescoes, a favorite baroque art form. Until his time, large ceiling paintings had been divided into compartments or sections, each illustrating a particular scene or episode. Cortona, in his vast ceiling fresco (1633–39) for the Gran Salone of the Palazzo Barberini in Rome, freed his frescoes from this restraint by mingling his scenes in one large composition unified by a background expanse of sky, thus creating a sense of movement, profusion, and limitless depth that epitomized the baroque.

As an architect, Cortona designed several churches in Rome, the most important being Santa Maria della Pace (1657); its convex semicircular portico, set between concave wings, gives a typical baroque impression of a stage set.

Cortona's painting influenced the course of European art for a century after his death; his architecture was influential for his contemporary, the Italian master Gian Lorenzo Bernini. Cortona died in Rome on May 16, 1669.

PIEZOELECTRIC EFFECT, appearance of an electric potential across certain faces of a crystal when it is subjected to mechanical pressure. Conversely, when an electric field is applied on certain faces of the crystal, the crystal undergoes mechanical distortion. Pierre Curie and his brother Jacques (1855–1941) discovered the phenomenon in quartz and Rochelle salt in 1880 and named the effect piezoelectricity (from Gr. *piezein,* "to press").

The piezoelectric effect occurs in several crystalline substances, such as barium titanate and tourmaline. The effect is explained by the displacement of ions in crystals that have a nonsymmetrical unit cell, the simplest polyhedron that makes up the crystal structure (*see* CRYSTAL).

When the crystal is compressed, the ions in each unit cell are displaced, causing the electric polarization of the unit cell. Because of the regularity of crystalline structure, these effects accumulate, causing the appearance of an electric potential difference between certain faces of the crystal. When an external electric field is applied to the crystal, the ions in each unit cell are displaced by electrostatic forces, resulting in the mechanical deformation of the whole crystal. Because of their capacity to convert mechanical deformation into electric voltages, and electric voltages into mechanical motion, piezoelectric crystals are used in such devices as the transducer, record-playing pickup elements, and the microphone (q.v.). They are also used as resonators in electronic oscillators and high-frequency amplifiers, because the mechanical resonance frequency of adequately cut crystals is stable and well defined.

PIG. *See* HOG.

PIGEON, common name for members of the bird family Columbidae; smaller species are commonly known as doves, but sizes of pigeons and doves overlap. The birds, almost worldwide in distribution, are most abundant in warm regions.

Pigeons have small heads, short necks, stout bodies with short legs, and sleek plumage and have a fleshy or waxy protuberance, the cere, at the base of the bill. They dwell in trees or on the ground and feed on seeds, fruit, acorns and other nuts, and insects. Pigeons fly rapidly and are noted for their cooing call. They build loose, almost flat, nests of twigs, bark, straw, and weeds; the female lays one or two tan or white eggs.

The best-known species is the common pigeon, *Columba livia,* whose wild ancestor, native to Europe and Asia, is called the rock dove. It is

Mourning dove, Zenaida macroura

Victoria crowned pigeon, Goura victoria

about 33 cm (about 13 in) long, bluish gray above, with black markings on the wings and a whitish rump; below, it is purplish on the breast and bluish on the abdomen. The sides of the neck, especially in males, are iridescent. The more than 200 domestic breeds as well as the variably colored street or feral pigeons are derived from this species. Homing pigeons (*see* HOMING PIGEON), which also vary in color, are bred for their navigational abilities and not for plumage characters. Among the other domestic breeds are the carrier pigeon, a tall, erect form with large wattles around the eyes and the base of the bill, whose name is commonly misapplied to the homing pigeon; the frills, characterized by forward curvature of the tips of the feathers of the neck and body, giving a ruffled appearance; the pouters, which can dilate the crop region into a swollen globe; and the jacobin (a favorite pet of Queen Victoria), whose elongated neck feathers form a hood over the head.

The appropriately named white-crowned pigeon, *C. leucocephala,* a Caribbean species that extends north to southern Florida, is the only wild member of the genus *Columba* found in the eastern U.S. The larger band-tailed pigeon, *C. fasciata,* about 39 cm (about 15 in) long, has a range extending from coastal British Columbia and the Rocky Mountains south to Argentina. The passenger pigeon (q.v.), *Ectopistes migratorius,* once common throughout the U.S., has been extinct since 1914.

Well-known pigeons of the Old World include the crowned pigeons of the genus *Goura,* which inhabit New Guinea and adjacent islands, and are characterized by an erect crest of modified feathers; the Australian bronze-wings, constituting *Phaps* and

An urban pigeon drinks from the pool outside the Seagram Building, New York City. UPI

allied genera and characterized by bronze spots on the wings; the Nicobar pigeon, *Caloenas nicobarica,* of islands in the East Indies, characterized by long, iridescent, dark-green hackle feathers of the neck that hang down over the back and shoulders; and the large (up to 50 cm/20 in long), fruit-eating imperial pigeons of the genus *Ducula,* with about 37 species in Asia and the Pacific islands, varying from multicolored to pure white.

Among the pigeons called doves, the members of the large genus *Streptopelia* are widely distributed in Eurasia and Africa. An Asian species, the spotted dove, *S. chinensis,* has been successfully introduced in many parts of the world, including southern California and Hawaii. A domestic form of uncertain wild origin, the ringed turtledove, *S. risoria,* has feral populations in California and Florida; usually buffy with a black ring on the hind neck, a pure white variety is a popular addition to movie scenes of large weddings. The most common North American dove is the mourning dove, *Zenaida macroura,* named for its plaintive call. It is about 30 cm (about 12 in) long, with a brown body, bluish-gray wings, and a long, white-tipped tail. Once found chiefly in open countryside, this species has become a familiar sight in urban residential areas. Smallest of the doves are the sparrow-sized ground doves, genus *Columbina,* of the southern U.S. and the New World Tropics.

For further information on this topic, see the Bibliography in volume 28, sections 463, 473.

PIG IRON. *See* IRON AND STEEL MANUFACTURE.

PIGMENT, in biology, any chemical molecule that reflects or transmits visible light, or both. The color of a pigment depends on its selective absorption of certain wavelengths of light and its reflection of others. For example, chlorophyll (q.v.), the plant pigment, absorbs light in the violet and the orange to red portions of the light spectrum, converting this light energy to chemical energy (*see* PHOTOSYNTHESIS), and reflects light in the green and yellow portions of the spectrum. Thus, chlorophyll appears green.

Chlorophyll and many other pigments act as catalysts, substances that accelerate or facilitate chemical reactions but are not used up in the reactions. The carotenoids, a group of red, orange, and yellow pigments that occur widely in living organisms, also contain many catalytic members. Some carotenoids, such as carotene, are involved in the synthesis of vitamin A, important in vision and growth, and others act as accessory pigments in photosynthesis, transferring the light energy that they absorb to chlorophyll for conversion to chemical energy. They are synthesized by all green plants and by many fungi and bacteria and are acquired secondarily by animals through their food.

Apparently, some substances with important biological functions are only coincidentally pigments as well. Thus, the oxygen-carrying molecules in the blood of higher animals also provide the blood's coloration. Some of these pigments have taken on secondary functions. Hemoglobin, for example, is also responsible for the brilliant red coloration, important in courtship, seen in the buttocks, genitals, and faces of baboons.

Other pigments, however, are important in providing concealing coloration in animals and plants. The function of such coloration is to deceive possible predators or prey. In some systems of coloration, the concealed organism mimics its background so closely that predators cannot distinguish it. The pigmentation patterns of many tropical moths and butterflies, for example, so closely match the background patterns of the tree trunks on which they usually rest that they cannot be distinguished from the trees from only a few centimeters away. Many insects also combine pigmentation with shape to facilitate concealment. Thus, some tropical mantises blend perfectly with the orchid flowers on which they occur, both because their pigments match those of the orchids and because their bodies are generally shaped like parts of the flowers; other mantises are pigmented and shaped like leaves.

Pigments also protect organisms by providing coloration that matches that of an inedible or otherwise undesirable organism. Viceroy butterflies, for example, are pigmented orange and black in patterns that resemble those of the undesirable monarch butterfly. (Because the monarch butterfly feeds on milkweed plants and ingests alkaloids and cardiac glycosides, its ingestion has severe effects on vertebrates.) *See* ADAPTATION; MIMICRY.

Chemically, pigments fall into a number of large groups, but these are often arbitrarily divided into two major groups. The first group comprises pigments that contain nitrogen; it includes hemoglobins, chlorophylls, bile pigments, and dark-colored pigments called melanin, widespread in many animal groups and the chemical that is responsible for variations in the color of human skin. Related to melanins are the indigoids, of which the well-known plant pigment indigo is an example. Riboflavin, which is also known as vitamin B_{12} (*see* VITAMIN), is one of a number of pale yellow to green pigments that are produced by several plant groups.

The second group is formed of pigments without nitrogen. Carotenoids are members of this group, as are the important plant pigments called flavonoids. In leaves, flavonoids selectively admit light wavelengths that are important to photosynthesis, while blocking out ultraviolet light, which is destructive to cell nuclei and proteins. Flavonoids are also important in flower color, in particular providing red and blue pigments. Bright fall colors are produced by the conversion of colorless flavonoids, called flavonols, into colored forms—anthocyanins. Quinones provide many yellow, red, and orange pigments, including several dyes derived from insects that feed on plants containing the quinones. Cochineal, for example, is a red pigment obtained from the fat cells of scale insects that feed on cactus plants.

For discussions of natural and synthetic pigments and their uses in technology and art, *see* DYEING; DYESTUFFS; OIL PAINTING; PAINT AND VARNISH; POTTERY; RUGS AND CARPETS; WATERCOLOR PAINTING. M.R.C. & P.H.R.

PIGNUT. *See* HICKORY.

PIGWEED. *See* AMARANTH; GOOSEFOOT.

PIKA, also cony or mouse hare, common name for any of about 14 species of small, herbivorous mammals that constitute the genus *Ochotona* and family Ochotonidae of the order Lagomorpha, which also contains the rabbits and hares. Pikas are native to mountainous regions of northern and central Asia and western North America. They have long, dense, usually grayish brown fur, short, rounded ears, and a vestigial tail that is not visible externally. Head and body length is from 12.5 to 30 cm (5 to 12 in). During the late summer and early fall, pikas cut grass and other vegetation, sometimes spreading it to dry in the sun, and then gather it into haystacklike piles near their rocky shelters for use as a reserve winter food supply.

PIKE, common name for several species of carnivorous, freshwater game fishes of the family Esocidae, characterized by elongated bodies and billlike snouts. The best-known member is the northern pike, *Esox lucius,* which grows to about 1.4 m (about 4.5 ft) and ranges through northern latitudes of North America, Europe, and Asia. The muskellunge (q.v.), a larger sport fish, is found in the northeastern U.S. and southeastern Canada. The smaller chain pickerel, *E. niger,* which grows to about 60 cm (about 2 ft), also ranges into the southeastern U.S.

Pike are small-scaled fish with many bones and large, sharp-toothed jaws. Their silver undersides and dark green or bronze backs help to conceal them in the weeds in which they lurk in wait for fish, frogs, and small mammals. Their dorsal and anal fins are of equal size and are set far back toward the tail. Pike are solitary hunters. They scatter their eggs about in weeds, where the newly hatched fry find protection. The so-called walleyed pike are not true pike but members of the perch (q.v.) family.

For further information on this topic, see the Bibliography in volume 28, sections 468, 813.

PIKE, Zebulon Montgomery (1779–1813), American explorer and army officer, born in Trenton, N.J. He entered the army about 1793 and became a second lieutenant in 1799. In 1805 he led an expedition to discover the source of the Mississippi River. The following year he set out on another expedition through the newly acquired Louisiana Territory, and in his travels he traversed Spanish territory. Historians are undecided as to whether Pike strayed or intended to spy. He was captured but released by the Spanish. Pikes Peak in Colorado, which was first sighted by him on this expe-

Pickerel, Esox niger, *a small species of the common pike.*

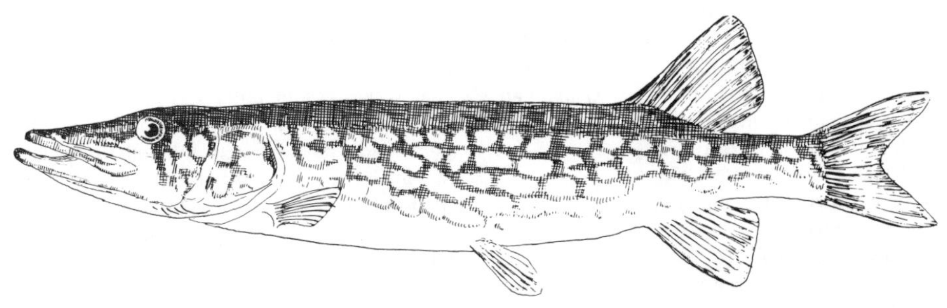

Pikes Peak Colorado Advertising & Publicity Committee

dition, bears his name. During the War of 1812, as a brigadier general, Pike directed the assault on the town of York (now Toronto), Canada, and was killed during the fighting.

PIKES PEAK, one of the most famous peaks in the Rocky Mts., located in the Front Range, central Colorado, near Colorado Springs. Although the elevation (4301 m/14,110 ft) of the peak is not the highest in the state, Pikes Peak is noted for a commanding view. Tourists can ascend the mountain by three different means: by horseback, by a cog railway approximately 14 km (9 mi) long, or by automobile over a well-constructed road. Two springs, Manitou and Colorado, are located near the foot of the mountain. On the summit of Pikes Peak is a meteorological station. The peak was discovered in 1806 by the American explorer and army officer Zebulon Montgomery Pike. It was first climbed in 1820.

PIKESVILLE. *See* BALTIMORE COUNTY.

PILATE, Pontius (fl. 1st cent. AD), Roman military governor, or procurator, of the imperial province of Judea from 26 to 36. The Jewish historian Flavius Josephus portrayed him as a harsh administrator who failed to understand the religious convictions and national pride of the Jews. Pilate is known mainly for his connection with the trial and execution of Jesus Christ; his culpability has been the subject of debate ever since.

The governor of Judea had complete judicial authority over all who were not Roman citizens, but many cases, particularly those relating to religious matters, were decided by the Sanhedrin, the Jewish supreme council and tribunal. According to the Gospel accounts, after the Sanhedrin found Jesus guilty of blasphemy, it committed him to the Roman court, having itself no power to pronounce the death sentence. Pilate refused to approve the judgment without investigation; the Jewish priests then made other charges against Jesus, and the governor had a private interview with him. Pilate appears to have been impressed with the dignity and with the frankness of Jesus' answers to his questions and to have tried to save him (see John 18:38–39, 19:12–15). Nevertheless, fear of an uprising in Jerusalem forced Pilate to accede to the demand of the populace, and Jesus was executed. Pilate was recalled to Rome in 36. According to the theologian and church historian Eusebius of Caesarea, he later committed suicide. Pilate is revered as a martyr by the Coptic church, which celebrates his feast day on June 25.

PILCHARD, European fish of the genus *Sardinops,* closely allied to the herring (q.v.). The pilchard swims in vast schools along the western coast of Europe and in the Mediterranean Sea, from which it is taken by seines for European markets and canning factories. It reaches nearly the size of the herring, but is thicker, and the outlines of the back and belly are straighter; the upper part of the body is bluish green, the sides and abdomen silvery white, cheeks and gill covers yellowish, dorsal fin and tail dusky. Young pilchards suitable for canning are called sardines.

PILCOMAYO, river, central South America, the longest tributary of the Paraguay R. It rises in S Bolivia and flows SE until it joins the Paraguay R. just below Asunción, Paraguay. In the lower course it forms the boundary between Argentina and Paraguay. The Pilcomayo is about 1125 km (about 700 mi) long.

PILE DWELLINGS. *See* LAKE DWELLINGS.

PILGRIM, one who visits some holy place with religious intent. Pilgrimages are characteristic of many religions, such as those of ancient Egypt, Persia in the Mithraic period, India, China, and Japan. The Greek and Roman custom of consulting the gods at local oracles, such as those at Dodona or Delphi, both in Greece, is widely known. In the early period of Hebrew history, pilgrimages were made to Shiloh and Dan (both in what is now Israel) and to Bethel (now Beitin, Jordan). The great Islamic pilgrimage to Mecca (now in Saudi Arabia), a survival of pagan times, is obligatory for every Muslim, and other Islamic devotional pilgrimages, particularly to the tombs of saints, are numerous. Kairouan in Tunisia, Ouezzane in Morocco, Karbala in Iraq, and Meshed (now An Najaf) in Iran are sacred Muslim cities. Benares (now Varanasi), India, is a renowned place of pilgrimage for Hindus.

The early Christians made pilgrimages to the scenes of the Passion of Christ in Jerusalem. Even after Jerusalem had been occupied by the Saracens, the liberty of pilgrimage, on payment of a tax, was secured by treaty; the necessity of protecting pilgrims gave rise to the medieval military orders, such as the Knights Templars.

The chief places of pilgrimage in the West included, in Italy, Rome, Loreto (near Ancona), and Assisi; in Spain, Santiago de Compostela, Guadalupe, and the monastery on Montserrat near Barcelona; in France, the churches of Notre Dame de Fourvière, at Lyon, and Saint-Denis; in Germany, Cologne and Trèves (now Trier); in Switzerland, Einsiedeln; in England, Walsingham Abbey, in eastern England, and Canterbury; in Scotland, Whithorn, Scone, Dundee, Paisley, and Melrose; and in Ireland, many places connected with the life or death of the early Irish saints. Gustavo A. Madero is the site of a celebrated shrine to the Virgin Mary, in central Mexico. In later times, pilgrims traveled in large numbers to Lyon, Le Puy, Paray-le-Monial, and Lourdes, all in France.

PILGRIM FATHERS, group of separatists from the Church of England who founded Plymouth Colony, the first permanent settlement in New England. The group, numbering 101 men, women, and children, left Plymouth, England, on Sept. 16, 1620, on the *Mayflower* (q.v.). On November 21, the *Mayflower* dropped anchor in the sheltered harbor off the site of present-day Provincetown, Mass. There the same day 41 of the adult males drafted and signed the Mayflower Compact, the first constitution written in the New World. The Pilgrim Fathers landed on the site of Plymouth on December 21, a date that is celebrated in New England as Forefather's Day.

PILLAR SAINTS. *See* SIMEON STYLITES, SAINT.

PILLARS OF HERCULES, name given by the ancient Greeks to two peaked rocks that flank the E entrance of the Strait of Gibraltar. They seem to have been first visited by the Phoenicians about 1100 BC. Ancient Calpe, the N pillar, is the modern Rock of Gibraltar, and ancient Abila, at Ceuta on the African coast, is now called Jebel Musa.

PILL BUG. *See* WOOD LOUSE.

PILLORY, former mechanism for public punishment of criminals, consisting of two parallel boards, joined by sliding hinges and fixed like a signboard on the top of a strong pole, supported on a wooden platform elevated above the ground. A large circular hole with its center in the line of junction of the two planks received the neck, and two corresponding holes of smaller size, one on each side of it, received the wrists. In France the pillory was abolished in 1832. It was abolished in Great Britain in 1837 and in the U.S., where early statutes had ordered it for some offenses, in 1839. In the state of Delaware, however, this form of punishment remained in effect until 1905. *Compare* STOCKS.

PILON, Germain (c. 1530–90), French sculptor, one of the most important and influential of the 16th century. Born and trained in Paris, he produced mainly tomb sculpture and portrait busts. Much of his early work was done under the direction of the Italian-born court artist Francesco Primaticcio. Most notable of this work was Pilon's tomb of Henry II and Catherine de Medici

(1563–70, Church of St. Denis, Paris), consisting of kneeling figures, recumbent effigies, and standing figures of the four Virtues; he achieved a naturalism and freedom of movement that went beyond the usual tense Mannerist style of the period. His mature work, exemplified by the *St. Francis in Ecstasy* of the Valois Chapel (c. 1585, Church of St.-Jean-St.-François, Paris), is characterized by an even greater freedom and relaxation in its modeling. His work represents an important step toward the emotional naturalism of the baroque style and was a strong influence on the next generation of French sculptors.

PÍLOS, also Pylos, town, W Greece, in Pelopónnisos Region, at the S entrance to Pílos (Navarino) Bay, near Kalámai. The main industries are fishing and livestock raising. Pílos Bay is one of the finest harbors in Greece.

Excavations near the N shore of the bay have yielded the remains of a 13th-century BC palace said to have belonged to Nestor, legendary king of Messenia. Ancient Pílos began to decline when Messenia was conquered by Sparta in the 8th century BC. Pílos Bay was the site of an Athenian victory over Sparta in 425 BC. In the Middle Ages ancient Pílos was called Palaeo Navarino; the present city developed on the S shore of the bay and was called Navarino. It was held by Turkey almost continuously from 1498 until 1827, when a Turkish-Egyptian fleet was defeated by a British-French-Russian fleet in the Battle of Navarino. The town was renamed Pílos in the late 19th century. Pop. (1981) 2017.

PILOT FISH, streamlined scavenging fish, *Naucrates ductor,* of the family Carangidae (*see* POMPANO), which accompanies large fish, notably sharks, and slow-moving vessels in temperate and tropical seas. Pilot fish often remain close to floating or moving objects for months. Blue-gray in color and reaching 61 cm (2 ft) in length, they have four small spines anterior to the dorsal fin and five or six dark vertical bands on the body. The young are conspicuously different, with large eyes, and spines about the head; they often seclude themselves beneath seaweed and jellyfish, including the Portuguese man-of-war. In Greek mythology the pilot fish was believed to guide lost ships to port and was held sacred.

PILOT SNAKE. *See* BLACKSNAKE.

PILOT WHALE. *See* DOLPHIN.

PILSEN. *See* PLZEŇ.

PIŁSUDSKI, Józef Klemens (1867–1935), Polish revolutionary, independence fighter, and national hero, who became a dictator of resurrected Poland.

Born at Zułow (near present-day Vilnius, Lithuania) on Dec. 5, 1867, Piłsudski was educated at the University of Kraków. During his student years he became sympathetic to the Socialist movement, which advocated the independence of Poland from Russian rule. In 1887 he was arrested on a charge of conspiring to assassinate Emperor Alexander III of Russia and, although innocent, was sentenced to five years of penal servitude in Siberia.

Józef Piłsudski UPI

Following his release in 1892, he became a leader of the Polish Socialist party; in 1894 he began to publish a secret party newspaper, *The Worker.* Piłsudski later organized a secret private army of about 10,000 Poles to fight for the freedom of Poland; when World War I broke out, he offered his force to the Austrians to fight the Russians. Late in 1916, the Central Powers proclaimed an independent Polish kingdom and formed a council of state, with Piłsudski as a member. When he refused, however, to order his troops to support the Central Powers against the Allies, Piłsudski was imprisoned by the Germans.

Released in November 1918, Piłsudski returned to Warsaw a national hero and proclaimed an independent Polish republic. He was immediately accepted as head of state and commander in chief of the Polish army; as such, he supervised the disarming of the remaining occupation armies of the Central Powers, and all Polish military commanders placed themselves under his command. As his aim was the restoration of the territories belonging to Poland at the time of the partition in 1772, Piłsudski came into conflict with the new Czechoslovak and Lithuanian states and with the Bolshevik regime in the newly established Soviet Union. During the Russo-Polish War of 1920, Piłsudski, who was made marshal of Poland, successfully defended Warsaw against invading Soviet armies. He resigned as chief of state in December 1922. On May 12, 1926, however, disappointed in the performance of the parliamentary system, he led a military revolt that overthrew the government and installed a regime controlled by him. Thereafter, until his death, he was the virtual dictator of Poland; he was uninterruptedly the minister of war and commander in chief of the army, and twice during this time, from 1926 to 1928 and again in 1930, he was premier of Poland. He died in Warsaw on May 12, 1935.

PILTDOWN MAN, scientific hoax involving the supposed discovery near Piltdown, England, of an apelike fossil ancestral to modern humans. Reported in 1912, the discovery included fragments of what were later proved to be a modern human cranium and an ape's jawbone. Piltdown man was assigned a genus, *Eoanthropus* ("dawn man"), and a species, *dawsoni*, named after the discoverer, Charles Dawson (1864–1916), an amateur naturalist. For many years the fossil was a subject of anthropological controversy. In 1953, scientific analyses proved it a forgery.

PIMA, North American Indian tribe of the Uto-Aztecan language family and of the Southwest culture area, living in the Salt and Gila river valleys in southern Arizona. Traditionally, the Pima lived near the riverbanks and practiced intensive agriculture. Their farming methods differed sharply from those of other southwestern U.S. Indians. The Pima, for example, dug irrigation canals using wooden tools. They lived in villages governed by an elected tribal chief and a council. Their homes were single-family domed huts of mud and brush.

The first contact with the tribe was made by a European, the Jesuit missionary Eusebio Francisco Kino, in 1697; at that time they numbered some 4000. In 1990 Pima descendants numbered 14,431, and most lived on the Salt River and Gila River reservations. *See also* AMERICAN INDIAN LANGUAGES; AMERICAN INDIANS.

PIMENTO, also allspice or Jamaica pepper, common name for the berry of *Pimenta dioica,* a small West Indian tree of the family Myrtaceae (*see* MYRTLE). The tree grows to a height of about 9 m (about 30 ft) and has aromatic, glossy green leaves and terminal cymes of white flowers. The fruit, when dried, is widely used as a spice. The name *pimento* is sometimes applied to the pimiento, a variety of sweet pepper, *Capsicum annuum* (Grossum group), also used as a spice. *See* CAPSICUM.

PIMPERNEL, common name for about 20 mostly creeping but also erect herb species of the genus *Anagallis,* of the primrose (q.v.) family, and found nearly worldwide. The scarlet pimpernel, *A. arvensis,* is a small, spreading annual native to Europe and now found in North America. It grows in fields as a weed, reaching from 6 to 30 cm (2.7 to 12 in) in height, and has red, pink, or blue bell-shaped flowers 6 mm (0.2 in) wide. The flowers close at the approach of rain and open in bright sunshine; therefore, the plant has been called shepherd's barometer and poor man's weatherglass. The blue pimpernel, *A. monelli,* is abundant in parts of Europe. The bog pimpernel, *A. tenella,* is common in bogs in England.

PINANG, also Penang, state, Malaysia, comprising Pinang Island (in the Strait of Malacca, off the W coast of the Malay Peninsula) and the former Province Wellesley (on the Malay Peninsula opposite Pinang Island). The capital of the state is the port of George Town, on Pinang Island. Rubber, cultivated on plantations, is a chief product of the state. Other agricultural products include rice, coconuts, coffee, spices, and a wide variety of tropical fruits. Poultry, hogs, cattle, and buffalo are raised. Fishing is an important industry. Located in the state is the University of Science of Malaysia (1968), at Minden.

The first British settlement in the Malay Peninsula was established on Pinang Island in 1786 by the English East India Co. Province Wellesley was acquired in 1798 and was incorporated with Pinang Island as a single administrative unit in 1800. The enlarged settlement of Pinang was united (1826) with the settlements of Malacca and Singapore under a single British colonial governor; in 1867 the three settlements became a crown colony with the name of the Straits Settlements. In 1946 Pinang became a member of the Malayan Union (which was superseded in 1948 by the Federation of Malaya) and in 1963 became part of Malaysia. Area, 1033 sq km (399 sq mi); pop. (1980 prelim.) 911,586.

PINAR DEL RÍO, city, W Cuba, capital of Pinar del Río Province, near the foot of the Sierra de los Órganos. It is a transportation center for the surrounding Vuelta Abajo agricultural region in which, along with tobacco, the principal crop, sugarcane, pineapple, and coffee are also cultivated. Major manufactures include tobacco products and furniture. A museum of marine fauna is located here. Pinar del Río is linked to Havana by railroad and highway. Its main growth began in the mid-19th century. Pop. (1981 prelim.) 95,476.

PINCHOT, Gifford (1865–1946), noted American forestry expert, conservationist, and public official, born in Simsbury, Conn. After graduating from Yale University in 1889, he studied forestry in several European countries. From 1898 to 1910 he served as chief of the Division of Forestry (now the Forest Service) of the U.S. Department of Agriculture. During that period Pinchot filed charges against Richard Achilles Ballinger (1858–1922), then secretary of the interior, accusing him of abandoning the nation's conservation policies. Ballinger was upheld by President William Howard Taft, who in 1910 dismissed Pinchot for insubordination. From 1903 to 1936 Pinchot was professor of forestry at the Pinchot School of Forestry, which he helped found at Yale University. In 1923 he was elected governor of Pennsylvania and soon afterward helped settle a strike that had paralyzed the anthracite coal mines. He was elected again in 1931 and served until 1935. His writings include *Primer of Forestry* (1899), *The Fight for Conservation* (1909), and *Breaking New Ground* (posthumously pub. 1947).

PINCKNEY, Charles (1757–1824), one of the framers of the U.S. Constitution, who was born in Charleston, S.C., and educated for the bar. A second cousin of Charles Cotesworth and Thomas Pinckney, he was a practicing lawyer when he became a lieutenant of militia during the American Revolution. Captured at Charleston in 1780, he remained a prisoner of the British until 1781. Pinckney served in the Continental Congress in 1777–78, and 1784–87. At the Constitutional Convention he submitted one of the plans that formed the basis for the Constitution; it has become known as the "Pinckney Draught." Minister to Spain (1801–5) under President Thomas Jefferson, he tried unsuccessfully to negotiate the acquisition of Florida from that country. Pinckney served four terms as governor of South Carolina and was a member of the U.S. Senate (1798–1801) and the House of Representatives (1819–21).

PINCKNEY, Charles Cotesworth (1746–1825), American statesman, born Feb. 25, 1746, in Charleston, S.C., and educated at the University of Oxford. He became prominent as an advocate of American independence and participated in several battles of the American Revolution, rising to the rank of brigadier general in the Continental army. In 1787 he was a delegate to the Federal Constitutional Convention, and in 1788 he was influential in securing ratification of the U.S. Constitution in South Carolina. He was appointed minister to France in 1796. The French government refused to receive him officially, and he left. He returned the following year with the American statesmen Elbridge Gerry of Massachusetts and John Marshall of Virginia. They were approached by three French emissaries, who offered to begin negotiations for settling the main differences between France and the U.S. in return for a loan to their government. Interpreting this as a demand for a bribe, the Americans refused. In their report to Congress, comprising the correspondence that had passed between them and the French envoys, the three American commissioners substituted the letters "X," "Y," and "Z" for the names of the Frenchmen. The incident later became famous as the XYZ affair (q.v.). Pinckney was an unsuccessful Federalist candidate for vice-president in 1800 and for president in 1804 and 1808.

PINCKNEY, Thomas (1750–1828), American statesman, born in Charleston, S.C., brother of the American statesman Charles Cotesworth Pinckney. Educated at the University of Oxford, he was admitted to the bar in 1774 in both Britain and South Carolina. He served as a major in the American Revolution and was wounded and captured at Camden, N.J. From 1787 to 1789 he was governor of South Carolina, doing much to restore order in the state after the war, and from 1792 to 1794 he served as U.S. minister to Great Britain. Acting as special commissioner to Spain in 1795–96, he negotiated a treaty with Spain that settled Mississippi River navigation rights and the southern U.S. boundary line with Spanish territories in North America. He was an unsuccessful candidate of the Federalist party for vice-president in 1796 and served as a congressman from 1797 to 1801. During the War of 1812 he was commissioned major general of a southern district. He remained deeply interested in agriculture during his life, publishing articles and importing improved breeds of cattle.

PINDAR (518–438 BC), Greek poet, who is generally regarded as the greatest lyric poet in Greek literature.

Life. Pindar was born in 518 BC in Cynoscephalae, near Thebes, of a distinguished aristocratic family, the Aegeidae. Pindar's wide geographical range, aristocratic tone, and truly Panhellenic spirit can probably be attributed, at least in part, to his family's influence throughout Greece.

He is said to have studied with the Boeotian poet Corinna and to have been defeated by her in a poetic contest, whereupon she advised the youthful poet "to sow with the hand, not with the whole sack," a reference to his excessive employment of mythological ornament in his early work. In later years, Pindar traveled widely to all parts of the Greek world, and his national reputation brought him numerous commissions. He spent two years in Sicily at the invitation of Hiero I, king of Syracuse, and he composed paeans or encomia for Hiero and other kings and for the noblest Greek families.

No other Greek poet so adequately expressed the underlying spiritual unity preserved by the common language and religion and by the tradition of the great Panhellenic games. So great was Pindar's fame in later years that Alexander the Great, when he sacked Thebes in 335 BC, spared the house of Pindar.

Works. Pindar represents the culmination of the Greek choral lyric, composed to be sung to a musical accompaniment by choruses of young people, as distinguished from the personal lyric, which is sung or chanted by a single voice. Pindar composed hymns to the gods, dithyrambs, processional odes, dancing songs, dirges, and encomia, but only fragments of these have survived. His extant works, believed to be about one-fourth of his total production, are 44 epinician, or triumphal, odes, composed in honor of the victors at the four great national games, the Olympian, Pythian, Isthmian, and Nemean. They display the intricate structure, the lofty moral sentiment, and the deeply religious feeling for which the Greek choral lyric was noted.

Pindar's regular procedure in praising the victors at the games was to insert into the central portion of the poem a myth, either expressing the dominant mood of the occasion or connecting the victorious hero with the mythical past. He shows the Greek myths in transition from their treatment by the epic poets to the forms they assumed in Attic tragedy. Pindar also introduces into his odes numerous moral and religious reflections, and he proclaims the immortality of the soul and a future judgment.

PINDUS MOUNTAINS, mountain system, NW Greece, separating Thessaly from Epirus and extending about 160 km (about 100 mi) from the border of Albania. The Pindus range is as high as 2546 m (8352 ft) in the Smólikas. A continuation of the Dinaric Alps, the range forms a protective barrier for the Plain of Thessaly on the E. Only one main highway crosses the Pindus Mts., through the Métsovon Gap. Several of the main rivers in the area rise in the Pindus, including the Piniós, the Aóös (in Albania, the Vijosë), the Akhelóös, and the Aliákmon. The region is inhabited by a Vlach (Romanian) minority, who are mostly shepherds.

PINE, common name for the family Pinaceae, a medium-size group of trees, mostly evergreens, of widespread distribution in the temperate areas of the northern hemisphere, and for its representative genus, *Pinus.* The family, which contains about 210 species placed in 10 genera, has enormous economic importance as a source of timber and pulpwood, among other products. Members of the family characteristically have helically arranged, needlelike leaves. In several genera—for example, pine, *Pinus;* cedar, (q.v.), *Cedrus;* and larch (q.v.), *Larix*—the leaves are borne in clusters that are actually short branches, or spurs, on which the leaves are arranged in tight helices.

The pine family belongs to the order Pinales,

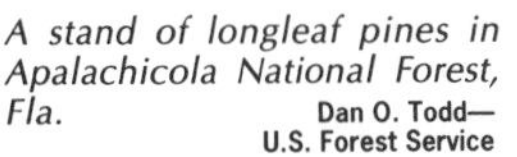

A stand of longleaf pines in Apalachicola National Forest, Fla. Dan O. Todd—U.S. Forest Service

phylum Pinophyta (*see* CONIFER). The plants have separate female and male cones; the former produce the seeds, and the latter, the pollen. Male and female cones are produced on the same plant; the seed-bearing cones are woody when mature; the seeds are winged. The family is distinguished from other conifers on the basis of its seed cones. Each of the flattened scales on which the seeds are borne is underlaid by a distinct, sterile bract (reduced leaf) that is usually shorter than the scale. The seed cones are drooping in all members of the family except the fir (q.v.), *Abies,* and *Keteleeria,* a small genus confined to South China and Southeast Asia. All members of the family have evergreen leaves except the golden larch, *Pseudolarix,* and the larch.

The pine genus itself is the largest in the family, with about 110 species, about 35 of which are in North America. Pines grow in a wide range of habitats, from sea level to altitudes of 4000 m (13,000 ft) and are distinguished from other members of the family by the leaves, which are in bundles. Each bundle contains a specific number of leaves, depending on the species, with a sheath of short, scalelike leaves at the base.

Pines are divided into two groups, based on the scale leaves and other characteristics. The soft pines have leaves in bundles of five, and the scale leaves fall away from mature leaf bundles. Their wood is soft and has a coarse grain. Well-known soft pines are white pine, *P. strobus,* of northeastern North America; pinyon pine, *P. edulis,* of the Southwest, the seeds of which are edible; and bristlecone pine, *P. aristata,* the Rocky Mountain species, and *P. longaeva,* the Great Basin bristlecone, which can live more than 4000 years and may be the oldest known living thing on the planet. Through analysis of bristlecone rings, scientists can tell what the climate was more than 10,000 years ago. The hard pines have leaves in clusters of two or three, and the scale leaves persist in mature clusters. The wood is usually hard, with a close grain. Well-known species include lodgepole pine, *P. contorta,* extending from Alaska to Baja California; longleaf pine, *P. palustris,* of the southeastern coastal plain; and ponderosa pine, *P. ponderosa,* of the American West. Both pine groups are economically important for their timber, pulp, tar, and turpentine and for their use as ornamentals. Other members of the pine family include Douglas fir, hemlock, and spruce (qq.v.). M.R.C.

For further information on this topic, see the Bibliography in volume 28, sections 456, 591, 631.

PINEAL BODY, small, cone-shaped projection from the top of the midbrain of most vertebrates,

An ancient bristlecone pine, Pinus aristata, *sculptured by wind, sand, and ice, in Inyo National Forest, Calif. On either side are living bristlecone pines.*
Leland J. Prater–U.S. Forest Service

arising embryologically as an outgrowth of the brain. The pineal body is absent in crocodiles and in mammals of the order Edentata (anteaters, sloths, armadillos) and consists of only a few cells in whales and elephants. In humans the structure develops until the seventh year, when it is slightly larger than a pea; thereafter, throughout life, small mineral particles, particularly calcium, may be deposited in the pineal body. The mineral deposits can sometimes be seen in skull X-ray photographs.

Named after a French psychologist, Philippe Pinel (1745–1826), who first described the gland in the human brain, it is only slowly beginning to be understood in its functions. It is known that the pineal body has both neural and endocrine properties. In simple vertebrates, such as the lamprey, the pineal body is mounted on a stalk close to an opening in the skull and functions as a photoreceptive organ. Photoreceptive structures linked with the pineal body are still observed in higher vertebrates such as reptiles and even some species of birds. In mammals the pineal body is not light-sensitive, but a neural connection remains between the eyes and the gland. Thus the functions of the pineal body in an animal are linked with surrounding light levels.

The isolation of the hormone melatonin in 1958 has led to a further understanding of the pineal body. Animal studies show that the gland synthesizes and secretes melatonin almost entirely at night, and that it ceases this function during the day. Melatonin, in turn, affects the functions of other endocrine organs such as the thyroid, adrenals, and gonads. Further experiments demonstrate that changes in the level of melatonin in the bodies of seasonally breeding animals affect their reproductive cycle, and that decreases in melatonin brought about by artificial lighting can prolong breeding activity. The role of the pineal body in the control of these biorhythms is only beginning to be elaborated, but the suggestion remains that even nonseasonal breeders such as human beings are affected by its daily functions. The onset of puberty may, in fact, be triggered by changes in melatonin level.

For further information on this topic, see the Bibliography in volume 28, sections 493–94.

PINEAPPLE, common name for the flowering plant family Bromeliaceae, characterized by unique water-absorbing leaf scales and regular three-parted flowers. The leaves are spirally arranged sheaths or blades, usually occurring in layers. The plant embryos have one seed leaf (*see* MONOCOTS). The family, which contains more than 2000 species placed in 46 genera, is almost exclusively confined to the Tropics and subtropics of the New World, with one species occurring in western Africa. The most economically important species is *Ananas comosus,* the familiar pineapple. A few species are sources of fiber; others are cultivated for their showy flowers or foliage. The family constitutes the order Bromeliales, and the term bromeliad is used for its members.

Bromeliads exhibit an interesting gradation from relatively primitive to highly evolved forms, with tremendous variations in size and adaptations to their environments. Primitive members include the genus *Puya,* which reaches a height of 10 m (30 ft) and grows high in the Andes. Plants of this genus are terrestrial and have elongated stems, fully developed roots, leaves with narrow petioles (leafstalks), and hairs that retard water loss by providing a dense covering. A second stage in bromeliad advancement is the pineapple, *Ananas comosus,* native to South America but now widely cultivated in tropical areas, primarily for its sweet, juicy fruit. Pineapples are terrestrial, growing to about 1 m (about 3 ft), but the stems are short and the petioles are expanded, fitting together to form a water-holding tank at the base of the plant. The leaves act as catchment basins and the tanks as reservoirs. Water is absorbed from the tank as needed by adventitious roots or leaf hairs. An extreme form of bromeliad adaptation is reached in Spanish moss (q.v.), *Tillandsia usneoides;* it has roots only when young, water absorption being taken over by specialized leaf scales. Spanish moss occurs throughout the range of the order as an epiphyte, growing on other plants for support.

Pineapple, Ananas comosus. *The fruit is a type of cone composed of small fused fruits.* Hawaiian Pineapple Co.

Bromeliads with water-holding bases have developed complex relationships with other organisms. Within these reservoirs live ecological communities ranging from unicellular algae and protozoans to aquatic flowering plants and insects, crabs, and frogs. Bromeliads receive dissolved nutrients from their wastes and decomposing remains and are thereby less dependent on roots in the soil.

The pineapple was probably first domesticated in the high plateaus of central South America; it was widely planted for its fiber before Europeans first saw it in the Caribbean. Thereafter, cultivation spread to warm regions around the globe. Hawaiian plantations produce almost a third of the world's crop and supply 60 percent of canned pineapple products. Other leading producers are China, Brazil, and Mexico.

For further information on this topic, see the Bibliography in volume 28, section 452.

PINE BARRENS, wilderness area, S New Jersey, about 3370 sq km (about 1300 sq mi) in extent. It is largely covered by a forest of pine, oak, and juniper and contains a diversity of flowering plants and wildlife. An unusual feature is two extensive tracts of unique pygmy pine forests, reaching maximum heights of 1.5 m (5 ft). Soils are sandy, and much of the area is underlaid by a vast groundwater reserve. Bog iron was mined here from the mid-18th to mid-19th century. Part of the area is protected in a state nature preserve; several other areas are state forests.

PINE BLUFF, city, seat of Jefferson Co., central Arkansas, a port on the Arkansas R.; inc. 1849. It is a manufacturing and commercial center in an area of cotton, rice, and soybean farms. Manufactures include paper products, fabricated metal products, and transformers. A federal toxicology research center and the University of Arkansas at Pine Bluff (1873) are here. Pine Bluff Arsenal is nearby. Settled in 1819 as Mount Marie, the community was renamed in 1832 for a forest of pines overlooking the river. Union forces held the city during the American Civil War, successfully repulsing a Confederate attack in October 1863. Pop. (1980) 56,636; (1990) 57,140.

PINELLAS PARK, city, Pinellas Co., W Florida, near Saint Petersburg; inc. as a city 1959. It is chiefly residential; manufactures include tools and dies, boats, clothing, and electronic equipment. The community was founded (1909–10) as a sugarcane processing center. Its name refers to the pine trees that once abounded here. Pop. (1980) 32,811; (1990) 43,426.

PINERO, Sir Arthur Wing (1855–1934), British author of popular farces and social dramas, born in London. As a young man he studied law, but at the age of 19 he became an actor; he continued in that profession until 1882. Pinero began his career as dramatist with the farcical comedy *£200 a Year* (1877); he received wide acclaim with *The Money Spinner* (1881) and after 1882 devoted himself to writing plays. Pinero was a prolific writer of farces and comedies, but he also wrote melodramas dealing with ethical and social problems. Among Pinero's plays that are still performed are *The Second Mrs. Tanqueray* (1893), the first to win recognition outside England; *Trelawney of the "Wells"* (1898), about life in a theatrical company; and the farces *The Magistrate* (1885) and *Dandy Dick* (1887). Pinero was knighted in 1909.

PINES, ISLE OF. *See* JUVENTUD, ISLA DE LA.

PINE SNAKE. *See* BULL SNAKE.

PING-PONG. *See* TABLE TENNIS.

P'INGTUNG, town, S Taiwan, near the Lower Tanshui R. It is an industrial center in a rich agricultural area. Major manufactures include sugar, machinery, chemicals, and alcoholic beverages. A nearby military installation is also important to the city's economy. Pop. (1980 est.) 185,142.

PINK, common name for the family Caryophyllaceae, a group of mostly herbaceous flowering plants, and for its representative genus, *Dianthus.* The family contains more than 2000 species placed in about 89 genera. *Dianthus,* with about 300 species of annual and perennial herbs, mostly natives of Europe and temperate Asia, contains the carnation, *D. caryophyllus,* and sweet william, *D. barbatus.* Other members of the family include chickweed (q.v.), genus *Stellaria*; soapwort, *Saponaria officinalis*; and catchfly or campion, *Silene.* Pinks occupy habitats ranging from salt marshes and beach areas to mesic forests.

The family Caryophyllaceae is placed in the order Caryophyllales, which consists of 12 families and about 10,000 species. Other families in the order are Phytolaccaceae (*see* POKEWEED), with about 65 species placed in 65 genera; Nyctaginaceae (*see* FOUR-O'CLOCK), with about 350 species in 34 genera, including Bougainvillea (q.v.); Chenopodiaceae (*see* GOOSEFOOT), with about 1300 species in 120 genera, including *Beta* (*see* BEET) and *Spinacia* (*see* SPINACH); Amaranthaceae (*see* AMARANTH), with about 800 species in 71 genera; Cactaceae (*see* CACTUS), with about 1650 species in 130 genera; Portulacaceae (*see* PORTULACA), with about 400 species in 21 genera; and Aizoaceae, with about 2400 species in 114 genera, including *Cryophytum* (*see* ICE PLANT).

Carnation, Dianthus caryophyllus

The order is most common in moist areas of the temperate and tropical zones. Many members, however, are adapted to alkaline areas, for example, the Chenopodiaceae, or to dry areas, for example, the Aizoaceae and Cactaceae.

Botanically, the order varies considerably, but nearly all members have leaves that lack stipules (leaflike appendages at the base of the leafstalk). Pinks also exhibit a distinctive form of growth in the stems and roots. In most dicots, growth of tissue for conducting food and water is localized in specialized cells called cambial cells, which form a single, continuous ring near the surface of the stems and roots. In most members of the pink order, however, this growth takes place in several layers of cambial cells at various depths within the roots and stems.

Flowers of the order have sepals (outer floral whorls). What appear to be petals in many members of the order, such as carnations and four-o'clocks, are actually highly modified sepals, and what appear to be sepals are actually bracts (leaves borne on the floral axis). The flowers have one to three whorls of stamens (male floral organs), and the styles of the pistil (female floral organ) are separate rather than united. The pigments responsible for the red to blue and yellow to orange colors in the Caryophyllales are most mostly betalains, namely betacyanins and betaxanthins, while, in most flowering plants, the pigments are flavonoids, namely anthocyanins and anthoxanthins.

Plants in the Caryophyllales are members of the class Magnoliopsida (*see* DICOTS) in the division Magnoliophyta (see Angiosperm). M.R.C.

For further information on this topic, see the Bibliography in volume 28, sections 452, 592.

PINKERTON, Allan (1819–84), Scottish-American detective. Born in Glasgow, Scotland, Pinkerton came to the U.S. and settled near Chicago in 1842. While engaged in business as a barrel maker in 1846, he captured a gang of counterfeiters and was consequently elected county sheriff. In 1850 he organized Pinkerton's National Detective Agency and was appointed the first city detective in Chicago. The recovery of a large sum of money stolen from the Adams Express Co. and the discovery of a plot to murder Abraham Lincoln in 1861 made his reputation. During the American Civil War he organized the secret service of the U.S. Army. During the railroad strikes of 1877, his agency provided strikebreakers. His books include *Strikers, Communists and Tramps* (1878) and *Thirty Years a Detective* (1884).

PINKEYE. *See* CONJUNCTIVITIS.

PINNACLES NATIONAL MONUMENT. *See* NATIONAL PARK SERVICE.

PINOCHET UGARTE, Augusto (1915–90), military dictator of Chile (1973–90), born in Santiago, and educated at Chile's military academy. Rising steadily through army ranks, he was appointed brigadier general during the administration of Eduardo Frei Montalva. Under President Salvador Allende he became commander of the Santiago garrison, and in 1972 he was made commander in chief of the army. He was one of the leaders of the U.S.-supported coup that deposed Allende in 1973, the first time the Chilean army had intervened in civil affairs. By 1974 he had emerged as head of state and quickly curtailed political activity. His regime was condemned by the UN Human Rights Commission (1977) for its torture of detained persons "as a regular practice." Pinochet was confirmed in office for an 8-year term in 1980. After an assassination attempt on him in 1986, Pinochet dealt even more harshly with dissidents. A plebiscite in October 1988 denied him the right to continue as president beyond March 1990, although he retained his post as army commander.

PINOCHLE, card game played by two, three, or four persons with a special pack of 48 cards—two ordinary packs—from which all the cards below the nine have been removed.

Two-Handed Pinochle. In this game each player gets 12 cards, 4 at a time. The 25th card is turned up, and its suit is declared trumps for that hand; the card is then placed faceup under the closed pack. If the turned-up card is a nine, the dealer scores 10 points; if any other card, either player who has a nine of trumps may, after he or she has taken a trick, substitute it for the turned-up card, scoring 10 points. The rank of the cards in descending order is ace, ten, king, queen, jack, and nine. The player who receives the cards from the dealer begins the game by placing one card of his or her hand faceup on the table. The other player wins the trick by playing a card of higher rank in the same suit, or a trump card; or loses the trick by playing a card of the same or lower rank in the suit, or a card of any other suit but trumps. After each trick, each player draws one card from the closed pack.

The hand is won by the player who scores the most points. Play usually ends when a player scores 1000 points. Scoring is done by melding and counting. Melding consists of turning faceup various combinations of cards that have specific values. The combinations include: ace, king, queen, jack, and ten of trumps, the so-called flush, 150 points; four aces of different suits, 100 points; four kings of different suits, 80; four queens of different suits, 60; four jacks of different suits, 40; the king and queen of trumps, the so-called royal marriage, 40; the jack of diamonds and the queen of spades (known as pinochle), 40; the king and queen of any suit but trumps, the so-called common marriage, 20; and the nine of trumps, 10. A player melds only after a trick is taken. The values of the cards are generally as follows: ace, 11 points; ten, 10 points; king, 4 points; queen, 3 points; and jack, 2 points. When the players have reached the end of the closed pack, the person who loses the last trick takes the faceup card. Both players then pick up their own melds and add them to the cards they already possess, which still number 12 cards. The second part of the hand is then played, the winner of the last trick leading. In this portion of the game suit must be followed. If one of the players no longer possesses the suit led, he or she must trump. If trumps are led, the other player must play a higher trump card if possible. The player who wins the last trick also adds 10 additional points to his or her score. The total number of points a player can win, counting the 10 for the last trick, but exclusive of melds, is 250. The player who wins the majority of points (melds plus count of tricks) wins the hand. The game may be for each hand; the player scoring the greater number of points wins the hand.

Three- and Four-Handed Pinochle. In three-handed pinochle, 16 cards are dealt to each player. The dealer turns up his or her last card as trumps; each player in turn, beginning with the one to the dealer's left, has the right to exchange the nine of trumps for the turned-up trump card; the nine becomes part of the dealer's hand. After the trump card has been redeemed by the nine, the players meld, and then play goes on as in the second part of the two-handed game, the player to the left of the dealer playing first.

In four-handed pinochle two players are partners against the other two; a single score is kept for each partnership, which is credited with the points scored by both players of the side. Twelve cards are dealt to each player, and the game then proceeds as in three-handed pinochle.

Auction Pinochle. A popular variety, auction pinochle, is for three or four players. When played by four, in each game one player deals but does not participate in the play. Each player receives 15 cards; 3, called the widow, are left facedown. The players bid for the privilege of naming trumps, the minimum bid usually being 250 and sometimes 300. The highest bidder names trumps and takes the widow. This player then melds as many of the 18 cards as possible and discards 3, which are later added to the trick total. Play for tricks ensues. At the end of the game, if the sum of what the highest bidder melds plus the trick count equals or exceeds the amount bid, that player wins; if it falls below, the player loses. The game is usually played for a specified sum for each 50-point bid; starting at 300 the sum is doubled for each extra 50 points, and the entire sum is doubled if spades are trumps. At the end of the hand, if the bidder has won, prefixed stakes are collected from each of the others; if the bidder has lost, each of the others is paid double the stakes. The loser may pay into a kitty the same amount paid to a winning player. The player who wins a 350 hand or higher collects a specified bonus from the kitty in addition.

For further information on this topic, see the Bibliography in volume 28, section 773.

PINSCHER. *See* DOBERMAN PINSCHER; MINIATURE PINSCHER.

PINTER, Harold (1930–), English playwright, born in London. He studied briefly at the Royal Academy of Dramatic Art, London, in 1948 and for the next ten years was an actor with various repertory companies touring the British Isles. His first short play, *The Room,* appeared in 1957. Full-length plays by Pinter include *The Birthday Party* (1958), *The Caretaker* (1960), *The Homecoming* (1964), *Old Times* (1971), *No Man's Land* (1975), and *Betrayal* (1979). He also wrote many short plays for television, radio, and the theater. Among his screenplays is *The French Lieutenant's Woman* (1981); he has appeared in other films for which he wrote scripts. His works, cryptic and original, have been described as comedies of menace. In a typical work, the characters communicate obliquely as they react to the threat of an invasion of their narrow lives.

Pinter also served as director in London (1967) and New York City (1968) of the plays *The Man in the Glass Booth* and *Butley* (1971). His *Poems and Prose: 1949–1977* was published in 1978.

PINTO, name of a two-color pattern of coat that occurs in various horses; also the name of a breed recognized in the U.S. since 1963. The name derives from the Spanish word meaning "painted." Piebald pintos are white and black; skewbald pintos are white and any color other than black.

PINTURICCHIO, real name BERNARDINO DI BETTO DI BIAGO (1454–1513), Italian painter of decorative frescoes. He was born in Perugia. An assistant to Perugino, he worked on the frescoes in the Sistine Chapel at Rome and then painted (c. 1485) frescoes in Santa Maria in Aracoeli in Rome illustrating the life of Saint Bernardino of Siena. After executing two works in the cathedral at Orvieto, he painted (1492–94) six frescoes in the Borgia apartments (now the library) of the Vatican. His last and most important works are the ten frescoes he painted (1502–7) in the Piccolomini Library of the Cathedral of Siena depicting the life of Pope Pius II, a member of the Piccolomini family, in brilliant color and realistic detail. Among Pinturicchio's few surviving easel paintings are the *Madonna in Glory* (1510, Municipal Museum, Barbiano) and *Christ Carrying the Cross* (1513, Borromeo Collection, Milan).

PINWORM, nematode worm, *Enterobius vermicularis,* parasitic in the intestines of human beings, occurring in most parts of the world (*see* ROUNDWORM). Pinworm is the most common roundworm infestation in the U.S., infecting children more often than adults. It occurs among all economic classes and in urban as well as rural areas. The pinworm is about 1 cm (about 0.4 in) long. Human beings become infected after drinking water or eating food contaminated by the eggs of the pinworm. The adult worm develops in the intestine and lays its eggs in the anal region. Reinfection occurs if the eggs are swallowed. Symptoms of infection, which are usually mild, include itching, intestinal upset or vomiting, and nervousness. Various drugs are used to treat the infection, in addition to stringent hygiene and the disinfecting of eating utensils and bed linens.

PINYIN. *See* CHINESE LANGUAGE.

PINZÓN, name of a family of Spanish navigators who accompanied Christopher Columbus on his first voyage to the New World. The most important were the following two brothers.

Martín Alonzo Pinzón (c. 1440–93), commander of the ship *Pinta* in Columbus's first expedition to America. Historians are uncertain why Pinzón became separated from Columbus for more than six weeks, but Columbus later accused him of treasonable conduct. As Pinzón was returning to Spain, his ship was again separated from Columbus's command in a storm; however, both reached Palos de la Frontera on March 15, 1493.

Vicente Yáñez Pinzón (c. 1460–1524), commander of the ship *Niña* in Columbus's first expedition to America. When Columbus's ship *Santa Maria* was wrecked near Hispaniola, Columbus joined Pinzón on the *Niña* to complete the voyage. Pinzón then (1499–1500) led an expedition from Spain to Brazil, during which he discovered the mouth of the Amazon River. In 1505 he was named governor of Puerto Rico. In 1508, with the Spanish navigator Juan Diaz de Solís (1470?–1516), he sailed along the coasts of Yucatán (now in Mexico) and Honduras, and in 1509 he sailed along the coast of Venezuela.

PION *or* **PI MESON.** *See* ELEMENTARY PARTICLES.

PIOTRKÓW TRYBUNALSKI (Rus. *Petrokov*), city, central Poland, capital of Piotrków Trybunalski Province, near Łódź. It is a textile center and also has tanneries, flour mills, sawmills, and factories producing mining equipment, agricultural machinery, chemicals, bricks, and glass. The city was founded in the 12th century and still contains the ruins of a medieval castle built by King Casimir III. From 1815 to 1919, the city belonged to Russia. Pop. (1988 est.) 80,000.

PIPAL. *See* BO TREE; FIG.

PIPE, in technology, tube used to transport liquids, liquid-solid mixtures, or fragmented solids from one point to another. Water, steam, and gas pipes are familiar in homes, and large systems of pipes include those used in municipal water supplies and for sewage disposal. Pipe systems known as pipelines may extend long distances, such as the 1300-km (800-mi) Trans-Alaska Pipeline used to carry petroleum from the Arctic Ocean to the Gulf of Alaska (*see* ALASKA).

Pipes have been used since ancient times and have been made of many materials, such as the bamboo pipes used in China and the lead and stone piping of Rome's aqueduct (q.v.) system. Pipe materials include clay, concrete, wrought and cast iron, steel, aluminum, and plastic.

PIPEFISH, common name applied to all of the small, gasterosteiform fishes of the family Syngnathidae, except the species in the genus *Hippocampus,* which are commonly known as sea horses (*see* SEA HORSE). Pipefishes are common in all warm and temperate seas; several freshwater species are found in India, China, Central America, and northern South America. Pipefishes are elongated, slender animals, ranging in length from 2.5 to 46 cm (1 to 18 in). The pipefish has a long, tubular snout terminating in a small, cylindrical mouth equipped with tiny jaws. The body is covered with an armor of bony plates arranged in rings. Pelvic fins are absent, and the remaining fins are minute. The tail is long, slender, and often prehensile. Pipefishes feed on minute crustacea. The fishes change color under varying conditions of light.

The male worm pipefish, Nerophis lumbriciformis, *carrying eggs in a groove along his belly. The pipefish lives among seaweed where it can easily camouflage itself to avoid predators.* Jane Burton–Bruce Coleman, Inc.

The breeding habits of pipefishes are curious: the female deposits its eggs in a marsupiallike brood pouch on the abdomen of the male; the eggs develop attachments to the abdominal wall and obtain nourishment from the bloodstream of the male; and about two weeks after the eggs are laid, the brood pouch of the male ruptures, liberating the young into the water. The common pipefish of the American Atlantic coast is *Syngnathus fuscus,* which attains the length of about 20 cm (about 8 in) long.

PIPE SPRING NATIONAL MONUMENT. *See* NATIONAL PARK SERVICE.

PIPESTONE NATIONAL MONUMENT. *See* NATIONAL PARK SERVICE (table).

PIPIT, common name for more than 40 species of small songbirds (*see* PASSERINE) of the genus *Anthus,* family Motacillidae (*see* WAGTAIL), found over most of the world. All are brownish in color, more or less streaked with black, often with white outer tail feathers and long hind claws. They resemble many larks in color and in habits, being chiefly birds of open grasslands or rocky areas and often singing while in flight. Pipits build their nests in hollows on the ground, using mostly grass and some moss, sometimes lining the nest with hair; they lay from three to seven eggs in a clutch.

Only two species are found widely in North America. The American pipit, *A. rubescens,* breeds on the arctic tundra and above the timberline on western mountains, and winters south to northern Central America. It is about 18 cm (about 7 in) long. The back is olive-brown and the underparts are buffy, variably streaked with black; streaks are often absent in the breeding birds of the Rockies. The outer tail feathers are edged with white. While walking on the ground, this pipit, like many others, constantly bobs its tail. Sprague's pipit, *A. spragueii,* a prairie species, is slightly smaller, at 16 cm (6.5 in) long. It differs from the American pipit in having the back and crown streaked with black, and pale, rather than black, bill and legs. Males tower high in the air in their song display.

Of the many Eurasian pipits, three species occasionally wander to Alaska. These are the brown tree pipit, *A. trivialis;* the olive tree pipit, *A. hodgsoni;* and the Pechora pipit, *A. gustavi.* The primarily Asian red-throated pipit, *A. cervinus,* breeds in Alaska and migrates south to California.

PIRACICABA, city, SE Brazil, in São Paulo State, on the Piracicaba R., near Campinas. A road and rail hub, it lies in an area in which sugarcane, coffee, rice, cotton, and cattle are produced. Industries include the milling of sugar, rice flour, and paper and the distilling of brandy. An agricultural college was founded in the city in 1901. Pop. (1980) 179,395.

PIRACY, in international law, the crime of robbery, or other act of violence for private ends, on the high seas or in the air above the seas, committed by the captain or crew of a ship or aircraft outside the normal jurisdiction of any nation, and without authority from any government. The persons who engage in acts of piracy are called pirates. International treaties and national legislation have sometimes applied the term *piracy* to attacks on the high seas authorized by a government, in violation of international law; to actions by insurgents acting for political purposes; or to violent acts on board a vessel under control of its officers. Such acts, however, are not regarded as piracy under the law of nations. Piracy is distinguished from privateering (*see* PRIVATEER) in that the latter is authorized by a belligerent in time of war; privateering was legally abolished by the Declaration of Paris of 1856, but the U.S. and certain other nations did not assent to the declaration. *See* INTERNATIONAL LAW.

Piracy is recognized as an offense against the law of nations. It is a crime not against any particular state, but against all humanity. The crime may be punished in the competent tribunal of any country in which the offender may be found, or carried, although the crime may have been committed on board a foreign vessel on the high seas. The essence of piracy is that the pirate has no valid commission from a sovereign state, or from an insurgent or belligerent government engaged in hostilities with a particular state. Pirates are regarded as common enemies of all people. In that nations have an equal interest in their apprehension and punishment, pirates may be lawfully captured on the high seas by the armed vessels of any state and brought within its territorial jurisdiction for trial in its tribunals.

Piracy is of ancient origin. The Phoenicians often combined piracy with more legitimate seafaring enterprise. From the 9th through the 11th century the Vikings (q.v.) terrorized western European coasts and waters. The Hanseatic League (q.v.), formed in the 13th century, was created partially to provide mutual defense against northern pirates roaming the North and Baltic seas. Muslim rovers, meanwhile, scourged the Mediterranean Sea, commingling naval war on a large scale with thievery and the abduction of slaves. In the 17th century the English Channel swarmed with Algerian pirates, operating out of northern Africa; Algiers continued to be a piratical stronghold until well into the 19th century (*see* BARBARY COAST; CORSAIR). The buccaneers (*see* BUCCANEER) were pirates who, during the 16th and 17th centuries, preyed mainly on Spanish commerce with the Spanish American colonies. Piracy waned with the development of the steam engine and the growth of the British and American navies in the latter part of the 18th and early 19th centuries.

In municipal law (q.v.), the term *piracy* has been extended to cover crimes other than those defined above, such as slave trading (*see* SLAVERY). An independent state has the power to regulate its own criminal code, and it may declare offenses to be piracy that are not so regarded by international law. These municipal laws can have binding force only in the jurisdiction creating them. Although similar regulations may be adopted by other states, in the absence of special agreement between two states, the officers of one may not arrest or punish subjects of the other for offenses committed beyond its jurisdiction. *See also* SMUGGLING.

PIRAIÉVS *or* **PIRAEUS,** city, central Greece, in Attikí (Attica) Department, on the Saronic Gulf, near Athens. It is a major port and industrial center of Greece. The city has shipyards, flour mills, and factories in which agricultural equipment, textiles, rugs, glass, and chemicals are produced. It also has a school of industrial studies (1938). Piraiévs was laid out about 450 BC, at which time it already served Athens as a port. In 86 BC, it was totally destroyed by the Romans, and it resumed importance only after Greece became independent in the 19th century. In 1834 the site was chosen as the port for modern Athens. Pop. (1981) 196,389.

PIRANDELLO, Luigi (1867–1936), Italian writer and Nobel laureate, who is considered the most important Italian dramatist of the period between the two world wars.

Pirandello was born June 28, 1867, in Agrigento, Sicily, and educated at the universities of Rome and Bonn. He taught Italian literature at the Normal College for Women, Rome, from 1897 to 1921, when his growing reputation as a writer enabled him to devote himself entirely to a literary career. He became internationally known in 1921 through his play *Six Characters in Search of an Author* (1921; trans. 1922) and was awarded the 1934 Nobel Prize in literature. Pirandello died Dec. 10, 1936, in Rome.

Pirandello's writings, of which his plays are the most outstanding, deal mainly with people of the lower middle class, such as teachers, boardinghouse proprietors, and clerks. He is concerned with philosophic ideas, such as that humans, because of the conflict within them between instinct and reason, are doomed to an existence full of grotesque inconsistencies; that specific actions are not right or wrong in themselves, but only in the way we regard them; and that an individual has not one definite personality but many, depending on how that person appears to the people with whom he or she comes in contact. Without faith in any fixed standards of ethics, morality, politics, or religion, characters in Pirandello's tales and plays find reality only in themselves, and then discover that they themselves are unstable and inexplicable phenomena.

Pirandello expressed his deep pessimism and his pity for the confusion and suffering of the human condition in humorous terms. The humor is, however, singularly grim and disturbing. The laughter it excites comes from the embarrassing, sometimes acutely painful, recognition of the absurdities of existence. Pirandello was an important innovator in stage technique. Ignoring the canons of realism, he made free use of fantasy to create the effect he wanted. He exerted great influence in liberating the contemporary theater from outworn convention.

Luigi Pirandello Bettman Archive

Among Pirandello's other plays are *The Pleasure of Honesty* (1917; trans. 1923), *Right You Are If You Think So* (1917; trans. 1922), *Henry IV* (1922; trans. 1922), and *As You Desire Me* (1930; trans. 1931). He also wrote the short-story collection *Better Think Twice About It* (1933; trans. 1935) and the novel *The Outcast* (1901; trans. 1925).

PIRANESI, Giovanni Battista (1720–78), Italian graphic artist, famous for his engravings and etchings during his lifetime—more than 2000 prints of real and imaginary buildings, statues, and ornaments. He contributed to 18th-century neoclassicism by his enthusiastic renderings of ancient Roman monuments, which included both accurate portrayals of existing ruins and imaginary reconstructions of ancient buildings. One of Piranesi's earliest and most lastingly renowned collections is his *Carceri d'Invenzione* (Imaginary Prisons, 1745; 2d ed. 1760), in which he transformed Roman ruins into fantastic, immeasurable dungeons dominated by immense, gloomy arcades, staircases rising to incredible heights, and bizarre galleries leading nowhere.

These engravings became an important influence on 19th-century romanticism and also played a role in the development of 20th-century surrealism. *See also* PRINTS AND PRINTMAKING.

PIRANHA, also caribe, any of about 12 species of carnivorous fish of the genus *Serrasalmus,* family Characidae, found in rivers of South America. Piranhas are compressed, oval-shaped, fine-scaled fishes, 25 to 60 cm (10 to 24 in) long. They have blunt heads and powerful jaws with sharp, wedge-shaped teeth that mesh like cutting shears and enable the fish to cut the flesh from prey, which consists mostly of other fish but also amphibians, birds, and mammals. Piranhas associate in large schools and are attracted by commotion and the scent of blood. Once aroused, they can quickly reduce a large mammal to a skeleton, although such incidents are rare. About four species are considered dangerous. Piranhas are also scavengers, and they are considered fine food fish.

PISA, city, central Italy, capital of Pisa Province, in Tuscany Region, on the Arno R., near the Ligurian Sea. The city is a rail and road junction and a tourist and industrial center. Important manufactures include textiles, machinery, processed foods, pharmaceuticals, and glass. Among the educational institutions are the University of Pisa (1343), a teachers college, an engineering school, a veterinary institute, and an agricultural school.

The principal landmarks of Pisa are grouped in the area of the Piazza del Duomo (Cathedral Square) and include the cathedral, the baptistery, and the bell tower (campanile). The cathedral, a great white marble edifice in the Romanesque style, was begun in 1063. The richly decorated facade was added in the 12th century. The baptistery, begun in 1153, is a circular building in the Romanesque style crowned with a great dome and lavishly ornamented in the 14th century in the Gothic style. The bell tower is known as the Leaning Tower of Pisa. Construction began in 1174 but was suspended when the builders became aware that the shallow foundation would be inadequate in the soft soil. The structure was nevertheless completed by the second half of the 14th century. The Leaning Tower is cylindrical in shape, with eight arcaded stories.

An Etruscan town, Pisa became a Roman col-

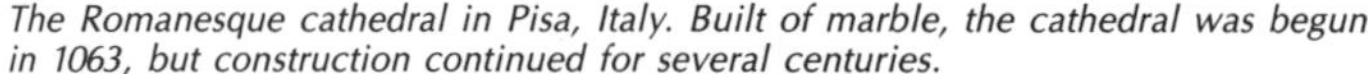

The Romanesque cathedral in Pisa, Italy. Built of marble, the cathedral was begun in 1063, but construction continued for several centuries.

ony in the 2d century BC. In the 9th century AD the city was a naval power. Pisa and its ally Genoa drove the Saracens from the islands of Sardinia and Corsica in the 11th century. Thereafter commercial rivalry between Pisa and Genoa led repeatedly to war. In the 12th and early 13th centuries Pisa attained its greatest power in commerce. During the political struggles that occurred in Italy during the Renaissance, Pisa belonged to the Ghibelline faction, which supported the Holy Roman emperors against the papacy. The opposing Guelphs were led by Florence, which wanted control of Pisan trade. Pisa was weakened in 1284, when the Genoese defeated its navy. In the next century Pisa won some victories on land, but in general its military situation worsened. In 1406 the city fell to Florence. Pisa regained its liberty in 1494 but in 1509 fell again to Florence. For later history, *see* FLORENCE.

Among the notable citizens of Pisa were Galileo and the sculptors Nicola and Giovanni Pisano and Andrea Pisano.

Pop. (1988 est.) 103,500.

PISAN, Christine de. *See* CHRISTINE DE PISAN.

PISANELLO (c. 1395–1455), Italian painter, draftsman, and medallist, who was the last and most brilliant artist of the ornate, courtly International Gothic style (q.v.). Originally named Antonio Pisano, he studied under Gentile da Fabriano, whose graceful, detailed style he inherited. Pisanello produced paintings, frescoes, drawings, and portrait medallions for the courts of Milan, Rimini, Naples, Mantua, Ferrara, and Verona. His well-known small painting, *Princess of the House of Este* (c. 1443, Louvre, Paris), exemplifies his style; it shows a woman in profile against a tapestrylike floral background and is characterized by elegant long lines, clear colors, and exquisite drawing of details.

His frescoes, such as his masterpiece *Saint George and the Princess* (1438, Sant'Anastasia, Verona), show to the greatest extent his precise and loving representation of the natural details of human figures, animals, flowers, and objects. His numerous drawings are also fastidiously detailed, and in some of them, particularly those of female nudes, he achieves a strength of three-dimensional modeling that establishes an important link between the Gothic and Renaissance styles.

PISANO, name of two 13th- and 14th-century Italian sculptors and architects, father and son, who were the preeminent figures of the 13th-century Italian revival of the classical Roman sculptural style. Working mainly in northern Italy in the cities of Pisa, Perugia, Siena, Pistoia, and Padua, the Pisanos created carved pulpits, cathedral facades, municipal fountains, and church sculpture.

Nicola Pisano's great sculptural masterpiece, the marble pulpit (1260) of the Baptistery in Pisa, Italy. The classically inspired carving consists of five bas-relief scenes of the life of Christ. Alinari

Nicola Pisano (c. 1220–c. 1284). Nicola, the father, is thought to have been trained in the Italian workshops of the Holy Roman emperor Frederick II, who encouraged a Roman revival. Nicola's carved reliefs for the pulpit of the Pisa Baptistery (1260) were derived from figures on Roman sarcophagi in the Camposanto of Pisa: A nude Hercules was rendered into a personification of Christian fortitude; a Phaedra became the Virgin Mary. These carvings are outstanding for their assimilation of the solid, three-dimensional Roman style as well as for their corresponding emphasis on the individuality and dignity of the human figure. They mark a turning point in Italian sculpture analogous to that represented in painting by the work of Giotto.

Giovanni Pisano (c. 1250–c. 1314). In Nicola's later work, and that of his son, Giovanni, the

Detail of the south door of the Baptistery of San Giovanni in Florence, executed by Andrea Pisano.

classical style often shows an increasing integration of Gothic motifs and stylistic elements. This uniquely Italian assimilation of French Gothic influences can be seen in Nicola and Giovanni's Siena pulpit (1268), Giovanni's sculptures and architectural design for the facade of the Siena Cathedral (c. 1285), and his later pulpit for Pistoia (1301). In these sculptures the carved figures take on the Gothic elements of violent movement, animated detail, angular and oblique arrangements, and deep-cut shadowy carving. His later pulpit for the Pisa Cathedral (1310) shows a return to classical motifs, tempered by certain Gothic elements. Giovanni's designs were some of the most powerful and expressive in Italian art at the end of the 13th century, and they were a dominant influence on Italian sculptors of the early Renaissance, among them Jacopo della Quercia, Lorenzo Ghiberti, and Donatello.

PISANO, Andrea, real name ANDREA DA PONTADERA (c. 1290–c. 1349), Italian sculptor, born in Pontadera, and probably trained in nearby Pisa. Considered the founder of the Florentine school of sculpture, he is best known for his relief panels on the bronze south door (1330–36) of the Florence Baptistery; their narrative scheme and naturalist style were influenced by Giotto's fresco cycles. As assistant to Giotto, and from 1340 Giotto's successor as master of the works of the Florence Cathedral, Pisano carved stone reliefs for the lower register of the campanile. In 1347 he became master of works for Orvieto Cathedral.

PISCES (Lat., "fishes"), in astronomy and astrology, zodiacal constellation lying on the ecliptic, the apparent path of the sun. The sign of this constellation is 12th in order on the zodiac and is usually symbolized by two fishes whose tails are bound together by a wavy band. The constellation does not include any notable stars but does contain the point through which the sun passes at the vernal equinox.

PISISTRATUS (c. 600–527 BC), Athenian general and statesman, tyrant of Athens from 560 to 527 BC, the son of Hippocrates, and a kinsman and friend of the celebrated legislator Solon. In the war against the Megarians, about 570–565 BC, Pisistratus acquired considerable military distinction, and subsequently came forward as the leader of Athenian subjects from northeast Attica (the region around Athens) who were fighting for political equality.

In 560, when he had sufficient political power, he seized the Acropolis and made himself tyrant. The leaders of the rich aristocratic party fled from the city, but returned in 554 and two years later drove Pisistratus into exile on the island of Euboea. Supported by Thebes and Argos, he was able to return to Athens and defeat his enemies in 541. Thereafter he lived in undisturbed possession of power, transmitting his supremacy to his sons, Hippias and Hipparchus (c. 555–514 BC).

Pisistratus' rule as tyrant was mild and beneficent. He reduced taxes, granted lands and needed resources to the poorer citizens, and provided for the aged and disabled. He united Attica, extended Athenian influence abroad by recovering Sigeum, which commanded the entrance to the Hellespont, and by acquiring the Thracian Chersonese. His administration is famous for his encouragement of literature and the arts. He adorned Athens with many beautiful buildings, and he was probably responsible for one of the first written versions of the works of Homer.

Camille Pissarro, a self-portrait.
Frank J. Darmstaedter–Jewish Museum

PISSARRO, Camille Jacob (1830–1903), French impressionist painter, whose friendship and support provided encouragement for many younger painters. Pissarro was born in Saint Thomas, Virgin Islands, and moved to Paris in 1855, where he studied with the French landscape painter Camille Corot. At first associated with the Barbizon school (q.v.), Pissarro subsequently joined the impressionists and was represented in all their exhibitions (*see* IMPRESSIONISM). During the Franco-Prussian War (1870–71), he lived in England and made a study of English art, particularly the landscapes of Joseph Mallord William Turner. For a time in the 1880s Pissarro, discouraged with his work, experimented with pointillism (*see* NEO-IMPRESSIONISM); as it proved unpopular with collectors and dealers, Pissarro returned to a freer impressionist style.

A painter of sunshine and the scintillating play of light, Pissarro produced many quiet rural landscapes and river scenes; he also painted street scenes in Paris, Le Havre, and London. An excellent teacher, he counted among his pupils and associates the French painters Paul Gauguin and Paul Cézanne, his son Lucien Pissarro (1863–1944), and the American impressionist Mary Cassatt. Of Pissarro's great output (including paintings, watercolors, and graphics), many works hang in the Luxembourg Gallery, Paris, and in the leading galleries of Europe. The Metropolitan Museum of Art, New York City, has his *Bather in the Woods* (1895).

PISTACHIO, common name for the plant genus *Pistacia,* of the family Anacardiaceae (*see* CASHEW), members of which have dioecious flowers without petals, and a dry drupe with a bonelike stone. The pistachio, or pistacia, tree, *P. vera,* is a small tree about 6 m (about 20 ft) high; native to Iran and Syria, it is now cultivated in all parts of the south of Europe and the north of Africa and in many other places. Pistachio nuts are much esteemed as food and also yield an oil used for cooking. The turpentine tree, *P. terebinthus,* yields the turpentine known in commerce as Cyprus turpentine. It has a greenish-yellow color, an agreeable odor, and a mild taste; in its properties it resembles the turpentine (q.v.) obtained from conifers.

Leaves and fruit of the pistachio, or pistacia, tree, Pistacia vera.

PISTOIA (anc. *Pistoria*), city, central Italy, capital of Pistoia Province, in Tuscany Region. Pistoia is a commercial center for fruit, flower, and vegetable growers. Manufactures include firearms, iron, steel, glass, footwear, and textiles. Among the city's outstanding 12th-, 13th-, and 14th-century buildings are the cathedral, the baptistery designed by the Italian sculptor Andrea Pisano, the Pretorio Palace, the town hall, and the Ceppo Hospital (founded 1277), with a terra-cotta frieze by the Italian sculptor Giovanni della Robbia.

Pistoia was a Roman colony from the 6th century BC. In 62 BC the Roman conspirator Catiline was slain near Pistoia. By the end of the 11th century AD the city was a free commune of commercial and cultural importance. It came under Florentine rule early in the 14th century; with Florence it became part of Tuscany in 1530, and in 1860 part of the kingdom of Italy. It is believed that the first pistols (Ital. *pistola*) were manufactured in Pistoia. Pop. (1990 est.) 90,000.

PISTOL, small close-range firearm that, unlike other small arms (q.v.), is intended to be fired with one hand. Three varieties are available: single shot, multiple-barrel repeating, and single-barrel repeating pistols.

Pistols or handguns, as they are also known, were not popular until after the development of the wheel lock, the first practical mechanical ignition device, in the first half of the 16th century. Most early pistols were too cumbersome to be carried in a holster by anyone on foot, and the short barrels and method of holding pistols limited their accuracy and the distance they could propel bullets. As a result, pistols were primarily used by cavalry troops in what amounted to hit-and-run tactics. As ignition systems were improved, it became possible to reduce the overall size and weight of pistols, until during the 18th century they became equally popular for use by foot soldiers, for the most part in a defensive role. From the last half of the 17th century to the first quarter of the 19th century most European and U.S. military pistols had flintlock ignition and barrels 23 to 30 cm (9 to 12 in) in length; smaller pocket pistols were also made for civilian use. No significant improvements were made, however, until after 1836, when the American inventor Samuel Colt (1814–62) patented a revolver (q.v.) design combining the metal percussion cap (which replaced the flintlock), interchangeable mass-produced parts, and the revolving cylinder that rotated and locked automatically when the hammer was cocked.

Improvements in ammunition were introduced with the development of the self-primed metallic cartridge in the mid-19th century. Minor improvements in revolver design continued until the beginning of the 20th century, when emphasis in development was redirected to the magazine-loaded automatic pistol. Since then the automatic has steadily gained in popularity and is now the primary military handgun of the world. It is gradually replacing the revolver for police use.

Modern automatic pistols carry two or three times more ammunition than revolvers and are faster to reload. Their flat configuration generally makes them easier to conceal. Even with the increased ammunition capacity, using newly developed lightweight materials makes their loaded weight about the same as that of older designs. Proponents of revolvers claim greater accuracy, reliability, and safety, however, so it is unlikely that automatics will totally replace revolvers. In fact, muzzle-loading pistols and revolvers continue to be used for sport and specialized worldwide competition. R.W.Fi.

For further information on this topic, see the Bibliography in volume 28, sections 552–53.

PISTON, Walter Hamor (1894–1976), influential American composer and teacher. Born in Rockland, Maine, he studied at the Massachusetts School of Art and began working as an artist. He later studied music at Harvard University and composition in Paris with the eminent French teacher Nadia Boulanger and the composer Paul Dukas. In Paris he came under the influence of the Russian-born composer Igor Stravinsky. Returning to the U.S., Piston taught music at Harvard from 1926 to 1960. Prime representatives of American musical neoclassicism, his compositions are characterized by radical harmonies often approaching the limits of tonality and by rigorously logical formal structure. He was chiefly a composer of orchestral and chamber works and often wrote for unusual combinations of instruments. Among his compositions are eight symphonies; the ballet *The Incredible Flutist* (1938); concertos for violin (1939, 1960) and viola (1958); and chamber music, including string quartets, the Sonata for Flute and Piano (1930), and the Violin Sonata (1943). Two of his symphonies (no. 3 and no. 7) won Pulitzer Prizes. His books *Principles of Harmonic Analysis* (1933), *Harmony* (1941), *Counterpoint* (1947), and *Orchestration* (1955) are standard texts.

PITCAIRN ISLAND, island in the central South Pacific Ocean, about midway between Australia and South America; area, 5 sq km (2 sq mi). With uninhabited Henderson, Ducie, and Oeno islands, it forms a dependency of Great Britain (area, 47 sq km/18 sq mi). Pitcairn Island is of volcanic origin and is characterized by steep basaltic cliffs that rise abruptly from the sea; it has fertile soil but no streams. Oranges, bananas, and other crops are grown here. Adamstown, the only village, is on the N coast, near Bounty Bay.

The uninhabited Pitcairn Island was discovered in 1767 by a British naval officer, Philip Carteret (d. 1796), and named for the sailor who first sighted it. In 1790 the island was occupied by mutineers of the HMS *Bounty* (q.v.) accompanied by a group of Tahitian men and women. The community was not discovered until 1808 when American whalers visited the island; at that time only one of the British sailors was still alive. In 1856, because of overpopulation, about 200 of the islanders were transferred at their own request to Norfolk Island although a number of them returned afterward. In 1957 the remains of the Bounty were discovered on the S end of the island. In 1970 Pitcairn was placed under the jurisdiction of the British high commissioner in New Zealand. Pop. (1989 est.) 56.

For further information on this topic, see the Bibliography in volume 28, section 1250.

PITCH, in music, highness or lowness of a musical tone as determined by the rapidity of the vibrations producing it. Standards of exact pitch have varied over the centuries. During the Renaissance, woodwind instruments usually were built so that A above middle C was about 446 Hz (vibrations or cycles per second), that is, about a half step higher than modern A. The pitches of organs varied widely, however. Woodwind instrument builders during the late 17th century, using the pitch of Parisian organs, effectively set the standard for the following century at about A = 415, or about a half step below modern pitch. In the late 18th and early 19th centuries, wind instruments for use in bands and orchestras were built to increasingly higher pitch specifications, reaching about A = 452 (Old Philharmonic Pitch) by the mid-19th century. Various efforts were made to fix the scale of pitch, the most influential being that of a French commission of musicians and scientists who met in 1858–59. This commission reported in favor of A = 435, the widely used French pitch. In 1887 this was formally adopted by the Vienna Congress, an international conference on pitch, and is now often called international pitch, or *diapason normal.* French pitch was not universally accepted, however, and Great Britain and the U.S. eventually adopted A = 440, which remains their standard pitch in the 20th century, despite some pressure to move it upward. G.V.

PITCHBLENDE, radioactive mineral composed of the mineral uraninite, UO_2; it is one of the main mineral ores of uranium (q.v.). It is historically important as the mineral in which the chemical elements polonium and radium were first discovered in 1898 by the French scientists Pierre and Marie Curie. Pitchblende was commercially important only as a source of radium until World War II, when it became extremely important as a source of uranium needed for the production of the atomic bomb.

Pitchblende is a black, opaque mineral with a dull, pitchlike luster. The hardness is 5.5, and the sp.gr., which is extremely high for a mineral, ranges from 9.0 to 9.7. It crystallizes in the isometric system (*see* CRYSTAL) and usually occurs in massive formations as a constituent of granite rocks and pegmatites or as a secondary mineral associated with silver, lead, or copper ores. Although the ores do not occur in large quantities throughout the world, the major sources of pitchblende are located in South Africa, the Czech Republic, Canada, Germany, and France. In the U.S. the most important source is a deposit found in Marysvale, Utah. Smaller deposits have been discovered in Connecticut, North Carolina, and Colorado.

PITCHER, Molly, real name MARY LUDWIG (1754–1832), famous heroine of the American Revolution, born near Trenton, N.J. In 1769 she married John Hays (d. 1789). She came to be called Molly Pitcher after carrying pitchers of water to her husband and other thirsty soldiers during the Battle of Monmouth (*see* MONMOUTH, BATTLE OF). According to some accounts, when her husband was overcome by heat, she fought in his place for the duration of the battle. In 1822, in recognition of her heroism, she was given a pension by the Pennsylvania legislature.

PITCHER PLANT, common name for three families of flowering dicot plants (*see* DICOTS), members of which have leaves modified as pitchers for trapping and digesting insects. Two families,

The tips of the leaves of an East Indian pitcher plant, Nepenthes rafflesiana, *extend to form insect-trapping "pitchers" filled with a sticky digestive liquid.*
M. P. L. Fogden–Bruce Coleman, Inc.

Sarraceniaceae (pitcher plant) and Nepenthaceae (East Indian pitcher plant), are in the order Nepenthales; the third family, Cephalotaceae (Australian pitcher plant), is in the unrelated order Rosales (*see* ROSE). The entire leaves of all these plants are tubular and hollow and lined with downward-pointing hairs. When an insect enters, it cannot climb back out against the hairs and ultimately falls to the bottom of the leaf, to be digested by juices contained there. Pitcher plants typically occur in poor soils and depend partly on nutrients obtained from the digested insects.

The most common pitcher plants are the members of the genus *Sarracenia* (8 species), found in eastern North America, and the California pitcher plant, *Darlingtonia californica,* native to northern California and the coastal Pacific Northwest. Nepenthaceae contains only the genus *Nepenthes* (about 75 species), found in tropical Asia. Cephalotaceae contains a single species, *Cephalotus follicularis,* which is native to Australia. *See* INSECTIVOROUS PLANTS. M.R.C.

For further information on this topic, see the Bibliography in volume 28, section 452.

PITHECANTHROPUS ERECTUS. *See* JAVA: *History.*

PITMAN, Sir Isaac (1813–97), English phonographer. He devised a system of shorthand (q.v.) based on phonetic rather than orthographic principles; adapted to more than 15 languages, it is still one of the most used shorthand systems in the world. Pitman explained the system in his 1837 publication *Stenographic Soundhand.* In 1842 he established the weekly *Phonographic Journal,* afterward named the *Phonetic Journal,* which he edited for more than 50 years. Pitman founded a publishing house, which issued *Pitman's French Weekly* and many pamphlets advocating radical reform in English spelling. He was knighted in 1894. Pitman's system was introduced in the U.S. by his brother, Benn Pitman (1822–1910), who immigrated to the country in 1852 and founded the Phonographic Institute in Cincinnati, Ohio, a place to teach and publish work on the shorthand.

PITT, William (1759–1806), prime minister of Great Britain (1783–1801 and 1804–6), who restored British confidence and prosperity after the American Revolution and was a resolute leader of the nation in war against revolutionary France.

Born in Hayes in Kent on May 28, 1759, Pitt, known as the Younger, was the second son of William Pitt, 1st earl of Chatham. He was educated for a political career at the University of Cambridge and Lincoln's Inn. In 1781 he entered Parliament, linking himself with William Petty, earl of Shelburne, leader of the political group

William Pitt the Younger

formerly connected with his father. In 1782 Shelburne took office with Charles Watson-Wentworth, marquess of Rockingham, and became prime minister when Rockingham died three months later. Pitt became chancellor of the Exchequer under Shelburne and was occupied with proposals for parliamentary and administrative reform. He left office with Shelburne in April 1783, but in December King George III named him prime minister, a post he held for 18 years.

First Ministry. Pitt's goal was to revive the national spirit through peace and economy. He was an excellent financial manager, improving the revenue, cutting expenditure, consolidating the accounts, and beginning systematic reduction of the national debt. In foreign policy he restored Britain's prestige in Europe and negotiated a favorable trade treaty with France. Some of his proposals—parliamentary reform, free trade between Britain and Ireland, abolition of the slave trade—were rejected by Parliament. When George III became temporarily insane in 1788, Pitt blocked an attempt by his political rival, Charles James Fox, to gain power by having the prince of Wales appointed regent. Pitt's Canada Act (1791) established representative institutions for English- and French-speaking Canada. The need for a place to settle convicts led to the establishment (1788) of a colony in Australia. Political control over the British territories in India was established by Pitt's India Act (1784).

The outbreak of the French Revolution in 1789, followed by general European war, removed the conditions that favored Pitt's policies of peace and economy. Britain declared war on France in

1793, and Pitt became the leader of a nation determined to resist the spread of French power and ideas. Pitt's policy was to attack French trade and colonies, while subsidizing allies to fight the French on land. In 1793-94 Pitt's ministry was strengthened when most of the Whigs came to his support, leaving only a small opposition led by Fox. Fear of radicalism led to legislation to suppress dissidents and restrict political discussion. The war in Europe went badly and brought many hardships at home, but British seapower remained, and Pitt continued the struggle.

A major problem was Ireland, where Irish patriots rose in rebellion (1798), encouraged by French promises of help. Pitt's solution to the Irish problem was the Act of Union (1800), which incorporated Ireland into one United Kingdom with Great Britain. He also proposed equal political rights for Roman Catholics as essential to making the Act of Union work. Opposition to Roman Catholic emancipation by the king and by many of Pitt's own supporters caused him to resign in 1801.

Second Ministry. Pitt was succeeded by Henry Addington (1757-1844), who made peace with Napoleonic France. War was soon resumed, however, and the nation again turned to Pitt, who returned to office in 1804, forming another coalition against France. Pitt had lost many of his former supporters, and weary determination replaced the vitality of his former years. The Battle of Trafalgar (1805) confirmed British supremacy at sea, but Napoleon continued victorious on land. When Pitt died at Putney on Jan. 23, 1806, his last words were, "Oh, my country! How I leave my country!"

Pitt was intelligent, receptive to new ideas, a superb speaker, and well informed on all aspects of government. His policies were moderate, for his political support came primarily from a king and parliamentary majority who were conservative in outlook. His long tenure of power and his determination to control all aspects of government were important contributions to the developing concept of a prime minister. E.A.Re.

PITT, William, 1st Earl of Chatham (1708-78), prime minister of Great Britain, who led the country to victory over France in the Seven Years' War.

Pitt was born on Nov. 15, 1708, in Westminster. The importance of the Pitt family had been established by Thomas Pitt (1653-1726), his grandfather, who gained a fortune in India. He was educated at Eton Public School and the University of Oxford and entered Parliament in 1735, representing a borough controlled by his family. He was an intense, forceful orator and became a prominent spokesman for the opposition during the ministry of Sir Robert Walpole. In 1739 the opposition pushed Walpole into war with Spain, and when Walpole failed to provide aggressive leadership, Pitt contributed to the political pressure that forced his resignation in 1742. King George II refused to give Pitt important political office, but in 1746 he was made paymaster of the army.

Pitt's First Ministry. Pitt's principal goal was imperial power. His opportunity came when war broke out with France in America in 1754 (*see* FRENCH AND INDIAN WAR), becoming a general European war in 1756. Britain did badly at first, but in 1757 Pitt and Thomas Pelham-Holles, duke of Newcastle, joined to form a ministry that combined Newcastle's long political experience with Pitt's dynamic energy. Pitt attacked the French Empire boldly, giving commands to able and ambitious young officers. In a series of remarkable victories the British conquered Canada, the area between the Appalachian Mountains and the Mississippi River, the French West Indies, and the French trading posts in West Africa. The British East India Co. destroyed French power in India. In the meantime Pitt used British gold to support Frederick II of Prussia, who was able to hold out against France, Austria, and Russia until an exhausted France was ready for peace.

The death of George II in 1760 changed the political situation, for his successor, the young George III, distrusted both Newcastle and Pitt and was determined to assert his own personal power. Pitt resigned in 1761 when his advice to

William Pitt, 1st earl of Chatham

attack Spain was rejected by the king and the cabinet. The following year Spain declared war, and the mighty forces that Pitt had assembled captured Florida, Havana, and Manila. Although the Treaty of Paris (1763) made Great Britain the dominant imperial power, Pitt criticized the treaty severely.

Later Career. The rest of Pitt's life was marked by political frustration and ill health. In 1765 he defended American resistance to the Stamp Act. The following year George III made him earl of Chatham and turned to him to form a nonpartisan government that would end dissensions at home and unrest in the colonies. His second ministry was a failure; it fell apart in 1768, and his influence after that was negligible. In 1778 Pitt collapsed in the House of Lords while delivering a speech opposing American independence. He died at Hayes in Kent on May 11, 1778.

Evaluation. Pitt was at his best leading the nation in war. His appeals to national pride and public opinion have led some historians to see him as a prototype of later democratic leaders, such as David Lloyd George and Sir Winston Churchill.

E.A.Re.

PITTSBURG, city, Contra Costa Co., W California, an inland port and industrial center at the confluence of the San Joaquin and Sacramento rivers; inc. 1903. Manufactures include steel products, chemicals, and roofing materials. A junior college is here. The community was founded as New York of the Pacific in 1849 and grew in the 1850s as a shipping point for coal mined (1855–1902) at Mt. Diablo. It was renamed for Pittsburgh, Pa., in 1911 following the development of the steel industry here. Pop. (1980) 33,034; (1990) 47,564.

PITTSBURGH, city, seat of Allegheny Co., SW Pennsylvania, situated at the point where the Allegheny and Monongahela rivers join to form the Ohio R.; inc. 1816.

Economy. The second largest city in Pennsylvania, Pittsburgh is a major financial and transportation center. Although it is the nation's busiest inland river port, Pittsburgh is also served by several railroads, inland-water carriers, major highways, and the nearby Greater Pittsburgh International Airport. The headquarters of several major corporations are located here.

Following the collapse of the domestic steel industry, Pittsburgh's economy was successfully transformed from one centered around manufacturing, particularly steel, iron, and glass, to one balanced among high technology, health, and business services. Pittsburgh is a world leader in organ transplants. As a result, many research and testing laboratories are located in the city. Major products include industrial automation,

Aerial view of Pittsburgh, where the Allegheny and Monongahela rivers meet to form the Ohio River. F. Dam–Leo de Wys

software engineering, and biomedical technology.

The Urban Landscape. The city, about 142 sq km (about 55 sq mi) in area, is located on an upland plateau dissected by rivers, which form narrow valleys delineated by steep bluffs or undulating highlands. Pittsburgh's main business section, called the Golden Triangle, occupies the level peninsula formed by the confluence of the two rivers. The city's manufacturing industries are concentrated in areas contiguous to the riverfronts. Principal residential sections are located on the highlands. Pittsburgh, which contains more than 720 bridges, is known as the City of Bridges.

Educational and Cultural Institutions. Included among the city's institutions of higher education are the University of Pittsburgh, Carnegie-Mellon University, Duquesne University (1878), Carlow College (1929), Chatham College (1869), La Roche College (1963), Point Park College (1960), the Pittsburgh Theological Seminary (1794), the Reformed Presbyterian Theological Seminary (1810), and several junior colleges.

Noted points of interest include the Frick Art Museum; the Museum of Art, the Sarah Mellon Scaife Gallery, the Science Center, and the Museum of Natural History, which are all operated by the Carnegie Institute; the Institute of Popular Science; Fort Pitt Blockhouse (1764) and Fort Pitt Museum, in Point State Park; the Pittsburgh Zoo, in Highland Park; Phipps Conservatory, in Schenley Park; Allegheny Observatory, in Riverview Park; and the Aviary-Conservatory, in West Park.

Among the sports, entertainment, and meeting facilities in the city are Three Rivers Stadium, used by major league baseball and football teams; Heinz Hall, home of the Pittsburgh Symphony Orchestra; the Benedum Center, which houses the Pittsburgh Ballet Theater, the Pittsburgh Opera, and the Civic Light Opera; and the David L. Lawrence Convention-Exhibition Center.

History. The area surrounding the confluence of the Allegheny and Monongahela rivers was claimed by both the British and the French. On the recommendation of George Washington, who had visited here in 1753, a detachment of Virginia militia occupied the area at the fork of the rivers in 1754 and started to construct a fort. Less than three months later they were attacked by a force of French and Indians and were compelled to withdraw. The French soon completed the construction of the fortification, calling it Fort Duquesne. In late 1758 a British expedition led by Gen. John Forbes (1710–59) moved against Fort Duquesne. Forbes occupied the site only after the French had destroyed the fort. A temporary fort was built and subsequently was replaced by a larger and more permanent fortification (1761). The structure was named Fort Pitt in honor of the then British prime minister, William Pitt, 1st earl of Chatham.

Following the American Revolution, Pittsburgh grew as an outfitting point for settlers heading west. In about 1792, George Anshutz (1753–1837) built a blast furnace here, the initial step in developing the city's great iron and steel industry, the main growth of which came after 1850. In 1797 Pittsburgh's first glass factory was constructed, and in 1804 the first cotton-textile factory was established in the city. In 1834 the opening of the Pennsylvania Canal and the Portage Railroad, both of which linked the city with Philadelphia, brought increased commerce to Pittsburgh. A fire destroyed much of the city in 1845, and a flood in 1936 caused much damage.

Since the 1950s Pittsburgh has undergone large-scale redevelopment; blighted areas, including the Golden Triangle section, have been rebuilt or restored, and major programs dealing with smoke-pollution control, flood prevention, and sewage disposal have been implemented. Pop. (1980) 423,959; (1990) 369,879.

PITTSBURGH, UNIVERSITY OF, state-related institution of higher learning, in Bradford, Greensburg, Johnstown, Pittsburgh, and Titusville, Pa., founded in 1787 as the Pittsburgh Academy. Its name was changed to the Western University of Pennsylvania in 1819, and the present name was adopted in 1908. Students pursue programs in business administration, dentistry, education, engineering, health professions, law, liberal arts and sciences, library science, medicine, nursing, nursing education, pharmacy, public administration, public and international affairs, public health, and social work. The degrees of bachelor, master, and doctor are conferred.

Many courses are given at the Cathedral of Learning, a 42-story neo-Gothic structure at the center of the Pittsburgh campus. The schools of dentistry, engineering, medicine, nursing, pharmacy, and public health surround the cathedral. Adjacent to the campus is the university's medical center, including the Children's Hospital, Eye and Ear Hospital, Falk Clinic, Presbyterian University Hospital, Western Psychiatric Institute and Clinic, and the graduate school of public health. One of the most notable campus buildings at the university is the Stephen Collins Foster Memorial, a neo-Gothic structure next to the cathedral. The memorial houses a large collection of material relating to the life and works of the American composer.

PITTSFIELD, city, seat of Berkshire Co., W Massachusetts, on headstreams of the Housatonic R., in the Berkshire Hills; settled 1761, inc. as a city 1890. A winter and summer resort area, the city contains facilities for the research and development of plastics. Paper is also manufactured here. The city is home to a community college. Nearby attractions include Hancock Shaker village (inhabited 1790–1960); "Arrowhead," the home of the writer Herman Melville from 1850 to 1863; and Tanglewood, site of a noted summer music festival. The city is named for the British statesman William Pitt, 1st earl of Chatham. Pop. (1980) 51,974; (1990) 48,622.

PITUITARY GLAND, master endocrine gland in vertebrate animals. The hormones secreted by the pituitary stimulate and control the functioning of almost all the other endocrine glands in the body. Pituitary hormones also promote growth and control the water balance of the body. *See* ENDOCRINE SYSTEM; HORMONE.

The pituitary is a small bean-shaped, reddish-gray organ located in the saddle-shaped depression (sella turcica) in the floor of the skull (the sphenoid bone) and attached to the base of the brain by a stalk; it is located near the hypothalamus. The pituitary has two lobes—the anterior lobe, or adenohypophysis, and the posterior lobe, or neurohypophysis—which differ in structure and function. The anterior lobe is derived embryologically from the roof of the pharynx and is composed of groups of epithelial cells separated by blood channels; the posterior lobe is derived from the base of the brain and is composed of nervous connective tissue and nervelike secreting cells. The area between the anterior and posterior lobes of the pituitary is called the intermediate lobe; it has the same embryological origin as the anterior lobe.

The Anterior Lobe. Concentrated chemical substances, or hormones, which control 10 to 12 functions in the body, have been obtained as extracts from the anterior pituitary glands of cattle, sheep, and swine. Eight hormones have been isolated, purified, and identified; all of them are peptides, that is, they are composed of amino acids. Growth hormone (GH), or the somatotropic hormone (STH), is essential for normal skeletal growth and is neutralized during adolescence by the gonadal sex hormones. Thyroid-stimulating hormone (TSH) controls the normal functioning of the thyroid gland; and the adrenocorticotropic hormone (ACTH) controls the activity of the cortex of the adrenal glands and takes part in the stress reaction (*see* HYDROCORTISONE). Prolactin, also called lactogenic, luteotropic, or mammotropic hormone, initiates milk secretion in the mammary gland after the mammary tissues have been prepared during preg-

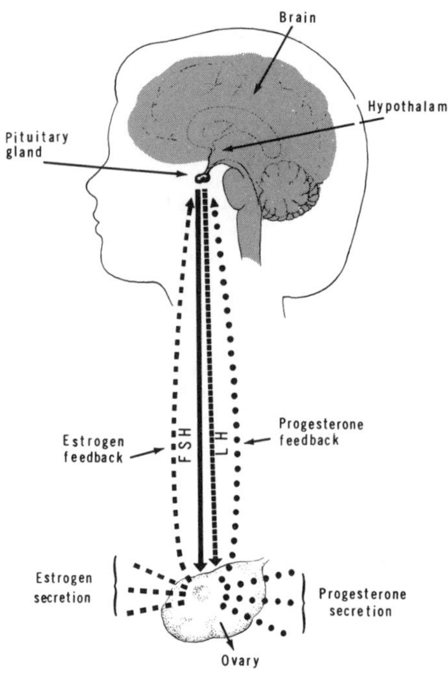

The Pituitary and Related Organs

nancy by the secretion of other pituitary and sex hormones. The two gonadotropic hormones are follicle-stimulating hormone (FSH) and luteinizing hormone (LH). Follicle-stimulating hormone stimulates the formation of the Graafian follicle in the female ovary and the development of spermatozoa in the male. The luteinizing hormone stimulates the formation of ovarian hormones after ovulation and initiates lactation in the female; in the male, it stimulates the tissues of the testes to elaborate testosterone. In 1975 scientists identified the pituitary peptide endorphin, which acts in experimental animals as a natural pain reliever in times of stress. Endorphin and ACTH are made as parts of a single large protein, which subsequently splits. This may be the body's mechanism for coordinating the physiological activities of two stress-induced hormones. The same large prohormone that contains ACTH and endorphin also contains short peptides called melanocyte-stimulating hormones. These substances are analogous to the hormone that regulates pigmentation in fish and amphibians, but in humans they have no known function.

Research has shown that the hormonal activity of the anterior lobe is controlled by chemical messengers sent from the hypothalamus through tiny blood vessels to the anterior lobe. In the

1950s, the British neurologist Geoffrey Harris (1913–71) discovered that cutting the blood supply from the hypothalamus to the pituitary impaired the function of the pituitary. In 1964, chemical agents called releasing factors were found in the hypothalamus; these substances, it was learned, affect the secretion of growth hormone, a thyroid-stimulating hormone called thyrotropin, and the gonadotropic hormones involving the testes and ovaries. In 1969 the American endocrinologist Roger Guillemin (1924–) and colleagues isolated and characterized thyrotropin-releasing factor, which stimulates the secretion of thyroid-stimulating hormone from the pituitary. In the next few years his group and that of the American physiologist Andrew Schally (1926–) isolated the luteinizing hormone-releasing factor, which stimulates secretion of both LH and FSH, and somatostatin, which inhibits release of growth hormone. For this work, which proved that the brain and the endocrine system are linked, they shared the Nobel Prize in physiology or medicine in 1977. Human somatostatin was one of the first substances to be grown in bacteria by recombinant DNA.

The presence of the releasing factors in the hypothalamus helped to explain the action of the female sex hormones, estrogen and progesterone, and their synthetic versions contained in oral contraceptives, or birth-control pills. During a woman's normal monthly cycle, several hormonal changes are needed for the ovary to produce an egg cell for possible fertilization. When the estrogen level in the body declines, the follicle-releasing factor (FRF) flows to the pituitary and stimulates the secretion of the follicle-stimulating hormone. Through a similar feedback principle, the declining level of progesterone causes a release of luteal-releasing factor (LRF), which stimulates secretion of the luteinizing hormone. The ripening follicle in the ovary then produces estrogen, and the high level of that hormone influences the hypothalamus to shut down temporarily the production of FSH. Increased progesterone feedback to the hypothalamus shuts down LH production by the pituitary. The daily doses of synthetic estrogen and progesterone in oral contraceptives, or injections of the actual hormones, inhibit the normal reproductive activity of the ovaries by mimicking the effect of these hormones on the hypothalamus.

The Intermediate Lobe. In lower vertebrates this part of the pituitary secretes melanocyte-stimulating hormone, which brings about skin-color changes. In humans, it is present only for a short time early in life and during pregnancy, and is not known to have any function.

The Posterior Lobe. Two hormones are secreted by the posterior lobe. One of these is the antidiurectic hormone (ADH), vasopressin. Vasopressin stimulates the kidney tubules to absorb water from the filtered plasma that passes through the kidneys and thus controls the amount of urine secreted by the kidneys. The other posterior pituitary hormone is oxytocin, which causes the contraction of the smooth muscles in the uterus, intestines, and blood arterioles. It stimulates the contractions of the uterine muscles during the final stage of pregnancy to stimulate expulsion of the fetus, and it also stimulates the ejection, or let-down, of milk from the mammary gland following pregnancy. Synthesized in 1953, oxytocin was the first pituitary hormone to be produced artificially. Vasopressin was synthesized in 1956.

Pituitary Disturbances. Pituitary functioning may be disturbed by such conditions as tumors, blood poisoning, blood clots, and certain infectious diseases. Conditions resulting from a decrease in anterior-lobe secretion include dwarfism, acromicria, Simmonds's disease, and Fröhlich's syndrome. Dwarfism occurs when anterior pituitary deficiencies occur during childhood; acromicria, in which the bones of the extremities are small and delicate, results when the deficiency occurs after puberty. Simmonds's disease, which is caused by extensive damage to the anterior pituitary, is characterized by premature aging, loss of hair and teeth, anemia, and emaciation; it can be fatal. Fröhlich's syndrome, also called adiposogenital dystrophy, is caused by both anterior pituitary deficiency and a lesion of the posterior lobe or hypothalamus. The result is extensive obesity, dwarfism, and retarded sexual development. Glands under the influence of anterior pituitary hormones are also affected by anterior pituitary deficiency.

Oversecretion of one of the anterior pituitary hormones, somatotropin, results in a progressive chronic disease called acromegaly (q.v.), which is characterized by enlargement of some parts of the body. Posterior-lobe deficiency results in diabetes insipidus (q.v.).

For further information on this topic, see the Bibliography in volume 28, sections 493–94.

PIT VIPER, name applied to more than 120 species of venomous snakes of the family Crotalidae. The snakes are distinguished by the presence of deep pits on each side of the head between the eye and the nostril. Like true vipers, of the family Viperidae, pit vipers, which are sometimes placed in the same family, have a pair of elongated fangs that may be folded back against the palate. The pit vipers are the only snakes, however, possessing facial pits. Research indicates that the pits react with great sensitivity to radiant heat, thereby enabling the snake to detect the presence of warm-blooded prey in the dark. Among the pit vipers are the rattlesnake, the moccasin, the copperhead, the fer-de-lance, the bushmaster, and the palm viper. Most pit vipers inhabit the western hemisphere; a few are native to Asia. The bushmaster is the only New World pit viper that lays eggs; most other species bring forth their young alive.

For further information on this topic, see the Bibliography in volume 28, sections 461, 471.

PIURA, city, NW Peru, capital of Piura Department, on the Piura R. and the Pan-American Highway. It is a commercial center for the irrigated Piura Valley, where cotton, rice, sugarcane, and corn are cultivated. The National University of Piura (1962), the National Technical University of Piura (1962), and a school of music are here. The community of San Miguel de Piura, the oldest Spanish settlement in Peru, was established nearby by the Spanish explorer Francisco Pizarro in 1532. In 1588 the settlement was moved to its present site. Pop. (1988 est.) 297,200.

PIUS II (1405–64), pope (1458–64), who was a noted humanist writer and scholar and who, as pontiff, tried to organize a Crusade against the Turks. Born Enea Silvio Piccolomini in Corsignano (now Pienza), near Siena, Italy, and called Aeneas Silvius, he became secretary to the bishop of Fermo and lived (1431–35) in Basel, Switzerland; later, after undertaking various secret diplomatic missions to England and Scotland on behalf of the church, he became a lay member of the Council of Basel (*see* BASEL, COUNCIL OF). In 1422 he was sent by the council to Germany to take part in the diet of Frankfort am Main. There he became poet laureate and private secretary to Frederick III, Holy Roman emperor, and wrote several witty literary works, including a novel in the style of the Italian writer Giovanni Boccaccio. In 1446 he took holy orders and was created a cardinal in 1456. He was elected to the papacy in 1458. Pius's primary concern as pope was to organize a Crusade against the Turks, who had taken Constantinople in 1453 and were threatening new conquests in Europe. He was unable to gain support until 1464, however, because of quarrels of a political and doctrinal nature with various European monarchs, including King Louis XI of France. When, in 1464, he finally set sail with the Crusade for the East, Pius died of fever at Ancona, Italy, during the journey.

PIUS IV (1499–1565), pope (1559–65), who presided over the conclusion of the Council of Trent. Born Giovanni Angelo Medici in Milan, Italy (he was not related to the famous Medici family of Florence), he was trained as a lawyer. He entered the service of Pope Paul III in 1534, took holy orders in 1545 on being created archbishop of Ragusa, Sicily, and was made a cardinal in 1549. After his election to the papacy he reversed some of the policies of his unpopular predecessor, Paul IV, particularly that of papal hostility to Spain; he also extended support to King Philip II of France and recognition to Holy Roman Emperor Ferdinand I. In 1562 he reconvened the Council of Trent, which had been suspended since 1552 (*see* TRENT, COUNCIL OF). A patron of the arts, he gave a number of commissions to Michelangelo.

PIUS V, Saint (1504–72), pope (1566–72), whose austere reforms and repressive measures against dissenters strengthened the Roman Catholic church (q.v.) at the time of the Counter Reformation (q.v.). Born Antonio Ghislieri near Alessandria in northern Italy, he became a Dominican friar at the age of 14 and subsequently worked zealously for the Inquisition (q.v.), eventually rising to the position of grand inquisitor; he was made a cardinal in 1557. As pope he enforced the reforming decrees of the Council of Trent (*see* TRENT, COUNCIL OF); aided French Roman Catholics in their persecution of the Huguenots (q.v.); expelled many Jews from the Papal States (q.v.); excommunicated Queen Elizabeth I of England; and used the Inquisition relentlessly to punish heretics. In 1570 he formed the Holy League in alliance with Spain and Venice against the Turks, and the league won a great naval victory in the Battle of Lepanto (1571). His personal asceticism, opposition to nepotism, and severe reforms raised the morale of the church; and his reliance on the Inquisition virtually eliminated Protestantism from Italy. His intolerance and harshness, however, were often counterproductive in foreign relations, and he antagonized France and the Holy Roman Empire as well as England. He was canonized in 1712; his feast day is April 30.

PIUS VI (1717–99), pope (1775–99), whose reign, ending in captivity by the French, marked the low point of the modern papacy. Born Giovanni Angelo Braschi in Cesena, Italy, he became secretary to Pope Benedict XIV and later treasurer of the apostolic chamber and cardinal under Pope Clement XIII (1693–1769); he succeeded Pope Clement XIV. His reign was marked by struggles with the rulers of Naples, Tuscany, Austria, and France over their efforts to restrict papal jurisdiction over church administration. At the outbreak of the French Revolution, all church property in France was confiscated and when the revolutionary regime demanded an oath of fidelity from the clergy, Pius denounced (1791) the revolution as unholy. He supported the antirevolutionary coalition of European powers, and, in 1797, after the invasion of Italy by Napoleon, Pius was forced to surrender papal territories to the newly created Cisalpine Republic (q.v.). In 1798 French armies under Gen. Louis Alexandre Berthier marched on Rome, which had been declared a republic by Roman revolutionaries in league with the French, and demanded that Pius renounce his temporal sovereignty. At his refusal the pope was taken prisoner and held first at Siena and ultimately at Valence, France, where he died.

PIUS VII (1742–1823), pope (1800–23), who struggled with Napoleon to preserve the traditional prerogatives of the church, which he largely succeeded in restoring after Napoleon's downfall. Born Luigi Barnaba Chiaramonti in Cesena, Italy, he became a member of the Benedictines and was made an abbot and cardinal by his relative Pius VI. Soon after his election as pope he negotiated the Concordat of 1801 with Napoleon's government (*see* CONCORDAT), by the terms of which the church was reestablished in France. In 1804 Pius anointed Napoleon in the ceremony in which the latter declared himself Emperor Napoleon I, but relations between the two deteriorated as Napoleon sought increased control over the French church, leading to the breaking off of diplomatic relations between France and the Papal States. In 1809 Napoleon decreed the Papal States a part of the French Empire and took Pius prisoner, keeping him in Savona, Italy, and later in Fontainebleau, France. The pontiff courageously resisted Napoleon's efforts to make him exercise papal authority in the emperor's political behalf. Indeed, his steadfast resistance to Napoleon did much to restore the prestige and moral stature of the papacy. Pius did not return to the Vatican until the spring of 1814, when military setbacks convinced Napoleon to free him. He subsequently repealed much of the legislation enacted under French occupation, restored the Jesuits, revived the Inquisition, and suppressed the Carbonari, a liberal secret society.

PIUS IX (1792–1878), pope (1846–78), whose pontificate, the longest in history, encompassed the First Vatican Council (*see* VATICAN COUNCIL, FIRST), the promulgation of several important dogmas, and the loss of the Papal States (q.v.).

Born Giovanni Maria Mastai-Ferretti, May 13, 1792, in Senigallia, Italy, Pius was ordained in 1819, became archbishop of Spoleto in 1827, and was created cardinal in 1840 by Pope Gregory XVI (1765–1846), whom he succeeded. The first years of his pontificate were marked by liberalism and political reforms in the administration of the Papal States; the constitution granted by Pius in 1848 merely satisfied demands for popular representation, however, and did not quiet the nationalism rising throughout Italy. The revolution of 1848 caused the pope to flee in exile to Gaeta, in the kingdom of Naples. Two years later, after the newly established Roman Republic had been dissolved by the intervention of France, Pius returned to the Vatican and thereafter devoted himself to opposing all liberalism, both ecclesiastical and political.

Pius affirmed church control of science, education, and culture in the Papal States and adamantly resisted demands for constitutional government and the unification of Italy. He supported Ultramontanism, a doctrine asserting papal authority in the international church. The triumph of this doctrine at the First Vatican Council resulted in the proclamation of the infallibility (q.v.) of the pope. In a bull published in 1854 he proclaimed the dogma of the Immaculate Conception (q.v.). In 1864 he issued a syllabus condemning 80 errors, among them the belief that the pope should reconcile himself to "progress, liberalism, and modern civilization." The temporal power of the papacy had already been greatly diminished when, in 1860, the new Italian Kingdom absorbed all the territory of the Papal States except for Rome. It was ended altogether in 1870, when the French troops protecting papal rule were withdrawn and Rome itself became the capital of a united Italy. Pius, refusing to accept the parliamentary act of 1871 defining the relations between the papacy and the Italian government, retired voluntarily to the Vatican. He remained there until his death, on Feb. 7, 1878, regarding himself a prisoner within its confines, as did his successors until the conclusion of the Lateran Treaty (q.v.) in 1929.

PIUS X, Saint (1835–1914), pope (1903–14), who opposed the Modernist movement in Roman Catholicism. Born Giuseppe Melchiorre Sarto in Riese, Italy, he was educated in the college at Castelfranco and the seminary at Padua; he was ordained in 1858. In 1903, while cardinal-patriarch of Venice, he was elected pope.

Conservative in both religion and politics, Pius stressed the inner life of the church and firmly opposed intellectual liberalism. He opposed Modernism (q.v.), a reinterpretation of religious doctrine in the light of 19th-century scientific thought. In 1907 he issued a decree condemning 65 Modernist propositions and placed several Modernist works on the Index of Forbidden Books (q.v.).

During Pius's reign the church was weakened by anticlerical legislation in France and Portugal. Pius condemned the seizure of church property and the prohibition of religious education in those countries.

Pius initiated the recodification of canon law, restored Gregorian chant to the liturgy, and established a new breviary as the standard for the whole church. Anticipating the Roman Catholic Action movement, he encouraged the laity to undertake church-supervised social action programs. Pius was canonized in 1954. His feast day is August 21.

PIUS XI (1857–1939), pope (1922–39), who navigated a tortuous path for the church during the turbulent years before World War II. Born Ambrogio Damiano Achille Ratti in Desio, Italy, on May 31, 1857, he was educated at the Lombard College and the Gregorian University in Rome. He was professor of dogmatic theology at the seminary of Milan from 1882 to 1888, a staff member and ultimately director of the Ambrosian Library of Milan from 1888 to 1910, and subprefect and later prefect of the Vatican Library in Rome from 1911 to 1918. The following year he became papal nuncio in Poland and in 1921 was made a cardinal and archbishop of Milan. He succeeded Benedict XV as pope in 1922.

During his reign Pius XI issued several social encyclicals, including *Casti Connubii* (Christian Marriage), of Dec. 30, 1930, discussing marriage and family life; the notable *Quadragesimo Anno* (Forty Years) of May 15, 1931, devoted to his view of the need for reconstruction of the social order; and *Nova Impendet* (Threatening News), of Oct. 2, 1931, examining the worldwide economic crisis of the 1920s and early 1930s. Pius XI's pontificate is also notable for the signing of the Lateran Treaty with Benito Mussolini, whereby the 59-year retirement of the popes in the Vatican was brought to an end and the temporal authority of the papacy over Vatican City in Rome was established. Although Pius negotiated a treaty with the government of Mexico in 1929, whereby Roman Catholic churches in that country were permitted to resume services, relations between church and state later deteriorated once again. In 1933 he signed a concordat with Germany that protected the rights of the church under the Third Reich but had the unfortunate effect of disarming certain opposition to Adolf Hitler both within and outside Germany. Thereafter, however, Pius repeatedly protested the offenses of National Socialism against both law and the church in Germany. An outspoken enemy of communism, he supported the regime of the Spanish dictator Francisco Franco during the Spanish civil war. Until 1938 the pope maintained friendly relations with the government of Mussolini but thereafter opposed the Italian and German governments and issued pleas against anti-Semitism and war. He died in Rome on Feb. 10, 1939.

PIUS XII (1876–1958), pope (1939–58) during World War II, respected especially for his efforts to persuade the contending nations to settle their differences peacefully.

Born Eugenio Pacelli in Rome, March 2, 1876, he was the son of Filippo Pacelli, dean of the college of Vatican lawyers. He departed from the family tradition of the practice of law and was ordained a priest in 1899. Subsequently he was a professor of canon law at the Pontifical Institute of the Apollinaire and of ecclesiastical diplomacy at the Academy of Noble Ecclesiastics in Rome. In 1901 he entered the papal secretariat of state and after 1904 assisted the Italian archbishop (later cardinal) Pietro Gasparri (1852–1934) in a new codification of canon law, issued in 1917. He succeeded Gasparri as secretary of the papal department of extraordinary ecclesiastical affairs in 1914 and three years later was consecrated titular archbishop of Sardes and also appointed apostolic nuncio to Bavaria. In the last-named post he attempted papal mediation for Pope Benedict XV to conclude World War I.

In 1920 he was appointed first papal nuncio to Germany and negotiated concordats between the Vatican and the German states of Bavaria and Prussia in 1924 and 1929, respectively. In the latter year he was recalled to Rome and created a cardinal and secretary of state to the Holy See. In this capacity he executed the policies of Pope Pius XI. He acquired a reputation as an able diplomat and established a precedent by traveling abroad in his official capacity, visiting France, Argentina, and Hungary. He visited the U.S. in an unofficial capacity and traveled extensively there. He ascended the papal throne as Pius XII on March 2, 1939.

During World War II, which through personal diplomacy he strove to prevent, Pius repeatedly issued pleas for peace and against totalitarianism and protested many actions of the German and Italian governments, particularly the bombing of Vatican City by the Germans in 1943. In his important encyclical *Mystici Corporis Christi* (The Mystical Body of Christ, 1943) Pius explained the theological doctrine that the church is the mystical body of Christ and condemned false mysticism. In the encyclicals *Divino Afflante Spiritu* (Inspiration of the Holy Spirit, 1943) and *Humani Generis* (Of the Human Race, 1950), he urged care in the interpretation of biblical texts and caution in adopting, uncritically, modern scientific teachings, without reference to the traditions of the church.

Pius XII

In 1946 Pius named 32 new cardinals to the Sacred College, including 5 from the U.S., bringing the college to 69 members (one short of the traditional complement of 70); for the first time it was composed of representatives of all continents. Pius continued and intensified the anti-Communist policies of his predecessor. In 1949 he issued a historic proclamation declaring that any Roman Catholic rendering support of any kind or degree to communism would automatically incur the penalty of excommunication. Pius opened the 25th Holy Year in the history of the church on Dec. 24, 1949. The following November he issued the apostolic constitution *Munificentissimus Deus* (Most Bountiful God), in which the assumption of the Blessed Virgin Mary was defined as a dogma of faith (*see* ASSUMPTION OF THE VIRGIN). In his Christmas message for 1950 Pius announced officially that the tomb of the apostle Peter had been found during excavations under the high altar of Saint Peter's Basilica in Rome. On Sept. 9, 1953, he proclaimed the Marian Year in celebration of the centenary of the definition of the dogma of the Immaculate Conception of the Virgin Mary. Pius XII died Oct. 9, 1958.

PIUTE, group of tribes of North American Indians who speak Uto-Aztecan languages. The Piute live on reservations in Oklahoma, Nevada, and California.

PIZARRO, Francisco (1476?-1541), Spanish explorer and conqueror of Peru, noted for his audacity, courage, cruelty, and unscrupulousness and for his abilities as a military and civil leader.

Pizarro was born in Trujillo. He came to America in 1510 and took part in a number of exploratory expeditions, including that of Vasco de Balboa, which resulted in the discovery of the Pacific Ocean in 1513. In 1519 Pizarro settled in Panama. Five years later he became a partner of the Spanish soldier and explorer Diego de Almagro and others in a project to explore and conquer territory to the south of Panama. In two expeditions (1524-25, 1526-28), Pizarro explored the west coast of South America and learned of the existence of the Inca Empire of Peru. In 1526 the partners contracted to cooperate in the conquest of Peru, and in 1528 Pizarro went to Spain to enlist royal aid for the venture. The following year Charles I, king of Spain, better known as Charles V, Holy Roman emperor, granted Pizarro the authority to conquer and rule Peru. Pizarro raised a military force in Spain and in 1530 sailed to Panama, where he enlisted additional recruits. In 1531, with about 180 men, Pizarro sailed for Peru, landing there in 1532. He conquered the empire of Peru, executed Emperor Atahualpa, and in 1535 founded the city of Lima as the capital of Peru in place of the native capital Cuzco.

After his conquest of Peru, conflicts over terri-

Francisco Pizarro Bettmann Archive

torial jurisdiction developed, and in 1537 civil war broke out between Pizarro and Almagro. Pizarro's followers defeated those of Almagro in 1538, and Almagro was put to death. In 1541 a group still loyal to Almagro assassinated Pizarro.

PLACEBO, in medicine, an inert substance, such as sugar, that is used in place of an active drug. In testing new drugs, placebos are used to avoid bias. That is, in a blind test, patients do not know if they have been given the active drug or the placebo; in a double-blind test, physicians observing the results also do not know. Placebos may be administered to some patients who have incurable illnesses in order to induce the so-called placebo effect: an improvement, at least temporarily, of the patient's condition. In a 1955 study by the American anesthesiologist Henry Knowles Beecher (1904–76), the condition of 35 percent of more than 1000 patients tested was improved by administering placebos. Little is understood of how this effect works, but one theory is that the patient's faith in a cure may be related to the release of brain chemicals called endorphins, the body's natural opiates. The effect may be negative, however, if hopes have been raised too high.

PLACENTA. *See* Fetus.

PLACENTIA, city, Orange Co., SW California; inc. 1926. It is primarily a residential suburb of Los Angeles and has some industry. Aerospace concerns in the area are a major source of employment for the city's residents. The community, once part of Rancho San Juan Cajon de Santa Ana (a Mexican land grant of 1837), was laid out in 1910 and developed as a center for citrus production. Its main growth as a residential center began in the 1950s. Pop. (1980) 35,041; (1990) 41,259.

PLAGUE, term applied indiscriminately in the Middle Ages to all fatal epidemic diseases, but now restricted to an acute, infectious, contagious disease of rodents and humans, caused by a short, thick, gram-negative bacillus, *Yersina pestis.* In humans, plague occurs in three forms: bubonic plague, pneumonic plague, and septicemic plague. Bubonic plague is the best-known form and is so called because it is characterized by the appearance of buboes, or enlarged, inflamed lymph nodes, in the groin or armpit or on the neck. Bubonic plague is transmitted by the bite of any of numerous insects that are normally parasitic on rodents, and that seek new hosts when the original host dies. The most important of these insects is the rat flea *Xenopsylla cheopis,* which is parasitic on the brown rat. Pneumonic plague, so called because the lung is the site of infection, is most often transmitted by droplets sprayed from the lungs and mouth of infected persons; the infection may spread from the lungs to other parts of the body, resulting in septicemic plague, which is infection of the blood. Septicemic plague may also be initiated by direct contact of contaminated hands, food, or objects with the mucous membranes of the nose or throat.

Untreated bubonic plague is fatal in 30 to 75 percent of all cases, pneumonic plague 95 percent of the time, and septicemic plague almost invariably. Mortality in treated cases is 5 to 10 percent.

Symptoms. In bubonic plague, the first symptoms are headache, nausea, vomiting, aching joints, and a general feeling of ill health. The lymph nodes of the groin or, less commonly, of the armpit or neck, suddenly become painful and swollen. The temperature, accompanied by shivering, rises to between 38.3° and 40.5° C (101° and 105° F). The pulse rate and respiration rate are increased, and the victim becomes exhausted and apathetic. The buboes swell until they approximate a chicken egg in size. In nonfatal cases, the temperature begins to fall in about five days, and approaches normal in about two weeks. In fatal cases, death results in about four days. In primary pneumonic plague, the sputum is at first slimy and tinted with blood; it later becomes free-flowing and bright red. Death occurs in most cases two or three days after the first appearance of symptoms. In primary septicemic plague, the victim has a sudden onset of high fever and turns deep purple in several hours, often dying within the same day that symptoms first develop. The purple color, which appears in all plague victims during their last hours, is due to respiratory failure; the popular name Black Death that is applied to the disease is derived from this symptom.

Prevention and Treatment. Many preventive measures, such as sanitation, killing of rats, and prevention of the transport of rats in ships arriving from ports in which the disease is endemic, are effective in reducing the incidence of plague. Famine, which reduces resistance to the disease, results in spread of plague. Individuals who have contracted the disease are isolated, put to bed, and fed fluids and easily digestible foods. Sedatives are used to reduce pain and to quiet delirium. During World War II, scientists using sulfa drugs were able to produce cures of plague; subsequently, streptomycin and tetracyclines were found to be more effective in controlling the disease.

History. Plague has been known for at least 3000 years. Epidemics have been recorded in China since 224 BC. The disease occurred in huge pandemics that destroyed the entire populations of cities throughout the Middle Ages; they have occurred sporadically since that time. The last great pandemic began in China in 1894 and spread to Africa, the Pacific islands, Australia, and the Americas, reaching San Francisco in 1900. Plague still occurs in Asia, Africa, South America, and Australia, but rarely appears in the U.S. In 1950 the World Health Organization initiated sanitation programs for plague control throughout the world.

For further information on this topic, see the Bibliography in volume 28, sections 505, 508.

PLAICE. *See* FLOUNDER.

PLAIN, THE. *See* MOUNTAIN, THE.

PLAINFIELD, city, Union Co., NE New Jersey, on a plain (hence its name) near the Watchung Mts.; settled by Friends about 1684, inc. as a city 1869. It is the commercial hub of ten associated communities (including North Plainfield, South Plainfield, Piscataway, and Scotch Plains) and contains industries producing pharmaceuticals, telecommunications equipment, machine parts, and furniture. A branch of a community college is here. Points of interest are the Drake House (1745), which was George Washington's headquarters in 1777 and which now houses a museum, and a Friends' meeting house (1788). The Plainfield Symphony Orchestra has performed here since 1899. Pop. (1980) 45,555; (1990) 46,567.

PLAINS, city, Sumter Co., SW Georgia; inc. as a city 1975. Known as the home of former President Jimmy Carter, the city is a commercial and processing center for a farm region in which peanuts, soybeans, corn, and peaches are grown. The community, founded nearby in 1840 as The Plains of Dura (after the biblical region), was moved to its present location in the 1870s to meet the railroad. Pop. (1980) 651; (1990) 716.

PLAINS OF ABRAHAM, also Heights of Abraham, plateau, S Québec Province, in Québec City, overlooking the Saint Lawrence R. During the French and Indian War, it was (Sept. 13, 1759) the scene of a decisive victory by British troops over French forces. The plateau is named for a riverboat pilot, Abraham Martin (1587–1664), who owned part of the land. A portion of the battlefield is preserved as a national historic park.

PLAINSONG, liturgical chant used in the Roman Catholic church, more commonly called Gregorian chant. The term is sometimes used in a broader sense to denote all types of Christian and non-Christian chant. *See* CHANT.

PLAINVIEW, city, seat of Hale Co., NW Texas, in the S Great Plains; inc. 1907. It is a commercial and processing center for an irrigated agricultural region in which cotton, grain, and livestock are produced. Manufactures include packed meat, flour, and farm supplies. Wayland Baptist University (1908) and the Museum of the Llano Estacado, a regional historic museum, are here. The main development of the community, settled in 1886 and named for the uninterrupted view across the Great Plains, began with the coming of the railroad in 1907. Pop. (1980) 22,187; (1990) 21,700.

PLANCK, Max Karl Ernst Ludwig (1858–1947), German physicist and Nobel laureate, who was the originator of the quantum theory.

Planck was born in Kiel on April 23, 1858, and educated at the universities of Munich and Berlin. He was appointed professor of physics at the University of Kiel in 1885, and from 1889 until 1928 filled the same position at the University of Berlin. In 1900 Planck postulated that energy is radiated in small, discrete units, which he called quanta. Developing his quantum theory further, he discovered a universal constant of nature, which came to be known as Planck's constant. Planck's law states that the energy of each quantum is equal to the frequency of the radiation multiplied by the universal constant. His discoveries did not, however, supersede the theory that radiation from light or matter is emitted in waves. Physicists now believe that electromagnetic radiation combines the properties of both waves and particles. Planck's discoveries, which were later verified by other scientists, were the basis of an entirely new field of physics, known as quantum mechanics, and provided a foundation for research in such fields as atomic energy. *See* ATOM AND ATOMIC THEORY; QUANTUM THEORY.

Planck received many honors for his work, notably the 1918 Nobel Prize in physics. In 1930 Planck was elected president of the Kaiser Wilhelm Society for the Advancement of Science, the leading association of German scientists, which was later renamed the Max Planck Society.

Max Planck UPI

He endangered himself by openly criticizing the Nazi regime that came to power in Germany in 1933 and was forced out of the society, but became president again after World War II. He died at Göttingen on Oct. 4, 1947. Among his writings that have been translated into English are *Introduction to Theoretical Physics* (5 vol., 1932–33) and *Philosophy of Physics* (1936).

PLANCK'S CONSTANT, fundamental physical constant, symbol *h,* first discovered (1900) by the German physicist Max Planck. Until that year, light in all forms had been thought to consist of waves. Planck noticed certain deviations from the wave theory of light on the part of radiations emitted by so-called blackbodies, or perfect absorbers and emitters of radiation. He came to the conclusion that these radiations were emitted in discrete units of energy, called quanta. This conclusion was the first enunciation of the quantum theory. According to Planck, the energy of a quantum of light is equal to the frequency of the light multiplied by a constant. His original theory has since had abundant experimental verification, and the growth of the quantum theory has brought about a fundamental change in the physicist's concept of light and matter, both of which are now thought to combine the properties of waves and particles. Thus, Planck's constant has become as important to the investigation of particles of matter as to quanta of light, now called photons. The first successful measurement (1916) of Planck's constant was made by the American physicist Robert Millikan. The present accepted value of the constant is $h = 6.626 \times 10^{-34}$ joule-second in the meter-kilogram-second system.

PLANE GEOMETRY, branch of elementary geometry dealing with the metrical and nonmetrical properties of the plane and of two-dimensional figures, such as the triangle or the circle. This branch is also known as Euclidean geometry, after the Greek mathematician Euclid, who first studied the subject in the 4th century BC, and whose comprehensive treatise *Elements* remained authoritative until the rise of so-called non-Euclidean geometry in the 19th century.

PLANET, any of the nine major celestial bodies that orbit the sun and shine by reflecting its light. Smaller bodies that also have the sun as their primary—that is, are not satellites of a planet—are called asteroids or planetoids. *See* EARTH; JUPITER; MARS; MERCURY; NEPTUNE; PLUTO; SATURN; SOLAR SYSTEM; URANUS; VENUS.

For further information on this topic, see the Bibliography in volume 28, section 384.

PLANETARIUM, term applied to any model or representation of the solar system, or to an optical device used for projecting celestial images, but particularly applied to structures that house projection instruments and the screens on which the images are displayed. The most widely used instrument for many years has been the one devised in 1923 by the Carl Zeiss optical company of Germany. Dumbbell-shaped and mobile on a structural axis, it projects optical images of celestial bodies on a large hemispherical dome, producing an artificial night sky. The principal motions of celestial bodies are demonstrated by operation of projectors at different speeds corresponding to the relative speeds of those bodies as seen from earth. Supplementary projectors and mechanisms make possible a wide range of shows, such as planetary tours and the representation of unusual celestial phenomena. Besides the Zeiss, other projectors have been designed for various dome sizes and special purposes, including cathode-ray systems and laser-light displays.

The first planetarium erected in the U.S. was the Adler Planetarium in Chicago. Other important planetariums in the U.S. include the Hayden Planetarium in New York City, the Fels Planetarium in Philadelphia, and the Griffith Planetarium in Los Angeles. Currently there are more than 1000 small planetariums serving public and private school systems, museums, and cultural centers in the U.S.

PLANE TREE, common name for the plant family Platanaceae, of the order Hamamelidales (*see* WITCH HAZEL), comprising a small group of large deciduous trees widely planted as ornamentals because of their quick growth and attractive scaly bark. The family contains only one genus, *Platanus,* which in turn contains about seven species found throughout temperate regions of the northern hemisphere. The leaves are simple and palmately lobed, with the base of the petiole (leafstalk) swollen. The flowers are small and individually inconspicuous but are clustered into globose heads, or inflorescences; separate male and female flowers occur on the same tree. The female flower clusters mature into globe-shaped structures that consist of many tightly packed separate fruits, each containing one seed.

The best known and most widely distributed species is *P. occidentalis,* usually known as American sycamore or buttonwood. Its natural range is throughout the eastern U.S., with scattered populations in northern Mexico. Typically, it grows in wet, poorly drained soils along the floodplains of streams. Although the American sycamore is widely planted as a street tree, the London plane tree, *P. acerifolia,* a hybrid between American sycamore and the Oriental plane tree, *P. orientalis,* is more tolerant of urban conditions. It is similar to the American sycamore, but its fruit clusters are borne in pairs rather than singly. M.R.C.

For further information on this topic, see the Bibliography in volume 28, sections 456, 675.

PLANK, Eddie, full name EDWARD STEWART PLANK (1875–1926), American professional baseball player, born in Gettysburg, Pa., and educated at Gettysburg College. Plank was one of the greatest left-handed pitchers in the history of baseball. He became a member of the Philadelphia Athletics of the American League immediately upon his graduation from college in 1901 and played with that team until 1915. In 1915 he played with the Saint Louis team of the Federal League, and from 1916 to 1918 with the Saint Louis Browns of the American League. He won 20 or more games a year eight times during his career. He took part in 623 games as a pitcher, winning 325 and losing 190, for a percentage of .631. Plank was elected to the Baseball Hall of Fame in 1946.

PLANKTON, collective term for a variety of marine and freshwater organisms that drift on or near the surface of the water. Their movement depends largely on tides, currents, and winds, because they are too small or weak to swim against the currents. That component of the plankton comprising bacteria and microscopic algae and fungi is called the phytoplankton. Important algal groups in the phytoplankton include diatoms, golden algae, green algae, and blue-green algae. The other component of the plankton, the zooplankton, comprises protozoa and small crustaceans, jellyfish, worms, and mollusks, together with the eggs and larvae of the many animal species inhabiting marine and fresh waters. Important protozoan groups in the zooplankton are dinoflagellates and foraminifera.

The density of plankton varies, depending on the availability of nutrients and the stability of the water. A liter of lake water may contain more than 500 million planktonic organisms. Marine plankton occasionally becomes so numerous that the organisms color the water; such sudden population increases are called tides. The so-called red tides are caused by billions of dinoflagellates of various species; such tides are sometimes dangerous, because they can poison both humans and fish. Red tides have occurred off the west coast of Florida and in the coastal waters of New England, southern California, Texas, Peru, eastern Australia, Chile, and Japan. In 1946 such a tide killed fish, turtles, oysters, and other marine organisms in the Gulf of Mexico near Fort Myers, Fla. The blue-green alga *Trichodesmus* sometimes, in dying off, imparts a reddish color to water; the Red Sea is so named because of this.

An estimated 90 percent of all photosynthesis and release of free oxygen takes place in the oceans. Marine phytoplankton is the first link in the vast aquatic food chain. The zooplankton, which feeds on the phytoplankton, is consumed in turn by larger animals such as fish and even by the largest mammal, the blue whale. The high protein content of plankton has stimulated research on it as a potential food source for humans.

See also MARINE LIFE.

For further information on this topic, see the Bibliography in volume 28, sections 448, 457, 464.

PLANNED ECONOMY, economic system in which the production and distribution of the wealth of a country are entirely or mainly controlled by the government. Formerly, the planned economy was essentially a theoretical concept advocated by Socialists, collectivists, and economic reformers. The first government to institute a planned economy was that of the USSR, which, in 1928, prepared its first five-year plan. After World War II planned economies were instituted by the Soviet satellite states.

PLANNED PARENTHOOD FEDERATION OF AMERICA, INC., also known as Planned Parenthood-World Population, U.S. organization dedicated to the principle that each individual has the right to decide when or whether to have a child. Known originally as the American Birth Control League, the organization was founded in 1921 by the American birth-control advocate Margaret Sanger to disseminate knowledge concerning contraception and to promote the distribution of contraceptive devices.

Now the largest network of voluntary family-planning providers in the U.S., the agency's 180 affiliates operate more than 800 clinics, providing contraceptive, abortion, and sterilization services; pregnancy testing and counseling; diagnosis and treatment of sexually transmitted diseases; and referrals for infertility and adoption. Planned Parenthood annually serves nearly 4 million Americans, many with marginal or low incomes. Through its Family Planning International Assistance division, the organization helps meet the family-planning needs of about 4 million people in the developing world.

Planned Parenthood Federation of America is a founding member and the U.S. affiliate of the International Planned Parenthood Federation, established in 1953. Headquarters of the international organization is in London; that of the American organization is in New York City.

PLANO, city, Collin and Denton counties, NE Texas, near Dallas; inc. as a city 1961. Situated in the blackland prairie, it is a commercial and manufacturing center; products include elec-

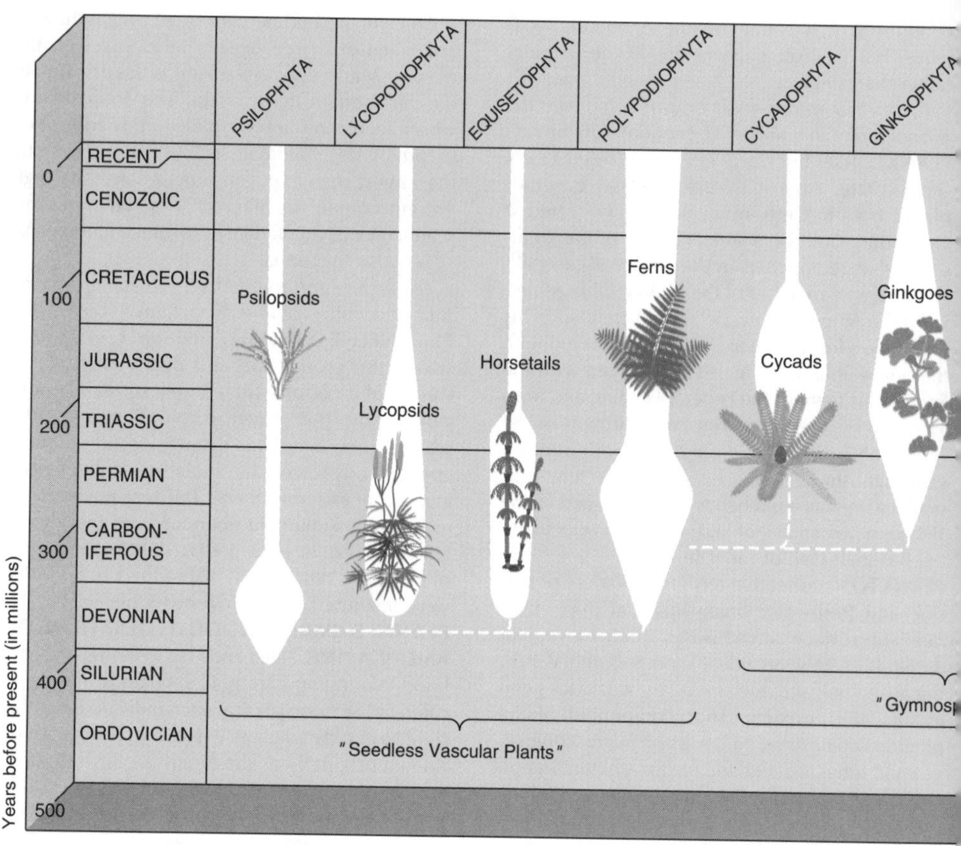

tronic, computer, and telecommunications equipment; brass items; compact disks; copper and aluminum wire; lighting fixtures; and printed materials. Several companies have corporate headquarters here. Pioneer cemeteries, the site of an Indian massacre (1844), and the Ammie Wilson House (1891), formerly part of a sheep farm and now a museum, are in the city. The community, settled in the 1840s, developed as a small agricultural center after the coming of the railroad in 1872. Its main growth began in the 1960s and accelerated in the '70s, when it annexed much territory. The city's name, chosen in 1850, was thought (incorrectly) to be Spanish for "plain," a reference to its geographical setting. Pop. (1980) 72,331; (1990) 128,713.

PLANT, any member of the kingdom Plantae, comprising about 260,000 known species of mosses, liverworts, ferns, herbaceous and woody plants, bushes, vines, trees, and various other forms that mantle the earth and are also found in its waters. Plants range in size and complexity from small, nonvascular mosses, which depend on direct contact with surface water, to giant redwood trees, the largest living organisms, which can draw water and minerals through their vascular systems to elevations of more than 100 m (more than 330 ft).

KINGDOM: PLANTAE

PHYLUM OR DIVISION

- **Bryophyta (mosses)**
- **Marchantiophyta (liverworts)**
- **Anthocerophyta (hornworts)**
- **Psilophyta (whisk ferns)**
- **Lycopodiophyta (club mosses)**
- **Equisetophyta (horsetails)**
- **Polypodiophyta (ferns)**
- **Cycadophyta (cycads)**
- **Ginkgophyta (ginkgoes)**
- **Pinophyta (conifers)**
- **Gnetophyta (gnetophytes)**
- **Magnoliophyta (flowering plants)**
  - **Class:**
    - **Magnoliopsida (dicots)**
    - **Liliopsida (monocots)**

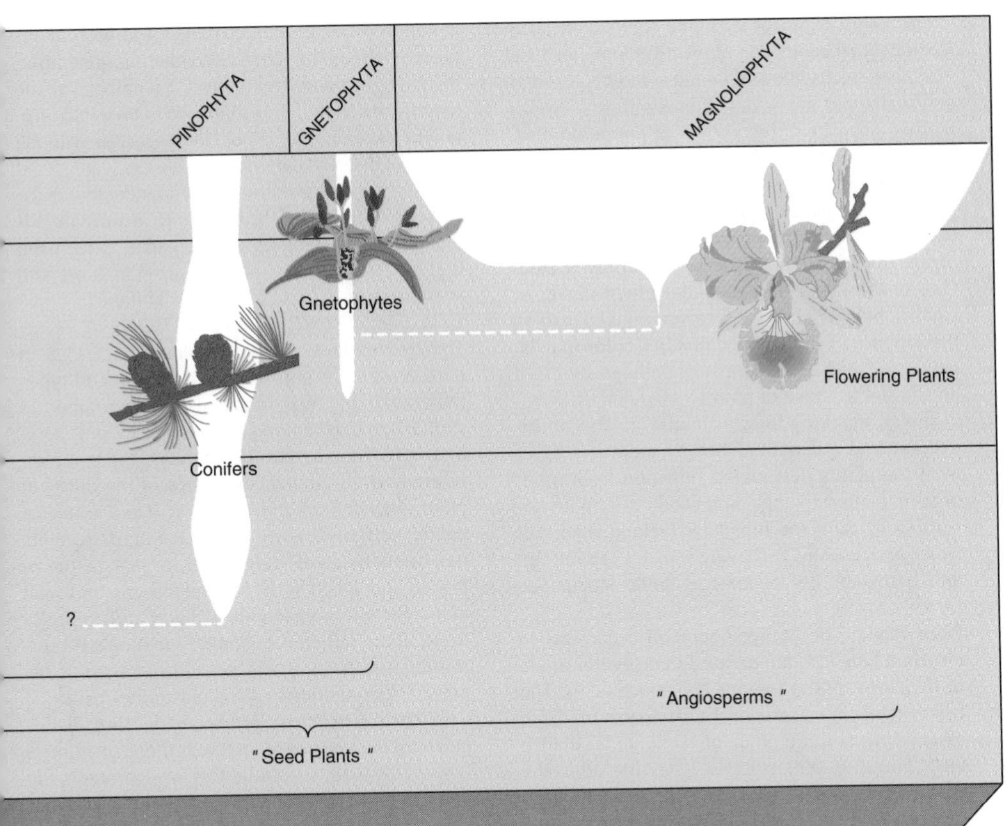

The evolution of tracheophytes, which encompass nine phyla of plants that have well-developed vascular systems. Dashed lines show probable evolutionary relationships, and widths of white areas indicate relative abundances of groups.

Only a tiny percentage of plant species are directly used by humans for food, shelter, fiber, and drugs. At the head of the list are rice, wheat, corn, legumes, cotton, conifers, and tobacco, on which whole economies and nations depend. Of even greater importance to humans are the indirect benefits reaped from the entire plant kingdom and its more than 3 billion years of carrying out photosynthesis (q.v.). Plants have laid down the fossil fuels that provide power for industrial society, and throughout their long history plants have supplied sufficient oxygen to the atmosphere to support the evolution of higher animals. Today the world's biomass is composed overwhelmingly of plants, which not only underpin all food webs (*see* FOOD WEB) but also modify climates and create and hold down soil, making what would otherwise be stony, sandy masses habitable for life.

Differentiation from Other Kingdoms. Plants are multicellular green organisms; their cells contain eukaryotic (nucleated) protoplasm held within more or less rigid cell walls composed primarily of cellulose (q.v.). The most important characteristic of plants is their ability to photosynthesize—that is, to make their own food by converting light energy into chemical energy—a process carried out in the green, chlorophyll-containing plastids (cellular organelles) called chloroplasts (*see* CHLOROPHYLL; CHLOROPLAST). A few plants have lost their chlorophyll and have become saprophytic or parasitic in nutrition—that is, they absorb their food from dead organic matter or living organic matter, respectively—but details of their structure show that they are evolved plant forms.

Fungi (q.v.), also eukaryotic and long considered members of the plant kingdom, have now been placed in a separate kingdom because they lack chlorophyll and plastids and because their rigid cell walls contain chitin rather than cellulose. Fungi do not manufacture their own food; instead they absorb it from either dead or living organic matter.

The various groups of algae (q.v.) were also formerly placed in the plant kingdom because many are eukaryotic and because most have rigid cell walls and carry out photosynthesis. Nonetheless, because of the variety of pigment types, cell wall types, and morphological expression found in the algae, they are now recognized as part of two separate kingdoms, Monera and Protista, containing a diversity of plantlike and other organisms that are not necessarily closely related. One of the phyla of algae—the green algae, or Chlorophyta—is believed to have given rise to the kingdom Plantae, because its chlorophylls, cell walls, and other details of cellular structure are similar to those of plants.

The animal kingdom, Animalia, is also multicellular and eukaryotic, but its members differ from the plants in deriving nutrition from other organic matter; by ingesting food rather than absorbing it, as in the fungi; by lacking rigid cell walls; and, usually, by having sensory capabilities and being motile, at least at some stage. *See* CLASSIFICATION.

Plant Phyla. The many species of organisms in the plant kingdom are divided into several phyla or divisions totaling about 260,000 species. The bryophytes (q.v.) are a diverse polyphyletic assemblage of three phyla of nonvascular plants, with about 16,000 species, that includes the mosses (q.v.), liverworts (*see* LIVERWORT), and hornworts. Bryophytes lack a well-developed vascular system for the internal conduction of water and nutrients and have been called nonvascular plants. The familiar leafy plant of bryophytes is the sexual, or gamete-producing, generation of the life cycle of these organisms. Because of the lack of a vascular system and because the gametes require a film of water for dispersal, bryophytes are generally small plants that tend to occur in moist conditions, although some attain large size under favorable circumstances and others (usually very small) are adapted to desert life.

The other phyla are collectively termed vascular plants or tracheophytes, (historically Tracheophyta). Vascular tissue is internal conducting tissue for the movement of water, minerals, and food. There are two types of vascular tissue: xylem, which conducts water and minerals from the ground to stems and leaves, and phloem, which conducts food produced in the leaves to the stems, roots, and storage and reproductive organs. Besides the presence of vascular tissue, tracheophytes contrast with bryophytes in that tracheophyte leafy plants are the asexual, or spore-producing, generation of their life cycle. In the evolution of tracheophytes, the spore-producing generation became much larger and more complex, whereas the gamete-producing generation became reduced and merely contained in the sporophyte tissue. This ability to evolve into larger and more diverse sporophytes, together with the ability of the vascular system to elevate water, freed tracheophytes from direct dependence on surface water. They were thus able to dominate all the terrestrial habitats of the earth, except the higher arctic zones, and to provide food and shelter for its diverse animal inhabitants.

CELL STRUCTURE AND FUNCTION

The tremendous variety of plant species is, in part, a reflection of the many distinct cell types that make up individual plants. Fundamental similarities exist among all these cell types, however, and these similarities indicate the common origin and the interrelationships of the different plant species. Each individual plant cell is at least partly self-sufficient, being isolated from its neighbors by a cell membrane, or plasma membrane, and a cell wall. The membrane and wall allow the individual cell to carry out its functions; at the same time, communication with surrounding cells is made possible through cytoplasmic connections called plasmodesmata.

Cell Wall. The most important feature distinguishing the cells of plants from those of animals is the cell wall. In plants this wall protects the cellular contents and limits cell size. It also has important structural and physiological roles in the life of the plant, being involved in transport, absorption, and secretion.

A plant's cell wall is composed of several chemicals, of which cellulose (made up of molecules of the sugar glucose) is the most important. Cellulose molecules are united into fibrils, which form the structural framework of the wall. Other important constituents of many cell walls are lignins, which add rigidity, and waxes, such as cutin and suberin, which reduce water loss from cells. Many plant cells produce both a primary cell wall, while the cell is growing, and a secondary cell wall, laid down inside the primary wall after growth has ceased. Plasmodesmata penetrate both primary and secondary cell walls, providing pathways for transporting substances.

Protoplast. Within the cell wall are the living contents of the cell, called the protoplast. These contents are bounded by a single, three-layered cell membrane. The protoplast contains the cytoplasm, which in turn contains various membrane-bound organelles and vacuoles and the nucleus, which is the hereditary unit of the cell.

Vacuoles. Vacuoles are membrane-bound cavities filled with cell sap, which is made up mostly of water containing various dissolved sugars,

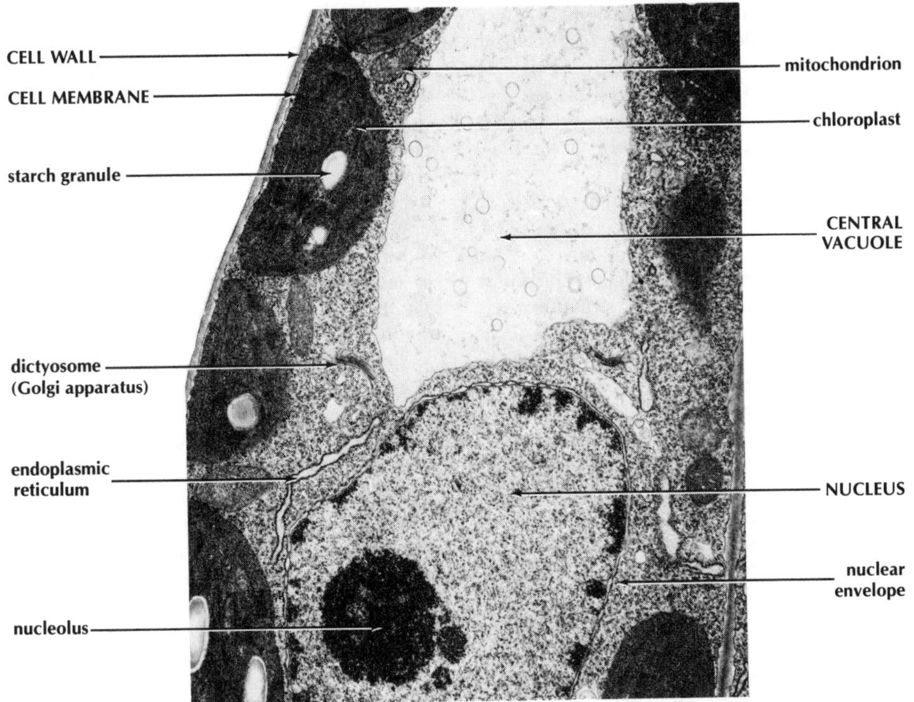

Main parts of the plant cell. Shown is a tomato-leaf cell, magnified 19,300 times. Chloroplasts are found in all photosynthetic cells. Brookhaven National Laboratory

salts, and other chemicals. Vacuoles are not found in animal cells.

Plastids. Plastids are organelles—specialized cellular parts that are analogous to organs—bounded by two membranes. Three kinds of plastids are important here. Chloroplasts contain chlorophylls and carotenoid pigments; they are the site of photosynthesis, the process in which light energy from the sun is fixed as chemical energy in the bonds of various carbon compounds. Leucoplasts, which contain no pigments, are involved in the synthesis of starch, oils, and proteins. Chromoplasts manufacture carotenoids.

Mitochondria. Whereas plastids are involved in various ways in storing energy, another class of cellular organelles, the mitochondria, are the sites of respiration. This process involves the transfer of chemical energy from carbon-containing compounds to adenosine triphosphate (q.v.), or ATP, the chief energy source for cells. The transfer takes place in three stages: glycolysis (in which acids are produced from carbohydrates), the Krebs cycle (*see* CITRIC ACID CYCLE), and electron transfer. Like plastids, mitochondria are bounded by two membranes, of which the inner one is extensively folded; the folds serve as the surfaces on which the respiratory reactions take place.

Ribosomes, Golgi apparatus, and endoplasmic reticulum. Two other important cellular contents are the ribosomes, the sites at which amino acids (q.v.) are linked together to form proteins, and the Golgi apparatus, which plays a role in the secretion of materials from cells. In addition, a complex membrane system called the endoplasmic reticulum runs through much of the cytoplasm and appears to function as a communication system; various kinds of cellular substances are channeled through it from place to place. Ribosomes are often connected to the endoplasmic reticulum, which is continuous with the double membrane surrounding the nucleus of the cell.

Nucleus. The nucleus controls the ongoing functions of the cell by specifying which proteins are produced. It also stores and passes on genetic information to future generations of cells during cell division. *See* CELL.

TISSUE SYSTEMS

There are many variants of the generalized plant cell and its parts. Similar kinds of cells are organized into structural and functional units, or tissues, which make up the plant as a whole, and new cells (and tissues) are formed at growing points of actively dividing cells. These growing points, called meristems, are located either at the stem and root tips (apical meristems), where they are responsible for the primary growth of plants, or laterally in stems and roots (lateral meristems), where they are responsible for secondary plant growth. Three tissue systems are recognized in vascular plants: dermal, vascular, and ground (or fundamental).

Dermal System. The dermal system consists of the epidermis, or outermost layer, of the plant body. It forms the skin of the plant, covering the leaves, flowers, roots, fruits, and seeds. Epidermal cells vary greatly in function and structure.

The epidermis may contain stomata, openings through which gases are exchanged with the atmosphere. These openings are surrounded by specialized cells called guard cells, which, through changes in their size and shape, alter the size of the stomatal openings and thus regulate the gas exchange. The epidermis is covered with a waxy coating called the cuticle, which functions as a waterproofing layer and thus reduces water loss from the plant surface through evaporation. If the plant undergoes secondary growth—growth that increases the diameter of roots and stems through the activity of lateral meristems—the epidermis is replaced by a peridermis made up of heavily waterproofed cells (mainly cork tissue) that are dead at maturity.

Vascular System. The vascular tissue system consists of two kinds of conducting tissues: the xylem, responsible for conduction of water and dissolved mineral nutrients, and the phloem, responsible for conduction of food. The xylem also stores food and helps support the plant.

Xylem. The xylem consists of two types of conducting cells: tracheids and vessels. Elongated cells, with tapered ends and secondary walls, both types lack cytoplasm and are dead at maturity. The walls have pits—areas in which secondary thickening does not occur—through which water moves from cell to cell. Vessels usually are shorter and broader than tracheids, and in addition to pits they have perforation—areas of the cell wall that lack both primary and secondary thickenings and through which water and dissolved nutrients may freely pass.

Phloem. The phloem, or food-conducting tissue, consists of cells that are living at maturity. The principal cells of phloem, the sieve elements, are so called because of the clusters of pores in their walls through which the protoplasts of adjoining cells are connected. Two types of sieve elements occur: sieve cells, with narrow pores in rather uniform clusters on the cell walls, and sieve-tube members, with larger pores on some walls of the cell than on others. Although the sieve elements contain cytoplasm at maturity, the nucleus and other organelles are lacking. Associated with the sieve elements are companion cells that do contain nuclei and that are responsible for manufacturing and secreting substances into the sieve elements and removing waste products from them.

Embryo enclosed in seed of the shepherd's purse, Capsella bursapastoris, *a dicot. The two seed leaves are well developed.* **Walker England–Photo Researchers, Inc.**

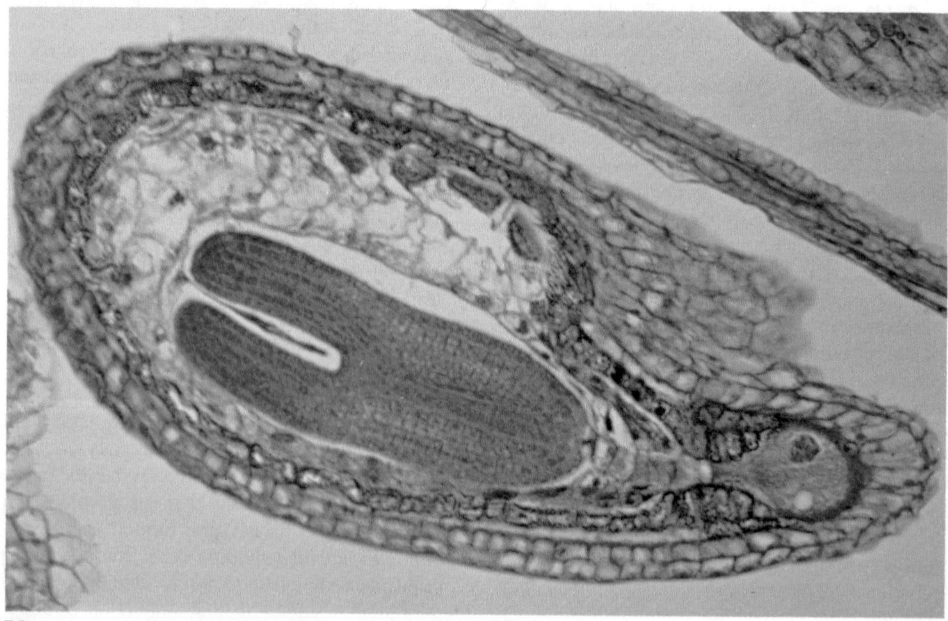

The redwoods that grow along parts of the Pacific coast of North America are the largest single organisms ever known to have lived. The vascular systems of these giants can draw nutrients up to heights of more than 100 m (330 ft).
Clyde H. Smith–Peter Arnold, Inc.

Ground System. The ground, or fundamental, tissue systems of plants consist of three types of tissue. The first, called parenchyma, is found throughout the plant and is living and capable of cell division at maturity. Usually only primary walls are present, and these are uniformly thickened. The cells of parenchyma tissue carry out many specialized physiological functions—for example, photosynthesis, storage, secretion, and wound healing. They also occur in the xylem and phloem tissues.

Collenchyma, the second type of ground tissue, is also living at maturity and is made up of cells with unevenly thickened primary cell walls. Collenchyma tissue is pliable and functions as support tissue in young, growing portions of plants.

Sclerenchyma tissue, the third type, consists of cells that lack protoplasts at maturity and that have thick secondary walls usually containing lignin. Sclerenchyma tissue is important in supporting and strengthening those portions of plants that have finished growing.

PLANT ORGANS

The body of a vascular plant is organized into three general kinds of organs: roots, stems, and leaves. These organs all contain the three kinds of tissue systems mentioned above, but they differ in the way the cells are specialized to carry out different functions.

Roots. The function of roots is to anchor the plant to its substrate and to absorb water and minerals. Thus, roots are generally found underground and grow downward, or in the direction of gravity. Unlike stems, they have no leaves or nodes. The epidermis is just behind the growing tip of roots and is covered with root hairs, which are outgrowths of the epidermal cells. The root hairs increase the surface area of the roots and serve as the surface through which water and nutrients are absorbed.

Internally, roots consist largely of xylem and phloem, although many are highly modified to carry out specialized functions. Thus, some roots are important food and storage organs—for example, beets, carrots, and radishes. Such roots have an abundance of parenchyma tissue. Many tropical trees have aerial prop roots that serve to hold the stem in an upright position. Epiphytes (*see* EPIPHYTE) have roots modified for quick absorption of rainwater that flows over the bark of the host plants.

Roots increase in length through the activity of apical meristems and in diameter through the activity of lateral meristems. Branch roots originate internally at some distance behind the growing tip, when certain cells become meristematic.

Stems. Stems usually are above ground, grow upward, and bear leaves, which are attached in a regular pattern at nodes along the stem. The portions of the stem between nodes are called internodes. Stems increase in length through the activity of an apical meristem at the stem tip.

This growing point also gives rise to new leaves, which surround and protect the stem tip, or apical bud, before they expand. Apical buds of deciduous trees, which lose their leaves during part of the year, are usually protected by modified leaves called bud scales.

Stems are more variable in external appearance and internal structure than are roots, but they also consist of the three tissue systems and have several features in common. Vascular tissue is present in bundles that run the length of the stem, forming a continuous network with the vascular tissue in the leaves and the roots. The vascular tissue of herbaceous plants is surrounded by parenchyma tissue, whereas the stems of woody plants consist mostly of hard xylem tissue. Stems increase in diameter through the activity of lateral meristems, which produce the bark and wood in woody plants. The bark, which also contains the phloem, serves as a protective outer covering, preventing damage and water loss.

Within the plant kingdom are many modifications of the basic stem, such as the thorns of hawthorns. Climbing stems, such as the tendrils of grapes and Boston ivy, have special modifications that allow them to grow up and attach to their substrate. Many plants have reduced leaves or no leaves at all, and their stems act as the photosynthetic surface (*see* CACTUS). Some stems creep along the surface of the ground and serve to reproduce the plants through vegetative means; many grasses reproduce in this way (*see* VEGETATIVE REPRODUCTION). Other stems are borne underground and serve as food-storage organs, often allowing the plant to survive through the winter; the so-called bulbs of tulips and crocus are examples.

Leaves. Leaves are the primary photosynthetic organs of most plants. They usually are flattened blades that consist, internally, mostly of parenchyma tissue called the mesophyll, which is made up of loosely arranged cells with spaces between them. The spaces are filled with air, from which the cells absorb carbon dioxide and into which they expel oxygen. The mesophyll is bounded by the upper and lower surface of the leaf blade, which is covered by epidermal tissue. A vascular network runs through the mesophyll, providing the cell walls with water and removing the food products of photosynthesis to other parts of the plants.

The leaf blade is connected to the stem through a narrowed portion called the petiole, or

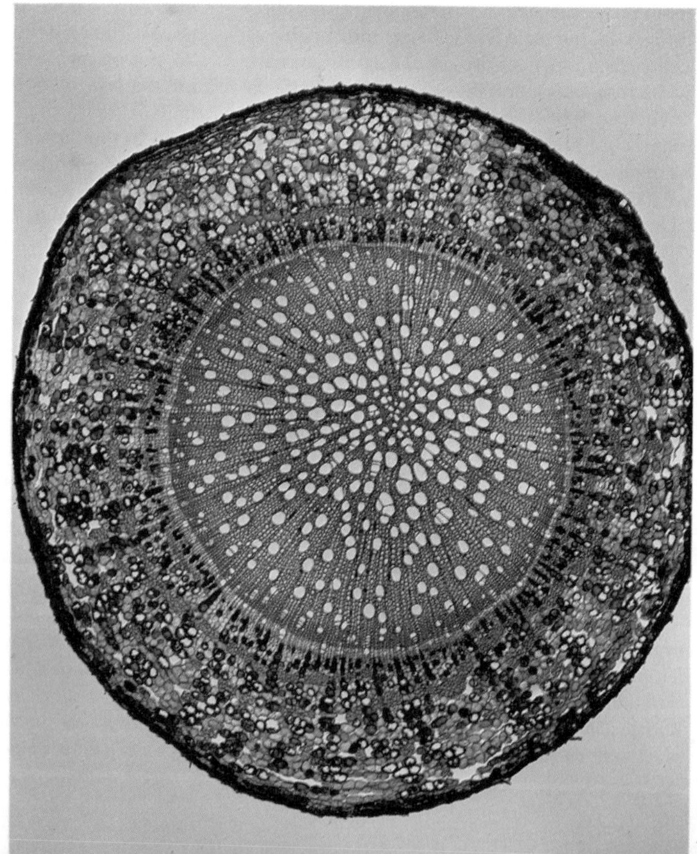

This cross section of a tree that is one year old reveals the central heartwood of dead supporting tissue surrounded by the living tissue, or sapwood, both of which are mainly xylem. The whole is surrounded by the vascular cambium and the protective bark, which contains the phloem.

Manfred Kage–Peter Arnold, Inc.

As with all bryophytes, or nonvascular plants, moss's leafy form is the sexual generation in its life cycle. Keith Gunnar–Bruce Coleman, Inc.

stalk, which consists mostly of vascular tissue. Appendages called stipules are often present at the base of the petiole.

Many specialized forms of leaves occur. Some are modified as spines, which help protect plants from predators. Certain groups of plants possess highly modified leaves that trap and digest insects, providing needed nutrients (*see* INSECTIVOROUS PLANTS). Some leaves are brightly colored and petallike, serving to attract pollinators to otherwise small, unattractive flowers; *Poinsettia* (*see* SPURGE) is a good example. Perhaps the most highly modified leaves are flowers themselves. The individual parts of flowers—carpels, stamens, petals, and sepals—are all modified leaves that have taken on reproductive functions. *See* FLOWER.

GROWTH AND DIFFERENTIATION

The growth and differentiation of the various plant tissue and organ systems are controlled by various internal and external factors.

Hormones. Plant hormones, specialized chemical substances produced by plants, are the main internal factors controlling growth and development (*see* HORMONE). Hormones are produced in one part of a plant and transported to others, where they are effective in very small amounts. Depending on the target tissue, a given hormone may have different effects. Thus, auxin, one of the most important plant hormones, is produced by growing stem tips and transported to other areas where it may either promote growth or inhibit it. In stems, for example, auxin promotes cell elongation and the differentiation of vascular tissue, whereas in roots it inhibits growth in the main system but promotes the formation of adventitious roots. It also retards the abscission (dropping off) of flowers, fruits, and leaves.

Gibberellins are other important plant-growth hormones; more than 50 kinds are known. They control the elongation of stems, and they cause the germination of some grass seeds by initiating the production of enzymes that break down starch into sugars to nourish the plant embryo. Cytokinins promote the growth of lateral buds, acting in opposition to auxin; they also promote bud formation. In addition, plants produce the gas ethylene (q.v.) through the partial decomposition of certain hydrocarbons, and ethylene in turn regulates fruit maturation and abscission.

Tropisms. Various external factors, often acting together with hormones, are also important in plant growth and development. One important class of responses to external stimuli is that of the tropisms—responses that cause a change in the direction of a plant's growth. Examples are phototropism, the bending of a stem toward light, and geotropism, the response of a stem or root to gravity. Stems are negatively geotropic, growing away from gravity, whereas roots are positively geotropic (*see* TROPISM). Photoperiodism, the response to 24-hour cycles of dark and light, is particularly important in the initiation of flowering. Some plants are short-day, flowering only when periods of light are less than a certain length (*see* BIOLOGICAL CLOCKS). Other variables—both internal, such as the age of the plant, and external, such as temperature—are also involved with the complex beginnings of flowering.

ECOLOGY

Rooted as they are in the ground, plants are commonly thought of as leading sedentary, vegetative, passive lives. A look, however, at the ingeniously developed interactions that plants have with their biological surroundings quickly corrects this notion.

Cooperation and Competition. Many plant species exist as separate male and female plants, and pollen from male flowers must reach the female flowers in order for pollination (q.v.) and seed development to take place (*see* SEED). The agent of pollination is sometimes the wind (a part of the physical environment), but in many cases it is an insect, bat, or bird (members of the biological environment). Plants may also rely on agents for dispersing their seed. Thus, after pollination, cherry trees develop cherries that attract birds, which ingest the fruit and excrete the cherry stones in more distant terrains.

Plants have evolved many other mutually beneficial relationships, such as the nitrogen-fixing bacteria that occur in the nodules on the roots of legumes. Many prairie grasses and other plants that flourish on open land depend on various herbivores to keep forests from closing in and shading them.

In the competition among plants for light, many species have evolved such mechanisms as leaf shape, crown shape, and increased height in order to intercept the sun's rays. In addition, many plants produce chemical substances that inhibit the germination or establishment of seeds of other species near them, thus excluding competing species from mineral resources as well as light. Walnut species, for example, use such an allelopathy, or chemical inhibition.

The Food Web. Because plants are autotrophic organisms—that is, they are able to manufacture their own food—they lie at the very foundation of the food web. Heterotrophic organisms (organisms that cannot manufacture their own food) usually lead less sedentary lives than plants, but they ultimately depend on autotrophs as sources of food. Plants are first fed upon by primary consumers, or herbivores, which in turn are fed upon by secondary consumers, or carnivores. Decomposers act upon all levels of the food web. A large portion of energy is lost at each step in the food web; only about 10 percent of the energy in one level is stored by the next. Thus, most food webs contain only a few steps.

Plants and Humans. From the prehistoric beginnings of agriculture until recent times, only a few of the total plant species have been taken from the wild and refined to become primary sources of food, fiber, shelter, and drugs. This process of plant cultivation and breeding began largely by accident, possibly as the seeds of wild fruits and vegetables, gathered near human habitations, sprouted and were crudely cultivated. Plants such as wheat, *Triticum aestivum,* which possibly originated in the eastern Mediterranean region more than 9000 years ago, were selected and replanted year after year for their superior food value; today many domesticated plants can scarcely be traced back to their wild ancestors or to the original plant communities in which they originated. This selective process took place with no prior knowledge of plant breeding but, rather, through the constant and close familiarity that preindustrial humans had with plants.

Today, however, the human relationship with plants is nearly reversed: An increasing majority of people have little or no contact with plant cultivation, and the farmers that do have such contact are becoming more and more specialized in single crops. The breeding process, on the other hand, has been greatly accelerated, largely through advances in genetics. Plant geneticists are now able to develop, in only a few years, such plant strains as wind-resistant corn, thus greatly increasing crop yields.

At the same time, humans have accelerated the demand for food and energy to the extent that entire species and ecosystems of plants are being destroyed before scientists can take proper inventory of the world's plant populations or develop an understanding of which plant species have the potential to benefit humanity. Most species remain little known; those that seem to offer the greatest hope exist in tropical areas where rapidly growing human populations can quickly reduce the land to arid, sandy wastes. A basic knowledge of plants is important in its own right, but it is also useful in attempting to solve many of the problems facing the human world today. *See* AGRICULTURE; FOOD SUPPLY, WORLD.

See also DICOTS; DISEASES OF PLANTS; FRUIT; MONOCOTS; NUT; PLANT BREEDING; PLANT DISTRIBUTION; PLANT PROPAGATION; POISONOUS PLANTS; and articles on major plant groups.

M.R.C. & P.H.R.

For further information on this topic, see the Bibliography in volume 28, sections 451–56.

PLANTAGENET, surname, originally nickname, of the English royal house of Anjou (q.v.) or the Angevin dynasty, founded by Geoffrey IV, count of Anjou (1113–51), husband of Matilda (1102–67), daughter of King Henry I of England. The name is derived from the Latin *planta* ("sprig") and *genista* ("broom plant"), in reference to the sprig that Geoffrey always wore in his cap. Reigning from 1154 to 1485, the Plantagenet kings, in the main line of descent, were Henry II, Richard I,

John, Henry III, Edward I, Edward II, Edward III, and Richard II; through the house of Lancaster, Henry IV, Henry V, and Henry VI; and through the house of York, Edward IV, Edward V, and Richard III.

PLANTAIN, common name applied to plants of the family Plantaginaceae, primarily natives of temperate regions. Plantains bear regular flowers, usually in elongated spikes. The calyx and corolla are each four-partite, and the petals are usually chaffy; the four stamens have long, threadlike filaments. Important genera include *Plantago, Littorella,* and *Bougueria.* Plantaginaceae constitutes the order Plantaginales, a dicot (*see* DICOTS) member of the division Magnoliophyta (*see* ANGIOSPERM).

The name plantain is also applied to a large-fruited, starchy variety of banana (q.v.), which belongs to a different order.

PLANTATION, city, Broward Co., SE Florida, near the South New River Canal; inc. 1953. It is primarily a residential suburb of Fort Lauderdale and has some light industry. The Everglades and a Seminole Indian reservation are in the vicinity. The community experienced a period of rapid growth in the 1960s and '70s. Pop. (1980) 48,653; (1990) 66,692.

PLANTATION, originally, a self-contained settlement or estate in the American South on which staple crops, chiefly cotton and tobacco, were planted by laborers or slaves. The first colonial plantations were established by farmers in the 17th century. At first they employed indentured white labor for growing tobacco. After the importation of black slaves into Virginia in 1619, the growth of plantations became inextricably connected with slavery (q.v.). The plantation system spread quickly from the eastern seaboard to the deep South in the 19th century after Eli Whitney invented (1793) the cotton gin. Large, often elegant, plantations growing cotton, sugar, tobacco, rice, and hemp flourished until the American Civil War and the emancipation of slaves in 1863. Exploitation of sharecroppers and laborers on so-called free-labor plantations continued, however, under a soil-exhausting, one-crop system. Since the 1930s federal programs, mechanization, and growing urbanization have made the institution of the plantation obsolete. The term is still used for large tropical farms with hired labor, particularly in South America, on which sugar-cane, cacao, rubber, coffee, cotton, and fruit are grown.

See AGRICULTURE; BLACKS IN THE AMERICAS.

PLANT BREEDING, the practical application of genetic principles (*see* GENETICS) to the development of improved strains of agricultural and horticultural crops. Plant breeders can adapt old crops to new areas and uses; increase yields; improve resistance to disease; enhance the nutritional quality and flavor of fruits and vegetables; and develop traits that are useful for storage, shipping, and processing of foods. Improved wheat and rice varieties sparked the green revolution in the developing world during the 1960s and '70s. In ornamental plants, breeders have developed larger and showier flowers, greater plant vigor, and myriad types, shapes, and colors.

History. Stone Age farmers improved crops through selection, choosing at each harvest the largest seeds from the best plants for sowing the following year. In so doing, over thousands of years, they converted favored wild grass and legume species into such crops as corn, wheat, and soybeans. In the 18th and 19th centuries farmers attempted to speed up crop improvement. Some advances were made, partly through selection and partly through trial and error, such as in the procedures used by the American horticulturist Luther Burbank. Through the work of Gregor Mendel, Hugo De Vries, and others, the development of the science of genetics at the beginning of the 20th century established a firm scientific base for plant breeding. Since that time it has continued to develop in both sophistication and accomplishments, enabling professional plant breeders to achieve predictable results and uniform quality.

Plant breeders use numerous methods to develop new varieties, but their primary techniques of development are selection, hybridization, and the use of mutations.

Selection. Individuals within a species vary widely in a number of characteristics. Many of these traits are heritable and can be passed on to their progeny. In practicing selection, plant breeders choose plants with desirable traits for further propagation and discard plants that are inferior for that trait. By doing so, plant breeders can select and reselect for the trait through successive generations, shifting the population in the desired direction.

Hybridization. Hybridization involves crossing plants of different strains or types to join in the progeny the desirable traits of both parents. Undesirable traits also enter the combination, however, so hybridization is usually followed by several generations of selection. This allows breeders to discard undesirable plants, choosing for further propagation only those plants with the desired combination of traits.

Backcrossing is a common variation on hybridization. This technique is often used to transfer into a desirable variety a beneficial trait from an otherwise undesirable parent. First the hybrid between the two parents is made; then the hybrid is crossed with the desirable parent. The progeny from this backcrossing normally segregate widely, with individual plants showing a mixture of the characteristics of both parents. By continued backcrossing and selection the plant breeder concentrates the qualities desired, and, if all goes well, in six or seven generations the variety once again breeds true but now exhibits its new trait. Backcrossing is valuable for adding single gene characteristics to crop plants, particularly for resistance to specific insects and diseases.

When desirable characteristics are fully developed in a hybrid plant, and the plant can be propagated asexually by budding, grafting, or cloning, then no further selection is necessary. A hybrid apple, for example, is propagated by grafting, so all resultant plants are identical.

Hybrids are often more vigorous than either parent. This phenomenon is called hybrid vigor and has been widely used by plant breeders to increase crop yields. Hybrid seeds have helped to double U.S. corn yields since the 1940s, and almost all the corn now grown in the U.S. and Europe is started annually from hybrid seed. Hybrid breeding has expanded in recent years, and hybrid varieties are now common in grain crops (corn, sorghum), vegetables (cabbage, tomatoes, squash), and many flower species.

Mutation. Occasionally an individual plant shows an important change in one or more traits arising from a spontaneous mutation. Usually a change in a single gene is involved. Most mutations are deleterious, but occasionally one has a distinct advantage. The plant showing the mutation may be used directly as a variety, a common practice in apples and other fruits, or the new trait may be added to existing varieties through hybridization and backcrossing. Plant mutations caused by single-gene changes have found wide use in ornamentals, resulting in double-flowered forms, weeping stems, dwarfism or unusual growth habits, and a wide diversity of color variations. Mutations can be induced artificially by X rays or ultraviolet light.

Doubling the number of chromosomes is another plant-breeding technique that has been useful in improving some flower and crop plants, sometimes producing forms with increased vigor and with larger leaves, flowers, and fruits. The chemical colchicine, an alkaloid extracted from the autumn crocus, is useful for this purpose.

New Techniques. Developments in plant tissue culture and genetic engineering (q.v.) are opening up new opportunities for plant breeders. In tissue culture, a single laboratory dish of plant cells can be the equivalent of a field with thousands of plants from which to select improved strains. As genetic engineering techniques are perfected, breeders may be able to transfer a gene for pest resistance to a crop plant directly from a wild relative or even from an unrelated species, thus reducing the need for pesticides over vast fields of crops. Such attempts were meeting with only quite limited success by the late 1980s, however, and genetic modification through somoclonal variation techniques may prove more immediately useful.

See also PLANT PROPAGATION. W.D.P.

For further information on this topic, see the Bibliography in volume 28, section 453.

PLANT DISEASES. *See* DISEASES OF PLANTS.

PLANT DISTRIBUTION, also phytogeography, study of all factors that influence the distribution of plants. Such studies include determining the actual distribution of particular species, charting that information on maps that show the plants' natural range, and illustrating or listing plant species and associations that occur in a given region. The most important determinants of the distribution of plant species are geology, ecology, and the dispersal ability of the reproductive bodies of the plant itself. No two plant species have identical distribution patterns. *See* CLIMATE.

Geology. The many changes in land areas and climates during the past have greatly affected the survival and distribution of plant species. The most dramatic changes have come about as a result of continental drift (*see* PLATE TECTONICS). These movements of the earth's crust caused large landmasses to break apart, coalesce, form mountains, and move into new climatic zones, which also changed through geologic time. The most recent major land shift is thought to have begun some 200 million years ago during the Triassic period (q.v.), when a single large continent called Pangaea broke up into smaller landmasses. These geologic changes provide a plausible explanation for the puzzling distribution of many plant species, the ranges of which cannot otherwise be explained. The conifers of the genus *Araucaria,* for example, have very large seeds that do not float in seawater and can disperse only short distances, but they have been found either as fossils or as actively growing plants on all continents and on some islands that appear to be continental fragments. Other geologic events—the recurring ice ages (q.v.), for example—have also affected plant distribution. The most recent major glacial period, some 1 million years ago, froze or buried vast terrains and confined plant life to the downslopes of mountains and the lower latitudes.

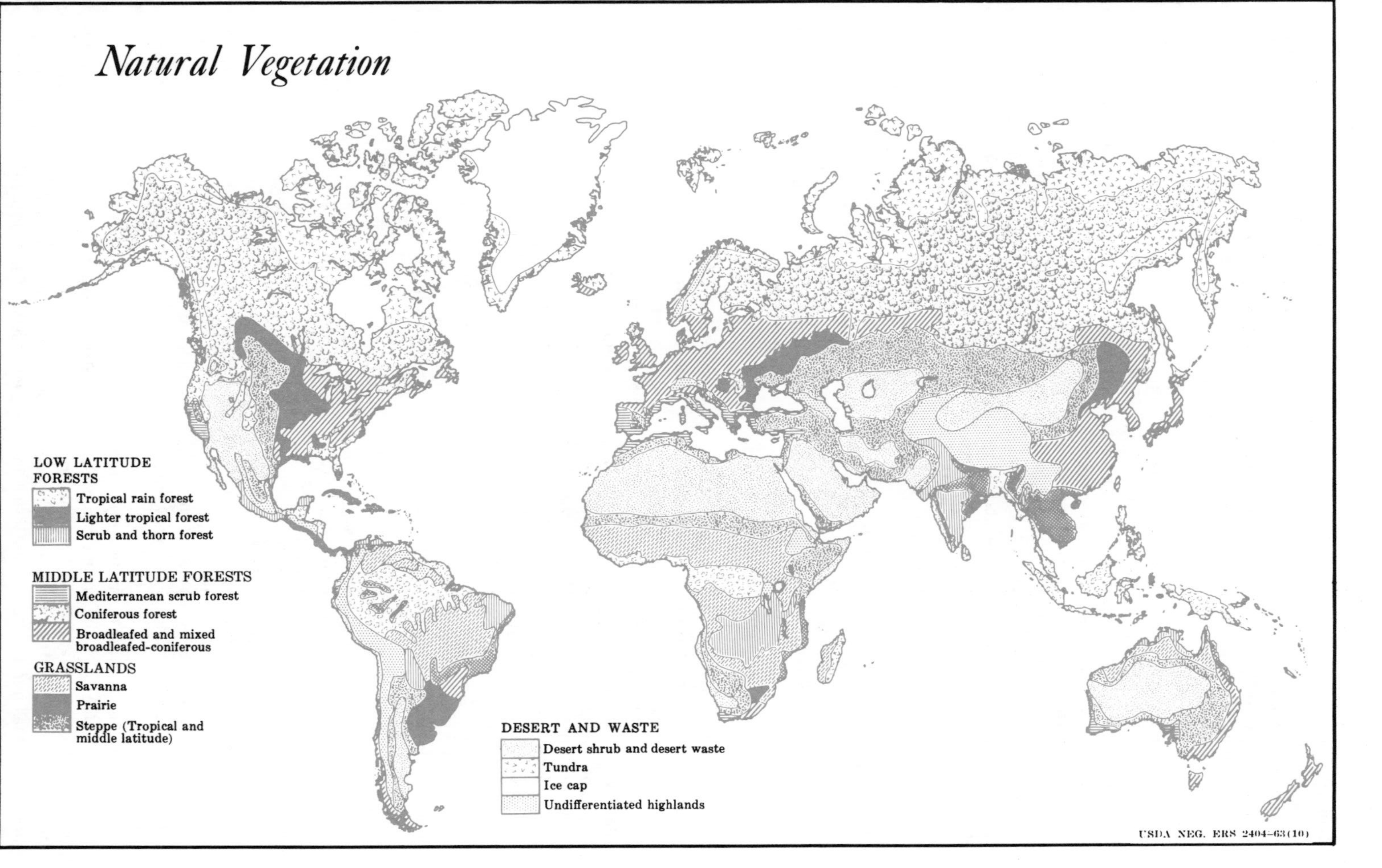
Natural Vegetation
LOW LATITUDE FORESTS
Tropical rain forest
Lighter tropical forest
Scrub and thorn forest
MIDDLE LATITUDE FORESTS
Mediterranean scrub forest
Coniferous forest
Broadleafed and mixed broadleafed-coniferous
GRASSLANDS
Savanna
Prairie
Steppe (Tropical and middle latitude)
DESERT AND WASTE
Desert shrub and desert waste
Tundra
Ice cap
Undifferentiated highlands
USDA NEG. ERS 2404-63(10)

Ecology. The tolerance of a plant species that lives and reproduces in a given geographic region must lie within the extremes of its climatic conditions, including temperature and precipitation, and the plant must be able to grow in the soil of the region. Plants known as xerophytes are able to survive very dry conditions. Desert shrubs are typical xerophytes, but plants that grow in alpine regions where the ground freezes—and thus water is unavailable to the plant roots—may also be xerophytes. Mesophytes are usually found in regions of moderate rainfall but may also grow as desert annuals that flower during the rainy season. Hydrophytes, plants that live in aquatic habitats, are adapted to conditions in which the oxygen and carbon dioxide gases essential to plant life are dissolved in water and thus are not readily available to the plant.

Plants found in widely separated geographic regions and belonging to different families often closely resemble one another in appearance because they have evolved similar adaptations to the ecological conditions of their range. Cacti of western hemisphere deserts, for example, look very much like the unrelated euphorbias, aloes, and succulents of deserts in southern Africa. Similarly, many unrelated rain-forest trees have the same general shape and similar foliage.

Dispersal Ability. The reproductive bodies of plants vary widely in their ability to disperse. The tiny spores of ferns and mosses disperse over a wide range because they can float for long distances in air currents. The seeds of beach plants can also disperse great distances because they have the ability to germinate after floating in ocean currents for many days. The seeds of plants adapted to rain forests (such as the mango and avocado) do not disperse very far, however, because they are usually large, fall close to the plant, and germinate almost at once.

The Hawaiian Islands are of volcanic origin and thus are an example of originally bare, isolated land that became populated with plants by means of long-distance dispersal. Many of the plants now considered native to these islands developed from seeds carried either by seawater or air currents or deposited in the droppings of fruit-eating migratory birds. Nearly all the rain-forest trees growing on volcanic islands were introduced by humans.

See also PALEONTOLOGY; PLANT; POLLINATION.

PLANT PROPAGATION, the art and science of establishing plant life and replacing plants that are used in daily life. The methods of propagation involved fall into two categories: sexual and asexual propagation.

Sexual Propagation. Sexual propagation by seed (q.v.) involves two individuals, male and female, in practically all instances. This makes for the possibility of endless combinations of genotypes; that is, in the process of fertilization, the genes of the parent plants recombine randomly, creating new genetic entities similar to but differing from one another and from the parents as well (*see* GENETICS). This diversity contributes to the development of new plant forms and species. It also protects a species from disaster in the form of disease or insect epidemics, or from gradual changes in the environment.

Most plant propagation is, in fact, from seed, including all annual and biennial plants. Among such plants are all the grains, most of the vegetable plants, and many of the horticultural and floral plants in the greenhouse trade. In addition, virtually all forest trees are produced from seed, as are those plants used for grafting (see below). Very occasionally, seeds can be produced apomictically—that is, without fertilization—but they do not have the genetic diversity found in seeds produced normally.

Seeds from most plants are ready to germinate when they ripen. Many of the woody perennials have some type of dormancy, however, which must be broken prior to planting. If the dormancy is of the embryo type—that is, if the embryo itself must go through a period of dormancy or maturing—the seed is placed in a cold room (1.6°-4.4° C/35°-40° F) in containers with abundant moisture. This process, called stratification, lasts for 30 to 120 days, depending on the species. If the dormancy is of the seed-coat type—that is, if the coat is tough and must be softened before germination can take place—the seed may be placed in a cement mixer with limestone chips or treated with concentrated sulfuric acid; this process is called scarification. Occasionally, seeds have both types of dormancy and must be treated by being both stratified and scarified.

Seeds are usually drilled (planted in rows), either by hand or mechanically, in a well-prepared soil. They are then covered with a light coat of soil, up to twice the diameter of the seed. Sowing usually is done in the spring, when environmental conditions for germination are most suitable. As soon as a sufficient amount of water is absorbed by the seed, biochemical changes take place, cell division begins, and germination occurs.

Asexual Propagation. When identical genotypes of a plant are to be reproduced, the plant must be propagated by asexual, or vegetative, means (*see* VEGETATIVE REPRODUCTION). In this way, for example, the Golden Delicious apple was per-

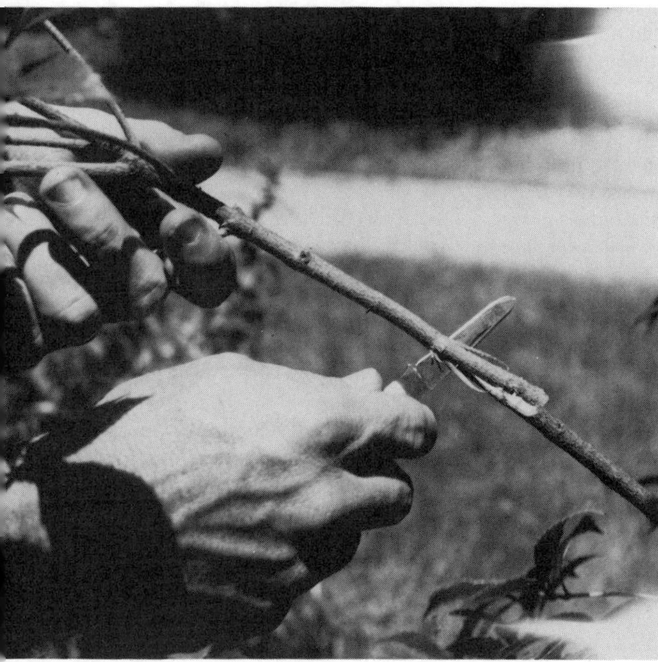

One method of rooting for propagation is by air layering. First, as shown here, a branch is cut with a slantwise slash; then a rooting compound is dusted into the wound, and the branch is wrapped with damp sphagnum moss and sealed with plastic film. Root growth eventually takes place at the site of the cut. USDA Photo

petuated and multiplied from the single branch where the mutation (q.v.), or "sport," first appeared, to thousands of other trees by the process called grafting.

Grafting. A graft is made by collecting a portion, or scion, of the plant to be propagated. The base of the scion is cut to a wedge-shaped point. A cut is also made into a seedling, or stock, of the same species, usually at a point where the diameter of the stock and the scion are equal. The scion is placed in the cut, matching the stock's cambium—the growth layer of lateral meristems (*see* PLANT: *Tissue Systems*)—with that of the scion. The two are held together by winding a grafting rubber band spirally from the bottom of the cut to the top. The whole graft area is then covered with grafting wax. In a relatively short period of time, often three to four weeks, the scion and stock plant will unite; the stock plant is then cut just above the graft union.

Many kinds of grafts can be made. The one described above, for example, is called a side graft; another common graft is the cleft graft. The basic principle of successful grafting, however, is the same in all cases, and certain conditions should always be met: The stock plant should be growing actively, the scion should be dormant, and the grafting knife should be sharp to make clean cuts.

Budding. In this variation of grafting, a dormant bud is used for scion material. The bud is removed from its stem along with a shield of bark and is inserted in a T-shaped cut at the base of the stock plant. The site is then wrapped with a grafting rubber band. When the bud breaks dormancy and is well established and growing, the part of the stock plant that is above the graft is removed.

Rooting cuttings. Some plant species can produce roots on an excised twig or leaf, if it is taken at the proper time. The cutting is inserted in the proper medium for rooting, such as vermiculite or a sand mixture, and provided with proper heat and humidity. Cuttings of some species such as willows and true poplars can be planted directly in the field.

Marcottage, or air layering. A process known as marcottage is successful with certain hard-to-root species. A branch tip is girdled—that is, a ring of bark is removed from around the branch, down to the xylem layer, cutting off the flow of nutrients to the branch tip. The area surrounding the girdle is then packed with moist sphagnum moss and wrapped in plastic. Eventually, a pronounced callus (thick new tissue) forms at the upper side of the girdle, and roots appear. These grow into the sphagnum moss. When a sufficient root mass is present, the twig is excised at the lower end of the girdle and potted.

Tissue culture. This newest and most technical method of vegetative propagation involves cloning (*see* CLONE). Any plant tissue with cells that can divide can be used for tissue culture. Although cultures have been started from fruit, endosperm, pollen, and embryos, tissues taken from the vascular area of stems or roots have been the most successful. A nutrient medium containing essential salts and amino acids is prepared in an agar solution, which is placed in a flask and sterilized. Sections of tissue are excised under aseptic (pathogen-free) conditions and placed on the surface of the medium. The flasks are stoppered with cotton (or some equivalent) and placed in a controlled environment. Within a short period of time the callus proliferates; it is then cut aseptically into small pieces and transferred to a medium rich in auxin, a plant chemical that promotes root formation, or kinetin, which promotes shoot initiation. Once roots and tops have developed, the plantlet is removed from aseptic conditions and planted under controlled conditions in a greenhouse. Tissue culture can be accomplished readily with such species as grapes, orchids, chrysanthemums, and carrots. With other species it is a very difficult procedure. F.C.C.

For further information on this topic, see the Bibliography in volume 28, section 453.

PLANTS, POISONOUS. *See* POISONOUS PLANTS.

PLASMA. *See* BLOOD.

PLASMA, in physics, usually gaseous state of matter in which a part or all of the atoms or molecules are dissociated to form ions (*see* IONIZATION). Plasmas consist of a mixture of neutral particles, positive ions (atoms or molecules that have lost one or more electrons), and negative electrons. A plasma is a conductor of electricity, but a volume with dimensions greater than the so-called Debye length exhibits electrically neutral behavior. At a microscopic level, corresponding to distances shorter than the Debye length, the particles of a plasma do not exhibit collective behavior but instead react individually to a disturbance, for example, an electric field.

On the earth, plasmas usually do not occur naturally except in the form of lightning (q.v.) bolts, which consist of narrow paths of air molecules of which approximately 20 percent are ionized, and in parts of flames. The free electrons in a metal can also be considered as a plasma. Most of the universe, however, consists of matter in the plasma state. The ionization is caused either by high temperatures, such as inside the sun and stars, or by radiation, such as the ionization of interstellar gases or, closer to the earth, the upper layers of the atmosphere (*see* IONOSPHERE), producing the aurora (q.v.).

Plasmas can be created by applying an electric field to a low-pressure gas, as in neon or fluorescent tubes (*see* NEON LAMP). A plasma can also be created by heating a neutral gas to very high temperatures. Usually the required temperatures are too high to be applied externally, and the gas is heated internally by the injection of high-speed ions or electrons that collide with the gas particles, increasing their thermal energy. The electrons in the gas can also be accelerated by external electric fields. Ions from such plasmas are used in the semiconductor industry for etching surfaces and otherwise altering the properties of materials.

In very hot plasmas the particles acquire enough energy to engage in nuclear reactions with each other during collisions. Such fusion reactions are the heat source in the sun's core, and scientists are trying to create artificial plasmas in the laboratory in which fusion reactions would produce energy for the production of electricity.

See also FUSION; NUCLEAR ENERGY; PHYSICS: *Developments in Physics Since 1930:* Plasma Physics.

PLASSEY, BATTLE OF (June 23, 1757), victory that led to British control of Bengal and marked the first stage in their conquest of India. In 1756 Siraj-ud-Dawlah (c. 1732–57), the nawab, or viceroy of Bengal, seized the British Fort William at Calcutta, where subsequently some British prisoners died in a dungeon known as the Black Hole of Calcutta (q.v.). Robert Clive, British governor of Fort Saint David (now Cuddalore), recaptured the fort in January 1757, and allied himself with Hindu leaders in Bengal who were dissatisfied with the Muslim Siraj-ud-Dawlah. After arranging for the defection of Mir Jafar (1691?–1765), one of the nawab's generals, he defeated a vastly superior Bengali army the following June at Plassey, a village near Krishnanager (Krishnagar), West Bengal. This victory, followed by that of Buxar (1764), secured British rule over the region.

PLASTER, a pasty composition (usually of sand, water, and a cementing agent such as gypsum, lime, or portland cement) that hardens on drying and is used for coating interior walls, ceilings, and partitions. Hair or fiber is mixed with the first and second coats to strengthen the plaster. Plasterboard, often used as a substitute for plastering, is a large sheet of prefabricated material made of fiberboard, paper, or felt with a hardened gypsum plaster core. The term *plaster* is sometimes also applied to molded ornamental walls and ceilings (*see* STUCCO, in art), and to plaster of Paris (*see* GYPSUM).

PLASTER OF PARIS. *See* GYPSUM.

PLASTICS, term applied to organic polymeric materials (those consisting of giant organic molecules) that are plastic—that is, they can be formed into desired shapes by extruding, molding, casting, or spinning. The molecules can be either natural—including cellulose, wax, and natural rubber—or synthetic—including polyethylene and nylon (q.v.). The starting materials are resins (q.v.) in the form of pellets, powders, or solutions.

Plastics are characterized by high strength-to-density ratios, excellent thermal and electrical insulation properties, and good resistance to acids, alkalies, and solvents. The giant molecules of which they consist may be linear, branched, or cross-linked, depending on the plastic. Linear and branched molecules are thermoplastic (soften when heated), whereas cross-linked molecules are thermosetting (harden when heated).

HISTORY

The development of plastics began about 1860, after Phelan and Collander, a U.S. firm manufacturing billiard and pool balls, offered a prize of $10,000 for a satisfactory substitute for natural ivory. One of those who tried to win this prize was U.S. inventor John Wesley Hyatt (1837–1920). He developed a method of pressure-working pyroxylin, a cellulose nitrate of low nitration (*see* CELLULOSE), that had been plasticized with camphor and a minimum of alcohol solvent. Although Hyatt did not win the prize, his product, patented under the trademark Celluloid (q.v.), was used in the manufacture of objects ranging from dental plates to men's collars. Despite its flammability and liability to deterioration under the action of light, Celluloid achieved a notable commercial success.

Other plastics were introduced gradually over the next few decades. Among them were the first totally synthetic plastics, the family of phenol-formaldehyde resins developed by the Belgian-American chemist Leo Hendrik Baekeland about 1906 and sold under the trademark Bakelite. Other plastics introduced during this period include modified natural polymers such as rayon (q.v.), made from cellulose products.

Breakthrough in Plastics Chemistry. Then, in 1920, an event occurred that set the stage for the future rapid development of plastic materials. The German chemist Hermann Staudinger (1881–1965) hypothesized that plastics were truly giant molecules. His subsequent efforts to prove this claim initiated an outburst of scientific investigation that resulted in major breakthroughs in the chemistry of plastics. This became evident in the 1920s and '30s, when large numbers of new products were introduced. Included were such materials as cellulose acetate, used in molding resins and fibers; polyvinyl chloride, used in plastic pipe, vinyl coatings, and wire insulation; urea-formaldehyde resins, used in tableware and

Neoprene latex, a polymer of chloroprene (C_4H_5Cl) with a structure similar to natural rubber, is used to manufacture durable, one-piece meteorological balloons. Neoprene resists weathering, ozone, and a variety of organic and inorganic substances.

electrical applications; and acrylic resin, developed as a binder for laminated glass.

One of the most familiar plastics developed in this period is polymerized methyl methacrylate, which, beginning in 1937, was marketed as Lucite and Plexiglas. This material has excellent optical properties and is suitable for eyeglass and camera lenses and for producing special effects in highway and advertising illumination. Polystyrene resins, also first produced commercially about 1937, are characterized by high resistance to chemical and mechanical alteration at low temperatures and by very low absorption of water. These properties make the polystyrenes especially suitable for radio-frequency insulation and for accessories used in low-temperature situations, as in refrigeration installations and in airplanes designed for high-altitude flight. Polytetrafluoroethylene, first made in 1938, was eventually produced commercially as Teflon in 1950. Another key development during the 1930s was the synthesis of nylon, the first high-performance engineering plastic.

World War II. During wartime, both the Allies and the Axis powers were faced with severe shortages of natural raw materials. The plastics industry proved to be a rich source of acceptable substitutes. Germany, for example, cut off early from sources of natural latex, initiated a major program that led to the development of a practical synthetic rubber (*see* RUBBER). Similarly, for the U.S., Japan's entry into the war eliminated most Far Eastern sources of natural rubber, silk, and many metals. The U.S. response was to accelerate the development and production of plastics. Nylon became a major source of textile fibers, polyesters were used in fabricating armor and other war matériel, and various types of synthetic rubber were produced in quantity.

The Postwar Boom. The scientific and technological momentum in the plastics industry carried over into the postwar years. Of particular interest were the advances in such engineering plastics as polycarbonates, acetals, and polyamides; other synthetics were used in place of metal for machinery, safety helmets, high-temperature devices, and many other products for environmentally demanding settings. In 1953 the German chemist Karl Ziegler developed polyethylene, and in 1954 the Italian chemist Giulio Natta (1903–79) developed polypropylene—two of today's most important plastics. A decade later, these two men shared the 1963 Nobel Prize in Chemistry for their studies of polymers.

KINDS OF PLASTICS

Three of the ways in which plastics can be categorized are by the polymerization process that

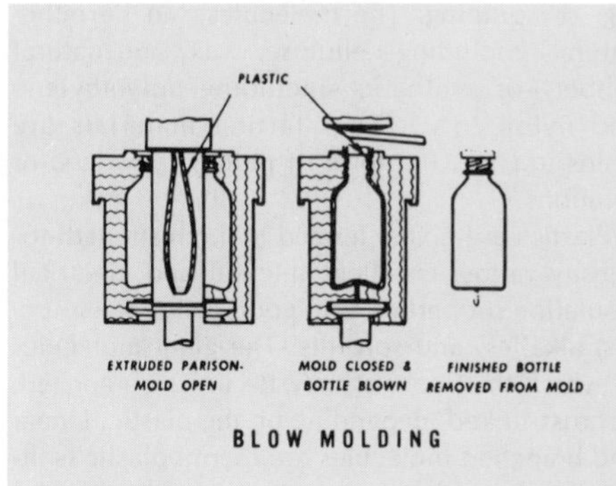

BLOW MOLDING

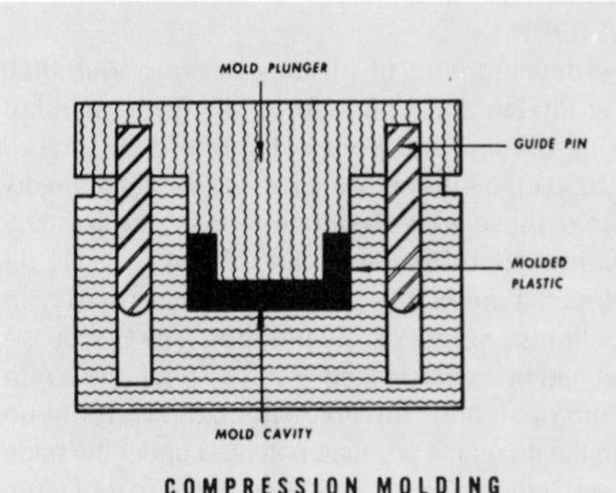

COMPRESSION MOLDING

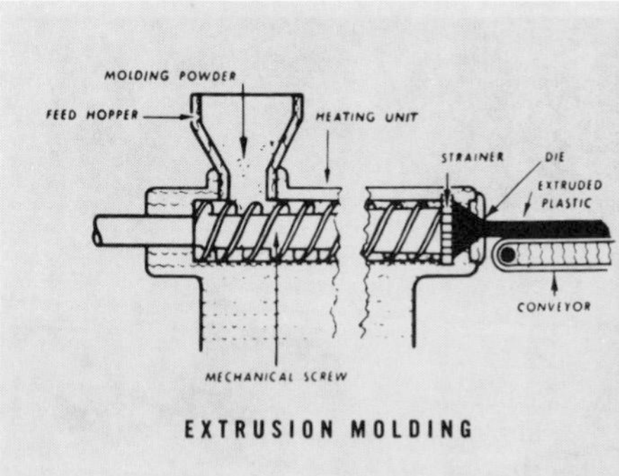

EXTRUSION MOLDING

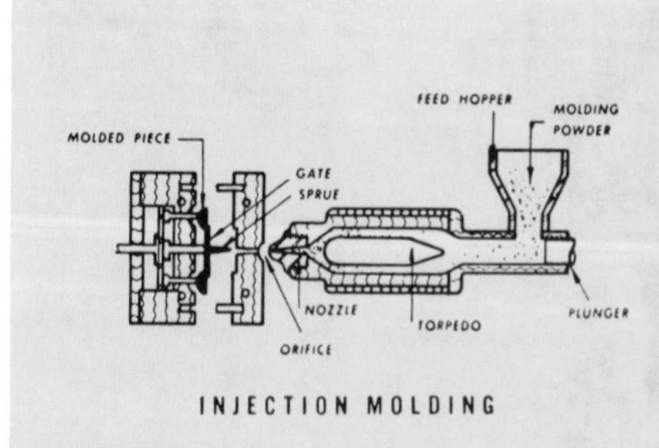

INJECTION MOLDING

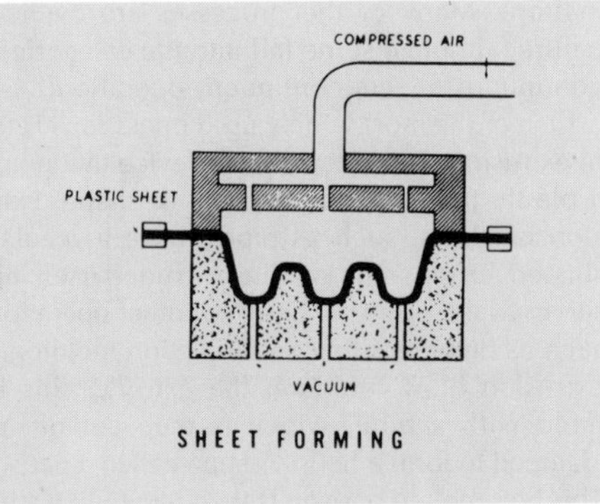

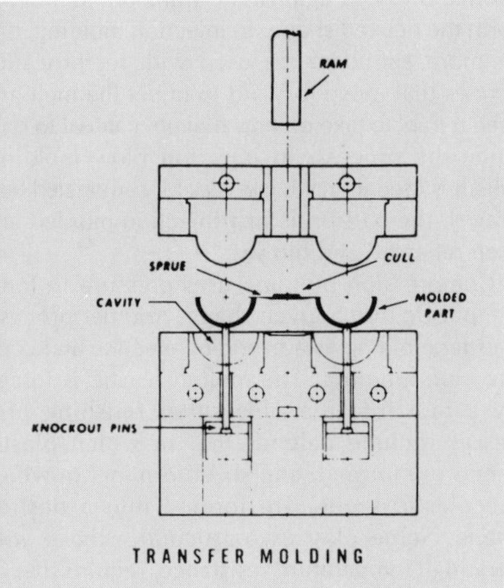

Fluid plastic materials are given form and shape in many different ways. The plastic is either shaped into intermediate sheets or is made directly into the final product by a process of molding. Six production methods are illustrated. Society of the Plastics Industry, Inc.

forms them, by their processibility, and by their chemical nature.

Polymerization. The two basic polymerization processes for producing resins are condensation and addition reactions. The former are stepwise reactions in which a variety of polymer chain lengths are formed, whereas addition reactions produce only specific lengths. Furthermore, condensation polymerizations produce small by-product molecules such as water, ammonia, and glycol, whereas no by-products are generated in addition reactions. Typical condensation polymers are nylons, polyurethanes, and polyesters. Addition polymers include polyethylene, polypropylene, polyvinyl chloride, and polystyrene. The average molecular weights for the addition polymers are generally orders of magnitude larger than those of condensation polymers.

Another polymerization process has more recently been developed, called group transfer polymerization (*see* POLYMER).

Processibility. The processibility of a plastic depends on whether it is thermoplastic or thermosetting. Thermoplastics, which are made up of linear or branched polymers (see diagram), are fusible: They soften when heated and harden when cooled. This is also true of thermosets that are lightly cross-linked. Most thermosets, however, harden when heated. This final cross-linking, which fixes the true thermosets, takes place after the plastic has already been formed.

Chemical Nature. The chemical nature of a plastic is defined by the monomer, or repeating unit, that makes up the chain of the polymer. For example, polyolefins, such as polyethylene, are made up of monomer units of olefins (open-chain hydrocarbons with at least one double bond—in the case of polyethylene, the unit being ethylene). Other categories, with examples, are acrylics (polymethylmethacrylate), styrenes (polystyrene), vinyl halides (polyvinyl chloride), polyesters, polyurethanes, polyamides (nylons), polyethers, acetals, phenolics, cellulosics, and amino resins.

MANUFACTURE

The manufacture of plastic and plastic products involves procuring the raw materials, synthesizing the basic polymer, compounding the polymer into a material useful for fabrication, and molding or shaping the plastic into its final form.

Raw Materials. Originally, most plastics were made from resins derived from vegetable matter, such as cellulose (from cotton), furfural (from oat hulls), oils (from seeds), starch derivatives, and coal, a solid fuel of vegetable origin. Casein (from milk) was among the nonvegetable materials used. Although the production of nylon was originally based on coal, air, and water, and nylon 11 is still based on oil from castor beans, most plastics today are derived from petrochemicals. These oil-based products are more widely available and less expensive than other raw materials. However, because most experts predict that the world supply of oil will be exhausted in the 21st century, other sources of raw materials, such as coal gasification, are being explored.

Synthesizing the Polymer. The first stage in manufacturing plastic is polymerization. As noted, the two basic polymerization methods are condensation and addition reactions. These methods may be carried out in various ways. In bulk polymerization, the pure monomer alone is polymerized, generally either in gaseous or liquid phase, though a few solid-state polymerizations are also used.

POLYMER STRUCTURES

(R represents a monomer)

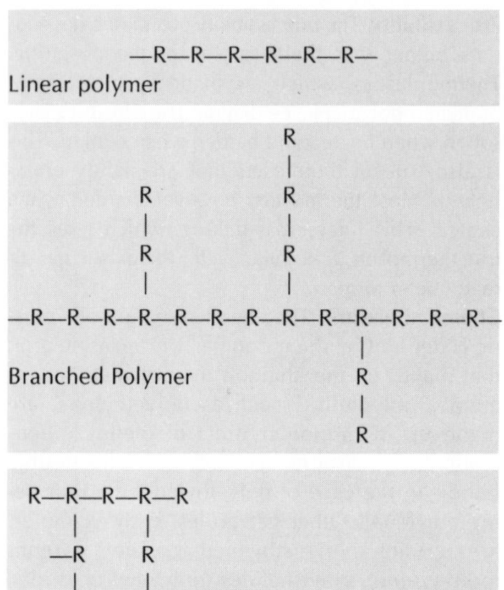

In solution polymerization, an emulsion is formed and then coagulated. In interfacial polymerization, the monomers are dissolved in two immiscible liquids, and the polymerization occurs at the interface of the two liquids.

Additives. Chemical additives are often used in plastics to produce some desired characteristic. For instance, antioxidants protect a polymer from chemical degradation by oxygen or ozone; similarly, ultraviolet stabilizers protect against weathering. Plasticizers make a polymer more flexible, lubricants reduce problems with friction, and pigments add color. Among other additives are flame retardants and antistatics.

Many plastics are manufactured as composites. This involves a system where reinforcements (usually fibers made of glass or carbon) are added to a plastic resin matrix. Composites have strength and stability comparable to that of metals but with generally less weight. Plastic foams, which are composites of plastic and gas, offer bulk with less weight.

Shaping and Finishing. The techniques used for shaping and finishing plastics depend on three factors: time, temperature, and flow (or deformation). Many of the processes are cyclic in nature, although some fall into the categories of continuous or semicontinuous operation.

One of the most widely used operations is that of extrusion. The extruder is a device that pumps a plastic through a desired die or shape. Extrusion products, such as pipes, have a regularly shaped cross section. The extruder itself also serves as the means to carry out other operations, such as blow molding and injection molding. In extrusion blow molding, the extruder fills the mold with a tube, which is then cut off and clamped to form a hollow shape called a parison. This hot, molten parison is then blown like a balloon and forced against the walls of the mold to form the desired shape. In injection molding, one or more extruders are used with reciprocating screws that move forward to inject the melt and then retract to take on new molten material to continue the process. In injection blow molding, which is used in making bottles for carbonated beverages, the parison is first injection molded and then reheated and blown.

Compression molding uses pressure to force the plastic into a given shape. Another process, transfer molding, is a hybrid of injection and compression molding: The molten plastic is forced by a ram into a mold. Other finishing processes include calendering, in which plastic sheets are formed, and sheet forming, in which the plastic sheets are formed into a desired shape. Some plastics, particularly those with very high temperature resistance, require special fabrication procedures. For example, polytetrafluoroethylene has such a high melt viscosity that it is first pressed into shape and then sintered—exposed to extremely high temperatures that bond it into a cohesive mass without melting it. Some polyamides are produced by a similar process.

USES

Plastics have an ever-widening range of uses in both the industrial and consumer sectors.

Packaging. The packaging industry is the leading user of plastics, accounting for about a third of total U.S. production. Applications can be either flexible or rigid; many foods are packaged in some form of thermoplastics. In the early 1990s, U.S. sales of low-density polyethylene (LDPE) exceeded ten billion pounds per year. The major use for LDPE is film marketed in rolls of clear-plastic wrap. High-density polyethylene (HDPE) is used for some thicker films, such as those used for plastic trash bags and containers. Other packaging plastics include polypropylene, polystyrene, polyvinyl chloride, and polyvinylidene chloride. The last is used primarily for its barrier properties, which can keep gases such as oxygen from passing into or out of a package. Similarly, polypropylene is an effective barrier for water vapor. In addition, it is often used in housewares and as a fiber for carpeting and rope.

Construction. The U.S. building industry is the second largest consumer of plastics, including many of the packaging plastics mentioned above. HDPE is used for pipes, as is polyvinyl chloride (PVC); PVC is also used in sheets for siding and similar components. Many plastics are used to insulate cables and wires, and polystyrene in the form of foam serves as insulation for walls, roofs, and other areas. Other plastic products are roofing, door and window frames, moldings, and hardware.

Other Uses. Many other industries, especially automobile and truck manufacturing, also depend on plastics. Tough engineering plastics are found in components like air-intake manifolds, fuel lines, emission canisters, fuel pumps, and electronic devices. Plastics are also used for interior paneling, seats, and trim. Many automobile bodies are made of fiberglass-reinforced plastic.

Among the other uses of plastic are housings for business machines, electronic devices, small appliances, and tools. Consumer goods range from sports equipment to luggage and toys.

HEALTH AND ENVIRONMENTAL HAZARDS

Because plastics are relatively inert, they do not normally present health hazards to the maker or user. However, some monomers used in the manufacture of plastics have been shown to cause cancer. Similarly, benzene, which is an important raw material for the synthesis of nylon, is a carcinogen. The problems involved in the manufacture of plastics parallel those of the chemical industry in general.

Most synthetic plastics are not environmentally degradable; unlike wood, paper, natural fibers, or even metal and glass, they do not rot or otherwise break down over time. (Some degradable plastics have been developed, but none has proven compatible with the conditions required for most sanitary landfills.) Thus, there is an environmental problem associated with the disposal of plastics. Recycling has emerged as the most practical method to deal with this problem, especially with products such as the polyethylene terephlalate bottles used for carbonated beverages, where the process is fairly straightforward. More complex solutions are being developed for handling the commingled plastic scrap that constitutes a highly visible, albeit relatively small, part of the problem of solid waste disposal.

See also SOLID WASTE DISPOSAL.

R.G.G.; REV. BY H.Mo.

For further information on this topic, see the Bibliography in volume 28, sections 415–16, 628.

PLASTIC SURGERY, branch of surgery, dealing with the remodeling of any portion of the human body that has been damaged or deformed. The malformation may have occurred congenitally, that is, at birth, as a child born with a cleft palate or a harelip (*see* BIRTH DEFECTS). Disfigurement may also be the result of injury or of deforming surgery required in treating such diseases as cancer. The primary objectives of plastic surgery are the correction of defects, the restoration of lost function, and the improvement of appearance of disfigured parts.

Plastic surgery is one of the oldest forms of surgery practiced. Nose-reconstruction operations were probably performed in ancient India as early as 2000 BC, when amputation of the nose was a form of punishment; the caste of potters eventually devised a method for rebuilding the nose by using a portion of the forehead, a technique still employed today. Some discussion of such surgery also appears in ancient Greek and Roman tracts. Significant further development of surgical techinques did not take place, however, until about the 16th century, particularly in the work of the Italian physician Gasparo Tagliacozzi (1546–99). In the 20th century the psychotherapeutic importance of plastic surgery was demonstrated following World War II; victims of war wounds and burns regained the use of the injured parts of their bodies and were spared the external disfigurement that normally results in a damaging loss of morale.

Reconstructive and Cosmetic Surgery. Reconstructive surgery involves the restoration of function to a damaged body part and the rebuilding of normal physical contours when parts of the body—such as the nose, jaw, ears, or fingers—are missing or disfigured. The large number of automobile accidents in modern times has resulted in many patients requiring reconstructive surgery of the face. Cancer patients who have undergone cures of the face and neck area may also need reconstructive surgery. Facial surgery is one of the most intricate aspects of plastic surgery, requiring artistic as well as technical skills. Surgery of the hand also involves complex techniques, because of the grafting of tendons and the transfer of muscles to restore usefulness to the disabled part.

Plastic surgery today is often done also for cosmetic reasons, to remove blemishes or to make unusual contours more normal. Among the most common of the cosmetic plastic surgery operations are rhinoplasty (remodeling of the nose), oroplasty (remolding of the external ear), blepharoplasty (removing excess skin and fatty tissue from eyelids and the eye area), and face-lifting, to remove the signs of aging. Another cosmetic technique is the removal of conspicuous scars by cutting out scar tissue and adjusting the wound edges. With the growing popularity of cosmetic surgery since the 1950s, plastic surgery has become misidentified with "beauty" surgery. In fact, only a small percentage of plastic surgeons have practices limited to cosmetic operations.

Grafting Techniques. A major technique used in plastic surgery is grafting, the transplanting or implanting of living tissue from one part of the body to another, or from one person to another, with the expectation that the tissue will adhere and grow to supply a missing part. Several techniques of skin grafting are commonly used. One is the transfer of tissue from an adjacent part to the defect by transposition or rotation of flaps of skin. Another frequently used technique, particularly in relatively minor facial defects, is full-thickness grafting, in which the full thickness of the skin is removed and transferred as a free transplant to the defective area. A third technique, called split-thickness grafting, is used especially for severe burn victims with deep burns covering large areas of the body. By means of an electrical device called a dermatome, a piece of skin at the donor site can be removed at a precise thickness that will contain enough living dermal cells to coalesce at the burn site, while leaving enough cells at the donor site for the skin to grow back. Sometimes a burn victim's life can be saved by temporarily covering the surviving dermal cells at the burn site with skin grafts from donors who are genetically incompatible; these grafts do not survive permanently and are eventually rejected by the patient (*see* IMMUNE SYSTEM; SKIN: *Skin Grafting*).

Other types of skin transfer are required in more complicated cases, such as those in which a full-thickness loss of the cheek or a loss of the entire nose occurs. The transplant must be nourished by blood vessels from its original site until established in its new position. In such cases, a tube—flap of skin with underlying tissue—is left to connect the transplant with its original blood supply. The procedure necessitates a two-step operation, the second step involving the removal of the connecting tube after the transplanted portion has acquired a new blood supply from the recipient site.

Other types of grafts are also employed in plastic surgery. For example, cartilage taken from a patient's rib may be sculpted to reproduce the shape of a missing ear. The cartilage is then transplanted at the site of the new ear. Bone grafts removed from the hipbone or from the rib are used to reconstruct various types of defects, for example, to replace a missing jawbone. Nerve grafts are used to alleviate facial paralysis if the facial nerve has been severed as a result of an accident.

Medical Training. The training requirements for a plastic surgeon include an M.D. degree, a minimum of five years of additional study and experience in an accredited general hospital, and two more years' experience as a resident in plastic surgery. The American Board of Plastic Surgery, founded in 1938, supervises the training of physicians specializing in plastic surgery and holds examinations for their certification to practice. J.M.Co.

For further information on this topic, see the Bibliography in volume 28, section 513.

PLATA, RÍO DE LA (Span., "Silver River"), also River Plate, estuary of the combined Paraná and Uruguay rivers, SE South America, forming a marine inlet between Uruguay and Argentina. It is about 230 km (about 143 mi) wide at its mouth and tapers gradually inland for a distance of about 274 km (about 170 mi) to the delta of the Paraná R. The best natural harbor on the estuary is at Montevideo, Uruguay. Artificial harbors have been constructed at La Plata and Buenos Aires, Argentina. The estuary was discovered in 1516 by the Spanish explorer Juan Díaz de Solís (1470?–1516) and received its present name from the Italian-born navigator Sebastian Cabot.

PLATAEA, ancient city of Greece, in Boeotia, at the base of Mt. Cithaeron, south of the ancient city of Thebes. Involved in a war with Thebes, the Plataeans placed themselves under the protection of Athens, apparently about 500 BC, and fought on the side of the Athenians against the Persians at Marathon in 490 BC. In 480 BC the Persians, under King Xerxes, retaliated by destroying the city. In the following year Plataea was the scene of a great victory by the Spartan Greeks, led by the generals Pausanias and Aristides, over the Persian armies commanded by Mardonius (fl. 500–479 BC); this battle ended the Persian invasion of Greece. The allegiance of the Plataeans to Athens angered the Thebans, and in 429 BC, the third year of the Peloponnesian War, the city was attacked by a combined force of Thebans and Spartans and razed to the ground. Restored after the Peace of Antalcidas, named for the Spartan naval commander Antalcidas in 386 BC, it was once more destroyed by the Thebans in 373 BC. Under Alexander the Great of Macedonia it was rebuilt, and it continued to be inhabited until the 6th century AD.

PLATEAU, extensive land formation. The top is flat or sloping; the elevation, from a few hundred to several thousand meters. A plateau is larger han a mesa (q.v.) or butte. Plateaus are often iven by erosion (q.v.) into deep canyons (*see* ANYON). A major plateau in North America is he Columbia Plateau. *See also* GEOLOGY.

LATERESQUE, in art, an ornate style of architecure and ornament that was important in Spain in he 15th and 16th centuries, and was also used in hat country's American colonies. The term *plateresque* means "in the manner of a silversmith"; he style is characterized by rich ornamentation, ncluding twisted columns and sinuous scrollvork, in heavy relief. Prime examples of the style nclude the cathedral of Granada (1523–1703), Monerrey Palace in Salamanca, and the facade of the Jniversity of Alcala de Henares (1541–53).

PLATE TECTONICS, theory of global tectonics geologic structural deformations) that has served as a master key, in modern geology, for understanding the structure, history, and dynamcs of the earth's crust. The theory is based on the observation that the earth's solid crust is broken up into about a dozen semirigid plates. The boundaries of these plates are zones of tectonic activity, where earthquakes and volcanic eruptions tend to occur.

Background. Although the plate-tectonics revolution in geologic thought occurred only recently (in the 1960s and '70s), the roots of the theory were established by earlier observation and deduction. In one such discovery, James Hall (1811–98), a New York geologist, observed that sediments accumulated in mountain belts are at least ten times thicker than those in continental interiors. This planted the seeds for the later geosynclinal theory (*see* GEOSYNCLINE) that continental crust grows by progressive additions that originate as ancient and folded geosynclines, hardened and consolidated into plates. This theory was well established by the 20th century. Another 19th-century discovery was that there was a midocean ridge in the Atlantic; by the 1920s scientists had concluded that this ridge was continuous almost all the way around the world.

In the period 1908–12, theories of continental drift were proposed by the German geologist Alfred Lothar Wegener and others, who recognized that continental plates rupture, drift apart, and eventually collide with each other. Such collisions crumple geosynclinal sediments, thus creating future mountain belts. Geophysical work on the earth's density and observations by petrologists had previously shown that the earth's crust consists of two quite different materials: sima, a silicon-magnesium rock, typically basalt, which is characteristic of oceanic crust; and sial, a silicon-aluminum rock, typically granitic and characteristic of continental crust. Wegener thought that the sialic continental plates sail across the simatic ocean crust like icebergs in the ocean. This reasoning was fallacious, because the melting point of sima is higher than that of sial. Geologists subsequently discovered the so-called asthenosphere, a layer of relatively low strength in the earth's mantle that underlies the crust at depths of 50 to 150 km (30 to 80 mi). First deduced hypothetically, it was later seismically demonstrated to be a low-velocity, plastic material capable of flowage (*see* EARTH).

One of Wegener's strongest arguments for continental drift was the geometric matching of continental margins, which he postulated had rifted apart. To support his theory, he pointed out that rock formations on opposite sides of the Atlantic—in Brazil and West Africa—match in age, type, and structure. Furthermore, they often contain fossils of terrestrial creatures that could not have swum from one continent to the other. These paleontological arguments were among the most persuasive to many specialists, but they did not impress others (mostly geophysicists).

Wegener's best examples of rifted continental borders, as mentioned, were along the two sides of the Atlantic Ocean. Sir Edward Crisp Bullard (1907–79), in fact, tested their precise fitting by computer-based analyses and presented his results to the Royal Society of London: The fit was perfect. Along many other ocean margins, however, no such match is found—for example, along the entire circum-Pacific belt or along the Burma-Indonesian sector of the Indian Ocean. This discrepancy points out a characteristic of continental margins that had been noted by a famous Viennese geologist, Eduard Suess, in the 1880s. He recognized an "Atlantic type" of margin, identified by abrupt truncation of former mountain belts and rifting structures, and a "Pacific type," marked by parallel cordillera-type mountains, lines of volcanoes, and frequent earthquakes. To many geologists, the Pacific-type coasts appeared to be located where geosynclines are in the process of becoming crumpled and uplifted to create mountains.

Seafloor Spreading. In the 1920s, the study of seafloors was advanced when sonar (q.v.), the echo-measuring device, was modified to measure ocean depths. With sonar, submarine topography could be surveyed and the seafloor mapped. Next, geophysicists adapted the airborne magnetometer so that it would record variations in geomagnetic intensity and orientation. Shipborne magnetometric traverses across the midocean ridges showed that the rocks on one side of the ridge produced a mirror-image geomagnetic pattern of the rocks on the other. Age dating of the basaltic crustal rocks of the seafloor showed that those nearest the ridge were distinctly younger (relatively recent, in fact) than those farther away (*see* DATING METHODS). In addition, no blanket of marine sediment was found at the ridge crest, but it appeared on either side and also grew older and thicker with increasing distance from the ridge. These observations, added to those of the high heat flow, led to the conviction that the ridge is where new ocean crust is being created; it is carried up by convection currents as hot lava, but is rapidly cooled and consolidated on contact with the cold deep-ocean water. To make room for this continual addition of new crust, the plates on either side of the ridge must constantly move apart. In the North Atlantic, the rate of movement is only about 1 cm (about 0.4 in) per year, while in the Pacific it amounts to more than 4 cm (almost 2 in) annually. It is these relatively slow rates of movement, driven by thermal convection currents originating deep in the earth's mantle, that have, over the course of millions of years, been generating the phenomenon of continental drift.

Detailed mapping of the ocean floor was collated in the 1960s and incorporated in physiographic maps in which the submarine landforms were artistically rendered by scientists at Columbia University's Lamont Geological Observatory. They noticed that the crest of the midocean ridge is in the form of a rift, or cleft, a few kilometers across, that coincides with the ridge center. They also found that in the Red Sea the rift enters the African continent to become an integral part of the famous Great Rift, which runs from the Jordan Valley and Dead Sea through the Red Sea to Ethiopia and East Africa. Evidently, the rift marks a split in the continental crust, as well as that of the ocean.

The new physiographic maps of the ocean floor also revealed, for the first time, that the crest of the midocean ridge is extensively offset by deep cracks, which have been called fracture zones (*see* OCEAN AND OCEANOGRAPHY: *Ocean Basin Structure*). These cracks mark the course of transform ("strike-slip") faults that have developed to accommodate strain generated by uneven rates of seafloor spreading. Although most of these faults are hidden below the ocean, one of them, the quake-prone San Andreas fault (q.v.), emerges from the Pacific near San Francisco and crosses hundreds of miles of land.

Volcanic Arcs and Subduction. Dynamic problems unique to Pacific-type coasts were recognized as early as the 1930s by American seismologists, who showed that earthquakes associated with these belts are at shallow depths near the outer (ocean) side of volcanic island arcs, but that the depth of seismic shocks increases until it reaches a maximum of about 700 km (about 430 mi) at a distance of 700 km landward from the front of the arc. By close analysis of a single instance, the American seismologist Hugo Benioff (1899–1968) concluded that this geometry represented a fault plane extending through the crust into the upper mantle and inclined downward toward land, at an angle of about 45°. A similar underthrusting, of the Southern Alps beneath the Northern Alps, had been proposed in 1906, and in the 1950s the process was named subduction.

The existence of similar subduction planes has now been demonstrated along almost all Pacific-type coasts. (Those where the zone is absent possess geologic evidence to show that a zone of this type formerly existed, but that it is simply inactive today.) Most of these belts disclose a major fault system that runs parallel to the general mountain system. At long intervals, the movement on the fault changes from gradual to abrupt, and a shift of about 1 to 5 m (about 3 to 15 ft) may be produced by just a single earthquake. Such faults are found in Chile, Alaska, Japan, Taiwan, the Philippines, New Zealand, and Sumatra.

During subduction, ocean crust is constantly being drawn down into the mantle and melted. Because it is continually recycled, no part of the modern ocean crust is more than 200 million years old. Indeed, crustal blocks are constantly moving and jostling as they are carried by the various plates.

An important effect of the melting of subducted ocean crust is the production of new magma. When subducted ocean crust melts, the magma that forms rises upward from the plane of subduction, deep within the mantle, to erupt on the earth's surface. Eruption of magma melted by subduction has created long, arc-shaped chains of volcanic islands, such as Japan, the Philippines, and the Aleutians. Where an oceanic tectonic plate is subducted beneath continental crust, the magma produced by subductive melting erupts from volcanoes situated among long, linear mountain chains, such as the Cordillera (q.v.), up to 100 km (60 mi) inland from the zone of subduction. (The zone itself is located along a submarine trench offshore of the continent.) In addition to creating and feeding continental volcanoes, melting of subducted ocean crust is responsible for the formation of certain kinds of ore deposits of valuable metallic minerals.

Integrated Plate-Tectonics Theory. With this knowledge of seafloor spreading and subduction zones, all that remained was for the ideas to be melded into an integrated system of geodynam-

1 TRIASSIC
about 200 million years ago

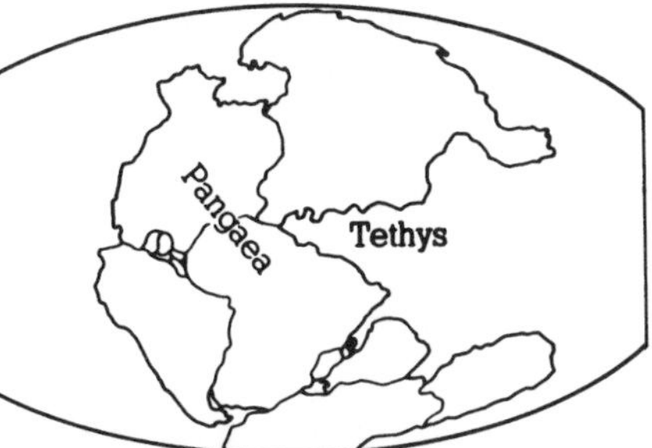
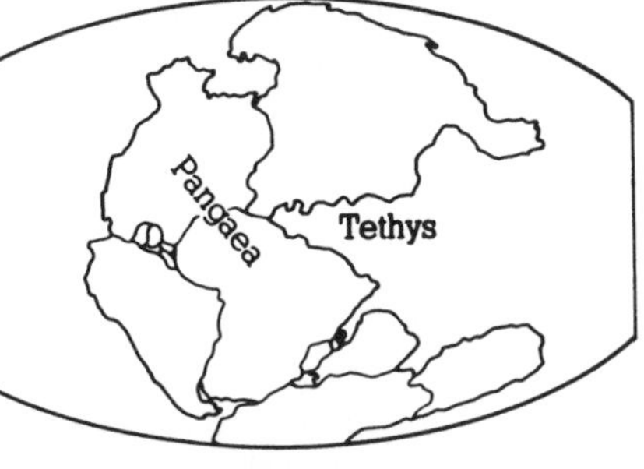

2 EARLY JURASSIC
about 180 million years ago

3 EARLY CRETACEOUS
about 130 million years ago

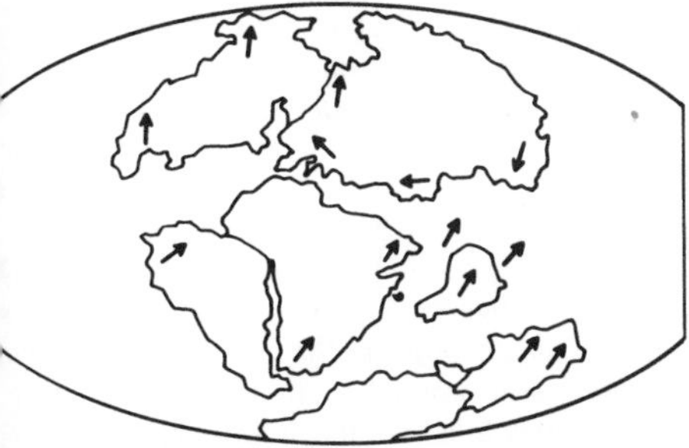

4 PALEOCENE
about 50 million years ago

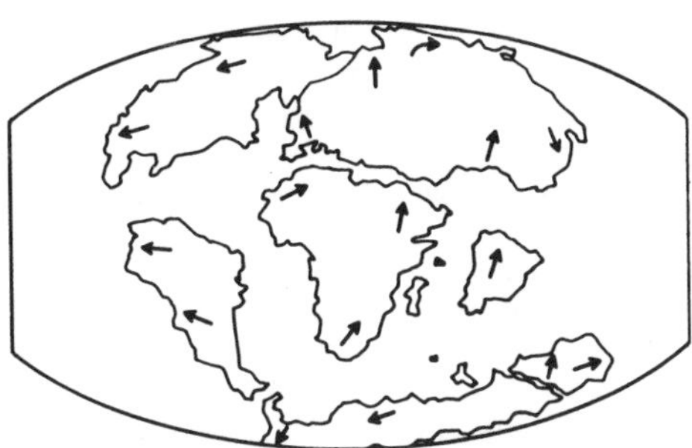

5 PRESENT

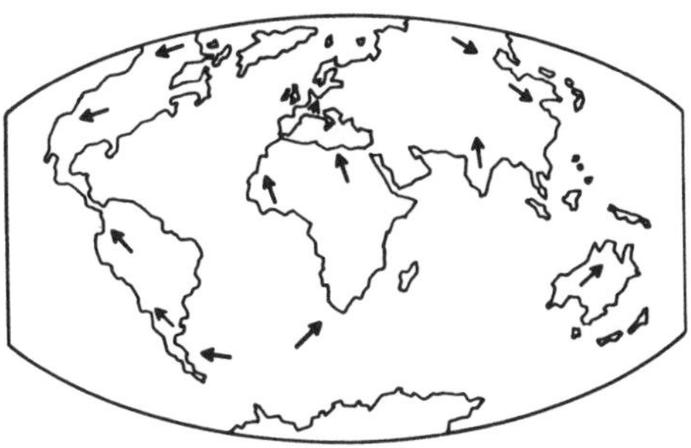

← **Indicates direction and distance of drift**

A series of maps indicating the probable distribution of landmasses on the earth's surface during different geological periods up to and including the present time. Currents of molten material, rising up through the rifts in the earth's crust, split Pangaea, the single continental landmass, into many parts distributed unevenly across the surface of the earth.

Oxford Illustrated Encyclopedia, Volume 1: Physical World, ed., Sir Vivian Fuchs (p. 135). © 1985 Oxford University Press. Used by permission.

An immense convection current is thought to have formed beneath early "supercontinents," left. Lava forced from deep in the earth gradually pushed the landmass apart, right, forming the continents known today. New material still flows outward from midocean ridges, and continents "float" on the creeping seafloor.

© 1968 by Scholastic Magazines, Inc. Reprinted by permission

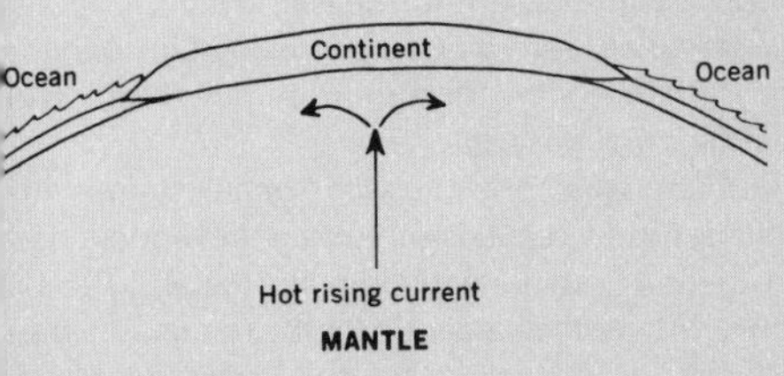

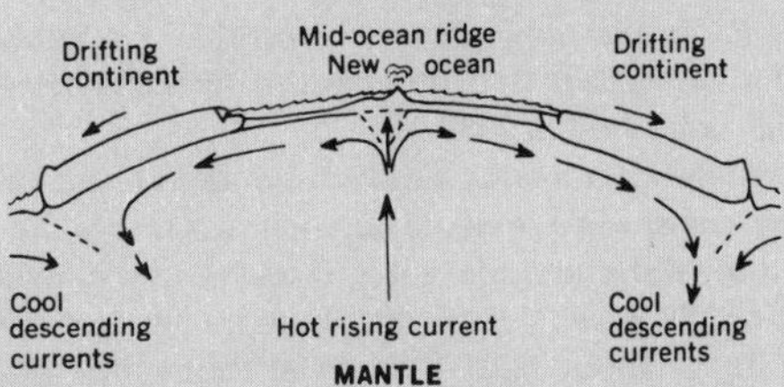

ics. In the 1950s, the Canadian geophysicist J. Tuzo Wilson (1908–93) demonstrated the global continuity of the subduction zones, rather like the stitching on a baseball. The American geologist Harry Hammond Hess (1906–69) argued that if the ocean floor were rifted apart in one part of the globe, the expansion that would result there had to be accommodated by subduction in another part; otherwise the earth would grow larger and larger. Xavier LePichon (1937–), a French student of seismology at Lamont, worked out the geometry of the plates from seismic evidence, and the American geophysicist Robert Sinclair Dietz (1914–) took Wegener's evidence of continental drift and reconstructed the positions of the continents and oceanic plates in successive stages back in time to about 200 million years ago. Since then, the theory of plate tectonics has been debated, tested, and expanded and has become both a paradigm and a center of controversy for the geological sciences.

For a review of the geological history of plate movements, *see* GEOLOGY: *The Geologic Time Scale,* and individual entries on geological eras and periods. R.W.Fa.

For further information on this topic, see the Bibliography in volume 28, sections 421–22.

PLATH, Sylvia (1932–63), American poet. Plath, who began writing poetry as a child, was educated at Smith College and at the University of Cambridge, where she was a Fulbright scholar. Her first publication, *The Colossus* (1960), gave evidence of her meticulously crafted, intensely personal style. *Ariel* (1965) is considered to contain her finest poems; like her subsequent verse (published after her death by suicide) they reflect an increasing self-absorption and obsession with death. Her Pulitzer Prize-winning (1982) *Collected Poems,* edited by her husband, the British poet Ted Hughes, was published in 1981. *The Bell Jar* (1963), a novel published under the pseudonym Victoria Lewis, is an autobiographical account of a young woman's mental breakdown. Plath's correspondence, *Letters Home, 1950–1963,* edited by her mother and published in 1975, gives further insight into the sources of Plath's inspiration and despair. Other works, published posthumously, include *Crossing the Water* (1971) and *Winter Trees* (1972), both collections of poetry, and *Johnny Panic and the Bible of Dreams* (1977), a book of short stories and other prose. Her *Journals* was published in 1982.

PLATINUM, metallic element, symbol Pt, one of the transition elements (q.v.) in group 10 (or VIIIb) of the periodic table (*see* PERIODIC LAW); at.no. 78, at.wt. 195.09. Platinum melts at about 1772° C (about 3222° F), boils at about 3827° C (about 6921° F), and has a sp.gr. of about 21.45.

It is the most important of the group of elements called the platinum metals, the other members of which are ruthenium, rhodium, palladium, osmium, and iridium (qq.v.). Platinum metals were probably used in alloyed forms in ancient Greece and Rome and were first mentioned in European literature in the early 16th century. The separation of the other platinum metals from platinum and from each other was accomplished in the early 19th century.

Properties and Occurrence. Platinum is a grayish-white metal with a hardness (q.v.) of 4.3. It has a high fusing point, is malleable and ductile, expands slightly upon heating, and has high electrical resistance. Chemically the metal is relatively inert and resists attack by air, water, single acids, and ordinary reagents. It dissolves slowly in aqua regia, forming chlorophatinic acid, H_2PtCl_6; is attacked by halogens; and combines upon ignition with sodium hydroxide, sodium nitrate, or sodium cyanide. Platinum ranks about 72d in natural abundance among the elements in crustal rock. Except for the mineral sperrylite, which is platinum arsenide and is found only sparingly in a few localities, platinum occurs in the metallic state, often alloyed with other platinum metals. Nuggets of the metal weighing up to 9.5 kg (21 lb) have been found.

Uses. Because of its chemical inertness and high fusing point, platinum is valuable for laboratory apparatus, such as crucibles, tongs, funnels, combustion boats, and evaporating dishes. Small amounts of iridium are usually added to increase its hardness and durability. Platinum is also used for contact points in electrical apparatus and in instruments used for measuring high temperatures. Finely divided platinum in the form of platinum sponge or platinum black is used extensively as a catalyst in the chemical industry. A considerable amount of the platinum used in the U.S. goes into jewelry, in which it is often alloyed with gold. It is also used for dental fillings.

Platinum is mined all over the world; in the late 1980s the USSR and South Africa were the leading producers. Canada, with mines in Ontario, where platinum is associated with nickel ore, ranked third in world production. Other leading producers are Colombia and the U.S.

PLATO (c. 428–c. 347 BC), Greek philosopher, one of the most creative and influential thinkers in Western philosophy.

Life. Plato was born to an aristocratic family in Athens. His father, Ariston, was believed to have descended from the early kings of Athens. Perictione, his mother, was distantly related to the

6th-century BC lawmaker Solon. When Plato was a child, his father died, and his mother married Pyrilampes, who was an associate of the statesman Pericles.

As a young man Plato had political ambitions, but he became disillusioned by the political leadership in Athens. He eventually became a disciple of Socrates, accepting his basic philosophy and dialectical style of debate: the pursuit of truth through questions, answers, and additional questions. Plato witnessed the death of Socrates at the hands of the Athenian democracy in 399 BC. Perhaps fearing for his own safety, he left Athens temporarily and traveled to Italy, Sicily, and Egypt.

In 387 Plato founded the Academy in Athens, the institution often described as the first European university. It provided a comprehensive curriculum, including such subjects as astronomy, biology, mathematics, political theory, and philosophy. Aristotle was the Academy's most prominent student.

Plato with a student at the Academy, a painting by Pierre Cécile Puvis de Chavannes. Bettmann Archive

Pursuing an opportunity to combine philosophy and practical politics, Plato went to Sicily in 367 to tutor the new ruler of Syracuse, Dionysius the Younger, in the art of philosophical rule. The experiment failed. Plato made another trip to Syracuse in 361, but again his engagement in Sicilian affairs met with little success. The concluding years of his life were spent lecturing at the Academy and writing. He died at about the age of 80 in Athens in 348 or 347 BC.

Works. Plato's writings were in dialogue form; philosophical ideas were advanced, discussed, and criticized in the context of a conversation or debate involving two or more persons. The earliest collection of Plato's work includes 35 dialogues and 13 letters. The authenticity of a few of the dialogues and most of the letters has been disputed.

Early dialogues. The dialogues may be divided into early, middle, and later periods of composition. The earliest represent Plato's attempt to communicate the philosophy and dialectical style of Socrates. Several of these dialogues take the same form. Socrates, encountering someone who claims to know much, professes to be ignorant and seeks assistance from the one who knows. As Socrates begins to raise questions, however, it becomes clear that the one reputed to be wise really does not know what he claims to know, and Socrates emerges as the wiser one because he at least knows that he does not know. Such knowledge, of course, is the beginning of wisdom. Included in this group of dialogues are *Charmides* (an attempt to define temperance), *Lysis* (a discussion of friendship), *Laches* (a pursuit of the meaning of courage), *Protagoras* (a defense of the thesis that virtue is knowledge and can be taught), *Euthyphro* (a consideration of the nature of piety), and Book I of the *Republic* (a discussion of justice).

Middle and late dialogues. The dialogues of the middle and later periods of Plato's life reflect his own philosophical development. The ideas in these works are attributed by most scholars to Plato himself, although Socrates continues to be the main character in many of the dialogues. The writings of the middle period include *Gorgias* (a consideration of several ethical questions), *Meno* (a discussion of the nature of knowledge), the *Apology* (Socrates' defense of himself at his trial against the charges of atheism and corrupting Athenian youth), *Crito* (Socrates' defense of obedience to the laws of the state), *Phaedo* (the death scene of Socrates, in which he discusses the theory of Forms, the nature of the soul, and the question of immortality), the *Symposium* (Plato's outstanding dramatic achievement, which contains several speeches on beauty and love), the *Republic* (Plato's supreme philosophical achievement, which is a detailed discussion of the nature of justice).

The works of the later period include the *Theaetetus* (a denial that knowledge is to be identified with sense perception), *Parmenides* (a critical evaluation of the theory of Forms), *Sophist* (further consideration of the theory of Ideas, or Forms), *Philebus* (a discussion of the relationship between pleasure and the good), *Timaeus* (Plato's views on natural science and cosmology), and the *Laws* (a more practical analysis of political and social issues).

Theory of Forms. At the heart of Plato's philosophy is his theory of Forms, or Ideas. Ultimately, his view of knowledge, his ethical theory, his psychology, his concept of the state, and his perspective on art must be understood in terms of this theory.

Theory of knowledge. Plato's theory of Forms and his theory of knowledge are so interrelated that they must be discussed together. Influenced by Socrates, Plato was convinced that knowledge is attainable. He was also convinced of two essential characteristics of knowledge. First, knowledge must be certain and infallible. Second, knowledge must have as its object that which is genuinely real as contrasted with that which is an appearance only. Because that which is fully real must, for Plato, be fixed, permanent, and unchanging, he identified the real with the ideal realm of being as opposed to the physical world of becoming. One consequence of this view was Plato's rejection of empiricism (q.v.), the claim that knowledge is derived from sense experience. He thought that propositions derived from sense experience have, at most, a degree of probability. They are not certain. Furthermore, the objects of sense experience are changeable phenomena of the physical world. Hence, objects of sense experience are not proper objects of knowledge.

Plato's own theory of knowledge is found in the *Republic,* particularly in his discussion of the image of the divided line and the myth of the cave. In the former, Plato distinguishes between two levels of awareness: opinion and knowledge. Claims or assertions about the physical or visible world, including both commonsense observations and the propositions of science, are opinions only. Some of these opinions are well founded; some are not; but none of them counts as genuine knowledge. The higher level of awareness is knowledge, because there reason, rather than sense experience, is involved. Reason, properly used, results in intellectual insights that are certain, and the objects of these rational insights are the abiding universals, the eternal Forms or substances that constitute the real world.

The myth of the cave describes individuals chained deep within the recesses of a cave. Bound so that vision is restricted, they cannot see one another. The only thing visible is the wall of the cave upon which appear shadows cast by models or statues of animals and objects that are passed before a brightly burning fire. Breaking free, one of the individuals escapes from the cave into the light of day. With the aid of the sun, that person sees for the first time the real world and returns to the cave with the message that the only things they have seen heretofore are shadows and appearances and that the real world awaits them if they are willing to struggle free of their bonds. The shadowy environment of the cave symbolizes for Plato the physical world of appearances. Escape into the sun-filled setting outside the cave symbolizes the transition to the real world, the world of full and perfect being, the world of Forms, which is the proper object of knowledge.

Nature of Forms. The theory of Forms may best be understood in terms of mathematical entities. A circle, for instance, is defined as a plane figure composed of a series of points, all of which are equidistant from a given point. No one has ever actually seen such a figure, however.

What people have actually seen are drawn figures that are more or less close approximations of the ideal circle. In fact, when mathematicians define a circle, the points referred to are not spatial points at all; they are logical points. They do not occupy space. Nevertheless, although the Form of a circle has never been seen—indeed, could never be seen—mathematicians and others do in fact know what a circle is. That they can define a circle is evidence that they know what it is. For Plato, therefore, the Form "circularity" exists, but not in the physical world of space and time. It exists as a changeless object in the world of Forms or Ideas, which can be known only by reason. Forms have greater reality than objects in the physical world both because of their perfection and stability and because they are models, resemblance to which gives ordinary physical objects whatever reality they have. Circularity, squareness, and triangularity are excellent examples, then, of what Plato meant by Forms. An object existing in the physical world may be called a circle or a square or a triangle only to the extent that it resembles ("participates in" is Plato's phrase) the Form "circularity" or "squareness" or "triangularity."

Plato extended his theory beyond the realm of mathematics. Indeed, he was most interested in its application in the field of social ethics. The theory was his way of explaining how the same universal term can refer to so many particular things or events. The word *justice,* for example, can be applied to hundreds of particular acts because these acts have something in common, namely, their resemblance to, or participation in, the Form "justice." An individual is human to the extent that he or she resembles or participates in the Form "humanness." If "humanness" is defined in terms of being a rational animal, then an individual is human to the extent that he or she is rational. A particular act is courageous or cowardly to the extent that it participates in its Form. An object is beautiful to the extent that it participates in the Idea, or Form, of beauty. Everything in the world of space and time is what it is by virtue of its resemblance to, or participation in, its universal Form. The ability to define the universal term is evidence that one has grasped the Form to which that universal refers.

Plato conceived the Forms as arranged hierarchically; the supreme Form is the Form of the Good, which, like the sun in the myth of the cave, illuminates all the other Ideas. There is a sense in which the Form of the Good represents Plato's movement in the direction of an ultimate principle of explanation. Ultimately, the theory of Forms is intended to explain how one comes to know and also how things have come to be as they are. In philosophical language, Plato's theory of Forms is both an epistemological (theory of knowledge) and an ontological (theory of being) thesis.

Political Theory. The *Republic,* Plato's major political work, is concerned with the question of justice and therefore with the questions "what is a just state" and "who is a just individual?"

The ideal state, according to Plato, is composed of three classes. The economic structure of the state is maintained by the merchant class. Security needs are met by the military class, and political leadership is provided by the philosopher-kings. A particular person's class is determined by an educational process that begins at birth and proceeds until that person has reached the maximum level of education compatible with interest and ability. Those who complete the entire educational process become philosopher-kings. They are the ones whose minds have been so developed that they are able to grasp the Forms and, therefore, to make the wisest decisions. Indeed, Plato's ideal educational system is primarily structured so as to produce philosopher-kings.

Plato associates the traditional Greek virtues with the class structure of the ideal state. Temperance is the unique virtue of the artisan class; courage is the virtue peculiar to the military class; and wisdom characterizes the rulers. Justice, the fourth virtue, characterizes society as a whole. The just state is one in which each class performs its own function well without infringing on the activities of the other classes.

Plato divides the human soul into three parts: the rational part, the will, and the appetites. The just person is the one in whom the rational element, supported by the will, controls the appetites. An obvious analogy exists here with the threefold class structure of the state, in which the enlightened philosopher-kings, supported by the soldiers, govern the rest of society.

Ethics. Plato's ethical theory rests on the assumption that virtue is knowledge and can be taught, which has to be understood in terms of his theory of Forms. As indicated previously, the ultimate Form for Plato is the Form of the Good, and knowledge of this Form is the source of guidance in moral decision making. Plato also argued that to know the good is to do the good. The corollary of this is that anyone who behaves immorally does so out of ignorance. This conclusion follows from Plato's conviction that the moral person is the truly happy person, and because individuals always desire their own happiness, they always desire to do that which is moral.

Art. Plato had an essentially antagonistic view of art and the artist, although he approved of certain religious and moralistic kinds of art. Again, his approach is related to his theory of Forms. A beautiful flower, for example, is a copy or imitation of the universal Forms "flowerness" and "beauty." The physical flower is one step removed from reality, that is, the Forms. A picture of the flower is, therefore, two steps removed from reality. This also meant that the artist is two steps removed from knowledge, and, indeed, Plato's frequent criticism of the artists is that they lack genuine knowledge of what they are doing. Artistic creation, Plato observed, seems to be rooted in a kind of inspired madness.

Influence. Plato's influence throughout the history of philosophy has been monumental. When he died, Speusippus (407?–339BC) became head of the Academy. The school continued in existence until AD 529, when it was closed by the Byzantine emperor Justinian I, who objected to its pagan teachings. Plato's impact on Jewish thought is apparent in the work of the 1st-century Alexandrian philosopher Philo Judaeus. Neoplatonism (q.v.), founded by the 3d-century philosopher Plotinus, was an important later development of Platonism. The theologians Clement of Alexandria, Origen, and St. Augustine were early Christian exponents of a Platonic perspective. Platonic ideas have had a crucial role in the development of Christian theology and also in medieval Islamic thought (*see* ISLAM).

During the Renaissance (q.v.), the primary focus of Platonic influence was the Florentine Academy, founded in the 15th century near Florence. Under the leadership of Marsilio Ficino, members of the Academy studied Plato in the original Greek. In England, Platonism was revived in the 17th century by Ralph Cudworth and others who became known as the Cambridge Platonists (q.v.). Plato's influence has been extended into the 20th century by such thinkers as Alfred North Whitehead, who once paid him tribute by describing the history of philosophy as simply "a series of footnotes to Plato."

See also GREEK PHILOSOPHY; IDEALISM; METAPHYSICS; PHILOSOPHY. R.M.B.

For further information on this topic, see the Bibliography in volume 28, section 41.

PLATT AMENDMENT, popular title of an amendatory law drafted by U.S. Senator Orville Hitchcock Platt (1827–1905) of Connecticut and passed by Congress as an amendment to the Army Appropriations Bill of 1901. It specified conditions under which the federal government might intervene in the internal affairs of Cuba; it was included in the Cuban constitution, adopted in 1901, and in the treaty between Cuba and the U.S. concluded in 1903. Many Cuban liberal statesmen denounced the interventions of 1906, 1912, 1917, and 1920 as undemocratic and imperialistic. Renegotiations of the treaty led to the abrogation of the Platt Amendment in 1934. *See* CUBA.

PLATTE, river, Nebraska, affluent of the Missouri R. It is formed by the junction, near the city of North Platte in central Nebraska, of the North Platte and South Platte rivers, which rise in the Rocky Mts. in Colorado. The Platte generally flows E in a wide, shallow stream until it reaches the Missouri, near Omaha. The length of the main stream is about 500 km (about 310 mi); including the North Platte, the total length is some 1595 km (some 990 mi) and the drainage area is about 233,100 sq km (about 90,000 sq mi).

PLATTSBURGH, city, seat of Clinton Co., NE New York, on the W shore of Lake Champlain, at the mouth of the Saranac R.; inc. as a city 1902. It is a summer resort, and manufactures here include paper products, plastics, and iron castings. Plattsburgh Air Force Base, the State University of New York College at Plattsburgh (1889), and a community college are here. Of interest is the Kent-Delord House (1797) and the Clinton County Historical Museum (c. 1807). Both buildings were occupied by the British during the War of 1812. The community was founded about 1784 by a colonial statesman, Zephaniah Platt (1735–1807), for whom it is named. The offshore waters were the scene of a decisive U.S. naval victory over the British in September 1814. Led by Commodore Thomas Macdonough (1783–1825), the Americans captured four British vessels and forced the enemy land forces to retreat to Canada. Pop. (1980) 21,057; (1990) 21,255.

PLATYHELMINTHES. *See* FLATWORM.

PLATYPUS (Gr. *platys,* "broad"; *pous,* "foot"), also duckbill, semiaquatic, egg-laying mammal, *Ornithorhynchus anatinus,* native to Tasmania and southern and eastern Australia, which with the echidnas (*see* ECHIDNA) forms the order Monotremata (*see* MONOTREME). The animal has a ducklike bill and webbed feet. The body of the platypus is egg shaped and is about 36 cm (about 14 in) long; the flattened tail measures about 13 cm (about 5 in) in length. The body and tail are covered with a thick, soft, woolly layer of fur, from which long, flat hairs protrude. The most conspicuous feature of the small head is the bill, which is about 6 cm (about 2.5 in) long and 5 cm (2 in) wide and which the animal uses for stirring up mud at the bottom of rivers in order to uncover the insects, worms, and shellfish on which it feeds. The head is joined directly to the body without an apparent neck. The platypus's eyes

Platypus, Ornithorhynchus anatinus
Australian News & Information Bureau

are small, and it has no external ears. Young platypuses have rudimentary teeth, but in adults the teeth are replaced by a few horny plates. Adult males have a hollow, horny spur on the inner side of the hind leg, from which a toxic fluid is ejected and which may be used as a weapon of defense. The call of the platypus is a throaty, clucking sound; the platypus also emits a low growl. Duckbills are shy, nocturnal animals and are seldom observed, even in localities where they abound. They are excellent swimmers and divers, but as they are otherwise not equipped to defend themselves against enemies, they live in long, winding burrows, which are usually dug by the females in the banks of rivers or streams. The burrows are blocked with earth in several places as fortification against intruders. At the end of the burrow, which may be from about 9 to 15 m (about 30 to 50 ft) in length, the female constructs a bed of weeds, leaves, and grass, which it uses as a nest for the eggs and young, and for a retreat. The male is excluded from the nesting burrow. The female lays usually two but sometimes as many as four eggs in a clutch. The young animals have no fur when they hatch. The female uses its tail to clasp the young to its abdomen, enabling them to lick the milk that flows onto it through pores. Platypuses are captured as biological curiosities, but the hunting of platypuses is forbidden by law.

PLAUEN, city, E central Germany, in Saxony, on the Elster R., near Zwickau. The city is a textile-milling center and has plants manufacturing machine tools, cables, steel products, electrical and electronic equipment, musical instruments, and lamps. A 17th-century castle and a Gothic church are two of the architectural features of Plauen. Founded in the 12th century by Slavs, the city passed to Bohemia in 1327 and to Saxony in 1466. Pop. (1989 est.) 77,600.

PLAUTUS, (Titus Maccius) (254?–184 BC), Roman comic dramatist, who enjoyed immense popularity among the Romans and greatly influenced post-Renaissance European dramatic literature.

Plautus was born in Sarsina, Umbria. According to legend he went to Rome as a youth, made money doing backstage work, lost it in business, and began to write comedies while employed in a mill. More than 100 comedies were ascribed to him, but of these only 20 and the very fragmentary *Vidularia* have been preserved; almost all were composed in the last 20 years of his life. The extant comedies of Plautus are all plays with costumes, characters, plots, and settings modeled upon original comedies written by Menander, Philemon (c. 361–263 BC), Diphilus (c. 360–289 BC), and other playwrights of the Greek New Comedy. Plautus added numerous local allusions, introduced the elements of song and dance, and, with his broad sense of humor and his mastery of colloquial Latin, produced farces that, although less polished, were often more amusing than the plays of the Greek New Comedy. The plots were usually based upon love affairs, with complications arising from deception or mistaken identity, and the characters were the standard types inherited from Greek comedies, such as parasites and braggart warriors. The comedies of Plautus, however, display variety and inventiveness in the treatment of both theme and character, and range from mythological parody (*Amphitruo*) to romance (*Rudens*), and from burlesque (*Casina*) and farce (*Menæchmi*) to refined comedy (*Captivi* and *Trinummus*).

PLAYING CARDS. *See* CARDS AND CARD GAMES.

PLEASANT HILL, city, Contra Costa Co., W California, a residential suburb of Oakland; inc. 1961. Diablo Valley College (1949), a large community college, is here. The area was settled in 1844 but remained rural until the early 1940s. Pop. (1980) 25,124; (1990) 31,585.

PLEASANTON, city, Alameda Co., W California, near Oakland; inc. 1894. Many firms engaged in research are located in Pleasanton, as well as wine and cheese manufacturers. The county fairgrounds and several old homes are here, and Pleasanton Racetrack is nearby. The community was named in 1867 for Gen. Alfred Pleasonton (1824–97), a Union officer during the American Civil War. Pop. (1980) 35,160; (1990) 50,553.

PLEASURE RIDGE PARK, unincorporated community, Jefferson Co., N Kentucky. It is primarily a residential suburb of Louisville, near the Ohio R. and Standiford Field Airport. Pop. (1980) 27,332; (1990) 25,131.

PLEBISCITE, a vote by the electorate of a nation, region, or locality on a specific question. In modern times, plebiscites have been held to determine the wishes of the inhabitants of a country or area as to their choice of sovereignty and have constituted an important political means of self-determination for a number of peoples and nations. The use of plebiscites in this sense originated at the time of the French Revolution, supposedly as an alternative to forcible annexations and wars of conquest. The plebiscites held after 1793, however, in areas including Belgium and the Rhineland, were accompanied by the intimidation of voters in order to assure decisions desired by the French government.

As democratic instruments, plebiscites were used after the resurgence of nationalistic sentiments in Europe in 1848. They played a prominent role, for example, in the long struggle for the independence and unification of Italy. In 1852 a notable plebiscite was held in France by Napoleon III to give the appearance of popular approval to the coup d'état by which he had overthrown the republic. In the 20th century, important plebiscites resulted in the separation of Norway from Sweden in 1905 and in the reacquisition of the Saarland by Germany in 1935. More recently, they have been used in Africa to learn the preferences of newly independent peoples for their national sovereignty.

PLEBS, common people of ancient Rome; one of the two elements making up the Roman nation, the other being the patricians or members of the original Roman family groups. The origin of the plebs is in dispute. Some scholars believe they were persons considered to be of inferior birth who flocked to the city as employees, hangers-on, or clients of the patrician families and whose number was constantly increased by the subjugation of the surrounding cities and states. Other scholars maintain that the plebs, native to Liguria, existed at Rome from the beginning of the city and were conquered by the Sabines.

During the Roman Republic (509–44 BC) the plebs gradually acquired a variety of new privileges and, after a long struggle with the patricians, eventually gained access to all civil and religious offices. A new aristocracy of *nobiles,* based upon wealth and office and composed of both patricians and plebs, was established. Thereafter the term *plebs* was loosely used to denote the multitude, in opposition to the senators and the knights.

PLEDGE OF ALLEGIANCE TO THE FLAG OF THE UNITED STATES, oath of loyalty to the U.S. national emblem and to the nation it symbolizes. The idea for such a pledge is said to have originated with one of the editors of *The Youth's Companion,* a magazine for children. By proclamation of President Benjamin Harrison, the pledge was first used on Oct. 12, 1892, during Columbus Day observances in the public schools. The original wording was as follows:

> I pledge allegiance to my flag and to the republic for which it stands: one nation, indivisible, with liberty and justice for all.

The pledge was amended subsequently by the substitution of the words "the flag of the United States of America" for the phrase "my flag." The newly worded pledge was adopted officially on Flag Day, June 14, 1924. By joint resolution of Congress the pledge was further amended in 1954 by the addition of the words "under God." This is how the pledge now reads:

> I pledge allegiance to the flag of the United States of America and to the republic for which it stands: one nation under God, indivisible, with liberty and justice for all.

When reciting the pledge of allegiance, civilians should stand at attention or with the right hand over the heart. Men should remove their hats. Armed services personnel in uniform face the flag and give the military salute.

PLEIAD, name sometimes applied to any group, usually seven in number, of illustrious figures, such as philosophers or poets. In ancient times the term was applied to a group of 6th-century BC philosophers (*see* SEVEN WISE MEN OF GREECE) and to a group of seven poets who flourished in the 3d century BC at Alexandria, Egypt, including Apollonius of Rhodes, Callimachus, and Theocritus. In modern times the term has been used to designate a group of seven 16th-century French poets, the Pléiade, of whom the most important was Pierre de Ronsard. The group attempted to raise the level of French literature by introducing into the French language words derived from Greek and Latin and by imitating many of the forms of classical literature. Influenced by the great 14th-century Italian poet Petrarch, the members of the Pléiade idealized love in their poems. Composers, such as the French Claude Le Jeune (c. 1528–1600), set their poems to music.

PLEIADES, in Greek mythology, seven daughters of Atlas and of Pleione, the daughter of Oceanus. Their names were Electra, Maia, Taygete, Alcyone, Celaeno, Sterope, and Merope. According to some versions of the myth, they committed suicide from grief at the fate of their father, Atlas, or at the death of their sisters, the Hyades. Other versions made them the attendants of Artemis, goddess of wildlife and of hunting, who were pursued by the giant hunter Orion, but were rescued by the gods and changed into doves. After their death, or metamorphosis, they were transformed into stars, but are still pursued across the sky by the constellation Orion.

PLEIADES, in astronomy, loose cluster of 400 to 500 stars, about 415 light-years from the solar system in the direction of the constellation Taurus (q.v.). The stars are about 1 light-year apart, on the average, and photographs show them to be surrounded by a nebulosity that shines by their reflected light. The cluster was named by the ancient Greeks after the "Seven Sisters" of mythology. Observers have claimed to be able to see with the naked eye as many as 12 of the stars in the cluster.

PLEIKU, town, central Vietnam, in the Annamese highlands. Pleiku was at the center of many critical actions of the war in Vietnam, including a guerrilla attack on a U.S. special forces camp in 1965, which provoked the first sustained U.S. air raids of the war. Pop. (1989) 75,810.

PLEISTOCENE EPOCH. *See* QUATERNARY PERIOD.

PLESIOSAUR, any of a group of carnivorous ocean-dwelling reptiles that flourished during the Age of Reptiles, from late Triassic times to the end of the Cretaceous Period, about 65 million years ago. Two major types of plesiosaur existed, one with a long neck and relatively small head, and the other with a short neck and a large head. Both types were more than 12 m (40 ft) long, depending on the species, but the head of the short-necked types could account for about a fourth of the total length. The limbs of plesiosaurs were like flippers; the tail was short.

PLEURA. *See* MEMBRANE.

PLEURISY, inflammation of the pleura membrane that lines the chest cavity and contains the lung. Most cases are due to infection and many are associated with pneumonia in the underlying lung. Some cases are due to viral infections. Occasionally pleurisy may occur in other diseases such as tuberculosis, systemic lupus erythematosis, rheumatic fever, and kidney failure. Pleurisy may develop in conjunction with a blood clot on the lung; it may also be associated with the development of fluid in the pleural space between the chest wall and the lung.

The characteristic symptom of pleurisy is sharp pain brought on by breathing and coughing. The patient breathes shallowly. If considerable fluid accumulates, the pain may subside, but the underlying lung may be compressed by the fluid and the patient may feel short of breath. On examination the doctor can usually hear the inflamed surfaces of the pleura rubbing together and producing a rough sound.

Treatment of pleurisy attempts to cure the underlying disease causing it; the pain is controlled with analgesic drugs.

PLEVEN, also Plevna, city, N Bulgaria, capital of Pleven Province. A trade in cattle and wine is carried on, as are vegetable canning, vegetable-oil extracting, tanning, flour milling, and the manufacturing of cotton, linen, and woolen textiles. Pleven was the site of a major battle of the Russo-Turkish War (1877–78). It was defended by the Ottoman Turks against Russian and Romanian troops, but in 1877 it fell to the Russians after four months of fighting. The fall of Pleven caused the Turks to seek an armistice early in 1878. Pop. (1985) 129,766.

PLINY THE ELDER, full name GAIUS PLINIUS SECUNDUS (23?–79), Roman writer and encyclopedist, who was the foremost authority on science in ancient Europe.

Pliny was born in Novum Comum (now Como, Italy) but went to Rome at an early age. When he was about 23 years old he entered the army, serving in a campaign in Germany. Returning to Rome in 52, he studied jurisprudence, but, being unsuccessful as a pleader, he devoted himself to scholarly study and writing. From about 70 to 72 he served in Spain as procurator, or collector of imperial revenues. In 79, when the great eruption of Vesuvius overwhelmed and destroyed Herculaneum and Pompeii, he was stationed at Misenum, near Naples, in command of the western Roman fleet. Eager to examine the volcanic phenomenon more closely, he sailed across the bay of Naples to Stabiae, where he was suffocated by the vapors from the eruption.

Pliny wrote many historical and scientific works, including *De Laculatione Equestri,* a treatise on the use of the javelin by cavalrymen; *Studiosus,* 3 books on the training of a young orator, written apparently for the guidance of his nephew Pliny the Younger; *Dubius Sermo,* an 8-book treatise on declensions and conjugations; a 20-book history of the Germanic Wars; and 31 books of Roman history covering 41 to 71.

Pliny's great encyclopedia of nature and art in 37 books, the *Historia Naturalis,* is the only one of his works that has been preserved. It embraces, as he states in his dedicatory epistle to the Roman emperor Titus, 20,000 important facts, extracted from about 2000 volumes by 100 authors. The first ten books were published in 77

Pliny the Elder Bettmann Archive

and the remainder after his death, probably by Pliny the Younger. The encyclopedia concerns astronomy, geography, ethnology, anthropology, human physiology, zoology, botany, horticulture, medicine and medicaments from plant and animal substances, mineralogy and metallurgy, and the fine arts, and also contains a valuable digression on the history of art.

PLINY THE YOUNGER, full Latin name GAIUS PLINIUS CAECILIUS SECUNDUS (62–113), Roman official, whose letters give a valuable description of life in the 1st century AD. He was a nephew of Pliny the Elder, by whom he was adopted and whose name he took in 79; his name was originally Publius Caecilius Secundus. He was born in Novum Comum, and studied in Rome under the famous teacher and rhetorician Quintilian. Pliny was distinguished both for his literary accomplishments and for his oratorical ability. He held numerous official appointments. As a young man he served as military tribune in Syria, where he frequented the schools of the Stoics; he was quaestor Caesaris at the age of 25, then praetor, and then consul in 100, in which year he wrote the *Panegyricus,* a eulogy of the emperor Trajan. About 111 he was appointed governor of the province of Bithynia, where he remained about two years. Whether his death occurred in Bithynia or soon after in Rome is not known. He was married three times, but died childless.

Pliny himself collected and published nine books of *Epistulae* (Letters), and a tenth book, containing his official correspondence as governor of Bithynia with the emperor Trajan, was published after his death. To these letters Pliny owes his place in literature as one of the masters of the epistolary style. The private letters, most of which were undoubtedly written or revised with a view to publication, give a valuable picture of the life of the writer and of his friends and contemporaries. Pliny himself appears in the letters as a genial philanthropist, devoted to literary pursuits and to improving his estates by architectural adornment. The most interesting letters include two of his friend the historian Publius Cornelius Tacitus on the eruption of Vesuvius—one letter describing in detail his villa at Laurentum, the other relating the story of a haunted house in Athens—and one to the Roman emperor Trajan, concerning the policy against the Christians.

PLIOCENE EPOCH, fifth and most recent division of the Tertiary period of the Cenozoic era (q.v.) on the geologic time scale (*see* GEOLOGY), spanning an interval from about 12 million to 2 million years ago. Like the Miocene, which preceded it, the Pliocene was named and defined by the British geologist Sir Charles Lyell on the basis of the percentage of modern species of shellfish found in the fossil record. In western North America, subduction of the Pacific tectonic plate margin helped elevate the Sierra Nevada and the volcanic Cascade Range. In Europe, the Alps continued to rise as tectonic plate motion buckled the crust across a wide swath of that continent (*see* PLATE TECTONICS). The climate became cooler and drier with the approach of the Ice Ages (q.v.) of the Pleistocene Epoch. Mammals had long since established themselves as the dominant terrestrial life form, and the rapid evolution of one group, the primates, produced species considered direct ancestors of *Homo sapiens.*

For further information on this topic, see the Bibliography in volume 28, sections 417, 436.

PLISETSKAYA, Maya Mikhaylovna (1925–), Soviet dancer, the leading ballerina of the Bolshoi Ballet, known for her technical skill, dramatic insight, and the supple, expressive use of her body. Born into a family of dancers in Moscow, she studied at the Bolshoi ballet school and joined the company in 1943, immediately dancing solo roles. Her greatest portrayal is considered Odette-Odile in *Swan Lake.* In addition to classical roles, she performed in modern Soviet ballets such as *The Stone Flower* (1954). In 1964 she received the Lenin Prize.

PLOIEŞTI, city, S Romania, capital of Prahova District, near Bucharest. It is the center of the country's petroleum production; other products include textiles, hats, drilling equipment, hardware, paper and cardboard, glass and leather goods, furniture, and rubber and clay products. During World War II, Ploieşti was repeatedly bombed by planes of the U.S., Britain, and the USSR. The first U.S. raid on the oil refineries at Ploieşti, on Aug. 1, 1943, was one of the largest of the war; it destroyed nearly 50 percent of their productive capacity. Pop. (1986 est.) 234,900.

PLOTINUS (AD 205–70), Roman philosopher, who founded Neoplatonism (q.v.). Plotinus was born in Asyut, Egypt. He studied with the Alexandrian philosopher Ammonius Saccas (fl. 1st half of 3d cent.) at Alexandria for ten years and about 244 went to Rome, where he established a school. Plotinus spoke on Pythagorean and Platonic wisdom and on asceticism; such was the impression made upon his hearers that some of them gave their fortunes to the poor, set their slaves free, and devoted themselves to lives of study and ascetic piety. At the age of 60, with the permission of the Roman emperor Gallienus, Plotinus planned to establish a communistic commonwealth on the model of *The Republic* by Plato, but the project failed because of the opposition of Gallienus's counselors. Plotinus continued to teach and write until his death. His works comprise 54 treatises in Greek, called the *Enneads*, 6 groups of 9 books each, an arrangement probably made by his student Porphyry (AD 232–c. 304), who edited his writings.

Plotinus's system was based chiefly on Plato's theory of Ideas, but whereas Plato assumed archetypal Ideas to be the link between the supreme deity and the world of matter, Plotinus accepted a doctrine of emanation. This doctrine supposes the constant transmission of powers from the Absolute Being, or the One, to the creation through several agencies, the first of which is *nous,* or pure intelligence, whence flows the soul of the world; from this, in turn, flow the souls of humans and animals, and finally matter. Human beings thus belong to two worlds, that of the senses and that of pure intelligence. Inasmuch as matter is the cause of all evil, the object of life should be to escape the material world of the senses, and hence people should abandon all earthly interests for those of intellectual meditation; by purification and by the exercise of thought people can gradually lift themselves to an intuition of the *nous,* and ultimately to a complete and ecstatic union with the One—that is, God. Plotinus claimed to have experienced this divine ecstasy on several occasions.

PLOVDIV (anc. *Philippopolis*), city, S Bulgaria, capital of Plovdiv Region, on the Maritsa R. It is a trading center and market for the Plovdiv Basin and an agricultural area producing tobacco and livestock. A manufacturing center, it has cigarette-making, food-processing, and woodworking industries; textiles, metal, leather, and chemicals are also produced. The city has an ancient gate and walls, a Catholic cathedral, old churches and mosques, and the ruins of a Turkish market and baths. It also has a university (1961) and institutes of food, agriculture, and music.

Originally the Greek settlement of Eumolpias, Plovdiv was captured in 341 BC by Philip II, king of Macedonia, and renamed Philippopolis. The city was the site of many battles and was ruled successively by the Goths, Byzantines, Bulgarians, Greeks, Ottoman Turks, and Russians. It was made the capital of Eastern Rumelia under the Congress of Berlin (1878) and was joined to Bulgaria in 1885. Pop. (1985) 342,131.

PLOVER, common name for members of the family Charadriidae, a group of widely distributed shorebirds consisting of more than 60 species. Two groups are usually recognized: the typical plovers, subfamily Charadriinae, and the lapwings (*see* LAPWING), subfamily Vanellinae. Plovers are distinguished from their similar shorebird relatives the sandpipers (family Scolopacidae) by their relatively short bills, which are enlarged and hardened at the tip. The plumage of sandpipers is relatively subdued in color and pattern, whereas many of the plovers are strikingly patterned.

The American golden plover, Pluvialis dominica, *migrates long distances.* © Rod Planck–Photo Researchers, Inc.

Plovers typically stand immobile, then run rapidly to the next food source, preying on a variety of small invertebrates. Although relatively sociable, they seldom form the large flocks typical of sandpipers in the nonbreeding season. Many are true shorebirds, but several of both the typical plovers and the lapwings inhabit upland areas, on fields or plains. Tropical plovers are sedentary, but the northernmost and southernmost breeding species are highly migratory. The nests are on the surface of the ground or in a small depression, sometimes lined with pebbles, shells, or grass. Clutch size is usually four in northern species, but fewer in the tropical plovers.

The largest genus is *Charadrius,* with about 30 species, many of which have dark "rings" or "belts" across their upper breasts. In the Americas the best-known species, and the only one with two breast rings, is the primarily upland killdeer (q.v.), *C. vociferus.* Sandy beaches of lakes and rivers east of the Rockies and of the Atlantic coast south to Virginia are the home of the piping plover, *C. melodus;* the small Great Lakes populations are considered endangered. It is about 16 cm (about 6.3 in) long, and its pale colors blend perfectly with dry beach sand. Similar in size but matching wet sand in color is the darker semipalmated plover, *C. semipalmatus,* a breeding bird of Alaska and much of northern Canada. It is a familiar sight in spring and fall along its migration route to southern South America. A similar species, the common ringed plover, *C. hiaticula,* nests principally in northern

Eurasia; the populations nesting in the eastern Canadian Arctic and Greenland migrate to Europe. It is larger (about 19 cm/7.5 in) and has a broader breast band than the semipalmated plover. Taking the place of the piping plover on the Gulf coast and much of western North America is the similar snowy plover, *C. alexandrinus,* which also ranges into South America and much of the Old World, where it is known as the Kentish plover. Other members of *Charadrius* nest on every continent.

The four members of the genus *Pluvialis* are among the most highly migratory shorebirds. In the breeding season, all four have black underparts and mottled backs. The black underparts are lost in the post-breeding molt. The largest is the black-bellied plover, *P. squatarola,* called grey plover in the Old World, which is about 33 cm (about 13 in) long. Its back is speckled with black and white, slightly tinged yellowish in winter. The three golden plovers have brightly mottled yellow and black upperparts. The American golden plover, *P. dominica,* about 26 cm (about 10.5 in) long, has one of the longest migrations known, a round trip of almost 13,000 km (about 8000 mi) from its arctic nesting areas to the southern tip of South America; part of this route takes it about 3860 km (about 2400 mi) over open ocean from Nova Scotia to northeastern South America. Equally impressive is the migration of the closely similar Pacific golden plover, *P. fulva,* which leaves its Siberian and Alaskan summer home and crosses the trackless Pacific Ocean annually to find the same islands on which to winter. The larger Eurasian golden plover, *P. apricaria,* 28 cm (11 in) long, occasionally strays across the Atlantic to Newfoundland.

For further information on this topic, see the Bibliography in volume 28, section 473.

PLOW, agricultural implement used to break and turn over soil. An important agricultural tool, the plow has been used since prehistoric times. The first plows were probably forked tree boughs, the points used for stirring the soil, the branches as handles. The implement could be pushed, or it might be pulled by ropes attached to a person or animal. Such simple plows are still used in light soil in some parts of the developing world. The Romans used a light scratch plow with an iron share, or blade, drawn by oxen. The heavy wheeled plow was developed in the Middle Ages to turn over the heavier soil of northwest Europe. It had a sharp point of iron or steel to cut under the soil; this sharp vertical cutter, or colter, was located directly in front of the share, making a preliminary cut that the share deepened and widened. It also had a moldboard behind the share to heave up the cut sod, and a tongue in front of the plow that could be attached to a team of from two to eight oxen.

The Eagle plow, used in Massachusetts throughout much of the 19th century. Made of cast iron, the plow worked well in the gravelly soil of New England.

Smithsonian Institution

Wheeled or wheelless, the plow changed little until the 1830s, when the heavy prairie soils of the North American Midwest brought about the invention of the steel plowshare by the blacksmith John Deere. The two-wheeled sulky plow, which had a seat for the rider, appeared during the American Civil War. During the 1890s, steam-powered tractors were successfully used on a few large farms; after 1900 cheaper gasoline-powered tractors began to replace horses as plow traction. Tractors were not widely adopted, however, until the introduction of the small all-purpose tractor in 1924 and the development of low-pressure rubber tires in 1932.

Modern plows may have as many as five sets of plowshares and moldboards, which can be raised and lowered hydraulically. Disk plows, for use in tough soils, are equipped with several concave disks. Rotary plows (rototillers) have cutters mounted on a rotating horizontal shaft. Deep plowing is done by subsoilers, with long steel-pointed shanks that can penetrate the soil up to about 1 m (about 3 ft), or by chisel plows, with several shanks carrying double-ended shovels that can plow about 50 cm (about 20 in) deep.

PLUM, borough, Allegheny Co., SW Pennsylvania, on the Allegheny R., near Pittsburgh; founded 1788, inc. as a borough 1956. Pharmaceuticals, office furniture, and industrial control devices are manufactured here. The community is named for the wild plum trees that once abounded in the area. Pop. (1980) 25,390; (1990) 25,609.

PLUM, common name for certain trees of the genus *Prunus,* of the family Rosaceae (*see* ROSE), and for their edible fruit, a drupe (hard-pitted fruit). The genus also contains the other trees that produce drupes: peach, cherry, almond, and apricot. About 12 plum species are cultivated throughout temperate regions for their fruit and as flowering ornamentals. The trees are rarely more than 10 m (33 ft) high. The plum varieties, which are suited to both warm and cool climates, exceed the other drupes.

The common European plum, or prune, *P. domes-*

tica, which is the most important species, has been cultivated since ancient times and probably originated near the Caspian Sea. It was introduced into North America, possibly by the Pilgrims, and is now mostly cultivated in the western U.S. Fruits of varieties of this species range in color from yellow or red to green, but purplish blue is most common. Dried plums, or prunes, are made from the varieties that are richest in sugar and solids. Before its dissolution Yugoslavia led the world in plum production; a plum brandy called slivovitz was produced there.

The Japanese plum, *P. salicina,* probably originating in China, was introduced into the U.S. in 1870. The fruit is more pointed at the apex than that of *P. domestica,* and its varieties are yellow or light red but never purplish blue. The Damson plum, *P. institia*—a small, oval, sweet fruit used mostly in jams—was first cultivated in ancient times in the region of Damascus.

For further information on this topic, see the Bibliography in volume 28, sections 456, 675.

PLUMBING, systems of piping within a building, for water supply and sewage. To protect public health, every inhabited building must have a supply of safe water for drinking and for the operation of the plumbing fixtures and appliances therein, and a sanitary drainage system for wastewater disposal. To provide the facilities required, local government authorities are responsible for establishing regulations known as plumbing codes, which govern design and installation requirements and the minimum number of fixtures needed, based on building use and the number of occupants.

History. The word *plumbing* is derived from *plumbum,* Latin for the metallic element lead (q.v.), the material most often used for ducts and piping until it was superseded by cast iron in the 19th century. Archaeologists have found evidence of systems for disposal of human waste in dwellings 10,000 years old. Waste disposal and running water were commonly incorporated in the palaces of royalty and priests from the time of the Indus Valley civilization through the Minoan civilization, and these systems were well developed during the Roman Empire. After a long decline and slow recovery, plumbing was a firmly established feature in dwellings of even the less affluent by the end of the 19th century.

Today at least 26 different systems are included in plumbing design, although not all are found in any one building. Basic modern plumbing fixtures include toilets, urinals, sinks, bathtubs, showers, laundry tubs, and drinking fountains (water coolers). In addition, hospitals require many specialized types of fixtures. Plumbing-connected appliances include dishwashers and laundry washers. All of the above fixtures, except for toilets, urinals, and drinking fountains, require both hot and cold water. Fixtures today are made of impervious materials such as vitreous china, enameled cast iron or steel, stainless steel, and plastic. Piping materials include cast iron, steel, brass, copper, stainless steel, aluminum, plastic, vitrified clay (tile), and concrete.

Water Supply and Drainage Systems. In developed communities, water under pressure is secured from street water mains and piped into the buildings. In other areas, water must be obtained from on-site wells or adjacent streams or lakes, in which case great care must be taken that the water is of potable quality. Where available street pressure is insufficient to serve a building because of its height, equipment within the building, such as a gravity tank above the roof, a pressure tank, or a booster pumping system must be installed. Hot water can be generated by heaters using gas, electricity, boiler water, oil, steam, or solar energy. In hospitals and laboratories, in addition, special water systems such as distilled, demineralized (deionized), and reverse osmosis (RO) water systems are usually required. *See* WATER SUPPLY AND WATERWORKS.

Drainage systems are of two basic types: sanitary and storm water. Sanitary drainage systems carry bodily and other wastes from the plumbing fixtures and appliances by gravity through a sewer to a sewage treatment facility outside the building. Sanitary drainage piping inside the building must be provided with a parallel system of vent piping, to keep the pressures in the drainage piping minimal and equalized in order to prevent the siphoning or blowing of water in the traps (U-shaped dips in the piping), which would allow sewer gas to enter the building. Storm-water drainage systems carry rainwater from the roof by gravity through a sewer to an outfall in a body of water or to a dry well. Basement drainage must be collected in a sealed and vented pit or tank and pumped up into the gravity system. Hospitals and laboratories often require additional special drainage systems for removal of acid waste, radioactive waste, and infectious waste. *See* SEWAGE DISPOSAL.

Safety Devices and Special Systems. Both water supply and drainage systems must be carefully designed to prevent serious contamination of the water and to stop sewer gas from entering the building. All water connections to fixtures and appliances must be provided with devices that prevent contaminants from being siphoned or forced back into the water piping, a condition known as backflow or back siphonage. Temperature and pressure-relief valves must be provided on all water heaters to prevent explosion in the event of malfunctioning controls. All fixtures and appliance and equipment connections to the sanitary drainage system must be provided with water-filled sewer-gas traps.

In developed communities, natural gas may be piped into a building from utility company street mains and distributed to appliances and equipment for cooking and heating. In rural areas, propane gas is piped into buildings from high-pressure tanks on the site. Hospitals require special medical gases such as oxygen, nitrous oxide, and nitrogen, which are piped from high-pressure cylinders. Both hospitals and laboratories also require compressed air from air compressors and negative pressure, or vacuum, from vacuum pumps. J.C.C.

PLUTARCH (AD 46?–120), Greek biographer and essayist, born in Chaeronea in Boeotia. He was educated in Athens and is believed to have traveled to Egypt and Italy and to have lectured in Rome on moral philosophy. He frequently visited Athens and was a priest in the temple at Delphi. He spent the later years of his life at Chaeronea, where he held municipal office. Many of the treatises he wrote are probably based on his lecture notes. To his students, Plutarch was regarded as a genial guide, philosopher, and spiritual director.

His extant works, written in a modified Attic, a so-called common dialect, fall into two principal classes: the didactic essays and dialogues, grouped under the title of *Moralia;* and the biographies, the *Parallel Lives* of famous Greeks and Romans. The more than 80 essays are charmingly written and enlivened by anecdotes and quotations. The essays treat matters of ethics and religion. Some are philosophical works supporting the teachings of Plato in opposition to the doctrines of the Stoics and the Epicureans, and nine books contain *Symposiaca,* or *Table Talks,* by wise men on various subjects.

Best known are Plutarch's *Parallel Lives,* a series of 4 single biographies and 23 pairs of biographies. Many of the pairs, such as those on the legendary lawgivers Lycurgus and Numa Pompilius (715–673 BC), the generals Alexander the Great and Julius Caesar, and the orators Demosthenes and Marcus Tullius Cicero, are followed with a brief comparison. Composed with great learning and research, the *Lives* are not only historical works of great value, but they are also, and purposely, character studies with a moral. The first translation of the *Lives* into English was by Sir Thomas North (1535?–1601) in 1579; this is the translation Shakespeare followed closely in the composition of his plays based on Roman history, such as *Coriolanus, Julius Caesar,* and *Antony and Cleopatra.*

PLUTO, in Roman mythology, god of the dead, the husband of Proserpine. The Latin counterpart of the Greek god Hades, Pluto assisted his two brothers, Jupiter and Neptune, in overthrowing their father, Saturn. In dividing the world among them, Jupiter chose the earth and the heavens as his realm, Neptune became the ruler of the sea, and Pluto received as his kingdom the lower world, in which he ruled over the shades of the dead. He was originally considered a fierce and unyielding god, deaf to prayers and unappeased by sacrifices. In later cults and popular belief the milder and more beneficent aspects of the god were stressed. Believed to be the bestower of the blessings hidden in the earth, such as mineral wealth and crops, Pluto was also known as Dis or Orcus, the giver of wealth.

PLUTO, in astronomy, ninth planet from the sun and outermost known member of the solar system (q.v.). Pluto was discovered as the result of a telescopic search inaugurated in 1905 by the American astronomer Percival Lowell, who postulated the existence of a distant planet beyond Neptune as the cause of slight perturbations (*see* ORBIT) in the motions of Uranus. Continued by members of the Lowell Observatory staff, the search ended successfully in 1930, when the American astronomer Clyde William Tombaugh (1906–) found Pluto near the position Lowell had predicted. The new planet's mass, however, seemed insufficient to account for the perturbations of Neptune, and the search for a possible tenth planet continues.

Pluto revolves about the sun once in 247.7 years at an average distance of 5.9 billion km (3.67 billion mi). The orbit is so eccentric that at certain points along its path Pluto is closer to the sun than is Neptune. No possibility of collision exists, however, because Pluto's orbit is inclined more than 17.2° to the plane of the ecliptic (q.v.) and never actually crosses Neptune's path.

Visible only through large telescopes, Pluto is seen to have a yellowish color. For many years very little was known about the planet, but in 1978 astronomers discovered a relatively large moon orbiting Pluto at a distance of only about 19,000 km (about 12,000 mi) and named it Charon. The orbits of Pluto and Charon caused them to pass repeatedly in front of one another from 1985 through 1990, enabling astronomers to determine their sizes fairly accurately. Pluto is about 2284 km (1420 mi) in diameter, and Charon is about 1192 km (740 mi) in diameter, making them even more closely a double-planet system than are the earth and its moon. Pluto was also

BRIEF SURVEY OF PLUTO

Distance from sun	
Perihelion	4.4 billion km (2.75 billion mi)
Mean	5.9 billion km (3.67 billion mi)
Aphelion	7.4 billion km (4.58 billion mi)
Eccentricity of orbit	0.25
Inclination of orbit	17.2°
Period of revolution	247.7 earth years
Rotation period	6.39 earth days (estimated)
Diameter	2284 km (1420 mi)
Mass (earth = 1)	0.004
Mean density (water = 1)	1.99 (estimated)
Known natural satellites	1

found to have a thin atmosphere, probably of methane, exerting a pressure on the planet's surface that is about 100,000 times weaker than the earth's atmospheric pressure at sea level. The atmosphere appears to condense and form polar caps during Pluto's long winter.

With a density about twice that of water, Pluto is apparently made of much rockier material than are the other planets of the outer solar system. This may be the result of the kind of cold-temperature/low-pressure chemical combinations that took place during the formation of the planet. Many astronomers think Pluto may be a former satellite of Neptune, knocked into a separate orbit during the early days of the solar system. Charon would then be an accumulation of the lighter materials resulting from the collision.

For further information on this topic, see the Bibliography in volume 28, sections 382, 384.

PLUTONIUM, radioactive metallic element, symbol Pu, one of the transuranium elements (q.v.) in the actinide series (q.v.) of the periodic table (*see* PERIODIC LAW); at.no. 94, at.wt. (most important isotope, plutonium-239) 239.12. Plutonium melts at about 641° C (about 1186° F), boils at about 3232° C (about 5850° F), and has a sp.gr. of 19.84.

Isotopes of plutonium were first prepared and studied by the American chemist Glenn T. Seaborg and his associates at the University of California, Berkeley, in 1941. Trace amounts of the element have since been found in uranium ores, but plutonium is prepared in relatively large quantities today in nuclear reactors.

Chemically, plutonium is reactive, its properties somewhat resembling those of the rare earth elements (q.v.). The silvery metal, which becomes slightly yellow through oxidation caused by exposure to air, exists in six varying crystalline forms and has four different oxidation states. The metal gives off heat because of its radioactivity (q.v.); 15 different isotopes of plutonium, ranging in mass number from 232 to 246, are known.

The most important isotope, plutonium-239, has a half-life of 24,360 years, and is produced by bombarding uranium-238 with slow neutrons. This forms neptunium-239, which in turn emits a beta particle and forms plutonium-239. Plutonium is the most economically important of the transuranium elements, because plutonium-239 readily undergoes fission and can be both used and produced in quantity in nuclear reactors (*see* NUCLEAR ENERGY). It is also used in making nuclear weapons. It is an extremely hazardous poison due to its high radioactivity (*see* RADIATION EFFECTS, BIOLOGICAL). Plutonium-238 has been used to power equipment on the moon by means of the heat it emits.

PLYMOUTH, city, Devon, SW England, on Plymouth Sound and the Plym and Tamar rivers. Plymouth possesses a fine natural harbor and is the site of the Royal Naval Dockyard, a major employer in the city. It is also an important fishing port and handles passenger traffic to the Continent. Manufactures include machine tools and chemicals. The city has an aquarium, a zoo, several museums, and a polytechnic college. Originally named Sutton, the town received a charter and its present name in 1439. During the 16th century it became a base for the expeditions of, among others, the navigator Sir Francis Drake. In 1588 the English fleet sailed from Plymouth Harbor to meet the Spanish Armada, and in 1620 the Pilgrims embarked from Plymouth aboard the *Mayflower.* During World War II the city was bombarded by the Germans; it has since been extensively rebuilt. Pop. (1991 prelim.) 238,800.

PLYMOUTH, town, seat of Plymouth Co., SE Massachusetts, on Plymouth Bay; founded 1620. The town has industries producing metal items, textiles, cordage, and processed food. Plymouth also is a fishing center and has summer-resort facilities, but its main focus is as a tourist spot, the site of the famous landing (1620) of the Pilgrims, who founded here the first permanent European settlement in New England. Among the many attractions are Plymouth Rock, the Pilgrims' legendary landing spot; Burial Hill cemetery, which contains the graves of several of the Pilgrims; and many preserved and restored 17th-century homes. Also of great interest are Plimoth Plantation, containing a re-creation of the Pilgrim village as it was in 1627 and the *Mayflower II,* a full-scale replica of a boat similar to the Pilgrims' *Mayflower;* Pilgrim Hall, a museum featuring a fine collection of Pilgrim artifacts; the Plymouth National Wax Museum, noted for its historical tableaux; The Mayflower Experience, a museum containing a multimedia depiction of the Pilgrims' ocean voyage; and the 25-m (81-ft) high National Monument to the Forefathers

(1889), a granite memorial known also as the Pilgrim Monument. Also notable are the Jenney Gristmill (a reconstructed water mill) and the Cranberry World Visitor's Center (with exhibitions on cranberry cultivation).

Plymouth was founded in December 1620 by the Pilgrims, who selected the site after an exploratory voyage along Cape Cod from what is now Provincetown, Mass. They named the community for their point of departure, Plymouth, England. The community was recognized as the seat of Plymouth Colony in 1633 and became part of Massachusetts Bay Colony in 1691. Pop. (1980) 35,913; (1990) 45,608.

PLYMOUTH, city, Hennepin Co., SE Minnesota; inc. as a city 1974. It is a residential and industrial suburb of Minneapolis. Manufactures include telecommunications equipment, food processing equipment, and air conditioners. Insurance and marketing industries are also important to the city's economy. Settled in the 1880s, Plymouth developed rapidly after World War II. Pop. (1980) 31,615; (1990) 50,889.

PLYMOUTH, city, SW Montserrat, in the parish of Saint Anthony, the country's capital and a port on the Caribbean Sea. It is the administrative and distribution center for the island. Major exports include hot peppers, tomatoes, and sea-island cotton. Tourism is an important aspect of Plymouth's economy; of interest are the nearby remains of Fort Barrington. Pop. (1985 est.) 3500.

PLYMOUTH BRETHREN, Christian sect founded in Dublin in the 1820s. The first church to be organized (1831) in England was at Plymouth. The movement rejected the formal ritual of the established church and preached the second coming of Christ. Churches soon appeared throughout the British dominions; in some parts of the continent of Europe, particularly France, Switzerland, and Italy; and in the U.S. The British clergyman John Nelson Darby (1800–82) became the most prominent leader of the sect, and the Brethren on the continent of Europe were generally known as Darbyites. The Brethren believe in the literal interpretation of the Bible and have no ordained, salaried clergy. They prefer to be called simply Believers, Christians, or Brethren. According to the latest available figures, the sect has about 1100 churches and 98,000 members in the U.S.

PLYMOUTH COLONY, in full The Colony of New Plymouth, colony founded in the New World by the Pilgrim Fathers. The foundation of this colony was one of the major events in the early history of the American colonies. In the reign of Elizabeth I, queen of England, one of the sects of Puritans known as Brownists separated from the new Protestant Church of England and after much persecution took refuge in the Netherlands. They finally determined to immigrate to America. A group of London investors financed them in exchange for most of their produce from America during their first six years. Their ship, the *Mayflower,* taking on many other passengers to fill the boat, sailed from Plymouth, England, for America on Sept. 16, 1620. When they reached the American coast, strong winds drove the *Mayflower* into Provincetown Harbor, at the end of Cape Cod. They wrote and signed the Mayflower Compact, forming the first constitutional American political democracy. After some exploration they settled on the site of what is now Plymouth, Mass. The Plymouth Colony later united with

A feast of thanksgiving after the hardships of settlement in the Plymouth Colony.
The Dicksons–Pilgrim Hall, Plymouth, Mass.

other New England colonies to form the Massachusetts Bay Colony in 1691.

PLYMOUTH COMPANY, one of two joint-stock companies chartered in England, April 10, 1606, to colonize in North America. The other company was the London Company (q.v.). The Plymouth Co. was formed by George Popham and Sir Ferdinando Gorges. A first band of colonists set out from England and was captured by the Spanish. The second group of colonists, numbering 120, left England in 1607 and settled on the west bank of the Kennebec River, near what is now Popham Beach, Maine. The death of Popham and a severe winter forced them to return to England in October 1608, and the company founded no permanent settlements. In 1620 the Plymouth Co. was reorganized as the Council for New England, which was disbanded in 1635.

PLYWOOD. *See* WOOD.

PLZEŇ (Ger. *Pilsen*), city, W Czech Republic, at the confluence of the Mže and Radbusa rivers, capital of Western Bohemia Region. Plzeň is famous for the brewing of Pilsner beer. The city is a center for the production of armaments, aircraft, locomotives, automobiles, and machinery. Clothing, ceramics, chemicals, hardware, and paper also are manufactured in Plzeň. Some of the major architectural features of the city include a Gothic church that was built in the 13th century and a 16th-century Renaissance town hall. Plzeň has a college of mechanical and electrical engineering (1949). Pop. (1991 prelim.) 173,129.

PNEUMATIC POWER. *See* COMPRESSED AIR.

PNEUMONIA, term applied to any of about 50 distinct inflammatory diseases of the lungs, characterized by the formation of a fibrinous exudate in the lungs. Pneumonia can be caused by bacteria, viruses, rickettsia, mycoplasma, funguses, protozoa, or by aspiration of vomitus.

Bacterial Pneumonia. Before the advent of antibiotics, the most common cause of death in adults was lobar pneumonia, an acute infection caused by the pneumococcus, a gram-positive bacterium formally known as *Streptococcus pneumoniae.* Pneumococcal lobar pneumonia often occurs in winter, after an acute viral upper respiratory infection. Usual symptoms include a single, shaking chill, followed by a fever of about 40° C (about 104° F), pain in the chest on breathing, cough, and blood-streaked sputum. The pneumococcus usually attacks an entire lobe or a portion of a lobe of the lung; in double pneumonia, it attacks both lungs.

Prompt treatment with penicillin can cure pneumococcal pneumonia within a few days. About 500,000 cases of pneumococcal pneumonia still develop in the U.S. each year; about 10 percent of these cases are fatal, particularly in older people. In 1977 a vaccine that confers immunity against the most virulent forms of pneumococcus was licensed. It is now used in persons over the age of 50 and in those with chronic heart, lung, or liver disease.

Most other types of bacterial pneumonias are bronchopneumonias, which are distinguished from lobar pneumonia clinically in affecting the regions of the lung close to the bronchioles. The pneumococcus occasionally can produce bronchopneumonia, and the disease can also be caused by Friedländer's bacillus, by *Klebsiella pneumoniae,* by *Hemophilus influenzae,* or by various staphylococci and streptococci. The onset of bronchopneumonia is less rapid than that of lobar pneumonia, and the fever does not rise as high. In 1976 scientists identified an additional form of bacterial pneumonia called Legionnaires' disease (q.v.), caused by *Legionella pneumophilia.* Most forms of bacterial pneumonia can be effectively treated with antibiotics.

Viral Pneumonia. Pneumonia can be caused by many different viruses, including those that cause upper respiratory infections, such as the influenza virus, adenoviruses, and rhinoviruses. Most cases of pneumonia seen now are viral in origin; they are usually mild and resolve spontaneously without specific treatment.

Mycoplasma Pneumonia. One common type of pneumonia, formerly called primary atypical pneumonia, is caused by *Mycoplasma pneumoniae,* a tiny prokaryotic organism that is neither a bacterium nor a virus. Epidemics of mycoplasma pneumonia occur in schools and in the military. The disease usually resolves spontaneously, but treatment with antibiotics can be helpful.

***Pneumocystis carinii* Pneumonia.** Pneumonia due to *Pneumocystis carinii,* a normally harmless protozoan, is the most common cause of death in people with acquired immune deficiency syndrome (q.v.), and can also occur in people with leukemia or others with impaired immune responses.

M.A.

PO (anc. *Padus*), river, N Italy, the longest in the country. Rising in the NW near the border with France, on Monte Viso in the Cottian Alps, it flows E for a distance of about 670 km (about 417 mi), past the cities of Turin, Chivasso, Trino, Piacenza, Cremona, Casalmaggiore, Viadana, Ferrara, and Porto Tolle, into the Adriatic Sea. Its drainage basin covers a large portion of the region. Its tributaries are the Tanaro, Dora Baltea, Dora Riparia, Ticino, Adda, Oglio, Mincio, Trebbia, Taro, Panaro, and Secchia rivers. The surface of the river along its lower course is high, and the land is protected by canals, levees, and dikes. The river is navigable for some 555 km (some 345 mi), from the Adriatic Sea to Casale Monferrato, a city in Piedmont; it is also used for irrigation. Deposits of silt, brought by many tributaries, are enlarging the delta of the Po at the mouth of the river to the extent that the delta is advancing into the Adriatic Sea at the rate of about 60 m (about 200 ft) per year.

POCAHONTAS, Indian name Matoaka (1595?–1617), American Indian princess, daughter of Powhatan, ruling chief and founder of the Powhatan confederacy of Algonquian Indian tribes; born in Virginia. According to legend, in 1608 she saved the life of Capt. John Smith by holding his head in her arms as he was about to be clubbed to death by her father's warriors. Many historians doubt the story, which is not found in Smith's detailed personal narrative written at the time. The story first appeared in Smith's *Generall Historie of Virginia* (1624). In 1612 Pocahontas was captured by the English, taken to Jamestown, and baptized Rebecca. In 1614 she married John Rolfe, one of the colonists, with the blessings of both the governor and her father. Eight years of peace between the Indians and the English followed the marriage. In 1616 Pocahontas went to England, where she met the king and queen and was received with royal honor. She died on the eve of her return to Virginia and was buried in the chapel of the parish church in Gravesend, England. She and her husband had one son, Thomas (1615–before 1678), from whom many prominent Virginians claim descent.

For further information on this person, see the section Biographies in the Bibliography in volume 28.

POCATELLO, city, seat of Bannock Co., SE Idaho, on the Portneuf R.; inc. 1893. It is a distributing and commercial center for an irrigated farm area producing potatoes, grain, and dairy products. Manufactures include fertilizer, electronic equipment, machinery, and processed food. Idaho State University (1901) is here, and American Falls Reservoir and other outdoor-recreation spots are nearby. The city was founded as a railroad center in 1882 and is named for Pocatello (c. 1814–84), a local Bannock Indian leader. Its main industrial growth began in the 1940s. Pop. (1980) 46,340; (1990) 46,080.

PO CHÜ-I (772–864), Chinese poet and government official. He held various posts, starting in the palace library and rising to become a provincial governor; he retired from public life as mayor of Luoyang (Loyang), the eastern capital. One of the greatest writers of the T'ang dynasty, which was renowned for its poetry, Po Chü-i was much influenced by his predecessor Tu Fu. Believing that literature should have a social purpose, Po Chü-i employed satire and humor in his work to protest against contemporary evils. His poetry was extremely popular in his own time; its elegantly simple style still attracts readers.

POCKET MOUSE, any of about 25 species of nocturnal, burrowing rodents of the genus *Perognathus,* which, with the kangaroo rat, kangaroo mouse, and spiny pocket mouse, form the family Heteromyidae. The pocket mouse, like others of this family, has hair-lined, external cheek pouches used to carry food. Special cheek muscles enable these pockets to be emptied by turning them inside out and then drawing them back into place. Pocket mice live in the desert or arid plains of the western U.S. and Mexico. All of the moisture they need is derived through the seeds, green vegetation, and insects they eat, and they have specially adapted kidney systems to conserve water.

Pocket mouse, genus Perognathus
A.W. Ambler–National Audubon Society

POCONO MOUNTAINS, also the Poconos, low mountain range, NE Pennsylvania. The Poconos, located chiefly in Monroe and Pike counties, are an upland of the larger Allegheny Plateau. Forming a 3108-sq km (1200-sq mi) escarpment overlooking the Delaware Valley and Delaware Water Gap to the E, the mountains are bordered on the N by Lake Wallenpaupack, on the W by the Wallenpaupack and Tobyhanna creeks, and on the S by the Wyoming Valley. The region has a maximum elevation of about 640 m (about 2100 ft). On the NE, the Pocono plateau joins the Catskill Mts. in New York State. The wooded hills and valleys have long been a popular vacation area, many communities having resort hotels with fishing, hunting, skiing, and other sports facilities. The area is also noted for its mountain laurel and about a dozen waterfalls.

POD. *See* FRUIT.

PODGORNY, Nikolay Viktorovich (1903–83), Soviet Communist leader, who served as titular head of state of the USSR from 1965 to 1977. He was born in Karlovka, the Ukraine, and was educated as a food industry technician in Kiev. He joined the Communist party in 1930 and was made deputy commissar of the Ukrainian and USSR food industries during World War II. After the war he advanced through the party ranks, becoming a full member of the Politburo in 1960. Succeeding Anastas Mikoyan as president of the USSR in 1965, he was removed from that position in favor of Communist party leader Leonid Brezhnev in 1977, at which time he was also dropped from the Politburo.

PODIATRY, also chiropody, profession of health sciences that deals with the examination, diagnosis, and treatment of conditions and functions of the human foot by medical and surgical methods. Because many diseases are often first manifested by symptoms in the feet, the podiatrist is frequently called upon to point out a patient's possible affliction with other disorders, among them, diabetes, arthritis, and circulatory problems. The podiatrist is also trained to recognize and correct congenital malformations of the foot in infants. With the increase in the number of people taking part in exercise, many podiatrists now practice sports medicine (q.v.), such as the fitting of foot supports, called orthotics, for runners. The podiatrist must complete a minimum of three years of undergraduate study and four years of podiatry college before receiving the degree of doctor of podiatric medicine and becoming eligible to take the state board examination, which is necessary for entering practice. Many graduates obtain advanced training during a residency at a general hospital, a requirement by many states to obtain a license. A few teaching hospitals also admit podiatric graduates to residencies, such as the orthopedic surgery program at the University of Chicago. Podiatrists are licensed to prescribe drugs and perform surgery, both in hospitals and in their offices. Colleges of podiatric medicine are located in Chicago, Cleveland, New York City, Philadelphia, and San Francisco.

POE, Edgar Allan (1809–49), American writer, known as a poet and critic but most famous as the first master of the short-story form, especially tales of the mysterious and macabre.

Poe was born in Boston on Jan. 19, 1809. His parents, touring actors, both died in Poe's early childhood, and the boy was raised by John Allan, a successful businessman of Richmond, Va. Taken by the Allan family to England at the age of six, he was placed in a private school. Upon returning to the U.S. in 1820 he continued to study in private schools and attended the University of Virginia for a year, but in 1827 his foster father, displeased by the young man's drinking and gambling, refused to pay his debts and forced him to work as a clerk.

Poe, disliking his new duties intensely, quit the job, thus estranging Allan, and went to Boston. There his first book, *Tamerlane and Other Poems* (1827), was published anonymously. Shortly afterward Poe enlisted in the U.S. Army and served a 2-year term. In 1829 his second volume of verse, *Al Aaraaf,* was published, and he effected a reconciliation with Allan, who secured him an appointment to the U.S. Military Academy. After only a few months at the academy Poe was dismissed for neglect of duty, and his foster father disowned him permanently.

Poe's third book, *Poems,* appeared in 1831, and the following year he moved to Baltimore, where he lived with his aunt and her 11-year-old daughter, Virginia Clemm (1822–47). The following year his tale "A MS. Found in a Bottle" won a contest sponsored by the *Baltimore Saturday Visitor.* From 1835 to 1837 Poe was an editor of the *Southern Literary Messenger.* In 1836 he married his young cousin. Through the next decade, much of which was marred by his wife's long illness, Poe worked as an editor for various periodicals in Philadelphia and New York City. In

Edgar Allan Poe American Museum of Photography

1847 Virginia died and Poe himself became ill; his disastrous addiction to liquor and his alleged use of drugs, recorded by contemporaries, may have contributed to his early death in Baltimore, on Oct. 7, 1849.

Poetry and Essays. Among Poe's poetic output, some dozen or so poems are remarkable for their flawless literary construction and for their haunting themes and meters. In "The Raven" (1845), for example, the author is overwhelmed by melancholy and omens of death. Poe's extraordinary manipulation of rhythm and sound is particularly evident in "The Bells" (1849), a poem that seems to echo with the chiming of metallic instruments, and "The Sleeper" (1831), which reproduces the state of drowsiness. "Lenore" (1831) and "Annabel Lee" (1849) are verse lamentations on the death of a beautiful young woman.

In the course of his editorial work, Poe functioned largely as a book reviewer, producing also a significant body of criticism; his essays were famous for their sarcasm, wit, and exposure of literary pretension. His evaluations have withstood the test of time and earned for him a high place among American literary critics. Poe's theories on the nature of fiction and, in particular, his writings on the short story, have had a lasting influence on American and European writers.

Stories. Poe, by his own choice, was a poet, but economic necessity forced him to turn to the relatively profitable genre of prose. Whether or not Poe invented the short story, it is certain that he originated the novel of detection. Perhaps his best-known tale in this genre is "The Gold Bug" (1843), about a search for buried treasure. "The Murders in the Rue Morgue" (1841), "The Mystery of Marie Rogêt" (1842–43), and "The Purloined Letter" (1844) are regarded as predecessors of the modern mystery, or detective, story.

Many of Poe's tales are distinguished by the author's unique grotesque inventiveness in addition to his superb plot construction. Such stories include "The Fall of the House of Usher" (1839), in which the penetrating gloominess of the atmosphere is accented equally with plot and characterization; "The Pit and the Pendulum" (1842), a spine-tingling tale of cruelty and torture; "The Tell-Tale Heart" (1843), in which a maniacal murderer is subconsciously haunted into confessing his guilt; and "The Cask of Amontillado" (1846), an eerie tale of revenge.

For further information on this person, see the section Biographies in the Bibliography in volume 28.

POET LAUREATE, formal title used in both Great Britain and the U.S. The term *laureate* is derived from the Latin word *laurea* ("laurel"); in ancient times the laurel wreath was sacred to Apollo, the Greek god of poetry and music. In Great Britain, the poet laureate is named by the sovereign as a member of the royal household and charged with the preparation of suitable verses for court and state occasions. Although Ben Jonson apparently fulfilled this role as early as 1616 under James I, the first official British poet laureate was John Dryden in 1668. The post is a lifetime appointment. The longest tenure, 1850–96, was held by Alfred, Lord Tennyson. In 1985 the U.S. Congress created the office of poet laureate as poetry consultant to the Library of Congress. The poet laureate holds the title for one year, during which he or she is required to give one public poetry reading and lecture. Robert Penn Warren was named first poet laureate in February 1986. In 1992 Mona Van Duyn became the first woman to hold the office; all the British laureates have been men.

POETRY, form of imaginative literary expression that makes its effect by the sound and imagery of its language. Poetry (the word is often used synonymously with the term *verse*) is essentially rhythmic and usually metrical, and it frequently has a stanzaic structure. It is in these characteristics that the difference between poetry and other kinds of imaginative writing can be discerned.

The Nature of Poetry. Poetry is one of the most ancient and widespread of the arts. Originally fused with music in song, it gained independent existence in ancient times—in the Western world, at least as early as the classical era. Where poetry exists apart from music, it has substituted for lost musical rhythms its own purely linguistic one. It is this rhythmic use of language that most easily distinguishes poetry from imaginative prose, the other great division of literature, and that forms the basis of the dictionary definition of poetry as "metrical writings." This definition does not, however, include cadenced poetry (as in the Bible) or modern free verse; both types of verse are rhythmic but not strictly metrical. Nor does it take into account the unwritten songs of many cultures past and present. It is, however, a useful starting point for considering what is now commonly meant by the word *poetry*.

Poetry generally projects emotionally and sensuously charged human experience in metrical language. Meter, the highly regular component of verse rhythm, depends basically on the relative strength and weakness of adjacent syllables and monosyllabic words. Whether a syllable is strong or weak, stressed or unstressed, may be a matter of length—longer or shorter, as in Arabic verse or classical Greek and Latin verse; and, in Greek verse at least, pitch as well as syllable length played a role in determining stress. It may also be a matter of intensity—louder or softer, as in medieval Latin verse and English and Germanic verse generally. Not all languages have such marked differences in syllabic emphasis, however; nor do all poets choose to exploit these differences to create rhythmic patterns. In many languages, poetic rhythm depends less on differences between syllables than on line length. This is traditionally determined by the total number of syllables in a line (syllabic verse), as in French, Italian, Chinese, Japanese, and Welsh poetry; or by the number of stressed syllables in a line (accentual verse), as in Old English alliterative poetry; or by some combination of number and stress, as in the foot verse that has been characteristic of English poetry since the time of the medieval poet Geoffrey Chaucer. *See* VERSIFICATION.

Poetic Forms. Most poetry in English is iambic, that is, made up of divisions, or feet, that alternate a weak and a strong syllable (designated here by x or /, respectively) in rising rhythm (softer followed by louder): "The Bustle in a House," or "We shall not want to use again." The meter of the first example is formally described as iambic trimeter (three iambic feet per line); that of the second as iambic tetrameter (four such feet per line). The most frequently used meter in English is iambic pentameter (in its unrhymed form this is called blank verse), which has five iambic feet in each line, as in the opening line of "Ode on a Grecian Urn," by the English poet John Keats: "Thou still unravish'd bride of quietness." The other most common feet are two in falling rhythm, the trochee (/x) and the dactyl (/xx); and another in rising rhythm, the anapest (xx/).

Lines in poetry are frequently interlocked by rhyme (q.v.) into stanzas, as in this poem by the 19th-century American poet Emily Dickinson:

> The Bustle in a House
> The Morning after Death
> Is solemnest of industries
> Enacted upon Earth—
>
> The Sweeping up the Heart
> And putting Love away
> We shall not want to use again
> Until Eternity.*

Here, not only can the lines be metrically described—as iambic trimeter and tetrameter—but the stanzas also follow a traditional form. Dickinson is using one of the meters of the hymnals, short meter: a four-line stanza in which the first, second, and fourth lines are iambic trimeter and the third line iambic tetrameter; and in which the second line rhymes with the fourth (and, sometimes, the first with the third). In Dickinson's poetry, rhymes are sometimes full, or exact (*May/day*) and sometimes, as here, near rhymes, called off-rhymes or slant rhymes (*Death/Earth, away/Eternity*).

Poets writing in other languages use other kinds of sound echoes besides rhyme to structure their stanzas. They may, for instance, use assonance (the repeating of a vowel) and consonance (the repeating of a consonant), and they may choose not to limit these effects to the ends of lines. Again, a poet writing in a language in which syllables show either level or deflected (changing) pitch, as in Chinese, can create patterns of contrast and repetition impossible in English. In nonstanzaic poetry, particularly accentual verse, the stressed syllables may be linked by the repetition of their initial consonants, one form of alliteration: "In a Summer Season when Soft was the Sun."

To return to Dickinson's poem and its more familiar prosodic principles (prosody being the study of versification, especially of meter), it can be noted that all the metrical elements influence the overall rhythm of the poem—fairly regular alternation of softer and louder syllables, the grouping of feet into lines of a specific length (with a pause at the end of each line, unless the meaning absolutely forbids it), and the further grouping of lines into stanzas with patterned sound echoes. In reciting a poem, it is necessary to remember the constant interplay between the rhythm of ordinary speech (prose rhythm) determined by the meaning, and the independent working of these underlying metrical patterns that add, shorten, or lengthen pauses, speed up some words and phrases and slow down others, and throw particular words and phrases into prominence. In poetry, the sound shapes the sense to a much greater degree than in prose. The position of a word in the line, a shift in meter, and the use of rhyme and other sound echoes to highlight key words are tools relatively unavailable to the prose writer; so is the simple control over speed and emphasis provided by the division into lines and stanzas.

A poem, then, generally has a very different rhythm from that of ordinary literary prose, although it is true that the two art forms exist on a continuum and metrical patterns are discernible, irregularly, in good prose. An excellent example may be found in the highly concentrated rhyth-

*Reprinted by permission of the publishers and the Trustees of Amherst College from *The Poems of Emily Dickinson*, edited by Thomas H. Johnson, Cambridge, Mass.: The Belknap Press of Harvard University Press, Copyright 1951, © 1955, 1979 by the President and Fellows of Harvard College.

mic sentences in *Ulysses* by the Irish novelist James Joyce. Poetic craft capitalizes on these rhythmic possibilities. Dickinson's poem, for example, is actually only one sentence; but its two stanzas and rhyme scheme provide the formal opportunity for four discrete, yet closely related, units of thought, feeling, and awareness within a single complex curve of movement. Thus, the first two lines conjure up the bustle of domestic tidying up, while the second pair complicates this busyness with the suggestion of a gravely special importance to all this activity related somehow to the death of a loved one. (Note the stately formality of the words "solemnest" and "Enacted.") Neither the activity nor its unique importance is made clear until the second stanza, however. Here, introducing specifically housework-related imagery, the poem launches into metaphor. What is being tidied up—discarded or shelved—is not trash or unneeded furnishings, but the "Heart" and "Love." (Dickinson's capitalization and punctuation are idiosyncratic.) The poem's full bite, bitterness, and desolate sense of loss, presented ironically in terms of such familiar daily activity, are brought home only in the last two lines. In very short compass, then, Dickinson's poem has made vivid to the imagination an exact quality and intensity of feeling.

Types of Poetry. Compression, extensive use of imagery (*see* FIGURES OF SPEECH), and a strong emotional—and frequently sensuous—component are characteristic of the great grab bag of poems called lyric. The other major divisions of poetry, narrative (epics, ballads, metrical romances, verse tales) and dramatic (poetry as direct speech in specified circumstances), are more amenable to characterization. Lyric poetry, however, covers everything from hymns, lullabies, drinking songs, and folk songs to the huge variety of love songs and poems; from savage political satires to rarefied philosophical poetry; from verse epistles to odes; and from 2-line epigrams or 14-line sonnets to lengthy reflective lyrics and substantial elegies. The content of lyric poetry is as varied as the concerns of human beings in every period and in every corner of the globe.

A clear distinction exists between poetry as pure art form and most so-called didactic poetry, which at its extreme is merely material that has been versified as an aid to memory ("Thirty days hath September") or to make the learning process more pleasant. Where the emphasis is on communication of knowledge for its own sake or on practical instruction, the designation *poetry* is rather a misnomer; in his *Georgics,* Vergil actually tried to teach readers how to farm. In such works, the rules of ordinary discourse apply, rather than those of poetic art. Clarity, logical arrangement, and completeness of presentation are valued over the poetic projection of human experience, although didactic materials, like any others, can serve this poetic end if handled properly. This distinction between poetry as art and poetry as versified discourse is part of the larger question of the boundaries of imaginative literature, a problem treated with particular incisiveness by the American philosopher Susanne K. Langer. Her *Feeling and Form* (1953) provides an excellent discussion of the difference between the use of language for ordinary communication as in expository writing, and its use as an artistic medium.

Among lyric poets, the Japanese are unequalled in the extreme compression of their poetry. Two favorite forms are the tanka, which has had a continuous tradition of some 1300 years and the haiku, which dates from the 16th century and had a marked effect on Western poets at the beginning of the 20th century. Both forms are unrhymed and in syllabic meter: The tanka is five lines of five, seven, five, seven, and seven syllables, and the haiku is three lines of five, seven, and five syllables. (Longer poems also use these five- and seven-syllable lines, and shorter poems are frequently linked into sequences or are carefully arranged in anthologies to provide a cumulative effect.)

Some of the short poems by one of the major 20th-century American poets, Ezra Pound, capture much of the haiku quality. His "Fan-Piece, for Her Imperial Lord," for instance, although based on a 1st-century BC Chinese poem (much longer in the original but still terse by Western standards), is quite Japanese in its prosody and effect:

> O fan of white silk,
>   clear as frost on the grass-blade,
> You also are laid aside.*

Two simple yet emotionally and sensuously powerful images—one evoking a courtly, gracious style of living, the other suggesting both the end of summer and the frosting over of vibrant life (which applies to the woman's sense of her own situation)—are associated here. They join with the lightly sketched motion of laying the fan aside—as the woman "also" has been laid aside by her "Imperial Lord." The three short lines exquisitely suggest, without any direct comment, the poignant end of a relationship and of a

---

*Ezra Pound, *Personae.* Copyright 1926 by Ezra Pound. Reprinted by permission of New Directions Publishing Corp.

whole way of life. The original Chinese poem also allows the images, for the most part, to speak for themselves, with little direct comment, and it was this aspect that especially struck European poets. Also, the rhymeless Japanese tradition that Pound was following in his translation-adaptation gave an added impetus to the development of free verse in English. Pound's "Fan-Piece" may therefore be considered either as a syllabic (five, seven, seven) poem, or as one alluding specifically to the haiku tradition in its content and number of words (five, seven, five), or as an outstanding example of free verse of the imagist school.

Poetic Tradition. Such cross-fertilization takes place frequently in the arts, and poetry is no exception; in their turn, European poets such as the 19th-century French symbolists have influenced both Japanese poets and poets writing in English. Another example is recent North American poetry, which has been enriched by the surrealist and associative techniques and revolutionary cast of poems by such Latin American poets as the Peruvian César Vallejo (1893-1938) and the Chilean Pablo Neruda. Earlier cross-cultural influences include the impact of French on English poetry (not to mention that of the French language on Old English) in the wake of the Norman conquest, of Chinese on Japanese over the centuries, and of Greek on Latin in the 3d century BC.

Many poems have vanished over the millennia, either because they existed only in the oral tradition and were eventually forgotten, or because so many manuscripts disintegrated or were destroyed. Some of the destruction was by natural processes; some occurred in the wanton pillaging of libraries and centers of learning; and some—as in the case of one of history's greatest lyric poets, the Greek Sappho—because of bigotry. During the Christian era Sappho's writings were condemned to be burned, and only about 700 lines remain—saved because they were included in uncondemned anthologies, or were quoted by other writers whose works survived, or because Egyptian embalmers chanced to wrap their mummies with strips of papyrus on which her verses were written. Of some other Greek writers only the names survive, but not a line of poetry. Closer to the present, the Old English epic *Beowulf,* the most important poem extant from Anglo-Saxon England, exists in but one manuscript; indeed, from centuries of Old English alliterative poetry only five manuscripts are known to have survived. The invention of printing in the 15th century enormously improved the chances of a book's survival, and the technological advances of the 20th century in data storage and retrieval make it theoretically possible to preserve any poem. Compared with what is extant from the last 5000 years, future generations of readers will have access to a tremendous quantity of verse from the past.

The Origin of Poetry. Enough poetry has come down from ancient times, however, to suggest certain enduring aspects of poetic expression, whatever the time or culture. In Egyptian hieroglyphic inscriptions of about 2600 BC are found kinds of poetry (evidently songs, although only the text, not the music, is preserved) still familiar today: laments, odes, elegies, hymns. The many songs relating to religion (an emphasis true also of such other ancient poetries as Sumerian, Assyro-Babylonian, Hittite, and Hebrew) support the hypothesis that the origins of poetry can be found in the communal expression, probably originally taking the form of dance, of the religious spirit. Thus, the dance rhythm could be marked not only by clapping, stamping, or rhythmic cries, but by chanting or otherwise intoning or singing words. Song, then, became the progenitor of both poetry and instrumental music. Work songs (a type also found in Egyptian tomb inscriptions of the 3d millennium BC), lullabies, play songs, and other songs accompanying rhythmic activity probably developed nearly simultaneously with religious songs. The ritual aspect of poetry is still evident in the songs of many native cultures, as in this Navajo incantation for rain, translated by the Irish-born American ethnologist Washington Matthews (1843-1905).

The corn grows up.
The waters of the dark clouds drop, drop.
The rain descends.
The waters from the corn leaves drop, drop.
The rain descends.
The waters from the plants drop, drop.
The corn grows up.
The waters of the dark mists drop, drop.

Not just lyric poetry but narrative verse as well may have had its origins in the religious impulse. The earliest narrative songs, or epics, tell the myths of creation and of the gods; later epics treat the lives of godlike heroes; and still later ones deal with the lives of historical heroes. The range is from the Babylonian creation myth and the Gilgamesh epic to the Greek *Iliad* and *Odyssey* of Homer, from the Indian *Ramayana* and *Mahabharata* to the medieval French *Song of Roland* and the Anglo-Saxon *Beowulf.* It is interesting that dramatic poetry was twice born in the West, both times in a religious context: first in ancient Greek festivals, then in medieval church ritual (perhaps with the assistance of much older surviving folk rituals).

As the earliest examples of poetry make clear, however, such ritual origins were expanded on very early. Not all songs existed solely for the practical purposes of propitiating the gods, smoothing the course of the soul's voyage after death, assuring the outcome of a battle, or influencing natural phenomena ("The waters of the dark clouds drop, drop"). When the tradition of the sung poem yielded to the written tradition—that is, when words were selected and ordered apart from melodic needs—greater complexities of content, syntax, form, and sound became possible. At the other extreme from music, sound all but vanishes in the new emphasis on the visual, or written, aspect of poetry. Concrete poetry is a contemporary graphic art that extends the millennia-old tradition of pattern poetry—verse that appears in shapes alluding to its subject. The work of the 20th-century American poet E. E. Cummings provides sophisticated and witty instances of the exploitation of the visual component of poetry. In his grasshopper poem (1935), for example, the scrambled spelling of the opening line ("r-p-o-p-h-e-s-s-a-g-r") mimics the erratic movements of the grasshopper.

The Future of Poetry. Technological advances such as the computer will probably change the shape of poetry, but not its importance, for poetry has shown itself to be as adaptable as any other art. While this is less obvious in restrictive societies, where poetry may be perverted for propaganda purposes and where the best work often goes underground, the achievements of poets in many countries in the 20th century augur well for the future. Works by poets in the U.S. and Great Britain, and in Latin America and Spain—to mention only a few areas where poetry continues to flourish—testify to its durability. In the U.S., numerous small magazines are devoted to publishing new poetry, many universities have a "poet-in-residence" on the faculty, and poetry readings by established and new writers are a feature of cultural life on and off campus.

For additional information, see articles on the types and forms of poetry and on poetic movements; see also biographies of individual poets and articles on national literatures. S.M.G.

For further information on this topic, see the Bibliography in volume 28, sections 819–20.

POGGIO, full name GIAN FRANCESCO POGGIO BRACCIOLINI (1380–1459), Italian humanist and calligrapher. While working in Florence, copying ancient manuscripts, Poggio devised the rounded, formal Humanistic script that served later as a model for the typeface known as Roman. While traveling in Italy and France, he discovered and recopied a number of manuscripts of important classical Latin texts—among them works of the rhetoricians Cicero and Quintilian and the poet Publius Papinius Statius (c. 40–c. 96). He himself wrote many works in Latin, including a large body of correspondence and, toward the end of his life, a history of Florence.

POGONOPHORE, also beardworm, any wormlike animal of the phylum Pogonophora. Pogonophores live in tubes they secrete in deep-ocean oozes, sometimes near hydrothermal vents. The animals may be more than 30 cm (1 ft) long but are never more than about 2 mm (0.08 in) in diameter. The body has no digestive tract, and food is absorbed directly through a front region bearing up to 250 tentacles. The sexes are separate. Pogonophores were first discovered in the 20th century, and their relationship to other phyla is not yet certain. *See* TUBE WORM.

POGROM (Rus., "devastation"), organized massacre of Jews. The first pogrom occurred in czarist Russia in 1881, following the assassination of Czar Alexander II by revolutionary terrorists. A massacre of Jews took place in 1903 in the Bessarabian city of Kishinev. After the failure of the Revolution of 1905 in Russia, pogroms occurred in about 600 villages and cities; thousands of Jews were slaughtered, and the property of many of the victims was looted and destroyed. Ostensibly, these pogroms were spontaneous uprisings of Christians outraged by alleged Jewish religious practices, especially the supposed ritual murder of Christian children in connection with the festival of Pesach, or Passover. As established by documentary evidence, however, the pogroms were deliberately organized by the czarist government to divert into channels of religious bigotry and ethnic hatred the Russian workers' and peasants' discontent with political and economic conditions. During the civil war that followed the Bolshevik Revolution of 1917, pogroms, which claimed hundreds of thousands of victims, were organized in the Ukraine by the White Guard leaders. A vast pogrom, the "night of broken glass" *(Kristallnacht),* took place in Germany in 1938. Undoubtedly the worst of all pogroms was the genocide perpetrated during World War II by the Nazi government of Germany, which systematically exterminated more than 5 million Jews. *See also* ANTI-SEMITISM; HOLOCAUST; JEWS; NATIONAL SOCIALISM.

POINCARÉ, Jules Henri (1854–1912), French physicist and one of the foremost mathematicians of the 19th century.

Poincaré was a cousin of the French statesman

and author Raymond Poincaré. He was born in Nancy and educated at the École Polytechnique and the École Supérieur des Mines in Paris. He taught at the University of Caen from 1879 to 1881 and was lecturer at the University of Paris from then until 1885, when he became professor there of physical mechanics, mathematical physics (1886), and celestial mechanics (1896).

Poincaré made important original contributions to differential equations, topology, probability, and the theory of functions. He is particularly noted for his development of the so-called Fuchsian functions and his contribution to analytical mechanics. His studies included research into the electromagnetic theory of light and into electricity, fluid mechanics, heat transfer, and thermodynamics. He also anticipated chaos theory. Among Poincaré's more than 30 books are *Science and Hypothesis* (1903; trans. 1905), *The Value of Science* (1905; trans. 1907), *Science and Method* (1908; trans. 1914), and *The Foundations of Science* (1902–8; trans. 1913). In 1887 Poincaré became a member of the French Academy of Sciences and served as its president in 1906. He also was elected to membership in the French Academy in 1908.

POINCARÉ, Raymond (1860–1934), strongly nationalist French statesman, who served five times as prime minister and was president of France from 1913 to 1920. Born in Bar-le-Duc, Poincaré was educated at the University of Paris and was elected to the Chamber of Deputies in 1887. A right-wing Republican, he served as education and finance minister in various governments, beginning in 1893, before heading his own first cabinet in 1912–13. As premier, he strengthened France's alliance with Great Britain and Russia in the tense period before World War I. As president during the war, he worked for national unity in the struggle against Germany; he even appointed (1917) his former political enemy Georges Clemenceau as premier because Clemenceau, like himself, staunchly opposed a negotiated peace. As head of two consecutive governments from 1922 to 1924, Poincaré insisted on complete payment of reparations by the Germans and, when they defaulted, ordered the occupation of the Ruhr by French troops in 1923. Defeated by a leftist coalition in 1924, he was recalled to the premiership two years later. Heading two more ministries between 1926 and 1929, he succeeded in stabilizing the French franc, the value of which had declined sharply under his predecessor.

POINSETTIA. *See* SPURGE.

POINT BARROW, point, N Alaska, the northernmost point of the U.S., on the Arctic Ocean. It has been important in Arctic exploration and aviation. The city of Barrow is located to the SW. The point was first sighted in 1826 by the British explorer Frederick W. Beechey (1796–1856), who named it for the British geographer Sir John Barrow (1764–1848).

POINTE-À-PITRE, town, E Guadeloupe (an overseas department of France), on SW Grande-Terre Island, in the West Indies. Situated on an ocean channel that separates Grande-Terre Island and Basse-Terre Island, it is the largest town, principal seaport, and leading commercial center of Guadeloupe. Pointe-à-Pitre is the seat of the University Center of Antilles-Guyane (1970) and the Pasteur Institute of Guadeloupe (1948), which has medical-research laboratories. The community was settled by the French in the mid-17th century. Pop. (1982) 25,310.

POINTE-AUX-TREMBLES, former city, Île-de-Montréal Co., S Québec Province, on the Saint Lawrence R.; inc. as a city 1958; became part of Montréal in 1982. Major manufactures included petroleum and paper products, clothing, lamps, and sanitary goods. The community was settled in 1674 and named for the trembling leaves of local aspen trees.

POINTE-CLAIRE, city, Île-de-Montréal Co., S Québec Province; inc. as a city 1958. The city is located on the S shore of Montréal Island, overlooking a wide portion of the Saint Lawrence R. known as Lake Saint Louis. It is a residential and industrial suburb of Montréal, with manufactures that include motor-vehicle parts, chemicals, electrical equipment, and metal and plastic products. The community was founded in the early 18th century. Pointe-Claire remained essentially an agricultural town until experiencing rapid growth in the 1950s. Pop. (1986) 26,026; (1991) 27,647.

POINTE-NOIRE, city, SW Congo, capital of Kouilou Region, on Pointe-Noire Bay (an arm of the Atlantic Ocean). The city is the chief port of the country and also a center for sport fishing. Timber, palm products, rubber, cotton, tobacco, gum, ivory, coffee, cacao, livestock, copper, diamonds, manganese, lead, and zinc are shipped. Industries include fishing, sawmilling, woodworking, palm-oil refining, food processing, and soap manufacturing. The city serves as the seaport for Brazzaville, with which it is linked by railroad.

Pointe-Noire is the site of Victor Augagneur College, the J. B. Lamarck Zoo, the Georges Brousseau Museum, and Notre Dame Cathedral. Now included within the city limits is Loango, former port and capital of an African state. Although the area came under French control in

1883, the city was not developed until 1921, nor the port until the 1930s. Pointe-Noire was capital of the Middle Congo from 1950 to 1958. Pop. (1985) 297,392.

POINTER, breed of large sporting dog that hunts by scent; it is trained in locating game to indicate the place of concealment of the quarry by standing rigid with its nose pointing in the direction of the spot. It was once believed that the breed originated in Spain several centuries ago and then spread into various other countries. It is now known, however, that pointers came into general use in Spain, Portugal, eastern Europe, and the British Isles at about the same time. The first pointers of which reliable records exist date from the middle of the 17th century in England. It is believed that the breed, sometimes specified as the English pointer, was established by crossing the foxhound, greyhound, bloodhound, and probably the spaniel. The English pointer was crossed with the Spanish pointer at the beginning of the 18th century in order to improve the former's pointing instinct, and during the 19th century with various breeds of setters in order to make it more tractable. The modern pointer is an

English pointer

ideal hunting dog, lean and lithe, with a smooth, shorthaired coat that is white with patches or spots of either liver, orange, black, or lemon. The dog weighs from 20 to 34 kg (45 to 75 lb) and stands from 58 to 71 cm (23 to 28 in). It has a long, moderately wide skull; a long, square muzzle; wide nostrils; long, silky ears that lie flat to the cheeks; medium-sized eyes that are either black or various shades of brown; a deep chest; a strong back; and a moderately long, tapering tail. The German shorthaired and German wirehaired pointers are related breeds.

POINT FOUR PROGRAM, popular designation given the foreign-aid program projected (Jan. 20, 1949) by President Harry S. Truman in his inaugural address as the fourth of "four major courses of action" (hence the name) of U.S. foreign policy. The program was administered by the Technical Cooperation Administration, created by Congress in 1950 with responsibility for furthering the political stability and economic and social progress of peoples living in developing areas of the world. Through Point Four the U.S. participated in the planning, realization, and evaluation of technical cooperation projects in agriculture, health, education, resources development, and transportation. Foreign-aid activities of the U.S. are currently carried out by the Agency for International Development.

POINTILLISM, in art, a late 19th-century method of painting, consisting of depositing small "points" (dots or strokes) of pure color on the canvas; seen from a distance, they blend and give the effect of a different color and heightened luminosity. The style, a development of impressionist color theories, was originated by the French painters Georges Seurat and Paul Signac. *See* IMPRESSIONISM; NEOIMPRESSIONISM.

POINT PELEE NATIONAL PARK, SE Ontario, Canada, established in 1918. The park occupies the southernmost point of the Canadian mainland, a peninsula extending into Lake Erie. Located on two major flyways (bird migration routes), the park has beaches, marshes, and ponds that harbor extraordinarily diverse birdlife. Area, 16 sq km (6 sq mi).

POISON, any substance that produces disease conditions, tissue injury, or otherwise interrupts natural life processes when in contact with or absorbed into the body. Most poisons taken in sufficient quantity are lethal. A poisonous substance may originate as a mineral, vegetable, or an animal, and it may assume the form of a solid, liquid, or gas. A poison, depending on the type, may attack the surface of the body or, more seriously, internal organs or the central nervous system. *See also* OCCUPATIONAL AND ENVIRONMENTAL DISEASES; POISONOUS PLANTS; RADIATION EFFECTS, BIOLOGICAL; TOXIN; VENOM.

Kinds of Poison. Poisons in humans are usually classified according to their effects as corrosives, irritants, or narcotics; the last named are also known as systemic or nerve poisons.

Corrosives include strong acids or alkalies that cause local tissue destruction, externally or internally; that is, they "burn" the skin or the lining of the stomach. Vomiting occurs immediately, and the vomitus is intermixed with blood. Common or so-called household corrosive poisons include hydrochloric acid, carbolic acid, bichloride of mercury, and ammonia.

Irritants such as arsenic, mercury, iodine, and laxatives act directly on the mucous membrane, causing gastrointestinal irritation or inflammation accompanied by pain and vomiting; diluted corrosive poisons also have these effects. Irritants include cumulative poisons, those substances that can be absorbed gradually without apparent harm until they suddenly take effect.

Narcotic poisons act upon the central nervous system or upon important organs such as the heart, liver, lungs, or kidneys until they affect the respiratory and circulatory systems. These poisons can cause coma, convulsions, or delirium. Narcotic poisons include alcohol, opium and its derivatives, belladonna, turpentine, potassium cyanide, chloroform, and strychnine. Also included in this category is one of the most dangerous poisons known, botulin toxin, a potent bacterial toxin that is the cause of acute food poisoning (*see* BOTULISM).

Blood poisoning, also bacterial in nature, is a condition that occurs when virulent microorganisms invade the bloodstream through a wound or an infection. Symptoms include chills, fever, prostration, and often infections or secondary abscesses in various organs (*see* SEPTICEMIA). Most poison gases also affect the bloodstream. Because these gases restrict the body's ability to absorb oxygen, they are often considered in a separate category called asphyxiants, to which group ordinary carbon monoxide belongs. Gas poisons, however, may also be corrosives or irritants (*see* CHEMICAL AND BIOLOGICAL WARFARE).

About 50 percent of all human poisoning cases in the U.S. involve commonly used drugs or household products such as aspirin, barbiturates, insecticides, and cosmetics. Because barbiturates are easily available, toxic effects resulting from their misuse are not infrequent. Acute poisoning may result from overdosage or interaction with other drugs, especially alcohol. The victim of acute barbiturate poisoning may become agitated and nauseated, or may pass into a deep sleep marked by increasingly shallow respiration. Coma and heart failure may follow. Chronic barbiturate poisoning, caused by prolonged use of the drugs, is usually marked by gastrointestinal irritation, loss of appetite, and anemia. In advanced stages of chronic barbiturate poisoning the victim may show mental confusion.

Treatment. One of the mainstays of treatment of accidental poisoning is the local or regional poison control center. Approximately 85 percent of cases of poisoning are handled in the home after telephone consultation with a center.

Various treatments may counteract the effect of a poison. In most cases the use of dilution is advisable, that is, the ingestion of large quantities of water or milk. In other cases it is advisable to use an emetic, a substance that induces vomiting and rids the stomach of certain poisons. An emetic may act locally, as on the gastric nerves, or systematically on the part of the brain that causes the vomiting. Household emetics, which act locally, include a tablespoon of salt dissolved in warm water or two tablespoons of mustard dissolved in a pint of water. Emetics must not be given to a person who has swallowed a corrosive poison. An antidote (q.v.), unlike an emetic, is a remedy that counteracts the effects of a poison chemically, although it may result indirectly in vomiting. An antidote may work against a poison by neutralizing it, rendering it insoluble, absorbing it, isolating it, or producing an opposite physiological effect generally. In any instance of poisoning, it is imperative that remedial treatment be started immediately. *See* FIRST AID.

For further information on this topic, see the Bibliography in volume 28, sections 452, 461, 506, 508.

POISON IVY, POISON OAK, AND POISON SUMAC, common names applied to three plants of the genus *Toxicodendron,* of the family Anacardiaceae (*see* CASHEW), capable of producing an allergic reaction in persons who have become sensitized to them. Poison ivy and poison oak are variants of *T. radicans* (sometimes treated as separate species by botanists), different mainly in the

Poison ivy and poison oak, Toxicodendron radicans. *Top: Fruit and leaves. Bottom: Variations in leaves of poison ivy (left and center) and poison oak (right).*

Poison sumac, Toxicodendron vernix. *Left: Detail of leaf, with leaflets. Right: Fruiting branch.*

shape of their leaflets. Both are woody perennial plants of roadsides, thickets, hedgerows, and open woods, and one or the other is found throughout the U.S. and southern Canada. They may take the form of vines climbing up tree trunks to considerable height, shrubs or sub-shrubs standing erect by themselves, or vines trailing on the forest floor, sometimes also trailing out into meadows from hedgerows. Distinguishing characteristics include the regular grouping of three leaflets in each leaf, and stiff clusters of small, yellowish or white berries that appear in summer and fall. Other characteristics vary considerably, especially size of leaflet, notching, whether the surface is shiny or dull, or color.

Poison sumac, *T. vernix,* is a tall, smooth-stemmed shrub of swamps throughout the eastern U.S. and Canada. It bears pinnately compound leaves with about 7 to 13 leaflets, including one at the tip. The fruits are white or yellowish berries in clusters similar to those of poison ivy. *See* SUMAC

Poison ivy, poison oak, and poison sumac contain a lacquerlike resin in their sap. The resin is composed of active substances that provoke a sensitizing reaction in most, if not all, persons the first time effective contact occurs. Contact may be made by brushing past the leaves or the bare stems. Contact with exposed pets, clothing, or garden tools many induce a reaction. Smoke from burning ivy plants may carry the resin and affect all uncovered parts of the body.

After a person has become sensitized, subsequent contact with the resin produces the typical allergic reaction of ivy poisoning. The effects do not become apparent for some hours. First, the skin reddens and begins to itch. Small watery blisters soon appear, often in lines indicating the point of contact with the plant, and the itching becomes intense. Finally, in severe cases, large watery swellings appear and coalesce. The condition is self-limiting, and recovery takes place in one to four weeks, even without treatment. A physician should be consulted in severe cases or if sensitive parts of the body, such as the eyelids, become involved. Scratching slows healing, invites infection, and may spread the resin from one location to another; the watery fluid in the blisters does not spread the reaction. Boric acid solution or calamine lotion are commonly used to relieve itching. Some or all of the resin may be removed by prompt and vigorous scrubbing with strong soap. Persons whose occupation exposes them to poison ivy, poison oak, or poison sumac should consider desensitization. *See also* ALLERGY.

For further information on this topic, see the Bibliography in volume 28, sections 452, 461.

POISONOUS PLANTS, plants containing substances that, taken into the body of humans or animals in small or moderate amounts, provoke a harmful reaction resulting in illness or death. Possibly as many as one out of each 100 species of plants is poisonous, but not all have been recognized as such. Dangerous plants are widely distributed in woods (baneberry) and fields (star-of-Bethlehem), swamps (false hellebore) and dry ranges (scrub oak), roadsides (climbing bittersweet) and parks (kalmia), and may be wild (celandine) or cultivated (wisteria). Many ornamental plants, such as oleander, lily of the valley, and mistletoe, are poisonous.

Botanists have no set rules to determine accurately whether any given plant is poisonous. Toxic species are scattered geographically, in habitat, and in botanical relationship. They contain more than 20 kinds of poisonous principles, primarily alkaloids, glycosides, saponins, resinoids, oxalates, photosensitizing compounds, and mineral compounds such as selenium or nitrates accumulated from the soil. The poisonous compound may be distributed throughout all parts of the plant (poison hemlock), or it may accumulate in one part more than any other, such as the root (water hemlock), berry (daphne), or foliage (wild cherries). A plant may vary in toxicity as it grows, generally becoming more toxic with maturity;

certain plants, however, can be highly toxic when young and harmless later (cocklebur).

Some active principles cause skin irritation directly (nettle); others bring about an allergenic reaction (poison ivy). Most poisons, however, must enter the body before they act, and in almost all cases this happens when they are eaten. Usually more than 57 g (2 oz) of the poisonous portion of the plant must be eaten by an average adult before poisoning will result (the amount is proportionately less for children). Some plants, however, are toxic in small amounts; for instance, one or two castor beans, the seeds of the castor-oil plant, may kill a child.

After ingestion, the poison may act immediately on the digestive tract (dumbcane, euphorbia, nightshade), producing severe abdominal pain, vomiting, and possibly internal bleeding, or it may be absorbed into the bloodstream. If so, it passes first to the liver, which may be injured. Oxalates crystallize in the kidneys (rhubarb), rupturing the tubules. Some plants affect the heart (oleander). Small amounts of principles in some of these (digitalis) may be used in medicine. Plants containing alkaloids often produce unpleasant or dangerous reactions in the nervous system. Examples are paralysis (poison hemlock), hallucinations (jimsonweed), or heart block (yew). A few poisons act directly within the cells of the body. The best example is cyanide, released from a glycoside in the plant (wild cherries), which prevents cells of the body from using oxygen. In contrast, unusually high levels of nitrates in plants combine with the hemoglobin of the blood so that it can no longer carry oxygen to the body cells. Some reactions are highly specific. Bracken destroys bone marrow, in which blood cells are formed. Saint-John's-wort contains a poison that, when ingested by animals, reacts with sunlight to produce severe sunburn and lesions on exposed skin.

Poisonous plants are too numerous to eradicate, and many are highly prized as houseplants or garden ornamentals. If poisoning is suspected, a physician or the local poison control center should be consulted immediately. J.M.K.

For further information on this topic, see the Bibliography in volume 28, sections 452, 461.

POITIERS (anc. *Limonum*), city, W central France, capital of Vienne Department, in Poitou. It is a commercial, manufacturing, and transportation center; products include machinery, metal goods, chemicals, electrical equipment, and processed food. Among the points of interest are Roman ruins; the Baptistery of Saint Jean (begun 4th cent.), one of the oldest Christian structures in France; and the Romanesque Church of Notre Dame la Grande and the Angevin-Gothic Cathedral of Saint Pierre, both begun in the 12th century. The University of Poitiers, established in 1432 by Charles VII of France, is in the city.

Founded in pre-Roman times, Poitiers was a residence of Visigoth kings in the 5th century AD. In 732, Charles Martel, ruler of the Franks, checked the advance of the Saracens into W Europe at a site between Poitiers and Tours. Poitiers was held by the English from 1152 to 1204, and in 1356, during the Hundred Years' War between England and France, the English, under Edward, the Black Prince, won a notable victory over the French near Poitiers. The city suffered considerable damage during the Wars of Religion of the late 16th century, when it was besieged by Huguenots. Its modern economic development dates from the 19th century. Pop. (1982) 82,884.

POKER, any of several card games in which players bet on the value of their hands for the purpose of winning the pool, or "pot," formed by the money that is wagered. Poker is universally popular, not only for its suspenseful betting, but because it challenges one's ability to conceal emotion and one's daring to "bluff," or deceive opponents. The basic form is called draw poker.

Draw Poker. This is so named for the "draw" by which players take new cards from the deck. It is played by two to seven persons, as a rule, using a 52-card deck. Cards are dealt one at a time to form hands of five cards each. From high to low, the cards rank ace, king, queen, jack, and ten through two, or deuce; the ace may also count as low, in forming a straight with the two, three, four, and five. The combinations of cards in a poker hand are, in ascending order of value, a pair, as two tens; two pairs; three of a kind, as three tens; a straight, or sequence of five cards of mixed suits; a flush, or five cards of the same suit and not in sequence; a full house, or three of a kind and one pair; four of a kind; a straight flush, or a sequence of five cards in the same suit; and a royal flush, or the sequence ten to ace in one suit. Each deal initiates a game.

Before the cards are dealt, the first player to the left of the dealer places in the pot an initial stake, of a fixed amount agreed on beforehand, known as the "ante." The dealer then distributes the cards starting with the player at the left. The game is begun by the person to the left of the one who has "anted." This player may either "open" the game by placing a bet in the pot or may "check" or "pass." To "check" means to declare one does not desire to bet at the moment but still desires to remain "in," that is, in the hand, pending betting by the other players. To "pass" means to "drop out," that is, to retire from the hand. Each player in turn, proceeding clockwise, may bet, check, or pass. If all players check or pass, the ante is returned and a new hand is dealt. After the game is opened, a player who wishes to remain must "call" the bet of the opener, that is, bet an equal amount; or "raise" the opening bet or the bet of any preceding player, that is, bet a larger amount; a player may also "reraise" any previous raise. When it is their turn again to play, the players who have checked must either bet or drop out; no player may check after a bet has been made. Bets, raises, and reraises are in the same amount as that fixed for the ante.

When the betting has come to an end by the calling of the highest bet, the players still remaining in the game may attempt to improve their hands by means of the draw. This consists of discarding from one to three cards and obtaining a like number, off the top of the facedown pack, from the dealer; in some variations only the player who has anted is permitted to discard and to draw (sometimes up to four cards). After the draw, a second round of betting takes place; it is begun by the player who opened the game, who may bet, check, or pass. The stakes are frequently doubled for the betting after the draw. Betting ends when all who wish to call the highest bet have done so, or when all but one player have dropped out. In the first case, a "showdown" follows, and the pot is won by the player holding the best hand. In the second case, the one player remaining wins, whatever the value of the hand, which need not be shown. Sometimes in draw poker, one or two additional cards called "jokers," or four cards from the regular 52-card pack, usually the deuces, are called "wild"; that is, they are designated as open in value, from ace to deuce, in any suit that the holder desires. The use of wild cards makes possible the existence of one added poker combination, five of a kind, which ranks higher than a royal flush and therefore is the supreme poker hand.

Jackpots. A variant of draw poker is known as "jackpots." In this game each player places an ante in the pot, and no player may open unless a pair of jacks or better is held. If no player can open, a new deal is made, all the money remaining in the pot. A three-card draw is the maximum permitted in jackpots. In all other respects, jackpots follows the rules of draw poker.

Stud Poker. Probably the most widely played form of poker is stud, or open, poker. In this game all cards but the first are dealt faceup, and four rounds of betting take place, beginning when the second card has been dealt. Stakes may be doubled when an open pair or better shows; in any case, stakes may be doubled for the fourth round of betting. At the end of the betting, the players still remaining turn up the first, or "hole," card, and the best hand wins the pot. A popular form of stud poker is seven-card stud, in which seven cards are dealt to each player, the first two and the last card down. The best poker hand of five cards chosen from the seven in a player's hand wins the game. In all other respects the game is the same as five-card stud poker.

For further information on this topic, see the Bibliography in volume 28, section 773.

POKEWEED, common name for the plant family Phytolaccaceae, of the order Caryophyllales (*see* PINK), and for its representative genus, *Phytolacca.* The family comprises about 18 genera and 65 species. Phytolacca contains about 25 species of herbs, shrubs, and trees that occur in tropical and subtropical regions. The small flowers lack petals, have many stamens (male floral organs), and produce fleshy berries at maturity. The common pokeweed, or pokeberry, *P. decandra,* native to the eastern U.S., may grow 3 m (10 ft) tall. Its young leaves are used as a substitute for greens and spinach; the young shoots, properly prepared, taste like asparagus; but the large, perennial root produces a cathartic poison, phytolaccin. The purple berries contain a dye. M.R.C.

POLAND, in full, Republic of Poland (*Polska Rzeczpospolita*), country, central Europe, bordered on the N by the Baltic Sea and Russia; on the E by Lithuania, Belarus, and Ukraine; on the S by the Czech Republic and Slovakia; and on the W by Germany. The area of the country is 312,677 sq km (120,725 sq mi).

In the 15th and 16th centuries, Poland was one of the major European powers under the Jagiełłon dynasty. With the end of the dynasty in 1572, Poland entered a long period of decline, culminating in the partition of the country among Russia, Austria, and Prussia in 1772, 1793, and 1795. Poland was again established as a sovereign state after World War I. It was partitioned a fourth time in 1939 by Germany and the USSR.

After World War II, Polish territory suffered a net loss of about 76,000 sq km (about 29,344 sq mi), as the land ceded to the USSR in the E was nearly double that acquired from Germany in the W. A Communist-dominated government ruled Poland from 1947 to 1989.

The name Polska (Poland), applied in the early 11th century, comes from an ancient Slavic tribe known as the Polanie (field or plains dwellers), who settled in the lowlands between the Oder (Odra) and Vistula (Wisła) rivers sometime in the early Middle Ages.

View of the old city of Kłodzko (Glatz), showing the Town Hall and (in the background) the Neisse River.
Kurt Scholz–Shostal Associates

LAND AND RESOURCES

Poland is a predominantly lowland country situated, for the most part, in the North European Plain.

Physiographic Regions. Although Poland appears as an unbroken plain on a relief map, it has considerable diversity and complexity. The average elevation is only about 175 m (about 575 ft) above sea level, as compared with the overall European average of some 290 m (some 950 ft), but elevations reach as high as 2499 m (8199 ft), atop Mt. Rysy in the High Tatra Mts. in the S, and as low as 1.8 m (5.9 ft) below sea level in the Vistula delta in the N. Poland is divided into a number of distinct parallel physiographic regions that run from E to W. A marked contrast exists between the N two-thirds of the country and the S one-third.

The N zone is a vast region of plains and low hills, divided into the Central Polish Lowlands, the Baltic Heights, and the Coastal Plain. The Central Lowlands are traversed from E to W by a series of large, shallow valleys. To the N of the Central Lowlands is the Baltic Heights region, dotted with hills and lakes. A narrow coastal lowland, about 40 to 100 km (about 25 to 60 mi) wide, runs nearly the entire length of the Baltic Sea. The coastline, 694 km (431 mi) long, is remarkably smooth and regular, the major exceptions being the Pomeranian Bay in the W and the Gulf of Danzig (Gdańsk) in the E. A few good natural harbors are along the Baltic.

The S one-third of Poland consists of a number of well-marked regions, comprising upland areas of various kinds and adjacent or intervening lowlands. A narrow belt of mountains occurs in the extreme S and SW. The Western Carpathian mountain system, which includes the High Tatra Mts. and the Beskids, contains the highest elevations in the country. In the SW, the Sudeten Mts. reach a maximum elevation of 1602 m (5256 ft) in Poland. N of the mountains are a zone of foothills, the Silesian Plain, and the Little Polish Upland.

Rivers and Lakes. Almost all Poland is drained N into the Baltic Sea by way of the Vistula and Oder river systems. The remainder is mostly drained by other rivers flowing into the Baltic. Poland has about 9300 lakes with an area of 1 ha (2.5 acres) or more. Lakes are concentrated in the Baltic Heights and Coastal Plain regions. Two lakes, Śniardwy (Spirding) and Mamry (Mauer), exceed 100 sq km (39 sq mi) in size. Poland has some 120 artificial reservoirs, which are situated mainly in the Baltic Heights and in the S mountains.

Climate. Poland's climate has features of both the moderate climate of Western Europe and the more severe continental climate of Eastern Europe. The climate of the W part may be classified as marine west coast, and the E part as humid continental with cool summers. Weather conditions are highly variable, particularly in the winter.

In January, mean temperatures range from –1° C (30.2° F) in the W to –5° C (23° F) in the S mountains. In summer, average temperatures decrease in a NW direction, from about 20° C (about 68° F) in the SE to about 17° C (about 63° F) near the Baltic. During the year, the warmest temperatures may exceed 40° C (104° F), and the lowest may drop below –42° C (–43.6° F).

Average annual precipitation in Poland as a whole amounts to only some 610 mm (some 24 in), but it ranges from about 1195 to 1500 mm (about 47 to 59 in) in the mountains to between 450 and 600 mm (18 to 24 in) in the lowlands. Summer precipitation is about double winter precipitation.

Mineral Resources. Poland has varied mineral deposits. Mineral wealth is heavily concentrated in the S upland regions and adjacent areas. Of greatest importance are the deposits of hard coal. Reserves are estimated at 80 billion metric tons, three-fourths of which are located in Upper Silesia. Poland, in addition, has more than 10 billion metric tons of lignite. The major deposits are in the Turoszow, Konin, and Belchatów basins. The country also has insignificant reserves of petroleum and natural gas.

Sulfur and copper are the most important of the country's nonfuel mineral resources. Some of the world's largest sulfur deposits occur near Tarnobrzeg in the SE, and large reserves of copper are located in Lower Silesia. Important reserves of zinc and lead occur in Upper Silesia. Other minerals of economic consequence are rock salt, potash, iron ore, and gypsum.

Plants and Animals. Forest covers about 28% of Poland. About four-fifths of the woodland is made up principally of spruce or pine. A few forests in the NE contain old and scarce species, such as dwarf birch and Lapp willow, which are unique in Europe. Much of Poland's forest has been cut down to create farmland or has been damaged by pollution.

Poland's animals are of limited variety. Most wildlife is typical of that found in other parts of Europe. Poland also has species that are either absent or extremely rare elsewhere in Europe. Those animals include chamois, bison, lynx, wildcat, elk, wolf, and brown bear. Wolf, bear, boar, and wildcat live in the higher mountains, and elk and deer are fairly numerous in the lake districts. Grouse, heathcock, and black stork inhabit grain-producing areas, lake marshes, and forests. The inland lakes and streams support considerable fish populations.

The rural region northeast of Warsaw is noted for its peasant cottages ornamented with decorative shutters, scrollwork, and diagonally laid wall planks. UPI

POPULATION

According to official Polish sources, ethnic Poles make up about 99% of the country's population. Of the approximately 500,000 people reported as members of ethnic minority groups, the Ukrainians and Belarussians form the largest communities, with much smaller groups of Slovaks, Czechs, Lithuanians, Germans, Russians, Gypsies, and Jews.

Population Characteristics. The population of Poland (1989 est.) was 37,875,000. The country has a moderate overall population density of 121 persons per sq km (314 per sq mi), with the highest densities in the S upland areas and the lowest in the NW and NE. The average annual rate of population increase was less than 1% from the mid-1960s through the 1980s.

The rate of urbanization has accelerated since the end of World War II; in the late 1980s, with about 60% of its population living in urban centers, Poland was a moderately urbanized country. Although the population is comparatively youthful, the average age has been steadily increasing. The proportion of the population aged 15 years or less is about 26% and that of people aged 60 years or more is about 14%. Poland has about 105 females for every 100 males.

Since the end of the massive population transfers in the early post-World War II period, the size and composition of the Polish population has been little affected by migration. Emigration since 1950 has consisted mainly of Germans and Jews, whereas immigration has consisted primarily of Polish repatriates from the former USSR.

Principal Cities. In the mid-1980s 40 cities had an estimated population of more than 100,000, but only 5 of those cities had more than 500,000 inhabitants. The major cities are Warsaw (pop., 1985 est., 1,659,400), the capital; Łódź (847,900); Kraków (740,100); Wrocław, formerly Breslau (637,200); Poznań, formerly Posen (575,100); Gdańsk, formerly Danzig (468,600); Szczecin, formerly Stettin (392,300); Bydgoszcz (366,400); Katowice (363,300); and Lublin (327,700).

Language. Polish is the official language of Poland and is used by nearly the entire population. It is spoken in several dialects, some of which depart considerably from standard Polish. *See* POLISH LANGUAGE.

Religion. Roman Catholicism is, at least nominally, the religion of some 95% of Poles, and it exerts an important influence on many aspects of Polish life. In 1978, Cardinal Karol Wojtyła, a Pole, became the Roman Catholic pope as John Paul II. The country has about 35 other churches and religious denominations with a combined membership of some 800,000. Of these, 8 are members of the Polish Ecumenical Council, the largest being the Polish Autocephalous Orthodox church (about 560,000 members) and the Evangelical Augsburg church (about 75,000 members). Before World War II, some 3.5 million Jews lived in Poland; the great majority of them were killed during the German occupation in the war. Others emigrated after 1945. As the 1980s ended, only about 10,000 Jews lived in Poland.

EDUCATION AND CULTURE

Poland has a long tradition of educational attainment, and education today occupies an important position in Polish culture.

Education. During the period of foreign rule of Poland, education was limited to a privileged elite. After World War I, when Poland's independence was restored, a centralized educational system was established. After World War II, the Communist government installed a school system patterned on the Soviet model. Virtually the entire population aged 15 years or more was literate in the 1980s.

Education is free and compulsory between the ages of 7 and 14. On completion of the 8-year elementary school, almost all children enter the secondary school system. About 20% of these

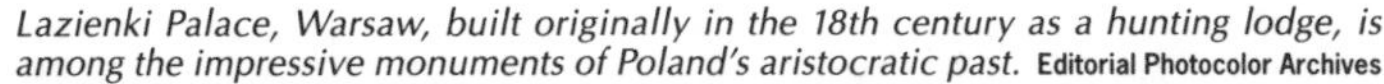

Lazienki Palace, Warsaw, built originally in the 18th century as a hunting lodge, is among the impressive monuments of Poland's aristocratic past. **Editorial Photocolor Archives**

INDEX TO MAP OF POLAND

Cities and Towns

Aleksandrów Łódzki . . . D 3
Andrespol . . . D 3
Andrychów . . . D 4
Augustów . . . F 2
Bartoszyce . . . E 1
Będzin . . . B 3
Biała Podlaska . . . F 3
Białogard . . . C 1
Białystok . . . F 2
Bielawa . . . C 3
Bielsk Podlaski . . . F 2
Bielsko-Biała . . . D 4
Biłgoraj . . . F 3
Błonie . . . E 2
Bochnia . . . E 4
Bogatynia . . . B 3
Bogusżów-Gorce . . . B 3
Bolesławiec . . . B 3
Braniewo . . . D 1
Brodnica . . . D 2
Brzeg . . . C 3
Brzeg Dolny . . . C 3
Brzesko . . . E 3
Busko-Zdrój . . . E 3
Bydgoszcz . . . C 2
Bytom . . . A 3
Bytów . . . C 1
Chełm . . . F 3
Chełmno . . . D 2
Chełmża . . . D 2
Chodzież . . . C 2
Chojnice . . . C 2
Chojnów . . . B 3
Chorzów . . . B 4
Choszczno . . . B 2
Chrzanów . . . B 4
Ciechanów . . . E 2
Cieplice Śląskie-Zdrój . . . B 3
Cieszyn . . . D 4
Cracow (Kraków) . . . E 4
Czechowice-Dziedzice . . . D 4
Czeladź . . . B 4
Czerwionka . . . A 4
Częstochowa . . . D 3
Dąbrowa Górnicza . . . B 3
Darłowo . . . C 1
Dębica . . . E 3
Dęblin . . . E 3
Dębno . . . B 2
Działdowo . . . E 2
Dzierżoniów . . . C 3
Elbląg . . . D 1
Ełk . . . F 2
Gdańsk . . . D 1
Gdynia . . . D 1
Gizycko . . . E 1
Gliwice . . . A 4
Głogów . . . C 3
Głowno . . . D 2
Głubczyce . . . C 3
Głuchołazy . . . C 3
Gniezno . . . C 2
Goleniów . . . B 2
Gorlice . . . E 4
Gorzów Wielkopolski . . . B 2
Gostyń . . . C 3
Gostynin . . . D 2
Grajewo . . . F 2
Grodziec . . . B 3
Grodzisk Mazowiecki . . . E 2
Grójec . . . E 3
Grudziądz . . . D 2
Gryfice . . . B 2
Gubin . . . B 3
Hajnówka . . . F 2
Hrubieszów . . . F 3
Iława . . . D 2
Inowrocław . . . D 2
Janów Lubelski . . . F 3
Jarocin . . . C 3
Jarosław . . . F 4
Jasło . . . E 4
Jastrzębie-Zdrój . . . D 3
Jawon . . . C 3
Jaworzno . . . B 4
Jędrzejów . . . E 3
Jelenia Góra . . . B 3
Kalisz . . . D 3
Kamienna Góra . . . B 3
Kartuzy . . . C 1
Katowice . . . B 4
Kędzierzyn . . . D 3
Kępno . . . C 3
Kętrzyn . . . E 1
Kęty . . . D 4
Kielce . . . E 3
Kłobuck . . . D 3
Kłodzko . . . C 3
Kluczbork . . . D 3
Knurów . . . A 4
Koło . . . D 2
Kołobrzeg . . . B 1
Konin . . . D 2
Końskie . . . E 3
Konstantynów Łódzki . . . D 3
Kościan . . . C 2
Kościerzyna . . . C 1
Kostrzyń . . . B 2
Koszalin . . . C 1
Kowary . . . B 3
Koźle . . . D 3
Kraków . . . E 4
Krapkowice . . . D 3
Kraśnik . . . F 3
Kraśnik Fabryczny . . . F 3
Krasnystaw . . . F 3
Krosno . . . E 4
Krotoszyn . . . C 3
Krynica . . . E 4
Kutno . . . D 2
Kwidzyn . . . D 2
Łańcut . . . F 3
Łaziska Górne . . . A 4
Lębork . . . C 1
Łęczyca . . . D 2
Lędziny . . . B 4
Legionowo . . . E 2
Legnica . . . C 3
Leszczyny . . . A 4
Leszno . . . C 3
Libiąż . . . D 3
Lidzbark Warmiński . . . E 1
Lipno . . . D 2
Łódź . . . D 3
Łomża . . . F 2
Łowicz . . . D 2
Lubań . . . B 3
Lubartów . . . F 3
Lubin . . . C 3
Lublin . . . F 3
Lubliniec . . . D 3
Luboń . . . C 2
Lubsko . . . B 3
Łuków . . . F 3
Malbork . . . D 1
Międzyrzec Podlaski . . . F 3
Międzyrzecz . . . B 2
Mielec . . . E 3
Mikołów . . . B 4
Mińsk Mazowiecki . . . E 2
Mlawa . . . E 2
Mrągowo . . . E 2
Myślenice . . . E 4
Mysłowice . . . B 4
Myszków . . . D 3
Nakło nad Notecią . . . C 2
Namysłów . . . C 3
Nidzica . . . E 2
Nisko . . . E 3
Nowa Ruda . . . C 3
Nowa Sól . . . B 3
Nowy Dwór
  Mazowiecki . . . E 2
Nowy Sącz . . . E 4
Nowy Targ . . . E 4
Nysa . . . C 3
Oborniki . . . C 2
Oława . . . C 3
Olecko . . . F 1
Oleśnica . . . C 3
Olkusz . . . D 3
Olsztyn . . . E 2
Opoezno . . . E 3
Opole . . . C 3
Ostróda . . . E 2
Ostrołęka . . . E 2
Ostrowiec
  Świętokrzyski . . . E 3
Ostrów Mazowiecka . . . F 2
Ostrów Wielkopolski . . . C 3
Oświęcim . . . D 3
Otwock . . . E 2
Ozorków . . . D 3
Pabianice . . . D 3
Piaseczno . . . E 2
Piekary Śląskie . . . B 3
Piła . . . C 2
Piotrków Trybunalski . . . D 3
Pleszew . . . C 3
Płock . . . D 2
Płońsk . . . E 2
Police . . . B 2
Poznań . . . C 2
Prudnik . . . C 3
Pruszcz Gdański . . . D 1
Pruszków . . . E 2
Przasnysz . . . E 2
Przemyśl . . . F 4
Pulawy . . . F 3
Pułtusk . . . E 2
Pyskowice . . . A 3
Rabka . . . D 4
Racibórz . . . C 3
Radom . . . E 3
Radomsko . . . D 3
Radzionków . . . A 3
Rawicz . . . C 3
Ruda Śląska . . . A 4
Rumia . . . D 1
Rybnik . . . D 3
Rydułtowy . . . D 3
Rypin . . . D 2
Rzeszów . . . F 4
Sandomierz . . . E 3
Sanok . . . F 4
Siedlce . . . F 2
Siemianowice Śląskie . . . A 4
Sieradz . . . D 3
Sierpc . . . D 2
Skarzysko-Kamienna . . . E 3
Skawina . . . D 4
Skierniewice . . . E 3
Sławno . . . C 1
Słubice . . . B 2
Słupsk . . . C 1
Sochaczew . . . D 2
Sokółka . . . F 2
Solec Kujawski . . . D 2
Sopot . . . D 1
Sosnowiec . . . B 4
Śrem . . . C 2
Sroda Wielkopolska . . . C 2
Stalowa Wola . . . F 3
Starachowice . . . E 3
Stargard Szczeciński . . . B 2
Starogard Gdański . . . D 2
Strzegom . . . C 3
Strzelce Opolskie . . . D 3
Strzemieszyce Wielkie . . . B 3
Suwałki . . . F 1
Swarędz . . . C 2
Świdnica . . . C 3
Świdnik . . . F 3
Świebodzice . . . C 3
Świebodzin . . . B 2
Świecie . . . D 2
Świętochłowice . . . A 4
Świnoujście . . . A 2
Szamotuły . . . C 2
Szczecin . . . B 2
Szczecinek . . . C 2
Szczytno . . . E 2
Szprotawa . . . B 3
Tarnobrzeg . . . E 3
Tarnów . . . E 4
Tarnowskie Góry . . . A 3
Tczew . . . D 1
Tomaszów Lubelski . . . F 3
Tomaszów
  Mazowiecki . . . E 3
Toruń . . . D 2
Trzcianka . . . C 2
Trzebinia-Siersza . . . C 4
Turek . . . D 2
Tychy . . . B 4
Ursus . . . E 2
Wadowice . . . D 4
Wągrowiec . . . C 2
Wałbrzych . . . C 3
Wałcz . . . C 2
Warsaw (Warszawa)
  (cap.) . . . E 2
Wejherowo . . . C 1
Wieluń . . . D 3
Włocławek . . . D 2
Wodzisław Śląski . . . D 4
Wołomin . . . E 2
Wołów . . . C 3
Wrocław . . . C 3
Września . . . C 2
Wschówa . . . C 3
Wyszków . . . E 2
Ząbki . . . E 2
Ząbkowice Śląskie . . . C 3
Zabrze . . . A 4
Żagań . . . B 3
Zagórze . . . B 4
Zakopane . . . D 4
Zambrów . . . E 2
Zamość . . . F 3
Żary . . . B 3
Zawiercie . . . D 3
Zduńska Wola . . . D 3
Zgierz . . . D 3
Zgorzelec . . . B 3
Zielona Góra . . . B 3
Złocieniec . . . C 2
Złotoryja . . . C 3
Złotów . . . C 2
Żyrardów . . . E 2
Żywiec . . . D 4

Other Features

Baltic (sea) . . . B 1
Beskids (mts.) . . . D 4
Brda (river) . . . C 2
Brynica (river) . . . B 3
Bug (river) . . . F 2
Danzig (gulf) . . . D 1
Dukla (pass) . . . E 4
Dunajec (river) . . . E 4
Gwda (river) . . . C 2
Hel (pen.) . . . D 1
High Tatra (mts.) . . . D 4
Kłodnica (river) . . . A 4
Łyna (river) . . . E 1
Mamry (lake) . . . F 1
Masurian (lakes) . . . E 2
Narew (river) . . . E 2
Neisse (river) . . . B 3
Noteć (river) . . . B 2
Nysa Kłodzka (river) . . . C 3
Nysa Łuzycka (Neisse)
  (river) . . . B 3
Oder (Odra) (river) . . . B 2
Orava (res.) . . . D 4
Pilica (river) . . . D 3
Pomeranian (bay) . . . B 1
Prosna (river) . . . C 3
Przemsza (river) . . . B 4
Rysy (mt.) . . . D 4
San (river) . . . F 3
Słupia (river) . . . C 1
Śniardwy (lake) . . . E 2
Sudeten (mts.) . . . B 3
Uznam (Usedom)
  (island) . . . B 1
Vistula (river) . . . D 2
Warmia (reg.) . . . D 1
Warta (river) . . . B 2
Wieprz (river) . . . F 3
Wisła (Vistula) (river) . . . D 2
Wkra (river) . . . E 2
Wolin (island) . . . B 2

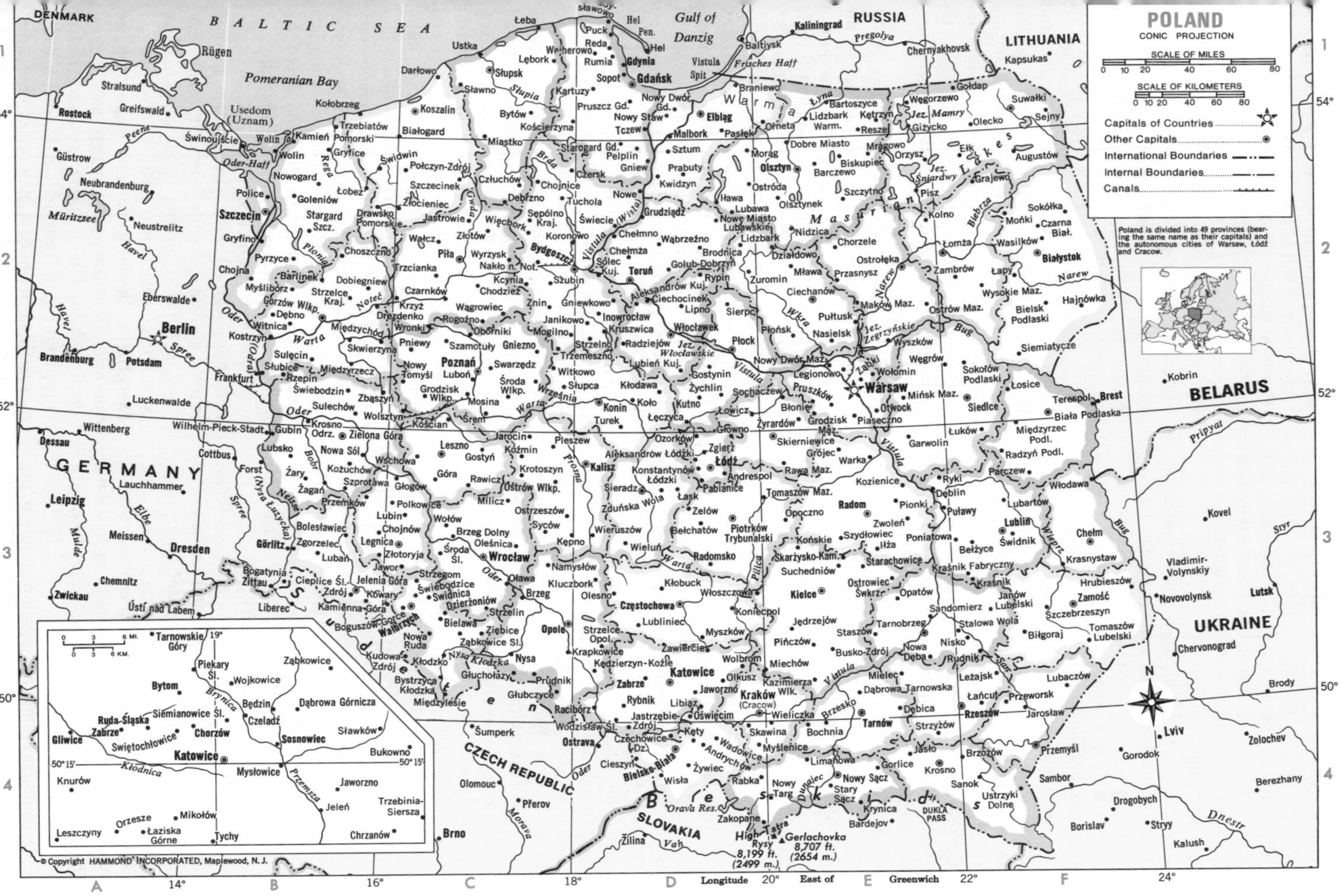
POLAND
CONIC PROJECTION
SCALE OF MILES
0 10 20 40 60 80
SCALE OF KILOMETERS
0 10 20 40 60 80
Capitals of Countries
Other Capitals
International Boundaries
Internal Boundaries
Canals
Poland is divided into 49 provinces (bearing the same name as their capitals) and the autonomous cities of Warsaw, Łódź and Cracow.
DENMARK
B A L T I C S E A
Pomeranian Bay
Gulf of Danzig
RUSSIA
LITHUANIA
BELARUS
UKRAINE
G E R M A N Y
CZECH REPUBLIC
SLOVAKIA
Vistula
Oder
Warta
Bug
Narew
Warsaw
Gdańsk
Kraków (Cracow)
Łódź
Poznań
Wrocław
Szczecin
Katowice
Lublin
Białystok
Berlin
Gerlachovka 8,707 ft. (2654 m.)
Rysy 8,199 ft. (2499 m.)
Longitude 20° East of Greenwich
© Copyright HAMMOND INCORPORATED, Maplewood, N.J.

students attend general secondary schools that prepare them for college or university entrance. In the late 1980s about 5.1 million pupils attended primary schools each year, and about 1.8 million were enrolled in secondary, vocational, and teacher-training institutions.

Poland has a long history of higher education. The University of Kraków (Jagiełłonian University), established in 1364, was the second university founded in central Europe. Of the 92 Polish institutions of higher education in the late 1980s, 11 were universities and 14 were technical universities. The universities were located in Kraków, Warsaw, Poznań, Wrocław, Lublin, Łódź, Toruń, Gdańsk, Szczecin, and Katowice.

Cultural Life. The great periods of Western cultural and intellectual expression are paralleled by the history of Polish creativity. The Italian Renaissance inspired a great burst of culture. The Reformation speeded the development of a Polish vernacular literature, and in the 18th and 19th centuries Poles were greatly influenced by French culture. After World War II artistic freedom was severely circumscribed during the Stalinist period from 1949 to 1955. After 1956 the government cultural policy generally became much more liberal.

Poland has attained its highest artistic recognition in the field of literature. The greatest literary period is generally regarded as the Romantic period of the 19th century, the chief figures being Adam Mickiewicz, Juliusz Słowacki (1809–49), Zygmunt, Count Krasiński (1812–59), and Cyprian Kamil Norwid (1821–83). Romanticism in drama and poetry was followed by realism, most notably in the novels of Bolesław Prus (1847–1912), Henryk Sienkiewicz, and Władysław Stanisław Reymont (1867–1925). Stanisław Wyspiański (1869–1907) is regarded as the founder of modern Polish drama. Among the many prominent figures after 1945 were Jerzy Andrzejewski (1909–83), Tadeusz Rózewicz (1921–), Stanisław Lem (1921–), Leon Kruczkowski (1900–62), and Zbigniew Zaluski (1926–). The émigré Polish poet Czesław Miłosz (1911–) received the Nobel Prize in literature in 1980. *See* POLISH LITERATURE.

In music, the greatest and best-known Polish composer is Frédéric Chopin. Karol Szymanowski is regarded as the most important figure since Chopin. A school of composers emphasizing avant-garde music developed after World War II. Well-known Polish musicians have included the harpsichordist Wanda Landowska and the pianist Ignace Jan Paderewski.

In painting, Poland has developed little in the way of distinctive styles. Artists have been influenced by various Western styles and trends, although in the 20th century traditional peasant art has exerted some influence. The portrayals of scenes from Polish history by Jan Matejko (1838–93) are of some note. Several Polish filmmakers, including Andrzej Wajda (1926–) and Roman Polański (1933–), achieved international reputations after 1950.

Cultural Institutions. Poland has many museums, some of the most notable are the National Museum, the Technical Museum, and the State Archaeological Museum, all located in Warsaw; the National Museum and the Wawel State Art Collections, in Kraków; the Archaeological and Ethnographical Museum, in Łódź; the Polish Maritime Museum, in Gdańsk; and the Upper Silesian Museum, in Katowice. Major libraries include the National Library and the Public Library, both in Warsaw, as well as several university libraries.

Communications. Mass communications in Poland were nationalized in 1946 and, under the Communist regime, were subject to government supervision. In the late 1980s, Poland had 53 daily newspapers with a total circulation of about 8.5 million. *Trybuna Ludu,* published in Warsaw, was the official organ of the Communist party and, as such, the most important and influential newspaper in the country. *Trybuna Robotnicza,* issued in Katowice, also had considerable influence. The official news agency was the Polish Press Agency. Periodical publications were numerous and varied. *Przyjaciółka* (The Friend), a weekly for women, was one of the most widely read magazines. The more influential magazines included *Polityka* (Politics), *Zycie Gospodarcze* (a weekly journal of economics), and *Perspektywy* (Perspectives). The non-Communist government that came to power in 1989 ended subsidies to newspapers; in the freer economic and political climate, more than 500 newspapers began publication.

Most radio and television programming originates in Warsaw, although the country has several regional radio and television centers. In the late 1980s about 10.8 million radios and about 9.9 million television receivers were licensed.

GOVERNMENT

Poland is governed under a constitution adopted in 1952 and subsequently amended. Major revisions in Poland's governmental structure have been implemented since 1989.

Executive. Under the Communist regime, the two houses of the Polish parliament elected the president of the republic. Direct presidential elections, held in late 1990, required a runoff when no candidate received a majority of the vote in the first round of balloting.

Legislature. The national legislature of Poland is a bicameral body consisting of a lower house,

Unveiling (August 1989) in Warsaw of the monument to the Warsaw uprising during World War II. © 1989 Dyana VanCampen

or Sejm, of 460 members elected to 4-year terms, and a senate of 100 members, also elected to 4-year terms. In the general elections of June 1989, 65 percent of the seats in the lower house were reserved for the Communist party and its allies and 35 percent for the opposition, led by Solidarity; no such restrictions applied to the parliamentary election held in October 1991.

Judiciary. The administration of justice is carried out by the supreme court, voivodeship (provincial) courts, district courts, and special courts. The supreme court is the highest tribunal and supervises all lower courts.

Local Government. Poland is divided into 49 voivodeships (provinces), named after the towns from which they are administered. The voivodeships are divided into towns and communes (*gminas*). Free multiparty elections for local councils were held in May 1990.

Political Parties. The Polish United Workers' (Communist) party, founded in 1948, was the leading political force in Poland until 1989, when it yielded power to a government dominated by the labor union Solidarity. In January 1990 the Communist party reestablished itself as the Social Democratic party, with a minority splitting off to form the Union of Social Democracy. The United Peasants' party (1949) and the Democratic party (1939), which together with the Communist party had constituted the Patriotic Movement for National Rebirth, broke with the Communists in 1989 to give Solidarity its parliamentary majority. Candidates of more than 100 political parties, which included spin-offs of the former Communist party and several Solidarity splinter groups, contested the October 1991 election. The results were inconclusive, with more than two dozen parties winning seats in parliament.

Health and Welfare. Poland has an extensive system of social welfare, funded from the national budget. Welfare and social security benefits include pensions and various forms of health care. Health care is free. The health care system includes some 77,500 physicians, 17,700 dentists, and 202,200 hospital beds.

Defense. In the early 1990s Polish military forces on active duty totaled 296,500 personnel, including an army of 194,200, a navy of 19,300, and an air force of 83,000. The last contingent of Russian combat troops—remnants of a Soviet force that had been stationed for decades on Polish soil—withdrew from Poland in October 1992.

International Organizations. Poland is a member of the UN and UN specialized agencies, as well as the General Agreement on Tariffs and Trade.

ECONOMY

After World War II Poland adopted a Soviet-type socialist economy, and almost all important means of production, resources, transportation, finance, and trade were nationalized. Private ownership was limited mainly to the agricultural sector and certain services. Manufacturing became the dominant economic activity, followed by agriculture and construction. In the late 1970s and the '80s, Poland experienced considerable economic difficulties, resulting primarily from a series of poor harvests, unrest among industrial workers, lagging technology, rising inflation, and the highest debt to the West of any Communist-bloc nation. These economic problems, which worsened during the course of the 1980s, were responsible in large part for the collapse of the Communist regime and its replacement by a Solidarity-led coalition in 1989.

In December 1989, the government launched a reform program designed to change Poland from a centrally planned to a free-market econ-

Grain harvest near the village of Muchowka in southern Poland. Most Polish agricultural land consists of small family farms that produce grain and potatoes as the main crops.
George G. Grechowicz–Peter Arnold, Inc.

omy. The package called for removal of virtually all price controls, imposition of wage controls, and privatization of many state-owned companies. Ailing firms were allowed to lay off employees or go bankrupt; to cushion the blow to the workers, a system of unemployment insurance was introduced. The immediate effect on living standards was a 40 percent decline in purchasing power.

According to Western estimates, Poland's gross national product (GNP) in the late 1980s was $276.3 billion, or $7280 per capita. The annual national budget included $23 billion in revenue and $24 billion in expenditure.

Labor. The total labor force in Poland numbers about 17.1 million. Approximately 28% of the workers are employed in agriculture and another 28% in manufacturing and mining. Until 1980 all labor unions were part of the state-sponsored Central Council of Trade Unions. After the labor unrest of the summer of 1980, striking workers won the right to form independent trade unions, and such unions were established under the leadership of the Solidarity (Solidarność) union; in May 1981 the Polish government agreed to permit private farmers to create an independent union (Rural Solidarity). In December 1981, however, following the imposition of martial law in the country, independent union activity was sharply curtailed by the government. All existing unions were outlawed in October 1982, and new government-dominated unions were established. Solidarity regained full legal status in April 1989.

Agriculture. Although Poland ranks as one of the leading European agricultural countries, it is chronically unable to meet its needs for food, feed grains, and vegetable oils. Under the Communist government, Polish agriculture was organized into both socialized and private sectors. Small private farms accounted for more than 70% of all farmland and for 80% of yearly agricultural production. The largest area of cultivated land is found in the Central Lowlands, but much of the best farmland is in the low plateaus and foothills of S Poland. Climate limits the range of crops that can be grown, and periodic drought causes considerable fluctuation in yearly crop output. Farmers generally achieve low yields compared to those of other Eastern European countries. The principal Polish crops are grain (rye, wheat, barley, oats), sugar beets, potatoes and other vegetables, apples, strawberries, currants, rapeseed, inseed, and tobacco. Annual harvests in the late 980s included 34.7 million metric tons of potaoes, 14.1 million tons of sugar beets, 5.5 million ons of rye, 7.6 million tons of wheat, and 3.8 nillion tons of barley. Large numbers of chickens, ogs, cattle, and sheep are raised on Poland's arms, and livestock products include meat, eggs, nilk, butter, cheese, and wool. The country also as about 1.1 million horses, many of which are sed as work animals on small private farms.

orestry. The annual roundwood harvest was bout 22.5 million cu m (about 795 million cu t) in the late 1980s. About four-fifths of the harvest consists of softwoods. About one-third of the wood is sawed into lumber, and the rest is used as pit props in mining, as fuel, or to make paper.

Fishing. The annual Polish fish catch was 670,900 metric tons in the late 1980s. Freshwater fish accounted for about 6% of the catch. Since 1960 the major marine fishing activity has moved from the Baltic Sea to the Atlantic Ocean, which now supplies about 70% of the catch, consisting mostly of cod, hake, herring, and pilchard. Major fishing ports are Świnoujście, Kołobrzeg, Darłowo, Ustka, Władysławowo, Puck, and Hel.

Mining. The mining industry employs about 3% of the Polish labor force. Coal mining is the most important sector, and Poland ranks among the world's leading producers of hard coal. Polish coal production in the late 1980s was some 266.2 million metric tons annually. Poland also is a leading producer of native sulfur (4.9 million metric tons). In addition, the country produces substantial quantities of lignite, copper, lead, zinc, magnesite, and rock salt. In the late 1980s the annual output of petroleum was 1.1 million barrels; natural gas, 5.8 billion cu m (205 billion cu ft).

Manufacturing. Before World War II, Poland's manufacturing base was dominated by the textile, iron and steel, chemical, processed food, and machinery sectors. In the postwar period, these industries were expanded, but other products, such as petrochemicals, machine tools, electronic equipment, ships, fertilizer, and copper, also were given emphasis. Industrial investment is concentrated in the older centers of Upper Silesia and in Warsaw, Łódź, and Kraków, but an effort has been made to introduce industry to smaller cities and rural areas. Annual output in the late 1980s included cement, 16.1 million metric tons; crude steel, 17.1 million tons; passenger cars, 233,000; washing machines, 779,000; and refrigerators, 506,000.

Energy. In the late 1980s Poland had an installed electricity-generating capacity of about 30.1 million kw, and annual production was about 145.8 billion kwh. More than 95% of the electricity was

A highly automated modern automobile assembly plant in Poland. Chestnot–Sipa Press

generated in plants burning coal or lignite; the remainder was produced in hydroelectric facilities.

Transportation. Poland has a dense network of public roads totaling some 340,190 km (some 211,380 mi), about 63% of which have a hard surface. In the late 1980s some 4.2 million passenger cars and about 953,700 commercial vehicles were in use. The Polish railroad system includes about 26,640 km (about 16,550 mi) of operated track. More than one-third of the system is electrified. Poland has about 4000 km (about 2490 mi) of navigable inland waterways. The Vistula, Oder, Bug, Warta, Narew, and Noteć are the principal navigable rivers; about 1215 km (about 755 mi) of canals connect the river systems. Major inland ports are Gliwice, Wrocław, and Warsaw. Three major seaports, Gdańsk, Szczecin, and Gdynia, account for nearly all Poland's maritime commerce. The country's merchant marine numbered about 715 ships in the late 1980s.

The state airline, Polskie Linie Lotnicze (LOT), provides domestic and international flights, and the country also is served by many foreign airlines. Warsaw is the main hub of Polish air traffic.

Currency and Banking. The złoty, divided into 100 groszy, is the basic currency unit (9398 złotys equal U.S.$1; 1990). The Polish National Bank, founded in 1945, serves as the country's central bank. The Bank of Food Economy provides financing for the agricultural and food industries. Other banks are the Export Development Bank and the Commercial Bank of Warsaw.

Foreign Trade. In the late 1980s annual imports totaled about $6.9 billion and exports $7.7 billion. Principal imports are machinery and equipment, crude and refined petroleum, basic metals and ores, chemicals, consumer goods, and agricultural products. Major exports are machinery and equipment, basic metals, chemicals, textiles and clothing, and food products. During the Communist period, Poland's foreign trade was mainly with other Communist countries, particularly the USSR, East Germany, and Czechoslovakia, but substantial trade was also carried on with such Western countries as West Germany, the U.S., France, Great Britain, and Italy.

Tourism. Poland experienced a rapid increase in the annual number of foreign visitors in the 1970s, with 9 to 11 million persons each year visiting the country during 1977–79. Political unrest slowed the tourist boom, however, and in the early 1980s the annual number of visitors did not exceed 2 million; later in the decade the tourist trade rebounded. People from other Communist countries made up the great majority of the visitors; most came from the USSR, East Germany, and Czechoslovakia. West Germany was the most important source of tourists from the West. Major attractions in Poland are the beach resorts along the Baltic Sea, the lake district, the Carpathian and Sudeten mountains, and the country's numerous historic sites and cultural institutions. Annual receipts from tourism averaged more than $180 million in the late 1980s. W.W.H.

HISTORY

Virtually nothing is known regarding the early activities of the Slavic tribes that laid the foundations of the Polish nation. According to some authorities, a number of these tribes united, about AD 840, under a legendary king known as Piast, but Poland does not begin to figure in European history until the reign, from 962 to 992, of Mieszko (c. 922–92), reputedly a descendant of Piast.

The Piast Dynasty. Mieszko led the Poles into Christianity, probably in an attempt to appease the crusading and marauding Germans. During the reign (992–1025) of his son, Boleslav I, the Christian church was firmly established in Poland. Boleslav also conducted successful wars against Holy Roman Emperor Henry II and considerably expanded the Polish domain. He was crowned king by the pope in 1025. At his death, Poland extended beyond the Carpathian Mountains and the Odra (Oder) and Dnestr rivers.

During the next three centuries Poland met with repeated misfortunes from internal disorder and foreign invasions. In 1079 Boleslav II murdered the bishop of Kraków and Poland was placed under a papal interdict. Boleslav III, who reigned from 1102 to 1138, conquered Pomerania, defeated the pagan Prussians, and defended Silesia against Holy Roman Emperor Henry V. On the death of Boleslav III Poland was divided among his sons, and the kingdom subsequently disintegrated into a number of independent warring principalities.

In 1240–41 the Mongols invaded and ravaged Poland. The neighboring Baltic dominions of the pagan Prussians had been subjugated, meanwhile, by the Teutonic Knights, and German colonists, encouraged by the Polish princes, began to settle in the country. During the period of German colonization, large numbers of Jews, in flight from persecution in western Europe, took refuge in Polish territory.

Władysław I the Short, of the Piast dynasty, was crowned king of Poland in 1320. From 1305 to 1333, defeats were inflicted on the Teutonic Knights, and the kingdom was reunited. The power and prosperity of Poland increased tremendously during the reign, from 1333 to 1370, of his son Casimir III, one of the most enlightened rulers in Polish history and the last of the Piast dynasty. He initiated important administrative, judicial, and legislative reforms, founded the University of Kraków (1364), extended aid to the Jewish refugees from western Europe, and added Galicia to the Polish domains.

The Jagiełłon Dynasty. The second dynasty of Polish kings, the Jagiełłonians, was founded by Jagiełło, grand duke of Lithuania. In 1386 Jagiełło married Jadwiga (1374–99), queen of Poland, a grand niece of Casimir III, and ascended the throne as Władysław II Jagiełło. Christianity was introduced into Lithuania, a pagan country, by Władysław, who was converted on his accession. In 1410 Polish and Lithuanian armies under Władysław won a decisive victory at Tannenberg over the Teutonic Knights, thereby raising Poland to a leading position among European nations. Thereafter, until 1569, a single sovereign usually ruled both states.

Under the Jagiełłon dynasty, which lasted until 1572, Poland attained great heights of power, prosperity, and cultural magnificence. Casimir IV, who ruled from 1447 to 1492, conducted a protracted and successful war (1454–66) against the Teutonic Knights. In 1466, by terms of the Peace of Thorn, which terminated the conflict, he secured West Prussia, Pomerania, and other territories. The landed gentry and lesser nobility acquired extensive privileges during Casimir's reign, mainly at the expense of the peasantry. The Sejm, a parliamentary body that evolved out of earlier assemblies of nobles and other social groups, began to assume greater importance. The succeeding Jagiełłon kings, notably Sigismund I, were generally victorious in the military and diplomatic struggles of the period, despite some setbacks in the east. In 1569 Sigismund II Augustus united the two realms of Poland and Lithuania. Protestantism, which made many converts among the nobility in the middle years of the 16th century, ceased to be significant after 1600.

With the death of Sigismund II Augustus, last of the Jagiełłonians, in 1572, the Polish nobility successfully concluded a prolonged campaign for complete control of the country. A regime of elected kings was instituted with the power of election vested in the Sejm, then a bicameral body consisting of the lesser and greater nobility. One important aspect of this system was to be the *liberum veto,* which made it possible for any member of the Sejm to prevent the passage of legislation. The constitution also sanctioned the formation of military confederations of nobles.

Wars and Polish Decline. For two centuries after these developments, the political, economic, and military position of Poland deteriorated. Successive and generally disastrous wars with Sweden, Russia, the Ukrainian cossacks, Brandenburg, and the Ottoman Turks led to the loss of important Polish territories and the devastation of much of Poland. In 1683 Polish and German armies under the command of John III Sobieski defeated a vast Turkish army at the gates of Vienna, halting a serious threat to Christendom in central Europe, but his victory was virtually the sole outstanding Polish achievement of the entire period. Early in the 18th century the Russian Empire opened a systematic offensive against declining Poland. Supplementing military force with bribery and intrigue, the Russian rulers gradually reduced neighboring Poland to impotence. Widespread political corruption among the Polish nobility accelerated the drift toward national catastrophe. Through shameless bribery of a faction of the Sejm and armed Russian intervention, Frederick Augustus II, elector of Saxony, was placed on the throne of Poland in 1734 as Augustus III (1696–1763). These events brought on the conflict known in history as the War of the Polish Succession (1733–35). Although sections of the Polish nobility subsequently united around a program of national salvation, Poland was unable to withstand the next Russian onslaught. In 1764 Russian troops entered Poland and forced the enthronement of Stanislas II Augustus, a paramour of Catherine II, empress of Russia.

Partitions of Poland. Russian expansionism, as exemplified by these events, caused profound alarm among the European powers. The Turks immediately declared war on Russia. Prussia and Austria, fearful of a general European conflict and coveting Polish territory, submitted a proposal to the Russian government for the partition of Poland.

The first partition and the Polish commonwealth. The Russian government agreed, and in 1772 the treaty of partition was concluded at Saint Petersburg. By the terms of this document, Russia, Austria, and Prussia acquired large portions of Polish territory, amounting to about one-quarter of the total area of the country. A constitution, which established safeguards against Polish resurgence, was also imposed on the nation by the partitioning powers. The country was officially termed the Polish Commonwealth. Consent of the Sejm to the treaty was obtained largely by bribery.

Despite the political restrictions surrounding the Polish Commonwealth, the attenuated nation progressed in several domestic fields in the decade following partition. The national education system was secularized and completely modernized. A movement for constitutional reform also developed during this period, but the Polish nobility frustrated effective action. Relations between Russia and Prussia deteriorated rapidly after 1786. With encouragement from Prussia, Polish patriots in the Sejm instituted sweeping governmental reforms in 1788 and began the draft of a new constitution. The draft, which proclaimed Poland a hereditary monarchy and strengthened and liberalized the government, was adopted, in the face of violent opposition from a section of the gentry, on May 3, 1791.

The second and third partitions. Shortly afterward the leaders of the disgruntled nobility and Catherine II reached a secret agreement providing for the restoration of the old order. The Polish conspirators organized the Confederacy of Targowica in May 1792. Supported by Russian troops, this organization immediately began military operations against Poland. The Polish army, led by Prince Józef Poniatowski, resisted for more than three months, but the government, abandoned by Prussia and confronted by overwhelming odds, soon capitulated. Russian armies then occupied all of eastern Poland, and shortly thereafter, early in 1793, the Prussians occupied the western portion of the country. These territorial seizures, which further reduced the area of Poland by two-thirds, were formally sanctioned in a second territorial partition, ratified in September 1793.

In 1794 the Poles embarked on a revolutionary war for the recovery of their lost territories. Under the leadership of Thaddeus Kosciusko, who assumed dictatorial powers, the hastily formed Polish armies won a series of victories over the Russians. By the summer of 1794 large sections of Russian-occupied Poland had been liberated and the Russians had suffered a humiliating defeat at Warsaw. A variety of factors, however, including dissension among the Polish high command, overwhelming numerical superiority of the Russians, and Prussian and Austrian intervention, rendered the Polish cause hopeless. In October 1794 the Russians won a decisive victory at Maciejowice. Russian forces under Field Marshal Aleksandr Suvorov entered Praga, a suburb of Warsaw, in November and massacred much of the population. Warsaw then surrendered, and the remnants of the revolutionary armies surrendered within a few weeks. After settling sharp differences on division of the spoils, the victorious powers concluded treaties between 1795 and 1797 on the third partition of Poland. By the terms of the treaties, the Russian Empire received about half of the remaining Polish territory, and Prussia and Austria each received about a quarter. With these events, the Polish state disappeared from the map of Europe.

Poland Under Foreign Rule. The Polish people remained under the yoke of foreign masters for nearly 125 years after the third partition. During the Napoleonic Wars, Napoleon, who had promised to reestablish Poland, obtained substantial help from the Poles, thousands of whom served in his armies. In 1807, by the provisions of the Treaty of Tilsit, he created the duchy of Warsaw, consisting originally of the territory taken by Prussia in 1793 and 1795. Two years later Napoleon forced Austria to cede Western Galicia to the duchy. Aside from granting the state a liberal constitution, Napoleon did little else for the Poles.

In 1815 the Congress of Vienna, which drafted the general European peace settlement after Napoleon's downfall, created a kingdom of Poland, consisting of about three-quarters of the territory of the former duchy of Warsaw, with the Russian emperor as king; established Kraków as a city republic; and distributed the remainder of Poland among Russia, Austria, and Prussia. Alexander I, emperor of Russia, granted the new kingdom a liberal constitution in 1815, but Polish nationalists soon initiated a powerful movement for independence. On Nov. 29, 1830, this movement culminated in the outbreak of armed insurrection. The Poles expelled the imperial authorities and, in January 1831 proclaimed their independence. In the ensuing war, the Poles kept the Russians at bay for several months. The Russians won an important victory at Ostrołęka on May 26, 1831, however, and they took Warsaw on September 8.

The constitution, the Sejm, and the Polish army were abolished in Poland in the aftermath of the rebellion. The Poles were deprived of civil liberties, their country was robbed of literary and art treasures, and severe measures were taken to Russianize public institutions and administration. Other abortive insurrections and nationalist demonstrations occurred in various parts of Poland in 1846, 1848, 1861, and most notably in 1863. After the insurrection of 1863 the Russian Empire, intensifying its program for the Russification of the Polish lands under its rule, introduced the Russian language in the schools, restricted the use of the Polish language, and interfered with the activities of the Roman Catholic church. Culturally, politically, and economically, the parts of Poland under Russian rule were transformed into mere provinces of the Russian Empire, losing almost all vestiges of their former autonomy. The Poles in Prussian Poland were subjected to a policy of Germanization (although not as severe as in the Russian zone); Poles in Austrian Poland were treated more liberally.

Independence. Conscripted into the armies of Russia and the Central Powers, Poles fought against Poles in World War I. After the downfall in March 1917, of the Russian Empire, the provisional government of Russia recognized Poland's right to self-determination. A provisional Polish government was subsequently formed at Paris. In September 1917 the Germans, then in complete control of the country, created a regency council as the supreme governmental authority of the so-called Polish kingdom.

On the collapse of the Central Powers in the fall of 1918, the Poles moved swiftly toward statehood. The republic of Poland was proclaimed in November, and a government was installed in January 1919.

The Post-World War I Period. The Treaty of Versailles (June 1919) granted Poland a narrow belt of territory (the so-called Polish corridor) extending along the Vistula River to the Baltic Sea, and large sections of Posen (Poznań) and West Prussia. The treaty also awarded Poland important economic rights in the free city of Danzig. After a war with Soviet Russia (1920–21), Poland annexed parts of Belorussia and the Ukraine. In the west, the Poles acquired sections of Upper Silesia in 1921–22.

In the two decades following the war, the foreign policy of Poland was largely determined by fear of Germany and the USSR. A defensive alliance with France was arranged in February 1921, and alliances were subsequently signed with Romania, Czechoslovakia, Yugoslavia, Latvia, Estonia, and Finland. In 1932 Poland concluded a nonaggression pact with the USSR. A similar agreement, effective for ten years, was concluded with Germany in 1934. Both these treaties guaranteed Poland's borders.

In the realm of domestic politics, developments in Poland, after the adoption of a permanent constitution in March 1921, were marked by incessant strife between the conservative and leftist political factions. Failure of the new state to protect the economic and political rights of the Jews, Ukrainians, Belorussians, Germans, and other minorities included in its population also caused constant friction and turmoil. Some concessions to the demands of certain of the minorities were legislated in 1924. In December 1925 a measure was enacted providing for distribution to the peasantry of 20,234 hectares (50,000 acres) of land annually.

Dictatorship and the German Threat. Meanwhile, Poland had been in the throes of an almost continuous financial crisis. The general instability and confusion led to frequent changes of cabinet. Following a coup led by Józef Pilsudski in 1926, Ignacy Moscicki was installed as president; Pilsudski, as minister of war, gradually acquired dictatorial control over the government in the late 1920s and early '30s. In 1935 a new constitution was adopted formalizing his authoritarian regime. Pilsudski survived the inauguration of the new system by less than a month, and was succeeded by Gen. Edward Smigły-Rydz (1886–1943).

The triumph of National Socialism in Germany and the expansionist policy of Adolf Hitler in the late 1930s posed grave dangers to Polish security. After the Munich Pact and the ensuing destruction of the Czechoslovakian state (March 1939), Poland, which had received about 1036 sq km (about 400 sq mi) of Czech territory in the Munich settlement, became the next major target of German diplomacy. This development took the form of German demands, delivered late in March, that Poland consent to the cession of Danzig to Germany and yield important rights in the Polish corridor. Polish rejection of these demands was followed, on March 31, by an Anglo-French pledge of aid to Poland in the event of German aggression. On April 28, Hitler renounced the German-Polish nonaggression treaty. On Sept. 1, 1939, Germany attacked Poland, an act that marked the outbreak of the Second World War.

World War II. By mid-September 1939, little more than two weeks after the start of the German invasion, German armies had overrun most of western and central Poland. In the same month, Soviet troops invaded Poland from the east, and the two invading powers divided the country between them. Enormous reprisals were exacted against the Poles throughout the German-occupied region. In the Soviet-occupied area, many thousands of Poles were forcibly deported to Siberia.

Numerous members of the Polish government and the military forces succeeded in escaping from Poland during the final phases of German and Soviet military operation against the country. Most of the refugee Polish troops, numbering about 100,000, succeeded in reaching France, where they were regrouped into combat units. These units and others that were later organized in the Soviet Union rendered valiant service to the Allied war effort in Europe. In the meantime a government-in-exile had been organized in France. Following the collapse of France in 1940, the Polish government established headquarters in London.

The armed forces of the Third Reich occupied

all of Soviet-held Poland during the initial phase of their attack on the USSR in 1941. During their occupation of the country, the German armies pursued a policy of systematic extermination of the Polish people, particularly Jews, many of whom perished at Auschwitz (Oświęcim), Treblinka, Majdenek, and other concentration camps scattered throughout the country. At the expiration of hostilities the estimated total of civilian casualties numbered about 5 million, a large proportion of which was inflicted by the Germans. Polish military casualties in the war totaled about 600,000. The material losses suffered were similarly enormous. In April 1943 the Jews of the Warsaw Ghetto, rather than wait for destruction in the camps, rose in rebellion against hopeless odds. The Germans quelled the rising after three weeks of hard fighting.

The liberation. The liberation of Poland from German domination began shortly after the Anglo-American invasion of France in June 1944. During June, July, and August the Soviet armies, taking advantage of the situation, inflicted a series of devastating defeats on the Germans in the east. Before the beginning of September the Soviet army, aided by contingents of Polish troops, had begun operations on Polish territory. In August 1944 Polish resistance forces took control of Warsaw, but the Soviets were either unable or unwilling to support them. The Germans recaptured the city in October and burned it to the ground after evacuating the population. The remains of Warsaw were occupied by the Soviet army in January 1945, and the last of the German invaders were driven from the country in March. In July 1944 the Soviet government had sponsored the formation of a Polish Committee of National Liberation, an organization largely dominated by Communists. The Committee of National Liberation, which established headquarters at Lublin after the liberation of that city, proclaimed itself the provisional government of Poland in December 1944. After several attempts, a reconciliation between the London and Lublin Polish governments was accomplished, and in June 1945, after the Germans had been expelled, a coalition established a Polish Government of National Unity. This government was officially recognized by the British and U.S. governments in the following month.

Postwar Boundary Changes. At the Potsdam Conference, held after Germany's surrender in 1945, the Allied powers placed Upper and Lower Silesia, Danzig (Gdańsk), and parts of Brandenburg, Pomerania, and East Prussia under Polish administration pending the conclusion of a final peace settlement. Of a population totaling about 8,900,000 in the German areas assigned to Poland, more than 7 million were Germans. Most of the Germans were subsequently expelled to Germany. The eastern frontier of Poland was delimited by the terms of a treaty concluded by the Polish and Soviet governments on Aug. 16, 1945. On the basis of this document, which established the Polish-Soviet frontier considerably to the west of the prewar boundary, the USSR acquired a considerable amount of former Polish territory. The inhabitants of this territory totaled approximately 12,500,000. Of this number, nearly 4 million were Poles, most of whom were repatriated.

The Emergence of the Communist State. Communist-Socialist strength in the government grew steadily during 1946 and 1947. In the 1947 parliamentary elections—denounced by the U.S. as not "free and unfettered"—the two-party coalition won more than 85 percent of the vote.

Stalinist takeover. Beginning in September 1948 the Polish Communist party purged itself of many thousands of so-called national Communists who had approved Yugoslavia's defiance of the Soviet Union. Among those jailed in the purge was Władysław Gomułka, secretary-general of the party and first deputy premier. In December the Socialists and Communists merged to form the Polish United Workers' party, in which pro-Stalin Communists were dominant. Soviet Marshal Konstantin Rokossovsky (1896–1968) was installed as head of the Polish armed forces in 1949, and thereafter Poland became one of the most faithful satellites of the Soviet Union.

Pro-Soviet Communist leaders then sought to outline industrial and economic goals for Poland in conformity with the economic and social system of the USSR. The major problem was the effort to collectivize agriculture, which was unsuccessful and later abandoned.

Church-state conflict. After the Vatican excommunicated all Communists in 1949, the Polish government confiscated many church properties, ordered the closing of church schools, and established a youth organization to counteract the influence of the church.

In the 1950s the government assumed supervision over the appointment of clergymen, requiring a loyalty oath of each candidate. Cardinal Stefan Wyszynski (1902–81), archbishop of Warsaw and primate of Poland, resisted the measure and was suspended from office. He was allowed to retire to a monastery; in 1956 he returned to his clerical duties as a result of more lenient policies.

Gomułka's Return. During the postwar period, Poland became an active member of the Council for Mutual Economic Assistance and the Warsaw Pact, both Soviet-dominated organs. In 1952 Poland adopted a constitution modeled after that of the USSR but explicitly recognizing certain property rights.

In the "thaw" following the death of Soviet leader Joseph Stalin in 1953, Polish artists, intellectuals, students, and workers raised demands for government reforms and a greater measure of freedom from Soviet control. In June 1956 workers staged a demonstration in Poznań; the quelling of the protest left 53 people dead and several hundred wounded. Leaders of the demonstration received relatively light sentences. In October Gomułka, who had been readmitted to the party, was named first secretary. Rokossovsky and other Stalinist officials in high Polish posts were dismissed.

Gomułka then became the dominant figure in Poland, steering a careful course between pro-Soviet and nationalist sentiments. Limited political reforms were introduced in the 1957 elections. Slates included non-Communists and independents; moreover, there were nearly twice as many candidates as posts to be filled.

Popular discontent erupted once again in Poland in the spring of 1968, as demands by students and artists for greater freedom of expression were met by severe government repression. Student riots began in Warsaw in March, at the university and at the Polytechnic School, and soon spread to the universities in Poznań, Lublin, and Kraków. The students demanded liberal reforms similar to those instituted in Czechoslovakia at the time. Seeking to stifle dissent, the government launched an "anti-Zionist" campaign, which had anti-Semitic overtones. Hundreds of Jews were dismissed from government, party, university, and newspaper positions. During the conferences in Warsaw in June and Bratislava in August 1968, Poland joined the Warsaw Pact powers in a condemnation of the Czech reform program and on August 20 participated in the occupation of Czechoslovakia, sending a contingent estimated at 45,000 troops.

Reconciliation with West Germany. Early in 1970 economic problems prompted the government to make a major adjustment in its foreign policy. Hopeful of obtaining economic and technological aid from prosperous West Germany, the Poles opened political talks with West Germany in January, and the Polish and German foreign ministers reached agreement in November. In December Chancellor Willy Brandt of West Germany went to Warsaw to sign the resulting treaty, in which West Germany formally accepted the postwar loss of 103,600 sq km (40,000 sq mi) to Poland and the establishment of the Oder-Neisse line as Poland's western frontier. In return, Bonn received informal Polish assurances that Polish residents who claimed German nationality (thought to number several tens of thousands) would be permitted to emigrate from Poland. Both sides agreed to settle disputes "exclusively by peaceful means" and to move toward "full normalization" of relations. Full relations were restored after the West German parliament ratified the treaty in May 1972.

The Gierek Regime. An economic crisis assumed major proportions late in 1970. Polish industry had fallen short of planning goals. Bad weather again contributed to a poor harvest and resulted in the costly import of grain. In addition, the prices of coal, food, and clothing were drastically raised. Outraged at the increases, workers in half a dozen Polish cities staged demonstrations which led to riots, arson, and looting. A week-long state of emergency was declared, and the protests were forcibly suppressed.

In the aftermath of the rioting, party secretary Gomułka and other party leaders were removed from the Politburo. Edward Gierek, a Politburo member, became party secretary. Prices were frozen at their previous levels, and in 1972 the freeze was extended indefinitely.

Improving relations with the West were symbolized by visits to Poland by U.S. presidents Richard M. Nixon in 1972, Gerald R. Ford in 1975, and Jimmy Carter in 1977. Poland began the repatriation of some 125,000 ethnic Germans to West Germany in 1975.

In June 1976 the government announced a sharp increase in food prices, made necessary, in part, by poor harvests since 1974. The announcement touched off another wave of popular protests, which forced the regime to moderate the increases by maintaining costly price subsidies. The continued need to import much food helped raise Poland's foreign debt to a perilously high level.

Conditions failed to improve over the next few years, and, in response to rapidly rising food prices, hundreds of thousands of Polish workers went on strike in the summer of 1980. Led by shipyard workers in Gdańsk and other Baltic coast ports, the strike paralyzed the country for nearly three weeks and quickly took on a political character. Early in September the government, making unprecedented concessions, agreed to the strikers' demands for wage increases, recognition of an independent trade union federation—known as Solidarity—and of the right to strike, release of political prisoners, and curtailment of censorship. Discredited party

In mid-August 1980, workers of the Lenin Shipyard in Gdańsk struck and took over the yard. Spreading to other cities, the strike toppled the government and led to the foundation of Solidarity, the Polish labor union. Jean-Louis Atlan–Sygma

leader Edward Gierek stepped down in favor of Stanisław Kania (1927–).

Labor unrest continued in 1981, and the reformers demanded more freedoms. Under Soviet pressure, Gen. Wojciech Jaruzelski (1923–) was made party chief and premier to bring the situation under control. In December, when Solidarity proposed a national referendum on whether to retain the Communist system, Jaruzelski responded by imposing martial law, suspending the union's activities, and arresting its leader, Lech Wałesa, along with many others. Resistance, although generally nonviolent, remained very strong. It was led by unionists, with the active support of the Roman Catholic church, but reached far into the ranks of the Communist party. By mid-1982, some 45,000 party members had been either suspended or expelled. Martial law was formally lifted in 1983. By this time, however, many of the government's expanded emergency powers had been made permanent.

When economic conditions deteriorated and popular discontent intensified in the late 1980s, the Communists took a more conciliatory line. Negotiations between labor and government leaders resulted in the full legalization of Solidarity, the establishment of a freely elected senate with veto power over legislation, and the vesting of executive powers in an indirectly elected president. In the elections of June 1989, Solidarity candidates won control of the senate and became a powerful minority in the Sejm. In July, Gen. Jaruzelski was elected president with Solidarity's concurrence, and Mieczysław Rakowski (1926–), the former premier, was made party chief. In August the Communists' choice for prime minister, Czesław Kiszczak (1925–), was unable to put together a cabinet. Jaruzelski then called on Tadeusz Mazowiecki (1927–), a close aide to Lech Wałesa, to form a Solidarity-led coalition government in which the Communists would control the defense and interior ministries. Mazowiecki thus became Poland's first non-Communist premier in more than 40 years. A presidential candidate in the November-December 1990 elections, he lost to Wałesa, who moved to transform Poland to a free market economy. Numerous parties competed in the parliamentary election of October 1991, Poland's freest since World War II; the inconclusive outcome led to the installation of a minority coalition government.

For further information on this topic, see the Bibliography in volume 28, sections 855, 949–50.

POLARIS. *See* NORTH STAR.

POLARIZATION OF LIGHT. *See* OPTICS.

POLE, in geography, one of two extremities of the axis around which the earth revolves; situated on the north or south side of the equator, equidistant from all parts of it, lat 90° N or lat 90° S, called, respectively, the north and south poles. For a discussion of the north and south magnetic poles, *see* EARTH: *Terrestrial Magnetism.*

In astronomy, the denominated celestial poles are those points in the heavens toward which the axis of the earth is directed and around which the heavens seem to revolve. These celestial poles are valuable points of reference to astronomers and geographers, and the determination of their position in the heavens is important. Although no stars mark their exact situation, a few minute telescopic stars can be observed a few seconds from the north pole. *See* NORTH STAR.

POLE, Reginald (1500–58), English Roman Catholic prelate, who opposed the religious policies of King Henry VIII.

Pole was born on March 3, 1500, in Staffordshire. He was a member of the Tudor and Plantagenet families, and his mother, Margaret Pole, countess of Salisbury (1473–1541), was a niece of Edward IV, king of England. Pole was educated at the universities of Oxford and Padua and was awarded a position in the English church while still quite young. He was not, however, ordained a priest. He returned to England from Italy in 1525. In 1530 he was sent to Paris in an effort to obtain approval from church academics of the divorce of Henry VIII, king of England, his cousin. Soon afterward, he became disgusted with the policies of Privy Councillor Thomas Cromwell, refused the archbishopric of York, and again took up residence in Italy. England was, at the time, split politically and religiously by the attempts of King Henry to control the church.

In Italy, Pope Paul III made Pole a deacon and elevated him to cardinal. Sent as papal legate to the Low Countries, Pole conferred there with agents of the English opponents to Henry. This move meant an open break with the king and royal retaliation. Henry had a bill of attainder passed against Pole and set a price on his head; in 1541 his mother was executed.

In 1553, on the death of King Edward VI, Henry's son and successor, Pole was at once commissioned by Pope Julius III (1487–1555) to go to England to assist Mary I, Edward's sister and the new queen of England, in the reconciliation of the kingdom and the papacy. Mary restored Roman Catholic forms of worship in England, and on Nov. 30, 1554, Pole absolved the houses of Parliament and the country from their schismatic condition, reconciling the Church of England to Rome. After Archbishop of Canterbury Thomas Cranmer was martyred, Pole was ordained a priest on March 20, 1556, and two days later was consecrated archbishop of Canterbury. Pole's legation was canceled, however, by Pope Paul IV in 1558. The cardinal was summoned before the Inquisition, but Queen Mary intercepted the order; Pole died shortly thereafter in London, on Nov. 17, 1558.

In a life devoted to the political and ecclesiastical issues of the Reformation and Counter Reformation, Pole was prominent not only in the history of England but in that of the Roman Catholic church as a whole. He was a prominent candidate in the 1549 papal election that followed the death of Paul III, and he was one of three commissioners to preside at meetings of the Council of Trent.

POLECAT, common name for a European carnivore, *Mustela putorius,* of the family Mustelidae, which also contains the badgers, weasels, skunks, and otters. The domesticated ferret (q.v.) is a subspecies. Valued for its fur, which is marketed under the name of fitch, the polecat grows to about 51 cm (about 20 in) in length with a tail about 15 cm (about 6 in) long. It is usually buff-gray in color, overshadowed with black-tipped hairs; yellowish markings are found on the head. A close relative is the North American black-footed ferret, *M. nigripes,* which has yellow fur, brown legs, and black tail and feet; it feeds on prairie dogs. The black-footed ferret is extremely rare and is in danger of becoming extinct. The polecat is an expert swimmer and catches fish for food; its common diet, however, consists mostly of small mammals, reptiles, and any birds, especially poultry. Its habits in general are the same as those of the stoat (*see* WEASEL). When irritated or alarmed the animal emits a disagreeable odor from the anal scent glands, a characteristic that has caused the term polecat to be erroneously applied to the skunk.

POLESTAR. *See* NORTH STAR.

POLE VAULTING. *See* TRACK AND FIELD.

POLICE, agency of a community or government that is responsible for maintaining public order and preventing and detecting crime. The basic police mission—preserving order by enforcing rules of conduct or laws—was the same in ancient societies as it is now.

HISTORY OF POLICE FORCES

The conception of the police force as a protective and law enforcement organization developed from the use of military bodies as guardians of the peace, such as the Praetorian Guard (q.v.) of ancient Rome. The Romans achieved a high level of law enforcement, which remained in effect until the decline of the empire and the onset of the Middle Ages. Beginning in the 5th century, policing became a function of the heads of fiefdoms and principalities.

During the Middle Ages, policing authority, particularly in England, was the responsibility of local nobles on their individual estates. Each noble generally appointed an official, known as a constable, to carry out the law. The constable's duties included keeping the peace and arresting and guarding criminals. For many decades constables were unpaid citizens who took turns at the job, which became increasingly burdensome and unpopular. By the mid-16th century, wealthy citizens often resorted to paying deputies to assume their turns as constables; as this practice became widespread, the quality of the constables declined drastically.

Policeman and policewoman on duty in the police department offices of a large city. Women form a growing percentage of the total number of active police officers.
D. W. Funt–Editorial Photocolor Archives

In France during the 17th century King Louis XIV maintained a small central police organization consisting of some 40 inspectors who, with the help of numerous paid informants, supplied the government with details about the conduct of private individuals. The king could then exercise a kind of summary justice as he saw fit. This system continued during the reigns of Louis XV and Louis XVI. After the French Revolution, two separate police bodies were set up, one to handle ordinary duties and the other to deal with political crimes.

In 1663 the city of London began paying watchmen (generally old men who were unable to find other work) to guard the streets at night. Until the end of the 18th century, the watchmen—as inefficient as they were—as well as a few constables, remained the only form of policing in the city.

The inability of watchmen and constables to curb lawlessness, particularly in London, led to a demand for a more effective force to deal with criminals and to protect the populace. After much deliberation in Parliament, the British statesman Sir Robert Peel in 1829 established the London Metropolitan Police, which became the world's first modern organized police force. The development of the British police system is especially significant because the pattern that emerged not only became a model for the American police system but also had great influence on the style of policing in almost all industrial societies.

The Metropolitan Police force was guided by the concept of crime prevention as a primary police objective; it also embodied the belief that such a force depended on the consent and cooperation of the public, and the idea that police constables were to be civil and courteous to the people. The force was well organized and disciplined and, after an initial period of public skepticism, became the model for other police forces in Great Britain. Several years later the Royal Irish Constabulary was formed, and Australia, India, and Canada soon established similar organizations. Other countries, impressed by the success of the plan, followed suit until nations throughout the world had adopted police systems based on the British model.

In the U.S., the first full-time organized police departments were formed in New York City in 1845 and shortly thereafter in Boston, not only in response to crime but also to control unrest. The American police adopted many British methods, but at times they became involved in local partisan politics. The British police, on the other hand, have traditionally remained aloof from partisan politics and have depended on loyalty to the law, rather than to elected public officials, as the source of their authority and independence.

POLICE IN THE U.S.

The U.S. has a fragmented system of police administration comprising some 19,000 separate municipal and county law enforcement agencies and an estimated 21,000 additional federal, state, and local agencies with specialized jurisdictions of responsibility. Approximately half the local law enforcement agencies consist of fewer than 10 police officers.

Law Enforcement Agencies. The principal law enforcement agencies of the federal government are the Department of Justice, the Department of the Treasury, and the U.S. Postal Service. The jurisdiction of federal law enforcement agencies is limited to the government's power to regulate interstate commerce, impose taxes, and enforce constitutional and federal law. Department of Justice agencies include the Federal Bureau of Investigation (q.v.), which deals with bank robberies, kidnappings, and violation of other federal laws and provides training, identification, and laboratory services to local police; the Drug Enforcement Administration (q.v.), which investigates cases involving illicit narcotics and drugs; several branches of the Immigration and Naturalization Service (q.v.), which enforce alien-entry laws; and the U.S. Marshals Service (*see* MARSHALS SERVICE, UNITED STATES), with responsibilities for safeguarding and transporting federal prisoners and acting as marshals for U.S. courts. Agencies in the Treasury Department include the Bureau of Alcohol, Tobacco and Firearms, which investigates tax violations related to alcohol and tobacco, enforces the laws concerning prohibition or control of firearms, and provides investigation of bombings; the Secret Service (q.v.), whose primary responsibilities include protection of the president and vice-president and their families and investigation of counterfeiting; and the U.S. Customs Service (*see* CUSTOMS SERVICE, UNITED STATES), which investigates smuggling activities. The Postal Inspections Service deals with such crimes as mail fraud and misuse of the mails.

Basically, two kinds of state police agencies exist in the U.S.: those with general functions similar to local police and those with limited responsibilities, mainly involving highway patrol on state roads.

A city police force is usually organized as one of several departments within the local government. The police are part of the local criminal justice system, which is the means by which society deals with criminals. The system includes the prosecuting attorney's office, the courts, probation offices, and corrections agencies.

There are thousands of private and industrial security forces in the U.S. These organizations employ a substantial percentage of all persons engaged in police work, and the use of private security by both businesses and individuals is increasing rapidly. Large corporations often maintain security forces to curb internal thefts, shoplifting, robberies, and trespassing.

Dogs destined for use in police work undergo rigorous training before being assigned to a police officer for patrol duty. UPI

Personnel. The executive head of a police department—the commissioner, superintendent, or chief of police—is usually appointed by a mayor, city administrator, or legislative body. In larger agencies, executive officers may be selected through a civil service or merit system, after moving through the ranks from patrol officer to sergeant, lieutenant, captain, and (in still larger agencies) deputy or assistant chief.

At the county level, the head of the agency usually holds the title sheriff. The sheriff is almost always elected and has the power to appoint deputies. Sheriffs' departments often provide law enforcement services for unincorporated areas of counties and are usually responsible for functions not normally carried out by municipal police, such as operating the county jail, providing courtroom security, and serving legal documents, including subpoenas and court orders.

Police Operations. A police department's goals are to prevent crime, investigate crime and apprehend offenders, control traffic, maintain order, and deal with emergencies and disasters.

Prevention of crime. The patrol division, consisting of uniformed patrol officers and supervisors, provides basic police services. In addition to foot and automobile patrol, officers engage in a variety of activities in response to citizens' needs. The greater part of patrol today is carried out by officers in police cars assigned to specific beats, or designated areas of the community. In small agencies, one-officer patrol cars are prevalent; in larger cities, combinations of one- and two-officer cars are common. Use of women officers for patrol duty is increasing; before 1970 the practice was unknown.

Recent research has raised doubts about the effectiveness of preventive patrol to curb most kinds of crime. Crime prevention, however, also means activities related to improving the security of homes and businesses, and to educating citizens to protect themselves. Most large police departments maintain a crime prevention unit to provide these services.

Criminal investigation. After patrol officers have conducted preliminary investigations, detectives who work in plain clothes further investigate serious crimes. Most detectives are assigned to the criminal investigations division after several years on patrol duty. In large departments, detectives are organized into specialized units, such as homicide, robbery, and narcotics. Contrary to popular belief, many cases solved by detectives are based on arrests made by patrol officers, or on leads supplied by officers or victims as a result of preliminary investigations.

Traffic control. Most traffic law enforcement and accident investigation is carried out by patrol officers. In large cities, however, specialists may handle serious or hit-and-run accidents, and motorcycle patrols may be responsible for freeway traffic. In the largest jurisdictions, officers may be assigned to traffic direction at busy intersections. A recent trend in many cities has been toward the use of civilian employees to handle parking violations.

Special police units. Modern police service often includes special units to handle special problems. In major American cities, tactical units, highly trained and well equipped, are available to quell riots. Bomb squads are also on call; the bomb squad of the New York City Police Department, for example, is widely known for its outstanding work in handling bomb cases and scares. Other units specialize in dealing with hostage situations.

Noncriminal services. In most communities, about 60 to 70 percent of the time spent by patrol officers on operational activities is not crime related. Officers are called on to locate missing persons and lost children and to deal with marital disputes, crowd control, and ambulance calls.

Police Technology. Requests for police services are generally transmitted to headquarters by telephone and then by radio to officers in the field. Police have long operated on the theory that fast response time results in more arrests and less risk or injury to victims. The current trend is toward handling calls by priority, with emergency response reserved for cases involving an injured party or those in which a reasonable chance exists to prevent a crime or make an arrest at the scene. Modern computer-assisted dispatching systems permit automatic selection of the nearest beat officer in service. In some cities, officers can receive messages displayed on computer terminals in their cars, without voice communication from headquarters. An officer, for example, can key in the license number of a suspect vehicle and receive an immediate response from the computer as to the status of the vehicle and the owner's identity.

An increasing number of agencies are now using computers to link crime patterns with certain suspects. Fingerprints found at crime scenes can be electronically compared with fingerprint files. Other departments use computers for workload analysis, budgeting, and payroll systems.

In recent years technological advances have been made in such areas as voiceprint identification (q.v.), use of the scanning electron microscope, and serology (an important tool because only 2 persons in 70,000 have identical blood

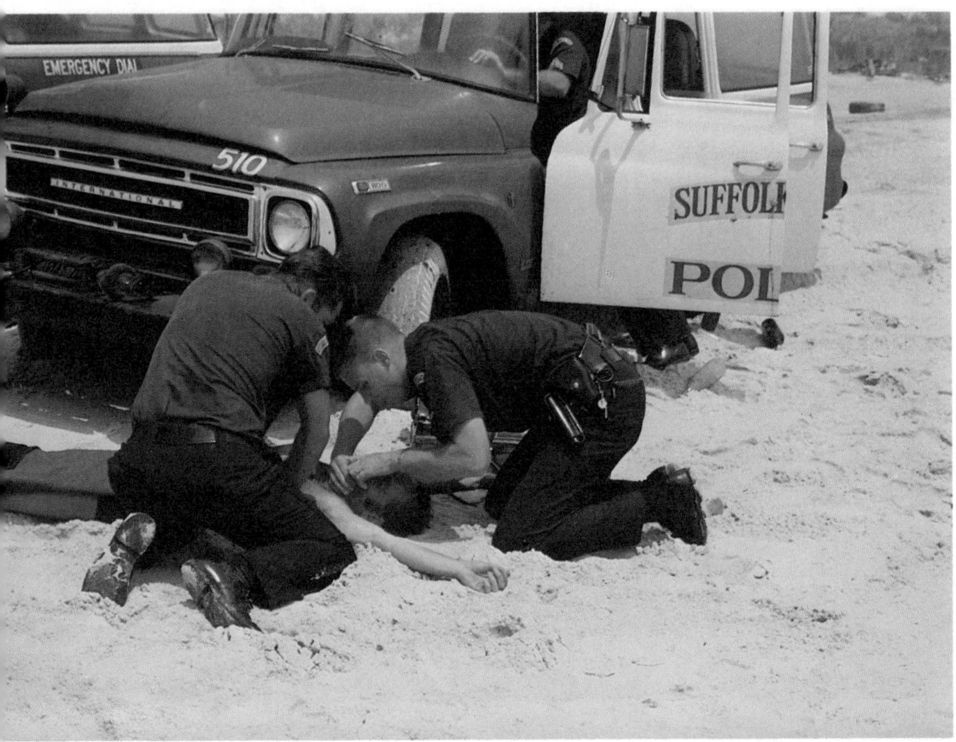

Two police officers aid a drowning victim on a New York beach. All police personnel are trained in first aid and emergency resuscitation techniques. Vance Henry–Taurus Photos

characteristics). Some of the new laboratory techniques, although highly effective, are extremely expensive, so their use is limited to the most challenging cases. *See* CRIME DETECTION.

Contemporary Issues and Trends. In the U.S. today, important and controversial issues have arisen regarding the administration and operations of police forces, especially in urban centers.

Police unions. In recent years, police unions, including groups associated with national labor organizations, have grown rapidly. Critics of this trend argue that unionized police forces are less likely to be neutral in controlling disorders that occur during labor strikes. Some people also believe that union affiliation will weaken official authority in maintaining discipline. Others argue that management deficiencies often prompt the need for unions and that unionization will lead to greater job satisfaction, higher morale, and increased tenure. Because police are public employees, laws restrict their right to strike or to participate in other job actions. The trend seems to be for police unions to engage in compulsory or binding arbitration when labor disputes arise.

Restraints on police methods. The police continue to rely on investigative methods that emphasize interviewing witnesses, interrogating suspects, developing sources of information through informants, carrying out surveillances, and making undercover purchases of narcotics and stolen property. These activities and the searches and arrests that result have received the full scrutiny of the courts. In recent decades, the U.S. Supreme Court has imposed conditions on police methods, such as the requirement that immediately after arrest a person must be informed of his or her rights, including the right to counsel and the right to remain silent. The Court has also banned the use of evidence obtained illegally or extralegally, such as information from unauthorized wiretapping (q.v.).

Police and civil disorders. The police are crucial in preventing and controlling civil disorders. In the aftermath of civil disturbances in the 1960s, for example, authorities recognized the importance of preventing police action from becoming a precipitating cause in itself, as well as the need for police to engage in positive community-related activities to alleviate tensions.

Use of deadly force. No issue provokes more intense controversy within minority communities than police policy concerning the use of force,

A San Mateo, Calif., policeman, on patrol in his car, uses a small computer to check a license plate number. Jim Balog–Black Star

especially deadly force. Some police officials and most minority community leaders believe that a police officer should use a firearm only in defense of a life (either that of the officer or of some other person) in immediate jeopardy. Others think that existing state laws, many of which permit an officer to use any force necessary to arrest a suspected felon, should not be limited by local policies.

Equal employment opportunities. In the past decades, prodded by changes in public attitudes and by court decisions, police departments have recruited increasing numbers of minority members and women. A movement away from arbitrarily determined eligibility requirements, such as minimum height and maximum ages, has also occurred.

Citizen policing. In some cities, volunteer citizen patrols have been formed to prevent crime. In a few cases, these patrols operate without an official relationship to the police department. Far more common, however, is the use of police-organized, uniformed citizen groups generally known as reserve or auxiliary police.

POLICE IN OTHER COUNTRIES

About 800 police forces operate in Canada today. Their operations resemble those of Great Britain and the U.S. Two provinces, Québec and Ontario, have provincial police with general law enforcement responsibilities. In the other provinces, rural policing is assumed by the Royal Canadian Mounted Police (q.v.).

Most European countries have police forces that are organized on a national basis. Policing in France, for example, is primarily the responsibility of two national law enforcement bodies: the Gendarmerie Nationale, which polices rural areas and small towns, and the Police Nationale, which is responsible for policing Paris and provincial urban jurisdictions with populations of more than 10,000. The French police system has influenced other countries, especially those that were formerly part of the French colonial empire.

After World War II, the Allied occupational forces introduced the British-American style of decentralized police forces to West Germany, partly to prevent a return to a national military force. The experiment was not totally successful, however, and a compromise currently exists between a national force and decentralization. Germany is organized into semiautonomous provinces or states, each with its own independently elected state government, judiciary, and police. There is also a federal investigative bureau, the

Bundeskriminalamt, which is renowned for its sophisticated computerized records system and technology.

In the Middle East, Israel has a single national police force that has been patterned after elements of the British Palestine Police. Following independence in 1948, attempts were made to demilitarize the force, but recurrent conflicts with neighboring Arab states have compelled the police to maintain security against terrorist actions, as well as carrying on the usual law enforcement activities. The battle-hardened Israeli police have developed highly effective investigative methods and technical capabilities.

Little is known about the operation or organization of the police in Communist nations, as details of the system are generally kept secret.

The International Criminal Police Organization (Interpol) was established after World War II, with headquarters in Paris. Interpol does not conduct worldwide criminal investigations; rather, it is a records clearinghouse that serves as a means of communicating information from the police of one country to those of another. The majority of nations in the non-Communist world, including all major Western powers, are members of Interpol.

See also CRIME; CRIMINAL LAW; CRIMINAL PROCEDURE; CRIMINOLOGY; PENOLOGY; POLICE POWER; PRISON; SECRET POLICE.

POLICE EXECUTIVE RESEARCH FORUM

For further information on this topic, see the Bibliography in volume 28, sections 298-99.

POLICE POWER, in U.S. domestic law, a term used to designate the power exercised by a state or municipal government to enact legislation regulating private interests for the protection of the safety, health, and morals of the people, the prevention of fraud and oppression, and the promotion of the public convenience, prosperity, and welfare.

The precise scope of police power is difficult to define. It covers, for example, the maintenance of the peace by the police; the licensing of some trades and professions; the regulation of rates charged by public service corporations; the regulation of security issues by so-called Blue Sky laws, which are statutes intended to prevent fraud in the sale of stocks and bonds; the regulation of hours of labor; and such health regulations as quarantine and compulsory vaccination.

The police power rests on the general legislative authority, and is limited only by express provisions contained in the U.S. Constitution or in state constitutions. Until 1936 the U.S. Supreme Court closely reviewed state and local police-power regulations to determine whether they were reasonable under the due process clause of the 14th Amendment; frequently the Court invalidated state and local social legislation. In recent decades the Supreme Court and other federal courts have declined to declare such legislation unconstitutional, except in the relatively few cases in which the police power has been exercised inconsistently with provisions of the Bill of Rights protecting freedom of speech or of religion or has failed to protect the procedural rights of citizens to a fair hearing.

The power of the federal government to legislate is neither inherent nor residual, but rests on grants of authority vested by the Constitution. Some of these are general, such as the power to regulate commerce; others are specific, as in the power to coin money and to establish post offices and post roads. Since the 1930s, when the Supreme Court upheld much of the federal legislation contained in the program known as the New Deal, the legislative powers of the federal government usually have been sustained by the courts, adding measurably to the ability of the national government to intervene in areas that were previously reserved for state and local governments through the exercise of the police power. N.D.

POLIOMYELITIS, infectious virus disease of the central nervous system, sometimes resulting in paralysis. The greatest incidence of the disease, also known as infantile paralysis, is in children between the ages of five and ten years. The disease was described in 1840 by the German orthopedist Jacob von Heine (1800-79). In its clinical form it is more prevalent in temperate zones.

Symptoms. The virus usually enters the body through the alimentary tract and spreads along nerve cells to affect various parts of the central nervous system. The incubation period ranges from about 4 to 35 days. Early symptoms include fatigue, headache, fever, vomiting, constipation, stiffness of the neck, or, less commonly, diarrhea and pain in the extremities. Because nerve cells that control muscular movement are not replaced once they are destroyed, poliovirus infection can cause permanent paralysis. When nerve cells in respiratory centers, which control breathing, are destroyed, the victim must be kept alive by an iron lung (*see* ARTIFICIAL RESPIRATION). For every paralytic case of poliomyelitis, however, there may be 100 nonparalytic cases.

Treatment. Because no drug developed so far has proved effective, treatment is entirely symptomatic. Use of moist heat coupled with physical therapy (q.v.) to stimulate the muscles was first initiated by the Australian nurse Elizabeth Kenny, and antispasmodic drugs are administered to

Dr. Jonas Salk, developer of a vaccine against poliomyelitis, checks a test of the effectiveness of vaccine inoculations in stimulating development of antibodies in the blood.
National Foundation

produce muscular relaxation. In the convalescent stage, occupational therapy (q.v.) is used.

Disease Control. Three broad types of the virus have been identified: the Brunhilde (type 1), Lansing (type 2), and Leon (type 3) strains. Immunity to one strain does not furnish protection against the other two.

Poliomyelitis control was made possible when, in 1949, the American bacteriologist John Franklin Enders and his coworkers discovered a method of growing the viruses on tissue in the laboratory. Applying this technique, the American physician and epidemiologist Jonas Salk developed a vaccine prepared from inactivated poliomyelitis viruses of the three known types. After field trials in 1954 the vaccine was pronounced safe and effective, and mass inoculation began. The American virologist Albert Sabin subsequently developed a vaccine containing attenuated, live polio virus that could be given orally. This vaccine, called trivalent oral polio vaccine (TOPV), was licensed in 1963 and has replaced the Salk injectable vaccine as the standard immunizing agent in the U.S. As a result of routine immunization, outbreaks of paralytic poliomyelitis declined dramatically from 57,879 cases in 1952 to only a few each year.

The vulnerability of a population that was not immunized was demonstrated in 1979, when 16 cases of paralytic poliomyelitis occurred among Amish people in the U.S. and Canada who had not been vaccinated.

For further information on this topic, see the Bibliography in volume 28, sections 448, 505, 508.

POLISH LANGUAGE, language spoken by most of the inhabitants of Poland and by several million native speakers in the U.S., several countries of the former USSR, Canada, and elsewhere. Polish belongs to the Western group of the Slavic branch of Indo-European languages and is thus closely related to Czech, Slovak, and the Sorbian language found in eastern Germany (*see* SLAVIC LANGUAGES). Polish dialects include Little Polish and Silesian (spoken in the south) and Mazovian and Great Polish (spoken in the north). Kashubian, or Cassubian, also heard in the north, is often treated as a dialect of Polish, although it evolved as a separate West Slavic language.

Phonetics and Grammar. Contemporary Polish has 7 vowel sounds and 35 consonant sounds, depicted by a modified Latin alphabet. Sounds that are not represented by the alphabet are indicated by digraphs such as *sz* and *cz* (resembling English *sh* and *ch*) and by diacritics such as *ż* and *ś* (resembling *zh* and a soft *sh*), derived from Czech. Unique to Polish is the *ł* (resembling English *w*). In the course of its evolution, Polish lost the distinction between long and short vowels, and word accent became fixed on the next-to-last syllable. Polish is the only Slavic language with nasal vowels (*ą* and *ę*), which are derived from Old Slavic nasal vowels. Of the original singular, dual, and plural, the dual has disappeared (as in most Slavic languages). The singular has three genders, masculine, feminine, and neuter; the plural developed a new category, personal masculine gender (for human males), which is distinguished from a common plural gender for all other categories. Polish is highly inflected and retains the Old Slavic case system: six cases for nouns, pronouns, and adjectives, plus a seventh case, the vocative (for direct address) for nouns and pronouns. Verbs are inflected according to gender as well as person and number, but the tense forms have been simplified through elimination of three old tenses (the aorist, imperfect, and past perfect). The so-called Slavic perfect is the only past tense form used in common speech. Word order remains highly flexible.

History. The oldest known examples of written Polish are names and glosses in Latin documents (notably a papal bull of 1136). Modern literary Polish emerged in the 16th century. Although the core of literary Polish has remained pure, loanwords were absorbed from medieval Czech and German, from Latin, and, more recently, from such languages as Belorussian, Ukrainian, French, and English.

POLISH LITERATURE, literature of the Polish people, written primarily in the Polish language. Polish literary activity began in pagan times with folk literature transmitted exclusively through oral tradition. This early literature falls into two main categories: lyric poetry, devoted to merriment and the joys of living; and epic poetry, consisting of fables, animal epics, apologues, religious legends, and historical tales.

The Medieval Period. In 966 Poland entered the sphere of Christian culture. The native pre-Christian culture of the Poles was rigorously suppressed, and, as was then customary throughout Europe, Latin literature and language became the chief subjects studied in all Polish schools. The most important early Polish works written in Latin include the *Chronica,* a biographical work written by an anonymous 12th-century author later called Gallus; the *Chronica Polonorum,* an allegorical chronicle by the 13th century Kraków bishop Wincenty Kadłubek (c. 1150–1223); and *Annales,* a historical work distinguished by the careful scholarship of its 15th-century author, Jan Długosz (1415–80). Vernacular works of this period include the *Kazania Święokrzyskie* (Sermons of the Holy Cross), fragments of prose sermons from the end of the 13th or the beginning of the 14th century; the *Kazania Gnieźnieńskie* (Gniezno Sermons), from the 15th century; and such biblical translations as the *Psałterz królowej Jadwigi* (Psalter of Queen Jadwiga, also called the Psalter of Saint Florian), from the late 14th or early 15th century, and the *Biblia królowej Zofii* (Bible of Queen Zofia), from the 15th century. Lives of saints, often rhymed, also survive from this period. The poetry of the era comprised historical, didactic, and religious songs, proverbs, and riddles, written in both Latin and Polish. *Bogurodzica* (Mother of God) is considered to be the oldest Polish religious song; it has served as a battle hymn and also as the Polish national anthem. An important example of Polish secular poetry is *Rozmowa mistrza ze Śmiercią* (Conversation of a Master with Death), a 15th-century work containing elements of social satire.

The Renaissance. At the end of the 15th century Polish literature began to significantly change, opening a new era, often called the golden age, of Polish literature. This was the Polish Renaissance, which lasted from about 1500 to 1600. The tradition of the medieval historians was carried on during this period by Maciej of Miechów (c. 1456–1523) in two Latin works, *Tractatus de Duabus Sarmatiis* (Treatise on the Two Sarmatias, 1517) and *Chronica Polonorum.* The same tradition was continued by Marcin Kromer (1512–89) in his Latin *De Origine et Rebus Gestis Polonorum* (On the Origins and Deeds of the Poles, 1555), and by Marcin Bielski (1495–1575) and Maciej Stryjkowski (1547–82), who wrote chronicles in Polish. The social and political thought of the time was manifested in the famous Latin treatise *De Republica Emendanda* (On the Reform of the State, 1551–54), by Andrzej Frycz Modrzewski (c. 1503–72). The production of sermons and lives of saints continued during this period; the outstanding writer of these was the Jesuit Piotr Skarga (1536–1612), who followed the great tradition of classical rhetoric.

Poetry developed during this period as never before in Polish history. In the early years of the Polish Renaissance notable poetic works were written in Latin by Paweł of Krosno (d. 1518), Andrzej Krzycki (1482–1537), Jan Dantyszek (1485–1548), Mikołaj Hussowski (1475 or 1485–c. 1533), and Klemens Janicjusz (1516–43). By the middle of the 16th century, Polish had begun to supplant Latin as the literary language of the country.

Among the leading Polish writers of this era was Mikołaj Rej (1505–69), who produced, in prose as well as verse, dramatic dialogues and moralistic and didactic works including *Wizerunek własny żywota człowieka poczciwego* (A Faithful Image of an Honest Man, 1558), *Zwierciadło* (The Mirror, 1567–68), and *Zwierzyniec* (Bestiary, 1562). The most significant figure in Polish poetry, however, and especially in lyric poetry, was Jan Kochanowski (1530–84), who translated the *Psałterz Dawidów* (David's Psalter, 1578) and wrote songs, epigrams, and the notable *Treny* (1580; *Laments,* 1920), a cycle of poems in which he mourned the loss of his daughter. Kochanowski also wrote a famous play based on classical motifs, *Odprawa posłów greckich* (1578; *The Dismissal of the Grecian Envoys,* 1918).

Other poets achieved eminence in this area, among them Sebastian Fabian Klonowic (c. 1545–

1602), who wrote the Latin poems *Roxolania* (Ruthenia, 1584), describing the life of the Ruthenians, and *Victoria Deorum* (Victory of the Gods, 1587), dealing with educational and moral problems. He also wrote in Polish *Flis* (1595; *The Boatman,* 1958) and *Worek Judaszów* (Judas's Sack, 1600), portraying particular social classes. Szymon Szymonowic (1558-1629) wrote a collection of idylls in the vernacular, and Mikołaj Sęp Szarzyński (1550-81) wrote a collection of lyric poetry, *Rytmy* (Rhythms, 1601), in the baroque style.

The 17th and Early 18th Centuries. In the 17th century Polish literature began to exhibit considerable diversity. The stormy political and military history of the period found expression in numerous diaries, notably the colorful and lively *Pamiętniki* (Memoirs, 1690-95) of Jan Chryzostom Pasek (c. 1636-1701). Many poetical works had historical themes; for example, *Niepróżnujące prożnowanie* (Non-idle Idling, 1674) by Wespazjan Kochowski (1633-1700) described the military triumphs and defeats of the era. Inspired by the events of his time, Kochowski also wrote *Psalmodia polska* (Polish Psalmody, 1695), a prose work composed in a biblical style, and a history in Latin, *Annales* (1683). The patriotic epic *Wojna Chocimska* (The War of Khotim, 1670) by Wacław Potocki (1621-96) celebrated the victory over the Turks in 1621, and his *Ogród fraszek* (A Garden of Trifles, 1690-91) provides an insight into the life of the Polish gentry of the time. Samuel Twardowski (c. 1595-1661) wrote the long rhymed chronicles *Władysław IV* (1649) and *Wojna Domowa z Kozaki i Tatary* (A Civil War with the Cossacks and the Tartars, 1681) and also *Dafnis* (Daphne, 1638), a dramatic idyll. Another poet, Maciej Kazimierz Sarbiewski (1595-1640), wrote Latin lyrics that earned him the name of "the Christian Horace." Lyrical poems in Polish were produced by Szymon Zimorowic (1609-29), a writer of erotic idylls, and by Jan Andrzej Morsztyn (c. 1613-93), a master of poetic form who wrote the collections of verses *Kanikuła* (Dog Days, 1647) and *Lutnia* (Lute, 1661).

The 17th century in Poland was also marked by the production of comedies, such as those by Stanisław Herakliusz Lubomirski (1642-1702). Many satires were written as well, sharply criticizing the social and political scenes; foremost among the writers of these were Krzysztof (1609-55) and Łukasz Opaliński (1612-62).

The Enlightenment. Polish literature of the Enlightenment period (about 1764 to 1795) was rationalistic, stressing empirical knowledge and promulgating social and political reforms. Among the thinkers who dealt with problems of education were Hugo Kołłątaj (1750-1812) and Stanisław Staszic (1755-1826). Fables, satires, and comedies of manners had particular significance in this era, and they were produced by almost all the prominent writers of the Polish Enlightenment. Franciszek Bohomolec (1720-84) wrote comedies based on French models. Franciszek Zabłocki (1754-1821) wrote plays about contemporary social customs; these included *Fircyk w zalotach* (The Fop-Suitor, 1781) and *Sarmatyzm* (Sarmatism, 1785). Other noteworthy playwrights were Julian Ursyn Niemcewicz (1757-1841), author of the famous political comedy *Powrót Posła* (The Return of the Deputy, 1790), and Wojciech Bogusławski (1757-1829), renowned as the creator of the comic opera, *Cud mniemany czyli Krakowiacy i górale* (A Supposed Miracle or Krakówians and Mountaineers, 1794).

Memorable satires were produced by Tomasz Kajetan Węgierski (1755-87), Adam Naruszewicz (1733-96), and Ignacy Krasicki (1735-1801). Naruszewicz and Krasicki also wrote fables influenced by classical and French models. The versatile Krasicki was the author as well of two mock heroic poems criticizing social evils, *Myszeida* (Mousiad, 1775) and *Monachomachia albo wojna mnichów* (Monachomachia or The War of the Monks, 1778). He also wrote the first Polish modern novels, *Mikołaja Doświadczyńskiego przypadki* (The Adventures of Nicholas Doświaczyński, 1776) and *Pan Podstoli* (Mr. Pantler, 1778), using them to advance his program for social reform. Several poets in Poland, expressing attitudes somewhat similar to those of the French philosopher Jean Jacques Rousseau, stressed the life of the emotions and an interest in nature. These tendencies found expression in songs, odes, and idylls by such writers as Franciszek Dyonizy Kniaźnin (1750-1807) and Franciszek Karpiński (1741-1825).

Romanticism. From 1795 to 1831 Polish literature exhibited such general European trends as classicism and romanticism. In the classical mode was the work of Alojzy Feliński (1771-1820), who wrote the verse tragedy *Barbara Radziwiłłowna* (1820) about 16th-century history, and the writings of Kajetan Koźmian (1771-1856), who produced descriptive poems and odes. Numerous romances, songs, and idylls were written in a sentimental vein during this period. Especially popular was the idyll *Wiesław* (1820) by Kazimierz Brodzinski (1791-1835).

The new romantic literature was influenced first by German writers and later by English poets, particularly Lord Byron. Polish romanticism reached its full maturity between 1831 and 1864. The major romantic poet who gained an endur-

Adam Mickiewicz, a portrait by the 19th-century Polish artist Walenty Wankowicz.

Polish Research and Information Service

ing position in world literature was Adam Mickiewicz. Among his works were several that played the decisive role in the ultimate victory of romanticism in Poland, such as *Ballady i romanse* (Ballads and Romances, 1822), which used folklore motifs; *Sonety Krymskie* (Crimean Sonnets, 1826), describing exotic scenes; and *Dziady* (1823-32; *Forefathers,* 1968), containing folkloric and patriotic elements. In addition, Mickiewicz produced a Polish national epic, *Pan Tadeusz* (1834; *Master Thaddeus,* 1885), a poetic work of great artistic value. Juliusz Słowacki (1809-49) wrote masterpieces of lyric poetry including the impressive mystical-historical poem *Król-duch* (King-Spirit, 1847), and the digressive poem *Beniowski* (1841). He also wrote historical and symbolic dramas, among them *Mazepa* (1840; trans. 1929), *Maria Stuart* (1830; trans. 1937), and *Kordian* (1834). The third of the great Polish romantic poets, Zygmunt Krasiński (1812-59), earned renown for the poetic dramas *Nieboska komedia* (1835; *The Undivine Comedy,* 1924), which dealt with problems of social revolution, and *Irydion* (1836; trans. 1927), set in late antiquity.

Other noteworthy Polish romantic poets were Bohdan Zaleski (1802-86), author of *Duch od stepu* (Spirit from the Steppe, 1841); Seweryn Goszczyński (1801-76), who wrote *Zamek Kaniowski* (Castle of Kaniow; 1828), dealing with peasant rebellion; and Antoni Malczewski (1793-1826), author of the verse tale *Maria* (1825; trans. 1935). Cyprian Kamil Norwid (1821-83), writing late in the romantic period, produced the lyrical cycle *Vade-Mecum* (1865-66), a work significantly ahead of its time in philosophical content and artistic technique.

The romantic period led to the emergence of several literary genres. The gentry tale in prose and in verse was produced by Wincenty Pol (1807-72), Władysław Syrokomla (1823-63), and Henryk Rzewuski (1791-1866). The historical novel found an unusually prolific author in Józef Ignacy Krazewski (1812-87), who wrote *Stara baśń* (An Ancient Tale, 1876), *Hrabina Cosel* (1874; *The Countess Cosel,* 1901), *Brühl* (1875; *Count Brühl,* 1911), and the romantic novels *Ulana* and *Resurrecturi.* Aleksander Fredro (1793-1876) wrote works that were more classical in spirit, including the comedies *Śluby panieńskie* (1833; *Maidens' Vows,* 1940), *Zemsta* (1834; *The Vengeance,* 1969), and *Pan Jowialski* (Mr. Jowialski, 1832).

Polish Positivism. The second half of the 19th century is called the era of Polish positivism. The literature of this period was chiefly prose, characterized by critical realism and a concern with current patriotic and social problems. In the latter part of the era, naturalistic tendencies emerged. Bolesław Prus (pseudonym of Aleksander Głowacki, 1847-1912) wrote excellent short stories and novels, including *Placówka* (1886; *The Outpost,* 1921), *Lalka* (The Doll, 1890), *Emancypantki* (The Emancipationists, 1893), and *Faraon* (1897; *The Pharaoh and the Priest,* 1902). Eliza Orzeszkowa (1841-1910) wrote many stories and novels, among them *Meir Ezofowicz* (1878; trans. 1898) and the epic *Nad Niemnem* (On the Banks of the Niemen, 1888). Maria Konopnicka (1842-

Zygmunt Krasiński Polish Research and Information Service

1910) wrote lyrics, stories protesting social wrongs, and *Pan Balcer w Brazylii* (Mr. Balcer in Brazil, 1910), a long epic poem concerning Polish emigrants.

The historical novel played an important role in Polish positivism. Henryk Sienkiewicz, who received the 1905 Nobel Prize, the first Polish writer so honored, wrote a notable trilogy, set in the 17th century and comprising *Ogniem i mieczem* (1884; *With Fire and Sword,* 1890), *Potop* (1886; *The Deluge,* 1891), and *Pan Wołodyjowski* (1887–88; *Pan Michael,* 1893). He also wrote *Krzyżacy* (1900; *The Knights of the Cross,* 1899), dealing with relations between Poland and the Teutonic Order in the 15th century, and the celebrated *Quo Vadis* (1896), a novel about early Christians in Rome.

Young Poland. In the history of Polish literature, the years from 1890 to 1918 are called the period of Young Poland. It was a time of intellectual crisis and of *fin de siècle* sophistication and disillusionment in the cultural world. Miriam (pseudonym of Zenon Przesmycki, 1861–1944), a translator and critic as well as the editor of the periodical *Chimera,* played a large role in the spreading of ideological and artistic slogans during this period, as did the novelist and playwright Stanisław Przybyszewski (1868–1927), who wrote in German as well as in Polish. Notable among the poetry of this era were the subtle lyrics of Kazimierz Przerwa-Tetmajer (1865–1940) and the symbolical, pessimistic poems of Jan Kasprowicz (1860–1926).

In fiction, one of the most prominent artists of the Young Poland period was Władysław Stanisław Reymont (1867–1925), author of the novel *Ziemia obiecana* (The Promised Land, 1899) and of *Chłopi* (1902–09; *The Peasants,* 1942), a vast epic depicting one year in the life of a Polish village. Reymont was awarded the 1924 Nobel Prize in literature. Stefan Żeromski (1864–1925) produced stories and novels emphasizing patriotism and social criticism, among them *Popioły* (1904; *Ashes,* 1928), a historical novel of the Napoleonic Wars, and *Wierna Rzeka* (1913; *The Faithful River,* 1943). Stanisław Wyspiański (1869–1907) was the most eminent dramatist of the Young Poland era. His works, often symbolic, contained an original vision of the history of Poland and a penetrating analysis of the contemporary social situation. Among his plays are *Warszawianka* (Varsovienne, 1898), *Wyzwolenie* (Liberation, 1903), *Noc listopadowa* (November Night, 1904), and *Wesele* (The Wedding), first staged in 1901.

Contemporary Developments. After World War I Poland, which had been divided among other

Henryk Sienkiewicz Polish Research and Information Service

European powers since the 18th century, regained its independence. Poetry and prose were transformed by contact with new tendencies in world literature. World War II weakened literary activity but did not succeed in suppressing it completely. During the last 50 years Poland has, in fact, produced a literature of notable richness and diversity, both in artistic and in ideological terms.

Among the most prominent writers of this time was the poet-philosopher Leopold Staff (1878–1957), who began to write in the period of Young Poland, later producing several collections of verse in the classical spirit, such as *Uśmiechy godzin* (Smiles of the Hours, 1910) and *Wysokie drzewa* (High Trees, 1931). Another outstanding poet, Julian Tuwim (1894–1954), was particularly interested in linguistic phenomena. He left several collections of lyrics characterized by dynamism and spontaneity, including *Czyhanie na Boga* (Ambushing God, 1918), *Sokrates tańczący* (Dancing Socrates, 1920), and a digressive poem *Kwiaty polskie* (Polish Flowers, 1949). An English translation of his work, *The Dancing Socrates and Other Poems,* was published in 1971. Konstanty Ildefons Gałczyński (1906–53) based his poem *Niobe* (1951) on classical motifs, also producing many ironic and grotesque lyrical works. Jan Lechoń (pseudonym of Leszek Serafinowicz, 1899-1956) wrote *Karmazynowy poemat* (Crimson Poem, 1920) as a reaction to World War I. Władysław Broniewski (1898-1962) continued the tradition of revolutionary poetry in the verse collections *Troska i pieśń* (Heavy Heart and Song, 1932) and *Krzyk ostateczny* (The Last Cry, 1938).

Among the younger generation of Polish poets the most notable figures are the moralist poet and playwright Tadeusz Różewicz (1921-), who is noted for his protests against the cruelties of war, and Zbigniew Herbert (1924-), one of the greatest modern Polish poets, who deals with problems of modern civilization and history. He is particularly known for his poem "The Elegy of Fortinbras," translated and published in *Selected Poems* (1977).

The other great Polish poet today is Czesław Miłosz (1911-), now living in exile in the U.S. *Selected Poems,* translated by various hands, was published in 1973. *The Separate Notebooks* (1984) is a bilingual edition of more recent poetry and some from the war years. Miłosz was awarded the Nobel Prize in literature in 1980 for his erudite, challenging verse, which reflects the spiritual pain of exile. The prose work, *The Land of Ulro* (1977; trans. 1984) continues his examination of his plight. Miłosz's *Issa Valley* (1955; trans. 1978) is a semiautobiographical novel distinguished for its poetic mythical evocation of a Lithuanian childhood.

Pope John Paul II (Karol Jozef Wojtyła) is also a distinguished writer in his native Polish. Among his several published works are religious poetry such as *Easter Vigil and Other Poems* (1978; trans. 1979) and some drama.

The leading prose writers include Maria Dąbrowska (1892-1965), author of the roman-fleuve *Noce i dnie* (Nights and Days, 1932-34), a vast family chronicle from the years preceding World War I; Zofia Nalkowska (1885-1954), writer of novels on social and psychological themes, such as *Granica* (Boundary Line, 1935) and *Medaliony* (Medallions, 1946), about the Nazi occupation of Poland; and Jerzy Andrzejewski (1909-83), author of *Popiół i diament* (1948; *Ashes and Diamonds,* 1962), a novel (later made into a film) dealing with Polish reality after World War II, and also of the satirical novel *Idzie skacząc po górach* (1963; *A Sitter for Satyr,* 1965.) Also important are Jarosław Iwaszkiewicz (1894-1980), creator of the autobiographical novel *Sława i chwała* (Glory and Vainglory, 1956-62), known also as a poet and a short-story writer; and Kazimierz Brandys (1916-), author of a cycle of psychological novels *Między wojnami* (Between the Wars, 1947-51), about the Polish intelligentsia, and of a novel in the form of a diary, *Listy do Pani Z* (*Letters to Madam Z,* 1958-60). Teodor Parnicki (1908-) wrote such historical novels as *Słowo i ciało* (The Word and the Flesh, 1959) and *Tylko Beatrycze* (Only Beatrice, 1962), dealing with the interplay of various cultures, mostly in antiquity.

Parody, absurd humor, and the grotesque are a distinct phenomenon in contemporary Polish literature, particularly in the works of Stanisław Ignacy Witkiewicz (1885-1939), author of many novels and grotesque plays, including the political parable *Szewcy* (The Cobblers, 1948); Witold Gombrowicz (1904-69), whose novels expose ideological stereotypes, as in *Ferdydurke* (1937; trans. 1961) and *Kosmos* (1965; *Cosmos,* 1967); and Sławomir Mrożek (1930-), author of plays that reveal the truth about contemporary human reality through surrealistic deformation, as in *Policja* (1958; *The Police,* 1967), *Na pełnym morzu* (1960; *Out at Sea,* 1967), and *Tango* (1965; trans. 1968).

Science fiction is also popular in Poland today, the works of Stanisław Lem (1921-) being particularly outstanding. Lem's work, based on a solid scientific and philosophical training, is represented in *The Cosmic Carnival of Stanisław Lem: An Anthology of Entertaining Stories by the Modern Master of Science Fiction* (1981). A later work, *Imaginary Magnitude,* published in translation in 1984, is a learned satire on cultural history and critical writing.

In addition to the production of longer works, contemporary Polish literature is characterized by the popularity of such genres as the fable, the philosophical parable, the essay, and the aphorism; the most prominent writer in the last genre is Stanisław Jerzy Lec (1909-66). An anthology of his work—*Unkempt Thoughts* (1959; trans. 1967)—has been issued. E.S.-T. & W.We.

For further information on this topic, see the Bibliography in volume 28, section 855.

POLISH SUCCESSION, WAR OF THE (1733-35), European conflict caused by the two rival claims to the throne of Poland asserted on the death in 1733 of Augustus II, elector of Saxony and king of Poland (1670-1733), by his son Augustus (1696-1763), and by the Polish nobleman Stanislas Leszczyński. Augustus II had been king of Poland from 1697 to 1704, maintaining his office largely through Russian support. In 1704 Stanislas, with the help of Charles XII, king of Sweden, had deposed Augustus II and then had been elected king by the Polish nobility. In 1709, however, Augustus reassumed the throne with Russian aid. On Augustus's death in 1733, Stanislas again claimed the throne and a majority of the Polish nobles, influenced by Louis XV, king of France, who was the son-in-law of Stanislas, reelected the Polish nobleman as king. At the same time Augustus's son also claimed the Polish throne, and a minority of the Polish nobility, influenced by Russia and Austria, then ruled respectively by Anna Ivanovna and and Holy Roman Emperor Charles VI, elected him Augustus III, king of Poland, and demanded that Stanislas abdicate. Stanislas refused, and in 1733 a large Russian army invaded and drove him out of Poland. He took refuge in the fortress of the free city of Danzig, to which the Russians laid siege. A French naval and military expedition to raise the siege was a failure. Stanislas maintained his position until June of the following year, when his army surrendered, and he fled to Prussia.

In the meantime, in retaliation for the Austrian support of Augustus III, France in 1733 had declared war on Charles VI. Spain and Sardinia, viewing the war as an opportunity to make territorial gains in Italy at the expense of Austria, which then held large parts of the peninsula, allied themselves with France. Spanish forces invaded Austrian-held Lombardy, Naples, and Sicily. The French invaded the duchy of Lorraine, then part of the Holy Roman Empire, and also engaged in indecisive fighting with the forces of Charles VI on the upper Rhine River.

The war was terminated by the Treaty of Vienna, negotiated in 1735, but not ratified until 1738. The treaty had four principal provisions: (1) Stanislas was to renounce the Polish throne, which was to remain in possession of Augustus III; in return Stanislas became duke of Lorraine and Bar, both of which duchies were to revert to France after his death; (2) the deposed Francis Stephen, duke of Lorraine (later Francis I, Holy Roman emperor), was compensated by being made grand duke of Tuscany; (3) Austria ceded Naples and Sicily to Spain and in exchange received the duchies of Parma and Piacenza, which had come into Spanish possession in 1731; and (4) France, at the instance of Charles VI, guaranteed the Pragmatic Sanction, the agreement, formulated by Charles in 1713, which declared that in default of male issue on his part, the hereditary Habsburg territories, which included the duchy of Austria and the kingdoms of Bohemia and Hungary, were to descend to his daughter Maria Theresa.

POLITBURO. *See* COMMUNISM; UNION OF SOVIET SOCIALIST REPUBLICS.

POLITIAN, full name ANGELO POLIZIANO (1454–94), Italian humanist scholar, teacher, and poet of the Renaissance. Born in Montepulciano in Tuscany and originally named Angelo Ambrogini, he was educated in Florence. He became tutor to the sons of the Florentine statesman Lorenzo de' Medici, and by the age of 30 was a professor of Greek and Latin literature in Florence. He attracted pupils from all the cities of Italy and from distant parts of Europe, among them Michelangelo, the German scholar Johann Reuchlin, and the English humanists Thomas Linacre and William Grocyn (1446?–1519).

Although Politian died at the age of 40, his writings are numerous. He translated into Latin various Greek works, including the *Enchiridion* of Epictetus, the *Charmides* of Plato, and the history of Rome by the Greek historian Herodian (d. after AD 238). He composed Latin poems, called *Sylvae,* on Greek and Latin authors and declaimed these poems in his lectures. His most learned production was the *Miscellanea* (1489), critical observations on ancient authors, which greatly influenced succeeding scholars. Politian was as accomplished a poet in Italian as in Latin. His many works include *Orfeo,* a lyrical drama with musical accompaniment, one of the earliest dramatic compositions of Renaissance Italy.

POLITICAL CONVENTION, in the U.S., assembly or convention of delegates, representing the membership of a political party, that meets to nominate candidates for elective public office. The national convention of a party, notably the Democratic party and the Republican party, is held during the summer of a presidential election year. The body nominates candidates for president and vice-president of the U.S., formulates and presents a platform or declaration of party policy, and elects the national committee of the party. The national convention may also adopt rules governing the organization of the party. Delegates to the national convention are usually chosen either by a state convention or in a primary election.

The conventions of the two major U.S. political parties are traditionally clamorous and emotional. The colorful, sometimes unruly atmosphere in large convention halls has often been likened to a rally or circus; but few people are unaware of the importance of the factional campaigning, conferring, and political strategies that underlie the seeming disorder. Common practices at conventions include demonstrative chanting, singing, sign waving, general noisemaking, and parading by delegations, both to support favorite candidates and to express state pride. Outside the main convention auditoriums, much political planning and negotiating is conducted during meetings of party leaders and representatives of the candidates.

Supporters of Ronald Reagan and George Bush parade down the aisles through cheering onlookers during the 1984 Republican Convention in Dallas.

Randy Taylor–Sygma

Procedure. At the opening of a national convention, the members of important committees, such as the credentials, rules, and platform committees, are appointed, and a temporary convention chairperson is elected. The chairperson gives the keynote address and usually presides until the delegates have been seated by the credentials committee. The permanent chairperson of the convention is then elected, and he or she presides during the adoption of the party platform and the balloting on presidential and vice-presidential candidates.

In voting for candidates, the roll of the states is called alphabetically, and the vote of each delegation reported by its chairperson; the votes of any state may be divided among two or more candidates. Several roll calls, or ballots, during which delegates may change their votes, are sometimes necessary before a candidate wins a majority for election.

The vice-presidential nomination follows the presidential nomination. Often the presidential nominee has determined the vice-presidential nominee before the formal nominations for a running mate begin. This decision is based on the advice of other party leaders, and often the vice-presidential candidate is a compromise choice, selected for an appeal to voters whom the presidential nominee might not otherwise attract in the national election.

After the formal acceptance speeches of the nominees, a national committee is selected consisting of one national committeeman and one national committeewoman from each state. In the Republican party, a state chairperson may also be a member of the national committee. The presidential candidate chooses a chairperson for the national committee. The committee decides contested issues within the party. Prior to the next national election, it determines the site and date of the next national convention and manages the national campaign. State committees throughout the country are subordinate to the national committee of their party.

History. In the early 19th century the informal party caucus was the customary nominating device for presidential and vice-presidential candidates. The caucus system was replaced in 1824 by the national convention system because of popular feeling that the caucus choices were not truly representative of the will of the people. Both factions of the Democratic-Republican party held small nominating conventions in 1824, but the first national and systematically representative convention was held in Baltimore, Md., in 1831 by the Anti-Masonic party. The first national convention of the Democratic party took place in 1832, at which Andrew Jackson became the first successful, or subsequently elected, presidential candidate to be nominated by a national convention. During this first meeting of the Democratic party many procedural rules for governing the party's national conventions were adopted. Among them were the two-thirds rule, requiring that each candidate receive two-thirds of the convention votes to be nominated, and the unit rule, requiring state delegates to cast their votes as a unit for a single candidate. The two-thirds rule was abandoned in 1936, but the unit rule was not abolished until 1968.

In recent conventions a presidential candidate has usually been nominated on the first ballot, as was, for example, Richard Nixon in 1968 and 1972. Earlier voting procedures, especially before the Democrats adopted the majority rule, often resulted in lengthy balloting. In 1860, for example, Senator Stephen Douglas was nominated on the 59th ballot, and in 1912 Governor Woodrow Wilson of New Jersey was nominated on the 46th ballot. Lengthy voting procedures can result in a stalemate, which has led to an American political phenomenon known as the "dark horse" candidate, an individual who succeeds in gaining the nomination in spite of having had little or no formal support before the convention opens. James Polk, the former governor of Tennessee who was nominated in 1844, is the most famous Democratic dark-horse candidate. He received the nomination on the ninth ballot, although his name had not been entered until the eighth ballot, and he went on to win the presidency.

In recent years open campaigning by willing candidates prior to the national conventions has helped the voters to evaluate the appeal of the candidates. Extensive media coverage of such preconvention campaigns also helps to clarify specific issues for the voters. Public-opinion polls, charting popular response to the candidates, reveal probable voting patterns in forthcoming elections. Many states now hold preconvention primary elections; the outcome of these primaries usually determines the presidential nominees.

In rare instances, such as the nomination of the incumbent presidents Franklin D. Roosevelt in 1936 and Lyndon B. Johnson in 1964, the candidate is nominated by acclamation without the formality of a roll-call vote.

Candidates of major parties usually have extensive political experience. The majority of party nominees have been senators or governors, but occasionally national heroes, such as Gen. Dwight D. Eisenhower, are drafted by a party.

The acceptance speech of the presidential nominee, now a standard feature, did not appear until 1932, when Franklin Roosevelt flew to Chicago to accept the Democratic nomination in person. He thus set a precedent for what has come to be the climax of the national political convention. Radio coverage of national conventions began in 1924, and today every major television network covers the national conventions of the Democratic and Republican parties. Chicago is the most popular site for national conventions of both major parties; since 1860, when Abraham Lincoln was nominated by the Republican party, 26 national Republican or Democratic conventions have been held in the city.

For further information on this topic, see the Bibliography in volume 28, section 185.

POLITICAL ECONOMY. *See* ECONOMICS.

POLITICAL OFFENSE, in criminal law, act declared by a state to involve a threat to its safety or existence, as treason or sedition, or declared to constitute an interference with the organization and processes of government, as bribery of public officials. Such offenses are distinguished from ordinary crimes that disturb the public peace, such as murder, arson, or larceny, but that are not directed against the government. The definition of a political offense has varied in different times and in different countries. For example, sabotage was never considered a political offense in the U.S., but was so considered in the USSR.

In modern times the tendency has been to deal leniently with political offenders, other than those guilty of treason, with the exception of such totalitarian governments as those of Germany from 1933 to 1945, of Italy from 1922 to 1945, and of the USSR and other Communist-controlled nations, where counterrevolutionary activities, terrorism, and espionage were political crimes punishable by death. (By 1991 most Communist governments had been overthrown, resulting in greater freedom for political dissidents.) In Great Britain and the U.S., persons charged with a political offense are not included in extradition treaties. Persons who leave a country because of fear of punishment for the commission of a political offense are generally received as refugees and protected by the country receiving them.

POLITICAL PARTIES IN THE UNITED STATES, in general, the two-party system that has usually prevailed in the U.S.

Early Nonpartisanship. The framers of the U.S. Constitution made no provision in the governmental structure for the functioning of political parties because they believed that parties were a source of corruption and an impediment to the freedom of people to judge issues on their merits. James Madison argued in his "Federalist Paper #10" against a system in which "factions" (his word for parties) might be able to seize control of the government (*see* FEDERALIST, THE). George Washington, in accordance with the thinking of his fellow Founding Fathers, included in his cabinet men of diverse political philosophies and policies.

Federalist and Republican Parties. Within a short time informal parties did develop, even though their adherents still insisted they disapproved of parties as a permanent feature in American politics. One faction, commonly identified with Secretary of the Treasury Alexander Hamilton and Vice-President John Adams, became known as the Federalist party (q.v.). Federalists favored an active federal government, a Treasury that played a vital role in the nation's economic life, and a pro-British foreign policy. It drew especially strong support from merchants, manufacturers, and residents of New England. The other faction, whose central figures were Secretary of State Thomas Jefferson and fellow Virginian James Madison, became known as the Republican party. The Republicans advocated a limited federal government, little government interference in economic affairs, and a pro-French foreign policy. They were particularly popular with debt-ridden farmers, artisans, and southerners.

The structure of government itself in the U.S. was conducive to the formation of political parties. The carefully elaborated system of checks and balances, established by the Constitution, makes executive and legislative cooperation necessary in the development of policy. Further, the division of legislative powers between the federal and state governments, as provided in the Constitution, makes it necessary for advocates of such policies as the regulation of commerce to seek representation or strength in both the federal and state legislatures. As these ends were too complex and difficult to achieve by impermanent groupings, the formation of permanent political organizations was inevitable.

The Republican party held power for 28 years following the inauguration of President Jefferson in 1801. During this period, the Federalist party became increasingly unpopular. It ceased functioning on the national level after the War of 1812, leaving the Republican party as the only national political organization.

New Political Alignments. Far-reaching changes in the U.S. economy and social structure resulted in the gradual formation of new political alignments within a one-party system. The principal changes behind these developments were the expansion of the country westward, with an accompanying development of a large class of pioneer farmers, whose frontier communities represented a type of democratic society never before seen in any country; the agricultural revolution in the southern states, following the invention of both the cotton gin by Eli Whitney and textile machinery, which resulted in the dynamic growth of the slave system producing cotton; and a considerable growth in the wealth and influence of manufacturers, merchants, bondholders, and land speculators of the northern states. The ideas of limited government that became known as Jeffersonian democracy appealed strongly to the sectional and class interests of the western frontier and the South, and also to the growing class of urban workers. The policies once advocated by the defunct Federalist party, however, were still popular with the minority of Americans who favored a more active economic role for the federal government.

Revived Two-Party System. The second two-party system developed gradually as Republicans began quarreling over several issues. The followers of Henry Clay and John Quincy Adams, who asserted that the federal government should actively promote economic development, became known as National Republicans. Their opponents, who eventually united behind the presidential candidacy of Andrew Jackson, were first known as Democratic-Republicans (*see* DEMOCRATIC-REPUBLICAN PARTY), and by 1828 as the Democratic party (q.v.).

During Jackson's tenure as president, his controversial policies and contentious personality prevented any reconciliation with the National Republicans. By the middle of Jackson's second term, his opponents began to call themselves the Whig party (q.v.). Leaders of the party included Daniel Webster and Henry Clay.

During the 1830s a radical splinter group of the Democratic party in New York City, the Locofocos, opposed monopolies and private bankers. The name was derived from a popular brand of matches used by the group to continue a crucial meeting in 1835, at which probank opponents turned off the gas. Later known as the Equal Rights party, the Locofocos were conciliated and reabsorbed into the Democratic party in 1838 with the election of Martin Van Buren.

The Democrats controlled the national government for most of the years between 1828 and 1860, although they lost two presidential elections to Whig military heroes. After 1840 the Democratic party became more and more the mouthpiece of the slaveholders. Northern Democratic leaders were often called "doughfaces," or northern men with southern principles, by opponents. Opposed to the Democrats were the Whigs and a variety of minor parties, such as the Liberty party, the political arm of the abolitionists (q.v.), and the Free-Soil party (q.v.).

In 1854 the party system dominated by Whigs and Democrats collapsed due to the controversy sparked by the Kansas-Nebraska Act (q.v.), which made it possible to establish slavery in western territories, where it had previously been banned. This act outraged northerners and convinced many Democrats and Whigs in that region to abandon their parties. Many of these voters initially joined the Know-Nothing party, an anti-Catholic, anti-immigrant organization whose antislavery reputation in the North helped it attract more than 1 million members (*see* KNOW-NOTHINGS).

The creation of a new Republican party (q.v.) was the most important result of the Kansas controversy. Organized in some places as early as July 1854, the party promised not only to prevent the admission of new slave states to the Union, but also to diminish slaveholders' influence in the federal government. The appeal of this platform quickly enabled the Republican party to overpower the Know-Nothings. Although the Republicans lost their first campaign for the presidency in 1856, they triumphed in 1860 with former Congressman Abraham Lincoln. The Republican victory resulted in part from the division of the Democratic party into northern and southern factions, each of which ran its own presidential candidate, and in part from their success at attracting Whigs and Know-Nothings who had opposed the Republicans in 1856. During the Civil War, the Republicans temporarily called themselves the Union party in an attempt to win the votes of prowar Democrats.

Post–Civil War Period. After the Civil War, as U.S. industrialization proceeded at great speed, the Republican party became the champion of the manufacturing interests, railroad builders, speculators, and financiers of the country, and to a lesser extent, of the workers of the North and West. The Democratic party was revived after the war as a party of opposition; its strength lay primarily in the South, where it was seen as the champion of the lost Confederate cause. Support also came from immigrants and those who opposed the Republicans' Reconstruction policies.

The socialist leader Norman Thomas addresses New Yorkers as presidential candidate in 1932. Thomas won nearly 900,000 votes for his party. Wide World Photos

In 1872 Republicans dissatisfied with the reelection of President Ulysses S. Grant formed the short-lived Liberal Republican party and nominated as their candidate the journalist Horace Greeley. Although he was also endorsed by the Democrats, Greeley was defeated, and his new party collapsed.

The chief political tactic of both parties during the postwar period was "waving the bloody shirt," by which Republicans in the North and Democrats in the South charged that a vote for the opposition was unpatriotic. Serious policy issues also separated the two parties. The most significant points of disagreement included the advocacy of high tariffs by the Republicans and of low customs duties by the Democrats, and the emphasis laid by the Democrats of the rights of states in contrast to Republican nationalism.

A number of minor parties emerged during the postwar period. In the long years of agricultural depression, from the conclusion of the Civil War to the end of the 19th century, discontent among farmers, particularly in the western plains but also in the South, constituted a fertile source of political activity, giving rise to the Granger and Populist movements (*see* GRANGER MOVEMENT; POPULISM). From these movements evolved a considerable number of organizations, constituted for the most part on a regional and state basis (*see* FARMERS' ALLIANCES; GREENBACK PARTY; GREENBACK-LABOR PARTY; PEOPLE'S PARTY). In industrialized regions, a large class of wage workers developed, whose protests against poor working conditions, low pay, and discriminatory and abusive treatment induced the formation of other parties independent of and opposed to the dominant Republican and Democratic parties. One of the first was the Socialist Labor party, founded in 1877 but unimportant until it came under the leadership of Daniel De Leon. Of far more significance was the Socialist Party of America (SPA), founded in 1901 by socialists unable to accept the autocratic De Leon (*see* SOCIALIST PARTY). The greatest leader of the SPA was Eugene V. Debs. In 1919 a split in the SPA led to the formation of the Communist party (CP), which had close ties with the Soviet Union. Although small, the CP had considerable influence at times, especially in the labor movement during the 1930s. These par-

A political cartoon satirizes the presidential campaign of 1912. Theodore Roosevelt, running on the Progressive party ticket, diverted votes from the Republican candidate, William Howard Taft, thereby enabling Woodrow Wilson to win on the Democratic ticket.

Library of Congress

ties of agrarian and working-class protest frequently raised issues that were taken up in subsequent years by leaders of the major parties; their own successes in elections, however, were mostly local and minor.

Progressivism. The various movements to improve industrial working conditions and curtail the power of big business, known by the early 20th century as Progressivism, caused divisions within both parties between Progressives and conservatives. The most serious split occurred in the Republican ranks, where the renomination of President William Howard Taft in 1912 caused Progressives to bolt and form the Progressive party (q.v.), which nominated former President Theodore Roosevelt. Although he lost the election, Roosevelt polled the highest percentage of the vote ever attained by a third-party candidate. The Republican split in that contest helped Woodrow Wilson become only the second Democrat to win the presidency since the Civil War. The Progressives made another strong bid for the presidency in 1924, when their candidate was Sen. Robert M. La Follette of Wisconsin, a veteran of the 1912 campaign, who won about 16 percent of the votes.

The New Deal and After. Although the Republican party regained control of the presidency during the 1920s, complex changes in political alignments were wrought by the Great Depression of the 1930s. The Democratic party, led by President Franklin D. Roosevelt, became the sponsor of the most far-reaching social-reform legislation in the history of the U.S. (*see* NEW DEAL). Many of its policies were supported by representatives of the Republican party, as well as by those who had previously supported La Follette. The attraction of Roosevelt's party was so great that such nominally independent political organizations as the American Labor party and the Liberal party (qq.v.) in New York State became, in effect, mere adjuncts of the Democratic party.

Roosevelt managed to break the stranglehold that Republicans had held over the presidency by drawing various new forces into the Democratic party. These included blacks, who traditionally had voted Republican because that party had ended slavery, but now supported the Democrats out of gratitude for New Deal unemployment relief. The other key addition was organized labor, which recognized that New Deal policies had helped unions achieve a status unprecedented in U.S. history.

When Roosevelt died in 1945, he was succeeded by Vice-President Harry S. Truman. Democratic unity appeared to unravel, however, when two dissident groups opposed him in the 1948 election—the anti–cold war Progressives under Henry A. Wallace and the anti–civil rights Dixiecrats under Strom Thurmond (1902–)—but Truman won despite them, and the Democrats remained in power until 1952.

The Republicans were returned to power that year, carried to victory by their popular candidate, Gen. Dwight D. Eisenhower. During Eisenhower's two terms, his moderate supporters came into conflict with the more conservative Old Guard Republicans. From 1955 onward the Democrats were in control of Congress, and their leaders often cooperated with the moderate Republicans.

The Decline of Party Influence. The New Deal combination of the South and the industrial North came together again to win the presidency for Democrat John F. Kennedy in 1960 and again for Lyndon B. Johnson in 1964, but widespread dissatisfaction with Johnson's military intervention in Vietnam brought the Republicans back into office under Richard M. Nixon in 1968. Although he was reelected with strong support from the South and West in 1972, Nixon was later forced to resign as a result of his involvement in a conspiracy to obstruct justice (*see* WATERGATE). The Democrats bolstered their declining strength in the South by nominating the former governor of Georgia Jimmy Carter in 1976. Carter defeated the Republican president Gerald R. Ford in that year, but failed to win reelection against Ronald Reagan in 1980. Under Reagan's leadership, conservative Republicans were firmly in control of their party in the 1980s, and the Republicans held a majority in the U.S. Senate from 1981 through 1986, when the Democrats regained control (they had maintained their majority in the House since the mid-term election of 1954). After Carter's defeat and the apparent breakup of the New Deal

Ross Perot's independent candidacy for the presidency in 1992, financed largely from his personal fortune, took votes from both the Republican incumbent, George Bush, and the ultimate winner, Democrat Bill Clinton.

coalition, the Democrats did not have the strong leadership necessary to regain the presidency during the 1980s.

Third-party movements were significant in 1968, in 1980, and especially in 1992, when a billionaire businessman, Ross Perot (1930–), drew almost 19 percent of the popular vote, the highest for a third-party presidential candidate since Theodore Roosevelt's run in 1912; however, despite Perot's appeal to voters disenchanted with "politics as usual," he gained no electoral votes, and Democrat Bill Clinton defeated President George Bush. The party system itself seemed to have been weakened, as voters became disillusioned with politicians and appeared to be influenced more by a candidate's overall message or positions on the issues than by party affiliation. Campaign techniques were changed by the increasing use of television advertisements and appearances. Media advisers became more prominent, often eclipsing traditional party leaders. In addition, the role of party conventions in selecting candidates was reduced by the growing prevalence of primary elections. R.E.Bu.

For further information on this topic, see the Bibliography in volume 28, sections 204–7.

POLITICAL SCIENCE, academic discipline, the focus of which is the systematic study of government in the largest sense, encompassing the origins of political regimes; their structures, functions, and institutions; all the ways in which governments discover and deal with socioeconomic problems—from dog licensing to diplomacy; and the interactions of groups and individuals that play a part in establishing, maintaining, and changing governments.

Nature of the Discipline. Political science usually is viewed as one of the social sciences, which also include anthropology, economics, history, psychology, and sociology. Its relationship to these disciplines can be seen from two perspectives. Some say that political science occupies a central position because the human and social concerns of the other social sciences must take place within—and be affected by—the political beliefs, practices, and authority that exist everywhere. The opposite view is that political science is the "handmaiden" of the other social sciences because it depends on them for its concepts, methods, and understandings. Whichever side one takes, it remains true that throughout the nearly 100-year history of political science as an academic field, first one and then another of the other social sciences has been seen as the key to comprehension of political matters.

The precursors of political science were concerned with the attainment and securing of ideal ends. Questions about the best form of government are now widely considered outside the scope of the discipline, which is regarded as being concerned not with what ought to be but, rather, with what actually is. Although the question of the ideal usually is placed in the field of political philosophy, some scholars argue that because value questions are implicit in all political inquiry, they need to be squarely faced.

Today most published research and formal study in political science deal primarily with tangible topics such as political campaigns and elections, the legislative process, executive power, administrative regulations, tax and welfare policies, international relations, comparative politics, judicial decision making, and the actions and effects of groups involved in business, labor, agriculture, religion, ethnic cultures, the military, and the media.

Early History. Strong interest in the nature of the state, its organs of control, and the place of the citizenry within its boundaries existed as far back as ancient Greece. Most scholars would agree that Aristotle was the earliest forerunner of the political scientist. Among other things, his treatment of types of regimes in his *Politics* presaged countless efforts to classify forms of government and has remained a major influence on the discipline. Plato's *Republic,* with its theoretical development of a utopia, or perfect city, was another important early work.

Over the centuries, other classics of the field were written by the Roman statesman Cicero, by St. Augustine and St. Thomas Aquinas, by the Italian statesman Niccolò Machiavelli, by the British philosophers Thomas Hobbes and John Locke, by the French writers Jean Jacques Rousseau and the Baron de Montesquieu, and by the German philosophers Immanuel Kant, G. W. F. Hegel, Friedrich Wilhelm Nietzsche, and Karl Marx. *The Federalist* (1787–88), a series of essays, most of them by the American statesmen Alexander Hamilton and James Madison, is a classic of early U.S. political thought (*see* FEDERALIST, THE). Almost all of these authors dealt with the possibility that a society could provide the conditions for a good life for all its people. These works are still read, largely because they go beyond material comfort to treat such higher values as justice, equality, liberty, and the promotion of human excellence.

Development in the U.S. As an academic discipline, political science is a part of higher-education curricula all over the world, although it is more prevalent in the U.S. than anywhere else. Political science emerged in the U.S. as a separate field of study in the late 19th century. Before then, young American scholars interested in the subject went to European universities for advanced graduate work.

The European emphasis on rigorous research, especially in Germany, won many American adherents. On their return to the U.S., these scholars worked to turn the study of government away from what they saw as sterile preoccupation with documents in archives and toward the political activities of actual human beings in everyday life. The fact that real power was frequently quite different from the formal authority set down in written constitutions and statutes was perhaps their main conviction. The new breed of political scientists, often college professors, insisted that a genuine understanding of governments could be gained only through study of the actual process of politics, using careful methods to observe, gather, organize, and explain the facts.

The successes achieved in the natural sciences led many political scientists to the belief that in time, if they borrowed the orderly analysis and methodology of physics, chemistry, and biology, and if they, too, developed explanatory theories, the study of government and politics could become as much a scientific endeavor as were the established laboratory sciences. In their efforts to achieve this scientific credibility, these scholars allied themselves primarily with researchers in the fields of sociology and psychology. From sociologists they borrowed statistical methods of collecting and analyzing data on people's political behavior. From psychologists they took definitions, propositions, and concepts to help in understanding why human beings act in certain ways. History was used as a source of facts to be analyzed by the political scientist. Economics also was relegated to a supplementary position, although the economists' ability to collect quantifiable data became the envy of many students of politics. As a result of these borrowings from other social sciences, political science came to be seen as an important field in its own right; no longer was it considered merely an adjunct to the fields of moral philosophy, law, political economy, or history.

Contemporary Political Science. Despite this early call for a completely realistic and independent discipline based on an objective approach and using the tools of science, the older, library-based, speculative, and normative study of politics remained standard until the mid-20th century, when the scientific approach finally began to dominate the field. The experience of academics who returned to the campus after government service in Washington, D.C., during the New Deal years and later, during World War II, had a profound effect on the entire discipline. Employment in agencies such as the Office of War Information polished their skills in applying the methods of social science, including public opinion surveys, content analysis, statistical techniques, and other means of collecting and systematically analyzing political data. Having seen firsthand how the game of politics is really played, these professors often came back to their research and to college classrooms eager to use these tools to determine precisely who gets political power in a society, why and how they get it, and what they do with it.

This movement developed into what has been described as the new orthodoxy of the study of politics. It came to be called "behavioralism" because its proponents insisted that objective observation and measurement be applied to the full range of human behavior as it manifests itself in the real world.

Opponents of behavioralism, although a minority within the discipline, have maintained that there can be no true science of politics. They contend, for example, that any form of experimentation in which all the variables are controlled in a political situation is not legal, ethical, or even possible with human subjects. To this argument, the behavioralists have replied that small increments of systematically gathered knowledge will add up, over time, to broad-gauged theories that can be used to explain human behavior.

Some behavioralists developed sophisticated models of human activity to guide their research, frequently drawing on computer technology for concepts as well as hardware. The widespread study of politics as a system—with "inputs," "outputs," and "feedback"—is a major example of the influence of computers on the discipline of political science.

Other behavioralists created a burgeoning subfield of policy analysis, which they promoted as an independent discipline. It calls for the mastery of rigorous scientific methods in order to put the policy analysts in a position to judge what would and would not work among the alternatives proposed to cope with public problems.

The debate about what political science is or should be continues to the present time. For all the differences that exist concerning methodology and approach, however, no one disputes that the study of government and politics is both proper and necessary. To the extent that the vitality of any scholarly discipline may be measured by how much its members care and argue about what should constitute its core, political science remains vigorous indeed.

See also ELECTION; GOVERNMENT. For additonal information on persons mentioned, see their individual biographies. F.J.R.

For further information on this topic, see the Bibliography in volume 28, sections 171–87.

POLITICAL THEORY, subdivision of political science (q.v.) traditionally concerned with the body of ideas expressed by political philosophers who have asked not only how politics work but how they should work. These philosophers have been concerned with the nature and justification of political obligation and authority and the goals of political action. Although their prescriptions have varied, and some have been utopian in concept, they have shared the conviction that it is the political philosopher's duty to distinguish between what is and what ought to be, between existing political institutions and potentially more humane institutions. The term *political theory,* in the past century, has come to be used as well to denote descriptive, explanatory, and predictive generalizations about political behavior regardless of the morality involved. This approach is more concerned with mathematical, statistical, and quantifiable techniques than with normative concerns.

The State. The central concern of political theorists throughout history has been the theory of the state (q.v.). Plato contributed to the founding of this theory in his discourse the *Republic,* which attempted to reconcile moral theory and political practice by projecting a community in which property was to be owned in common and which was to be governed by an aristocracy of philosopher-kings who would train the young. Such doctrines, in highly distorted form, have been used in modern times as the basis of the system of government known as totalitarianism (q.v.), which, in contrast to democracy (q.v.), asserts the supremacy of the state over the individual. A variant of this system, known as absolutism, vests the ruling power in a limited number of persons or in institutions, such as a priesthood, supporting certain fixed and generally immutable principles.

Aristotle is generally regarded as the founder of the scientific approach to political theory. His *Politics,* which classified governments as monarchies, aristocracies, and democracies, according to their control by one person, a select few, or many persons, successfully combined an empirical investigation of the facts and a critical inquiry into their ideal possibilities, thus providing a challenging model of political studies.

Church and State. Important shifts of emphasis have usually been related to the challenges of concrete historical and social problems. In the Middle Ages, for example, much political writing dealt with the outstanding political issue of the time, the protracted struggle for supremacy between the Roman Catholic church and the Holy Roman Empire. The Italian philosopher St. Thomas Aquinas defended the role of the church in his *Summa Theologica* (1265–73), while Dante argued in *De Monarchia* (On Monarchy, c. 1313) for a united Christendom under emperor and pope, each supreme in his appropriate sphere. In *The Prince* (1513) the Italian statesman Niccolò Machiavelli transcended the traditional church-state debate by realistically evaluating the problems and possibilities of governments seeking to maintain power.

The Social Contract. The English philosopher Thomas Hobbes also stressed governmental power. His major work, *Leviathan* (1651), argued that the sovereign's power should be unlimited, because the state originated in a so-called social contract, whereby individuals accept a common superior power to protect themselves from their own brutish instincts and to make possible the satisfaction of certain human desires. Another 17th-century English philosopher, John Locke, accepted much of Hobbes's social-contract theory but argued that sovereignty resided in the people for whom governments were trustees and that such governments could be legitimately overthrown if they failed to discharge their functions to the people.

The ideals and rhetoric of Locke later contributed to the establishment of the U.S. through their expression in the Declaration of Independence and *The Federalist,* two major documents of the American Revolution. Important contributions to republican and democratic ideals were also made by the French philosophers Jean Jacques Rousseau, who expressed ideas similar to those of Locke, and the Baron de Montesquieu, who proposed a separation of governmental powers in prerevolutionary 18th-century France similar to that later embodied in the U.S. Constitution. The political theories of Locke and the early Americans, constituting the attitude generally known as liberalism (q.v.), were further refined by the 19th-century British philosopher John Stuart Mill.

Marxism and Other Forms of Totalitarianism. Karl Marx was in many respects the most influential political theorist of the 19th century. He sought to combine factual analysis and political prescription in a thorough survey of the modern economic system. Arguing that "the history of all hitherto existing society is the history of class struggles," and that liberal governments and ideology were merely agents of the exploiting owners of property, Marx advocated the abolition of private property and predicted the demise of capitalism after a series of recurring crises. The abolition of property, and therefore of class exploitation, would make possible a situation in which individuals would contribute according to their abilities and take according to their needs. The state, following a transitional period in which the working class would rule, would eventually wither away. In the 20th century, Marxism has been the subject of conflicting interpretations. It served as the official ideology of a number of totalitarian states, and it was also the inspirational credo of many revolutionary and nationalist movements throughout the world (*see* COMMUNISM; SOCIALISM).

Another type of political theory, also constituting a form of totalitarianism, emerged after World War I in the political movements known as fascism and National Socialism (qq.v.). Both asserted, in varying degrees, the doctrine of the total supremacy of the state and justified the use of force to achieve political ends.

See also GOVERNMENT; HISTORY AND HISTORIOGRAPHY; PHILOSOPHY. I.K.

For further information on this topic, see the Bibliography in volume 28, section 172.

POLIZIANO, Angelo. *See* POLITIAN.

POLK, James Knox (1795–1849), 11th president of the U.S. (1845–49), under whose leadership the country fought a victorious war with Mexico and greatly increased its territory by annexing Texas and all the land west of the Rocky Mountains.

Early Life. Polk was born on Nov. 2, 1795, to a comparatively wealthy and influential family in Mecklenburg Co., N.C. His mother was a descendant of the famous Scottish religious reformer John Knox. When he was 11 years old, Polk and his family moved to Tennessee, the state in which he achieved prominence. After graduating from the University of North Carolina, he developed a lucrative law practice in the Nashville, Tenn., area. His career received a strong boost when he married the socially prominent Sarah Childress (1803–91). An ardent supporter of President Andrew Jackson, Polk rose steadily within the ranks of the Democratic party of Tennessee. He served two years in the state legislature and then, between 1825 and 1839, in the U.S. House of Representatives. He was Speaker of the House during the last four years of his congressional term.

Rise to National Prominence. As a congressman, Polk remained unswervingly loyal to Jackson, even when the administration's shifting policies caused him some embarrassment. Young Hickory, as Polk came to be called, was not widely loved, but he was respected for his dedication to the Democratic party and for his prowess as a speaker and politician.

In 1839 Polk retired from Congress to become governor of Tennessee. An ambitious man, he tried unsuccessfully to win the Democratic vice-presidential nomination as Martin Van Buren's running mate in 1840. Four years later, however, he exceeded this ambition when he unexpectedly became the party's choice for the presidency.

Polk was the nation's first "dark horse" candidate for the highest office. Little known outside Tennessee and the nation's capital, he was chosen only after the 1844 Democratic National Convention became deadlocked. Van Buren was supported by the majority of the delegates, but he failed to receive the two-thirds vote required by the rules of the convention. After other, more prominent men were rejected, the party turned to Polk. He was so obscure that the opposing

James Knox Polk

Whigs tried to score propaganda points during the campaign by regularly asking, "Who is James K. Polk?" He was named by the Democrats primarily because he was known to favor the annexation of Texas. Polk's cause was helped by the popular belief that the U.S. had a "manifest destiny" to occupy the whole continent from the Atlantic to the Pacific. Nevertheless, the 1844 presidential election was extremely close: Polk managed to defeat his Whig opponent, Henry Clay, but only by a few thousand votes.

The Polk Administration. Polk's goals as president were to achieve a lower tariff, to separate the federal government and the U.S. Treasury from the banking industry, and to acquire Texas, California, and Oregon for the U.S. One of his objectives was achieved a few days before he took office, when President John Tyler signed the bill providing for the annexation of Texas.

Achievements. If the greatness of a presidency depends on the extent to which a president succeeds in accomplishing goals, Polk's administration was indeed great. He astutely won congressional support for the measures he favored and used the veto effectively to block those he opposed. Questions have nevertheless been asked about the wisdom and morality of his major policies. The independent treasury was essentially a negative policy that left private and state bankers unregulated. The Walker Tariff Act of 1846—named after Secretary of the Treasury Robert J. Walker (1801–69)—pleased the South more than it did the nation as a whole. Also, Polk's foreign policy created a storm of controversy. The vast territorial acquisitions of his administration were achieved at great cost, not only in dollars and lives but in political bitterness that helped pave the way to the American Civil War.

Polk was a nationalist, and he reminded Europe that he would enforce the Monroe Doctrine and permit no intervention in the western hemisphere by non-American powers. When he demanded during the election campaign that Great Britain cede the whole of the disputed Oregon Territory up to the 54°40′ line, Polk may have pleased U.S. expansionists, but his claim was of dubious legality. After assuming office, he settled for a compromise that gave the U.S. land up to the 49th parallel, the northern border of the present-day state of Washington.

The Mexican War. Polk was so intent on acquiring California, which belonged to Mexico, that he was prepared in early May 1846 to make war on Mexico with or without a pretext. The pretext that he did seize occurred when Mexican troops fired on American soldiers in territory claimed by both nations north of the Rio Grande. Although U.S. troops may actually have been sent into the disputed area with the deliberate aim of provoking a conflict, Congress approved Polk's request that it recognize that a state of war existed between the U.S. and Mexico, raising the troops and appropriating the money and supplies necessary to fight the war. The vote in favor of war was overwhelming, but in reality Congress was bitterly divided. Many northerners believed the Mexican War was a southern plot designed to expand slavery into the new territories to be taken from Mexico. Some southerners, such as Alexander H. Stephens, joined with northern Whigs, such as Abraham Lincoln, to condemn what they believed were devious methods used by Polk to provoke hostilities.

The conduct of the war was marred by political intrigue and bickering that affected relations between Polk and his leading generals, Zachary Taylor and Winfield Scott. On the other hand, U.S. forces won a complete military victory that resulted in the annexation of what became the states of California, Nevada, Utah, Arizona, and New Mexico. Although Polk's foreign policy can be judged a success, it also raised questions about the nation's honor, divided the country over the issue of slavery's expansion, and poisoned relations between the U.S. and Mexico.

Polk died in Nashville on June 15, 1849, a few weeks after leaving office. E.P.

For further information on this person, see the section Biographies in the Bibliography in volume 28.

POLKA, lively couple dance, originally a folk dance from Bohemia (now in the Czech Republic). It became a ballroom craze in the mid-19th century, spreading throughout Europe and the Americas in many versions. Characteristically, couples circle the ballroom, often at reckless speed, using a simple "step, close, step, hop." The music is in $\frac{2}{4}$ time with a strong upbeat. The Czech composer Bedřich Smetana included notable polkas in his opera *The Bartered Bride* (1866).

POLLACK, also pollock, coalfish, saithe, Boston bluefish, or green cod, a commercially important food and game fish, *Pollachius virens,* of the cod (q.v.) family, Gadidae. Found in cooler coastal waters on both sides of the North Atlantic Ocean, the pollack can reach a length of about 1 m (about 3 ft) and weigh up to 11 kg (25 lb), but it usually weighs about 3.6 kg (about 8 lb). Its lower jaw projects beyond a pointed snout, and the tail is forked. The plump body is olive to brown above, with paler sides, and is silvery below. A closely related species, the European pollack, *P. pollachius,* is popular as a game fish in Europe. Pollacks prey on other fish and on crustaceans.

POLLAIUOLO, surname of two Italian artists of the Renaissance, who, as brothers, shared a busy workshop in Florence. Patronized by the Medici family, the firm produced articles of gold, bronze sculpture, paintings, and decorative work.

Apollo and Daphne, *by Antonio Pollaiuolo.*
National Gallery, London

Antonio Pollaiuolo, real name ANTONIO DI JACOPO D'ANTONIO BENCI (c. 1431–98), was a painter, sculptor, goldsmith, and engraver. His imposing silver relief *The Beheading of St. John the Baptist* and sumptuous embroideries woven after his design still survive in the museum of the cathedral of Florence. Among his better-known works are the bronze tomb (1484–93) of Pope Sixtus IV and the monument (1493–97) to Innocent VIII (1432–92), both in Saint Peter's, Rome. Others include the bronze *Hercules and Antaeus* (c. 1475, National Museum, Florence) and his famous *Battle of the Nudes* (c. 1470, Uffizi, Florence), the first important Italian engraving.

Piero Pollaiuolo (1443–96) was a painter. He did three of the paintings known as the *Seven Virtues* (1469–70, Uffizi, Florence), and probably collaborated with Antonio on three others.

POLLEN. *See* FLOWER; POLLINATION.

POLLINATION, transfer of pollen from the stamen, or male structure of a flower (q.v.), to the stigma of the pistil, or female structure, of the same or a different flower. In self-pollination, or autogamy, the pollen is transferred from the stamen to the stigma of the same flower; in cross-pollination, or allogamy, pollen is transferred from one flower to another on the same plant (geitonogamy) or to a flower of another plant of the same species (xenogamy).

Self-pollination is the simpler and more certain of the two fertilization processes, especially for many species that colonize by copiously repeating the same parental strain. A species producing such uniform offspring, however, runs the risk of having its entire population wiped out by a single evolutionary event. Cross-pollination produces more varied offspring that are better able to cope with a changed environment. Cross-pollinating plants also tend to produce more and better-quality seeds.

The advantages of cross-pollination are such that plants have evolved elaborate mechanisms to prevent self-pollination and to have their pollen carried to distant plants. Many plants ensure against self-pollination by producing chemicals that prevent pollen from growing on the stigma of the same flower, or from developing pollen tubes in the style. Other plants, such as date palms and orchard trees, have become dioecious, producing only male (staminate) flowers on some plants and female (pistillate) flowers on others. Some plants are dichogamous, that is, the pistil ripens before or after the stigma in the same flower becomes receptive.

Wind is the most common pollen carrier for cross-pollination. Because wind scatters pollen indiscriminately over wide areas, such trees as

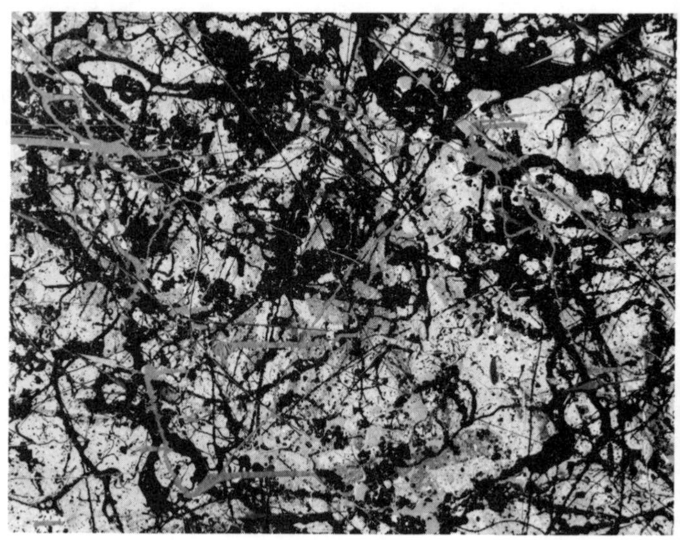

A detail of the painting Lucifer *(1947), by Jackson Pollock.*
Geoffrey Clements–Museum of Modern Art–Collection of Joseph H. Hazen

conifers must produce huge quantities of pollen to ensure fertilization, often enveloping pine forests in a haze of pollen. The date palm is wind-pollinated in nature but has been hand-pollinated in the Middle East for many centuries.

Bees, other insects, birds, and bats are more discriminate pollen carriers because each flies from flower to flower of the same species. The relationship between some plants and bees is very specific; for example, only certain bumblebees, entering such flowers as Scotch broom, *Cytisus scoparius,* cause the stamens to spring up and dust the underside of the bees with pollen. Perhaps the most important cross-pollinators of flowers are honeybees, whose hives are placed in orchards for this purpose. Species of big-tongued tropical bats are drawn to specialized flowers that attract the animals by nocturnal odors, abundant nectar, and protein-rich pollen.

See also PLANT; PLANT PROPAGATION.

For further information on this topic, see the Bibliography in volume 28, sections 451, 453.

POLLOCK. *See* POLLACK.

POLLOCK, (Paul) Jackson (1912–56), American painter, who was a leader of the abstract expressionist movement. He was born in Cody, Wyo., and studied at the Art Students League, New York City, with Thomas Hart Benton. Pollock spent several years traveling around the country and sketching. In the late 1930s and early '40s he worked in New York City on the WPA Federal Art Project. His early paintings, in the naturalistic style of Benton, depict the American scene realistically. Between 1943 and 1947 Pollock adopted a freer and more abstract style, as in *The She-Wolf* (1943, Museum of Modern Art, New York City).

After 1947 Pollock worked as an abstract expressionist, developing the action-painting technique of dripping paint and commercial enamels from sticks or trowels onto huge canvases stretched on the floor. By this method he produced intricate interlaced patterns of color, such as *Full Fathom Five* and *Lucifer* (both 1947, Museum of Modern Art). After 1950 his style changed again, as he crisscrossed raw white canvas with thin lines of brown and black pigment; *Ocean Grayness* (1953, Guggenheim Museum, New York City) is from this last period.

POLL TAX, term used for a tax levied on an individual, usually as a prerequisite for voting. Poll taxes are the same for all persons subject to them, regardless of their income, property, or other taxes paid (*see* TAXATION).

Poll taxes were originally levied on conquered people by the ancient Greeks and Romans. In England a poll tax was first imposed in 1377 and was reimposed at intervals until 1698. In the 17th century this tax was an important source of revenue for financing wars with rival nations. A notable poll tax was imposed on the entire male peasant population of Russia by Czar Peter the Great in 1718. One result of that tax was the institution of a census (q.v.) in order to provide a basis for financial calculations in connection with the tax and to aid in enforcement of the tax.

In the U.S., poll taxes were levied infrequently until after the American Civil War. They were then adopted by the southern states as a way of circumventing the 15th Amendment to the U.S. Constitution, which guaranteed former slaves the right to vote. Blacks without the means to pay the tax were refused the voting right. In later imes, payment of the current year's tax was ometimes coupled with the requirement that all elinquent poll taxes also be paid before a person ould vote. In this way the poll tax continued to isfranchise many blacks.

Subsequently poll taxes were repealed in several tates. Further efforts to eliminate them centered, ationally, on the enactment of a constitutional mendment. Not until 1964, however, was the 24th mendment ratified, finally prohibiting poll taxes n federal elections. In 1966 the U.S. Supreme Court uled that under the "equal protection" clause of the 14th Amendment, all poll taxes required for tate elections were unconstitutional. *See* CIVIL RIGHTS AND CIVIL LIBERTIES.

POLLUTION, contamination of air, water, or soil by materials that interfere with human health, the quality of life, or the natural functioning of ecosystems. For pollution of the atmosphere by emissions from industrial plants, incinerators, internal-combustion engines, and other sources, *see* AIR POLLUTION. For contamination of water, rivers, lakes, and seas by domestic, municipal, nuclear, and industrial waste products, *see* NUCLEAR ENERGY; SEWAGE DISPOSAL; WATER POLLUTION. *See also* CONSERVATION; SOLID WASTE DISPOSAL.

For further information on this topic, see the Bibliography in volume 28, sections 566, 568–70.

POLLUX, also Beta Geminorum, southernmost of the two stars in the zodiacal constellation Gemini, called the heavenly twins, the other twin being Castor. Pollux is a star of the first magnitude and is 33 light-years away from the earth.

POLO, game in which two opposing teams of players mounted on horseback attempt to drive a small ball through each other's goal by means of mallets. A goal counts as 1 point.

Equipment and Play. Outdoors, the game is played on a field no more than 300 yd (274.3 m) long and from 160 to 200 yd (146.3 to 182.9 m) wide. A goal, consisting of two uprights 8 yd (7.3 m) apart, is set up at the center of each end line of the field. Indoor polo is played mainly in the U.S., in large arenas such as armories or riding academies; the size of the field varies according to the floor space available, although 300 ft (91.5 m) in length by 150 ft (45.1 m) in width is considered ideal. The ball used outdoors, formerly made of wood, is now plastic; it is 3 to 3.5 in. (7.6 to 8.9 cm) in diameter and 3.5 to 4.5 oz (99 to 127.5 g) in weight. The ball used indoors is leather-covered and inflated, about 4.5 in. (11.4 cm) in diameter. The mallet has a wooden head and a thin, flexible, bamboo or graphite handle from 47 to 54 in. (119 to 137 cm) long. Protective equipment consists of helmets

Action is fast and competition brisk in polo.
Marvin E. Newman

and kneepads, and leg bandages for the horses. An outdoor polo team has four players; indoors, three make a team. A game is divided into periods, or chukkers, of 7.5 min each. The usual American game consists of six periods outdoors or four indoors. In international play, as many as eight periods may be played. Ties are resolved in an extra, "sudden-death" period (or periods), in which the first team to score wins.

Players are ranked, or "handicapped," according to their ability and value to a team; the higher the handicap, the better the player. An American, Thomas Hitchcock, Jr. (1900–44), is generally credited with having been the greatest player in the history of modern polo.

Many years of training are required to develop a speedy, maneuverable polo "pony," which is often a horse of Thoroughbred breeding with racetrack experience. Good polo ponies are central to the success of any team.

History. The origin of the game of polo is not definitely known, but authorities generally believe that it was first played in Persia hundreds of years before the Christian era and subsequently spread to other Oriental countries, including Tibet, India, China, and Japan. The game was particularly popular in India in the 16th century. Modern polo was originated in the 1850s by British army officers stationed in India. The game was introduced into England in 1869 and into the U.S. about 1876. Today polo is played throughout the world, including Argentina, the U.S., Great Britain, Australia and New Zealand, Mexico, India and Pakistan, and parts of Africa. The Cup of the Americas, played between the U.S. and Argentina from 1928 on, ranks as the best-known international polo match.

For further information on this topic, see the Bibliography in volume 28, section 786.

POLO, Marco (1254?–1324), Italian traveler and author, whose writings gave Europeans the first authoritative view of life in the Far East.

Polo was born in Venice. His father and uncle were Venetian merchants and business partners. In the course of their trading operations, they made (1260) an overland journey from Bukhara, Uzbekistan, to China. They remained for some years at Kaifeng, the eastern capital of the Mongol emperor Kublai Khan, returning to Venice in 1269. Two years later, taking Marco along with them, they began a second journey to China. Their route led from Acre (now in Israel) overland to Hormuz, at the mouth of the Persian Gulf; northward through Iran to the Oxus River (present-day Amu-Darya), in central Asia; up the Oxus to the Pamir and across the Pamir to the Lob Nor region of Sinkiang Province (present-day

Marco Polo (from a 16th-cent. German woodcut).

Xinjiang Uygur Autonomous Region), China; and finally across the Gobi Desert to the court of Kublai Khan, then at Shangdu (Shang-tu), China, which they reached in 1275. The Polos were the first Europeans to visit most of the territory they traversed in this journey, particularly the Pamir and the Gobi Desert.

Marco Polo entered Kublai Khan's diplomatic service, acting as his agent on missions to many parts of the empire, and was for three years governor of the Chinese city of Yangzhou (Yangchow). His father and uncle served as military advisers to Kublai Khan. The Polos stayed in China until 1292, when they left the country as escorts for a Mongol princess traveling by sea to Iran; they reached that country by way of Sumatra, south India, the Indian Ocean, and the Persian Gulf. They then proceeded overland past Tabriz in northwest Iran, along the east coast of the Black Sea, and past Constantinople. They arrived in their home city of Venice in 1295.

In 1298 Marco Polo was captain of a Venetian galley that participated in a battle between the fleets of Venice and Genoa, and he was taken prisoner. During his imprisonment in Genoa, he dictated to a fellow prisoner the detailed account of his travels. He was released from prison in 1299 and returned to Venice.

Marco Polo's literary work, *The Travels of Marco Polo* (first published in French), is perhaps the most famous and influential travel book in history. With a wealth of vivid detail, it gave medieval Europe its first consequential knowledge of China and its first information concerning other Asian countries, including Siam (Thailand), Japan, Java, Cochin China (now part of Vietnam), Ceylon (now Sri Lanka), Tibet, India, and Burma. For a long time it was the only existing source in Europe for information on the geography and life of the Far East. The book became the basis for some of the first accurate maps of Asia made in Europe. It helped to arouse in Christopher Columbus an interest in the Orient that culminated in his exploration of America in 1492 while attempting to reach the Far East of Polo's description by sailing due west from Europe, and suggested the all-sea route from Europe to the Far East around Africa finally accomplished in 1497–98 by the Portuguese navigator Vasco da Gama.

POLONAISE, national dance of Poland, known since at least 1645. It is a courtly processional dance for couples arranged in line by rank. The step is slow and gliding, and the dance has several figures, including the exchange of partners. The music is usually in stately $\frac{3}{4}$ time. As concert music, polonaises have been composed by Johann Sebastian Bach, Wolfgang Amadeus Mozart, and Frédéric Chopin.

POLONIUM, radioactive metalloid element, symbol Po, in group 16 (or VIa) of the periodic table (*see* PERIODIC LAW); at.no. 84, at.wt. (naturally occurring isotope) 210. Polonium melts at about 254° C (about 489° F), boils at about 962° C (about 1764° F), and has a sp.gr. of 9.4. The first element to be discovered by means of its radioactivity (q.v.), polonium was found in pitchblende (q.v.) in 1898 by the French chemist Marie Curie, who named it for her native country, Poland. Polonium is one of the elements in the uranium-radium series of radioactive decay, the first member of which is uranium-238. It occurs in radium-containing ores and is found in isotopic forms with mass numbers ranging from 192 to 218. Polonium-210 (also called radium-F), the only naturally occurring isotope, has a half-life of 138 days.

Because most polonium isotopes disintegrate by emitting alpha particles, the element is a good source of pure alpha radiation. It is also used in nuclear research with elements such as beryllium that emit neutrons when bombarded by alpha particles. In printing and photography equipment, polonium is used in devices that ionize the air to eliminate accumulation of electrostatic charges.

POL POT, also Pol Porth or Tol Saut, pseudonym of SALOTH SAR (1928–), Cambodian guerrilla commander and political leader, generally considered responsible for the devastation of his country. Born in Kompong Thom Province, he joined the outlawed Indochinese Communist party in 1946, later studied in Paris, and taught school in Phnom Penh. In 1963 he went into the jungle, where he organized the guerrillas known as the Khmer Rouge; in the open civil war following Lon Nol's coup in 1970, he was allied with Prince Sihanouk. After the Khmer Rouge ousted Lon Nol in 1975, Pol Pot directed the emptying of Cambodian cities, forcing virtually the entire population into the countryside to work as peasants. During the next three years, when he was prime minister, between 2 million and 4 million people are estimated to have perished by execution, disease, starvation, and overwork. Pol Pot was deposed by the invading Vietnamese in January 1979 and thereafter waged a guerrilla war against the regime they installed. In 1982 he formed a common front with opposition leaders Prince Sihanouk and former Prime Minister Son Sann (1911–); he resigned as Khmer Rouge commander in 1985.

POLTAVA, city, E central Ukraine, capital of Poltava Oblast, on the Vorskla R. The city is the trade and transportation center of a fertile agricultural district; its manufactures include processed food, motor vehicles, machinery, and leather goods. Several institutions of higher education, theaters, and a museum are located in the city. Settled by the 9th century, Poltava was first mentioned in 1174 and was captured by Lithuania in 1430. The advancing troops of Charles XII of Sweden were defeated (1709) near Poltava by Peter I, thus ending the Northern War. Pop. (1987 est.) 309,000.

POLYANDRY, form of marriage in which a woman has more than one husband or mate at the same time. Polyandry has been practiced by many peoples in all parts of the world since ancient times. At present, however, polyandry is prohibited by law in most countries.

Two principal forms of polyandry exist today. Among the Nair people, who inhabit the Malabar Coast of India, a woman may marry several men of equal or superior rank. Known by anthropologists as the "Nair Family," this system also includes a matrilineal social structure in which children are included in the mother's clan and property is inherited in the female line.

Another distinct type of polyandry is practiced in areas of Tibet. In this form, a woman may marry the eldest brother of a family and then take his brothers as mates also.

Either of these principal forms of polyandry may occur in more or less complex forms of group marriage, in which polyandry and polygyny (*see* POLYGAMY) coexist.

POLYBIUS (203?–120? BC), Greek historian, born in Megalopolis. He was one of the thousand noble Achaeans who, after the conquest of Macedonia in 168 BC, were sent to Rome as hostages. At Rome, Polybius was received into the home of the Roman general Lucius Aemilius Paulus (229?–160 BC) and became the tutor of his two sons, the younger of whom was adopted into the Scipio family, becoming known as Scipio Africanus the Younger. Scipio and Polybius became close friends. In 151 BC, after 16 years in Italy, the surviving Achaean exiles were permitted by the Roman Senate to return to Greece. Polybius, however, soon rejoined Scipio, followed him in his African campaign, and was present at the destruction of Carthage in 146 BC. The outbreak of the war between the Achaeans and the Romans called him again to Greece, where he was of the greatest service, through his influence with the Romans, in procuring favorable terms for the vanquished.

The latter part of his life was devoted to the composition of his great work, *Universal History* (40 vol.). His purpose was to show how and why all the civilized countries of the world fell under the dominion of Rome. The work covers the period between 220 and 146 BC, the year that Corinth fell. Although much of the greater part of the work has perished—only the first five books are fully preserved—the plan of the whole is fully known. As a historian Polybius tried not merely to present facts but to discover the causes of these facts and to draw from them lessons valuable for the future. His tone is frequently didactic, and the continuity of his narrative is often interrupted by digressions. His style is simple and clear. In the history of Greek literary style his work is significant for its employment of the so-called common dialect, a modified Attic, which came into use about 300 BC.

POLYCARP, Saint (69?–155?), Christian prelate, one of the apostolic fathers, bishop at Smyrna (now İzmir, Turkey) during the first half of the 2d century. He received a visit and an epistle from another of the apostolic fathers, Ignatius of Antioch, just prior to Ignatius's martyrdom (perhaps in 116). Toward the end of his life he represented the churches of Asia Minor in meetings with Pope Anicetus (r. 155–66), in Rome; one topic of the talks was the dating of Easter. Polycarp was martyred at Smyrna at the age of 86. According to the Christian martyr and theologian Irenaeus, who was his pupil, Polycarp spoke with the apostle John the Evangelist. Polycarp was probably a disciple of John and acquainted with the other disciples of Christ; this fact, as well as his gift of preaching and his devout character, gave him a position of great authority among the Asian churches. His feast day is February 23.

POLYCLITUS (fl. about 450–420 BC), Greek sculptor of the Classical Period. He was born in Argos or Sicyon. Polyclitus (Polycleitus) made a colossal gold and ivory statue of Hera, goddess of marriage and childbirth, which stood in the temple of Hera near Argos, but he was most renowned for his bronze statues of human subjects. He made a careful study of the proportions of the human body and is said to have written the *Canon,* a treatise on the subject. His figures are marked by powerful muscular frames, and the faces are square rather than oval, with broad brows, straight noses, and small chins, the lines of which are sharply defined. He was praised by his contemporaries for his technical skill, delicacy of finish, and beauty of line. Marble replicas exist of several of his famous statues, such as the *Doryphorus,* or youth carrying a spear (Naples Museum); the *Diadumenus,* or youth binding a fillet around his brow (National Museum, Athens); and the *Amazon* (Metropolitan Museum, New York City).

POLYGAMY, form of marriage in which a person has more than one mate. The practice of polygamy includes polyandry (q.v.), or marriage with more than one husband, as well as polygyny, the specific term for marriage with a plurality of wives.

Polygyny has been widely practiced at various times by many peoples throughout the world, and it is still common in Muslim countries and some parts of Africa. Polygyny has never been the only form of marriage in any nation or tribe; usually only the rich and powerful men have maintained polygynous families, while the majority of the people have lived in monogamous relations. Polygamy, both in its polygynous and polyandrous forms, is illegal in most of the world.

POLYGNOTUS, Greek painter, who dominated Athenian art in the period between 470 and 450 BC. Although none of his paintings remains, contemporary descriptions establish that he was an unusually influential innovator. He introduced landscape and simple perspective into painting, freed composition from the convention of placing figures along a rigid baseline, and broke away from the rigidity of archaic Greek art by expressing emotion in the features of the face.

POLYGON, in geometry, closed plane figure formed by the joining of three or more straight lines. The best-known polygons are the triangle, which has three sides; the quadrilateral, which has four sides and includes squares, rectangles, and parallelograms; the pentagon, which has five sides; and the octagon, which has eight sides. A regular polygon is one that has equal sides and equal interior angles.

POLYGRAPH, any of various scientific recording devices designed to register a person's bodily responses to being questioned. Popularly known as a lie detector, the polygraph has been used chiefly in criminal investigations, although it is also used in employment and security screening practices. Because no machine can unerringly recognize when a person is lying, the polygraph results are used in conjunction with other evidence, observations, and information. Emotional stress reflected by this test, for instance, need not be due to lying. On the other hand, a subject may be a pathological liar and therefore show no measurable bodily responses when giving false answers. Ordinary nervousness, individual physical or mental abnormalities, discomfort, excessive pretest interrogation, or indifference to a question also affect test accuracy. The polygraph can, however, provide a basis for an evaluation of whether or not the subject's answers are truthful. This test has also been helpful in exonerating innocent persons accused of crimes.

A polygraph is actually several instruments combined to simultaneously record changes in blood pressure, pulse, and respiration (qq.v.). The electrical conductivity of the skin's surface can also be measured—increased sweat-gland activity reduces the skin's ability to carry electrical current. The Reid polygraph, devised in 1945 by the American criminologist John Edward Reid (1910–), also records muscular movement.

Apparatus worn by the seated subject includes a so-called pneumograph tube around the chest, an ordinary blood-pressure cuff, and electrodes on the fingers and surfaces of the hand. The actual physiological changes are transmitted, through a small panel unit, into synchronized readings on moving graph paper; these parallel graphs are then correlated and interpreted to determine whether the subject is lying.

Proper conditions and procedure are essential in polygraph testing. The room used should be plain, quiet, comfortable, and private; two-way mirrors and microphones are sometimes used as legal precautions. The examiner's role is also important. He must be consistently objective and should be thoroughly trained in scientific interrogation to reduce the inherent human error.

Polygraph results are generally considered inadmissible as legal evidence (q.v.) in U.S. courts, except where mutual agreement is given by the opposing parties in a case, and the use of the device in private employment procedures was severely restricted by federal law in 1988. The chief objections to the polygraph are that its use is unconstitutional, that it constitutes an invasion of privacy, and that it is still too inconclusive scientifically to be considered valid as evidence. In several countries the use of the polygraph is prohibited by their governments on the basis of violation of free will.

For further information on this topic, see the Bibliography in volume 28, section 299.

POLYHYMNIA. *See* MUSES.

POLYMER, substance consisting of large molecules that are made of many small, repeating units called monomers, or mers. The number of repeating units in one large molecule is called the degree of polymerization. Materials with a very high degree of polymerization are called high polymers. Polymers consisting of only one

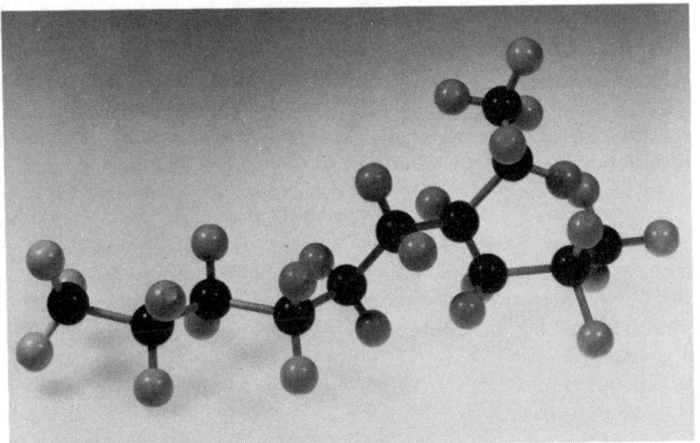

This molecular model of polyethylene, or polymerized ethylene, a plastic used to make films, tubing, molded objects, and electrical insulation, consists of a chain of carbon atoms to which hydrogen atoms are attached at all the available positions. The special properties of different polymers depend on the atoms and groups that make them up and on the cross-linkages and branchings in the molecules.

Dow Chemical Company

POLYMER STRUCTURES (R and S represent two different monomers.)

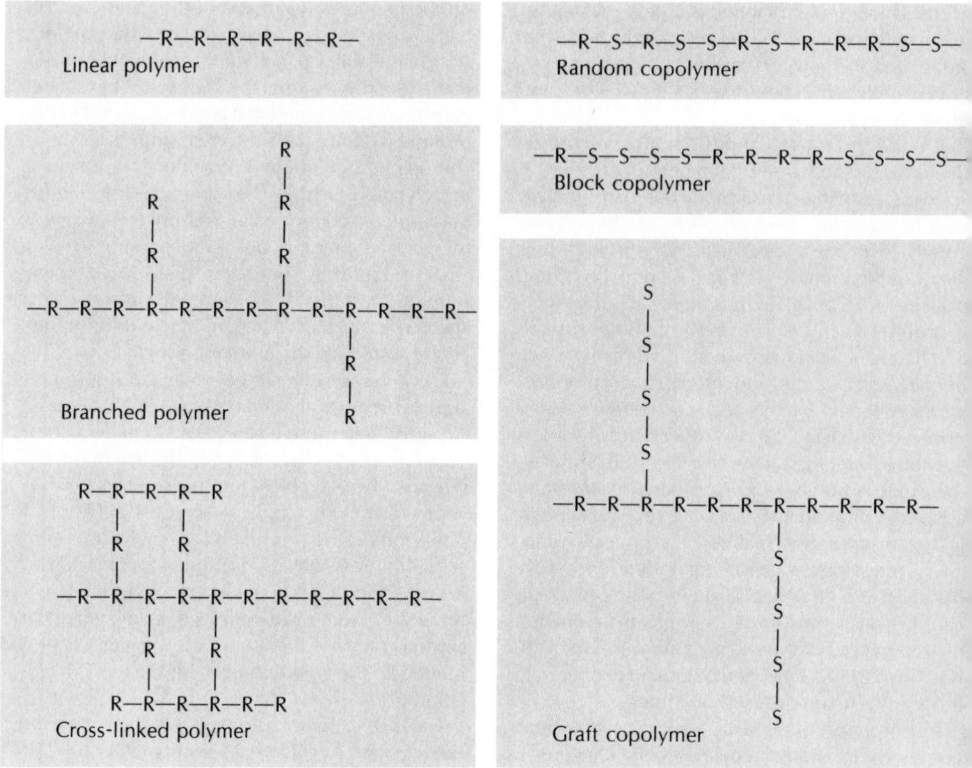

```
—R—R—R—R—R—R—
Linear polymer
```

```
—R—S—R—S—S—R—S—R—R—R—S—S—
Random copolymer
```

```
                         R
                         |
            R            R
            |            |
            R            R
            |            |
—R—R—R—R—R—R—R—R—R—R—R—R—R—
                             |
                             R
                             |
Branched polymer             R
```

```
—R—S—S—S—S—R—R—R—R—S—S—S—S—
Block copolymer
```

```
  R—R—R—R—R
  |   |
  R   R
  |   |
—R—R—R—R—R—R—R—R—R—R—R—
      |   |
      R   R
      |   |
    R—R—R—R—R—R
Cross-linked polymer
```

```
        S
        |
        S
        |
        S
        |
        S
        |
—R—R—R—R—R—R—R—R—R—R—R—
                |
                S
                |
                S
                |
                S
                |
                S
Graft copolymer
```

kind of repeating unit are called homopolymers. Copolymers are formed from several different repeating units.

Most of the organic substances found in living matter, such as protein, wood, chitin, rubber, and resins, are polymers. Many synthetic materials, such as plastics, fibers (*see* NYLON; RAYON), adhesives, glass, and porcelain, are also to a large extent polymeric substances.

Structure of Polymers. Polymers can be subdivided into three, or possibly four, structural groups. The molecules in linear polymers consist of long chains of monomers joined by bonds that are rigid to a certain degree—the monomers cannot rotate freely with respect to each other. Typical examples are polyethylene, polyvinyl alcohol, and polyvinyl chloride (PVC).

Branched polymers have side chains that are attached to the chain molecule itself. Branching can be caused by impurities or by the presence of monomers that have several reactive groups. Chain polymers composed of monomers with side groups that are part of the monomers, such as polystyrene or polypropylene, are not considered branched polymers.

In cross-linked structures, two or more chains are joined together by side chains. With a small degree of cross-linking, a loose network is obtained that is essentially two dimensional. High degrees of cross-linking result in a tight three-dimensional structure. Cross-linking is usually caused by chemical reactions. An example of a two-dimensional cross-linked structure is vulcanized rubber, in which cross-links are formed by sulfur atoms (*see* RUBBER). Thermosetting plastics (*see* PLASTICS) are examples of highly cross-linked polymers; their structure is so rigid that when heated they decompose or burn rather than melt.

Synthesis. Two general methods exist for forming large molecules from small monomers: addition polymerization and condensation polymerization. In the chemical process termed addition polymerization, monomers join together without the loss of atoms from the molecules. A typical example is the formation of polyethylene, a homopolymer:

$$n(CH_2{=}CH_2 \rightarrow H{-}(CH_2{-}CH_2)_n{-}H$$

Other addition polymers are polypropylene,

polystyrene, polyvinyl acetate, and polytetrafluoreothylene (Teflon).

In condensation polymerization, monomers join together with the simultaneous elimination of atoms or groups of atoms. An example is the reaction between a diamine and a diabasic acid to form a polyamide (a nylon):

$$nH_2N(CH_2)_6NH_2 + nHO\text{—}\overset{\overset{\displaystyle O}{\|}}{C}(CH_2)_4\overset{\overset{\displaystyle O}{\|}}{C}\text{—}OH \rightarrow$$

H H O O

|| || || ||

Typical condensation polymers are polyamides, polyesters, and certain polyurethanes.

In 1983 a new method of addition polymerization called group transfer polymerization was announced. An activating group within the molecule initiating the process transfers to the end of the growing polymer chain as individual monomers insert themselves in the group. The method has been used for acrylic plastics; it should prove applicable to other plastics as well. R.G.G.

For further information on this topic, see the Bibliography in volume 28, section 416.

POLYNESIA, one of the three major divisions (with Melanesia and Micronesia) of Oceania, encompassing islands in the central and S Pacific Ocean. Polynesia comprises the Hawaiian Islands, Kiribati, Tuvalu, Samoa, the Marquesas Islands, French Polynesia, and Easter Island. Ethnological descriptions sometimes include New Zealand because of the presence in that country of the Maori, a Polynesian people.

For further information on this topic, see the Bibliography in volume 28, section 1250.

POLYNESIA, FRENCH. *See* FRENCH POLYNESIA.

POLYNESIAN ART AND ARCHITECTURE. *See* OCEANIAN ART AND ARCHITECTURE.

POLYNESIAN LANGUAGES. *See* MALAYO-POLYNESIAN LANGUAGES.

POLYNESIANS, people speaking Polynesian languages (*see* MALAYO-POLYNESIAN LANGUAGES) and inhabiting a widely scattered group of islands, collectively known as Polynesia, in the South Pacific Ocean. Polynesians constitute one of the tallest and most robust races of humankind. The Polynesians are brown or olive in complexion; their faces have a distinct Caucasian cast; and they have wavy black or brown hair (*see* RACES, CLASSIFICATION OF). The largest number of Polynesians displaying these typical characteristics are found in Hawaii, New Zealand, Samoa, Tahiti, Tonga, and the Marquesas Islands. Other Polynesians appear to have mixed with neighboring peoples such as those of Melanesia and Papua. The Polynesians are not indigenous to Polynesia; ethnologists differ as to their origin, but the most accepted view is that they were established in the Malay Archipelago about the 2d century BC, when they were driven eastward by Malayan invaders. By the 13th and 14th centuries AD they occupied the territory they now inhabit.

Early Polynesian economy was based on cultivation of taro and yams, gathering of fruit and coconuts, fishing, and rearing of pigs. Polynesians were expert in canoe building and navigation. They used wood and plant fibers to make fishing nets, ropes, and cloth for clothing. Their houses, built of hardwood posts, were walled with lengths of bamboo and plaited palm leaves and roofed with reed thatch. Metal was unknown, but, in New Zealand especially, stone was used for utensils and carved into axes, lance points, and religious figures. Wood carving in intricate geometrical patterns was highly developed on many of the islands.

The religion of the Polynesians, still practiced, is a form of animism—worship of animals and natural objects believed to possess supernatural powers. A supreme deity, Io, is also revered. The practice of religion as a moral code is largely conditioned by the system of taboo. Cannibalism was once almost universal as a ceremonial rite. In areas where the original social structure is maintained, organization is on the basis of the family, with an active head chosen by the elders through a system of mixed heredity and adoption. The family is patriarchal and polygamous.

For further information on this topic, see the Bibliography in volume 28, section 1250.

POLYNOMIAL. *See* EQUATION; EQUATIONS, THEORY OF.

POLYP. *See* HYDRA.

POLYPHEMUS, in Greek mythology, a Cyclops, the son of Poseidon, god of the sea, and of the nymph Thoösa. During his wanderings after the Trojan War, the Greek hero Odysseus and his men were cast ashore on Polyphemus's island home, Sicily. The enormous giant penned the Greeks in his cave and began to devour them. Odysseus then gave Polyphemus some strong wine and when the giant had fallen into a drunken stupor, bored out his one eye with a burning stake. The Greeks then escaped by clinging to the bellies of his sheep. Poseidon punished Odysseus for blinding Polyphemus by causing him many troubles in his subsequent wanderings by sea. In another legend, Polyphemus was depicted as a huge, one-eyed shepherd, unhappily in love with the sea nymph Galatea.

POLYPHONY, music consisting of two or more simultaneously sounding parts (in contrast to monophony, or music consisting solely of a single melodic line). Ethnomusicologists use the term *polyphony* to mean all instances of simultaneous parts (such as a drone and melody; or Western homophony; or African choral music), the one exception being simultaneous variations of a single melody (called heterophony).

In Western music history, polyphony often is given a narrower meaning: The simultaneous parts must be rhythmically distinct from one another. Polyphony in this sense overlaps somewhat with counterpoint (the technique of combining simultaneous parts or melodies), and the word *polyphony* often refers to the contrapuntal vocal music of the Middle Ages and the Renaissance. In this narrower, contrapuntal sense, polyphony is also contrasted with another musical texture—homophony, in which the simultaneous parts all have the same rhythm and create successions of chords, each chord being heard as a unit (as in typical four-part hymns).

For further information on this topic, see the Bibliography in volume 28, section 722.

POLYTECHNIC UNIVERSITY. *See* NEW YORK, POLYTECHNIC INSTITUTE OF.

POLYTHEISM, belief in the existence of many gods or divine beings. It has been widespread in human cultures, past and present, and has taken many forms. Natural forces and objects—celestial, atmospheric, and earthly (such as stars, rain, mountains, and fire)—have often been identified with divinities. Gods have also been worshiped in the form of vegetation (especially trees and cultivated plants) and animals (for instance, the monkey in India and the hummingbird among the Aztecs). The assumption of human forms and characteristics by divine beings (anthropomorphism), as in the emphatically human passions and behavior of the Greek and Roman gods, is virtually a universal feature of polytheism.

Polytheism is clearly related to a belief in various kinds of demons and spirits, as in animism, totemism, and ancestor worship (qq.v.), but in polytheism the spirits are distinct, personified deities who belong to a cosmic hierarchy described in myths or sacred writings. Scholars have proposed several theories to account for its emergence. It has been attributed, for instance, to the need for supernatural moral sanctions or to the awe inspired by (and the desire to appease) the uncontrollable forces of nature. It has also been associated in some theories with the development of a social structure characterized by specialization and class distinctions.

Many polytheistic religions, such as Hinduism and ancient Egyptian religion, have exhibited a clear tendency toward monotheism (q.v.), the belief in and worship of one god or divine power, and polytheistic beliefs and practices sometimes coexist with an essentially monotheistic theology. *See also* RELIGION. J.A.Sa.

POMBAL, Sebastião José de Carvalho e Mello, Marquês de (1699–1782), Portuguese statesman, who was the virtual ruler of the country during the reign (1750–77) of Joseph Emanuel (1715–77).

Pombal was born in Lisbon on May 13, 1699, and educated at the University of Coimbra. In 1738 he was appointed ambassador to London and seven years later was sent to Vienna in a similar capacity. In 1750 King Joseph appointed him minister of state, and he soon proved his administrative talents. When a devastating earthquake struck Lisbon in 1755, he organized the relief efforts and planned its rebuilding. He was made chief minister in 1756, and from then on his powers were practically absolute.

Pombal abolished slavery in Portugal, reorganized the educational system, and published a new code of laws. In addition he effected the reorganization of the army, the introduction of new colonists into the Portuguese settlements, and the establishment of an East India Co. and other companies for trade with Brazil. Agriculture, commerce, and finances were all improved. His reforms, however, encountered much opposition and his power much enmity, especially among the Jesuits and the nobles. When an attempt was made on the king's life in 1758, Pombal managed to implicate both the Jesuits and the nobility; some nobles were then tortured to death and the Jesuits banished (1759). The king created him a marquis in 1770.

Pombal's power ended with the death of the king, and he was later declared guilty of abuse of power. Banished from court, he retired to Pombal, where he died on May 8, 1782.

POME. *See* FRUIT.

POMEGRANATE, common name for a small tree or thorny shrub, *Punica granatum,* of the family Punicaceae, in the order Myrtales (*see* MYRTLE); its fruit is also called pomegranate. *Punica,* the only genus, is native to tropical Asia and is characterized by large solitary flowers with numerous stamens and pistils. The pomegranate is of bushy growth with glossy leaves and red flowers. The fruit is about the size of a large orange and is filled with seeds, the fleshy outer seed coats of which consist of a sweet, acid, edible, orange-red pulp. The astringent rind is used in medicine and in tanning. The tree is cultivated for its fruit in warm regions throughout the world; dwarf varieties afford ornamental blossoms.

POMERANIA (Pol. *Pomorze;* Ger. *Pommern*), former maritime province of Prussia, on the Baltic Sea. Following the defeat of Germany in World War II, Pomerania was partitioned into two areas divided by the Oder River. The part of Pomerania west of the Oder was included in the new state of Mecklenburg, in the Soviet Zone of Occupation (later East Germany—1949–90). With German unification in 1990, this area became part of the German state of Mecklenburg-West Pomerania. The territory east of the river, comprising most of Pomerania, was placed under Polish administration pending the final peace settlement with Germany; the territory was formally ceded to Poland by the terms of an agreement reached in 1970.

The region called Pomerania during the Middle Ages was originally the Baltic coast territory between the Vistula and Oder rivers, inhabited, about AD 600, by the Pomerani (Pomorzanie), a Slavic tribe. The frontier was gradually moved west, as the territory was conquered by the Teutonic Knights, and the district between the Vistula and Prośnica rivers became known as Pomerellen, a part of Poland. By the Peace of Westphalia (1648), ending the Thirty Years' War, Pomerania was partitioned between Brandenburg and Sweden. Brandenburg (after 1701, the kingdom of Prussia) received part of Swedish Pomerania in 1720 and annexed Pomerellen in 1772. In 1815 the Congress of Vienna united all of Pomerania under Prussian rule.

POMERANIAN, breed of toy dog that is believed to have originated in Pomerania, Germany, from a type of large white spitz dog that itself is descended from the sledge dogs of Iceland and Lapland. It became popular in England in the late 19th century and in the U.S. in the early 20th century. The Pomeranian has a foxlike head; medium-sized, slightly oblique dark eyes; small ears that are carried erect; and a short neck with a profuse mane. It has a short, compact body and a tail, covered with long hair, that turns up over the back and is carried flat along the top of the body. The dog weighs about 2.3 to 3.2 kg (about 5 to 7 lb). It has two coats: a soft, fluffy undercoat, and outer coat of long, lustrous hair. The animal may be any of a variety of colors: black, white, brown, red, orange, or blue; or it may be particolored. The Pomeranian is noted for its docility, vivacity, and alertness; it is valued as a pet and as a show dog, and makes a good watchdog.

POMONA, city, Los Angeles Co., SW California; inc. 1888. It is a residential and industrial community near Los Angeles. Major manufactures in Pomona include processed food, electronic equipment, building materials, and paper products. Pomona is the site of the California State Polytechnic University-Pomona (1938). The annual Los Angeles County Fair is held here. The community, established in 1875, is named for Pomona, the Roman goddess of fruit. Pop. (1980) 92,742; (1990) 131,723.

POMPADOUR, Marquise de, *née* JEANNE ANTOINETTE POISSON (1721–64), influential mistress of Louis XV, king of France, known for her patronage of art and literature. She was born in Paris on Dec. 29, 1721. After her marriage in 1741, her name was Madame Lenormand d'Étoiles. In 1745 she attracted the favorable notice of the king and was installed in the palace of Versailles. Soon afterward she was ennobled by the title of marquise de Pompadour, from the manor of Pompadour, purchased for her by the king. She had great influence with Louis, for whom she acted in many ways as an executive secretary. For nearly 20 years her influence was predominant in all important affairs of state, and no one was appointed to office without her consent. She acted as an intermediary between the ministers and the king. Largely through the influence of the marquise de Pompadour a diplomatic arrangement was made so that, in the Seven Years' War, France fought on the side of its hereditary enemy, Austria. The marquise made and unmade ministers, and the French statesman Duc Étienne François de Choiseul owed his influence to her support. She was instrumental in confining in the Bastille, and other prisons, many persons who questioned her right to the enormous drafts on the public treasury made by the king. She died at Versailles on April 15, 1764, probably of lung cancer.

Marquise de Pompadour **Archives Photographiques**

POMPANO, common name for any of several deep-bodied fishes of the family Carangidae of the perch order, Perciformes; the family also includes the jacks. The pompano's mouth is small and toothless. Its tail is deeply forked and set on a narrow base. Carangids are distributed worldwide and vary greatly in size and shape. Their color is a metallic blue, green, silver, or gold, and they are fast swimmers. The Florida pompano, *Trachinotus carolinus,* considered a delicacy, is an important commercial fish in the southeastern U.S., Mexico, and Brazil. The soft-rayed part of its dorsal fin typically is as long as the anal fin. Most pompanos have a lateral line that arches at the anterior end, but in some species the line is interrupted by horny plates. The fishes are often heavy-bodied—for example, the amberjack—and some have a raised, often sharp ridge at the back of the head. The Atlantic horse mackerel is torpedo-shaped.

POMPANO BEACH, city, Broward Co., SE Florida, on the Atlantic Ocean and the Intracoastal Waterway, near Fort Lauderdale; inc. 1947. It is a diversified tourist, commercial, and manufacturing center; winter vegetables are grown in the area. Manufactures include precision and electronic equipment, boats, and plastic and metal goods. A large farmers market is here. Settled in 1884, the city is named for the fish (pompano) found in nearby waters. In 1947 the beach area merged with the town of Pompano (inc. 1908) to form the city of Pompano Beach. Pop. (1980) 52,618; (1990) 72,411.

POMPEII, ancient city of Italy, in the Campania Region, built at the mouth of the Sarnus River (now Sarno), a few miles south of Mount Vesuvius, between Herculaneum and Stabiae. The city was founded about 600 BC by the Oscans, who were later conquered by the Samnites. Under the dictator Lucius Cornelius Sulla it became a Roman colony in 80 BC and later a favorite resort for wealthy Romans, reaching a population of about 20,000 at the beginning of the Christian era. It was also a place of considerable trade and was the port town of Nola and other inland cities of the fertile valley of the Sarnus. The city was much damaged by an earthquake in AD 63 and was completely demolished in AD 79 by an eruption of Vesuvius that overwhelmed the towns of Pompeii, Herculaneum, and Stabiae. The eruption also changed the course of the Sarnus and raised the sea beach, placing the river and the sea at a considerable distance from the ruined city and obscuring the original site.

Archaeological Finds. For more than 1500 years Pompeii lay undisturbed beneath heaps of ashes and cinders, and not until 1748 were excavations undertaken. The importance of the discoveries first came to the attention of the world through the work of the German classical archaeologist Johann Joachim Winckelmann. New discoveries continued to be made throughout the 19th century and into the 20th. In 1912, in a street that connects the Strada dell' Abbondanza with the amphitheater, several houses were found, each

Remains at Pompeii of a textile works with vats for cleaning such materials as wool and silk. Alinari

Cast of a victim of the eruption of Mt. Vesuvius. It was made by pouring plaster of paris into the cavity left in hardened ash after the body had disintegrated. Alinari

with a balcony on the second floor that was 6 m (20 ft) long and 1.5 m (5 ft) deep. This section of the city is known to tourists as the Nuovi Scavi (New Excavations). Some of the ruins were badly damaged by air raids during World War II and had to be restored. Additional excavations are continuously made. More than one-fourth of the city remains to be excavated, and much of this area lies beneath piles of earth heaped up from earlier excavations.

Among the most significant aspects of the discoveries at Pompeii is the remarkable degree of preservation of the ancient objects. The showers of wet ashes and cinders that accompanied the eruption formed a hermetic seal about the town, preserving many public structures, temples, theaters, baths, shops, and private dwellings. In addition, remnants of some of the 2000 victims of the disaster were found in the ruins of Pompeii, including several gladiators who had been placed in chains to prevent them from escaping or committing suicide. Ashes, mixed with rain, had settled around the bodies in molds that remained after the bodies themselves had turned to dust. Liquid plaster was poured into some of these molds by the excavators, and the forms of the bodies have thereby been preserved; some of these figures are exhibited in the museum erected at Pompeii near the Porta Marina, one of the eight gates of the city.

Most of the inhabitants escaped the eruption, carrying with them their movable assets. After the eruption they tunneled into and around the houses and public buildings, and carried off almost everything of value, even to the extent of stripping marble slabs from the buildings. For this reason few objects of great value have been discovered at Pompeii. Most of the movable objects that were found, and some of the best-executed wall paintings and floor mosaics, have been removed to the National Museum in Naples. Taken together, the buildings and objects provide a remarkably realistic and complete picture of life in an Italian provincial city of the 1st century AD. The surviving edifices, representing a transition from the pure Greek style to the building methods of the Roman Empire, have been especially important for the study of Roman architecture.

For further information on this topic, see the Bibliography in volume 28, section 888.

POMPEY THE GREAT, full name GNAEUS POMPEIUS MAGNUS (106–48 BC), Roman general and statesman, the erstwhile ally and son-in-law of Julius Caesar, but later his arch-rival for power.

Pompey was born in Rome on Sept. 29, 106 BC, into a senatorial family; his father, Gnaeus Pompeius Strabo (d. 87 BC), was consul in 89 BC. At the age of 17 Pompey fought, along with his father, on the side of Lucius Cornelius Sulla against the faction of Gaius Marius and Lucius Cornelius Cinna. In 84 BC he raised three legions and defeated the Marian party, and he was later sent to destroy the remnants of the Marian faction in Africa and Sicily. On his triumphant return to Rome he was honored with the title Magnus, or the Great. Pompey subsequently defeated the followers of Marcus Aemilius Lepidus, a one-time Sulla partisan, whom he drove out of Italy, and destroyed the Marian party in Spain (76–71 BC). Returning to Italy, Pompey brought an end to the Servile War instigated by the slave Spartacus. He was now the idol of the people and was elected consul for the year 70 BC, serving with Marcus Licinius Crassus.

In 67–66 BC, Pompey cleared the Mediterranean Sea of pirates and was subsequently given control of the provinces in the east and put in

Pompey the Great

charge of the war against Mithradates VI of Pontus. Between 65 and 62 BC, Pompey conquered not only Mithradates but also Tigranes the Great, king of Armenia (c. 140–55 BC), and Antiochus XIII of Syria (r. 69–64 BC), annexing the territory of the latter to the Roman dominions. He also subdued the Jews and captured Jerusalem. On his return to Italy he disbanded his army and in 61 BC entered Rome in triumph for the third time. After his return he was anxious that his acts in Asia should be ratified by the Senate and certain lands be apportioned among his veterans. The Senate, however, declined to accede to his wishes, and Pompey, turning against the aristocratic party, now formed a close alliance with Julius Caesar, and the two men, together with Crassus, formed in 60 BC the coalition commonly called the First Triumvirate. Caesar's daughter Julia (83?–54 BC) was given in marriage to Pompey, and the following year Caesar repaired to Gaul, and there for nine years carried on a career of conquest while Pompey spent his time at Rome.

Jealousies, however, arose between the two leaders. Julia died in 54 BC, and Crassus was slain in Syria the following year. Pompey then returned to the aristocratic party, whose members desired to check Caesar's ambitions and deprive him of his command. Caesar consented to the order to lay down his office and return to Rome, provided that Pompey, who had an army near Rome, would do the same. The Senate insisted on an unconditional resignation, but Caesar crossed the Rubicon in 49 BC, thus defying the Senate and its armies, which were under Pompey's command. Pompey withdrew his forces to Brundisium (now Brindisi) and then to Greece. Caesar meanwhile made himself master of Italy and defeated a strong army in Spain commanded by Pompey's legates and then crossed the Adriatic to attack Pompey. The latter, who had gathered a strong army, was victorious at first, but was defeated at Pharsalus in 48 BC. He escaped to Egypt, where he was murdered on Sept. 28, 48 BC.

POMPIDOU, Georges (Jean Raymond) (1911–74), second president (1969–74) of the Fifth French Republic. He was born on July 5, 1911, in Montboudif and educated at the École Normale Supérieure and the École Libre des Sciences Politiques, Paris. He taught literature in Marseille and Paris until 1939, when he joined the French army. After France capitulated to Germany in 1940, he served in the Resistance. From 1944 until 1946 he was a member of the staff of Gen. Charles de Gaulle and then head of the provisional government of France. During de Gaulle's retirement, beginning in 1946, Pompidou served first on the council of state, the highest judicial body of France, and later as a director of the Rothschild Frères bank. Upon de Gaulle's return to power in 1958, Pompidou was for one year chief of his cabinet. In 1962 de Gaulle, as president, named Pompidou premier; Pompidou held the office for six years, resigning in 1968. In the following year de Gaulle himself resigned and Pompidou was elected to succeed him. In general, he continued his predecessor's policies, but he helped in the negotiations leading to Great Britain's entry into the European Community in 1973, something to which de Gaulle had strongly objected. Pompidou died in Paris on April 2, 1974.

PONAPE, now POHNPEI, formerly ASCENSION ISLAND, island, Federated States of Micronesia, E Caroline Islands, W Pacific Ocean. It is a hilly, volcanic island, about 335 sq km (about 130 sq mi) in area, and is surrounded by barrier reefs that enclose smaller islands. Ponape has considerable fertile soil. It was formerly in the U.S.-administered Trust Territory of the Pacific Islands. Pop. (1980 prelim.) 22,319.

PONCA CITY, city, Kay Co., N Oklahoma, on the Arkansas R.; inc. 1899. It is a commercial and manufacturing center in a region in which wheat, livestock, and petroleum are produced. Products include refined petroleum, oil-field equipment, and fabricated metals. Among the points of interest are the Pioneer Woman Statue and Museum, an Indian museum, and the Marland Mansion and Conference Center. The community, named for the Ponca Indians (who settled nearby in 1879), was founded in 1893 during the Cherokee Strip land rush. Pop. (1980) 26,238; (1990) 26,359.

PONCE, city, Ponce Municipality, S Puerto Rico, on the Caribbean coast. One of Puerto Rico's largest cities, it is a commercial and distribution center for the surrounding region. Principal industries include tourism; sugar refining; food processing; the manufacture of clothing and paper; and publishing. Its port, Playa de Ponce, is one of the island's major seaports. An airport is nearby. Ponce is the site of the Catholic University of Puerto Rico (1948), the Ponce School of Medicine (1976), and the Technological University College (1970). Points of interest include the Ponce Art Museum, a fire house (1882), and a restored 19th-century coffee plantation. Founded in 1692, Ponce is named for the Spanish explorer Juan Ponce de León. It received a royal title from Spain in 1877 and became a city. Pop. (1980) 161,739; (1990) 159,151.

PONCE, Manuel María (1882–1948), influential Mexican composer. He spent his early career composing, conducting, teaching, and writing music criticism in Mexico. After study in Paris with the French composer Paul Dukas in the 1920s, Ponce abandoned the genteel salon-music style then prevalent in Mexico, and began applying an impressionistic idiom to works with concise structures and skilled counterpoint. His guitar works in this style—notably *Folias de España*—became standards in the modern guitar repertoire. His other compositions include orchestral, chamber, and piano music and songs, the most famous of which is *Estrellita* (1914).

PONCE DE LEÓN, Juan (1460–1521), Spanish explorer, born in San Servos, León. In 1493 he accompanied Christopher Columbus on his second voyage to America. Later Ponce de León conquered Boriquen (Puerto Rico) for Spain and was governor of the island from 1510 to 1512. From the Indians he heard tales of an island called Bimini, located somewhere north of Cuba, which reputedly possessed the fountain of youth, a spring whose waters had the power to restore youth. Believing these tales, Ponce de León in 1512 obtained permission from the Spanish king to find, conquer, and colonize Bimini. The next year Ponce de León sailed from Puerto Rico at the head of an exploratory expedition. On March 27 he sighted the eastern shore of the present state of Florida, which he believed to be the legendary Bimini. He landed north of the site of present-day Saint Augustine on April 2 and named the region Florida because he sighted it on Easter Sunday (Span. *Pascua Florida,* "flowery Easter"). Believing Florida was an island, he tried to sail around it, going south to what is now Key West, up the west coast of Florida, then south again. He reached Puerto Rico again in September 1513. From 1515 to 1521 he engaged in subduing the rebellious natives of that island. In 1521 he set out to colonize Florida; the expedition included about 200 people and many domestic animals. The party landed on the west coast of Florida, where it was fiercely attacked by Indians. Ponce de León was severely wounded; the expedition withdrew and sailed to Cuba, where he died.

PONDICHERRY *or* **PONDICHÉRY,** city, SE India, capital of the Union Territory of Pondicherry, a seaport on the Coromandel Coast. Besides shipping, the chief industry of the city is the manufacture of cotton textiles. It was the capital of former French India.

The French colonies in India were founded shortly after 1664. During the War of the League of Augsburg (1689–97), Pondicherry, acquired by France in 1674, was captured (1693) by a Dutch force; it was restored to France in 1697 by terms of the Peace of Ryswick. The British seized it three times during the 18th century, but after periods of occupation ranging from 2 to 11 years, they restored it to France. Great Britain took the settlement again in 1803 and held it until 1814. France relinquished Pondicherry in 1954, and it then came under the central administration of the republic of India. A formal treaty of cession was signed in 1956 by India and France. Pondicherry was constituted a portion of the Indian state of Madras, now Tamil Nadu State. In 1962 it became part of the Union Territory of Pondicherry. Pop. (1981 prelim. greater city) 251,471.

POND LILY. *See* WATER LILY.

PONDWEED, any of about 100 species of perennial water plants of the genus *Potamogeton,* found in lakes, streams, and coastal waters. Pondweeds branch upward from their beds, usually extending some of their straight to elliptical leaves above the surface. The small green to brown flowers are borne in clusters on spikes, and the fruits are hard, tiny nuts. Pondweeds are a food source for ducks and other waterfowl.

PONS, Lily (1904–76), French-born American coloratura soprano, admired for her pure, expressive voice and classical technique. Born in Draguignan, she made her debut in 1929 and sang primarily with the Metropolitan Opera in New York City and the Chicago Civic Opera. Her principal roles were in operas such as *Lakmé,* by the French composer Léo Delibes, and *Daughter of the Regiment,* by the Italian composer Gaetano Donizetti. From 1938 to 1958 she was married to the Russian-born U.S. conductor André Kostelanetz (1901–80).

PONSELLE, Rosa Melba, professional name of ROSE MELBA PONZILLO (1897–1981), celebrated American dramatic soprano, born in Meriden,

Conn. She sang for a time in vaudeville before turning to opera. From 1918 until her retirement in 1936 she sang at the Metropolitan Opera House in New York City. With her in the principal roles, the Metropolitan revived many operas, such as the Italian composer Giuseppe Verdi's *Don Carlos; William Tell* and *Norma* by the Italians Gioacchino Rossini and Vincenzo Bellini, respectively; and *Oberon* by the German composer Carl Maria von Weber.

PONTCHARTRAIN, LAKE, shallow brackish lake, SE Louisiana, covering about 1620 sq km (about 625 sq mi). It is about 64 km (about 40 mi) long and 40 km (25 mi) wide; its depth varies from 3 to 5 m (10 to 16 ft). Many resorts and two state parks are on the shore of the lake. The Pontchartrain Causeway, across the lake, links the New Orleans area on the S shore with the N shore.

PONTIAC (1720–69), chief of the Ottawa Indians and leader of the confederate tribes of the Ohio Valley and Lake Region against the British in 1763–65. He distinguished himself in the French service at an early age and is said to have led the warriors of his own tribe against the British army officer Edward Braddock in 1755. With the object of driving the British from their frontier possessions and reestablishing Indian autonomy, Pontiac organized a confederacy that embraced virtually all the tribes from the head of Lake Superior almost to the Gulf of Mexico. According to the arrangement the warriors of each tribe, on a concerted day, early in May 1763, were to attack the garrison in their immediate neighborhood. Pontiac himself was to lead the assault at Detroit.

In the great wilderness extending from the Pennsylvania frontier to Lake Superior were 14 British posts, of which the most important were Fort Pitt, Detroit, and Mackinaw. The Indians captured all but four of the posts, Niagara, Pitt, Ligonier, and Detroit. Mackinaw was taken by a stratagem, and the entire garrison was killed. A plot for the capture of Detroit seems to have been betrayed to the commanding officer by an Indian woman, and failed, but Pontiac at once began a siege that lasted for five months. Reinforcements finally succeeded in entering Detroit; Pontiac's men began to desert him, and the news of the signing of a peace treaty between France and Great Britain removed all hopes of French aid. Pontiac thereupon raised the siege and on Aug. 17, 1765, entered into a formal peace treaty, which he confirmed at Oswego in 1766. Three years later he was murdered by an Illinois Indian.

PONTIAC, city, seat of Oakland Co., SE Michigan, on the Clinton R., near Detroit; inc. 1861. A residential and industrial community, the city also serves as a warehouse and distribution center. Major manufactures include motor vehicles and components and glass products. Because of its numerous scenic lakes, Pontiac is also a summer resort. Located here is the Pontiac Silverdome, an enclosed stadium that is the home of the Detroit Lions professional football team. The community, established in 1818, is named for Pontiac, the famous chief of the Ottawa Indians. In the late 1880s Pontiac became one of the largest producers of wagons and carriages in the U.S., and during the 20th century the city developed into a major motor-vehicle production center. Pop. (1980) 76,715; (1990) 71,166.

PONTIANAK, city, W Indonesia, on the island of Borneo, capital of West Kalimantan Province, at the junction of the Little Kapuas and Landak rivers, near the South China Sea. Pontianak is a leading port and trading center of W Borneo, and its exports include copra, rubber, timber, and palm oil. Pepper is grown here, and gold deposits lie in the vicinity. Tanjungpura University (1963) is in the city. Pontianak was the capital of a former sultanate; a Dutch trading station was established here in 1778. Many persons of Chinese descent live in the city. Pop. (1980) 304,778.

PONTINE MARSHES, swamp district, central Italy, in Latium, extending SE from Velletri to the Tyrrhenian Sea at Terracina. About 775 sq km (about 300 sq mi) in area, the district is separated from the sea by sand dunes and is traversed by the Appian Way. Throughout history the marshes have been a breeding place for disease, notably malaria. Gaius Julius Caesar attempted to make the surrounding area healthful, but he died before his plan to turn the Tiber R. into the marshes could be effected. Other Roman emperors attempted to reclaim the land, and after them a succession of popes. In 1899 the Italian government set aside funds for the project. Under the government of Benito Mussolini, more than 20,230 ha (50,000 acres) were reclaimed and put under cultivation from 1928 to 1932. Since that time, the towns of Latina and Terracina have been founded in the area.

PONTIUS PILATE. *See* PILATE, PONTIUS.

PONTOPPIDAN, Henrik (1857–1943), Danish novelist, born in Fredericia, and educated as an engineer at the Polytechnic Institute in Copenhagen. He worked as a journalist until he turned (c. 1880) to writing fiction. In his novels he was an accurate observer of social and political life among the Danish peasantry. He shared the 1917 Nobel Prize in literature with the Danish writer Karl Gjellerup. Pontoppidan's first novel cycle, *Det Forjättede Land* (1891–95), is about the life of a Danish clergyman; it includes *Emanuel, or*

Children of the Soil (1896), *The Promised Land* (1896), and the untranslated *Dommens Dag* (Day of Judgment, 1895). His major work, the autobiographical *Lykke-Per* (Lucky Peter, 5 vol., 1898–1904), reflects his dissatisfaction with his bourgeois Protestant upbringing. *De Dödes Rige* (Kingdom of the Dead, 5 vol., 1912–16) describes the decade from 1900 to 1910 in Denmark.

PONTORMO, Jacopo da, real name JACOPO CARRUCCI (1494–1557), Italian painter, born in Pontormo, who worked chiefly in Florence. He was initially influenced by the calm, balanced High Renaissance styles of Piero di Cosimo and Leonardo da Vinci and of Andrea del Sarto, whom he assisted. These influences shaped such early works (1514–15) as the *Visitation, Madonna with Four Saints,* and other frescoes for the Florentine church of SS Annunziata. From 1518 on, Pontormo did much work for the Medici, including frescoes for their villa at Poggio and, later, their family church, San Lorenzo. About 1518 he developed a new Mannerist style, partly inspired by Michelangelo and Albrecht Dürer, marked by elongated forms, heightened emotion, and tension between figures and space. Among his Mannerist works are *Joseph in Egypt* (1518?, National Gallery, London), *Holy Family and Saints* (c. 1518, San Michele, Vizdomini), and the *Deposition* (1526, Santa Felicità). He also did portraits, such as *Alessandro de Medici* (c. 1525, Pinacoteca Nazionale, Lucca).

PONTUS, ancient district in northeastern Asia Minor (in what is now Turkey) on the Black Sea, or Pontus Euxinus, from which it received its name, and extending from Paphlagonia on the west to Armenia on the east. Its southern limits were the Anti-Taurus Mountains, and its territory corresponded to the modern Trabzon and Sivas, Turkey. The name Pontus does not occur in records before the 4th century BC and did not come into common use until after the time of Alexander the Great of Macedonia. Before Alexander's conquest of Persia in 330 BC, Pontus was governed by a satrap for the Persian Empire. The foundation of the powerful kingdom of Pontus was laid by Mithradates I Ctistes (d. about 301 BC). His son, Mithradates II (d. about 265 BC), gained control of Paphlagonia and northern Cappadocia. The most important king of Pontus was Mithradates VI. On his overthrow in 66 BC by the Roman general Pompey the Great, the kingdom was divided, the western portion being joined to the province of Bithynia in a Roman province known as Pontus and Bithynia and the eastern region being assigned to native princes. The eastern territory was constituted a Roman province in 62 AD and at first was joined to Galatia, but in the 4th century AD, under the Roman emperor Constantine I, it became a separate province with the name Pontus Polemoniacus.

PONY. *See* HORSE.

PONY EXPRESS, mail service operating between Saint Joseph, Mo., and Sacramento, Calif., inaugurated on April 3, 1860, under the direction of the Central Overland California and Pike's Peak Express Co. The mail was carried rapidly overland on horseback between St. Joseph and Sacramento; the schedule allowed ten days for the trip. The mail was then carried by boat to San Francisco. Stations averaging at first 40 km (25

An armed rider on the Pony Express. Bureau of Public Roads

mi) apart were established, and each rider was expected to cover 120 km (75 mi) a day. Eventually, the Pony Express had 100 stations, 80 riders, and between 400 and 500 horses. The regular Pony Express service was discontinued on the completion of the line of the Pacific Telegraph Co. in October 1861. The express route was extremely hazardous, but only one mail delivery was ever lost.

POODLE, breed of dog, believed to have originated in Germany as a water retriever. It appeared in various parts of the world long ago; bas-reliefs dating from the 1st century in southern Europe represent such an animal. Although the poodle has been particularly popular in France since the beginning of the 19th century, its intelligence and adaptability have made it a universal favorite.

Three varieties of the breed exist: the standard, which is 38 cm (15 in) or more in height at the shoulder and weighs 9kg (20 lb) or more; the miniature, from 25 to 38 cm (10 to 15 in) high at the shoulder and weighing from 5 to 9 kg (12 to 20 lb); and the toy, which is 25 cm (10 in) or less at the shoulder and weighs under 5 kg (12 lb). The standard variety is used in the country as a water retriever, watchdog, and pet; the miniature and toy varieties are used as pets chiefly in urban surroundings. All three types have a moderately peaked skull; a long, straight muzzle; dark, oval-shaped eyes; ears thatare set low and hang close to the head; a strong neck; a deep chest; straight forelegs and muscular hind legs; and a tail that is carried high. The dog has a woolly undercoat and a topcoat that consists either of wiry, curled hair, or long, silky hair hanging in cords. The dog may be of any solid color. The coat of the poodle is generally clipped in one of two principal styles, the Continental or the English saddle. The custom of clipping apparently originated as a means of facilitating swimming. In the Continental style, the hindquarters of the dog are shaved down to the skin, with rosettes of hair usually left on the hips and hocks. In the English saddle style, the hindquarters are clipped to leave a blanket ofshort hair. In both styles each leg is clipped, leaving only a bracelet of hair near the foot; the face and tail are also clipped, except for a pom-pom of hair at the end.

A championship toy poodle. The poodle is an ancient breed of dog, originally raised as a large hunting animal. Three varieties of the breed are distinguished by size: the standard (the largest), the miniature, and the toy (the smallest). Creszentia Allen

POOL. *See* BILLIARDS.

POOLE, borough, Dorset, S England, on the English Channel. Poole has a large, nearly landlocked harbor and is a naval supply station and a yachting center. Its port handles mainly imports of petroleum products. Pottery is manufactured, and the borough has an oyster fishery. Poole was first mentioned in the records of the 14th century; it received county status in 1586. Pop. (1991 prelim.) 130,900.

POONA, also Pune, city, W India, in Maharashtra State, at the confluence of the Mutha and Mula rivers. The city is part of an important agricultural and manufacturing region. It is also noted as the site of several institutions of higher learning, including the University of Poona (1949) and Bhandarkar Oriental Research Institute (1917). Several 17th- and 18th-century palaces and temples are in Poona. Pop. (1981 prelim., greater city) 1,685,300.

POOR RICHARD'S ALMANACK. *See* FRANKLIN, BENJAMIN.

POP ART, visual arts movement of the 1950s and '60s, principally in the U.S. and Great Britain. The images of pop art (shortened from "popular art") were taken from mass culture. Some artists duplicated beer bottles, soup cans, comic strips, road signs, and similar objects in paintings, collages, and sculptures. Others incorporated the objects themselves into their paintings or sculptures, sometimes in startingly modified form. Materials of modern technology, such as plastic, urethane foam, and acrylic paint, often figured prominently. One of the most important artistic movements of the 20th century, pop art not only influenced the work of subsequent artists but

Modern Painting with Clef *(1967); oil, synthetic polymer, and pencil on canvas, by Roy Lichtenstein, an American painter and innovator in the field of pop art.*
Lee Stalsworth–Hirshhorn Museum and Sculpture Garden, Smithsonian Institution

also had an impact on commercial, graphic, and fashion design.

The historical antecedents of pop art include the works of Dadaists such as the French artist Marcel Duchamp, as well as a tradition, in U.S. painting of the 19th and early 20th centuries, of trompe l'oeil pictures and other depictions of familiar objects. Moreover, a number of pop artists had at times earned their living by working as commercial artists.

The pop art movement itself, however, began as a reaction against the abstract expressionist style of the 1940s and '50s, which the pop artists considered overly intellectual, subjective, and divorced from reality. Adopting the goal of the American composer John Cage—to close the gap between life and art—they embraced the environment of everyday life. In using images that reflected the materialism and vulgarity of modern mass culture, they sought to provide a perception of reality even more immediate than that offered by the realistic painting of the past. They also worked to be impersonal, that is, to allow the viewer to respond directly to the object, rather than to the skill and personality of the artist. Occasionally, however, an element of satire or social criticism can be discerned.

In the U.S., Robert Rauschenberg and Jasper Johns provided the initial impetus—Rauschenberg with his collages constructed from household objects such as quilts and pillows, Johns with his series of paintings depicting American flags and bull's-eye targets. The first full-fledged pop work was *Just What Is It That Makes Today's Home So Different, So Appealing?* (1956, private collection) by the British artist Richard Hamilton (1922–); in this satiric collage of two ludicrous figures in a living room, the pop hallmarks of exuberance, incongruity, crudeness, and good humor are emphasized.

Pop art developed rapidly during the 1960s. In 1960 the British artist David Hockney produced *Typhoo Tea* (London, Kasmin Gallery), one of the earliest paintings to portray a brand-name commercial product. In the same year Rauschenberg finished his painted cast bronzes of Ballantine beer cans. In 1961 Claes Oldenburg, an American, constructed the first of his garish, humorous plastic sculptures of hamburgers and other fast-food items. At the same time Roy Lichtenstein, another American, extended the range of pop art with his oil paintings that mimic blown-up frames of comic strips. Several pop artists also produced happenings, or theatrical events staged as art objects in themselves.

In addition to appropriating the subject matter of mass culture, pop art appropriated the techniques of mass production as well. Rauschenberg and Johns had already abandoned individual, titled paintings in favor of large series of works, all depicting the same objects. In the early 1960s the American Andy Warhol carried the idea a step further by adopting the mass-production technique of silk-screening, turning out hundreds of identical prints of Coca-Cola bottles, Campbell's soup cans, and other familiar subjects.

Other important pop works by American artists are the white plaster casts of real people in real settings, by George Segal; pastries depicted in thick paint that resembles cake frosting, by Wayne Thiebaud (1920–); paintings imitating billboards, by James Rosenquist (1933–); the satiric Great American Nudes series of Tom Wesselmann (1931–); objects combined with paintings, by Jim Dine (1935–); and designs of words, numbers and symbols, by Robert Indiana (1928–). In Great Britain, Peter Blake (1932–) produced mock-serious publicity-shot images of popular heroes, and the American-born R. B. Kitaj (1932–) painted images often called "collages of ideas," incorporating obscure literary allusions but with a strong figurative basis.

For further information on this topic, see the Bibliography in volume 28, section 662.

POPAYÁN, city, SW Colombia, capital of Cauca Department, on the Cauca R. at the NW foot of Puracé Volcano of the Cordillera Central. A rail terminus and road hub, it is a trading center of the surrounding agricultural area. Sulfur mines are worked on Puracé Volcano. Industries in the city include flour milling, tanning, and the manufacture of fiber products, shoes, clothing, and bricks. A center of religious and intellectual life since colonial days, the city contains old monasteries, a cathedral, colonial houses, and three museums. It is renowned for Easter-week celebrations. The University of Cauca was founded here in 1827 on the site of an Indian village. Pop. (1985) 158,336.

POPCORN. *See* CORN.

POPE, in Latin, *papa,* from the Greek *pappas,* meaning "father," an ecclesiastical title expressing affection and respect and, since the 8th century, recognized in the West as belonging exclusively to the bishop of Rome, head of the Roman Catholic church. During the 4th and 5th centuries bishops were sometimes called pope. The title is still accorded the Coptic patriarch of Alexandria, Egypt. Priests of the Orthodox churches may also be called *pappa,* reflecting the sense of the original Greek word.

Besides the designation pope, the head of the Roman Catholic church also holds these titles: vicar of Christ; successor of St. Peter; supreme pontiff of the universal church; patriarch of the West; primate of Italy; archbishop and metropolitan of the Roman province; sovereign of the State of Vatican City; and servant of the servants of God. *See* PAPACY.

For further information on this topic, see the Bibliography in volume 28, section 79.

POPE, Alexander (1688–1744), English poet, who, modeling himself after the great poets of classical antiquity, wrote highly polished verse, often in a didactic or satirical vein. In verse translations, moral and critical essays, and satires that made him the foremost poet of his age, he brought the heroic couplet, which had been refined by John Dryden, to ultimate perfection.

Ice Bag-Scale A, *by Claes Oldenburg, made of polyvinyl and lacquered wood. This pop monument, 5 m (18 ft) in diameter, inflates and deflates mechanically.*
Gemini G.E.L., Los Angeles, © Gemini G.E.L. 1970.

Born on May 21, 1688, in London, Pope was the son of a cloth merchant. His parents were Roman Catholics, which automatically barred him from England's Protestant universities. Until he was 12 years old, he was educated largely by priests; primarily self-taught afterward, he read widely in English letters, as well as in French, Italian, Latin, and Greek. A devastating illness struck him in childhood, leaving him deformed. He never grew taller than 4 ft 6 in. and was subject to frequent headaches. Perhaps as a result of this condition, he was hypersensitive and exceptionally irritable all his life.

In 1717 Pope moved to a villa in Twickenham, west of London on the Thames River, where he lived for the rest of his life. The most celebrated personages of the day came to visit him there. He was a bitterly quarrelsome man and attacked his literary contemporaries viciously and often with-ut provocation. To some, however, he was ·arm and affectionate; he had a long and close ·iendship with the English writers Jonathan wift and John Gay.

Pope's literary career began in 1704, when the laywright William Wycherley, pleased by Pope's erse, introduced him into the circle of fashion-ble London wits and writers, who welcomed im as a prodigy. He first attracted public atten-on in 1709 with his *Pastorals.* In 1711 his *Essay n Criticism,* a brilliant exposition of the canons f taste, was published. His most famous poem, *he Rape of the Lock* (first pub. 1712; rev. ed. 714), a fanciful and ingenious mock-heroic ork based on a true story, established his repu-ation securely. In 1714 appeared his "The Wife f Bath," which, like his "The Temple of Fame" 1715), was imitative of the works of the same tle by the 14th-century English poet Geoffrey haucer. In 1717 a collection of Pope's works con-aining the most noteworthy of his lyrics was ublished. Pope's translation of Homer's *Iliad* as published in six volumes from 1715 to 1720; translation of the *Odyssey* followed (1725–26). Ie also published an edition of Shakespeare's lays (1725).

Pope and his friend Swift had for years written cornful and very successful critical reviews of hose whom they considered poor writers; in 727 they began a series of parodies of the same riters. The adversaries hurled insults at Swift nd Pope in return, and in 1728 Pope lampooned hem in one of his best-known works, *The Dun-iad.* He later enlarged the work to four vol-mes, the final one appearing in 1743. In 1734 he ompleted his *Essay on Man.* Pope's last works, *Imitations of Horace* (1733–39), were attacks on political enemies of his friends.

lexander Pope

Pope used the heroic couplet with exceptional brilliance, giving it a witty, occasionally biting quality. His success made it the dominant poteic form of his century, and his poetry was translated into many languages. He died on May 21, 1744, at Twickenham.

POPHAM, George (1550?–1608), early colonist of Maine, born in southwestern England. As an associate of the English colonizer Sir Ferdinando Gorges in a colonization scheme for a part of Maine, he sailed from Plymouth in 1607 with two ships and about 120 people and landed in August at the mouth of the Kennebec River. He established the first English settlement in New England, building a storehouse and a fortification that was called Fort Popham. Popham was elected president of the new colony but died the following year, and the colonists, becoming disheartened by the severity of the climate, returned in the spring to England.

POPISH PLOT. *See* OATES, TITUS.

POPLAR, common name for any of about 35 species of trees of the genus *Populus,* a member of the family Salicaceae (*see* WILLOW). Poplars are short-lived, fast-growing trees native mostly to the northern hemisphere. The soft wood of poplars is used for paper pulp, in light construction, and in crate making. Poplars are divided into three groups, or subgenera: aspens, balsam poplars, and cottonwoods, so-called because of the abundant, cottonlike seeds they produce. The Lombardy poplar, *P. nigra* var. *italica,* with close, erect branches, is planted as a windbreak. The black cottonwood, *P. trichocarpa,* of western North America is the largest poplar on the continent, attaining heights of more than 80 m (200 ft). *See also* ASPEN.

POPOCATÉPETL, volcano, S central Mexico, in Puebla State, near Mexico City. It is sometimes called Puebla Volcano after the state in which it is located. It is the second highest peak in Mexico, 5452 m (17,887 ft) above sea level. Although the volcano, which has a snow-covered cone, still occasionally emits smoke, there has been no recent major eruption. The crater is 612 m (2008 ft) across at the widest point and 400 m (1312 ft) across at its narrowest point and has a maximum depth of 505 m (1657 ft). Sulfur is obtained from the crater.

POPPER, Sir Karl Raimund (1902–), Austrian-born British philosopher of science, known for his theory of scientific method and for his criticism of historical determinism. He was born in Vienna and received a Ph.D. degree from the University of Vienna in 1928. Although not a member of the so-called Vienna school of philosophy (*see* POSITIVISM), Popper was sympathetic with their scientific attitude, but critical of certain of their beliefs. From 1937 to 1945 he taught at Canterbury University, New Zealand, and then at the University of London.

Popper's most significant contribution to the philosophy of science was his characterization of the scientific method. In *The Logic of Scientific Discovery* (1934; trans. 1959), he criticized the prevailing view that science is fundamentally inductive in nature. Proposing a criterion of testability, or falsifiability, for scientific validity, Popper emphasized the hypothetico-deductive character of science. Scientific theories are hypotheses from which can be deduced statements testable by observation; if the appropriate experimental observations falsify these statements, the hypothesis is refuted. If a hypothesis survives efforts to falsify it, it may be tentatively accepted. No scientific theory, however, can be conclusively established.

In *The Open Society and Its Enemies* (1945), Popper defended democracy and advanced objections to the totalitarian implications of the political theories of Plato and Karl Marx. He criticized the view that discoverable laws of the development of history render its future course inevitable and thus predictable. R.M.B.

POPPY, common name for the family Papaveraceae, a small group of herbaceous flowering plants occurring principally in the North Temperate Zone, and for its representative genus, *Papaver.* The family contains about 23 genera and 210 species; many are important as ornamentals, and one species is the source of opium (q.v.). Members of the family occupy varied habitats, but they are more common in open, well-drained areas. This preference helps explain why several members of the family, especially poppies, are bothersome weeds in cultivated fields. *See also* BLOODROOT.

The genus *Papaver* contains about 50 species. The Oriental poppy, *P. orientale,* is widely cultivated as an ornamental, and many color forms have been developed. The opium poppy, *P. somniferum,* produces several useful products. Its tiny seeds, produced in huge quantities in each of the plant's dry fruits, or capsules, are used in baking and produce an important drying oil. Opium is the dried sap, or latex, that is harvested from the capsules while they are still young. It contains many alkaloids, including morphine and codeine (q.v.), that are useful in medicine. Heroin is synthesized from the morphine purified from the complex mixture of alkaloids in opium (*see* DRUG DEPENDENCE).

The family Papaveraceae shares the order Papaverales with the family Fumariaceae (*see* FUMITORY). This family contains about 16 genera and 400 species, also mostly found in the North Temperate Zone with a few species located in mountainous regions of tropical Africa and South Africa. The most familiar member of the family

A field of wild Oriental poppies, Papaver orientale. *The Oriental poppy, native to Asia Minor and eastern Europe, is the ancestor of many highly developed garden varieties of poppy.*
Werner H. Müller–Peter Arnold, Inc.

is the bleeding heart (q.v.); others are of minor ornamental importance.

The leaves are usually deeply divided and arranged in a rosette around the base of the short stem. The flowers have two to four sepals (outer floral whorls) and twice as many petals (inner floral whorls). The stamens (male floral organs) vary in number from six to many more, and the ovary (female floral organ) is superior (borne above and free from the other flower parts). The order characteristically has sap that isrich in alkaloids. The sap is clear and watery in the fumitory family, milky in the poppy family.

Plants in the order Papaverales are members of the class Magnoliopsida (*see* DICOTS) in the phylum or division Magnoliophyta (*see* ANGIOSPERM).

M.R.C.

For further information on this topic, see the Bibliography in volume 28, sections 452, 503–4, 592.

POPULAR MUSIC, musical forms and styles that are generally listened to and performable by persons with little or no musical training; that are commercially marketed; and that are disseminated by mass media. More loosely, popular music can also refer to any musical genre used for entertainment. In its narrower definition, popular music especially encompasses the most widespread forms and styles in Europe and North America; some non-Western cultures, however, possess different genres of popular music.

Music in all these styles circulates primarily by the printed page (sheet music), recordings (disks, tapes, films), and broadcasts (radio, television, public-address systems) and is thus reproducible upon demand. In contrast to popular music, folk music is usually disseminated noncommercially, by word of mouth; and classical music is usually performed by trained musicians and is often noncommercial.

European popular music emerged with 18th-century urbanization and industrialization; it developed distinctive characteristics to meet the tastes of all but the extreme upper or lower class.

Precursors. In nearly all cultures, some music with popular elements has served for entertainment. In the Middle Ages, secular songs with frivolous or love texts, composed by troubadours and trouvères in France and by minnesingers in Germany, were performed by professional minstrels. In the 15th century, a growing merchant and upper class supported composers of secular vocal part music, such as the chanson in France and the madrigal in Italy; theater music; and instrumental music, notably for lute and keyboard. Even the church embraced secular elements. In the 16th century, Martin Luther set vernacular religious texts to secular melodies; Roman Catholic composers from the 14th century on have written masses on secular tunes; 20th-century gospel songs meet all criteria for popular music.

Music was first printed in multiple copies about 1500; thereafter, the sale and circulation of printed music made wider popularization possible and began to replace private patronage as the chief source of income for composers. Performers, too, gained public patronage with the growth of public concerts in the 18th century. In England, from the 16th century on, itinerant singers sold ballad texts printed as broadsides (loose sheets) to be sung to a familiar tune such as "Greensleeves."

18th and 19th Centuries. With the coming of the Industrial Revolution in the 18th century, the distribution of wealth to a broader level of society allowed more families to purchase musical instruments. Manufacturers began mass-producing instruments in the late 18th century, and the piano and guitar soon became standard commercial products. Songs and arrangements of orchestral and operatic selections were sold as sheet music for the home parlor, and popular songs were introduced in concerts and stage shows. Music became part of the curriculum in public schools. The quantity of music in print increased throughout the 19th century, with publishers in every major city. After about 1880, music publishers in the U.S. were concentrated in New York City, where the district and the music they produced were called "Tin Pan Alley."

20th Century. The invention of the phonograph by the American Thomas Edison made music even more accessible in the home, because consumers needed no training to have music on demand. Coin-operated phonographs (forerunners of the jukebox) appeared before 1900, and by World War I many popular entertainers and even concert musicians were making recordings. Radio in the 1920s and television in the late 1940s began broadcasting live and recorded music directly into the home. In public places, sound films after the late 1920s introduced many popular entertainers; and public-address systems were used to broadcast music that was designed to ease stress subconsciously—offering the least objectionable styles possible, although allowing listeners no choice in what they heard.

As the popular music industry expanded, it increasingly involved the financial, legal, and social professions. Composers and publishers sought protection of their commercial rights through copyright and performing-right laws, and professional performers formed unions to protect wages and regulate working conditions.

The Beatles, the most popular singing group of the 1960s, were a dominating influence on modern popular music. Wide World Photos

The rise of popular music changed the role of music in daily life. Music in the home, formerly either a diversion of the wealthy elite or a form of folk life, became a customary part of middle-class home life. Song texts came to reflect the fundamental concerns of the family, portraying hope, despair, heroism, humor, frustration, nostalgia, and, above all, love. As cities overtook rural areas in population, popular music styles served psychological needs more strongly as bearers of cultural values and as buffers against the inescapable presence of other people.

Cross-Cultural Influences. The 20th-century mass media facilitated the mixing of elements among popular, folk, and classical styles as music traveled freely from one part of the world to another. American jazz and black-derived social dances swept Europe during and after World War I. The radio and phonograph introduced European and U.S. styles to Africa, resulting in *kwela* music in South Africa and highlife in Ghana and Nigeria. In highlife, the ensemble was modeled on British dance bands, and the musical style was borrowed from U.S. jazz. In the 1960s, soul music replaced highlife. In Egypt and the Middle East, the recording industry fostered a pan-Arabic popular vocal style based on traditional folk idioms. Instrumental ensembles in Southeast Asia and the Pacific islands added Western guitars. In India, China, and Japan, European pianos and violins had a great impact, and popular music was increasingly arranged for distribution through films and recordings.

European and U.S. Trends. In the West, a pan-European style slowly eroded local and national distinctions, as European and U.S. performers cultivated international audiences. In the U.S. an influx of Latin American dances and instruments occurred in the 1930s, and the urban-based folk revival of the 1950s borrowed songs, instruments, and vocal styles from Anglo-American folk music. Opera and operetta provided models for Broadway musicals, and selections from symphonies and ballets became popularized.

The "baby boom" and concomitant emphasis on youth culture following World War II produced a large teenage market that overwhelmed adult tastes. A new dominant genre developed: rock-and-roll, which amalgamated elements from two other popular genres, white country and western music and black rhythm-and-blues.

Style and Format. Some pieces of popular music ("standards") have become exceptionally familiar across several generations. But with performrs and public demanding fresh material, and ublishers finding it profitable to advertise in- reasing numbers of pieces, the majority of items reated have been frankly ephemeral. The media ave sometimes determined the format of popu- ar music; since lengthy works are not readily urchased and since bulky items are more costly or dealers to handle, sheet music usually has nly about six pages, and single recordings are nly two and a half or three minutes long.

Each popular song or instrumental piece is ar- anged to conform with one of various styles, uch as country, jazz, soul, gospel, rock, Jamaican eggae, or a Broadway tune. Each style's charac- eristics are conveyed in the text (if the piece is a ong) and in the musical elements of instrumen- ation, rhythm, melody, texture, harmony, and ocal style. Some examples of the musical ele- nents follow.

1. Instrumentation—South Sea music uses Ha- vaiian steel guitars; early rock-and-roll, the saxo- hone.

2. Rhythm—some kinds of rock set voices gainst rapid guitar and drum rhythms; "disco" nusic has repetitive, danceable rhythms; "easy istening" orchestral music has slow rhythms vith light accents.

3. Melody—"acid" rock has angular lines with vide intervals and abrupt breaks; gospel and country music have narrow ranges and more rep- etition.

4. Texture—in some jazz, each instrument has a different line; in "easy listening" music, chord- based arrangements blend all parts and empha- size the melody.

5. Harmony—gospel music uses a few chords, repeated in patterns; some rock and jazz have complex aggregates of notes following no pat- tern.

6. Vocal style—country emphasizes lower ranges, husky timbres, and nasality; singers of "standard" and show tunes employ more open, resonant vocal production.

See also AFRO-AMERICAN MUSIC; AMERICAN MU- SIC; BLUES; COUNTRY AND WESTERN MUSIC; JAZZ; MUSICAL; POPULAR AND SOCIAL DANCE; ROCK MU- SIC; SINGING. D.L.R.

For further information on this topic, see the Bibliography in volume 28, section 741.

POPULAR AND SOCIAL DANCE, overlapping terms referring to dances performed by the par- ticipants for their own enjoyment and not be- longing to any folk tradition; such dances characteristically emerged among the aristocratic or wealthy in past societies and developed in the urban, mass-media-influenced cultures of the 20th century.

Different scholars vary in their usage of the terms *popular dance* and *social dance.* Some ap- ply *popular dance* to dances of the 20th century. Some reserve *social dance* for the dances of the more urban and sometimes more affluent mem- bers of society who gather to see and be seen. Still others consider *social dance* to encompass not only urban or elite dances but also recrea- tional folk dances (as opposed to ceremonial or ritual folk dances). The focus here, however, is on nontraditional (that is, nonfolk) social dances popular among the elite of past centuries as well as among members of 20th-century, largely ur- ban, society. The steps and patterns of such dances tend to reflect the values and attitudes of society during a given period. The dances often cross geographic boundaries and, particularly in the 20th century, are enjoyed by large numbers of people. Many are rooted in folk dance (q.v.), and, like recreational folk dances, they can be contrasted with theatrical dance (which is meant for an audience and is performed by highly skilled and trained individuals). Like folk dances, however, popular social dances have often been employed and transformed by choreographers for use in the theater. Although popular and so- cial dance forms exist to some extent in non- Western cultures, they are particularly prominent in Western culture, and throughout their docu- mented history, they have influenced Western music and theater.

Middle Ages and Renaissance. The earliest spe- cific documentation of the social dances popular in Western Europe is from the Middle Ages. The predominant dance forms of the early Middle Ages were chain dances, in which the partici- pants, linked in a line, accompanied themselves with singing. Carol, reigen, branle, and farandole are the dances most frequently mentioned. In the later Middle Ages, members of the feudal no- bility concerned themselves with chivalry, knighthood, and troubadour songs about courtly love. In this environment, couple dances began to achieve popularity. The estampie was one of the first formal couple dances; it was a slow, stately dance performed to instrumental accom- paniment in the courts of Europe.

During the Renaissance (14th–16th cent.), the nobility were joined as cultural leaders by a pow- erful mercantile class. As humanism and an inter- est in classical Greece and Rome became powerful ideas, dances tended to reflect secular values. In their ordered patterns, the dances of the Renaissance seem to mirror the contempo- rary philosophical fascination with the harmoni- ous movements of the planets and other celestial bodies. Many of these dances were created by

Couples in courtly costume (one dancer in a winged disguise) progress slowly forward in this basse danse, illustrated in a 13th-century manuscript. The slow forward and backward steps and swaying pauses of the basse danse lent it an air at once intimate and ceremonial. New York Public Library Picture Collection

professional dancing masters hired by the nobility. For the first time, instruction manuals became available, showing the steps and patterns of the various court dances—the trend-setting dances of the 15th through the 18th century. The 15th-century manuscripts of such dancing masters as the Italians Domenico da Piacenza (d. about 1470) and Guglielmo Ebreo (c. 1425–after 1480) are available for study, along with a dance manual published in the late 1490s by the French printer Michel de Toulouze (fl.1482–1505). The dances taught were balli and balletos, the *bassadanza,* and its northern counterpart, the *basse danse.* Danced with simple movements and gentle shifts of weight by couples who touched hands at arm's length, the *basse danse* proceeded around a hall in quiet, stately manner, led by the highest-ranking couple. When the Italian noblewoman Catherine de Médicis became queen of France in 1547, she brought to the French royal court not only Italian influences, but also her Italian dancing master.

The dance manuals published between 1550 and 1630, written by the Frenchman Thoinot Arbeau (1519–96), the Italian Cesare Negri (c. 1536–c. 1604), and other dancing masters, describe dances such as the pavane, galliard, allemande, courante (qq.v.), saltarello, and volta, as well as circular branles and progressive longways dances (for a line of couples, in which each couple re-

Aristocratic, precisely patterned, and quietly flirtatious, the minuet dominated court dance for more than a century. New York Public Library Picture Collection

›eats the pattern with one new couple after an-›ther; *see* COUNTRY DANCE). The sense of order ›nd harmony so important during the Renais-›ance gave rise to formalized suites of dances; ›avanes, for example, were followed by gal-liards. The pavane replaced the *basse danse* as :he usual processional dance. The galliard, with ts springy leaps and kicks, became a dance of nale display to a more subdued female partner. *See also* SUITE.

17th Through 19th Centuries. In 1643 Louis XIV became king of France, then the center of world power. Pavanes and galliards began to die out, and dances such as the sarabande, chaconne, gavotte, musette, hornpipe, (qq.v.), gigue (*see* JIG), rigaudon, and bourrée became prominent. During the 1660s at the French court the minuet (q.v.) appeared; its hierarchical format, complex patterning, and contained elegance reflected a world of order, convention, and extreme empha-

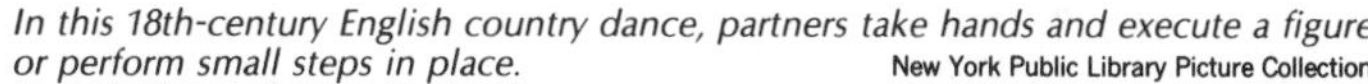

In this 18th-century English country dance, partners take hands and execute a figure or perform small steps in place. New York Public Library Picture Collection

sis on detail. It was danced by one couple at a time, in order of rank; with erect posture, small, precise steps that sank and rose at the knee and foot, and small, precise hand and arm movements, the dancing couple outlined a specific floor pattern (at first an *S,* later a *Z*).

The minuet had a lengthy popularity, and its demise overlapped with the beginnings of the waltz (q.v.) and with significant historical events—the American and French revolutions, the Industrial Revolution, and the rise of the middle class. In parallel with the fascination of literary and musical romanticism with folk music and folk life, the waltz was derived from a folk dance (the Austrian ländler), as were other 19th-century couple dances such as the mazurka and polka (qq.v.). Everything about the waltz was new and different—the impetuous tempo, couples dancing simultaneously with others in random patterning, partners facing each other instead of side by side, and the radically new embracing hand positions. It retained extensive popularity through the 1870s.

Ragtime Through World War II. Not long after the first performance in 1867 of the "Blue Danube" waltz, by the Austrian composer Johann Strauss the Younger, dominance in the development of popular dance shifted from Europe to America. Previously, American emphasis had been on imported English country dancing and the French contredanse and cotillion (q.v.). In 1889, however, the American bandmaster John Philip Sousa's "Washington Post March" gave birth to the two-step in $\frac{6}{8}$ meter, with a quick marching step with skips. Ragtime, with roots in black American music, emerged in the late 1890s. With its lively, syncopated rhythms, it gave rise (1911–15) to a popular craze for dances imitating animals, such as the turkey trot (in which syncopated arm gestures simulated wing movements, and the feet moved with one step to each beat), the grizzly bear, and the bunny hug. Also popular during this time were the tango (q.v.) and the maxixe. The radical changes in dance styles mirrored the changes in society—automobiles and airplanes, radios and telephones, woman suffrage, the rise of labor unions, the writings of Sigmund Freud, the Russian Revolution of 1905. The dances of the teens and '20s, such as the Charleston (q.v.), with its kicks, swinging arms,

The jitterbug, as danced by Sheila Rae and Ted Arkin in the motion picture Naughty But Nice *(1939). A lively, almost acrobatic dance, the jitterbug was the precursor of many rock dance steps.*
Culver Pictures

Ballroom dancers move gracefully around the floor at a dance studio where they have been learning basic steps. Despite the popularity of more strenuous forms, ballroom dancing enjoyed a revival in the late 1970s and early '80s.
Arthur Murray International, Inc.

mobile torsos, and blaring rhythms, reflected a euphoric sense of prosperity and freedom. The Jazz Age of the 1920s was brought to an end with the stock-market crash in 1929. In the 1930s swing emerged as the new musical sound, played by big bands led by musicians such as Benny Goodman and others. Wanting respite from the Great Depression, Americans eagerly watched movie extravaganzas by the dance director Busby Berkeley (1895–1976) as well as the movies of the dancers Fred Astaire and Ginger Rogers (1911-). To swing music, teenagers danced the jitterbug (q.v.), an outgrowth of the 1927 lindy. The fox-trot (q.v.), a fast, trotting dance from about 1913, came back in a slower, smoother version. In 1939 at the World's Fair a samba (q.v.) orchestra played at the Brazilian pavilion. Soon, popular culture was swept with a rage for South American dances such as the rumba (q.v.), mambo, cha-cha, and conga line. The Latin forms and sensual hip movements became popular at a time when women were gaining increased freedom, working in factories and managing homes and businesses while men were away at war during the 1940s.

Rock Music and Its Dances. In the 1950s the quietly sensuous movements of the Latin dances became the provocative hip rolls of the singer Elvis Presley, whose first major record was released in 1956. Also in the mid-1950s, rock and roll became a national phenomenon when Bill Haley (1927–81) and His Comets were featured in the film *Rock Around the Clock,* and the television show "American Bandstand" began its telecasts of dancing teenagers. American society underwent fundamental upheavals during this period and the following decade with the civil rights movement, protests against the war in Vietnam, and such events as the famous music festival at Woodstock, N.Y., in 1969. In 1960 the rock musician Chubby Checker (1941-) ushered in the twist, performed with gyrating hips and torso and a body attitude that seemed to express "do-

Break dancing became a fad among teenagers in the mid-1980s. Steve Hopkins–Black Star

ing your own thing." The dances of the 1960s—such as the fish, the hitchhiker, the frug, and the jerk—were free and individualistic. People danced in large masses, both sexes with long hair, all dancing by themselves and inventing as they went along. Several contradictory trends appeared in the 1970s and '80s. Couple dancing, enhanced by the individuality of the 1960s, returned in the 1970s with the hustle and other elaborately choreographed dances performed to disco music, a simple form of rock with strong dance rhythms. Alongside the disco movement, which dominated the 1970s and '80s, the more outrageous punk rock movement brought in its wake slam dancing, which involved leaping, jumping, and sometimes physical attack, and in the mid-1980s the acrobatic solo dance form known as break dancing. At the same time, in an impulse to nostalgia, the big-band sound was revived with foxtrots, waltzes, and jitterbugs.

See also DANCE. N.P.

For further information on this topic, see the Bibliography in volume 28, section 765.

POPULAR SOVEREIGNTY. *See* SQUATTER SOVEREIGNTY.

POPULATION, term referring to the total human inhabitants of a specified area, such as a city, country, or continent, at a given time. Population study as a discipline is known as demography. It is concerned with the size, composition, and distribution of populations; their patterns of change over time through births, deaths, and migration; and the determinants and consequences of such changes. Population studies yield knowledge important for planning, particularly by governments, in fields such as health, education, housing, social security, employment, and environmental preservation. Such studies also provide information needed to formulate government population policies, which seek to modify demographic trends in order to achieve economic and social objectives.

THE FIELD OF DEMOGRAPHY

Demography is an interdisciplinary field involving mathematics and statistics, biology, medicine, sociology, economics, history, geography, and anthropology. The field of demography has a relatively brief history. Its beginning often is dated from the publication in 1798 of *An Essay on the Principle of Population* by the British economist Thomas Robert Malthus. In this work Malthus warned of the constant tendency for human population growth to outstrip food production and classified the various ways that such growth would, in consequence, be slowed. He distinguished between "positive checks" to population growth (such as war, famine, and disease) and "preventive checks" (celibacy and contraception).

The development of demography has been tied closely to the gradually increasing availability of data on births and deaths from parish and civil registers, and on population size and composition from the censuses that became common in the 19th century (*see* CENSUS). The growth of behavioral sciences in the 20th century and advances in the fields of statistics and computer sciences further stimulated demographic research. Subfields of mathematical, economic, and social demography have grown rapidly in recent decades.

DEMOGRAPHIC DATA AND MEASUREMENTS

Modern national governments and international organizations place a high priority on the accurate determination of national and worldwide populations. Describing the present population and predicting those of the future with reasonable accuracy requires reliable data.

Methods of Research. National censuses, civil registration, and, since the 1960s, national sample surveys are the major sources of demographic data. They provide the raw materials for investigating the causes and consequences of population changes. The most common source is the population census, a count of all persons by age and with specified social and economic characteristics within a given area at a particular time. A register is a continuous record of births, deaths, migrations, marriages, and divorces, often maintained by a local government; reliability varies with the scrupulousness of citizens in reporting these data. In the sample survey, a statistically selected portion is used to represent the total population.

In the U.S., decennial censuses have been taken since 1790. Since the 1950s the U.S. Bureau of the Census has conducted an annual Current Population Survey, a highly detailed sample survey of many aspects of demographic behavior and related socioeconomic factors. International population data are compiled in systematic form by the United Nations Statistical Office, which prepares an annual *Demographic Yearbook;* by the UN Demographic Division, which issues biennial assessments and projections of world population; and by the International Bank for Reconstruction and Development.

Measures of Population. The numbers of births, deaths, immigrants, and emigrants over a specified time interval determine the change in population size. For comparative purposes, these components of change are expressed as proportions of the total population, to yield the birth rate, death rate, migration rates, and the popula-

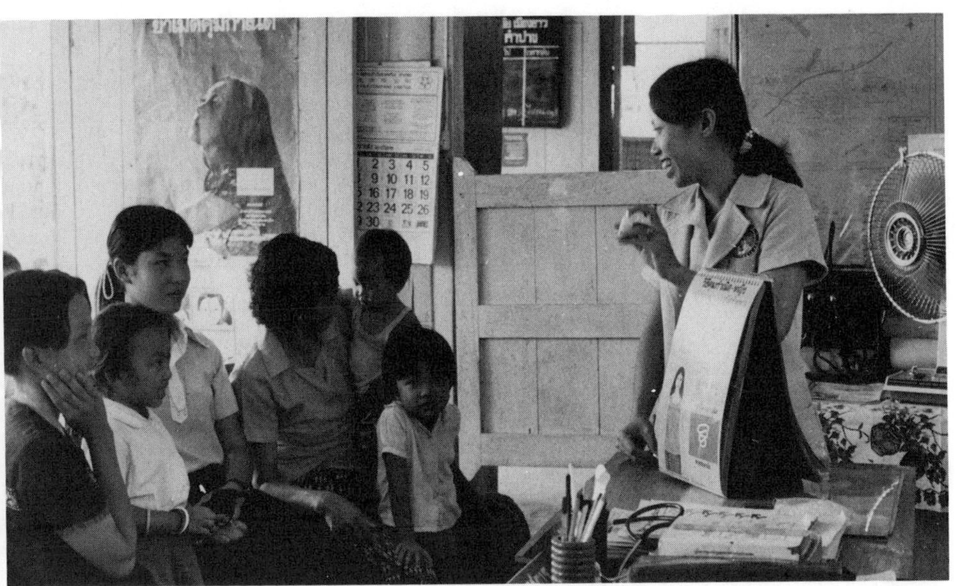

Family-planning programs are an essential part of the effort to stabilize world population growth. A community midwife in northern Thailand explains various forms of contraception to villagers. S. Surin–World Health Organization

tion growth rate. (Birth and death rates typically are stated as numbers per 1000 population per year.) These rates are affected by the age-composition of the population; for example, a very healthy population, which, as a result, has a relatively large proportion of old people, might have a death rate similar to that of a poor population made up of predominantly younger members. Demographers, therefore, often use measures that are free of this age-distribution influence. Two such widely used measures are the total fertility rate (TFR) and the life expectancy at birth.

The total fertility rate is the number of children a woman would have during her reproductive life if she experienced the prevailing rates of fertility at each age. High-fertility countries may have birth rates of 40 or even 50 per 1000 population (per year); corresponding levels of the TFR would be 5 to 7 children per woman. Low-fertility countries have birth rates of 15 to 20 per 1000 and TFRs of about 2. "Replacement level" fertility (the level at which each person on average has a single successor in the next generation) corresponds to a TFR of about 2.1 under low-mortality conditions.

The life expectancy at birth is the average length of life that would be observed in a population in which the currently prevailing mortality risks at each age continued indefinitely. Preindustrial populations were characterized by large fluctuations in mortality; long-run averages, however, would probably have shown death rates of 30 to 40 per 1000 and life expectancies of 25 to 35 years. Under modern health conditions, death rates below 10 per 1000 and life expectancies above 70 years are common.

Another important mortality measure is the infant mortality rate. This is the probability of death in the first year of life, usually stated as a number per 1000 births. Many less-developed countries have infant mortality rates above 100 per 1000—that is, more than 10 percent of the children die in their first year. In countries with effective health and educational systems, infant mortality rates are about 15 per 1000, or even lower.

WORLD POPULATION GROWTH AND DISTRIBUTION

The UN, an accepted authority on population levels and trends, estimates that the world population reached 5.3 billion in 1990, and is increasing annually by more than 90 million persons. The rate of increase, 1.7 percent per year, has fallen below the peak rate of 2 percent per year attained by 1970. However, absolute yearly increments are not expected to start declining until after the year 2000.

Past and Present Growth. Estimates of world population before 1900 are based on fragmentary data, but scholars agree that, for most of human existence, long-run average population growth approached approximately 0.002 percent per year, or 20 per million inhabitants. Growth was not steady but was marked by oscillations dictated by climate, food supply, disease, and war.

Starting in the 17th century, great advances in scientific knowledge, agriculture, industry, medicine, and social organization made possible substantial increases in population. Inanimate energy gradually replaced human and animal labor. People slowly acquired the knowledge and means to control disease. All continents shared in a fivefold population increase over a 300-year period—from about 500 million in 1650 to 2.5 billion in 1950—but increases were most striking in regions where new technologies were devised and applied.

Beginning about 1950, a new phase of population growth was ushered in when famine and disease could be controlled even in areas that had not yet attained a high degree of literacy or a technologically developed industrial society. This happened as a result of the modest cost of importing the vaccines, antibiotics, insecticides, and high-yielding varieties of seeds produced since the 1950s. With improvements in water supplies, sewage-disposal facilities, and transportation networks, agricultural yields increased, and deaths from infectious and parasitic diseases greatly declined. Life expectancy at birth in most developing countries increased from about 35–40 years in 1950 to 61 years by 1990. The rapid decline in deaths among people who maintained generally high fertility rates led to annual population growth that exceeded 3.1 percent in many developing nations—a rate that doubles population size in 23 years.

Regional Distribution. As of 1990, 1.2 billion people lived in the developed nations of the world, and 4.1 billion people lived in the less-developed countries. By region, over half the world's population is in East and South Asia; China, with more than 1.2 billion inhabitants, and India, with some 880 million, are the dominant contributors. Europe and the countries of the former USSR contain 15 percent, North and South America make up 14 percent, and Africa has 12 percent of world population.

Differences in regional growth rates are altering these percentages over time. Africa's share of the world population is expected to more than double by the year 2025, while the population of South Asia and Latin America remains nearly constant and the other regions, including East Asia, decline appreciably in relative size. The share of the present developed nations in world population—23 percent in 1990—is expected to fall to 17 percent by 2025. Nine out of every ten persons who are now being added to the world's population are living in the less-developed countries.

Urban Concentration. As a country develop from primarily an agricultural to an industrial economy, large-scale migration of rural residents to towns and cities takes place. During this process, the growth rate of urban areas is typically double the pace of overall population increase. Some 29 percent of the world population was living in urban areas in 1950; this figure was 43 percent in 1990, and is projected to rise to about 50 percent by the year 2000.

Urbanization eventually leads to a severe decline in the number of people living in the countryside, with negative population growth rates in rural areas. Rapid growth of overall population has deferred this event in most less-developed countries, but it is projected to occur in the early decades of the 21st century.

Most migrants to the cities can be assumed to have bettered themselves in comparison to their former standard of living, despite the serious problems of overcrowding, substandard housing, and inadequate municipal services that characterize life for many arrivals to urban centers. Dealing with these conditions, especially in very large cities, presents massive difficulties for the governments of less-developed countries.

Population Projections. Most of the potential parents of the next two decades have already been born. Population projections over this interval can, therefore, be made with reasonable confidence, barring catastrophic changes. Beyond two decades, however, uncertainties about demographic magnitudes and other characteristics of human societies build up rapidly, making any projections somewhat speculative.

The UN medium projections issued in 1990 show the world population increasing from 5.3 billion in 1990 to 6.2 billion in 2000, and 8.5 billion in 2025. "High" and "low" projections for 2025 are 9.1 billion and 7.9 billion respectively. The average world birth rate is projected to decline from the 1990 level of 26 per 1000 to 22 per 1000 at the end of the century and to 17 per 1000 in 2025 (corresponding to a fall in TFR from 3.3 in 1990 to 2.3 in 2025). Because of the expanding share of the population at high-mortality ages, the average world death rate is expected to decline only slightly; from 9 (per 1000) in 1990 to 8 in 2025. Average world life expectancy, however, is projected to rise from 65 years in 1990 to 73 years in 2025.

Wide variations in population growth will undoubtedly persist. In the developed world, population growth will continue to be very low and in some nations will even decline. Western Europe as a whole is projected to have a declining population after 2000. U.S. Census Bureau projections, assuming middle fertility and mortality levels and net immigration averaging 880,000 per year, show U.S. population increasing from 249 million in 1990 to 334 million in 2025 and 383 million in 2050. Thereafter, growth would be virtually zero.

The UN expects the less-developed countries to have steadily falling rates of population growth. For the less-developed world as a whole, the 1990 growth rate of 2.0 percent per year is projected to be cut in half by 2025. Africa will remain the region with the highest growth rate. In 1990 this rate was 3.1 percent; in 2025 it is projected to be about 2.2 percent. Africa's population would more than triple, from 682 million in 1990 to 1.58 billion in 2025, and then continue growing at a rate that would almost double the population size in another 35 years.

POPULATION POLICIES

Government population policies seek to contribute to national development and welfare goals through measures that, directly or indirectly, aim to influence demographic processes—in particular, fertility and migration. Examples include statutory minimum ages for marriage, programs to promote the use of contraception, and controls on immigration. (When such policies are adopted for other than demographic reasons, they can be termed implicit policies.)

Population Policy in the U.S. The early immigrants to North America found a vast continent with a relatively small indigenous population. Overcrowding was incomprehensible because of the expanse of land to the west.

In the mid-20th century, as the rest of the world awakened to the potential crisis brought on by unchecked population growth, the U.S. government examined the possible impact of overpopulation in the nation. The President's Commission on Population Growth and the American Future began a two-year study in 1970. Submitted to President Richard M. Nixon in 1972, it welcomed the prospect of zero population growth in the U.S., but did not propose that the government take strong measures to attain it. The commission did, however, advocate education on family planning and widely available access to contraception and abortion services. Primarily because of this, the president rejected the commission's recommendations.

Since then, U.S. fertility has fallen below replacement level. This is due in part to the implicit policies that, taken together, make bearing and raising children very costly to parents. Future policy concerns may reflect worry over population aging and the demographic aspects of funding social security. In addition, the conflicting interests involved in determining numbers and characteristics of migrants is likely to keep immigration policy on the political agenda.

Population Policies in Developed Nations. European countries did not address the issue of a national population policy until the 20th century. Subsidies were granted to expanding families by such disparate nations as Great Britain, Sweden, and the USSR. The Italian Fascists in the 1920s and the National Socialists (Nazis) in Germany during the 1930s made population growth an essential part of their doctrines.

Japan, with an economy comparable to those of the European nations, was the first developed country in modern times to initiate a birth-control program. In 1948 the Japanese government formally instituted a policy using both contraception and abortion to limit family size.

European pronatalist policies were conspicuously unsuccessful in the 1930s, and their milder variations over the past few decades (in, for example, France and many Eastern European nations) have apparently done little to slow a continuing fertility decline. Government control of migration is more straightforward. Short-term migration tied to labor demands (guest workers) has been a common practice in Western Europe, allowing the various nations the flexibility to curtail migration during economic recessions.

Population Policies in the Third World. In 1952 India took the lead among developing nations in adopting an official policy to slow its population growth. India's stated purpose was to facilitate social and economic development by reducing the burden of a young and rapidly growing population. Surveys to ascertain contraceptive knowledge, attitude, and practice showed a high proportion of couples wishing no more children. Few, however, practiced efficient contraception. Family-planning programs were seen as a way to satisfy a desire for contraception by a large segment of the population and also to confer health benefits from spacing and limiting births.

Asia's lowered growth rate can be attributed mainly to the stringent population policies of China. Although it has a huge population, China has successfully reduced both fertility and mortality. The government has recently been advocating one-child families to lower the nation's growth rate from a current estimate of 14 per 1000 annually to close to zero by the year 2000.

By 1979 more than 90 percent of the population in developing countries lived under governments that, in principle at least, supported access to contraceptives by their citizens, based on considerations of health and the right to choose whether and when to have children. Evidence indicates that progress toward the objectives of lowered fertility and national growth is being achieved in many nations, in part by government support for family-planning programs.

See also AGRICULTURE; FOOD SUPPLY, WORLD; HOUSING. THE POPULATION COUNCIL

For further information on this topic, see the Bibliography in volume 28, sections 167–68, 523–24, 586.

POPULATION BIOLOGY, the study of populations of animals and plants, a population being a group of interbreeding organisms in a specific region—for example, the members of a fish species in a lake. A given population is usually isolated to some degree from others of its species, whether geographically or in terms of behavioral or anatomical differences, but its boundaries may be vague; for example, the fish in a lake may also interbreed with the fish of interconnecting waterways. Nevertheless, a population is a useful, if occasionally artificial, unit for study.

Populations are analyzed in terms of their variability, density, and stability, and of the environmental and other processes and circumstances that affect these characteristics. Among such determinants of a given population are birth and death rates; the distribution of ages and sexes; behavioral patterns of competition and cooperation; predator-prey, host-parasite, and other relationships with different species; food supplies and other environmental considerations; and migration patterns. Population biologists try to develop mathematical models of the group under study that incorporate as many determinants as possible. Such models enable scientists to predict what effect a change in any one determinant may have on a population as a whole.

Although all populations are unique in some way, some general characteristics can be described. Thus isolation, by whatever means, tends to cause a population to develop locally useful traits through natural selection (q.v.). If the isolation persists, selection and random genetic drift—the introduction of mutations—may lead to the appearance of a new species, members of which are no longer likely or even able to interbreed with the original species.

Another characteristic of a population is its so-called environmental carrying capacity—that is, the maximum average number of individuals that the population can reach in its given setting. The degree to which this number affects and is affected by other changes in the population or its environment—that is, the population's dynamics—is yet another distinguishing characteristic. Long-term changes may result in the extinction of a population, its replacement by a better-adapted one, or a move by the population to a new environment. Finally, populations are characterized by a tendency to disperse from a region where the density of their numbers is high to a region of lower density. This is advantageous to those members that remain, and may also be advantageous to those that explore new territories, which may have greater food resources.

The study of population dynamics and of population genetics—the effects of heredity and evolution on populations—is important for all human interventions in the environment, from crop growing to attempts at pest and predator control. It also involves human populations themselves, in terms of population growth and the availability of food supplies (*see* POPULATION).

POPULISM, U.S. agrarian movement of the late 19th century that developed mainly in the area from Texas to the Dakotas and grew into a Farmer-Labor political coalition. The populist movement began during the economic depression of the 1870s, when there was a sharp decline in the income of farmers at a time when their living and operating costs were rising. The farmers began to organize early in the 1870s, and, during the ensuing two decades, large numbers of them joined such bodies as the National Grange and the Farmers' Alliances (qq.v.). The latter were cooperative organizations that hoped to lower farmers' costs by selling supplies at reduced prices, loaning money at rates below those charged by banks, building warehouses to store crops until prices became favorable, and taking political action to achieve these goals. Alliances were popular in the South, where many farmers existed in an almost endless cycle of debt. In some southern states, alliances even embraced black farmers, who had been ostracized from political life there since Reconstruction. By 1891 the movement had gained sufficient strength to warrant a national political party. The alliances joined with the Knights of Labor (q.v.) and other groups to form the People's party, whose members were called Populists.

The principal objectives of the Populists were the free coinage of silver and the issuance of large amounts of paper currency; such inflationary measures tended to raise farm prices and enable the farmers to pay off their debts, most of which had been contracted during the period of inflation following the American Civil War. Populists also sought to replicate their cooperative system on a national scale; to lower transportation costs by nationalizing the railroads; to achieve a more equitable distribution of the costs of government by means of a graduated income tax; to institute direct popular elections of U.S.

senators; and to inaugurate the 8-hour workday. The results of the first election in which the Populists took part, that of 1892, were promising; the Populist presidential candidate, James B. Weaver (1833–1912), received 1,029,846 votes. Populist influence peaked in 1896 when William Jennings Bryan, a Democrat who sympathized with the Populists' agenda, won his party's presidential nomination. The Populists endorsed Bryan, thus sacrificing their independent identity. After he was defeated, the Populist party faded steadily from the political scene, disappearing about 1908.

Despite the brevity of its existence, the Populist movement profoundly influenced subsequent U.S. political life; almost all the original Populist demands, once widely viewed as radical and contradictory to America's free enterprise system, were eventually enacted into law.

See also GREENBACK-LABOR PARTY; GREENBACK PARTY.

PORCELAIN. *See* POTTERY.

PORCUPINE, any herbivorous rodent (q.v.) of the families Hystricidae and Erethizontidae. Porcupines have long, pointed spines, or quills, growing from the back and sides. The quills, which have needle-sharp ends containing hundreds of barbs, are only loosely attached and can be erected by the muscles of the skin.

The Hystricidae, comprising the Old World porcupines, range through the forests of southern Europe and Asia, Africa, and Indonesia. The family is typified by the common porcupine, *Hystrix cristata,* which is thick-bodied, grizzled, and black in color; it grows to a length of 60 cm (24 in), with some of its quills exceeding 30 cm (12 in) in length. The Erethizontidae, comprising the New World porcupines, include four forms: the tree porcupine of Central and South America, which has a prehensile tail; the Canada porcupine, *Erethizon dorsatum;* the thin-spined porcupine of Brazil; and the Amazonian porcupine. The Canada porcupine is found in heavily wooded regions throughout North America, from Alaska to the northern extreme of Mexico. It grows to a length of about 65 cm (26 in) and has a short tail and brownish hair, which almost conceals its 5- to 15-cm (2- to 6-in) quills.

For further information on this topic, see the Bibliography in volume 28, sections 461, 475.

PORCUPINE FISH, any of about 15 species of fish, commonly found near tropical reefs, that constitute the family Diodontidae. The fish range from 30 to 90 cm (12 to 36 in) long. Their stout bodies are covered by spines that are normally relaxed in larger species but permanently erect in smaller ones. When threatened, the fish may swallow water or air, inflating its body into a bristling ball. The upper teeth are fused, as are the lower, producing a beaklike mouth used for feeding on coral and mollusks—hence the family name, meaning "two-toothed." The skin is often spotted. The fish is related to the puffer (q.v.).

PORGY, any of about 100 fishes of the family Sparidae. Porgies are carnivorous shore fish of tropical and temperate seas, abundant in American and European waters, and are highly esteemed as food fishes. The common American porgy, or scup, *Stenotomus chrysops,* is about 30 cm (about 12 in) long and is plentiful off the eastern coast of the U.S. south of Cape Cod. Several allied species occur about Florida and the West Indies. The European red porgy, *Pagrus pagrus,* is common in the Mediterranean and off the Atlantic coasts of Europe and America. Red, with blue spots, it is about 60 cm (about 24 in) long. *Besugo* and *pargo colorado* are other names for the red porgy. The name is also applied to several unrelated fishes, such as the menhaden (q.v.).

PORI (Swed. *Björneborg*), city, SW Finland, in Turku-and-Pori Province, on the Kokemäen R., near the Gulf of Bothnia. It is a seaport and a commercial center. Major manufactures include wood products, metals, machinery, and textiles. The Satakunnan Museum, housing archaeological and historical collections, is here. The city, chartered in 1564, was badly damaged by fire in the 19th century. Pop. (1988 est.) 77,400.

PORIFERA. *See* SPONGE.

PORK. *See* MEAT.

PORNOGRAPHY, written, graphic, or oral depictions of erotic subjects intended to arouse sexual excitement in the audience. Pornography is commonly divided into two categories: soft-core, in which the erotic material is more titillating than explicit; and hard-core, in which erotic content is explicit and intense. Although in common usage pornography is often equated with obscenity (q.v.), the latter is a legal term covering anything offensive to public morals, whereas the former refers exclusively to erotic materials.

Pornography is an age-old phenomenon. The ancient Greeks were familiar with it, as is evident in the derivation of the word, which is classical Greek for "writings about harlots." Until modern times, the most graphic and widely disseminated pornography appeared in the great Eastern civilizations. In the West, the Judeo-Christian view of sex as taboo in art and literature limited depictions of erotic subjects until the 20th century.

Historically, most objections to pornography have been based on religious grounds. Because in the Judeo-Christian tradition sex is considered primarily a means of procreation, any purely erotic treatment of the subject was looked on as perverse and immoral. With the recent proliferation of hard-core pornography, however, its possible social consequences have become the subject of intense debate. Proponents of a liberal attitude toward pornography argue that it is essentially a harmless diversion and may serve to relieve sexual tensions. Opponents of this view, including many feminists, contend that the hard-core pornography presents its overwhelmingly male audience with a degrading and socially harmful picture of women. Opponents are particularly concerned with the effects of pornography, especially that found in the mass media, on the ideas and values of young people.

Modern-day controversy over pornography's impact on society is the latest manifestation of a still-unresolved debate over the legal status of pornography. Basically, this debate centers on whether or not pornography should be considered a form of obscenity, and whether it should be subject to some form of censorship (q.v.).

PORPHYRINS, vital chemical substances, produced by almost all living organisms, necessary for cell respiration. Molecules of various porphyrins consist of a fundamental skeleton of four rings linked together to form a larger ring. The rings are basically of the pyrolle type, four carbon atoms and one nitrogen atom; depending on the porphyrin, various other atoms are connected to the large ring. Moreover, atoms of various metals positioned in the center of the large ring distinguish different porphyrins. A major component of hemoglobin, heme, is an iron porphyrin. Chlorophyll, the substance that gives green plants their color, is a derivative of a magnesium porphyrin.

PORPHYRY (Gr. *porphyros,* "purple"), term originally applied to an Egyptian rock composed of prominent crystals of feldspar embedded in a red or purple matrix, but now applied to any igneous rock having well-defined crystals embedded in a mass of relatively finer grained material. The fine-grained matrix is called the groundmass and the larger crystals, phenocrysts. Igneous rocks of any mineral composition may have porphyritic varieties. The substance known as porphyry copper consists of copper minerals distributed in a body of porphyry.

PORPOISE, common name applied to seven species of small whales, order Cetacea, closely related to dolphins (*see* DOLPHIN), and belonging to the same family, Delphinidae. Porpoises are generally smaller than dolphins and have rounded conical heads that lack the dolphin's characteristic beak. Porpoises have triangular rather than hooked dorsal fins, and instead of vaulting completely out of the water like dolphins do, they make wheellike rolls, surfacing about four times a minute to breathe.

The most frequently seen and most wide-ranging of the porpoises is the common, or harbor, porpoise, *Phocoena phocoena,* which inhabits cool and cold waters of the northern hemisphere, especially around tidal estuaries and inlets of large rivers. Unlike dolphins, these porpoises are rarely seen in the open ocean and do not play in the bow waves or wakes of ships. They grow from 1.2 to 1.8 m (4 to 6 ft) long and are usually bluish-black above and whitish below. They often travel in small schools that make explosive exhalations as they surface. After mating in the late spring, the female gives birth after about 11 months to a calf about half her length.

Other porpoises, which have more restricted ranges, include the Dall porpoise, *Phocoenoides dalli,* and the true porpoise, *P. trui,* both of which have distinctly white underbelly markings that rise high up the flank; they inhabit the cold waters of the North Pacific, as far south as Japan. The black finless porpoise, *Neophocoena phocoenoides,* which has no dorsal fin, inhabits estuarial waters of southern and eastern Asia.

For further information on this topic, see the Bibliography in volume 28, sections 476–77.

PORSENA (fl. late 6th cent. BC), also Lars (Lord) Porsena, in early Roman history, a semilegendary king of Clusium in Etruria, and last of the Etruscan kings. When Tarquinius Superbus, the seventh and last of the legendary kings of Rome, was expelled from the city, he is said to have appealed to Porsena, who then marched on Rome at the head of a great Etruscan army to restore Tarquinius to the throne. Porsena's attempt to cross the Pons Sublicius over the Tiber River was blocked by the legendary 6th-century Roman soldier Horatius Cocles, who held the Etruscan army at bay while his comrades behind him hewed down the bridge. This incident has been celebrated in the famous poem "Horatius at the Bridge" by the British writer Thomas Macaulay. Porsena then besieged Rome but later made peace and withdrew; according to many scholars, both ancient and modern, the account of the peace treaty was a contemporary attempt to conceal the actual conquest of the city by Porsena, and the Etruscans were later defeated and forced back into their own territories.

PORTAGE, city, Porter Co., NW Indiana, near Lake Michigan, in the townships of Portage and Westchester; inc. 1959. It is a residential and industrial suburb of Gary. Indiana Dunes State Park is nearby. Portage Township maintains a port on Lake Michigan with facilities for handling ocean-going vessels. Pop. (1980) 27,409; (1990) 29,060.

PORTAGE LA PRAIRIE, city, S Manitoba, on the Assiniboine R., near Lake Manitoba; inc. 1907. Portage La Prairie is a distribution center for the surrounding agricultural area, in which grain, vegetables, and cattle are raised. Major manufactures here include processed food, building materials, sporting goods, clothing, and machinery. Island Park and Crescent Lake are in the city, and the Long Plain Indian Reservation and Fort La Reine Pioneer Museum and Village are nearby. The settlement was originally established in 1851 near the site of Fort La Reine, a French fur-trading post built in 1738. Pop. (1986) 13,198; (1991) 13,186.

PORTALES, Diego (1793–1837), Chilean statesman. Portales was born on June 26, 1793, in Santiago, where his father was superintendent of the Royal Mint. In 1822, after Chile had won its independence from Spain, he started a trading company that later took over management of the *estanco,* the state tobacco monopoly. He gradually became leader of the conservative *estanquero* group that opposed Chile's Liberal government. In 1829 he joined forces with the supporters of the exiled dictator Bernardo O'Higgins and Gen. Joaquín Prieto (1786–1854), and together they decisively defeated the Liberal army in 1830.

Portales remained in Prieto's government as minister of war and vice-president until 1833; he helped form the constitution of 1833, which set the nation on a firm basis. Refusing the presidency for himself, he devoted his efforts to building an efficient governmental bureaucracy and briefly served as governor of Valparaíso (1832–33). He returned to the war ministry in 1835 when Chile was threatened by a newly formed Peru-Bolivia confederation. During the subsequent war, Portales was taken prisoner by a mutinous Chilean regiment and was killed on June 6, 1837.

PORT ARTHUR (China). *See* LÜDA.

PORT ARTHUR (Ontario). *See* THUNDER BAY.

PORT ARTHUR, city, Jefferson Co., SE Texas, a major deepwater port on Sabine Lake, near Louisiana; settled about 1835, inc. 1898. Linked to the Gulf of Mexico by the Sabine-Neches Canal (completed 1899), it is a major petroleum-shipping port; manufactures include refined petroleum, petrochemicals, and ships. A junior college is here. Pleasure Island, in Sabine Lake, is a nearby recreation area. Port Arthur was founded in 1895 by Arthur E. Stilwell (1859–1928), who selected the site as the S terminus of his Kansas City Southern Railway; the community is named for him. In 1901 oil was discovered nearby, at Spindletop, and subsequently the financier John W. Gates (1855–1911), known as "Bet-a-Million Gates," helped develop Port Arthur. Pop. (1980) 61,251; (1990) 58,724.

PORT-AU-PRINCE, city, central Haiti, capital of the country and of Ouest Department, on the Golfe de la Gonâve (Gulf of Gonaïves). It is the principal seaport and commercial center of Haiti. Major manufactures include processed food, beverages, tobacco products, textiles, and building materials. Tourism and construction are also important to the city's economy. Port-au-Prince is the site of the State University of Haiti (1920), the National Library, the National Museum, the Archaeological Museum, the Art Center, a technical institute, and a polytechnic college. Other points of interest include the National Palace, the Basilica of Notre Dame, and the French-built stone quay (1780).

The settlement was laid out by the French in 1749 and served as the capital of the French colony of Saint-Domingue from 1770 to 1804. When Haiti became independent in 1804, the city was chosen as the new nation's capital. The community has periodically suffered from earthquakes and from civil unrest. Pop. (1982 prelim.) 449,831.

PORT COQUITLAM, city, SW British Columbia, at the confluence of the Pitt, Coquitlam, and Fraser rivers, near Vancouver; inc. 1913. It is a commercial and distribution center for an area of diversified agricultural production. Major manufactures include refined metals, boats, processed food, and rubber, wood, and metal goods. The name of the community, which was established as a railroad junction in the mid-19th century, is derived from a Cowichan Indian term for "salmon." Pop. (1986) 29,115; (1991) 36,773.

PORT ELIZABETH, city, SE South Africa, in Cape Province, on Algoa Bay (an arm of the Indian Ocean). It is an important seaport and manufacturing center and a popular resort noted for its fine beaches. Major manufactures include motor vehicles, metal and wood products, footwear, processed food, and chemicals. Port Elizabeth is the site of the University of Port Elizabeth (1964); Port Elizabeth Technikon (1925), a technical university; the King George VI Art Gallery, featuring collections of British and South African art; the Port Elizabeth Museum, with natural history exhibits, an oceanarium, and a collection of reptiles; and Fort Frederick, built by the British in 1799. The community developed around Fort Frederick. It was laid out in 1820 by the British military leader and colonial official Sir Rufane Shaw Donkin (1773–1841) and named for his late wife, Lady Elizabeth (1790?–1818). The town grew rapidly after it was connected by railroad to Kimberley in 1873. Pop. (1985, greater city) 651,993.

PORTER, Cole (1893–1964), American songwriter, born in Peru, Ind., and educated at Yale and Harvard universities. Porter began to write popular songs in his youth, and in 1916 he completed his first professional score, for the musical revue *See America First.* His promising career was interrupted in 1917 when he enlisted in the French Foreign Legion; he was later transferred to the French army. After World War I he returned to the U.S., where his witty, sophisticated lyrics and subtle melodies soon made him one of the most notable figures in popular music; he wrote the words, as well as the music, for all his scores and songs. Among the musical comedies for which he wrote scores are *Fifty Million Frenchmen* (1929), *Anything Goes* (1934), *Kiss Me Kate* (1949), and *Can-Can* (1953). He also composed scores for several films. His songs include "Night and Day," "Begin the Beguine," "What Is This Thing Called Love," and "I've Got You Under My Skin."

PORTER, David Dixon (1813–91), American naval officer, born in Chester, Pa. He was the son of the American naval officer David Porter (1780–1843), who won fame during the War of 1812 as commander of the ship *Essex.* In his youth Porter served under his father, who held the successive posts of commander in chief of the West India Squadron and commander in chief of the Mexican navy. Beginning his naval career as a midshipman in 1829, Porter rose to the rank of commander by 1861. In 1862, during the American Civil War, he was placed in command of the mortar flotilla of the Union forces, joined the fleet of his adopted brother Capt. David Glasgow Farragut, and bombarded the New Orleans forts held by the Confederates. In command of the Mississippi squadron, he helped to bring about the fall of Vicksburg in 1863. Porter served as superintendent of the U.S. Naval Academy from 1865 to 1869. He became a vice admiral in 1866 and an admiral in 1870.

PORTER, Katherine Anne (1890–1980), American writer, who is generally regarded as one of the leading modern writers of short stories. She was born in Indian Creek, near San Antonio, Tex., and educated at private schools. She contributed articles to various newspapers while traveling in the U.S., Europe, and Mexico. Her first collection of short stories, *Flowering Judas* (1930), was quickly acclaimed. These stories, some with Mexican settings, were praised for their psychological insight and technical excellence. Among Porter's story collections are *Hacienda* (1934), *Noon Wine* (1937), *Pale Horse, Pale Rider* (1939), and *Collected Stories* (1965), which was awarded the 1966 Pulitzer Prize in fiction. The *Collected Essays and Occasional Writings of Katherine Anne Porter* appeared in 1970. Her only novel, *Ship of Fools* (1962), depicting a voyage on an ocean liner on the eve of World War II, was made into a motion picture in 1965.

PORTER, William Sydney. *See* HENRY, O.

PORT-GENTIL, city, W Gabon, capital of Ogooué-Maritime Prefecture, on an island in the Ogooué R. estuary E of Cape Lopez. The city is an important center of the Gabon petroleum industry as well as a sport and commercial fishing center. Exports include timber, petroleum, fish, cacao, and forest products from the interior. Local industries include fish processing, oil refining, sawmilling, and plywood fabricating. The community was originally a hunting camp called Mandji-Oroungou; a French post was established in 1885. The town developed after 1932 and was organized in 1956. Pop. (1983 est.) 123,300.

PORT HARCOURT, city, SE Nigeria, capital of Rivers State, on the Bonny R., in the Niger R. delta. The city is a leading port of the country, a road and rail hub, and a major industrial center, and its exports include palm oil, petroleum, coal, tin, columbite, palm products, cocoa, and peanuts. Industries of the area include sawmilling, auto assembly, food canning, flour milling, tobacco processing, and the manufacture of rubber, glass, metal, and paper products, cement, petroleum products, paint, enamelware, bicycles, furniture, and soap. Located in the city are the University of Port Harcourt (1975) and Rivers State University of Science and Technology (1971). Port Harcourt was established by the British in 1915 and serves E Nigeria and parts of N Nigeria. Pop. (1990 est.) 352,400.

PORT HURON, city, seat of Saint Clair Co., SE Michigan, a deepwater port on Lake Huron (from which its name is derived) and on the Saint Clair R.; inc. as a city 1857. It is a commercial, manufacturing, and tourist center; products include fabricated metal, paper, industrial lubricants, motor-vehicle parts, and rubber and wood items. A junior college is here. The Blue Water International Bridge (1937–38) and the International Train Tunnel connect the city with Sarnia, Ont., across the St. Clair R. Fort Saint Joseph was built here by the French about 1686, but permanent settlement began only after Fort Gratiot was constructed in 1814. Port Huron was created by the merger of five communities in 1837. It was a major lumbering center until the 1880s. Pop. (1980) 33,981; (1990) 33,694.

PORTLAND, city, seat of Cumberland Co., SW Maine, a deepwater port on Casco Bay; founded 1632, inc. as a city 1832. Largely situated on a peninsula, it is a major shipping, fishing, and commercial center; manufactures include printed materials, processed food, textiles,. forest products, and chemicals. The city is a gateway to the summer resort islands in Casco Bay and is linked by ferry with Nova Scotia. The University of Southern Maine (1878), Westbrook College (1831), the Portland School of Art (1882), and two junior colleges are here. The poet Henry Wadsworth Longfellow was born and lived in Portland; his house is now a museum.

The community, known by a number of different names, was destroyed by Indians in 1676 and by the French and Indians in 1690. In 1775, the settlement (then part of Falmouth), was severely damaged by the British. In 1786 it was separated from Falmouth and named for Portland, England. It served as the capital of Maine from 1820 to 1832. A great fire in 1866 leveled much of the central city. Pop. (1980) 61,572; (1990) 64,358.

PORTLAND, city, seat of Multnomah Co. and also in Clackamas and Washington counties, NW Oregon, on the Willamette R. near its confluence with the Columbia R., inc. 1851. It is Oregon's largest city, a major deepwater port, and an economic center for the surrounding region.

Economy. Portland has a diverse economy with a broad base of manufacturing, distribution, commercial trade, and regional government services. Manufactures include machinery, electronic equipment, metal products, transportation equipment, lumber, and wood products. The city is served by major interstate highways, railroad lines, light-rail and bus systems, and an international airport. The area is noted for its scenic beauty, with Mt. Hood and other snowcapped peaks of the Cascade Range visible from the city and the Columbia Gorge nearby. Tourism is, therefore, an important aspect of the city's economic base.

Educational and Cultural Institutions. Portland is the site of a number of institutions of higher education, including Lewis and Clark College (1867), the University of Portland (1901), Reed College (1909), Portland State University (1946), the Pacific Northwest College of Art (1909), the University of Oregon Health Sciences University (1974), Western States Chiropractic College (1907), Concordia College (1905), Warner Pacific College (1937), Columbia Christian College (1949), Multnomah School of the Bible (1936), Western Evangelical Seminary (1945), Western Conservative Baptist Seminary (1927); and three junior colleges. Points of interest in Portland include the Oregon Art Institute, which contains a collection of art and artifacts of the Indians of the Northwest; the Oregon Museum of Science and Industry, which includes a planetarium; the Metro Washington Park Zoo; the World Forestry Center; the

The famous International Rose Test Gardens in Portland, Oreg., have been the site of the annual Portland Rose Festival since 1907. In the background is Mt. Hood.
Greater Portland Convention and Visitors Association

Hoyt Arboretum; the Portland Center for the Performing Arts, home to the Portland Opera Association, the Oregon Symphony Orchestra, and the Oregon Ballet Theatre; and Memorial Coliseum, home of the Portland Trail Blazers, a major league basketball team. Popularly known as the City of Roses, Portland is the site of the International Rose Test Gardens of the American Rose Society and has been the scene of the annual Portland Rose Festival since 1907.

History. The community, laid out in 1845, is named for Portland, Maine, the hometown of one of its early residents. The settlement grew as a supply point and trading center for prospectors heading first for the California gold rush (1850s), then for the Alaska and Klondike gold rushes (1890s). Industrial growth was spurred by the completion in the early 1880s of the first transcontinental railroad connecting Portland to the East and by the construction in the 1930s of hydroelectric facilities on the Columbia and Willamette rivers. The Lewis and Clark Centennial Exposition of 1905, a world's fair, was held here. During the 1960s and '70s a program of urban redevelopment led to the modernization of the downtown area. In 1980 much volcanic ash fell on the Portland area as a result of eruptions of Mt. Saint Helens in nearby Washington State. Pop. (1980) 366,383; (1990) 437,319.

PORTLAND CEMENT. *See* CEMENT.

PORT LOUIS, city, NW Mauritius, capital of the country, located on the island of Mauritius. A port on the Indian Ocean, it is also the country's largest city and main commercial and administrative center. Major manufactures include processed food (especially sugar), wood products, and printed material. Port Louis is the site of the Mauritius Institute (1880), which operates a public library and the Port Louis Museum (featuring natural history collections), and the Citadel, a fortress built in 1838. Established by the French about 1735, the city grew as a deepwater port for ships traveling between Europe and Asia, but declined after the Suez Canal was opened in 1869. In 1968, when Mauritius became independent, Port Louis was chosen to be the nation's capital. Pop. (1988 est.) 139,000.

PORT MORESBY, city, SE Papua New Guinea, capital of the country and its Central District, located on New Guinea island, on Paga Point between Fairfax Harbor and Walter Bay of the Gulf of Papua. The city is in an area of plantations and experimental livestock and dairy farms. Its exports are copra, coffee, rubber, plywood, timber, and gold. Sawmilling, brewing, tobacco processing, and the manufacture of handicrafts and concrete are the principal industries, and fishing is of importance. Port Moresby is the site of government offices, the territorial museum, the University of Papua New Guinea (1965), the Institute of National Affairs, and sports facilities. Ela Beach, on the S side of the point, offers excellent bathing. Port Moresby was an important Allied military base during World War II. Pop. (1980) 123,624.

PORT NATAL. *See* DURBAN.

PORTO ALEGRE, city, SE Brazil, capital of Rio Grande do Sul State, a port on Lagoa dos Patos (an inlet of the Atlantic Ocean). Located at the junction of five rivers, Porto Alegre is the chief trade center of Brazil, S of São Paulo. Main industries include food processing, shipbuilding, and the manufacture of textiles. Exports are mainly agricultural and livestock products from the surrounding area. The city is the seat of the Federal University of Rio Grande do Sul (1934) and a Catholic university (1948). Porto Alegre was founded about 1742. Pop. (1980 prelim.) 1,108,883.

PORTO-NOVO, city, S Benin (formerly Dahomey), the capital of the country and of Ouémé Province, on Porto-Novo lagoon (an arm of the Gulf of Guinea). It is one of the country's largest cities, a major seaport, and the administrative and commercial center for the surrounding agricultural region. It is the site of the National Library, the National Archives, the Institute of Applied Research, and an old cathedral built by the Portuguese. The community was probably founded in the late 16th century as the capital of a small African state. In the 17th century the Portuguese built a trading post here; the settlement became a center for sending black Africans as slaves to the Americas. In the late 19th century the area came under the control of the French. It was made the capital of the French dependency of Dahomey in 1900, and in 1960, when the country became independent, it continued to serve as the administrative center of the new nation, which was renamed Benin in 1975. Pop. (1982 est.) 208,000.

PORTO RICO. *See* PUERTO RICO.

PORTRAITURE, representation in art of a person, suggesting his or her appearance, character, and personality. Portraits may be drawings, paintings, sculpture, engravings or other prints, or cut-paper silhouettes. They may range from a miniature painting, carved cameo, or struck coin to a larger-than-life-size statue. Some portraits are formal, idealized presentations, such as a tomb figure. Others may be spontaneous sketches or witty caricatures. The portrait artist's major concern is deciding how to combine his or her vision with the subject's ideas and actual appearance so as to create an effective work of art.

The Ancient, Byzantine, and Medieval Worlds. The first representations of persons as individuals

Bronze bust of Lucius Junius Brutus (3d-2d cent. BC, *Museo Capitolino, Rome), an example of Roman realistic portraiture.* Scala

were the funerary statues of rulers and nobles found in ancient Egyptian tombs. Those from the Old Kingdom (c. 2755–2255 BC) were highly stylized, emphasizing the dignity and eternal essence of the subject. More intimate, realistic portraits were sculpted in the New Kingdom (1570–1070 BC), notably those of the Pharaoh Ikhnaton and his family.

In Greece, individualized portraits were sculpted in the 5th and 4th centuries BC. They were generally idealized likenesses, which modified the actual appearance of the subject in conformity with the artist's idealized conception of what it should be, whether a youth, statesman, or some other figure. Late Greek sculpture of the Hellenistic period moved toward more realistic, emotionally expressive representation.

True realism in portraiture was the creation of the Romans, who executed exceptionally fine stone and bronze statues, life-size heads, and sepulchral monuments from late Republican times well into the 3d century of the empire. The Republican pieces appear austere, the imperial ones more subtly animated and expressive. Few specimens survive; of these, especially striking are the 2d and 3d century AD funerary portraits in encaustic, discovered in tombs at al-Fayyum, Egypt. Early Christian art was generally a symbolic treatment of religious subjects.

Byzantine art, which flourished from the 6th to the 15th century, further developed the spiritual aspects of Early Christian art. Byzantine portraiture found unique expression in brilliantly colored mosaic murals of religious and court figures in formal, ritualistic poses.

During the Middle Ages, most portraiture consisted of rulers, nobles, churchmen, and religious donors carved in stone on tombs or church facades, or depicted in paint on stained-glass windows and altarpieces and in murals and manuscript pages. In the Romanesque period, the figures tended to be stylized symbols; in the Gothic period, they gradually became more realistic representations of individuals.

Renaissance and Mannerism. During the Renaissance, portraiture flourished as a manifestation of humanism. Thus it revived the ancient classical interest in human affairs and emphasized development of the individual. In 15th-century Italy the Florentine sculptor Donatello revived portrait sculpture in stone, a style that was continued by Desiderio da Settignano and others. Pisanello struck fine portrait medals. Early Renaissance portrait painters of realistic murals and panels included Benozzo Gozzoli, Domenico Ghirlandaio, Sandro Botticelli, Andrea Mantegna, Giovanni Bellini, and Piero della Francesca. Celebrated masters of the High Renaissance, such as Leonardo, Raphael, Andrea del Sarto, Giorgione, and Titian, carried formal portraiture to new

Portrait of a Man *(15th cent.), by Dirk Bouts, an example of Flemish realism.*
Metropolitan Museum of Art–Bequest of Benjamin Altman

Raphael's Lady with a Unicorn *(1505-06, Galleria Borghese, Rome).* Scala

Louis David's unfinished portrait of Napoleon (1790s), in the neoclassical style. Scala

heights of refined perception and rich color and light.

Portraits by northern Renaissance painters show a preoccupation with realism and precise detail of physiognomy and costume. This approach is characteristic of panels by the Flemish masters Jan van Eyck, Rogier van der Weyden, and Hans Memling and the drawings and paintings of the later Germans Albrecht Dürer and Hans Holbein the Younger.

Mannerist portraits tended to exaggerate color, proportion, light, or expression in reaction to the balanced classicism of the High Renaissance. They include works by Agnolo Bronzino and Tintoretto in Italy and highly personal interpretations by El Greco in Spain.

The Baroque and Rococo Periods. Portraiture of the 17th century was dominated by the dramatic, exuberant baroque style. The Flemish painters Peter Paul Rubens and Sir Anthony van Dyck and Hyacinth Rigaud of France painted formal portraits in the grand manner, thus glorifying their aristocratic and richly appareled sitters. This approach was expressed in sculpture by Giovanni Lorenzo Bernini, an Italian, and continued by the 18th-century English painter Sir Joshua Reynolds. Rembrandt in the Netherlands, Philippe de Champaigne in France, and Diego de Velázquez and Francisco de Zurbarán in Spain concentrated on the inner condition of their subjects. Rembrandt, Franz Hals, Jan Steen, and other Dutch painters depicted middle- and lower-class sitters.

The decorative, intimate refinement of the late baroque style called rococo influenced 18th-century portraiture, as in paintings by François Boucher, Jean Baptiste Chardin, and Maurice Quentin de La Tour and the sculpture of Jean Antoine Houdon in France. Portraits by Thomas Gainsborough, George Romney, and Sir Henry Raeburn in England and Scotland flattered the aristocracy with a softened, idealized manner. William Hogarth did dignified yet realistic portraits and lively group scenes. John Singleton Copley, Gilbert Stuart, John Trumbull, and Charles Willson Peale painted simpler, realistic portraits of middle-class citizens of the American colonies and the new republic.

Modern Period. In the 19th century most major artists tried their hand at portraiture. The Spaniard Francisco de Goya painted with simplicity and psychological insight. Formal portraits in the disciplined neoclassical style were painted by Jacques Louis David in France and sculpted by Antonio Canova in Italy. Neoclassicism influenced the calm, realistic portraits of J. A. D. Ingres in France. Eugene Delacroix excelled in portraiture in the more dramatic, colorful romantic style. Gustave Courbet worked in a robust, realistic style. Elements of caricature and satire inspired the calligraphic drawings, paintings, and prints of Henri de Toulouse-Lautrec and especially of Honoré Daumier.

The development of photography (q.v.) in the mid-19th century made realistic portraiture less

David Hockney's A Visit with Christopher and Don, Santa Monica Canyon *(1984).* © David Hockney

Pablo Picasso's expressive portrait of Sabartes, Le Bock *(1901).* Scala

important. In France, where artists experimented with new approaches to art, portraits by the painters Edouard Manet and Mary Cassatt reflect impressionism. Vincent van Gogh and Paul Cézanne painted emotionally intense portraits. Auguste Rodin, combining romantic, realist, and impressionist influences, sought psychological understanding in sculpted form. This approach was continued in 20th-century England by Sir Jacob Epstein, who created dramatic portraits of prominent individuals in bronze.

In early 20th-century France, Amadeo Modigliani and Pablo Picasso painted portraits influenced by cubism and expressionism. The portraits done by Chaim Soutine in France and Oskar Kokoschka in Germany were especially psychologically expressive.

American portraiture tended to be more realistic. It was exemplified in the 19th century by the painter Thomas Eakins and the sculptors Daniel Chester French and Augustus Saint-Gaudens. In the early 20th century, John Singer Sargent, who was trained in Europe, painted brilliant, flattering portraits of fashionable society. Realism predominated, however, in the paintings of George Bellows and Grant Wood, and in the harsh, "new realist" nudes of Philip Pearlstein (1924-).

Non-Western Cultures. In societies that emphasize community life and religious ritual, portraiture generally does not flourish. Wooden masks of African and North American Indian tribal peoples represent stylized supernatural beings. Lifesize, naturalistic bronze heads of the kings of Benin, made in Nigeria in the 15th to the 17th century, were ritual objects rather than memorials of individuals. In pre-Columbian civilizations, Maya reliefs show stylized priests and nobles more important for their office than for their individuality. Pottery vessels of the Chavín, the Mochica, and other peoples are realistically modeled in a variety of faces, but they seem to have been created for ritual use.

Portraiture appears late in Muslim art. It began in the 16th and 17th centuries as album leaves and book illustrations depicting members of the Safavid court of Persia, where a tradition of figural art existed. Persian portraiture influenced the delicate, realistic portrayals of the members of the Ottoman Turkish court and the Mughal court in India. In non-Muslim India, monks, saints, and rulers were generally pictured in sculpture murals and coinage according to established canons of beauty.

China has a long tradition of realistic portrait painting. It began with murals of rulers and officials in the Eastern (Later) Han dynasty (AD 25-220) and continued into the 20th century in the form of pairs of funerary portraits of court officials and their wives.

Japanese portraiture, influenced by Chinese example, began in the Nara period (7th-8th cent.) with naturalistic statues of Buddhist monks in lacquer, clay, or wood. Portrait sculpture of monks and priests of the Kamakura period (12th–14th cent.) was powerful and naturalistic. The period also encompassed the emergence of realistic painted portraits of courtiers, poets, and military heroes, in scenes or as single figures. Woodblock printmakers in the Edo period (17th–19th cent.) perceptively portrayed courtesans, actors, and other inhabitants of Tokyo's pleasure quarters.

For further information on this topic, see the Bibliography in volume 28, section 714.

PORT SAID, city, NE Egypt, a port on the Mediterranean Sea, at the entrance to the Suez Canal. The city is built on low, sandy ground between Lake Manzilah and the Mediterranean Sea. The principal occupations in Port Said include fishing and the manufacture of chemicals, processed food, and cigarettes. It also has a large export trade, notably in cotton and rice, and is a fueling station for ships traveling the canal route. It is also a summer resort. Port Said was established in 1859, when work on the Suez Canal began. Pop. (1986 est.) 382,000.

PORTSMOUTH, city, Hampshire, S England, on Portsea Island, on the English Channel. Portsmouth is one of the most important naval stations in Great Britain; the Royal Dockyard here is the main source of employment. The city has some commercial wharves, and passenger traffic flows from here to the Continent; aerospace industries are also important to its economy. The Southsea section of the city is a popular seaside resort. Noteworthy structures include the cathedral (mostly 12th cent.); the HMS *Victory,* the flagship of Adm. Horatio Nelson at the Battle of Trafalgar (1805); and the house in which Charles Dickens was born. A polytechnic college is also here. Portsmouth was founded in 1194 by Richard I. In 1496 the Royal Dockyard was established and the world's first dry dock was built here. During World War II, because of its strategic military significance, Portsmouth was damaged by extensive German aerial bombings. Pop. (1991 prelim.) 174,700.

PORTSMOUTH, city, Rockingham Co., SE New Hampshire, a seaport on the Atlantic Ocean and on the Piscataqua R., opposite Kittery, Maine; settled 1623, inc. as a city 1849. It is a commercial, manufacturing, fishing, and tourist center. Products include processed seafood, footwear, electronic equipment, cable, gypsum goods, and industrial machinery. The great Portsmouth Naval Shipyard (situated in Kittery) is important to the local economy. Points of interest include Strawbery Banke, a restoration of the settlement as it was in colonial times; the Richard Jackson House (c. 1664); and the John Paul Jones House (1758), where the naval hero lived in 1777 while his ship, the *Ranger,* was being built. A junior college is in the city. The community, named for Portsmouth, England, was the capital of colonial New Hampshire. The Treaty of Portsmouth, ending the Russo-Japanese War, was signed at the Portsmouth Naval Shipyard in 1905. Pop. (1980) 26,254; (1990) 25,925.

PORTSMOUTH, city, seat of Scioto Co., S Ohio, at the confluence of the Ohio and Scioto rivers; inc. as a city 1851. It is a commercial, manufacturing, and transportation center; products include iron castings, wood products, mopeds, chemicals, and shoelaces. Shawnee State University (1986) is here, and many Indian mounds and a U.S. nuclear facility producing fissionable material are nearby. The community was founded in 1803 and is probably named for Portsmouth, N.H. It developed as a transshipment point after the completion (1832) of the Ohio Canal, which linked it with Cleveland; it grew as a rail center in the 1850s. The city suffered major river flooding in 1937. Pop. (1980) 25,943; (1990) 22,676.

PORTSMOUTH, independent city, SE Virginia, a major seaport on the Elizabeth R. and Hampton Roads, near Norfolk and Newport News; laid out 1752, inc. as a city 1858. It is the site of the great Norfolk Naval Shipyard, one of the leading facilities in the U.S. for shipbuilding and repair. Manufactures also include electronic equipment, chemicals, clothing, and processed food. A U.S. Navy hospital and a U.S. Coast Guard district headquarters are here. Tourist attractions include the Naval Shipyard Museum, the Light Ship Museum, Trinity Episcopal Church (1762), and Olde Towne, a section of the city containing many historic structures.

A private boatyard was built here in 1767, and during the American Revolution Portsmouth served as a British naval base. A U.S. naval shipyard was founded here in 1801. During the American Civil War the Confederates briefly held (1861–62) the shipyard, and here they converted the steamship *Merrimack* into an ironclad warship (rechristened *Virginia*); it engaged the Union ironclad vessel *Monitor* in a famous battle (March 9, 1862) in Hampton Roads. The city is named for Portsmouth, England. Pop. (1980) 104,577; (1990) 103,907.

PORT OF SPAIN, also Port-of-Spain, city, Trinidad and Tobago, capital of the country, a seaport on the NW coast of the island of Trinidad, located on the Gulf of Paria. It is the commercial center and leading port of the country. Major manufactures in the area include alcoholic beverages, tobacco products, building materials, processed food, textiles, chemicals, and plastic items. Tourism is also important to the city's economy. Port of Spain is the site of the Royal Botanical Gardens; the National Archives; the National Museum and Art Gallery, with a collection of historical and natural history items and fine art; an Anglican cathedral (1816–23); and a Roman Catholic cathedral (consecrated 1832). In the vicinity of Port of Spain are Piarco International Airport and the University of the West Indies (1946).

An Indian village known as Conquerabia occupied the site when the Spanish settled in the area in 1595 and renamed the community Puerto de España. After the British took control of the island in 1797, the settlement's name was Anglicized to Port of Spain. The city served as the capital of the Federation of the West Indies from 1958 to 1962, when the grouping was dissolved. Pop. (1984 est.) 60,700.

PORT SUDAN, city, NE Sudan, on the Red Sea. The only seaport of Sudan, it handles most of the foreign trade of the country. It is a commercial and shipping center for the rich cotton-growing regions of the valley of the Nile R. The principal exports are live cattle and sheep, hides and skins, gum arabic, and cotton. Port Sudan was founded in 1906 as a modern harbor to replace Suakin, which had become obstructed by rapidly growing coral reefs. Pop. (1983) 206,727.

PORT TALBOT, town, Port Talbot District, West Glamorgan, S Wales, on Swansea Bay of the Bristol Channel. It is the site of one of the largest steel-producing complexes in Europe. Other products include iron and tinplate; coal is mined in the vicinity. Its port was improved in 1970 to allow the docking of large ore-carrying vessels. The town is also a seaside resort and local trade center. Dock facilities were opened here in 1837, and the town developed as a coal-shipping center. Pop. (Port Talbot District, 1991 prelim.) 49,900.

PORTUGAL, republic, SW Europe, situated in the W portion of the Iberian Peninsula, bounded on the N and E by Spain and on the S and W by the Atlantic Ocean. The Azores and Madeira Islands in the Atlantic are considered integral parts of the republic. The total area of metropolitan Portugal, including the Azores (2335 sq km/902 sq mi) and the Madeira Islands (796 sq km/307 sq mi), is 92,082 sq km (35,553 sq mi). Portugal has one overseas territory, Macau (Macao), in E Asia near Hong Kong.

LAND AND RESOURCES

The frontiers of Portugal are defined by mountains and rivers, and the interior is largely mountainous. In the W and S the mountains descend to a large coastal plain that is intensively cultivated. The highest range is the Serra da Estrela in central Portugal, rising to almost 2000 m (almost 6562 ft). Portugal is traversed by three great rivers, which rise in Spain and empty into the Atlantic Ocean. The Tagus (Tejo), with Lisbon situated at its mouth, is the largest river; followed by the Douro, with Oporto at its mouth; and the Guadiana, which forms part of the E frontier. A fourth river, the Minho, forms part of the N frontier.

A view of Lisbon, capital of Portugal. The Aguas Livres aqueduct was constructed during the reign of King John V in the 18th century to bring water from the north to supply the city's public fountains.
Joachim Messerschmidt–Bruce Coleman, Inc.

The seacoast city of Nazaré is built on a hillside on the Atlantic, north of Lisbon. Most of Portugal is hilly or mountainous, with deep river valleys giving access to the coast. Bruce Coleman, Inc.

Climate. The climate varies according to altitude, and high temperatures occur only in the comparatively low regions of the S. The mean annual temperature N of the Douro R. is about 10° C (about 50° F); between the Tagus and Douro, about 15.6° C (about 60° F); and in the valley of the Guadiana, about 18.3° C (about 65° F). Rainfall is heavy, particularly in the N.

Natural Resources. The most valuable of Portugal's natural resources are its minerals. Much of this wealth was not developed until after World War II. Among the mineral resources are coal, copper, gold, iron ore, kaolin, tin, and wolframite, which is a source of tungsten. Although a substantial segment of the population supports itself by agriculture, the land is not particularly suited to this occupation. The plants and animals of Portugal are virtually identical with those of Spain. The most abundant trees are the evergreen oak, cork oak, poplar, and olive. Grapevines flourish in the arid soil, and port wine from Oporto and Madeira wine from Madeira are world famous. Wild animals include the wolf, lynx, wildcat, fox, wild boar, wild goat, deer, and hare. Birdlife and insects abound. Portugal also has an abundance of waterpower resources in its rivers and mountain streams.

POPULATION

The Portuguese are a combination of several ethnic elements, principally Iberians, Romans, Visigoths, and later Moors. The people still live, for the most part, in rural villages.

Population Characteristics. The population of Portugal, including the Azores and Madeira islands, was (1989 est.) 10,372,000. The overall population density was about 113 persons per sq km (292 per sq mi).

Political Divisions. Mainland Portugal is divided into 18 districts for administrative purposes: Aveiro, Beja, Braga, Bragança, Castelo Branco, Coimbra, Évora, Faro, Guarda, Leiria, Lisbon, Oporto, Portalalegre, Santarém, Setúbal, Viana do Castelo, Vila Real, and Viseu. The Azores and Madeira each constitute an autonomous region.

Principal Cities. Lisbon (pop., 1981 prelim., 812,385) is the capital, largest city, and leading seaport of Portugal. Other important cities include Oporto (329,104), the second-largest city and seaport; Coimbra (56,568), an industrial center; and Faro (20,687), in the Algarve resort area.

Religion and Language. Roman Catholicism is the faith of more than 94% of the Portuguese people. The constitution guarantees freedom of religion, and some Protestant churches have been established. The official language of the country is Portuguese.

Education. Elementary education is free and compulsory between the ages of 6 and 15. Secondary education is voluntary. In the late 1980s Portugal had about 12,700 primary schools annually attended by some 1,234,300 pupils and staffed by more than 75,400 teachers. The country's 1500 secondary schools were staffed by about 53,900 teachers and had about 647,400 students.

Approximately 109,200 students attended Portugal's institutions of higher education in the late 1980s. The University of Coimbra, in Coimbra, and the University of Lisbon, in Lisbon, were both founded in the 13th century in Lisbon.

Culture. Portuguese culture is closely related to Spanish culture and has been influenced by the three primary cultures from which it derives: the Latin, the Visigoth (*see* GOTHS), and the Muslim (*see* ISLAM).

A shepherd guides a flock of sheep along a winding road in the Portuguese countryside. UPI

Lisbon has a number of important libraries, including the Library of the Academy of Sciences, the Ajuda Library, the National Library, and the Military Library. The National Archives of Torre do Tombo, also in Lisbon, is noteworthy for its collection of historical documents dating from the 9th century. The provincial libraries in Oporto, Évora, Braga, and Mafra contain many rare old books and large manuscript collections. Various specialized libraries are attached to the universities.

Museums of archaeology, art, and ethnography are found in the principal cities and towns of each district. The art museum in Coimbra is famous for its collection of 16th-century sculpture; the museum in Évora is known for Roman sculpture and 16th-century paintings. The National Museum of Ancient Art, in Lisbon, houses decorative art and paintings from the 12th to the 19th century. Also in Lisbon are the National Museum of Contemporary Art; the National Museum of Natural History; the Calouste Gulbenkian Museum, with a collection of fine art dating from 2800 BC to the 20th century; the Ethnographical Museum; and the Archaeological Museum.

Some of the relics found in Portugal date from prehistoric times. Dolmens, ancient stone burial chambers, have been found along the Atlantic coast, and in the Algarve region, tombs dating from the Iron Age have been discovered. Some of the country's most important monuments were constructed during the Roman occupation of the Iberian Peninsula (2d cent. BC–5th cent. AD). The so-called Temple of Diana in the SE, the ruins of the city of Conimbriga on the W coast, and the bridge of Chaves in Trásos Montes e Alto Douro in the E are fine examples of Roman architecture. Subsequent occupations by the Visigoths in the 5th century and by the Muslim Moors in the 8th century can be discerned in the styles of many of Portugal's buildings and churches.

The 14th century was the golden age of Portuguese sculpture, at which time such notable monuments as the tombs of the kings at Alcobaça were produced. The sculptors of the Renaissance and baroque periods in Portugal did their finest work for the church.

The Portuguese are a musical people, and their folk music ranges from very lively songs and dances to sad laments. Similar to other music of the Iberian Peninsula, Portuguese music reflects three major influences: the Roman Catholic church, the troubadours of the kings, and the wandering minstrels who sang their stories across the countryside.

For a discussion of the literature of the country, *see* PORTUGUESE LITERATURE.

ECONOMY

Although the Portuguese economy grew by 5.3% annually during 1965–80, the economic growth rate slowed to less than 1% during the 1980s, and Portugal remains the least developed nation in Western Europe. The country's gross national product in the late 1980s was $29.6 billion, or about $2890 per capita. The estimated annual budget in the late 1980s included $8 billion in revenue and $11.1 billion in expenditure.

Agriculture. Agriculture engages some 20% of the employed civilian working population and accounts for about 8% of the yearly gross domestic product (GDP). Chief crops and annual production figures for the late 1980s were potatoes (795,000 metric tons), grapes (1.4 million), tomatoes (865,000), corn (663,000), wheat (401,000), and olives (149,000). Portugal is one of the world's leading producers of wine and olive oil. Livestock numbered approximately 1.4 million cattle, 5.2 million sheep, 2.8 million pigs, and 18 million poultry.

Forestry and Fishing. Approximately 40% of Portugal is forested. The country is one of the largest producers of cork in the world; in the mid-1980s the annual output of cork products exceeded 301,400 metric tons. The roundwood harvest in the late 1980s amounted to 9.4 million cu m (332 million cu ft) annually.

Commercial fishing is also important to the Portuguese economy. The annual fish catch in the late 1980s totaled about 395,250 metric tons, of which more than 25% was sardines.

Mining. Annual mineral production in Portugal in the late 1980s included 254,000 metric tons of coal, 279,100 metric tons of copper-bearing iron pyrites, 57,000 metric tons of kaolin, 2000 metric tons of tungsten concentrates, and smaller quantities of copper, gold, silver, and tin. Mining of uranium deposits was begun in 1979.

A typical coastal view. Traditional occupations, such as net-fishing, coexist in Portugal with a highly developed tourist industry.
Klaus D. Francke–Peter Arnold, Inc.

A beachfront scene at Estoril, a resort north of Lisbon.
American Export Lines

Manufacturing. Manufacturing is of increasing importance to the economy of Portugal, employing about 23% of the labor force. Major manufactures include processed food; textiles; machinery; chemicals; wood, glass and pottery items; refined petroleum; and building materials. Annual output in the mid-1980s included about 27,400 metric tons of processed sardines, 285,900 metric tons of refined sugar, 1.3 million metric tons of fertilizer, and 386,900 metric tons of steel ingots. An oil refinery and petrochemical complex opened S of Lisbon in 1979. Products of cottage industries, such as lace, pottery, and tiles, are world famous.

Energy. In the late 1980s, Portugal had an installed electricity-generating capacity of about 6.9 million kw, and annual production was some 20.1 billion kwh. About 46% of Portugal's electricity was generated by hydroelectric facilities.

Currency and Foreign Trade. The unit of currency in Portugal is the escudo, consisting of 100 centavos (150 escudos equal U.S.$1; 1990). In the late 1980s annual Portuguese imports totaled about $17.9 billion and exports about $12.8 billion. Principal imports included mineral fuels, machinery and transportation equipment, and food and livestock. Principal exports included clothing, textile yarns and fabrics, and wood and paper products. Among Portugal's chief trading partners were Germany, Great Britain, the U.S., France, Spain, and Italy. Foreign exchange receipts from tourism, amounting to more than $2 billion annually in the late 1980s, help to compensate for the chronic trade deficit.

Transportation. Portugal has about 61,600 km (about 38,280 mi) of paved roads and some 2.6 million registered passenger cars. The railroad system has a total length of about 3610 km (about 2240 mi). Most of the tracks are wide gauge to accommodate shipments from Spain. The merchant marine comprises more than 300 vessels. Major seaports include Lisbon, Leixões, Setúbal, and Funchal (Madeira). Transportes Aéreos Portugueses (TAP), the national airline, provides domestic and international service. A number of foreign airlines also have scheduled stops at Lisbon's international airport.

Communications. In the late 1980s Portugal had about 2.1 million telephones, 2.2 million radios, and 1.6 million television receivers. Daily newspapers numbered about 30 and had a combined circulation of more than 850,000.

Labor. In the late 1980s the total labor force in Portugal was about 4.7 million, of which labor unions, or syndicates, enrolled approximately 55%.

GOVERNMENT

Portugal is governed under a constitution promulgated in 1976 and revised in 1982. Although the constitution initially called for the creation of a "classless" state based on public ownership of land, natural resources, and the principal means of production, this socialist language was stricken in 1989. The right to strike and the right of assembly are guaranteed, and censorship and the death penalty are proscribed.

Executive. Portugal is a republic with a president, popularly elected to a 5-year term, as head of state. The president of the republic appoints the prime minister, who is the country's chief administrative official. The prime minister presides over a cabinet of about 15 ministers.

Legislature. Legislative power is vested in a unicameral parliament, the Assembly of the Republic. Members of the Assembly are elected under a system of proportional representation and serve 4-year terms. The Assembly had a total of 230 seats in the early 1990s.

Judiciary. The judicial system in Portugal is headed by the supreme court, which is made up of a president and 29 judges. Below the supreme court are courts of appeal and ordinary and special district courts.

Local Government. Local authority is vested in the district governors and district legislatures. Each district is further subdivided into parishes, each with an elected assembly and council.

Political Parties. The leading political parties in Portugal are the Socialist party (PS), the Social Democratic party (PSD), the United People's Alliance (APU), and the Social Democratic Center party (CDS). Running in coalition as the Democratic Alliance, the PSD and CDS together captured parliamentary majorities in the elections of 1979 and 1980. In 1983, however, with the Democratic Alliance dissolved, the PS swept into power in coalition with the PSD. The PSD led the vote in the parliamentary elections of 1985 and won clear majorities in 1987 and 1991.

Defense. Portugal, a member of the North Atlantic Treaty Organization, has modern, well-equipped armed forces. Military service is compulsory for male citizens for terms of 16 to 24 months. In the late 1980s the armed forces numbered about 75,300 people—44,000 in the army, 16,100 in the navy, and 15,200 in the air force.

HISTORY

Up to the Middle Ages, the history of Portugal is inseparable from that of Spain. Present-day Portugal became a part of the Roman province of Lusitania in the 2d century BC. In the 5th century AD control of the region passed to the Visigoths, and in the 8th century it was included in the area of Moorish Muslim conquest. In 997 the territory between the Douro and Minho rivers (now northern Portugal) was retaken from the Moors by Bermudo II, king of León (d. 999), and in 1064 the reconquest was completed as far south as present-day Coimbra by Ferdinand I, king of Cas-

INDEX TO MAP OF PORTUGAL

Districts*

Aveiro .... A 2
Azores .... B 5
Beja .... B 3
Braga .... A 2
Bragança .... B 2
Castelo Branco .... B 3
Coimbra .... A 2
Évora .... B 3
Faro .... A 4
Guarda .... B 2
Leiria .... A 3
Lisbon .... A 3
Madeira .... A 4
Oporto (Porto) .... A 2
Portalegre .... B 3
Santarém .... A 3
Setúbal .... A 3
Viana do Castelo .... A 3
Vila Real .... B 2
Viseu .... B 2

Cities and Towns

Abrantes .... A 3
Águeda .... A 2
Albufeira .... A 4
Alcácer do Sal .... A 3
Alcobaça .... A 3
Aldeia Nova .... B 4
Aljezur .... A 4
Aljustrel .... A 4
Almeirim .... A 3
Almodôvar .... B 4
Alpiarça .... A 3
Alportel .... B 4
Alter do Chão .... B 3
Alvalade .... A 4
Alvito .... A 3
Amadora .... A 3
Amarante .... A 2
Amareleja .... B 3
Anadia .... A 2
Arronches .... B 3
Aveiro .... A 2
Barcelos .... A 2
Barrancos .... B 3
Barreiro .... A 3
Batalha .... A 3
Beja .... B 3
Borba .... B 3
Braga .... A 2
Bragança .... B 2
Caldas da Rainha .... A 3
Campo Maior .... B 3
Cantanhede .... A 2
Cartaxo .... A 3
Cascais .... A 3
Castelo Branco .... B 3
Castelo de Vide .... B 3
Castro Daire .... B 2
Castro Marim .... B 4
Castro Verde .... A 4
Celorico da Beira .... C 2
Cercal .... A 4
Chamusca .... A 3
Chaves .... B 2
Coimbra .... A 2
Coruche .... A 3
Covilhã .... B 2
Crato .... B
Cuba .... B
Elvas .... B
Ericeira .... A
Espinho .... A
Esposende .... A
Estoril .... A
Estremoz .... B
Évora .... B
Fafe .... A
Faro .... A
Fátima .... A
Feira .... A
Ferreira do Alentejo .... A
Figueira da Foz .... A
Freixo .... B
Fronteira .... B
Fundão .... B
Gouveia .... B
Grândola .... A
Guarda .... B
Guimarães .... A
Idanha-a-Nova .... B
Ílhavo .... A
Lagoa .... A
Lagos .... A
Lamego .... B
Leiria .... A
Lisbon (Lisboa)(Cap.) ... A
Loulé .... A
Lourinhã .... A
Lousã .... A
Mafra .... A
Maia .... A
Mangualde .... B
Marinha Grande .... A
Marinhas .... A
Matosinhos .... A
Mealhada .... A
Melgaço .... A
Mértola .... B
Mira .... A
Miranda do Corvo .... A
Mirandela .... B
Mogadouro .... B
Monforte .... B
Montargil .... A
Montemor o Novo .... A
Montemor-o-Velho .... A
Montijo .... A
Moura .... B
Mourão .... B
Muge .... A
Nazaré .... A
Nelas .... A
Nisa .... B
Óbidos .... A
Odemira .... A
Oleiros .... B
Olhão .... B
Oporto (Porto) .... A
Ovar. .... A
Pampilhosa da Serra ..... B
Penafiel .... A
Penamacor .... B
Peniche .... A
Pombal .... A
Ponte de Sôr .... B
Ponte do Lima .... A
Portalegre .... B
Portimão .... A
Porto (Oporto) .... A

* Portugal is divided into 18 mainland districts bearing the same names as their respective capitals. The Azores and Madeira are offshore autonomous regions.

Porto de Mos . . . . .A 3
Póvoa de Varzim . . . . . .A 2
Proença-a-Nova . . . . . . .A 3
Redondo . . . . .B 3
Reguengos de Monsaraz. . . . . .B 3
Rio Maior. . . . . .A 3
Rosmaninhal. . . . . .B 3
Sabugal. . . . . .B 2
Salvaterra de Magos . . .A 3
Santarém. . . . . .A 3
Santiago do Cacém . . . .A 3
São Bras de Alportel (Alportel) . . . . .B 4
São Pedro do Sul. . . . . .B 2
São Teotónio . . . . .A 4
Serpa. . . . . .B 4
Sertã . . . . .A 3
Sesimbra. . . . . .A 3
Setúbal . . . . .A 3
Silves. . . . . .A 4
Sines . . . . .A 4
Sintra. . . . . .A 3
Soure. . . . . .A 2
Tavira. . . . . .B 4
Tomar . . . . .A 3
Torre de Moncorvo . . . .B 2
Torres Novas . . . . .A 3
Torres Vedras. . . . . .A 3
Vendas Novas. . . . . .A 3
Viana do Alentejo. . . . . .B 3
Viana do Castelo . . . . . .A 2
Vieira de Leiria. . . . . . . .A 3
Vila do Conde. . . . . .A 2
Vila Franca de Xira. . . . .A 3
Vila Nova de Fozcôa . . .B 2
Vila Nova de Gaia. . . . . .A 2
Vila Pouca de Aguiar. . .B 2
Vila Real . . . . .B 2
Vila Real de Santo António . . . . .B 4
Vila Velhao de Ródão . .B 3
Vila Verde . . . . .B 2
Vila Viçosa . . . . .B 3
Vimioso . . . . .B 2
Vinhais. . . . . .B 2
Viseu . . . . .B 2

Other Features

Alcántara (res.). . . . . . . .B 3
Azores (islands) . . . . . . .B 5
Douro (river). . . . . .B 2
Espichel (cape). . . . . . . .A 3
Estrela (mts.). . . . . .B 2
Estrela, Malhao da (peak). . . . . .B 2
Guadiana (river) . . . . . . .B 4
Lima (river) . . . . .A 2
Madeira (islands) . . . . . .A 5
Minho (river). . . . . .A 2
Mira (river) . . . . .A 4
Monchique (mts.). . . . . .A 4
Mondego (cape). . . . . . .A 2
Mondego (river) . . . . . . .B 2
Ossa (mts.). . . . . .B 3
Roca (cape) . . . . .A 3
Sado (river). . . . . .A 3
Santa Maria (cape). . . . .B 4
São Vincent (cape). . . . .A 4
Setúbal (bay). . . . . .A 3
Tagus (Tejo) (river) . . . .A 3
Tâmega (river) . . . . .B 2
Tejo (Tagus) (river) . . . .B 3
Xarrama (river). . . . . . . .A 3

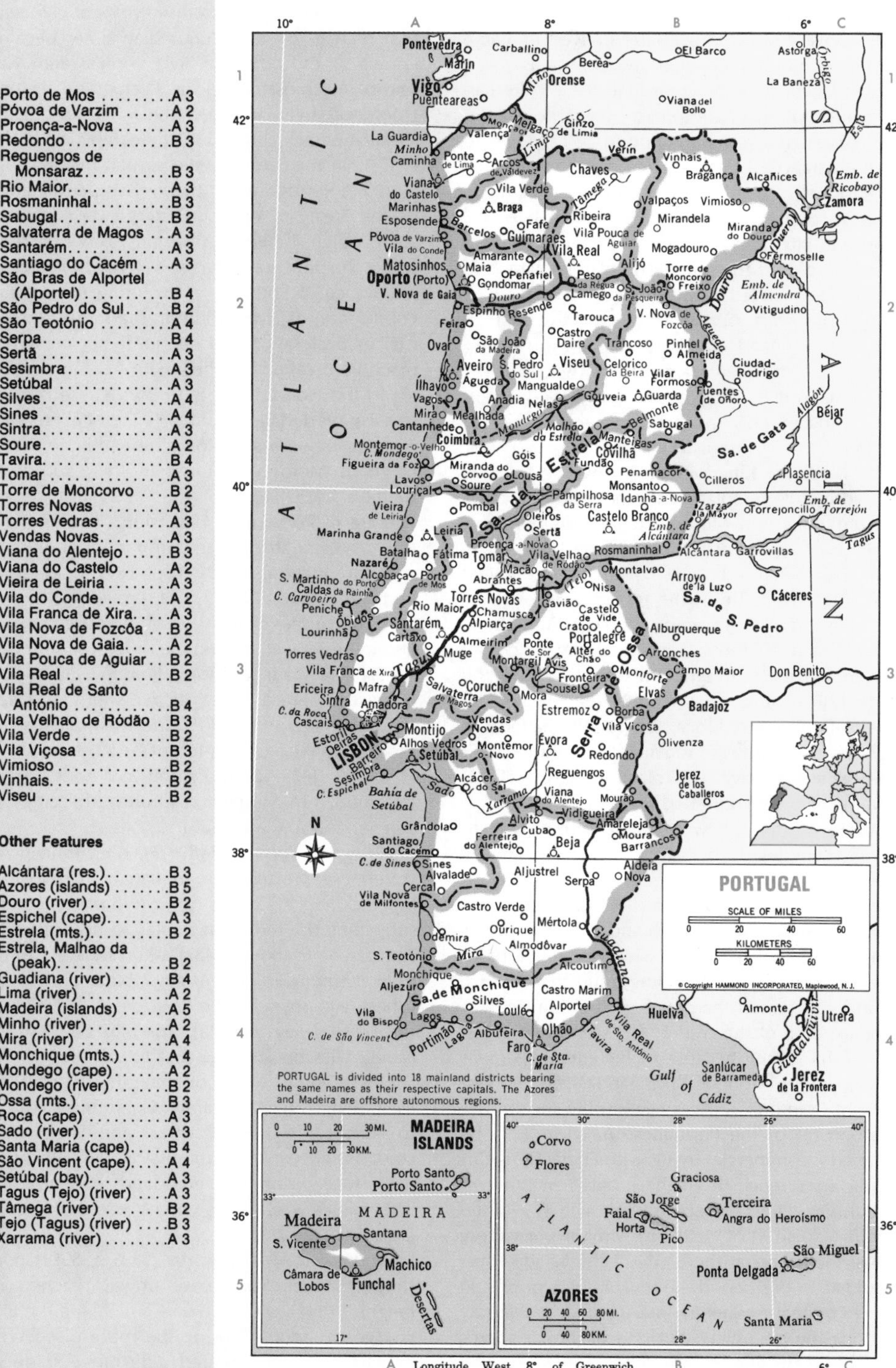

tile and León. The reconquered districts were then organized into a feudal county, composed of Spanish fiefs. Portugal later derived its name from the northernmost fief, the Comitatus Portaculenis, which extended around the old Roman seaport of Portus Cale (present-day Oporto).

In 1093 Henry of Burgundy (d. 1112) came to the assistance of Castile when it was invaded by the Moors. In gratitude Alfonso I of Castile made Henry count of Portugal. On the death of Alfonso in 1109, Count Henry, and later his widow, Teresa, refused to continue feudal allegiance to León. He invaded León and began a series of peninsular wars, but with little success. In 1128 his son, Alfonso Henriques, later Alfonso I, king of Portugal, rebelled against his mother. The Portuguese knights accepted Alfonso as king in 1143, and in 1179 the pope recognized the independence of Portugal.

The Medieval Kingdom of Portugal. Alfonso I, aided by the Templars and other military orders sworn to fight the Moors, extended the border of the new kingdom as far south as the Tagus River. His son Sancho I (r. 1185–1211) encouraged Christians to settle in the reconquered area by establishing self-governing municipalities there. The Cistercian monks occupied the land and promoted efficient agricultural methods. In the late 12th century, the Almohads, a Muslim dynasty from North Africa, temporarily halted the Christians' southward movement, but after their defeat at Las Navas de Tolosa in Castile (1212) the reconquest continued.

King Alfonso III, who reigned from 1248 to 1279, completed the expulsion of the Moors from the Algarve and moved the capital of Portugal from Coimbra to Lisbon. He also began the practice of governing with the aid of a Cortes (representative assembly), which included members of the nobility, the clergy, and the citizens, and he increased the power of the monarchy at the expense of the church. His son Diniz, called the Farmer King because of his encouragement of agriculture, founded the nation's first university at Coimbra and was responsible for the development of the Portuguese navy. In 1294 he signed a commercial treaty with England, beginning a sequence of alliances between the two countries. Diniz's successor, Alfonso IV, joined with Alfonso XI of Castile to win a major victory over the Moors at the Battle of the Salado River in 1340. In this period the royal houses of Castile and Portugal frequently intermarried, repeatedly raising the possibility that one of the kingdoms might be absorbed by the other.

After the death of Ferdinand I, the last of the legitimate descendants of Henry of Burgundy, his illegitimate half brother John I secured the Portuguese throne in 1385, after two years of civil war. His branch of the Burgundian line became known as the house of Aviz. John's reign was one of the most notable in Portuguese history. He successfully defended the kingdom against Castilian attack and in 1385 defeated Castile decisively in the Battle of Aljubarrota. In 1386 England and Portugal allied themselves permanently by the Treaty of Windsor. The greatest fame of John's reign, however, rests on the work done under the direction of his son Henry the Navigator, prince of Portugal, in exploring the African coast for an eastward route to the Indies. A century of exploration and conquest began, which made Portugal one of the greatest colonial powers in the world. In 1418–19 Portuguese navigators explored Madeira and in 1427 discovered the Azores. A successful Portuguese military campaign in Morocco resulted in the capture of Ceuta in 1415.

The Era of Portuguese Expansion. Madeira and the Azores rapidly became important centers of sugar production, and the capture of Ceuta gave Portugal a foothold in Africa, providing the impetus for further exploration of the African coast. Using the caravel, a new type of light sailing vessel especially adapted for Atlantic voyages, Portuguese mariners sailed as far south as Cape Verde in 1444, and by 1460 they had reached Sierra Leone. Meanwhile, John I's successors, King Duarte (r. 1433–38) and Alfonso V, sent further expeditions to Morocco, capturing the cities of Tangier and Arzila (Asilah).

The reign of John II (1481–95). King John II restored the prestige the monarchy had lost at home during the reigns of his two predecessors, subjecting the turbulent nobles to his authority. Abroad, he founded (1482) a Portuguese stronghold at Elmina, in present-day Ghana, and established relations with the kingdom of the Kongo (in present-day Angola). In 1487–88, Bartholomeu Dias became the first to sail around the southern end of Africa, opening the sea route to the Orient. After Christopher Columbus's voyage to America in 1492, Portugal and Spain concluded the Treaty of Tordesillas (1494), allocating to Portugal all undiscovered lands east of a line 370 leagues west of the Cape Verde Islands. *See* DEMARCATION, LINE OF.

Emanuel and his successors (1495–1580). Under King Emanuel, Portuguese power reached its height. In 1497–99 Vasco da Gama made the first voyage to India following the route discovered by Dias, and inaugurated a lucrative trade in spices and other luxuries between Europe and South Asia. Led by Alfonso de Albuquerque, the 'ortuguese occupied Goa, India, in 1510, Maacca (now Melaka, Malaysia) in 1511, the Moluc-as (in present-day Indonesia) in 1512–14, and lormuz Island in the Persian Gulf in 1515. During ie same period they opened up trade with China nd established relations with Ethiopia. As other ortuguese kings had done, Emanuel dreamed of niting Portugal and Spain under his rule and uccessively married two daughters of King Ferinand V and Queen Isabella I. Under pressure om his Spanish relations, he followed their example by expelling Jews and Muslims from his omains in 1497, thus depriving Portugal of much f its middle class. His son, John III, promoted e settlement of Brazil and (again influenced by e example of Spain) introduced (1536) the Inuisition into Portugal to enforce religious uniormity. By the time he died in 1557, Portugal ad begun to decline as a political and comercial power. This trend continued under King ebastian, who was killed during another expeition against Morocco in 1578. On the death of is successor, King Henry, in 1580, the Aviz dyasty came to an end.

he Habsburg and Braganza Dynasties. When lenry died, seven claimants disputed the succesion to the throne. The most powerful was Philip , king of Spain, who in 1580 became Philip I of ortugal. The annexation of Portugal to the Spanh Habsburg monarchy subjected it to the heavy xpenses of Spanish wars in a period known as e Sixty Years' Captivity. After 1600, Portuguese omination of trade with the East Indies was lost the Dutch and the English. Under Philip I, ortugal enjoyed considerable autonomy, but his ccessors, Philip II (Philip III of Spain) and Philip (Philip IV of Spain), treated it as a Spanish rovince, provoking widespread discontent. After nsuccessful revolts in 1634 and 1637, Portuguese onspirators with the support of France won inependence for their kingdom in 1640. John, uke of Braganza, was elected John IV, first king f the house of Braganza, which ruled Portugal long as the monarchy endured.

ohn IV and his successors. (1640–1816). King ohn expelled the Dutch from Brazil, which they ad occupied in 1630, and renewed the tradional tie with England. Although further weakned by conflicts with Spain in the second half f the 17th century, Portugal recovered a measure prosperity in the 18th century, after gold and iamonds were discovered in Brazil. Between 683 and 1750, during the reigns of Pedro II 648–1706) and John V (1689–1750), British merhants came to dominate Portuguese trade; the onarchy became more despotic and the Cortes ll into disuse. During the reign (1750–77) of Joseph Emanuel, the kingdom was controlled by the chief-minister, Sebastião José de Carvalho e Mello, marquês de Pombal, considered one of the greatest statesmen in modern Portuguese history. Although a ruthless dictator, he worked to weaken the power of the privileged nobility and the church, encouraged industry and education, and ended the foreign monopoly of trade. Pombal was dismissed, however, at the accession of Joseph Emanuel's daughter Maria I (1734–1816) in 1777. During the French revolutionary and Napoleonic wars, Portugal sided with Britain against France.

In 1807, when the armies of Napoleon threatened Portugal, the royal family withdrew to Brazil and made Rio de Janeiro the seat of government. A French army occupied Portugal but was defeated in 1808 by a British army under Sir Arthur Wellesley, 1st duke of Wellington. By the Convention of Sintra (Aug. 30, 1808), the French left the country, but they reinvaded a year later. Wellington again checked the French advance, and by 1811 Portugal was free of French influence. The Portuguese royal family chose, however, to remain in Brazil, which in 1815 was made a separate kingdom. In 1816 John VI succeeded to the two thrones, ruling Portugal through a council of regency.

The constitutional monarchy. In 1820 the Portuguese army headed a revolution designed to bring about a constitutional government. King John, who agreed to return to Portugal as constitutional monarch, made his son, Dom Pedro, regent of Brazil. Brazil proclaimed itself independent in 1822, and Pedro was made constitutional emperor Pedro I of that country. In Portugal, meanwhile, Pedro's brother, Dom Miguel (1802–66), appealed to the supporters of absolute monarchy to overthrow the constitutionalists, and an insurrection led by the prince almost succeeded on April 30, 1824. King John managed to remain in power, however, and Miguel went into exile in Vienna.

In 1826 Pedro I of Brazil succeeded to the throne of Portugal as Pedro IV. He put into effect a constitutional charter, providing for a parliamentary regime based on authorization of the monarchy rather than on popular will. He then abdicated in favor of his daughter, Maria II, called Maria da Gloria (1819–53), a 7-year-old child. Miguel returned from Vienna in 1828 and, ruling as regent for Maria II, seized the throne. A period of acute civil strife followed. With the help of England, France, and Spain, Maria was restored to the throne in 1834.

Political conflict characterized her reign as the Liberals, who supported the 1822 constitution, opposed the Chartists, who supported the 1826

The tower of Belem, overlooking Lisbon's harbor, was built in 1521 on the site at which Vasco da Gama and other great Portuguese navigators set sail. Heyward Associates

charter. Under her successors—Pedro V (1837–61), who reigned from 1853 to 1861, and Louis (1838–89), who reigned from 1861 to 1889—political strife became less pronounced.

The Republic. Republican and radical movements grew during the reign of Carlos I, and the appointment of João Franco (1855–1929), an antirepublican dictator, as prime minister in 1906 served to increase their strength. In 1908 Carlos and his eldest son were assassinated in Lisbon. The second son of Carlos ascended the throne as Manuel II, and although he restored constitutional government, his corruption equaled that of his father. In October 1910 the army and navy led a revolution that deposed Manuel and established a republic. A liberal constitution was put into effect in 1911, and one of its provisions separated church from state. Manuel José de Arriaga (1842–1917) was elected first president of the Portuguese republic.

For the next 15 years Portugal was shaken by political chaos. Ministry succeeded ministry, with an average duration of four months in office. Early in 1916 during World War I, Portugal, honoring its alliance with Great Britain, seized German ships in the harbor of Lisbon. On March 9 Germany declared war. Portuguese troops fought in France and in Africa. Internal disorder and political turbulence, however, continued, and in 1919 a Royalist uprising added to the confusion. In May 1926, an army coup deposed the 40th ministry since the proclamation of the republic. Within a few days of their success the military leaders selected Gen. António de Fragoso Carmona to head the new government. In 1928 Carmona was elected president in an election in which he was the sole candidate. In the same year he appointed António de Oliveira Salazar, a professor of economics at the University of Coimbra, as minister of finance. Salazar was given extraordinary powers in order to put Portuguese finances on a sound basis.

The Salazar regime. Salazar was successful in this task and rapidly became the most powerful political figure in Portugal. Profoundly religious, he restored much of the power of the church. In 1930 he founded the União Nacional (National Union), a political organization based on authoritarian principles. He became prime minister and dictator in 1932 and was influential in the promulgation of a new constitution in 1933. Portugal became a corporative state with a planned economy, its new regime being called the Estado Novo (New State). No opposition was countenanced. In 1936, with the beginning of the Spanish civil war, Salazar supported the insurgents, led by Gen. Francisco Franco. In 1939 Portugal signed a friendship and nonaggression pact with Spain, to which, on July 29, 1940, was added a protocol designed to ensure the neutrality of both countries during World War II. In October 1943, however, when the Axis powers were weakening, Portugal allowed the Allies to base planes and ships in the Azores.

The planned economy was considerably disturbed during the war years. The fishing industry declined, exports lessened, and refugees crowded the country. Moreover, the Japanese advance in the East Indies threatened Portuguese overseas territories in Asia, and Timor was captured in 1942. By the end of the war, unemployment and poverty were widespread. Political opposition to Salazar was suppressed, however, and National Union candidates monopolized the elections of November 1945. In May 1947, after crushing an attempted revolt, the government deported numerous labor leaders and army officers to the Cape Verde Islands. Marshal Carmona was reelected to the presidency without opposition in February 1949. He died in April 1951 and was succeeded in July by Gen. Francisco Lopes (1894–1964), a supporter of Salazar.

During the 1950s, Portugal developed close relations with the U.S., and in 1958 Salazar allowed an opposition candidate, Humberto Delgado (1904–65), to run for the presidency, but he was defeated by the government's candidate, Rear Admiral Américo Deus Tomás (1894–1987). Tomás was reelected in 1965 and 1971.

In the 1960s, Portugal faced opposition to its rule in the overseas territories. India annexed Portuguese Goa in 1961. In Africa, rebellion broke out in Angola in early 1961, in Portuguese Guinea in late 1962, and in Mozambique in the fall of 1964. The government mounted intensive military campaigns against each African rebellion. It also passed measures to improve political and economic conditions within the territories. In 1961 Portugal extended Portuguese citizenship to Africans in the territories; however, heavy fighting continued throughout the decade and into the 1970s. During these years the UN condemned Portugal for waging "colonial wars."

In the mid-1960s a number of foreign loans helped to finance major irrigation and construction projects, and some economic growth was gradually realized. Although several student demonstrations occurred during this period, political opposition to the Salazar regime remained uncoordinated.

Premier Antonio Salazar of Portugal (left) meets with Gen. Francisco Franco of Spain (right) in 1957 to discuss joint Iberian policies. Wide World Photos

Democratic reforms. On Sept. 29, 1968, Marcello Caetano (1906–80), a law professor and businessman and a longtime associate of Salazar, became prime minister, succeeding Salazar, who had been incapacitated by a cerebral stroke. Although Caetano called for reforms when he took office, he continued Salazar's repressive policies, especially in Africa.

A series of military and political advances made by African liberation movements threatened Portugal's economic stability and led to the overthrow of the Caetano government by a group of Portuguese army officers on April 25, 1974. A seven-man junta, under Gen António de Spinola (1910–), was installed and promised democracy at home and peace for the African territories. During 1974 and 1975, Guinea-Bissau, Mozambique, the Cape Verde Islands, São Tomé and Principe, and Angola became independent, and in 1975–76 Portuguese Timor was occupied by Indonesian forces. The return of troops and European settlers to Portugal from the newly independent nations aggravated Portugal's own problems of unemployment and political unrest.

On Sept. 30, 1974, Spinola resigned the presidency, warning of growing Communist influence. He was replaced by Gen. Francisco da Costa Gomes (1914–). Vasco Gonçalves (1921–), who had become prime minister in July, remained in office. Early in 1975, the Movement of the Armed Forces (Movimento das Forças Armadas, or MFA) assumed a formal role in the government, and steps were taken to reorganize the armed forces. The provisional government passed a law establishing a single trade union confederation and began to reform the economic and social life of Portugal. Among the first actions to be undertaken were the nationalization of certain types of heavy industry and banking, and the expropriation and redistribution of large agricultural holdings. In March a right-wing coup attempt, reportedly directed by Spinola, was suppressed. In April the Socialists led in the voting for a constituent assembly.

Gonçalves formed a new government, but it proved unstable. After a series of clashes between Socialists and Communists, followed by violent anti-Communist demonstrations, especially in the north, the MFA established a triumvirate consisting of Costa Gomes, Gonçalves, and Gen. Otelo de Carvalho (1934?–), Portugal's security chief. In September, at the army's insistence, Gonçalves was replaced as prime minister by Vice Admiral José de Azevedo (1917–83). Under the Azevedo government, relative stability was restored, and a new investment code was adopted to attract foreign capital. In parliamentary elections in April 1976, the Socialists won a plurality of the vote, and their leader, Mario Soares, became prime minister. In June Gen. António Ramalho Eanes (1935–) was elected president of Portugal. The country experienced severe economic problems during the next two years, and in mid-1978 Soares was dismissed. After the fall of two successive interim governments, the conservative Democratic Alliance, headed by Francisco Manuel de Sá Carneiro (1934–80), won a clear majority in parliamentary

In Lisbon, Prime Minister José de Azevedo (left), Mário Soares (center), Socialist leader, and Emidio Guerreiro (right), chief of the Popular Democrats, celebrate their election victory in September 1975. Wide World Photos

Pope John Paul II is greeted at the Lisbon airport by then Portuguese President António Ramalho Eanes as he arrives for a four-day visit, including a trip to the shrine of Fátima. Wide World Photos

elections held in December 1979. Sá Carneiro took office as premier in January 1980, but was killed in a plane crash the following December. He was succeeded in January 1981 by Francisco Pinto Balsemão (1937–), another conservative. On his initiative, the military Council of the Revolution was abolished in 1982 by constitutional amendment. Parliamentary elections in April 1983 brought Soares back into power as prime minister. Soares's government introduced an austerity program and conducted negotiations leading toward Portugal's entry into the European Community. Elections in October 1985 led to the formation of a minority government under a Social Democrat, Aníbal Cavaco Silva (1939–). Soares returned as president following elections in 1986; Portugal entered the European Community the same year. In the 1987 elections the Social Democrats won control of parliament, the first time a single party held the majority since 1975. President Soares won another 5-year term in January 1991, and the Social Democrats held their majority in parliamentary elections in October.

For further information on this topic, see the Bibliography in volume 28, sections 848, 967, 970.

PORTUGUESE INDIA, five districts on the Indian subcontinent, ruled by Portugal in 1505–1974. Three of the districts are coastal, namely, Goa (now a state) and adjacent islands off the Malabar Coast; Daman (formerly Damão), near Nasik; and Diu, an island S of the Kathiawar Peninsula and adjacent mainland territories. The other two districts, Dadra and Nagar Aveli, are inland. India seized the inland districts in 1954 and occupied the coastal ones in 1961. Portugal recognized the sovereignty of India over the districts in 1974. The capital of Portuguese India was Nova Goa, or Panjim.

PORTUGUESE LANGUAGE, one of the Romance languages. Like all other languages of the group, Portuguese is a direct modern descendant of Latin, the vernacular Latin of the Roman soldier and colonist rather than the classical Latin of the cultured Roman citizen. It developed in ancient Gallaecia (modern Galicia, in northwestern Spain) and in northern Portugal and then spread throughout present-day Portugal. Portuguese resembles Spanish more than it does any of the other Romance tongues. Like Spanish, it contains a very large number of words of Arabic origin, and like other modern languages, its vocabulary also contains a great many words of French and Greek origin. A very small number of words are derived from Carthaginian, Celtic, and Phoenician. Portuguese is spoken in Portugal; Galicia (in a dialect called Galician); Brazil; several islands in the Atlantic Ocean; Angola, Mozambique, and other former colonies in Africa and Asia; and parts of Indonesia.

The official language of Brazil is Portuguese, but technically, it is a dialect of Portuguese, with some differences in vocabulary, pronunciation, and syntax. It bears the same relationship to the Portuguese of Portugal as American English does to British English.

Portuguese retains many grammatical forms no longer found in other members of the Romance language group. The future subjunctive and future perfect subjunctive, for example, remain in use. As in Old Spanish, the endings of the future and the conditional in modern Portuguese may be detached from the stem to permit the interpolation of the object pronoun. Portuguese is the only Romance language with a personal or inflected infinitive. For example, *partir* ("to depart") may be conjugated *partir eu,* "for me to depart" or "that I may depart." In addition to the compound pluperfect, Portuguese has also a simple one developed from the Latin pluperfect; thus the pluperfect of *amara* means "I had loved" in addition to the conventional "I would love." Portuguese closely parallels Spanish in its grammar. Many nouns have the distinctive endings of *a* for the feminine form and *o* for the masculine form, corresponding to Latin nouns of the first and second declensions, respectively. The sign of the plural in Portuguese is regularly *s.*

The Portuguese language has proved of particular interest to linguists because of the complexity of its phonetic structure. The language contains 11 distinct vowel sounds, and a great difference in pronunciation exists between closed and open *a, e,* and *o.* All five vowels may be nasalized, although with less complete stoppage of the nasal passages than in French. The nasalization is indicated by a tilde placed over the vowel, or by an *m* or *n* placed after it. The language also contains a number of diphthongs, several of which may be nasalized.

Phonetic analysis of Portuguese reveals 25 separate consonantal sounds, which have almost the same value as in other Romance languages, with some variation from region to region. The most important variations are that *rr* is generally alveolar in Portugal and frequently uvular or guttural in Brazil, and that sounds corresponding to English *ch* and *dj* do not exist in Portugal but are found in Brazil represented by *ti* and *di. Lh* corresponds to Spanish *ll* and Italian *gl. Nh* corresponds to Spanish *ñ* and Italian *gn. Ch* and *j* are pronounced as in French.

The dental character of the consonants *d, t, n,* and *l* is more pronounced in Portuguese than in English, because in Portuguese pronunciation the tongue tends to touch the base of the upper teeth. The linking together in spoken Portuguese of syntactically related words in a sentence accounts for the variation in the sound of a number of consonants. This phenomenon is particularly evident in the case of the sibilant consonants *s* and *z.* One of the most distinctive features of Portuguese, compared with other Romance languages, is the loss of the so-called intervocalic *l* and *n.* Thus, *quaes* represents the Latin *quales* and *pessoa* the Latin *persona.* The Portuguese forms of the definite article *o, a* ("the") are due to the intervocalic position of the *l* in such syntactical combinations as *de-lo* and *de-la* ("of the"), from which have resulted the contracted forms *do* and *da,* and by a redivision of the compound, *d'o* and *d'a.* A word ending in *l* in the singular loses the *l* in the plural due to its intervocalic position. Thus, the singular of "sun" is *sol,* but the plural is *soes.* J.F.S.

PORTUGUESE LITERATURE, literature of Portugal, written in Portuguese and other languages. It is noted for the sweetness of its lyrical verse and the biting wit of its satirical prose. Portuguese literature may be divided into four periods: 1200 to 1415, the age of the troubadours; 1415 to 1580, the humanistic flowering, rivaling that of Castile; 1580 to 1820, a time of stagnation; and 1820 to the present, the romantic revival. Until the 14th century, Portuguese literature was a regional variety of that of the Iberian Peninsula, composed in the language of northwestern Spain by Galicians, Portuguese, and Castilians alike; down to the 17th century many Portuguese also wrote in Castilian. Thus, the Portuguese claim authorship of *Amadis of Gaul,* the greatest Spanish novel of chivalry.

Age of the Troubadours. Courtly troubadour poetry in Portugal began in the 13th century with the reign of Alfonso III and reached its height during the reign of his son Diniz, an excellent troubadour himself. A few authors stand out in the 13th century; the priests Airas Nunes and Joan Airas de Santiago, João Garcia de Guilhade, and the *jogral* (professional musician) Martin Codax. The songs of the troubadours were of three types: *cantigas de amor,* or plaintive love songs; *cantigas de amigo,* or songs about suitors, put into the mouths of women in delightful native forms still alive in oral folk tradition; and *cantigas de escarnho e de mal dizer,* or mocking and slanderous songs. More than 2000 songs of the troubadours survive. They are gathered in three *cancioneiros,* or songbooks, and a fourth book of a different character, containing legends in praise of the Virgin Mary by King Alfonso X of León and Castile. Portuguese prose of the 13th and 14th centuries consists of *livros de linhagens* (anecdotal registers of noble lineages); chronicles; saints' lives and other edifying literature translated from the Latin; and adaptations of the Arthurian romances about the knights of the Round Table.

Early Renaissance. In the late 15th century a second era of Portuguese cultural flowering began, resulting in part from overseas expansion around Africa and the accompanying growth of the Atlantic port cities. The curiosity about human nature that was characteristic of the Renaissance led to more world writing, although there occurred no radical break with the doctrines of the medieval church or with the troubadours. Classic and Italian influences, a greater variety of forms, and excitement over widening horizons characterize the best poetry in the *Cancioneiro geral* (General Songbook, 1516), compiled by Garcia de Resende (1470–1536) and encompassing the work of 300 poets. Four of these poets won renown: Resende himself for treating in verse one of the great romantic themes of European literature, the murder of the royal paramour Inés de Castro; Gil Vicente, who founded the Portuguese theater with the fine plays he wrote and performed for the royal court from 1502 on; Bernardim Ribeiro (1482-1552), the author of hauntingly melancholy poetry and *Livro dos saudades* (Book of Longings, 1554–57)—also known by its opening words, *Menina e moça* (Child and Maiden)—a sentimental novel combining pastoral and chivalrous features; and Francisco de Sá de Miranda (1481–1558), who, after a sojourn in Italy, revolutionized Portuguese poetry through the introduction of Italian meters. Vicente, the greatest of these four poets, excelled in such different veins as the spiritual, in *The Ship of Hell* (1516; trans. 1929); the romantic, in *Amadís de Gaula* (c. 1523); and the farcical, in *Auto da Índia* (Play of India, c. 1509). His works are peopled by the whole range of Portuguese society, from Gypsies and black slaves to prelates and princes, seen through the sympathetic eyes of a truly Christian humanist who, serious and gay in turns, sprinkles his scenes generously with songs inspired by the folk poetry of his country.

Golden Age of Literature. In the next generation, improving on the innovations of Sá de Miranda, António Ferreira (1528-69) wrote *Ignez de Castro* (1587; trans. 1825), a verse tragedy with a Greek chorus, and Jorge Ferreira de Vasconcelos (1515-85) wrote several prose comedies of manners, among them *Eufrósina* (1555), a moralized counterpart to the Spanish novel *La Celestina.* Prose fiction progressed little. Novels of chivalry remained in fashion, among them the verse and prose romance *Lusitania transformada* (Lusitania Transformed, 1595), by Fernão Álvares do Oriente (1540-95). Moral tales were written by Gonçalo Fernandes Trancoso (1515?-96?). In the 16th century, writers produced numerous moral or religious treatises, mostly in the humanistic form of dialogues, such as *Imagem da vida cristã* (Image of the Christian Life, 1563 and 1572), by Heitor Pinto (1528-83?); the impassioned *Consolação às tribulações de Israel (Consolation of Israel in Its Tribulations, 1553),* by the Portuguese Jewish writer Samuel Usque (1500?-60?); and a critique of colonial practices, *Soldado prático* (The Experienced Soldier, 1590), by Diogo do Couto (1542-1616).

Couto is best known as one in the series of splendid historians who grandly chronicled the rise and decline of the Portuguese Empire beginning with Gomes Eanes de Azurara (c. 1410-74), who wrote on the Portuguese prince Henry the Navigator. The peak was reached with João de Barros (c. 1496-1570) who, following the classical model of the Roman historian Livy, began an ambitious history of the overseas conquests in his *Décadas da Ásia* (Decades of Asia, 1552-1615). Couto continued the chronicle, and between them they covered the history and geography of the 16th century. Other historians were the cosmopolitan humanist Damião de Góis (1502-74), who chronicled the reign of King Emanuel and Gaspar Correia (1495-1561), who poured his experiences as secretary to Affonso de Albuquerque, the conqueror of Goa and Malacca, into the minutely detailed, vivid *Lendas da Índia* (Indian Memoranda, 1858-66). The prose works of this era that are the richest in exotic, dramatic, and picaresque scenes are the travel books. These include factual accounts of the discovery of the seaway to India in 1497-98 (written by Álvaro Velho in 1838) and of the coast of Brazil in 1500 (written by Pero Vaz de Caminha in 1817); a series of shipwreck stories collected in the 18th century as *The Tragic History of the Sea* (1735-36; trans. 1959 and 1967); and the adventures of Fernão Mendes Pinto (c. 1510-83) in the Far East as a trader, pirate, and slave, fictionalized in the posthumously published *Peregrinação* (Wanderings, 1614).

Camões and the Decline of the Golden Age. The high adventure and decline of the Golden Age in Portugal, along with its ideals of the gentleman, the Christian, and the lover, are summed up in the active life and literary works of the greatest writer of Portugal, the poet Luís de Camões. As a poor young nobleman he tried his luck first at court, then overseas in Africa and Asia. He returned home penniless and broken in health, but with one imperishable treasure, his national poem *Os Lusíadas* (The Lusiads, or sons of Lusus, that is, the Portuguese, 1572). It is perhaps the best of all Renaissance epics, praising the Portuguese leaders of the past and, by implication, the entire small but undaunted nation. Vasco da Gama's voyage to India provided the theme, which the poet heightened with the inclusion of ancient mythology. The work culminates in a timeless apotheosis of the human mind as conqueror over nature. Camões also excelled as a lyric poet (*Poems,* 1595; trans. 1803); his sonnets and canzones make him the rival of the 14th-century Italian Petrarch as a subtle philosophical poet. In the sweetest, purest language Camões wrote of ideal love and the absurdity of human fortunes. He also wrote a number of plays that deal with classic themes.

Camões overshadowed many worthy poets of his time and of the next two generations, among them Diogo Bernardes (1530-1605) and his brother Agostinho da Cruz (1540-1619), both of whom wrote of God revealed in the idyllic green countryside of Portugal, and Francisco Rodrigues Lobo (1580-1622), who also treated pastoral themes.

Camões inspired Portuguese writers for centuries. He sustained the national spirit during the era of stagnation when Portugal's exploitation by Castile and the ensuing struggles of the Portuguese to regain and maintain independence were offset only by the prosperity of one great colony, Brazil. Even so, this third era produced several remarkable writers. Manuel de Faria e

Sousa (1590–1649) was a poet, historian, and literary critic, whose commentary (1639) on *Os Lusíadas* was a monumental labor of love and eruditon. Francisco Manuel de Melo (1608–66) had the same talents, as well as experience in his positions and a clever wit that did not fail him in jail or exile. The wit shines brightly in his best poems, his letters to friends, and his four *Apólogos dialogais* (1721), dialogues on current topics. The other masters of baroque conceits were two clerics: Antonio das Chagas (1631–82), a soldier turned friar; and the internationally known Jesuit preacher António Vieira (1608–97), whose sermons, filling 15 volumes (1679–1748), are unique for imaginative power, ingeniousness, bold prophetic criticism, and enlightened patriotism.

18th Century. In the 18th century, in the name of "good taste," Franco-Italian classical academic regularity vanquished baroque exuberance. Poetic inspiration, thus repressed, found a precarious refuge in Brazil, and in its place didactic literature abounded. The *Verdadeiro método de estudar* (True Method of Study, 1746) of Luís António Verney (1713–92), an anti-Scholastic, anti-Jesuitic treatise on education, led to reforms typical of the Age of Enlightenment. In a lighter vein, António José da Silva (1705–39) produced burlesque puppet plays, and Francisco Xavier de Oliveira (1702–83), who fled to England, became the first Portuguese essayist with his chatty *Cartas familiares* (Letters to Friends, 1741–42). The romantic period was foreshadowed in the autobiographical and philosophical sonnets *Rimas* (Rhymes, 1791–99), which were written by a reckless bohemian, Manuel Maria Barbosa du Bocage (1765–1804), who spent his talent on improvisations and obscenities.

19th Century. The fourth era, that of the nationalist awakening, has yet to run its course. Portuguese nationalism grew out of French revolutionary ideology and the Napoleonic invasions of the Iberian Peninsula in the first quarter of the 19th century. Such young middle-class intellectuals as João Baptista da Almeida Garrett and Alexandre Herculano (1810–77) spent years of exile in France and England, where they imbibed romantic notions of liberty and nationalism at firsthand. Back in Portugal, Almeida Garrett undertook the revival of the national stage with historical dramas, such as *Brother Luiz de Sousa* (1844, trans. 1909). He met with more success as a poet, transmuting his loves into verse, romanticizing the misfortunes of genius in a long poem on Camões, or reworking Portuguese folk ballads. In *Viagens na minha terra* (Journeys in My Native Land, 1846) he created a whimsical tale mixing romance with satire and autobiography, written in

Camilo Castelo Branco Casa de Portugal

a refreshingly conversational style. Herculano made his reputation as a historian of medieval Portugal, but he also created historical fiction, including a novel about the Visigoths and Moors, *Eurico, o presbítero* (Euric the Presbyter, 1844), into which he introduced the issue of priestly celibacy.

Portuguese romanticism did not tend to extremes but was combined with neoclassical precepts. Thus, two "romantics" came to be considered models of pure Portuguese style: the blind poet António Feliciano de Castilho (1800–75) and his talented disciple Camilo Castelo Branco, who was more romantic in his living than in his writing. Castelo Branco created a gallery of country and small-town types from northern Portugal in stories and novels of manners, including *Amor de perdiçáo* (Love of Perdition, 1862) and *Contos do Minho* (Tales from the Minho Province, 1875–76). Castilho was displaced in 1865 by a group of bright university students, in the name of "modern ideas": German philosophies, French socialism, science, and realistic art. The most gifted (and the unhappiest) of the group was a poet from the Azores, Antero Tarquínio de Quental, who wrote philosophical sonnets alternating between high hopes for human progress and utter despondency (*Os sonetos completos, 1886*). Others in the group included the first Portuguese literary historian in the modern sense, Teófilo Braga (1843–1924); a brilliant cultural historian and economist, Joaquim Oliveira Martins (1845–94); the foremost social poet, Guerra Junqueiro (1850–1923), and the best writer of realistic fiction, José Maria de Eça de Queirós. Eça de Queirós showed himself to be a mocking genius and a master of subtle artistic prose in such novels as *The Relic* (1887; trans. 1887).

During the final quarter of the 19th century, these artists outshone a host of younger talents, among them the symbolist poets Camilo Pessanha (1867-1926), steeped in Chinese culture (*Clepsidra,* 1922); Eugénio de Castro (1869-1944), author of *Oaristos* (1890); and António Nobre (1867-1903). Nobre's single volume, *Só* (Alone, 1892), highlighted a return to the sentimental nationalism of Almeida Garrett, romanticizing the "folk," but, unlike Almeida Garrett, opposing any change. Prominent among traditionalists were António Correia de Oliveira (1879-1960), the popular versifier of *A minha terra* (My Land, 1915-17), and, towering above all poets since Almeida Garrett, Fernando Pessoa (1888-1935), intensely national but also anti-Roman Catholic and ironic, sophisticated, and mystical. He wrote under various names to express dramatically the conflicting personalities within his complicated soul. Only after he had drunk himself to death were his poems and literary essays widely read and acclaimed; typical of his writing is *Ode triunfal* (Triumphal Ode, 1914). Although Pessoa participated in the futurist movement, known as *modernismo* in Portugal, he remained a solitary figure. Unlike him, most intellectuals came to the defense of the democratic institutions, working in vain for reforms against the professional politicians. The leaders among these intellectuals were Aquilino Ribeiro (1885-1960), a novelist who created such true country tales as the roguish *Malhadinhas* (Little Corrals, 1922); the pantheistic poet Teixeira de Pascoaes (1877-1952); the patriotic poet-historian Jaime Cortesão (1884-1960); and the essayist António Sérgio (1883-1969), a foe of nationalistic myths. The dramatist and poet Júlio Dantas (1876-1962) became known for his wit and sense of atmosphere, especially in his most noted play, *A ceia dos cardeais* (The Bishop's Supper, 1907).

20th Century. A second generation continued the struggle for reform after the collapse of the republic in 1926: the poet Miguel Torga (1907-   ), author of a prose and verse *Diário* (Diary, since 1941), a unique commentary on current events, Portugal, the Portuguese, and his own psyche; the storywriter Irene Lisboa (1892-1958), a masterful observer of pathetic, obscure lives; Ferreira de Castro (1898-1974), made famous by his novel *The Jungle* (1930; trans. 1930), about a Portuguese emigrant to Brazil; and the subtle psychologist José Rodrigues Miguéis (1901-80), author of *A escola do paraíso* (School of Paradise, 1960), a novel evoking the Lisbon of 1910.

Júlio Dantas Casa de Portugal

These writers were joined by many who reacted against the introspective craftsmanship stressed by José Régio (1901-69) and José Gaspar Simões (1903-   ), editors of *Presença* (Presence, 1927-40). The writers of this group engaged in social realism, or *neorealismo*. This movement led to experimentation with new narrative techniques, particularly by the existentialist Vergílio Ferreira (1916-   ), author of the novel *Alegria breve* (Short-Lived Joy, 1965), and José Cardoso Pires (1925-   ), who wrote the novel *O hóspede de Job* (Job's Guest, 1963).

Neorealismo, together with writings from the northeast of Brazil, a region that has climatic and social similarities to Africa, encouraged a literary upsurge in Portuguese territories in Africa. This produced the regional and social fiction of the Cape Verdeans Baltasar Lopes (1904-   ) and Manuel Lopes (1907-   ); fiction on the relations between blacks and whites in Angola, in such works as *Terra morta* (Dead Land, 1949), by Castro Soromenho (1910-68); and such lyric, increasingly militant poems as those of Francisco José Tenreiro (1921-63), from São Tomé, the first Portuguese writer to espouse pride in African blackness.

Surrealist and concretist experimentation brought to the fore such Portuguese poets as Jorge de Sena (1919-78), master of association of ideas and images in both prose (*Andanças do demónio;* The Demon Abroad, 1960 and 1967) and verse (*Metamorfoses,* 1963). To a lesser extent than in poetry, new viewpoints are revitalizing Portuguese fiction, not only through such foreign ideas as existentialism and structuralism but also through the emancipation of women, who make up half the literate population. Modern Portuguese women writers include Agustina Bessa-Luís (1922–), who traced the incommunicability and psychological complexity of middle-class women in such novels as *A sibila* (The Sibyl, 1953); and poets such as the liberty-loving Sofia de Melo Breyner Andresen (1919–). In 1972 Maria Isabel Barreno (1939–), Maria Teresa Horta (1937–), and Maria Velho da Costa collaborated to produce a volume of essays, stories, and poetry, subsequently published in the U.S. as *The Three Marias; New Portuguese Letters* (1975). The work was inspired by a 17th-century classic, passionate love letters attributed to a Portuguese nun, Marianna Alcoforado (1640–1723). First published (1669) in French, they were issued in Portuguese in 1819 and translated into English as *Letters from a Portuguese Nun* in 1893. Because of its feminist content, and some erotic passages, *The Three Marias* was banned and the authors were put on trial, occasioning much international protest. When the new Portuguese revolutionary government took over in 1974, the authors were pardoned and the book released.

Hampered by the lack of support, modern Portuguese drama is confined mainly to amateur circles. One of the playwrights to come to wider attention, however, is Bernardo Santareno (1924–), who works psychological overtones into analyses of broader national problems—as in *O inferno* (1968).

See also BRAZILIAN LITERATURE.

For further information on this topic, see the Bibliography in volume 28, section 848.

Portuguese man-of-war, Physalia physalis UPI

PORTUGUESE MAN-OF-WAR, name commonly applied to coelenterate animals of the genus *Physalia,* belonging to the order Siphonophora. The animal is common in tropical seas, floating on the surface with an inflated brightly colored bladder crowned with a transparent sail. Actually a colony of specialized cells, it may reach a length of 15 cm (6 in) and trail tentacles that may be more than 30 m (about 100 ft) long. These tentacles are armed with thousands of poison-secreting cells called nematocysts. The toxin secreted, a mixture of enzymes, is a neurotoxin about 75 percent as powerful as cobra venom. Nematocysts remain active and may sting even when the Portuguese man-of-war is dying or dead. The cells also numb the animal's prey.

PORTUGUESE WATER DOG, working breed of dog that somewhat resembles a poodle but with a more spaniel-like face and more webbing between the toes. Developed in Portugal to retrieve fishing equipment from the water, the dog stands up to 55 cm (22 in) at the shoulder and weighs up to 25 kg (55 lb). The coat is black, white, brown, or grayish, often with white markings, and may be short and curly or long and wavy. The ears drop, and the tail is long and curved.

PORTUGUESE WEST AFRICA. *See* ANGOLA.

PORTULACA, common name for the family Portulacaceae, order Caryophyllales (*see* PINK), a small, widespread group of more or less succulent herbs and subshrubs, with concentrations of species along the Pacific Coast of North America and in southern Africa, and for its representative genus, *Portulaca.* About 21 genera and 400 species make up this family of dicots (q.v.). The leaves are opposite or alternate and bear stipules (appendages, usually leaflike, at the leaf base) that are often modified into membranous scales or hairs. The usually small flowers characteristically have only two green sepals, five petals and stamens, and a single ovary borne above and free from the other floral parts. The common purslane, *P. oleracea,* has long been used as a pot herb and in salads. Rose moss, *P. grandiflora,* is a bedding plant; several species of *Lewisia,* flame flower (*Talinum*), and rock purslane (*Calandrinia*) are also used as ornamentals. M.R.C.

POSEIDON, in Greek mythology, god of the sea, the son of the Titans Cronus and Rhea, and the brother of Zeus and Hades. Poseidon was the husband of Amphitrite, one of the Nereids, by whom he had a son, Triton. Poseidon had numerous other love affairs, however, especially with nymphs of springs and fountains, and was the father of several children famed for their wildness and cruelty, among them the giant

Orion and the Cyclops Polyphemus. Poseidon and the Gorgon Medusa were the parents of Pegasus, the famous winged horse.

Poseidon plays a prominent part in numerous ancient myths and legends. He contended unsuccessfully with Athena, goddess of wisdom, for the control of Athens. When he and Apollo, god of the sun, were cheated of their promised wages after having helped Laomedon, king of Troy, build the walls of that city, Poseidon sent a terrible sea monster to ravage the land, and during the Trojan War he helped the Greeks.

In art, Poseidon is represented as a bearded and majestic figure, holding a trident and often accompanied by a dolphin. Every two years the Isthmian Games, featuring horse and chariot racers, were held in his honor at Corinth. The Romans identified Poseidon with their god of the sea, Neptune.

POSEN. *See* POZNAŃ.

POSITIVISM, system of philosophy based on experience and empirical knowledge of natural phenomena, in which metaphysics and theology are regarded as inadequate and imperfect systems of knowledge.

Development. The doctrine was first called positivism by the 19th-century French mathematician and philosopher Auguste Comte, but some of the positivist concepts may be traced to the British philosopher David Hume, the French philosopher Duc de Saint-Simon, and the German philosopher Immanuel Kant.

Comte chose the word *positivism* on the ground that it indicated the "reality" and "constructive tendency" that he claimed for the theoretical aspect of the doctrine. He was, in the main, interested in a reorganization of social life for the good of humanity through scientific knowledge, and thus control of natural forces. The two primary components of positivism, the philosophy and the polity (or program of individual and social conduct), were later welded by Comte into a whole under the conception of a religion, in which humanity was the object of worship. A number of Comte's disciples refused, however, to accept this religious development of his philosophy, because it seemed to contradict the original positivist philosophy. Many of Comte's doctrines were later adapted and developed by the British social philosophers John Stuart Mill and Herbert Spencer and by the Austrian philosopher and physicist Ernst Mach.

Logical Positivists. During the early 20th century a group of philosophers who were concerned with developments in modern science rejected the traditional positivist ideas that held personal experience to be the basis of true knowledge and emphasized the importance of scientific verification. This group came to be known as logical positivists, and it included the Austrian Ludwig Wittgenstein and the British Bertrand Russell and G. E. Moore. It was Wittgenstein's *Tractatus Logico-philosophicus* (1921; German-English parallel text, 1922) that proved to be of decisive influence in the rejection of metaphysical doctrines for their meaninglessness and the acceptance of empiricism as a matter of logical necessity.

The positivists today, who have rejected this so-called Vienna school of philosophy, prefer to call themselves logical empiricists in order to dissociate themselves from the emphasis of the earlier thinkers on scientific verification. They maintain that the verification principle itself is philosophically unverifiable.

For further information on this topic, see the Bibliography in volume 28, section 35.

POSITRON, elementary nuclear particle having a mass equal to that of an electron and a positive electrical charge equal in magnitude to the negative charge of the electron. The positron is sometimes called a positive electron or anti-electron, and the electron is known as a negatron. Negatron-positron pairs are formed if cosmic rays or gamma rays of energies of more than 1 mev (million electron volts) are made to strike particles of matter. The reverse of the pairing process, called annihilation, is initiated when a negatron and a positron interact, losing their combined mass and producing gamma rays.

The existence of the positron was first suggested in 1928 by the British physicist Paul Dirac as a necessary consequence of his quantum-mechanical theory of electron motion. In 1932 the American physicist Carl Anderson confirmed the existence of the positron by observation. *See* ATOM AND ATOMIC THEORY; ELEMENTARY PARTICLES.

POSITRON EMISSION TOMOGRAPHY (PET), in nuclear medicine, technique for imaging internal body tissues. PET requires a cyclotron as an on-site source of short-lived positron-emitting isotopes. The isotopes are injected into the patient along with a glucose-related compound, and the positrons collide with electrons in body tissues to produce photons. The photons are tracked by a tomographic scintillation counter, and the information is processed by a computer to provide both images and data on blood flow and metabolic processes within the tissues observed. PET scans are particularly useful for diagnosing brain tumors and the effect of strokes and various mental illnesses. *See also* RADIOLOGY.

POST, Wiley (1899–1935), American aviator, born in Grand Plain, near Grand Saline, Tex. With the Australian-American aviator Harold Charles

Gatty (1903–57) as navigator, Post set a world record in July 1931 for flying around the world. The two men covered 15,474 mi (24,903 km) in 8 days, 15 hrs, 51 min in a Lockheed Vega monoplane, the *Winnie Mae.* Post made the first solo flight around the world, from July 15 to 22, 1933, in the same plane, completing a distance of 15,596 mi (25,099 km) in 7 days, 18 hr, 49 min, a new record for the distance. The American humorist Will Rogers was a passenger in his plane when both men were killed in a crash on Aug. 15, 1935, near Point Barrow, Alaska.

POSTAL SERVICE, UNITED STATES, independent agency within the executive department of the U.S. government, responsible for nationwide postal regulation and delivery. The postal system, formerly known as the Post Office Department, was reorganized as the U.S. Postal Service under the Postal Reorganization Act of 1970, which became effective in July 1971. The chief functions of the Postal Service are the collection and delivery of letters, parcel post, and printed matter, such as books, magazines, and newspapers, and the issuance of domestic and foreign money orders. The Postal Service handles more than 160 billion pieces of mail a year.

The changes in the postal system stemmed from four basic provisions of the Postal Reorganization Act: elimination of politics from postal management; adequate financing authority; establishment of a postal career service, allowing collective bargaining between management and employees; and creation of an independent commission for setting of postal rates.

The Postal Service is directed by an 11-member board of governors, 9 of whom are appointed by the president on a bipartisan basis with the advice and consent of the U.S. Senate. The nine governors appoint a tenth to be postmaster general; they then appoint a deputy postmaster general. The independent Postal Rate Commission has five members, appointed by the president. Tenure in these offices is decided on the basis of performance rather than political affiliation; one purpose of this stipulation is to avoid needless discontinuity of the postal system, which formerly occurred in presidential election years. The Postal Service is authorized to borrow up to $10 billion from the general public, that is, from the Department of the Treasury, and can propose to the Postal Rate Commission changes in rates or classification of mail.

Classifications of Postal Matter. Mailable matter in the domestic service is divided into four classes, for which different rates are charged. First-class mail includes letters, postcards, matter wholly or partly in writing, and matter sealed or closed against inspection; second-class mail comprises newspapers and periodical publications; third-class mail (less than 16 oz/170 g) includes books, circulars, matter wholly in print, and proof sheets; and fourth-class mail (domestic parcel post, 16 oz or over) covers merchandise and all matter not covered in the other three classes. Express mail, the newest service, provides overnight delivery for packages of up to 70 lb. Letters and postcards sent by airmail to foreign countries are considered first-class mail, as are parcels sent by air or as registered mail. Additional fees are charged for special delivery or special handling. No airmail category exists for first-class letters within the U.S.

Illegal Postal Matter. According to current regulations, liquor; poisons; medicines under certain restrictions; explosives; all articles likely to cause injury or damage; and seditious, obscene, defamatory, or threatening matter are excluded from the mails. Postal regulations also restrict unsolicited advertisements that are of a sexually explicit nature. The postmaster general is authorized to prevent mail delivery to persons conducting a fraudulent business.

Zip Code System. In 1963 the ZIP (Zoning Improvement Program) code system was introduced to simplify the patterns and procedures of mail distribution. The ZIP code is a five-digit number used on the last line of the address following the name of the city and state. The first digit, from 0 to 9, stands for one of the ten main geographical areas into which the U.S. and its possessions are divided; each area includes three or more states or possessions. The next four digits delimit localities further by subdividing the main area; the first three digits together represent a sectional or metropolitan area, with the next two numbers specifying an associated or branch post office. In October 1983 the Postal Service began using an expanded ZIP code system of nine numbers, consisting of the five-digit code plus four additional digits, which specify an individual delivery route. Use of ZIP codes is voluntary; however, reduced postage rates are offered to large-volume mailers employing the expanded nine-digit code.

History. The first American postal service was established in the colony of Massachusetts in 1639. From 1707 until the year before the American Revolution, the General Post Office in London controlled the postal service in America. In 1775 the Continental Congress resolved to have a postal system of its own, and Benjamin Franklin was elected to carry on the work. When a postal service was authorized by Congress in 1789 under the U.S. Constitution, the nation had 75 local

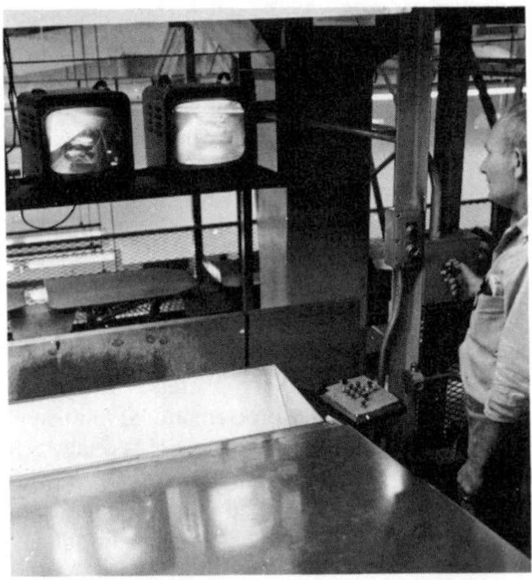

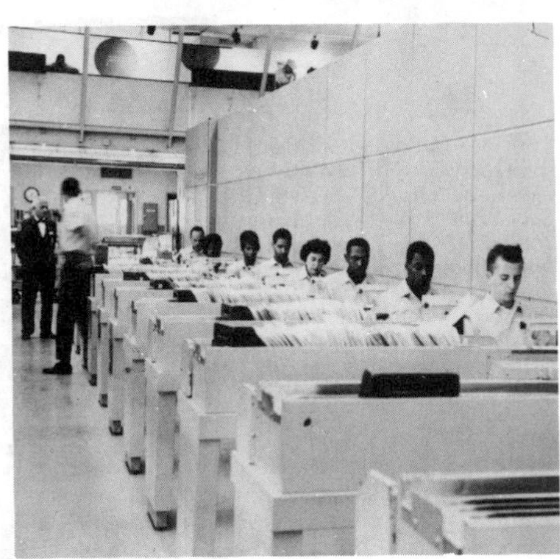

The mechanization of mail handling. Top, left: The edger-stacker receives a fast-moving flow of jumbled letters, places them on edge, and stacks them in preparation for canceling. Top, right: Closed-circuit television systems monitor postal machinery and enable employees to regulate the flow of mail and to detect obstruction in overhead equipment. Bottom, left: Optical ZIP code readers, attached to letter sorters, read and sort incoming and outgoing machine-printed mail. Bottom, right: High-speed letter sorting machines sort mail to about 300 separate destinations at speeds in excess of 36,000 pieces per hour.

post offices, and the mails were carried over 1875 mi (more than 3000 km) of postal routes.

The introduction of adhesive stamps in 1847 greatly simplified post office operations. The system of registering letters was first adopted in 1855. In cities, street letter boxes were introduced in 1858 and free mail delivery in 1863 under Postmaster General Montgomery Blair. The Pony Express began mail service between Saint Joseph, Mo., and San Francisco in 1860. The money order system was put into operation in 1864, and rural free delivery service was established in 1896. The parcel post system came into operation in the U.S. in 1913. The first regular service for airmail was established between New York City and Washington, D.C., in 1918. The Postal Savings System, established by Congress in 1911, was terminated in 1966.

From 1829 to 1971 the appointment as U.S. postmaster general carried with it a position in the president's cabinet. The postmaster general makes postal agreements with foreign governments, awards and executes contracts, and directs the foreign mail service.

For further information on this topic, see the Bibliography in volume 28, section 331.

POSTERS, mass-produced advertisements or announcements printed on large sheets of paper for public display. Posters ordinarily consist of a colorful picture or illustration along with a short identifying text or trademark. They usually have a commercial purpose—to advertise products or publicize entertainment events—but they also occasionally appear as public education announcements, propaganda instruments, or pure works of art with no overt message.

Posters came into existence in the 15th century with the invention of the printing press. Usually unillustrated, the earliest posters carried announcements of royal proclamations, municipal decrees, fairs and markets, and occasionally advertisements for books. Small woodcut illustrations were used somewhat more frequently in later centuries, but they were relatively difficult to produce and were never common. Not until the 19th century did posters begin to assume their modern look.

Beginnings of the Modern Period. Two events about 1800 gave birth to the modern era of poster production. One was the beginning of industrialization on a large scale, which created a need for extensive advertising. The other was the invention, in 1798, of a new printing method, lithography, that made it much easier for artists to include colored illustrations on posters. Poster production boomed throughout the first half of the 19th century, and posters were used to advertise everything from railroads to corsets to department stores. Also at this time, theatrical posters first appeared, often with realistic illustrations of scenes from the advertised plays, operas, or burlesques.

Eldorado-Aristide Bruant dans son cabaret *(1893), a poster by Henri de Toulouse-Lautrec, publicizing a Paris cabaret. In Toulouse-Lautrec's hands, the poster became a significant art form as well as a powerful advertising medium. With a minimum of text and the attention concentrated on the dashing figure of Bruant, this color lithograph makes its point clearly and forcefully.*

Joseph Martin–SCALA–Editorial Photocolor Archives

Most of these early posters were literal, straightforward, and relatively unimaginative. Not until the work of Jules Chéret (1836-1932), beginning in 1867, did the art of the poster begin to realize its full potential. Chéret revolutionized the look of posters. Whereas in earlier posters the illustrations were subordinate to the text, Chéret used the illustrations as the dominant features and reduced the text to a relatively minor explanatory role. His illustrations departed from literal depictions of the text. Instead of realistic scenes, he drew idealized figures, emphasizing prettiness, vitality, and movement. He specialized in theatrical posters, and a typical work (he produced nearly 1000) might feature an effervescent young woman in ruffles and flounces, performing a cancan step against a filmy, pastel background. The text was reduced to a minimum, usually a few words at the top or bottom of the poster announcing the name of the theater and the attraction presented.

Chéret's methods spread quickly throughout Europe and America. Applied to posters for commercial products as well as theatrical events, they gave rise to a visually charming poster art that appealed directly to the senses and was understandable even to the illiterate.

The new vitality of poster art led many well-known painters and artists to try their hands at the craft. The most important developments came in the 1890s, when the French painters Henri de Toulouse-Lautrec and Pierre Bonnard and various Art Nouveau artists introduced important innovations.

The 1890s. Toulouse-Lautrec, the supreme poster artist of the 19th century, made significant changes in both the content and the artistic style of posters. He abandoned the lyrical impressionism of earlier styles, using instead large areas of flat color in his posters, a technique borrowed from Japanese prints. The idealized female figures of earlier works were replaced with naturalistic, almost caricatured people depicted in telling vignettes—a woman drinking at a bar, a gentleman kissing a woman at a table. In his work, the text of the poster steadily decreased in prominence as he concentrated all attention on the picture. One of Toulouse-Lautrec's last works, *Jane Avril* (1899), eliminates the text entirely (except for the name of the entertainer herself); it is the prototype for all modern, purely pictorial posters.

The Art Nouveau artists introduced an alternative pictorial style to that of Toulouse-Lautrec. Their pictures employed flowing lines and elegant elongated forms to create exotic, stylized illustrations. The most important Art Nouveau poster artists were the English Aubrey Beardsley, the Czech-French Alphonse Mucha, the Belgian Henri van de Velde, the Scottish Frances MacDonald (1874-1921) and her sister Margaret MacDonald (1865-1933), the American Will Bradley (1868-1962), the Austrian Gustav Klimt, and the Dutch Jan Toorop (1858-1928). Van de Velde's *Tropon* poster (1899) was a landmark. He completely eliminated human figures from the picture, substituting an abstract design—to create a whole new category of poster design.

Bonnard, although not a prolific poster producer, made one highly influential innovation in his 1894 poster advertising the periodical *La Revue Blanche*. He used the text as an integral part of the illustration, intertwining the letters of the words with the painted picture and using small printed words to form the background. This new style had an invigorating effect on subsequent poster design well into the 20th century.

The 20th Century. With World War I, beginning in 1914, poster art underwent an abrupt change. Posters became propaganda instruments and were also used to encourage army enlistment and to sell war bonds. Artistically, they were usually crude and blunt compared to previous styles. The most famous was the American painter James Montgomery Flagg's *I Want You* (1917), showing a stern Uncle Sam pointing a finger directly at the viewer.

During the 1920s and '30s, in the hands of artists such as the French Cassandre (the professional name of Adolphe Mouron, 1901-68) and Jean Carlu (1900-) and the American E. McKnight Kauffer (1890-1954), posters absorbed a multitude of influences, including cubism, surrealism, Dada, and Art Deco. The best-known works were Cassandre's Art Deco advertisements for the French National Railroads, such as *Nord Express* (1927), featuring trains and railroad tracks portrayed in an elegant, semiabstract, geometrical style.

During these years, two new types of poster also became popular—movie and travel posters. The latter had first been produced in 1908 by the London Transport Co., but during the 1930s they began to be used by all major transportation companies. Movie posters boomed enormously in the wake of the popularity of silent films and, after 1929, sound films.

Also important in the 1920s and '30s were noncommercial posters produced by serious artists, especially in Germany and Russia. Dada artists in Berlin and Russia, notably John Heartfield, (1891-1968), George Grosz, and the Russian El Lissitzky (1890-1941), experimented with photographic (rather than painted) posters, often as-

Tigers dramatically communicate the idea of "circus" (cyrk in Polish) in this poster for the Polish circus by W. Gorka. Cepelia

sembling complex photomontages from pieces of several photographs. The German Bauhaus school of design in Weimar and Munich pioneered modern forms of graphic art, making the text of the poster an integral part of the design and in some cases using the words or letters of the text to create the entire design. The work of the Austrian-born American Herbert Bayer (1900–85) carried graphic design to a level of sophistication not equaled until the 1960s.

During World War II forceful propaganda posters were again produced, often by major artists such as the Russian-American Ben Shahn. Posters of the postwar period adapted and refined all earlier trends, attracting the attention of serious painters such as the Spaniards Pablo Picasso and Salvador Dali, the French Henri Matisse, the Swiss Max Bill, and the American Roy Lichtenstein, as well as several American graphic artists: Peter Max (1937–), Milton Glaser (1929–), and Tomi Ungerer (1931–). The principal artistic innovation of the postwar era has been the purely pictorial poster, which has no advertising or commercial purpose but carries an artistic or aesthetic message.

For further information on this topic, see the Bibliography in volume 28, section 716.

POSTIMPRESSIONISM, term designating generally the pictorial art movements that succeeded impressionism (q.v.). Initially the term was applied to the styles developed during the last 2 decades of the 19th century by the French painters Paul Cézanne, Paul Gauguin, Henri de Toulouse-Lautrec, and Georges Seurat, and by the Dutch painter Vincent van Gogh. It was first used in reference to an exhibition of paintings by Cézanne, Gauguin, and van Gogh held in London in 1910. In their work all of the painters named, except Seurat, stressed a subjective view of the visual world. Seurat is considered a postimpressionist because he used the color technique of the impressionists as a means of achieving structural unity in his work. Although the postimpressionists based their styles of painting on the color innovations of impressionism, they reacted against the naturalistic accuracy of impressionism and its attempt to depict light.

The work of the postimpressionists reveals a freely expressive use of color and form. They departed from certain features of impressionism, such as analysis of the effects of light and the illusionistic conventions of naturalism. Cézanne was more interested in rendering the structural qualities of his subject than in copying nature. He painted still lifes and landscapes in a manner emphasizing their cubic volume, as in *Pines and Rocks* (1895–98, Museum of Modern Art, New York City). His emphasis on the geometric forms and prismatic light inherent in nature anticipated cubism. Gauguin was concerned with developing flat, decorative surface patterns in an attempt to capture the pictorial boldness of folk art, as in *Calvary* (1889, Palais des Beaux-Arts, Brussels). His work influenced the style of the French painter Henri Matisse, one of the leaders of Fau-

Self-portrait (c. 1876) by Paul Cézanne. Bavarian National Gallery, Munich

Detail of D'où Venons-nous? Que Sommes-nous? Où Allons-nous? *(1897; Where Do We Come From? What Are We? Where Are We Going?), oil on canvas by Paul Gauguin. This powerful allegory, which clearly displays his vision of life, is Gauguin's largest and most famous painting.* Museum of Fine Arts, Boston–Tompkins Collection

Road With Cypress and Star *(1890), oil on canvas by Vincent van Gogh.*
Collection: State Museum Kroller-Muller, Otterlo, Netherlands

vism. Van Gogh used vivid, often strident, colors to evoke powerful spiritual and emotional meanings from his subjects. Representative of his subjective approach is *Starry Night* (1889, Museum of Modern Art). His paintings presaged expressionism. Seurat painstakingly applied his paints over the entire surface of the canvas in tiny points of pure color, which, when viewed from afar, would appear to blend, forming blocks of color and shadows. A fine example of his work is the large painting *Sunday Afternoon on the Island of la Grande Jatte* (1884–86, Chicago Art Institute). Toulouse-Lautrec, who is also famous for his work in color lithography, was influenced strongly by the linear compositions of Japanese prints. He frequently chose for subjects equestrian scenes and scenes of Paris nightlife, such as that depicted in *At the Moulin Rouge* (1889, Chicago Art Institute).

Other movements in 20th-century art, such as surrealism and futurism, as well as cubism, expressionism, and Fauvism, are referred to as post-impressionist because they developed as a result partly of the freedom achieved for the artist by impressionism and partly of a new emphasis upon mental conception in art. In the latter sense the 20th-century art movements reflect notably the innovations of Cézanne, Gauguin, and van Gogh. J.J.S.

For further information on this topic, see the Bibliography in volume 28, sections 659–60.

POTASH. *See* POTASSIUM.

POTASSIUM, metallic element, symbol K (from Lat. *kalium,* "alkali"), one of the alkali metals (q.v.) in group 1 (or Ia) of the periodic table (*see* PERIODIC LAW); at.no. 19, at.wt. 39.098. Potassium melts at about 63° C (about 145° F), boils at about 76° C (about 1400° F), and has a sp.gr. of 0.86.

Properties and Occurrence. Potassium was discovered and named in 1807 by the British chemist Sir Humphry Davy. The metal is silver-white and can be cut with a knife. It has a hardness (q.v.) of 0.5. Potassium exists in three natural isotopic forms, with mass numbers 39, 40, and 41. Potassium-40 is radioactive and has a half-life of 1.28 billion years. The most abundant isotope is potassium-39. Several radioactive isotopes have been artificially prepared. Potassium metal is prepared by the electrolysis of fused potassium hydroxide or of a mixture of potassium chloride and potassium fluoride. The metal oxidizes as soon as it is exposed to air and reacts violently with water, yielding potassium hydroxide and hydrogen gas. Because hydrogen gas produced in the reaction with water burns spontaneously, potassium is always stored under a liquid such as kerosene, with which it does not react.

Potassium is found in nature in large quantities, ranking eighth in order of abundance of the elements in the crust of the earth, in various minerals such as carnallite, feldspar, saltpeter (qq.v.), greensand, and sylvite. Potassium is a constituent of all plant and animal tissue as well as a vital constituent of fertile soil.

Uses. Potassium metal is used in photoelectric cells. Potassium forms many compounds resembling corresponding sodium compounds, based on a valence of 1. A few of the element's most important compounds follow. Potassium bromide, KBr, a white solid formed by the reaction of potassium hydroxide and bromine, is used in photography, engraving, and lithography, and in medicine as a sedative. Potassium chromate, K_2CrO_4, a yellow crystalline solid, and potassium bichromate (or potassium dichromate), $K_2Cr_2O_7$, a red crystalline solid, are powerful oxidizing agents used in matches and fireworks, in textile dyeing, and in leather tanning. Potassium iodide, KI, a white crystalline compound, very soluble in water, is used in photography for preparing gelatin emulsions and in medicine for the treatment of rheumatism and overactivity of the thyroid gland. Potassium nitrate, KNO_3, a white solid prepared by fractional crystallization of sodium nitrate and potassium chloride solutions, is used in matches, explosives, and fireworks and in pickling meat. It occurs naturally as saltpeter. Potassium permanganate, $KMnO_4$, a purple crystalline solid, is used as a disinfectant and germicide and as an oxidizing agent in many important chemical reactions. Potassium sulfate, K_2SO_4, a white crystalline solid, is an important potassium fertilizer and is also used in the preparation of potassium alum. Potassium hydrogen tartrate, $KHC_4H_4O_6$, commonly known as cream of tartar, is a white solid used in baking powder and in medicine.

The term *potash* originally designated potassium carbonate, obtained by leaching wood ashes, but is now applied in general to a number of potassium compounds. Potassium carbonate, K_2CO_3, a white solid, also called potash or pearl ash, is obtained from the ash of wood or other burned plant materials, and by reacting potassium hydroxide with carbon dioxide. It is used in making glass and soft soap. Potassium chlorate, $KClO_3$, called chlorate of potash, a white crystalline compound, is formed by the electrolysis of potassium chloride solution. It is a powerful oxidizing agent and is used in matches, fireworks, and explosives, as a disinfectant, and as a source of oxygen. Potassium chloride, KCl, a white crystalline compound, commonly called chloride of potash or muriate of potash, is a common constituent of potassium salt minerals, from which it is obtained by volatilization. It is an important potassium fertilizer and is also used in making other potassium compounds. Potassium hydroxide, KOH, called caustic potash, a white deliquescent solid (dissolved by the moisture in the air), prepared by the electrolysis of potassium chloride or by the reaction of potassium carbonate and calcium hydroxide, is used in the manufacture of soap and is an important chemical reagent. It dissolves in less than its own weight of water, liberating heat and forming a strongly alkaline solution.

POTATO, edible starchy tuber produced by certain plants of the genus *Solanum,* of the family Solanaceae (*see* NIGHTSHADE), especially the common white potato, *S. tuberosum.* The name is also applied to the plants. The white-potato tuber is a food staple in most countries of the temperate regions of the world. The plant is grown as an annual herb; the stem attains a length of up to almost 1 m (3 ft), erect or prostrate, with pointed leaves and white to purple flowers. The fruit is a many-seeded berry about the size of a cherry. Like the stems and the foliage, the fruit contains significant amounts of solanin, a poisonous alkaloid characteristic of the genus. The plant, native to the Peruvian Andes, was brought to Europe in the 16th century by Spanish explorers. The cultivation of the potato spread rapidly, especially in the temperate regions, and early in the 18th century the plant was introduced into North America. The earliest authentic record of its cultivation there was dated 1719, at Londonderry, N.H. Production in the U.S. during the mid-1980s involved a harvest of almost 500,000 ha (about 1.2 million acres) yielding about 16.1 million metric tons of potatoes annually. The principal potato-producing states are, in order, Idaho, Washington, Maine, Wisconsin, North Dakota, California, and Pennsylvania. The early crop is produced by California and the Gulf states; as the season advances, the harvest moves to the states of the Great Plains, the Pacific Northwest, and the Northeast.

In ordinary cultivation, propagation is accomplished by planting the tuber or a section of the tuber containing an eye, which is an undeveloped bud. New varieties are developed from seed produced after controlled pollination. Improved varieties may be propagated rapidly by using cuttings from the sprouts. Rich, sandy loams are most suitable for producing the light, mealy types favored by American and British taste; heavy, moist soils produce the firm type preferred by Europeans. Named varieties popular in the U.S. include Rose, Idaho, Cobbler, Early Ohio, Green Mountain, Hebron, Rural, and

Burbank. Freshly dug potatoes contain 78% water, 18% starch, 2.2% protein, 1% ash, and 0.1% fat. About 75% of the dry weight is carbohydrate. The potato is an important source of starch for the manufacture of adhesives and alcohol.

The most important disease of the potato is late blight, caused by the fungus *Phytophthora infestans,* which rots leaves, stems, and tubers. The early blight, caused by *Alternaria solani,* is not so destructive but causes lesions that permit entry of the various forms of bacterial rot. Several forms of mosaic disease and leaf curl are caused by infection with viruses. The Colorado potato beetle, *Leptinotarsa decemlineatum,* is the most destructive of the insect pests; others include the potato leafhopper, *Empoasca fabae,* the potato flea beetle, *Epitrix cucumeris,* and species of aphids and psyllids. *See also* SWEET POTATO.

For further information on this topic, see the Bibliography in volume 28, sections 453, 589, 592.

POTAWATOMI, North American Indian tribe of the Algonquian (q.v.) language family and of the Eastern Woodlands culture area. The Potawatomi, or Fire Nation, were closely related to both the Ojibwa (q.v.) and the Ottawa Indians (q.v.). When the Potawatomi first became known to Europeans in the early 17th century, they were settled around what is now Green Bay, Wis. Gradually they extended their territory until, by 1800, they dominated a large area from Wisconsin to Michigan and much of northern Indiana and Illinois. During the colonial period they fought with the French against the British, and in 1763 they took part in the uprising under the Ottawa Indian chief Pontiac. They were allied with the British against the Americans in the American Revolution and in the War of 1812.

Between 1815 and 1841 the Potawatomi sold their lands to the U.S. government, and most of them moved west, eventually settling on a reservation in southern Kansas. By the mid-20th century about 2000 Potawatomi lived in Kansas, with smaller bands in neighboring states. In 1990, 16,763 people in the U.S. claimed to be of Potawatomi descent.

See also AMERICAN INDIANS.

For further information on this topic, see the Bibliography in volume 28, sections 1105–8.

POTEMKIN, Grigory Aleksandrovich (1739–91), Russian field marshal and statesman, born in Smolensk, and educated at the University of Moscow. He came to the attention of Catherine the Great in 1762 after taking part in the coup d'état that made her empress. In 1774, after distinguishing himself in the Russo-Turkish War of 1768–74, Potemkin became a count, governor-general of the Ukraine, and the favorite of the empress. Their romance ended in 1776, but Potemkin remained the most powerful man in Russia almost until his death. In 1783 he played a major role in the Russian conquest of the Crimea and was created a prince. He became a field marshal in 1784 and introduced many reforms into the Russian army, built a fleet on the Black Sea, and founded a number of ports. In 1787 he organized Catherine's triumphant Crimean tour, which brought on her second war with Turkey (1787–92). Potemkin acted in the war as commander in chief. He died en route to peace negotiations.

POTENTIAL ENERGY, energy stored in a gravitational, magnetic, or electric field by virtue of an object being moved in that field. It equals the work (that is, the product of force times distance) that must be expended on the particle. Raising an object above ground, for example, will increase its potential energy by an amount that is identical to the work done to raise it.

If a piece of iron is placed within the field exerted by a magnet, it acquires an amount of potential energy equal to the work required to place it where it is within the field. In the same way, an electrical potential is the amount of energy (or voltage) acquired by an electric charge by virtue of the work done in placing the charge within the electric field. *See* ELECTRICITY; ENERGY; FIELD; FORCE; GRAVITATION; MAGNETISM; WORK.

POTENTIOMETER. *See* ELECTRIC METERS.

POTENZA (anc. *Potentia*), city, S Italy, capital of Potenza Province and of Basilicata Region. Located in the Apennines, Potenza is a commercial center for the surrounding agricultural region. Manufactures include processed food and machinery. A noted archaeological museum is here. Founded by the Romans in the 2d century BC, Potenza passed to the Lombards in the 6th century AD. The city had destructive earthquakes in 1273 and 1857. It was the first city in S Italy to expel (1860) the Bourbon rulers of the Kingdom of the Two Sicilies. Pop. (1988 est.) 67,400.

POTLATCH, a ceremonial distribution of gifts observed by North American Indian tribes of the Pacific coast from Oregon to Alaska. These tribes, such as the Kwakiutl, emphasized competitiveness and were acutely conscious of social standing.

Occasions for potlatches included weddings and deaths in the family of the host. The festivities began with dancing, feasting, and speechmaking. The host would then distribute gifts, usually in the form of food and blankets. The host might even destroy money and verbally abuse his guests to indicate his financial and social superiority.

Guests who received gifts were obliged to hold potlatches of their own at a later date. They would usually try to give gifts of an even greater value than those they had received in an attempt to establish their own superiority and wealth.

POTOMAC, river of the eastern U.S., formed by its own North Branch and South Branch, which rise in NE West Virginia and unite below Cumberland, Md. From this point the river winds about 460 km (about 285 mi) SE before emptying into Chesapeake Bay. It forms part of the boundary between West Virginia and Maryland and also separates Virginia from both Maryland and the District of Columbia. Large ships can go up the Potomac as far as Washington, D.C. The Potomac's principal affluents are the Shenandoah and Monocacy rivers. Mount Vernon (q.v.)—the home of George Washington—Anacostia, and other historic sites are located on its banks.

POTOSÍ, city, S Bolivia, capital of Potosí Department, in the Andes Mts., near Sucre. Set at more than 3960 m (more than 13,000 ft) above sea level, Potosí is one of the highest inhabited communities in the world. It is a mining center, and tin, copper, and lead are produced here. Manufactures include processed food, furniture, and beer. Within the city are Tomás Frías Bolivian University (1892), a cathedral, a mint built in 1572, and many colonial churches. Potosí was founded in 1546, a year after silver was discovered in the region. By 1611 Potosí was the leading silver center in the world and had a population of 150,000. By 1825, however, the silver was virtually exhausted, and the population fell to 8000. During the early 20th century, tin mining became important, and the city began to grow again. Pop. (1987 est.) 111,200.

POTSDAM, city, NE Germany, capital of the state of Brandenburg after the German unification in 1990 (formerly the capital of Potsdam District, East Germany). Potsdam is located on the Havel R. near Berlin. Among the manufactures are locomotives, textiles, and pharmaceuticals; motion pictures are produced in the suburb of Babelsberg. The Brandenburg Gate (1770) and several palaces, including Sans Souci Palace (1745–47) and the New Palace (1763–69), both built by Frederick II, are among the architectural features of the city. It is also the site of the College of Film and Television (1954), the Institute for International Relations and Legal Studies (1948), and a history museum. The city was badly damaged in World War II and in 1945 was the site of the Potsdam Conference. Pop. (1987 est.) 141,700.

POTSDAM CONFERENCE, meeting of the heads of government of the U.S., the USSR, and Great Britain, held in Potsdam, near Berlin, from July 17 to Aug. 2, 1945, following the unconditional surrender of Germany in World War II. The purpose of the conference was the implementation of decisions reached previously at the Yalta Conference. The U.S. was represented by President Harry S. Truman and the USSR by Premier Joseph Stalin. Great Britain was represented at first by Prime Minister Winston Churchill and later by the new prime minister, Clement Richard Attlee.

A communiqué issued at the close of the con-

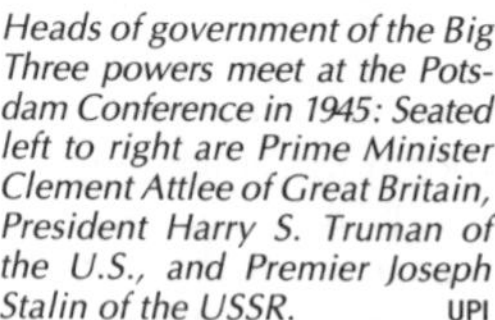

Heads of government of the Big Three powers meet at the Potsdam Conference in 1945: Seated left to right are Prime Minister Clement Attlee of Great Britain, President Harry S. Truman of the U.S., and Premier Joseph Stalin of the USSR. UPI

ference, and known as the Potsdam Agreement, contained the decisions reached by the participants. The principal decisions related to Germany. Administration of the country, until the establishment of a permanent new government, was transferred to the military commanders of the U.S., the USSR, Great Britain, and France, in their zones of occupation, and a four-power Allied Control Council was created to resolve questions pertaining to Germany as a whole. Pending definitive settlement in a peace treaty, all lands east of the Oder and Neisse rivers were placed under Polish and Soviet jurisdiction. It was agreed that the four occupying powers of Germany should take reparations from their respective zones of occupation; but, because the USSR had suffered greater loss than any of the other major powers, provision was made for additional compensation to the USSR. Rigid measures of control were decided on in the Potsdam Conference to prevent Germany from ever again becoming a threat to world peace. The conferees determined to disarm the country and prevent remilitarization; to outlaw the National Socialist (Nazi) party that had been led by Hitler; to decentralize the economy and reorganize it with emphasis on agriculture; and to encourage democratic practices.

On July 26, the U.S., British, and Chinese governments issued an ultimatum, called the Potsdam Declaration, to the Japanese government, confronting Japan with a choice between unconditional surrender and total annihilation; the USSR was not then at war with Japan and was not a party to the ultimatum. The representatives at the conference also set up a Council of Foreign Ministers to draft peace treaties and confirmed their intention to try Axis war criminals.

Although the Potsdam Conference was considered successful, many of the agreements reached were dishonored within a year as a result of the growing rift between the USSR and Western Europe.

POTTER, (Helen) Beatrix (1866-1943), English writer and illustrator of children's books, born in London, and privately educated. During most of her adult life, she lived in a farm cottage in Sawrey, Westmoreland Co., where she kept many animals as pets. Unsuccessful in attempts to publish her serious botanical work (watercolor studies of fungi), she wrote (1893) and published privately (1900) for an invalid child *The Tale of Peter Rabbit.* This story about the first of many animal characters she was to create became a children's classic throughout the world. Other diminutive animal characters created by her include Benjamin Bunny, Jemima Puddle-Duck, and Mrs. Tiggy-Winkle. Inseparable from her whimsical tales are her delicate but exact and detailed watercolor illustrations depicting her characters in domestic scenes. Potter's other works include *The Tailor of Gloucester* (1902) and *The Tale of Tom Kitten* (1907). Interested in the preservation of the natural landscape, she bequeathed her property in Sawrey to the National Trust, which also maintains her home as a museum.

POTTERY, clay that is chemically altered and permanently hardened by firing in a kiln. The nature and type of pottery, or ceramics (Gr. *keramos,* "clay"), is determined by the composition of the clay and the way it is prepared; the temperature at which it is fired; and the glazes used.

TYPES, PROCEDURES, AND TECHNIQUES

Earthenware is porous pottery, usually fired at the lowest kiln temperatures (900°-1200° C/1652°-2192° F). Depending on the clay used, it turns buff, red, brown, or black when fired. To be made waterproof, it must be glazed. Nearly all ancient, medieval, Middle Eastern, and European painted ceramics are earthenware, as is much contemporary household dinnerware. Stoneware, water-resistant and much more durable, is fired at temperatures of 1200°-1280° C (2191°-2336° F). The clay turns white, buff, gray, or red and is glazed for aesthetic reasons. (Pottery fired at about 1200° C/2192° F is sometimes called middle-fire ware; its earthenware or stoneware traits vary from clay to clay.) Stoneware was made by the Chinese in antiquity and became known in northern Europe after the Renaissance. Porcelain is made from kaolin, a clay formed from decomposed granite. Kaolin is a primary white clay—one found in the earth in the place where it was formed and not transported there by rivers; secondary clays, river borne to the site of deposit, contain impurities that give it various colors. Porcelain is fired at 1280°-1400° C (2336°-2552° F); it is white and often translucent. Porcelanous ware was first made in China, hence its common name china. Chinese porcelain is less vitrified (softer) than its modern European counterpart, which was developed in Germany in the early 18th century. Earthenware imitations of Chinese porcelain are also made; called soft-paste or frit porcelains, they are fired at about 1100° C (about 2012° F). In the mid-18th century, English potters invented bone china, a somewhat harder ware that gained whiteness, translucency, and stability through the inclusion of calcium phosphate in the form of calcined (fired, chemically altered) oxbones.

Preparing and Shaping the Clay. The potter can remove some of the coarse foreign matter natural

A potter models a spout on a jug, using a foot-driven potter's wheel. Saskatchewan Govt.

to secondary clays, or it can be used in various quantities for different effects. A certain amount of coarse grain in the clay helps the vessel retain its shape in firing, and potters using fine-grained clays often "temper" the clay by adding coarser materials such as sand, fine stones, ground shells, or grog (fired and pulverized clay) before kneading the clay into workable condition. The plasticity of clay allows pottery to be shaped in several traditional ways. The clay can be flattened and then shaped by being pressed against the inside or outside of a mold—a stone or basket, or a clay or plaster form. Liquid clay can be poured into plaster molds. A pot can be coil built: Clay is rolled between the palms of the hands and extended into long coils, a coil is formed into a ring, and the pot is built up by superimposed rings. Also, a ball of clay can be pinched into a desired shape. The most sophisticated pottery-making technique is wheel throwing.

The potter's wheel, invented in the 4th millennium BC, is a flat disk that revolves horizontally on a pivot. Both hands—one on the inside and the other on the outside of the clay—are free to shape the pot upward from a ball of clay that is thrown and centered on the rotating wheel head. Some wheels are set in motion by a stick that fits into a notch in the wheel (often activated by an assistant); called a handwheel, this is the classical wheel of Japanese potters. In 16th-century Europe, with the addition of a flywheel separate from the wheel head and mounted in a frame, the potter could control the wheel by kicking the flywheel. A kick bar, or foot treadle, was added in the 19th century. In the 20th century the electric wheel with a variable-speed motor allowed greater and more regulated rotating speed.

Drying and Firing. To fire without breaking, the clay must first be air dried. If the clay is thoroughly dry, porous, relatively soft pottery can be baked directly in an open fire, at temperatures of 650°-750° C (1202°-1382° F); primitive pottery is still made in this way. The first kilns were used in the 6th millennium BC. Wood fuels—and, later, coal, gas, and electricity—have always required careful control to produce the desired effect in hardening the clay into earthenware or stoneware. Different effects are achieved by oxidizing the flames (giving them adequate ventilation, producing a great flame) or by reducing the oxygen by partially obstructing the entrance of air into the kiln. For example, a clay high in iron will typically burn red in an oxidizing fire, whereas in a reducing fire it will turn gray or black; chemically, in reduction firing the clay's red iron oxide (FeO_2, or with two molecules, Fe_2O_4) is converted to black iron oxide (Fe_2O_3) as the pot gives up an atom of oxygen to the oxygen-starved fire.

Decoration. A pot can be decorated before or after firing. When the clay is half dry and somewhat stiffened ("leather hard"), bits of clay can be pressed into the pot; the body can be incised, stamped, or pressed with lines and other patterns; or clay can be cut out and the body pierced. The vessel walls can be smoothed by burnishing, or polishing, so that rough particles are driven inward and the clay particles are aligned in such a way that the vessel surface is shiny and smooth. (Some clays can be polished after firing.) Slip (liquefied clay strained of coarse particles) may be used: The bone-dry (completely dry) or half-dry pot can be dipped into slip of creamy consistency (to which color is sometimes added); or the slip can be brushed on or trailed on with a spouted can or a syringe. Designs can be drawn with a pointed tool that scratches through the slip to reveal the body, a technique known as sgraffito.

Glazes. Historically, unglazed pottery has always been more common than glazed pottery. Glaze is a form of glass, consisting basically of glass-forming minerals (silica or boron) combined with stiffeners (such as clay and fluxes) and melting agents (such as lead or soda). In raw form, glaze can be applied either to the unfired pot or after an initial unglazed, or biscuit, firing. The pot is then glaze fired; the glaze ingredients must melt and become glasslike at a temperature that is compatible to that required for the clay. Many kinds of glazes are used. Some heighten the color of the body; others mask it. Alkaline glazes, popular in the Middle East, are shiny and frequently transparent. They are composed mostly of silica (such as sand) and a form of soda (such as nitre). Lead glazes are transparent, with traditional types made of sand fused with sulfide or oxide of lead. They were used on earthenware by Roman, Chinese, and medieval European potters and are still employed on European earthenware. Tin glazes, opaque and white, were introduced by medieval Islamic potters and were used for Spanish lusterware, Italian majolica, and European faience and delftware. Eventually the Chinese and Japanese made such glazes for the European market.

Metal oxides give color to glazes. Copper will make a lead glaze turn green and an alkaline glaze turquoise; a reduction kiln will cause the copper to turn red. Iron can produce yellow, brown, gray-green, blue, or, with certain minerals, red. Feldspars (natural rocks of aluminosilicates) are used in stoneware and porcelain glazes because they fuse only at high temperatures. The effects of specific glazes on certain clay bodies depend both on the composition of each and on the potter's control of the glaze kiln.

Underglaze and Overglaze Decoration. Pottery can also be painted before and after firing. In Neolithic times, ochers and other earth pigments were used on unglazed ware. Metal oxides used in or under glazes require somewhat higher temperatures in order to fix the colors to the glaze or body—they include copper green, cobalt blue, manganese purple, and antimony yellow. If enamels (fine-ground pigments applied over a fired glaze) are used, the pot must be refired in a muffle (covered, indirect-flame) kiln at low temperatures to fuse the enamel and glaze. Transfer prints (designs printed on paper with oxides and, while wet, transferred to the pot, the paper burning away in the firing) are often used to decorate commercially manufactured pottery. In the 18th century the print plate was hand engraved, but now lithography and photography are used.

Potters' marks were used to identify ware in China from the 15th century on, and in Europe from the 18th, and famous pottery marks have always been easily forged. Greek potters and painters signed their work, as is true of a few Islamic potters and most 20th-century potters.

EAST ASIA

The leading pottery centers in East Asian history were China, Korea, and Japan.

China. In Neolithic China, pottery was made by coil building and then beating the shapes with a paddle; toward the end of the period (2d millennium BC) vessels were begun handbuilt, then finished on a wheel. At Kansu, in northwest China, vessels from the Pan-shan culture, made from finely textured clay and fired to buff or reddish-brown, were brush painted with mineral pigments in designs of strong S-lines converging on circles. They date from 2600 BC. The early Chinese kiln was the simple updraft type; the fire was made below the ware, and vents in the floor allowed the flames and heat to rise. Lung-shan pottery, from the central plains, was wheel made. Chinese Neolithic vessels include a wide variety of shapes—tripods, ewers, urns, cups, amphorae, and deep goblets.

The Shang period. The Neolithic prototypes became the basis for bronze vessels during the Shang period (c. 1766–c. 1027 BC), and Shang ceramic molds for bronze casting, made of high-quality clay, have been found. Shang pottery had four basic types, most of them found at the capital at Anyang, in present-day Henan (Ho-nan) Province. The first continued the Neolithic functional tradition in coarse gray clay, decorated with impressed cords or in incised geometric patterns; the second consisted of dark gray imitations of bronze vessels; the third, white pottery with finely carved decoration resembling bronze designs; the last, glazed stoneware.

Chou period through the Six Dynasties. Except for the white pottery, all the Shang types continued in the Chou period (c. 1027–256 BC). Coarse red earthenware with lead glazes was introduced in the Warring States era (403–221 BC); this ware too resembled bronzes. In the south, stoneware with a pale brown glaze was fashioned into sophisticated shapes.

The discovery in 1974 of the terra-cotta (q.v.) army of Shih Huang Ti, the first emperor of the Ch'in dynasty (221–206 BC)—an imperial bodyguard of more than 6000 life-size soldiers and horses buried in military formation—added new dimensions to modern knowledge of the art of the ancient Chinese potters. These handsome idealized portraits, each with different details of dress, were modeled from coarse gray clay, with heads and hands fired separately at high earthenware temperatures and attached later. Afterward, the assembled, fired figures were painted with bright mineral pigments (a procedure called cold decoration), most of which have now flaked.

Tomb figures and objects with molded and painted decoration continued to be made in the Han dynasty (206 BC–AD 220); these included houses, humans, and even stoves. Bricks were sometimes decorated with scenes of everyday animal and human activity. Also produced were gray stoneware with a thick green glaze, and reddish earthenware.

During the Six Dynasties period (AD 220–589), celadon-glazed stoneware, a precursor of later porcelain celadons, began to appear. (Celadons are transparent iron-pigmented glazes fired in a reducing kiln and yielding gray, pale blue or green, or brownish-olive.) Called Yüeh (or green) ware, they were less influenced than earlier pottery by the shapes of cast bronzes. Jars, ewers, and dishes became more delicate of line and classical in contour, and some had simple incised or molded ornament.

T'ang and Sung dynasties. Tomb figures and stoneware continued to be made during the T'ang dynasty (618–906), showing stylistic influences from Central Asia. Bowls and basins with carved decoration were exported to India, Southeast Asia, and the Muslim Empire. Two important ceramic types, however, characterized this period. One was a fine white earthenware covered with a lead glaze of glowing yellow and green tints, often in mottled patterns. The other, the most significant innovation of the T'ang potters, was porcelain—made into thin, delicate bowls and vases with clear, bluish or greenish glazes.

Porcelain was further refined in the Sung dynasty (960–1279), the age in which all art flourished, and the greatest era of Chinese pottery. Potters became adept at controlling glazes, a trend that began in the T'ang period. Vessels were elegantly shaped. Decoration—molded, carved, or painted—included dragons, fish, lotuses, and peonies, scholarly subjects of the court painters, each representing a virtue. Kilns were established throughout China, each kiln site having its own style.

In the Northern Sung, three outstanding styles emerged: Ting, Ju, and Chün. Ting ware was decorated with the previously mentioned motifs and covered with a smooth ivory glaze. It was admired by courtly patrons but was also used as everyday pottery. Ju was a coarse stoneware covered with a celadonlike light bluish-gray glaze with a subtle crackle. Chün glazes, thickly applied, ranged from blue to lavender, with added splashes of copper red or purple. Later, in the 12th century, Northern Sung celadons reached their height, with a gray stoneware body covered in transparent olive or light brown. Tz'u-chou, a popular stoneware used by all social classes,

Neolithic Chinese earthenware jar from the Pan-shan culture at Kansu, dating from c. 2600 BC. The fired surface was painted over with a characteristic S-scroll design.

Metropolitan Museum of Art, Purchase, Mrs. Richard Linburn Gift, 1980

The brilliant polychrome glazing of this realistically modeled terra-cotta horse characterizes it as a production of the T'ang dynasty (618–906) of China. Such pieces were designed for use as tomb figures.
Cleveland Museum of Art–Anonymous Gift

combined transparent glazes with bold slip painting, sgraffito, carving, incising, impressing, and molding, as well as polychrome overglaze enameling, all in a great variety of motifs. The Lung-ch'üan celadons of the Southern Sung—white porcelain with light bluish-green jadelike crackled glazes—were of even higher quality. The shapes were varied, some inspired by ancient bronzes, some by Middle Eastern metalwork and glass. Many were exported. Other famous wares were Chi-chou, white porcelain with a slightly bluish or greenish glaze (similar to the white Ch'ing-pai made later in the Sung era), exported to Indonesia, Southeast Asia, and the Philippines; and Chien ware, dark-bodied stoneware with a blackish-brown glaze scattered with metallic blue and black spots.

Yüan and Ming dynasties. The Mongol conquests of the mid-13th century brought new foreign influences. Under the Yüan dynasty (1279–1368) potters adjusted to produce for an expanding export market. The size of vessels increased, and potters experimented with bright enamel overglaze colors. Ch'ing-pai and Lung-ch'üan wares became heavier. White porcelain vases with blue underglaze painting were made.

This blue-and-white ware became a major export item in the Ming period (1368–1644). Under its clear glaze the porcelain body was painted with designs of great vigor and freedom of line in cobalt oxide (imported from Iran until a local source was substituted). These pieces became the favorites of 16th-century Europe, although Ming potters also made polychrome stoneware and monochromatic and white wares. New in the Ming era was the delicate Tou-ts'ai ware, a glassy porcelain with overglaze enamel painting. The court provided potters with a wide variety of new designs: scrolls, fruit, flowers, and scenes with people. Pottery was marked with dates of the emperors' reigns; the marks of successful pieces were imitated in later times.

Export to Europe reached its height in the late 17th century, when artistic standards were still high. A new enamel style, introduced from Europe and called *famille rose,* had as its principal color a delicate opaque pink, the metallic pigment for which was derived from colloidal gold. The *famille rose* colors could be mixed for shading and allowed miniature precision in drawing.

Ch'ing period. A vast number of fine porcelain vessels were produced in the Ch'ing dynasty (1644–1912), for both domestic and foreign markets, with potters concentrating on the refinement of glazes. Popular polychrome enamel styles were *famille verte* (green, yellow, and aubergine purple) and its derivatives, *famille noir* (black ground) and *famille jaune* (yellow ground). Monochromatic copper red glazes popular in Ming—both oxblood (*sang de boeuf*) and the paler peach bloom—were revived, as were Sung celadons. In the 18th century, European collecting of Chinese porcelain was at its peak; at times whole rooms were devoted to it. By the end of the century, however, the endless repetitions of old motifs and forms led to sterility, and the Chinese could no longer compete with European mass-produced porcelain.

Korea. Chinese pottery and porcelain always exerted a strong influence in Korea, but Korean potters introduced subtle variations on Chinese models. Gray stoneware, found in tombs, was typical of the Silla dynasty (57 BC–AD 935). Sung-influenced celadons characterize pottery of the

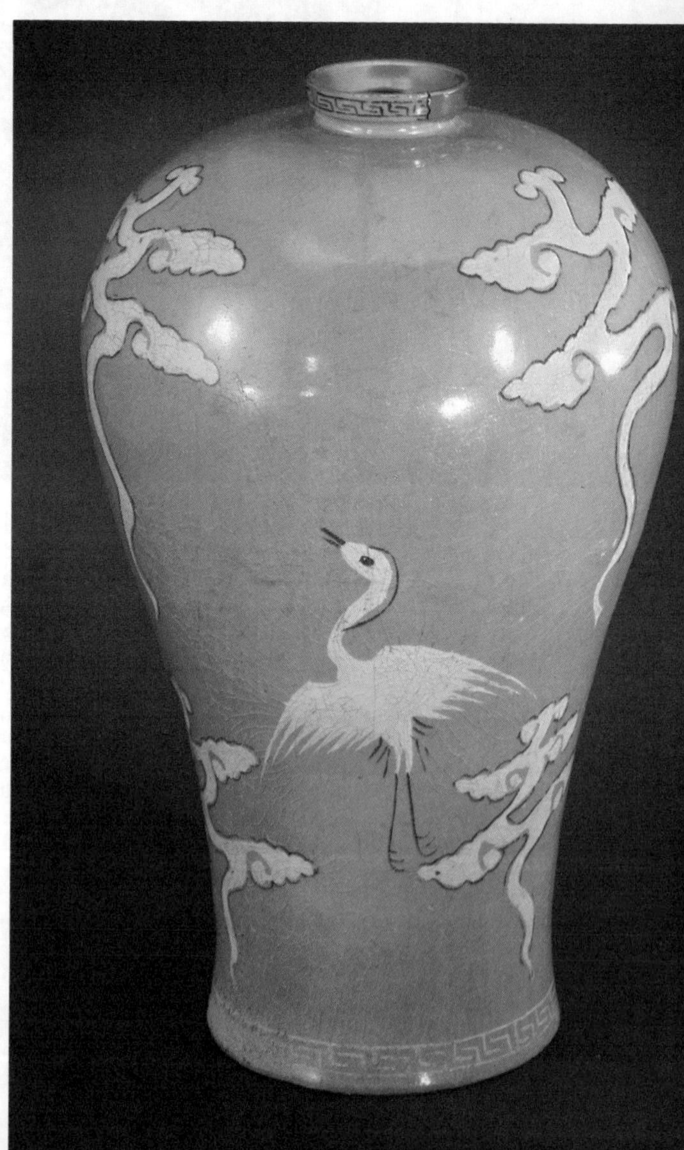

Gallipot (a vessel characterized by a very small mouth) from the Koryŏ dynasty of Korea (918–1392). The incised slip decoration typical of Koryŏ pottery was inspired by Chinese celadon ware of the Sung period. The Metropolitan Museum of Art, Fletcher Fund, 1927

A Korean bank, or climbing kiln, built into a mountain slope and accommodating multiple firing chambers. Firing takes up to two weeks. Here, workmen load finished pots onto a cart. W. H. Hodge–Peter Arnold, Inc.

Koryŏ dynasty (918–1392). Later work, although less refined, was admired for its straightforward dignity. Koreans, in turn, introduced their own and Chinese pottery into Japan.

Japan. The earliest ceramics of Neolithic Japan, those from the Jōmon period (c. 10,000–c. 300 BC), were shaped by hand, usually by the coil method. Decorated with impressions of cords and mats, they were baked in an open fire at a low temperature. Colors were reddish or ranged from gray to black. Some cult figures and utilitarian vessels were highly burnished or covered with a red iron oxide. The pottery of the Yayoi culture (c. 300 BC–c. AD 250), made by a Mongol people who came from Korea to Kyushu, has been found throughout Japan. The Yayoi used the wheel for their yellow and light brown earthenware, the smooth surface of which was at times painted bright red.

Two basic kiln types—both still in use—were employed in Japan by this time. The bank, or climbing, kiln, of Korean origin, is built into the slope of a mountain, with as many as 20 chambers; firing can take up to two weeks. In the updraft, or bottle, kiln, a wood fire at the mouth of a covered trench fires the pots, which are in a circular-walled chamber at the end of the fire trench; the top is covered except for a hole to let the smoke escape.

From the later Kofun, or Tumulus (Grave Mound), period (c. AD 250–552), pottery was found in the enormous tombs of the Japanese emperors. Called Haji ware, it resembled Yayoi pottery. More truly unique were the *haniwa,* delightful unglazed reddish earthenware figures that surrounded the tombs—houses, boats, animals, women, hunters, musicians, and warriors. Although the *haniwa* lack the grandeur of the Ch'in emperor's army, they compensate for it with their rustic vitality. Sué was another pottery of this period, a gray stoneware fired in a climbing kiln and decorated with a natural ash glaze (one formed during the firing as ash from the wood fuel fell on the pots). Originating in Korea, the natural ash glaze became characteristic of later Japanese wares made at Tamba, Tokoname, Bizen, and Shigaraki. Jars, bottles, dishes, and cups were made, some with sculpted figures. Sué ware continued to be made in the Asuka period (552–710), when Chinese cultural and religious influences were just beginning.

Nara through Kamakura periods. With the Nara period (710–84), Japan's first historical epoch, the full impact of T'ang China ware became obvious in Japan's production of high-fire pottery. Some glazes were monochromatic green or yellowish-brown; some were two-color, green and white; a few had three of these colors on rough grayish bodies. The glaze patterns were streaks and spots, not quite as refined as T'ang ceramics. Most examples of this work are preserved at the Shosoin imperial treasury at Nara.

In the early Heian period (794–894), natural ash glazes were further developed, and celadons were introduced to Japan. Then, because of disruptions in relations with China in the late Heian, or Fujiwara, period (894–1185), the quality of the pottery declined. Once contact with Sung China was renewed in the Kamakura period (1185–1333), the ceramics industry flourished, this time centered at Seto, near Nagoya. *Ki*-seto, or yellow Seto—still made today—was influenced by the popular Sung celadons; the Japanese equivalents, however, were fired in oxidizing kilns, which gave their glazes yellow and amber hues. Tokoname, a rustic pottery for everyday use, was also made in the Fujiwara period, as were other types that retain their primitive appeal.

Muromachi and Momoyama periods. Although the Ashikaga shoguns of the Muromachi period (1338–1573) did not encourage ceramic arts, the Chinese-influenced tradition of the tea ceremony, which began at that time, stimulated the manufacture of the beautiful vessels used in this elaborate ritual. The tea cult spread to the military and merchant classes in the Momoyama period (1573–1603). Its stoneware and porcelain implements reflected the tasteful, subtle beauty and elegance of the ceremony. Each shape had a specific function and name.

One sought-after variety of stoneware tea bowl, related to the Chien ware of China, was *temmoku,* with a thick purplish-brown glaze that is still popular. Seto kilns produced such fine pottery that the works of other kilns also came to be called Seto ware. Even more famous were the Raku wares, still made today by the 14th generation of the same family. Raku ware—tea ceremony vessels, other pottery, and tiles—is shaped by hand; its irregular forms follow a prescribed aesthetic of asymmetry. The glaze is brushed on in several thin layers, and the pot is fired at low temperatures. When the glaze is molten, the pot is pulled from the kiln with tongs; it cools quickly, and the glaze crackles under the thermal shock. Raku ware is admired by potters throughout the world for its rugged shapes and soft, somber lead glazes that sometimes drip downward in globs. Also prized for the tea ceremony was Oribe ware, typified by brown iron-oxide painted designs derived from motifs of textile decoration, juxtaposed with an irregular splash of runny, transparent green glaze.

Another Momoyama ware was Karatsu, influenced by Korean Yi ware. In *e*-Karatsu ("picture" Karatsu), freehand geometric patterns, grasses, and wisteria were painted in iron oxide on a whitish slip. Karatsu ware had several other styles, with different kinds of decoration. Bizen ware was at its best in the Momoyama period. Still made, it is a hard stoneware, basically brick red, but subject to irregular changes of color resulting from alternating oxidation and reduction in the firing. It is unglazed except for glaze formed by ash or straw packed around the pots in the kiln or by falling ash.

The Edo period and after. At the beginning of the Edo period, kaolin was discovered near Arita, in northern Kyushu, still a major pottery center. This discovery enabled Japanese potters to make their own hard, pure white porcelain. One type, Imari ware (named for its export port), was so popular in 17th-century Europe that even the Chinese imitated it. Its bright-colored designs were inspired by ornate lacquer work, screens, and textiles. By the late Edo period (1800–67) Imari ware declined. Kakiemon (persimmon) porcelain, made in Arita, was a far more refined, classically shaped ware, even when its motifs were similar to Imari ware. Both wares used overglaze enamels. Nabeshima ware, also of high quality and similar to silk textiles in its designs, was reserved for members of that family and their friends; only in the Meiji period (1868–1912) was it sold commercially and imitated. The designs were first drawn on thin tissue, and then in underglaze blue lines; the enamel colors were added and heat fused after the glaze firing. In eastern Japan in the Edo period, Kutani was the porcelain center. Kutani vessels were grayish in color because of impurities in the clay, and their designs were bolder than those of Arita and Imari wares. Kyoto, formerly a center for enameled pottery, became famous for its porcelain in the 19th century. In the Edo period, some 10,000 kilns were active in Japan.

The utilitarian works of folk potters, evaluated by contemporary taste, are as admired and re-

Japanese Raku ware tea bowl of the late 16th century.
Editorial Photocolor Archives

pected as the export items of earlier centuries. New influences from Europe came with the Meiji pottery, but native folk traditions were still appreciated within the country. Potters at the old centers remain active in the 20th century, working in the same styles as their ancestors, with the same local clays. Japan's most famous 20th-century potter is Hamada Shoji (1894–1978), important not only for his pottery but also as a forceful figure in the revival of folkcraft. Hamada favored iron and ash glazes on stoneware, producing shades of olive green, gray, brown, and black, and did not sign his pots (although he signed their wooden containers). In 1955 the Japanese government declared Hamada an Intangible Treasure of the country.

PRE-COLUMBIAN AMERICAS

Ancient American pottery—put to ritual, funerary, and domestic use—developed distinctive, sophisticated shapes and decorative styles, wholly unrelated to those of the Old World and executed on a high artistic level. Pots were built by coiling, hand modeling, and molding; the potter's wheel was unknown. Painted decoration was in clay slips colored with vegetable and mineral pigments.

South America. Pottery from about 3200 BC was found in Ecuadorian sites, but the foremost styles appeared in Peru. There, the Chavín style (fl. 900–400 BC), with its jaguar motifs, was succeeded in the Classic period (1st millennium AD) by one of the finest pre-Columbian potteries, that of the Mochica culture of the north coast. Molded buff-colored vases were painted in red with vivid narrative scenes; portraitlike jars were modeled in relief with great subtlety. Both had the characteristic Peruvian stirrup spout, a hollow handle with a central vertical spout. To the south the Nazca culture produced double-spouted polychrome jars with complex stylized animal motifs. The later Tiahuanaco and Inca polychrome styles were well crafted but were less dazzling.

Middle America. The earliest domestic Mexican ceramics come from the Formative period (1500–1000 BC) in the Valley of Mexico. On the Gulf coast the Olmec culture produced hollow, naturalistic figurines. During the Classic period, pottery figurines from the east showed lively freedom of expression; those from the west were often grouped in impressionistic scenes of daily life. At Teotihuacán in the central plateau, polychrome three-footed vessels were produced in molds. In the Post-Classic era the Toltecs occupied the central plateau, producing typical ceramics painted red on cream or orange on buff. Later, the Aztecs first assimilated earlier abstract

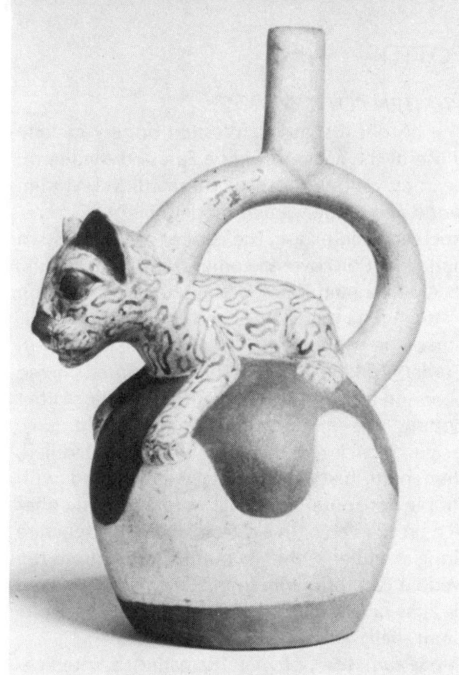

This stirrup-spout vessel from the Mochica culture of pre-Columbian Peru is decorated with the figure of an ocelot. Museum of the American Indian

decoration, then turned to red and orange bowls ornamented with birds and other life forms. Farther south, the Zapotecs and Mixtecs resisted Aztec influence. Besides modeled animals, humans, and gods, they made a highly burnished polychrome ware that influenced later Mexican pottery.

Mayan ware attained a variety and quality unique in Mesoamerican ceramics. Classic-era Mayan ware included delicate figurines, polychrome cylindrical vases with scenes and glyphs resembling those in Mayan manuscripts, and plaques containing whistles, with molded and modeled scenes of everyday life.

North America. In the Mississippi Valley the Mound Builders of the 1st millennium BC produced painted, modeled, and incised ware. In the Southwest fine pottery was made by the ancestors of the Pueblo Indians—notably the red-on-buff ware (about AD 600–900) of the Hohokam and the polychrome ware (1300 and later) of the Anasazi, both adorned with human and animal figures; and the delightful, distinctive Mimbres pottery (1000–1200) of the Mogollon culture, with black-on-white geometric designs, birds, bats, frogs, and ceremonial scenes. The ancient tradition has been carried on into modern Pueblo pottery, notably in the work of Maria Martinez (1887–1980), who is widely known for her burnished black ware.

WESTERN POTTERY

The historical styles of Western pottery include those of the ancient Middle East and Mediterranean as well as those of the medieval Muslim world and medieval and modern Europe.

Ancient Middle East. The earliest Middle Eastern pottery yet discovered comes from Çatal Hüyük, in Anatolia, and dates from 6500 BC. In addition to terra-cotta cult statues and painted clay statuettes, the ware from this site (near modern Çumra, Turkey) includes pieces painted in red ocher on a body covered with cream slip. Other pottery was monochromatic—buff, light gray, beige, or brick red. It was coil built and paddled, then burnished; some pots were incised with simple horizontal lines. The ware was fired either in a bread oven or in a closed kiln with a separate firing chamber. Other Neolithic pottery from the Middle East, primarily from Syria, had impressed designs or was combed with the edge of a cardium shell.

Persia and Mesopotamia. The earliest painted ceramics of northern Mesopotamia date from just before the 5th millennium BC. At Samarra, stylized human and animal figures were painted with colors ranging from red to brown and black on a buff background. Shortly thereafter, polychrome pottery of higher quality was made at Tell Halaf, where potters had learned more thorough control of their kilns.

At about the same time, Persian potters painted geometric designs on pots covered with light-colored slip. By the 4th millennium the potter's wheel was in use. People from the north migrated to Persia and introduced red and gray monochromatic pottery. At the height of the al-Ubayd period (4th millennium BC) a pottery industry around Susa produced many drinking vessels and bowls from refined clay. Coated with a greenish-yellow slip, they were decorated in a free style with painted geometric shapes, plants, birds, other animals, and stick-figure people.

Glazed pottery began to be produced about 1500 BC. The finest Mesopotamian ceramic work was not in domestic pottery, but rather in glazed brickwork used for architectural ornamentation. The tradition began in the 3d millennium at Uruk, where columns and niches were covered with a geometric mosaic of colored naillike ceramic cones. In Babylonia during the Kassite rule (mid-2d millennium BC), unglazed terra-cotta was used to face temples and palaces. Later, at Khorsabad, the capital of the Assyrian monarch Sargon II (r. 722–705 BC), a temple entrance was decorated with molded glazed brickwork depicting animals in procession. This tradition reached its climax in Babylon in the late 7th century BC. There the famous Sacred Way was lined with glazed bricks on which more than 700 bulls, dragons, and lions were carved and molded, then glazed in a palette ranging from white to yellow to brownish-black against a blue or greenish-blue ground. The facade of the royal throne room was decorated with lions on walls and with columns crowned and surrounded by stylized palmettos and lotus buds.

Glazed bowl from northern Iran (15th cent.), decorated with spiral designs and foliate motifs on a turquoise ground.

The Metropolitan Museum of Art, Bequest of Isaac D. Fletcher, 1917, Mr. & Mrs. Isaac D. Fletcher Collection

Egypt. In the 5th millennium BC Egyptian potters made graceful, thin, dark, highly polished ware with subtle cord decoration. The painted ware of the 4th millennium, with geometric and animal figures on red, brown, and buff bodies, was not of the same high standard. Dynastic Egypt was famous for its faience (not the same as the later European ceramics of that name). First made about 2000 BC, it is characterized by a dark green or blue glaze over a body high in powdered quartz, somewhat closer to glass than to true ceramics. Egyptian artisans made faience beads and jewelry, elegant cups, scarabs, and ushabti (small servant figures buried with the dead).

The Mediterranean, Greece, and Rome. Pottery from the islands of the Mediterranean and Aegean during the late Bronze Age (1500–1050 BC) and early Iron Age (1050–750 BC), especially from Crete and Cyprus, showed great imagination on the part of the artists, who painted bichrome ware with geometric, abstract, and figurative designs. At times, pottery shapes were fanciful and seemingly nonfunctional, at other times quite delicate in vessels used for ointments and cosmetics.

Greece. The fashioning and painting of ceramics was a major art in classical Greece. Native clay was shaped easily on the wheel, and each distinct form had a name and a specific function in Greek society and ceremonial: The amphora was a tall, two-handled storage vessel for wine, corn, oil, or honey; the hydria, a three-handled water jug; the lecythus, an oil flask with a long, narrow neck, for funeral offerings; the kylix, a double-handled drinking cup on a foot; the oenochoe, a wine jug with a pinched lip; the krater, a large bowl for mixing wine and water. Undecorated black pottery was used throughout Greek and Hellenistic times, the forms being related either to those of decorated pottery or those of metalwork. Both styles influenced Roman ceramics.

Even in the Bronze Age, the Greeks took advantage of oxidizing and reducing kilns to produce a shiny black slip on a cream, brownish, or orange-buff body, the shade depending on the type of clay. At first, decorative designs were abstract. By the Middle Bronze Age (2000–1500 BC), however, stylized forms from nature appeared. By the Late Bronze Age, plants, sea creatures, and fanciful animals were painted on pots of well-conceived shape by the Mycenaeans, who were initially influenced by Cretan potters. Athenian geometric style replaced the Mycenaean about 1000 BC and declined by the 6th century BC. Large kraters in the Geometric style, with bands of ornament, warriors, and processional figures laid out in horizontal registers, were found at the Dipylon cemetery of Athens; they date from about 750 BC.

Late Minoan vase (Crete, 15th cent. BC; National Museum, Athens). Jan Lukas–Editorial Photocolor Archives

Attic potters introduced black-figure ware in the early 6th century. Painted black forms adorned the polished red clay ground, with detail rendered by incising through the black. White and reddish-purple were added for skin and garments. Depictions of processions and chariots continued; animals and hybrid beasts (particularly in the Orientalizing phase that followed the Geometric period) were also shown, at times surrounded by geometric or vegetal motifs. Such decoration was always well integrated with the vessel shapes, and the iconography of Greek mythology can be identified. Beginning in the 6th century, the decoration stressed humans far more than animals. Favorite themes included people and gods at work, battle, and banquet; musicians; weddings and other ceremonies; and women at play or dressing. In some cases, events or heroes were labeled. Mythological and literary scenes became more frequent. Potters' and painters' names and styles have been identified, even when they did not sign their works.

Red-figure pottery was invented about 530 BC, becoming especially popular between 510 and

A representation of Venus rising from the sea forms an appropriate decoration for an Attic red-figure hydria, *or water jar (Archaeological Museum, Pegli, Italy).*
SCALA–Editorial Photocolor Archives

430. The background was painted black, and the figures were left in reserve on the red-brown clay surface; details on the figures were painted in black, which allowed the artist greater freedom in drawing. The paint could also be diluted for modulating the color. Secondary colors of red and white were less used; gold was sometimes added for details of metal and jewelry. Anatomy was rendered more realistically, and after 480, so were nuances of gesture and expression. Although Athens and Corinth were centers for red-figure pottery, the style also spread to the Greek islands. By the 4th century BC, however, it declined in quality. Another Greek style featured outline drawing on a white ground, with added colors imitating monumental painting; these vessels, however, were impractical for domestic use.

Rome. The Romans admired highly polished red-gloss earthenware—possibly in reaction against Greek and Hellenistic black pottery. The red-gloss technique developed in the eastern Mediterranean in the late Hellenistic period. This ware was made by dipping the pot in a suspension of fine particles of high-silica clay (which gave a higher gloss when polished) and firing it in an oxidizing kiln. Decoration was in raised designs: The pots were formed in clay molds that had been impressed along the edges with roulettes in repeat motifs, stamped with other designs and figures, and given further details that were hand-carved in the mold—hence the term *terra sigillata* ("stamped earth") for this ware. (The term is often also applied by extension to the clay suspension in which the pots were dipped.) Many designs and shapes were inspired by metalwork and cut glass. Arretium (modern Arezzo) was the center for red-gloss ware with relief decoration, and the best of this pottery, from the 1st centuries BC and AD, is thus called Arretine ware. Several areas of the Roman Empire made Arretine ware, but as manufacture moved farther from the capital, the quality of the red-gloss ware declined. The best was from southern France from the 1st century AD.

The black-gloss ware that the Greeks had made also spread through the Roman Empire. In England it resembled Celtic metalwork. At times the wet clay was pinched out to create a dotted effect; other pots were decorated with white slip or pigment. Roman potters also made lead glazes, a procedure that enabled them to add metal oxides for color. Lead-glazed earthenware became the major pottery of medieval Europe.

Islamic Pottery. The first Muslim potters of the Umayyad dynasty (AD 661–750) inherited the traditions of the Middle East: the blue- and green-glazed quartz fritwares known in Egypt since Roman times; the alkaline-glazed pottery of Syria, Mesopotamia, and Iran, known since Achaemenid times (6th–4th cent. BC); and the Roman lead-glazed ware, continued by Byzantine potters. Three successive waves of Chinese influence inspired change in Islamic pottery: in the 9th–11th century, T'ang stoneware; in the 12th–14th century, Sung white ware; and in the 15th–19th century, Ming blue-and-white ware.

Medieval Arabic styles. In the 9th century, caliphs of the Abbasid dynasty encouraged local artisans to imitate imported T'ang pottery with local clay and glazes. The Arab potters soon developed their own style—first in unglazed pottery with molded, stamped, and applied-relief decoration, then in underglaze sgraffito designs and in opaque white tin-glazed bowls with painted flowers and inscriptions, and finally in luster painting. Lusterware was earthenware with an opaque white tin glaze, fired once, then painted with metallic pigments and refired in a reduction kiln. The designs reflected metallic hues of red, bronze, lime, and yellow.

When potters emigrated from Iraq to the western Muslim world in the 10th century, the luster technique moved with them. As with tin glazes, lusterware ultimately influenced Europe by way of the Arab residence in Spain. It was also popular in Fatimid Egypt (969–1171) and Iran.

Iran and Turkey. The Seljuk dynasty that ruled Iran, Iraq, Asia Minor, and Syria in the 12th and 13th centuries found substitutes for porcelain, and the Iranian cities of Rayy and Kashan became centers for this white ware. Another fine Seljuk type was Mina'i ware, an enamel-overglaze pottery that, in its delicacy, imitated illuminated manuscripts. Kashan potters, after the 13th-century Mongol conquests, used green glazes influenced by Chinese celadons. Cobalt-blue glazes appeared in Iran in the 9th century, later falling from use. They were taken up again in the 14th to the 18th century in response to the popularity of blue-and-white ware with Chinese and European clients.

İznik was the center for Turkish pottery. There slip-painted pieces influenced by Persian and Afghanistani ware predated the Ottoman Turks' conquest of the region. Later, between 1490 and 1700, İznik ware displayed decorations painted under a thin transparent glaze on a loose-textured white body; in its three stages the designs were in cobalt blue, then turquoise and purple, then red.

During the Safavid dynasty, Kubachi ware, contemporary to İznik pottery, was probably made in northwestern Iran, and not at the town of Kubachi where it was found. Characteristic Kubachi pieces were large polychrome plates, painted underneath their crackle glazes. Gombroon ware, exported from that Persian Gulf port to Europe and the Far East in the 16th and 17th centuries, had incised decorations on translucent white earthenware bodies. Copper-colored Persian lusterware was fashionable in the 17th century, as was polychrome painted ware.

In general, Islamic pottery was made in molds. Shapes were either Chinese inspired or were the basic shapes of metalwork. In addition to lusterware, the most creative work was the manufacture of tiles for mosques.

Europe to 1800. Islamic tin-glazed pottery and lusterware became the ceramics of Spain from the 13th through the 15th century. At times called Hispano-Moresque ware, it had its center of manufacture at the Valencian town of Manises. It was exported from Majorca, and thus the extremely popular Italian Renaissance ceramics that it influenced were known as majolica, from the Italian name for Majorca.

Majolica, faience, and delftware. In majolica, painting over the white glaze was further developed, in yellow, orange, green, turquoise, blue, purplish-brown, and black. Frequently a transparent overglaze was added, as well as incised and molded-relief decoration. Made in many Italian cities in the 15th to 16th century, this ware bore

Italian majolica jar (Faenza, c. 1530).
The Metropolitan Museum of Art, Fletcher Fund, 1946

little resemblance to its Spanish namesake. After 1600 the name *faience* was applied to the French variation of this tin-glazed ware, as well as to 16th- and 17th-century French and Belgian majolica-influenced pottery. In Germany, where it flourished until the 18th century, it was called fayence. After the center of its manufacture shifted from Antwerp to Delft in the mid-17th century, the name *delftware,* even for its English variation, came into use. The English delftware was made in London, Liverpool, and Bristol and in Dublin, until creamware (*see* Stoneware and Lead-Glazed Earthenware, below) began to replace it in the 1770s.

Tin-glazed ware remained popular in Europe until the early 19th century. It was made by dipping the biscuit-fired pot into a basic lead glaze to which tin oxide (an opacifier and whitener) had been added. This produced a dense white that completely covered the color of the clay body, providing a surface for painting any glaze color successful at moderate to high earthenware temperatures. Silver and gold were used for Spanish lusterware, painted over the fired glaze and refired in a low-temperature reduction kiln. In the 18th century, the fired tin glaze was painted with overglaze enamels and the pottery refired in a muffle kiln.

The full impact of Ming porcelain was felt throughout Europe in the first half of the 17th century, particularly in the golden age of delftware (1630–1700). The pottery became thinner, its decoration more delicate. Manganese purple outlines were drawn on the clay before the biscuit firing; then the underglaze blue and the final lead-and-tin glaze were applied. Tiles, plates, jugs, and vases were made, and the different Delft factory marks were imitated, even by the Chinese.

Stoneware and lead-glazed earthenware. European stoneware was developed in Germany at the end of the 14th century. It was salt-glazed: Common salt (an alkali) was thrown into the kiln, and soda from the salt created a glassy layer on the pot's surface. Hafner ware, a lead-glazed earthenware, was popular in the 16th and 17th centuries, with many vessels imitating metal jugs and tankards. Traditional English earthenware was decorated with slips and lead glazed, as was central European peasant pottery, taken to America by emigrants.

English stoneware was made on a large scale only after the late 17th century. The best of Staffordshire white salt-glazed stoneware was made between 1720 and 1760. Staffordshire also was a center for creamware, a popular lead-glazed

This gaily painted figure of a cow was fashioned of tin-glazed Delftware (Holland, 18th cent.).

The Metropolitan Museum of Art, Gift of Henry G. Marquand, 1894

One of a pair of fan-shaped French Sèvres (soft-paste) porcelain vases, designed by Étienne Evans in 1758.
Metropolitan Museum of Art–Gift of R. Thornton Wilson, 1954, in memory of Florence Ellsworth Wilson

earthenware made of Devonshire white clay mixed with calcined flint. In 1754 the English ceramist Josiah Wedgwood began to experiment with colored creamware. He established his own factory, but often worked with others who did transfer printing (introduced by the Worcester Porcelain Co. in the 1750s). He also produced red stoneware; basaltes ware, an unglazed black stoneware; and jasperware, made of white stoneware clay that had been colored by the addition of metal oxides. Jasperware was usually ornamented with white relief portraits or Greek classical scenes. Wedgwood's greatest contribution to European ceramics, however, was his fine pearl ware, an extremely pale creamware with a bluish tint to its glaze.

European porcelain. The first soft-paste porcelains, cream rather than white in color, were made in Italy in the 16th century, and then in France, where at Sèvres soft porcelain flourished.

John Flaxman designed the decoration for this 18th-century Wedgwood jasperware recreation of an ancient oil lamp. The terra-cotta relief on the lid represents the Muses watering Pegasus on Mt. Helicon. Metropolitan Museum of Art, Rogers Fund, 1911

The first hard-paste porcelain factories were established in 1710 at Meissen, Germany, where white clay was available. By the 1750s it had spread to Dresden, Venice, and the rest of Europe. The English imported kaolin from America before discovering it in Cornwall in 1768; the French found it at Limoges at the same time. Fine chinas are still made in these places.

The best early English porcelain was made at Chelsea in 1745. After its factory was sold to one in Derby in 1769, neoclassical style dominated domestic ware and figurines. In the 1740s a patent was taken out by porcelain makers at Bow in London, using bone ash in the clay body. The Lowestoft factory in Suffolk (est. about 1757) used a similar formula. Glassy soft-paste porcelain was made at Staffordshire in the 18th century; Josiah Spode of that town was credited with having introduced the Staffordshire variety of Bow bone china.

Brown-glazed Bennington pottery statue, made in Vermont in the mid-19th century.
Metropolitan Museum of Art–Rogers Fund

19th and 20th Centuries. Inexpensive transfer-printed wares for mass sale were popular in 19th-century England and on the Continent, as were relief-decorated wares. These spread to the U.S., along with the manganese-brown Rockingham glazes developed in England in the early 19th century; the latter were popular with New Jersey and Ohio potteries. Mass-produced ware gradually displaced the dominant U.S. folk pottery, a vigorous salt-glazed stoneware.

Industrial ceramics after 1860 were of high quality. Some of the finest were and still are made by the Royal Porcelain factory in Copenhagen. Art Nouveau, the Paris Exhibition of 1900, and the Bauhaus in the 1920s all influenced industrial ceramic design.

The individual studio or artist potter has been as important to the history of modern pottery as the industrial potter. England's Arts and Crafts movement had its impact after 1861, as did the salt-glazed stoneware of the Doulton factories in Lambeth after 1871. In the U.S. the Rookwood factory (1880, Cincinnati, Ohio), the Grueby Faience Co. (1897, Boston), and the Pewabic Pottery Works (1900, Detroit) brought prestige to the artist-potter. The international reputation of

Fine pottery crafted by 20th-century American artisans. Below: A stoneware vase (1965) by Robert Spenny. Right: A stoneware teapot with a wooden handle.
Courtesy of American Craft Council

the English potters Bernard Leach—trained in Japan and inspired by Japanese and English folk potters—and Michael Ambrose Cardew (1901–83)—a leader in the 20th century revival of pottery—further enhanced the contemporary tradition of the artist-artisan in clay.

For further information on this topic, see the Bibliography in volume 28, sections 645, 647, 655, 669, 671, 673, 687–88.

POTTO, small, arboreal, slothlike African primate, *Perodicticus potto,* of the family Lorisidae (*see* LORIS). The common potto is about the size of a squirrel and has a blunt head with globular eyes and a short tail. The tips of some of its spinal bones project through the skin and serve as a defense; it can raise its thick brown fur to hide these sharp protuberances at will. The potto has three digits and a thumb that provide a powerful grip for hanging from trees; the short index finger is vestigial. It sleeps during the day curled up in a ball and hunts fruit, eggs, or insects at night, seldom leaving trees. The smaller golden, or Calabar, potto, *Arctocebus calabarensis,* known as the angwantibo, has less prominent spinal bones, golden fur, and webbed digits.

POTTSTOWN, borough, Montgomery Co., SE Pennsylvania, on the Schuylkill R.; inc. 1815. Manufactures include motor-vehicle parts, tires, metal goods, electronic and electric equipment, and processed food. The Hill School (a noted preparatory school) and a museum of antique cars are in Pottstown, and Valley Forge is nearby. One of the first ironworks in the U.S. was built here by Thomas Rutter (1667?–1730) in 1716 and, after his death, expanded by his associate Thomas Potts (1680–1752). An early iron-making village is preserved in Hopewell Village National Historic Site in nearby Elverson, Pa. A steel plant was opened here in 1732. The community was laid out in 1752 and was known as Pottsgrove until 1815. Pop. (1980) 22,729; (1990) 21,831.

POUGHKEEPSIE, city, seat of Dutchess Co., SE New York, on the Hudson R.; settled by the Dutch 1687, inc. as a city 1854. It is a commercial and financial center; manufactures include mainframe computers, printed materials, clothing, business machines, electronic equipment, chemicals, and pharmaceuticals. Vassar College (1861) and Marist College (1946) are here, and Hyde Park, where President Franklin D. Roosevelt lived, is nearby. During the American Revolution, Poughkeepsie was the temporary capital of New York State, and the U.S. Constitution was ratified here in 1788. The community was an important river port until the mid-19th century. The city's name is derived from an Algonquian Indian word, perhaps meaning "a little reed lodge by a water place." Pop. (1980) 29,757; (1990) 28,844.

POULENC, Francis (1899–1963), French composer and pianist, born in Paris. Poulenc studied piano with several noted teachers but taught himself composition. His first published work, *Rapsodie négre* (1917), for solo voice and chamber orchestra, appeared when the composer was serving in the French army during World War I. In 1920 Poulenc joined five other composers, in a group known as Les Six, in rebelling against the influence of such conservative French composers as Claude Debussy, Vincent D'Indy, and César Franck (*see* SIX, LES).

Poulenc's works are harmonically conservative, light, satiric, and tuneful. He wrote many highly esteemed songs, including the cycle *Le bestiaire* (The Zoo, 1919), and became noted for his ability to match his music to the rhythms of the language. Among his stage works are the ballet *Les biches* (The Does, 1924), produced by the Russian impresario Sergey Diaghilev; the comic opera *Les mamelles de Tirésias* (The Breasts of Tiresias, 1946); and the serious opera *Les dialogues des Carmélites* (1957). His cantata *Figure humaine* (1945) was inspired by the French Resistance to German occupation during World War II. His other works include the *Concert champêtre* (Pastoral Concerto, 1928); *Aubade* (1929), for dancer, piano, and chamber orchestra; and works for piano and for violin.

POULTRY FARMING, commercial raising of chickens, turkeys, ducks, and geese for their meat and eggs. Since the 1930s and '40s, the poultry industry has become one of the most efficient producers of protein for human consumption. It expanded rapidly during World War II because of the shortage of beef and pork, which

Six-week-old broiler chickens in a large-scale poultry-raising facility. Automatic feeders foster a rapid growth rate by making food continuously available to the birds. Donald Miller–Monkmeyer Press

require a much longer time to develop; only seven weeks are required to produce a broiler and five months to produce a laying hen. As a result of modern technological development, many poultry houses now provide excellent environmental control, and the management and marketing of the birds are finely regulated.

Chickens. For hundreds of years, chickens were kept in small flocks for home consumption of eggs and meat, with any surplus sold or exchanged for other produce. Not until the 20th century did poultry farming become commercialized. The production of eggs came first; for years the production of broilers was merely an offshoot, the male chickens being raised until about 10 to 16 weeks old and then sold for meat.

A modern poultry farm may have several hundred thousand or even more than a million laying hens. The U.S. poultry industry comprises somewhat fewer than 300 million such hens, but with modern production techniques they are supplying the nation with more eggs than did a larger hen population some years ago. A dozen eggs can be produced with less than 1.8 kg (less than 4 lb) of feed. Whereas egg-producing hens once produced about 100 eggs each year, such hens can now produce up to 280 eggs each year.

Advances in the broiler industry have been even more spectacular. The industry started on a commercial scale on the Delmarva (Delaware-Maryland-Virginia) Peninsula and then spread farther south and southwest. By the early 1990s the industry was producing approximately 5.9 billion broilers a year, most of them in the southern U.S., with an efficiency such that one unit weight of broiler was being produced with fewer than two unit weights of feed. Nearly all broilers are now the offspring of white Plymouth Rock females and dominant white Cornish males.

Today more than 85 percent of the laying hens in the U.S. are housed in wire cages containing from two to ten hens each. The cages may be in a single tier or in tiers of up to five cages. Most of these are automated to provide a constant supply of feed and water and to maintain control of the environment. With temperatures remaining at near-ideal conditions, the birds never suffer frozen feet, combs, or wattles. Mortality is consistently lower than in the times when hens were mainly housed on a litter floor, where they were constantly in contact with one another and with feces; the latter condition also required more antibiotics and drugs to prevent disease.

Objections have been raised to the use of cags, but in fact they provide greater comfort than o litter floors. The larger numbers of birds in a iven area produce sufficient heat to maintain omfortable temperatures, which allows for more entilation to provide a flow of fresh air. Litter oors, on the other hand, give rise to ammonia-ich air that can cause respiratory and other mal-dies. Lowered light levels and reduced contact etween birds also inhibit their natural tendency oward cannibalism. Finally, controlled temper-tures cause the birds to eat less to meet their nergy needs; the estimate has been made that f all laying hens were housed on litter floors, ggs would cost twice as much as they do now.

The U.S. is a leader of the worldwide poultry ndustry. In 1990, for example, it produced near-y 68 billion eggs. About 159 billion eggs were roduced in China, and 86 billion eggs by the uropean Community. The Soviet Union with 82 illion eggs was also a major producer. Within he U.S., California produces about 11 percent of he nation's eggs, followed by Indiana, Penn-ylvania, Ohio, and Georgia; the leading broiler-roducing states are Arkansas, Georgia, Alabama, nd North Carolina.

Turkeys. The turkey industry began to develop n a larger scale in the late 1930s and early '40s nd has since grown rapidly. At first the birds vere grown on ranges, but disease problems orced farmers to raise them on slats or wire latforms. This proved costly and labor ineffi-cient, so when controls were found for the dis-eases, turkey farms returned to the use of ranges r large houses. In 1990 about 283 million tur-keys were produced in the U.S.; North Carolina, Minnesota, California, Arkansas, Missouri, and Virginia are the leading states.

Ducks. In the U.S., the highly specialized duck ndustry was once concentrated almost entirely n Suffolk Co. on Long Island, N.Y., where more than 10 million ducks were grown each year in the 1960s. The industry has now spread to Wis-consin, Indiana, and Virginia. Ducks are often started at one end of their house and moved along progressively until they are ready for market at approximately seven weeks of age, when they weigh about 3.1 kg (about 7 lb). Usually they are started on wire and progress to litter and outside runs at three to four weeks of age.

Geese. In the U.S., most geese are produced in small farm flocks of up to a few hundred; few large operations exist. The birds are hardy and are usually grown on ranges, where they are good foragers and require little care after the first two or three weeks. Goose remains a specialty food, but the demand for goose down has increased in recent decades. The birds themselves are some-times used by farmers for weed control.

See DUCK; FOWL; GOOSE; TURKEY. C.E.O.

For further information on this topic, see the Bibliography in volume 28, section 594.

POUND *or* **POUND STERLING,** monetary unit of Great Britain, represented by the symbol £. On the basis of gold content, the pound as represented by a gold coin, the sovereign, contains 113.001 grains, or 7.32238 grams, of fine gold. Because of the position that Britain holds in world trade and as a major international banking center, the pound has been a major currency of foreign exchange. A sterling area or sterling zone designation indicates those countries, either former members of the British Empire or current members of the Commonwealth of Nations or countries that maintain a high percentage of their foreign trade with Great Britain, that hold substantial amounts of pounds as exchange reserves.

Historically, the terms *pound* and *pound sterling* originated in Anglo-Saxon Britain during the 8th century when the basic monetary unit, called a "sterling," was made equivalent to $\frac{1}{240}$ of a pound of silver and 240 sterlings became known as a "pound of sterling." The pound was convertible into silver until 1717, when the British government substituted gold in the amount cited above. In 1797 the government abandoned the gold standard; it was restored at the old rate in 1816. The gold standard was abandoned again during World War I, restored at the old rate in 1925, and finally abandoned in 1931.

Periodically, as the British economy fluctuated, the value of the paper pound was altered with respect to its parity with other currencies. In 1939, at the outbreak of World War II, the exchange value was $4.03, $0.73 less than the exchange value during World War I. In 1949 the pound was devalued to an exchange rate of $2.80, in 1967 to $2.40, and in 1971 officially pegged at $2.60. Since June 1972, the pound has floated free from its official parity at a rate determined by supply and demand. By 1985 the fluctuating pound had lowered to the $1.00 mark, but it regained strength later in the decade. By mid-1993 it was about $1.50.

On Feb. 15, 1971, the pound's coinage equivalent was changed to the decimal system, from 20 shillings to 100 pennies, replacing the traditional shillings and pence that had been used since 11th-century Anglo-Norman times.

POUND, Ezra Loomis (1885–1972), American avant-garde poet, critic, and translator, who exerted an enormous influence on the development of English and American poetry and criticism in the early 20th century.

Pound was born Oct. 30, 1885, in Hailey, Idaho, and educated at the University of Pennsylvania and Hamilton College. He went abroad in 1907 and from 1908 until 1930 lived in London, where he served as a foreign correspondent for the American magazines *Poetry* and *The Little Review.* Pound championed and in some cases edited the works of T. S. Eliot, William Butler Yeats, James Joyce, and other avant-garde authors writing in England. He also set forth the theories behind the literary movement that came to be known as imagism.

Pound's literary reputation was established very early, with the publication of *Personae,* a verse collection, in 1909. In 1920 Pound moved to Paris, where he became a leader of the American expatriate literary circle that included Gertrude Stein and Ernest Hemingway; he also worked for the American literary magazine *Dial,* translated from Italian, Chinese, and Japanese literature, and completed several books of criticism and poetry, including *Hugh Selwyn Mauberly* (1920). In 1924 he settled in Rapallo, Italy, and during World War II he broadcast Fascist propaganda from Rome to the U.S. He was arrested by the Americans in 1945, declared psychologically unfit to stand trial for treason, and confined to a mental hospital in Washington, D.C. On his release in 1958, he returned to Italy, where he died Nov. 1, 1972, in Venice.

Portions of Pound's major work, *Cantos,* were first published in 1925; the first complete English edition of all the published segments was issued in 1970 as *The Cantos of Ezra Pound.* Pound drew his themes from Confucian ethics, classical mythology, economic theory, and other seemingly disparate sources in his effort to interpret cultural history. His *Letters* and his *Collected Poems* were both published in 1950. His *Literary Essays* appeared in 1954 and *Translations* in 1963.

Ezra Loomis Pound Boris de Rachewiltz

POUSSIN, Nicolas (1594–1665), French painter who was the founder and greatest practitioner of the French neoclassical style. His work symbolizes the virtues of logic, order, and clarity, and it has influenced the course of French art up to the present day.

Poussin was of peasant extraction, born near Les Andelys, Normandy, in June 1594. He studied painting in Rouen and Paris, where he was first exposed to ancient Roman sculpture and to the work of the Italian master Raphael, two significant lifelong influences on his art. He went to Rome in 1624, where, except for an 18-month sojourn (1640–42) in Paris, he lived for the rest of his life. His early work in Rome reflects the crowded compositions and animated surfaces of mid-16th century Mannerism. About 1630 his style began to change as he drew away from the emerging exuberant baroque style and devoted himself entirely to his passion for the antique, concentrating on biblical and mythological subjects. At first his paintings, such as the *Plague at Ashdod* (1603–31, Louvre, Paris), had the rich glowing color of the Venetian artist Titian, but after 1633 Poussin moved steadily toward more sober, cool tonalities. His compositions became more serene and his figures more sculptural, echoing the later paintings of Raphael, while he attempted to depict emotion through easily readable gestures, poses, and facial expressions, as in his large *Triumph of Neptune* (c. 1636, Philadelphia Museum of Art).

Poussin journeyed to Paris in 1640 with some reluctance, although the trip earned him the enduring patronage of wealthy bourgeois collectors and also cemented his relations with the French Académie Royale, which later elevated his style to the status of formal doctrine. His paintings of the next decade (1643–53), such as *Holy Family on the Steps* (1648, National Gallery, Washington, D.C.), following his return to Rome, are the purest embodiment of French neoclassicism, characterized by calm composition, cool silvery colors, hard, clear lighting, and a feeling of solemnity. During his last years (1653–65), he concentrated on landscape scenes in which the actions and expressions of the human figures were drastically simplified and the human form took on an almost cubistic abstraction. Paintings like the *Arcadian Shepherd* (c. 1656, Louvre), in which he attained a monumental simplification and almost supernatural calm, went beyond the illustration of historical events to become symbols of eternal verities.

Poussin's belief that art should appeal to the mind rather than to the eye—that it should present the most noble and serious human situations

The Four Seasons: Autumn *(1660–64, Louvre, Paris) by Nicolas Poussin.* Scala/Art Resource

n an orderly manner devoid of trivial detail or sensuous allure—became the basis of the French academic style of the 17th century. Until the 20th century he remained the dominant inspiration of such classically oriented artists as J. L. David, J. A. D. Ingres, and Paul Cézanne. He died in Rome on Nov. 19, 1665.

POVERTY, economic condition in which people lack sufficient income to obtain certain minimal levels of health services, food, housing, clothing, and education generally recognized as necessary to ensure an adequate standard of living. What is considered adequate, however, depends on the average standard of living in a particular society.

In the U.S., the poverty level is normally based on an annual income figure. In 1986 a family of four with an income below $11,203 was defined as poor. The poverty line, however, varies by family size and is adjusted annually to allow for inflation (*see* INFLATION AND DEFLATION). By current U.S. standards, most people elsewhere in the world would be considered poor.

Poverty in the U.S. declined gradually during the 1950s and early '60s and then more rapidly in the 5-year period beginning in 1964. The proportion of Americans who were poor declined from 19 to 12 percent between 1964 and 1969, but by 1986 the poverty rate in the U.S. had increased to 13.6 percent.

Causes. Individuals who have a lower than average ability to earn income, for whatever reason, are likely to be poor. Historically, this group has included the aged, the disabled, the feeble-minded, single mothers, and members of some minorities. In the U.S. today, the largest group in the poverty-stricken population consists of single mothers and their children; these families account for about one-third of all poor people. Not only do working women generally earn less than men, but a single mother often has a difficult time caring for children, running a household, and earning an adequate income. Other groups disproportionately represented below the poverty threshold are the disabled and their dependents, very large families, and families in which the head is either unemployed or works for low wages. Despite recent progress, some minority groups, especially blacks and Hispanics, are also overrepresented below the poverty line.

Lack of educational opportunity is another cause of poverty. In the U.S., a larger percentage of blacks than whites are poor today, in part because of a heritage of inferior education. Not until after the U.S. Supreme Court declared segregated schools unconstitutional in 1954 were most black children allowed to attend the same public schools as white children and thus to obtain the same quality of education. *See* BLACKS IN THE AMERICAS; EDUCATION IN THE UNITED STATES.

Much of the world's poverty is due to a low level of economic development. China and India are examples of heavily populated, developing nations where poverty is rampant. Even in economically developed countries, widespread unemployment can create poverty. The Great Depression impoverished millions of Americans and Europeans in the 1930s. Less severe economic contractions, called recessions, cause smaller increases in the poverty rate (*see* BUSINESS CYCLE).

Effects. Tens of thousands of poor people throughout the world die every year from starvation and malnutrition. The effects of poverty in the U.S., although not so dramatic, are just as real. Infant mortality rates are higher and life expectancy lower among the poor. In 1968 a congressional investigation revealed widespread hunger and malnutrition in poor U.S. communities; in the late 1980s these conditions still existed in the rural counties of central Appalachia and in many other areas.

Poverty breeds crime. Most of the poor are not criminals, and many criminals are not poor, but people from environments dominated by poverty are more likely to commit crimes and to be punished. Other social problems, such as mental illness and alcoholism, are common among the poor, in part because they are causes as well as effects of poverty. Finally, poverty tends to breed poverty; in some cases, the handicap of poverty is passed from one generation to another.

Poverty Programs in the U.S. Many programs that help the poor are also beneficial to the majority of the American people. Federal, state, and local government expenditures for social-welfare programs such as social security, health care, education, and welfare amount to more than half of all government spending. Almost half of these expenditures went to people who would have been poverty stricken had they not received such benefits. Without these programs, estimates indicate that twice as many Americans would have incomes below the poverty line. Programs that benefit all Americans (for example, social security) cost much more and lift many more people out of poverty than programs for the poor alone.

Welfare programs are a relatively small part of total social-welfare expenditures; in a recent year they amounted to about $14 of every $100 spent. More than half of all welfare funds provide aid in kind—for medical care, food stamps, and housing—rather than cash to the recipients.

How much the government should spend on social welfare has always been a controversial issue. In 1964, after President Lyndon B. Johnson declared a "war on poverty," the U.S. Congress enacted many new laws and programs to increase expenditures and reduce poverty. The pace of reform slowed during the 1970s, however, and in the early 1980s cutbacks in poverty programs were being made by the government in an a tempt to balance the federal budget, curb infl tion, and build up the economy. By 1986 Congre had tightened eligibility requirements for mo benefit programs, including the food stamp pro gram, and had removed thousands of the workin poor from the welfare rolls. I.G.

For further information on this topic, see th Bibliography in volume 28, section 292.

POWDER METALLURGY. *See* ALLOY.

POWELL, Anthony Dymoke (1905–), Englis novelist, born in London, and educated at Eto and the University of Oxford. He worked for publishing firm, a film company, and as a journal ist, and he served in World War II.

Powell's earliest novels, including *Afternoo Men* (1931) and *What's Become of Waring?* (1939 deal wittily with the Bohemian life of Chelse and Bloomsbury. His partly autobiographical la er works depict the changing nature of the uppe class of British society from just before Worl War II through the postwar period. His majo work is *A Dance to the Music of Time* (1951–75 a series of 12 novels in which the experiences o the narrator Nicholas Jenkins, a writer, are con trasted with those of a ruthless political oppor tunist named Widmerpool. The tone grows mor somber and haunting as they age and societ changes. *To Keep the Ball Rolling* (4 vol 1977–83) is Powell's autobiography.

POWELL, Colin L(uther) (1937–), U.S. mili tary leader. The son of Jamaican immigrants Powell was born in New York City and attende City College of New York as a cadet in the Re serve Officers Training Corps. After serving tw tours of duty in Vietnam (1962–63; 1968–69), h held a succession of important U.S. military an civilian positions, becoming national securit adviser to President Ronald Reagan in 1987 Promoted to the rank of four-star general i April 1989, he was named chairman of the Join Chiefs of Staff in August. The first black office to hold the nation's highest military post, Powel had a pivotal role in planning and executing th invasion of Panama and the Persian Gulf Wa (q.v.).

POWELL, John Wesley (1834–1902), America ethnologist, geologist, explorer, and governmen administrator, known for his work as the firs major classifier of American Indian languages, a well as for his pioneering work as a geographica and geological surveyor of the Rocky Mountains

Powell was born on March 24, 1834, at Moun Morris, N.Y. When his family moved to Illinois he made long solo voyages on the Ohio and Mississippi rivers and became intensely interested in nature. After study at Oberlin and Wheaton coleges and service in the Union army during the American Civil War, he became a geology professor at Illinois Wesleyan College in 1865, and later he lectured at Illinois Normal University. In 1867 and 1868 he led geological expeditions into Colorado and Utah. The next year, with government backing, he explored and made a geological survey of the Green and Colorado river canyons. Between 1870 and 1879 he continued his survey of the Rocky Mountain region.

During Powell's travels he studied the Indians he encountered, and in 1879 he was appointed the first director of the U.S. Bureau of Ethnology. He also served (1881–92) as head of the U.S. Geological Survey, which under his direction became a highly effective organization. In 1891 he published the first complete classification and distribution map of the 58 language stocks of the Indians of the U.S. and Canada. He died in Haven, Maine, Sept. 23, 1902.

Powell's books include *Explorations of the Colorado River of the West* (1875), *An Introduction to the Study of Indian Languages* (1877), and *Report on the Lands of the Arid Region of the United States* (1878).

POWELL, LAKE, artificial lake, southwestern U.S., one of the largest in the world, in N Arizona and S Utah. It is formed behind Glen Canyon Dam (completed 1964) on the Colorado R., upstream from the Grand Canyon. The lake, which is some 300 km (some 185 mi) long, has an area of about 650 sq km (about 250 sq mi). It forms the core of the Glen Canyon National Recreation Area.

POWELL, Lewis Franklin, Jr. (1907–), American jurist and associate justice of the U.S. Supreme Court. He was born in Suffolk, Va., and educated at Washington and Lee and Harvard universities. He began his law practice in Richmond, Va., in 1931. As chairman of the Richmond school board from 1952 to 1961, he was largely responsible for that city's peaceful integration of the public schools. During the 1960s he served as president of three American legal associations, and in 1971 President Richard M. Nixon named him to the Supreme Court. In his years on the Court, he was considered to be a moderate who often cast the decisive vote in close decisions. He retired from the Court in June 1987.

POWER, in mathematics, product formed by successively multiplying a number, letter, or algebraic expression by itself. An exponent (another number, letter, or expression), appearing to the upper right of the base (number, letter, or expression) involved, indicates the number of times the base has been involved in this operation of self-multiplication. (For example, 3^2 means 3 times 3, or 9.) The product of two equal factors such as a base multiplied by itself is called the second power, or square, of that factor. The product of three equal factors such as a base multiplied by itself twice is called the third power, or cube, of that factor, and so on. The concept of powers underlies logarithms. *See* ROOT. J.Si.; REV. BY J.Le.B.

POWER, in physics and engineering, rate of performing work (q.v.) or transferring energy (q.v.). In the centimeter-gram-second system (*see* CGS SYSTEM), power is measured in units of ergs per second, and in the British system in foot-pounds per second. The basic electrical unit of power is the watt, equal to 1 joule/sec, the joule being equal to 10 million ergs. The power of 1 w is produced when an electromotive force of 1 V is applied across a resistor and a direct current of 1 amp flows (*see* ELECTRICAL UNITS; ELECTRICITY). Large amounts of electrical power are usually expressed in kilowatts (1000 w) or megawatts (1 million w). The amount of work done in an electric circuit (q.v.), such as a domestic electric system, is equal to power multiplied by time and is expressed in kilowatt-hours.

The power output of engines, electric motors, and other machinery is generally measured in horsepower (q.v.), abbreviated hp; it equals 550 ft-lb/sec, or 33,000 ft-lb/min, or 746 w.

POWER OF ATTORNEY, in law, written document, certified by a notary public, designating a person or party as an agent empowered to act for another person (principal) in a legal capacity. A general power of attorney authorizes the named agent to act on behalf of the principal or signer in any legal circumstance, whereas a special power of attorney specifies and restricts the province of an agent's responsibility. Most frequently, people will give another person power of attorney when they are ill or for other reasons are unable to conduct their own affairs, or when they are absent from home or business for a long period of time. A power of attorney is revocable under normal circumstances and becomes void on the death of the principal. *See* PRINCIPAL AND AGENT.

POWER PLANT, in physics and engineering, any system used to generate mechanical or electrical power that can be utilized to perform work; *see* ELECTRICITY; MECHANICS; POWER; WORK. For the different types of engines and systems employed, *see* ELECTRIC MOTORS AND GENERATORS; ELECTRIC-POWER SYSTEMS; INTERNAL-COMBUSTION ENGINE; JET PROPULSION; NUCLEAR ENERGY; ROCKET; SOLAR ENERGY; STEAM ENGINE; TURBINE; WATERPOWER. *See also* ENERGY; HORSEPOWER.

POWERS, Hiram (1805–73), American sculptor, born near Woodstock, Vt. His skill in making models for a wax museum attracted attention, and he received numerous commissions for portrait busts. In 1837 Powers went to Florence, Italy, where he spent the rest of his life. In 1843 he completed the work *Greek Slave,* of which many replicas were made. A marble figure of a nude woman in chains leaning against a draped pillar, it was one of the most celebrated statues of the time. He also made statues of American statesmen, including Benjamin Franklin and Thomas Jefferson for the Capitol in Washington, D.C.

POWER TRANSMISSION. *See* ELECTRIC POWER SYSTEMS.

POWHATAN, Indian name Wa-Hun-Sen-A-Cawh *or* Wahunsonacook (1550?–1618), father of the Indian princess Pocahontas. He was the chief of the Powhatan confederacy of Algonquian Indian tribes in what is now Virginia, at the time the English first settled there.

POWYS, county, E Wales; Llandrindod Wells is the administrative center. The county's terrain is largely mountainous. The economy is dominated by agriculture, chiefly livestock raising. Tourism is important, especially in the scenic Brecon Beacons National Park (1957) in the S. Powys was created in 1974 with the merger of the former counties of Montgomeryshire, Radnorshire, and most of Breconshire (qq.v.). Area, 5077 sq km (1960 sq mi); pop. (1991 prelim.) 116,500.

POZNAŃ (Ger. *Posen*), city, W Poland, capital of Poznań Province, a port on the Warta R. The city is a major railroad junction and an important industrial and commercial center. The chief industries are food processing and the manufacture of metals, engines, freight cars, machine tools, chemicals, and ceramics. Adam Mickiewicz University (1919), a technical university, a Gothic cathedral, a 16th-century city hall, and many historic churches and museums are in the city. Poznań is one of the most ancient cities of Poland; in 968 it became the first Roman Catholic bishopric in Poland. The city passed to Prussia in 1793, became part of the Grand Duchy of Warsaw in 1807, came under Prussian rule again in 1815, and reverted to Poland in 1919. In 1956 workers staged large-scale protest demonstrations here. Pop. (1985 est.) 575,100.

PRAETOR, also pretor, title of magistrate of the ancient Romans. The title was first applied to consuls. In 366 BC, when the Licinian-Sextian laws provided that the supreme authority should be in the hands of the two consuls, one of whom had to be of the common people, or plebs (q.v.), the praetorship was created as a separate office to provide for the jurisdiction of civil suits, and it seems at first to have been open only to patricians. The praetor, known as the urban praetor, was actually a third consul and was accompanied by six lictors. In 337 BC the praetorship was opened to plebeian men and made the stepping-stone to the consulate. The urban praetor presided over all litigation between citizens in the city of Rome proper.

A second praetor, known as the peregrine praetor, was appointed in 242 BC to conduct lawsuits in which one or both of the litigants were foreigners. More praetors were added for the administration of newly acquired provinces, until the number of praetors reached a total of 16. Of this group the urban praetor ranked first and, in the absence of the consuls from Rome, had the power to convoke meetings of the Senate. The praetorship was ordinarily of annual tenure, and the age requirement was 30 years. Magistrates of praetorian rank presided over the special courts of law established at Rome to deal with such crimes as extortion, bribery, treason, and murder.

The praetors, like the consuls, were elected by the Roman people assembled in the *comitia centuriata* (*see* COMITIA), and, also like the consuls, they possessed imperium, or military power, and went forth as propraetors, or military governors of the provinces, upon the expiration of their terms of office. Upon the reorganization of the provinces under the Roman Empire, all governors of the imperial provinces, being under the proconsular authority of the emperor, were designated as propraetors. They were so termed whether they were of consular or praetorian rank.

PRAETORIAN GUARD, bodyguard of the ancient Roman emperors. By the 2d century BC the bodyguard of a Roman general was known as the praetorian cohort, but Augustus, the first Roman emperor, in 27 BC instituted the Praetorian Guard as a separate force by organizing 9 cohorts, each consisting of 500 men, under the command of a prefect, who was called the praetorian prefect. The only large permanent body of troops allowed in Rome itself, or near the city, it soon acquired great political power. Members served 16 years, receiving special privileges and pay. They gradually began to exercise their political power in an unscrupulous manner, deposing and elevating emperors at their pleasure. In AD 193, after the assassination of Emperor Publius Helvius Pertinax (126–93), they sold the throne to Didius Severus Julianus (133–93). In the same year the Guard was reorganized by his successor, Emperor Lucius Septimius Severus. It was abolished by Emperor Constantine the Great in 312.

PRAETORIUS, Michael, real name MICHAEL SCHULTHEISS (1571–1621), German composer, theorist, and music publisher, who helped establish the style of early 17th-century German music. Born in Kreuzberg, he studied organ in Frankfurt, served Heinrich Julius, duke of Brunswick (1564–1613), after 1604, and became music director at Wolfenbüttel in 1612. His abundance of sacred choral compositions includes the *Musae Sioniae* (1605–10), a veritable encyclopedia of 1244 chorale arrangements. His major work is the three-volume *Syntagma musicum* (1614–20), a historical and descriptive treatise in Latin that is an invaluable source of information on early baroque music and musical instruments.

PRAGMATIC SANCTION, solemn ordinance or decree of a head of state, relating to a matter of primary importance and having the force of fundamental law. Pragmatic sanctions have included the instrument that limited (1438) papal authority in France; and the ordinance by which Charles VI, Holy Roman emperor, decreed (1713) that if he died without a male heir his eldest daughter, Maria Theresa, later archduchess of Austria and queen of Hungary and Bohemia, would inherit the Habsburg dominions.

PRAGMATISM, philosophical doctrine, developed by the 19th-century American philosophers Charles Sanders Peirce, William James, and others, according to which the test of the truth of a proposition is its practical utility; the purpose of thought is to guide action; and the effect of an idea is more important than its origin. Pragmatism was the first independently developed American philosophy. It opposes speculation on questions that have no practical application. It asserts that truth is relative to the time, place, and purpose of investigation and that value is as inherent in means as in ends.

The American philosopher and educator John Dewey developed pragmatism into a new philosophy, instrumentalism. The British philosopher Ferdinand Canning Scott Schiller (1864–1937) and the French philosopher Henri Louis Bergson contributed to the development of pragmatism. Like the older utilitarianism, pragmatism presents a working philosophy for the natural sciences. Many similarities have been noted between pragmatism and Sophist ideas.

PRAGUE (Czech *Praha;* Ger. *Prag*), city, W central Czech Republic, capital of the country, in central Bohemia, situated on both sides of the Vltava (Ger. *Moldau*) R. The largest city in the Czech Republic, Prague is the chief commercial and industrial center and the cultural capital of the country. Primary manufactures here are machine tools, electrical machinery, automobiles, chemicals, textiles, clothing, leather goods, and glassware. The city is also the main center of book publishing in the country. Educational institutions in Prague include Charles University (1348) and the Technical University of Prague (1707). The city also has many art, music, and professional schools, as well as museums, libraries, and theaters.

One of the most picturesque cities in Europe, Prague is built in a broad valley paralleling the banks of the Vltava R. and on the surrounding hills. The river is spanned by many bridges, of which the most famous is the Karlsbrücke (Ger., "Charles Bridge"), built in the 14th century and later embellished with statues of saints. The E bank of the river is the site of the Old Town, dating from the 13th century, and the New Town, built about a century later. In the Old Town, traversed by crooked streets and containing architectural relics of Bohemian grandeur, is the 14th-century Tyn Cathedral, a center of the religious revolt of the Hussites. The section also contains the University of Prague; Staroměstská Radnice, the 14th-century town hall; and the Municipal House. The New Town, primarily a commercial and industrial section, encompasses many public

Soldiers of the Praetorian Guard. Bettmann Archive

Wenceslas Square in Prague, with the National Gallery in the background. UPI

buildings, museums, and banks. On the W side of the river is the part of the city called the Lesser Town, with a number of baroque palaces. Above this section and dominating the entire city is Hradčany Castle; formerly the residence of the kings of Bohemia, it is now the residence of the president of the Czech Republic. Next to this vast structure is the Gothic-style Cathedral of Saint Vitus, with the tombs of many Bohemian kings.

The settlement of Prague dates from the 9th century, when it served as the site for several Bohemian castles. The city began to grow in the 13th century with the establishment of German communities by Wenceslas I, king of Bohemia (1205–53). The German colonists developed the city rapidly, building the Altstadt (Old Town) as a trading center in 1232 and, expanding to the SE, starting the Neustadt (New Town) a century later. Prague prospered as the capital of the powerful province of Bohemia and during the 14th century became the largest European city after Paris. In 1442 it was conquered by the Hussites yet continued to grow in wealth and power. It was severely damaged during several wars, notably in the Thirty Years' War. In 1744 the city surrendered to Frederick II, king of Prussia, who, during the Seven Years' War, defeated the Austrian forces at Prague. In 1848, Prague was bombarded by Austrian troops used to quell a Czech revolution, and in 1866 it surrendered to Prussian forces during the Seven Weeks' War. Upon the establishment of the republic of Czechoslovakia in 1918, Prague became its capital. During World War II the city was occupied by German forces from March 1939 until May 1945. The city was again the scene of turmoil when, in August 1968, Soviet troops invaded Prague and massive demonstrations ensued (*see* CZECHOSLOVAKIA: *The Prague Spring*). Prague also was the site of massive nonviolent demonstrations that led to the downfall of Czechoslovakia's Communist regime in 1989. When the country divided on Jan. 1, 1993, the city became capital of the independent Czech Republic. Pop. (1991 prelim.) 1,212,010.

PRAIA, city, S Cape Verde, capital of the country, on the SE shore of the island of São Tiago, which is in the Atlantic Ocean, off the coast of W Africa. It is a seaport and trading hub for the agricultural production of the islands and is the administrative center of the country. The city also has a tourist industry. Praia, made the capital of the Portuguese-controlled Cape Verde Islands in 1770, remained the capital when the country became independent in 1975. Pop. (1985 est.) 49,500.

PRAIRIE CHICKEN, common name for two of the three species of birds of the genus *Tympanuchus,* in the grouse (q.v.) subfamily Tetraoninae, family Phasianidae. Males of all three species have featherless sacs at the sides of the neck, inflated during courtship displays. The greater prairie chicken, *T. cupido,* formerly ranged throughout much of the grassland regions of the U.S. and central Canada. It was most abundant during the interim between the near-extinction of the bison and the proliferation of domestic cattle, when the ungrazed tall-grass prairie was at its greatest development. The isolated eastern population, known as the heath hen, *T. c. cupido,* ranged from Massachusetts to the Potomac River, but by 1835 it was confined to the island of Martha's Vineyard, where the last bird died in 1932. Attwater's prairie chicken, *T. c. attwateri,* of the coastal prairies of Texas and western Louisiana, is considered endangered. The shrinking range of the species as a whole is attributable primarily to habitat loss, although overhunting may also have been involved.

The male greater prairie chicken is about 47 cm (about 18.5 in) long, the female somewhat smaller. The upperparts are brown, the underparts buffy white, both heavily barred with dark brown. Both sexes have a tuft of stiff, elongated feathers at the sides of the neck. In the spring, groups of males congregate at dawn and perform their courting ritual while the females watch. The sacs at the sides of the neck, which are orange in this species, are inflated and deflated, producing a booming sound; the stiffened feathers just above the sacs are erected; the wings droop; and the feet patter while the head and neck bob.

The lesser prairie chicken, *T. pallidicinctus,* is slightly smaller (40 cm/16 in). Its plumage is paler and the male's sacs are plum-red in color. Formerly more widespread, it now occupies a limited range, principally in northern Texas and western Oklahoma.

The third species of *Tympanuchus* is the sharp-tailed grouse, *T. phasianellus,* in which the plumage is mottled rather than barred, and the male's sacs are purple. It inhabits open woodlands and grasslands over much of North America east to Michigan, and sometimes hybridizes with the greater prairie chicken.

For further information on this topic, see the Bibliography in volume 28, sections 473, 814.

PRAIRIE DOG, any of five similar species of small, ground-dwelling rodents of the genus *Cynomys,* once very common in the plains and plateaus of the western U.S. They are closely related to the marmot and ground squirrel (qq.v.) and belong to the squirrel family, Sciuridae. Prairie dogs, which grow to about 38 cm (about 15 in) long, emit a barklike yip as a warning cry, hence their name. Highly social rodents, they live in "towns" sometimes made up of thousands of individuals; they dwell in holes dug straight down 3 to 4 m (10 to 16 ft) to nest hollows. The animals surface during the day and spend much time identifying and grooming each other and defending family territorial boundaries, for which they have elaborate rituals. Prairie dogs build the earth from their holes into conical rings that prevent flooding. They feed on herbs and grasses within range of their holes; their methods of selective browsing and scattering the raw, excavated earth from their tunnels attracts a crop of fast-growing weeds, which they later eat.

The chief predators of prairie dogs are hawks, eagles, and coyotes, for which the rodents stay alert at their tunnel entrances, sounding special warning cries when danger threatens. Because prairie dogs compete with cattle for rangeland grasses, ranchers have severely reduced their numbers. Protected colonies are limited to national parks. A typical species is the common prairie dog, *C. ludovicianus,* which has short legs and a blunt, squirrellike head with short ears. Females produce two to ten pups in the spring.

PRAIRIE PROVINCES, general name for the Canadian provinces of Alberta, Manitoba, and Saskatchewan (qq.v.).

PRAIRIE SCHOONER, type of wagon, used in the 19th century by American pioneers for transportation across the western prairies and mountains to frontier settlements. The characteristic white canvas covering of the wagon resembled the sails of the maritime schooners of the period, hence the name. Canvas-covered wagons had been in common use during the early 19th century in the eastern U.S. as freight transports, particularly in the form of the Conestoga wagon. The prairie schooner, however, was lighter than any other covered wagons and was drawn by two or four horses or oxen in contrast to the six-horse teams needed for the heavier wagons. The prairie schooner consisted of a common farm wagon with a canvas top supported by horseshoe-shaped wooden arches and extending down both sides of the wagon. Oval-shaped openings were left in the front and rear to allow sun and air to enter the interior where passengers traveled and goods were stored. Frequently, large wagon trains of prairie schooners were organized to provide greater protection from marauders while crossing the open plains and prairies. Prairie schooners were supplanted in the late 19th century by the new transcontinental railroads.

PRAIRIE VILLAGE, city, Johnson Co., NE Kansas, a residential suburb of Kansas City, at the Missouri line; settled 1858, inc. 1951. A planned community, it was platted in 1941 by a private development firm and is named for its geographical location. Pop. (1980) 24,657; (1990) 23,186.

PRAKRIT LANGUAGES. *See* INDIAN LANGUAGES; SANSKRIT LANGUAGE.

PRAKRIT LITERATURE. *See* INDIAN LITERATURE.

PRASAD, Rajendra (1884–1963), Indian nationalist leader and first president of India (1950–62). Born in Bihar State and educated at Presidency College, Calcutta, and at the University of Allahabad, he later practiced and taught law in Calcutta. In 1917 he became a disciple of the Indian nationalist leader Mohandas K. Gandhi and joined his passive-resistance movement against British rule. After 1920, when Prasad gave up his law practice, he devoted full time to the struggle for Indian freedom. A prominent member of the Indian National Congress, he was its general secretary in 1922 and president in 1932, 1939, and 1947. He served several prison sentences between 1930 and 1932 for his activities in behalf of Indian independence and a 3-year term during World War II for opposition to the British war effort. He became a minister in Jawaharlal Nehru's government in 1947 and presided over the Constituent Assembly from 1946 to 1949. When India became a republic in 1950, Prasad was inaugurated the first president. He retired 12 years later.

PRASEODYMIUM, metallic element, symbol Pr, one of the rare earth elements (q.v.) in the lanthanide series (q.v.) of the periodic table (*see* PERIODIC LAW); at.no. 59, at.wt. 140.908. Praseodymium melts at about 931° C (about 1708° F), boils at about 3520° C (about 6368°F), and has a sp.gr. of 6.64.

It was discovered in 1885 by the German chemist Carl Auer von Welsbach (1858–1929), who separated it from neodymium. A mixture of the two elements had formerly been considered a single element, called didymium. Praseodymium is a paramagnetic, silvery metal that corrodes rapidly in moist air. It forms green trivalent salts.

Praseodymium is widely distributed in nature and ranks 37th in order of abundance of the elements in the crust of the earth. It is found in cerite and other rare earth minerals. It is used, with small amounts of other rare earth metals, in magnesium alloys and in misch metal, an alloy used for cigarette-lighter flints and as a dexoidizer in alloys and vacuum tubes. A mixture of praseodymium and neodymium is used to tint goggles for welders.

PRATO, city, central Italy, in Tuscany Region. A textile center since the Middle Ages, Prato is also an important wool-manufacturing center. Points of interest in the city include a cathedral, built between the 12th and 15th centuries, parts of which were designed by the Italian sculptors Donatello, Michelozzo, and Giovanni Pisano, and which contains frescoes by the Italian artist Fra Filippo Lippi. Prato became an independent commune in the 11th century. It fell to Florence in the 14th century. Pop. (1988 est.) 164,800.

PRAWN, common name applied to numerous species of shrimplike, ten-legged crustaceans, mostly of the family Palaemonidae (*see* SHRIMP). It is distinguished from the shrimp mainly by a long, serrated rostrum, or beak, that projects from the shell. Prawns are widely distributed in both fresh and brackish waters in temperate and tropical regions. The common European prawn, *Palaemon serratus,* occurs in great numbers along sandy shores. It averages about 10 cm (about 4 in) in length and is greatly esteemed as a table delicacy. Several American species of edible prawns exist, including *Palaemonetes vulgaris,* a small variety found off the Atlantic coast from Massachusetts to Florida, and *Panaeus setiferus,* a 15-cm (6-in) southern species often marketed as shrimp. Freshwater prawns native to the Tropics may attain a length of more than 60 cm (2 ft).

For further information on this topic, see the Bibliography in volume 28, section 464.

PRAXITELES (fl. 4th cent. BC), Greek sculptor, considered the greatest sculptor of his time. He is said to have lived in Athens about 360 BC. Praxiteles worked almost entirely in marble. Most scholars agree that one original work of his is extant, the *Hermes with the Infant Dionysus* (c. 340 BC), discovered in 1877 during the excavation of the Temple of Hera at Olympia, in Greece, where it had been seen in ancient times by the Roman traveler and chronicler Pausanias. It is now at the Archaeological Museum there. His other work is known only through Roman copies. The most famous is the *Aphrodite of Cnidus* (Museo Pio-Clementino, Vatican City). The work of Praxiteles shows a humanization in the ideals of the Attic period of Greek art. His subjects are either human beings or the more youthful and less awesome deities, such as Aphrodite, goddess of love, Apollo, god of music and prophecy, and Hermes, messenger of the gods. His portraits of

Resting Satyr *(Museo Capitolino, Rome), Roman copy of a work by Praxiteles.* Alinari

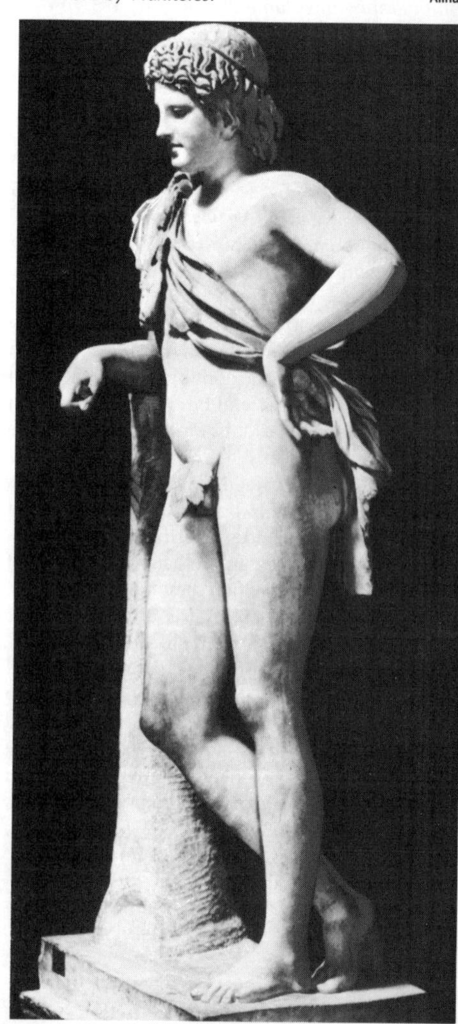

divinities do not possess the superhuman qualities of earlier Greek works, but instead are wrought with grace and charm. Praxiteles was celebrated for his satyrs; best known is the *Resting Satyr* (Roman copy, Museo Capitolino, Rome), immortalized by the American writer Nathaniel Hawthorne in *The Marble Faun* (1860).

See also GREEK ART AND ARCHITECTURE.

PRAYER, in religion, both a person's act of communion with God, or any other object of worship, and the words used. It is the natural result of a person's belief in God. Prayer may be individual or group, formal or spontaneous, silent or spoken. In one or more forms, it is at the center of worship. The inseparable accompaniment of sacrifice in most primitive religions, prayer occupied a central position in Jewish religion from earliest days. The Temple was "a house of prayer" (see Isa. 56:7) and the Psalms, or Psalter, became the prayer of liturgy of the Temple and the synagogue and formed the substance of prayers in early Christianity.

Christian prayer normally includes invocation, praise, thanksgiving, petition (for oneself and others), confession, and appeal for forgiveness. It follows the pattern of the Lord's Prayer (Lat. *Paternoster*) given by Jesus Christ to his disciples (see Matt. 6:9–13; Luke 11:2–4).

Prayer forms of corporate worship vary from the highly liturgical formalized prayers of the Divine Office in the Roman Catholic church and the Book of Common Prayer of the Church of England and other Anglican churches, through the extemporaneous spoken prayers of nonliturgical services, to the silent prayer of a Friends' Meeting. *See* FRIENDS, SOCIETY OF.

In its narrowest sense, prayer is understood as spiritual communion for the sake of requesting something of a deity. In its broadest sense, prayer is any ritual form designed to bring one into closer relation to whatever one believes to be the ultimate. In this sense, both the dance ceremonials of the American Indian and the meditation of the Buddhist seeking self-perfection are forms of prayer. At the highest level, sacrifice is absorbed into prayer in the sacrificial offering of self to God through total commitment.

Aids to prayer, evolved through the centuries, include prayer beads, which enable a worshiper to count the prayers he or she is praying; the prayer wheel, a cylindrical box containing written prayers believed to become effective as the box is revolved on its axis, used primarily by Lamaists; and the prayer rug, used by Muslims.

PRAYING MANTIS. *See* MANTIS.

PRECAMBRIAN ERA, in geology, earliest division of time for which rock strata are recognized. The era is taken to include the entire time interval beginning with the formation of the solid crust of the earth, more than 4 billion years ago, and ending 570 million years ago, when life in the seas had begun to flourish and evolve rapidly. Over the course of these billions of years, the earth's surface underwent many important changes. At some early stage of the Precambrian era, the crust became differentiated into the dark, heavy "simatic" rocks that floor the huge basins in which the first oceans began forming, and the lighter "sialic" rocks that float on the sima and form the continents. At the same time, the crust became broken into tectonic plates, giving rise to continental drift (*see* PLATE TECTONICS). The first oceans eventually became home to newly evolved aerobic bacteria and algae (*see* BLUE-GREEN ALGAE). These early marine life forms are thought to have been responsible for generating oxygen, pouring the gas into the primitive atmosphere for millions of years, thereby setting the stage for evolution of oxygen-dependent marine creatures in the following Cambrian period of the Paleozoic era (qq.v.).

Precambrian rocks consist in general of (1) an extensive series of metamorphosed igneous and sedimentary strata, such as gneisses, schists, slates, quartzites, and crystalline limestones; (2) igneous rocks, slightly altered; and (3) recognizable sedimentary rocks that contain fossils of primitive uni- and multicellular marine life such as algae, traces of more primitive life, such as bacteria, and (from the youngest Precambrian rocks) the Ediacaran fauna (q.v.), an assemblage of complex, soft-bodied marine invertebrates that may represent an evolutionary dead end (*see* PALEONTOLOGY). Precambrian rocks are rich in ores and other minerals: the iron ore of the Lake Superior region; gold, nickel, and copper; and quarries of building stone such as granite and marble. Other minerals of economic importance in Precambrian rocks include graphite, garnet, apatite, talc, emery, and feldspar.

See also GEOLOGY. P.R.Ma.

For further information on this topic, see the Bibliography in volume 28, sections 417, 436.

PRECESSION. *See* ECLIPTIC; GYROSCOPE.

PRECIPITATION, in physics and chemistry, process or phenomenon of formation of a second, visible phase or state of matter, within a first phase (*see* PHASE RULE). If, for example, air containing water vapor is cooled below its dew point, a precipitate of liquid water forms within the gaseous phase. This precipitate may adopt the final form of fog, rain, or condensate. If a solution becomes supersaturated in some component that is a solid at the temperature involved, that substance tends to nucleate and crystallize out, or precipitate spontaneously; it may settle as a sediment or may be separated from the liquid phase by the process of filtration or centrifugation. A precipitate of one solid phase may be also found within a second solid phase, as in the case of some metal alloys, where the precipitate results in a pronounced increase in hardness and tensile strength of the metal.

See also COLLOID; ELECTROSTATIC PRECIPITATOR.

PRE-COLUMBIAN ART AND ARCHITECTURE, the art and architecture of the indigenous civilizations of Mesoamerica and the Andes and of neighboring cultures before the 16th century AD. For the art of ancient indigenous cultures north of Mexico, *see* AMERICAN INDIANS.

For 3000 years before the European discovery and colonization of the western hemisphere, the Indians of Latin America developed civilizations that rivaled the artistic and intellectual accomplishments of ancient China, India, Mesopotamia, and the Mediterranean world. The quality of these accomplishments is even more impressive because much of the essential technology of eastern hemisphere civilizations was unknown to the American Indian. The wheel, for instance, was used in Mesoamerica only for toys and was never developed into the potter's wheel, wagon wheel, or pulley system. Metal tools were rarely used, and then only in the last stages of pre-Columbian history. The elaborate sculptures and intricate jade ornaments of the Maya, therefore, were accomplished by carving stone with stone.

Pre-Columbian and post-Columbian Indian art and architecture evince a concern with the relation both of the structure to its environment and of the object to its material. This regard for nature resulted in an aesthetic rooted in an awareness of natural dualities—day and night, sun and moon, land and water, life and death. The tension in most American Indian art, therefore, is derived from the contrast of opposing design elements such as light and dark, open and closed compositions, the static form and the mobile form, the realistic and the abstract, and the plain and the ornate.

Geographical Scope. Pre-Columbian cultures are grouped according to general geographic area. Although scholars sometimes differ in the precise regions they identify, their basic divisions are more or less the same. In this article the Mesoamerican Area includes the present countries of Mexico, Belize, Guatemala, Honduras, and El Salvador. Constituting the Intermediate Area are lower Central America and the northern South American nations of Venezuela, Colombia, and Ecuador. Peru and Bolivia make up the Central Andean Area, and the Peripheral Area comprise the rest of South America, as well as the Caribbean islands. Although these areas were initially regarded as entirely separate cultural entities, recent archaeological research has indicated substantial cultural cross-fertilization and relation rather than isolation. Cultural similarities, therefore, are now being as actively investigated as were differences in the past. Many anthropologists, archaeologists, and art historians are also now studying modern Latin American Indian cultures for vestigial manifestations of or similarities to pre-Columbian civilization.

Chronological Divisions. To distinguish the major characteristics of pre-Columbian civilizations, three general chronological divisions have been widely used: the Pre-Classic, or Formative, period (c. 1500 BC–c. AD 300); the Classic, or Florescent, period (c. 300–c. 900); and the Post-Classic period (c. 900–1540). Although the term *classic* suggests the height of a cultural development, current scholars and critics deny the once-common assumption that the finest pre-Columbian art and architecture were achieved in the Classic period. The art and architecture of the Post-Classic Mixtec and Aztec of Mexico and the Chimu and Inca of Peru are not less distinguished than those of their Classic predecessors, but only different in accomplishment and taste.

The Pre-Classic period was an age of experimentation and innovation, the achievements of which were expanded and refined by later civilizations. In this early period the Americas were primarily isolated into chiefdoms and small kingdoms that were largely independent of one another in their cultural development. Evidence exists, however, of some distribution of religious ideas and art motifs. The Olmec of Mexico, the San Agustín culture of Colombia, and the Chavín of Peru all worshiped a feline deity, and all shared a similar iconography (pictorial vocabulary) in their art.

During the Classic period complex empires developed. Their rulers were often priests, rather than the warrior-priests who were the principal administrators of Post-Classic civilizations, and cultures were more readily disseminated or assimilated. Although this is often considered a peaceful period, recent archaeology has demonstrated that most major Classic civilizations were warlike. Conquest and extensive trade resulted in wealth that was spent on constructing or elaborating ceremonial centers or cities, as well as creating increasingly luxurious personal effects and high-quality objects for funerary or ritual use.

The Post-Classic period was characterized by frequent wars resulting from the socioeconomic pressures of increased population and technological development. The terminal cultures and civilizations of this period are the best documented, because they were directly encountered by the Spanish, who recorded their personal impressions or had histories compiled of the conquered.

Cultural Traits. Pre-Columbian civilizations were primarily agricultural, with maize (corn) being developed as the dietary staple in Mesoamerica, and the potato in Andean Peru and Bolivia. Until the relative secularism of the Post-Classic period, religion was also central to the formulation and development of pre-Columbian American culture. Religious ideas and rituals, however, were largely determined by the concerns of agricultural societies for crop fertility. Much pre-Columbian art and architecture, therefore, is involved with astronomy, which helped the Indians determine appropriate times for planting and times for harvesting.

Essentially, two types of urban design were developed. The more common was the ceremonial center, a complex of structures primarily consisting of religious and administrative buildings constructed around plazas, but without common dwellings or streets. It is conjectured that only the secular and religious rulers and their courts lived in these centers, while the majority of the population resided on small farms in a surrounding suburban zone. Less common, especially outside the Central Andean Area, were true cities with streets organizing residences of rich and poor, as well as plaza-oriented temples and administrative buildings. (Recent excavations, however, suggest that some Mesoamerican sites once thought to be ceremonial centers may have been true cities.) Both ceremonial complexes and true cities served as centers for religion, government, and commerce. Important for supplying necessities and luxuries, commerce also provided the routes for transmitting ideas, technology, and art forms and motifs.

KINDS OF ART

Outstanding in pre-Columbian artistic development were architecture, sculpture, painting, and decorative arts such as pottery, metalwork, and textiles.

Architecture. The earliest pre-Columbian buildings were constructed from wood, bundled reeds, fiber matting or thatch, and other perishable materials. A permanent, monumental architecture using stone or adobe (sun-dried brick) was developed principally in Mesoamerica and the Central Andean Area.

Pre-Columbian architectural technology was rudimentary. Most structures were built with the post-and-lintel or trabeated (horizontal-beam, archless) system, although the Chavín of Peru and the Maya of Mesoamerica employed the corbeled, or false, arch, in which one stone was extended above another to form an archlike shape. Stone rather than metal tools were used, and human labor rather than machines was used for transporting and building such characteristic structures as pyramids, palaces, tombs, and platform temples (built on earth platforms).

Traditionally, the pre-Columbian pyramid has been regarded as different from its Egyptian counterpart because it was intended not as a burial structure but as a symbol of spiritual ascent and the residence of a deity. Recent excavations, however, increasingly indicate that tombs were sometimes incorporated into pyramids. Pictographs in Mesoamerican codices (screen-fold books of paper or deerskin) illustrate that pyramids were also used for military defense. The Aztec symbol for conquest was a burning pyramid of which the calli, or house of the god (the temple atop the pyramid), had been toppled by the conqueror. In order to make them more monumental or reflect current taste, many Mesoamerican pyramids were periodically rebuilt over a preexisting structure.

Sculpture. The majority of extant pre-Columbian sculptures are clay figurines and effigy pots. Stone sculpture is found primarily in Mesoamerica and only occasionally in the Central Andean and Intermediate areas, regions in which the use of metal was earlier and more extensive. Although metalworking technology was highly sophisticated, carving was done with stone rather than metal tools.

Painting. Archaeologists are continually excavating new examples of painted pre-Columbian architectural decoration. Teotihuacán in Mexico had buildings covered on both the interior and exterior with a thick plaster that was painted with either decorative patterns or narrative scenes. At the Mexican sites of Bonampak and Chichén Itzá, the Maya and Maya-Toltec painted their temple interiors with realistic frescoes that depict daily life and historical events. Although primarily found in Mesoamerica, architectural painting has been discovered in the Intermediate Area in the geometrically patterned underground tombs at Tierradentro in Colombia and the mythological murals at Panamarca in Peru. Also in Peru, Moche effigy pots of architectural structures indicate that the exteriors of buildings were often boldly painted with symbolic motifs.

Mesoamerican pictographic writing appeared in codices a thousand years before the Spanish conquest. Called glyphs, the pictographs demonstrate the refined drawing abilities of the Maya, Mixtec, and Aztecs. Most codices were destroyed during the 16th century by zealous Spanish missionaries, who regarded them as sources of paganism and the occult.

Another type of pre-Columbian painting was the decoration of pottery. Maya, Moche, and Peruvian Nazca ceramics provide many of the finest examples of design and technique.

Decorative Arts. Most objects recovered from pre-Columbian sites are associated with burial offerings and are utilitarian or ceremonial rather than decorative in function. Despite the lack of many technological advantages in their manufacture, these objects were equal in design and execution to any of the finest examples of preindustrial art in any part of the world.

Pottery. Possibly first developed in Colombia or Ecuador, pottery succeeded baskets and gourds as containers. Throughout the entire pre-Columbian world, pottery became the most common surviving artifact. Both hand-modeled and molded pots and clay objects were made. Decoration involved incising designs, carving or molding reliefs, and employing various techniques of painting and polishing. Although polychromed ceramics were produced, most pottery was painted with one or two colors or left unpainted.

Metalwork. From its probable origins in the northern Central Andean Area about 700 BC, metalworking spread to the Intermediate Area and finally was transmitted to Mesoamerica about AD 1000. Because of European greed for gold and silver, most unburied or unhidden objects of these materials were melted down by the Spanish conquerors and exported to Spain as ingots. Although iron and steel were unknown, copper was widely worked and the alloying of bronze was discovered about AD 1000. Tumbaga, an alloy of copper and gold, was employed in Peru, Colombia, and Ecuador. Many techniques were used for working metal, including the lost-wax process, soldering, and repoussé or embossing. Metalwork was frequently engraved, gilded, or inlaid with various stones and shells.

Textiles. Because of the extremely dry climate of the Peruvian coast, this is the only pre-Columbian region where major examples of early textiles have survived. Buried in desert tombs, especially in the Paracas Peninsula, 2500-year-old textiles have been perfectly preserved, as they were in the arid climate of ancient Egypt. Cotton was the most common fiber used for weaving cloth, although in the Central Andean Area llama, alpaca, and vicuña wool was also used. These materials were often colored with mineral and vegetable dyes. Besides woven patterns and images, textiles designs were achieved through painting, stamping, embroidering, and appliqué In Post-Classic Mesoamerica and Peru, fabric was also made of feathers.

MESOAMERICAN AREA

The majority of pre-Columbian Mesoamerican sites are located in present-day Mexico.

Pre-Classic Period. The major Pre-Classic cultures of Mexico were the Olmec and the western cultures of Colima, Jalisco, and Nayarit.

Olmec. Along the central coast of the Gulf of Mexico, the Olmec developed the first major Mesoamerican civilization, between about 1500 and 200 BC. Major ceremonial centers such as La Venta, Tres Zapotes, and San Lorenzo were located in the swampy jungle river deltas of the Mexican states of Veracruz and Tabasco. Many of the most characteristic elements of Mesoamerican civilization originated with the Olmec and are especially evident at La Venta, which appears to have been this culture's primary spiritual, intellectual, and administrative capital.

La Venta, like most later Mesoamerican sites, is planned with a north-south orientation so that building doors open east to west, corresponding to the daily passage of the sun. A mounded-earth pyramid 30 m (100 ft) high, possibly the earliest in Mesoamerica, was constructed as the focal point of an axial arrangement of platform temples and plazas. This urban arrangement would become the most common plan for later Mesoamerican ceremonial centers. The Olmec were the first to use stone architecturally and sculpturally, although it had to be laboriously quarried and transported from the Tuxtla Mountains 97 km (60 mi) to the west. Architectural stone mosaics also were created for the first time in the Americas.

The most impressive Olmec artifacts are colossal stone heads of males, about 2.7 m (about 9 ft) high, that are portraitlike in their realism. Large, detailed relief carvings depicting mythological deities or events have been discovered, as well as small, exquisitely carved, in-the-round sculptures of basalt or jade. Despite the importance of sculpture, however, it was not integrated with the architecture as it would be in later Mesoamerican civilizations. Isolated stone stelae, or slabs of rock, were erected to commemorate significant events, and they were inscribed with the first form of writing to be devised in the Americas.

Olmec art, like that of the Maya, is characterized by a high degree of naturalism. Emphasis is placed on the curvilinear rather than the rectilinear, thus encouraging fluid, rhythmic forms that seem more harmonious to a tropical locale than

Funerary figure (Pre-Hispanic Museum, Oaxaca, Mexico) from southern Mexico.
E. Peter Ayala–Editorial Photocolor Archives

the stylized angular art that is commonly found in the relatively austere mountain valleys of central and southern Mexico.

The Olmec established an empire extending from the Gulf of Mexico coast through the central Valley of Mexico to the western Mexican states of Morelos and Guerrero. Although pottery produced in the Olmec heartland was not distinguished, at the Olmec colonial sites of Tlatilco and Tlapacoya are found hollow clay figurines, probably the first made, which are among the finest examples of Mesoamerican ceramic sculpture. The indigenous culture of Tlatilco also produced vast numbers of very small individualized figurines of women with elaborate hairstyles and detailed body ornamentation. Their exaggerated female anatomy seems to indicate use as fertility images.

In the western Mexican states of Morelos and Guerrero, Olmec influence is seen in Xochipala clay figurines and in the small, highly stylized stone sculptures of the Mezcala. The cave painting at Oxtotitlan, in Guerrero, and the reliefs carved on the cave walls at Chalcatzingo, in Morelos, are examples of pure Olmec art in this region. Both sites are dedicated to the cult of the jaguar deity, whose power and exploits were the subject of most Olmec art.

Colima, Jalisco, and Nayarit. In the late Pre-Classic and early Classic periods, major cultures developed in western Mexico. Once mistakenly called Tarascan, they are now referred to by the names of the Mexican states in which the sites are located: Colima, Jalisco, and Nayarit.

No major architectural sites were constructed, and little stone sculpture was made, but some of the most accomplished Mesoamerican clay effigy pots and figurines were produced. At Ixtlán del Rio in Nayarit, artisans created detailed genre sculptures depicting all aspects of village life. These negative-painted scenes (with unpainted figures defined by the painted background) possess the clarity and immediacy of photographs. Although less naturalistically dynamic and spontaneous, Colima figurines are also realistic, but are more monumental in form and essential in contour. Jalisco figurines are the most naive stylistically but are characterized by an arrestingly bold presence. The vital realism of western Mexican clay sculpture has made these artifacts among the most popular examples of pre-Columbian art. Because they were buried in deep underground shaft-and-chamber tombs, an unusually large number of pieces have survived.

Classic Period. Teotihuacán, the Mayan cities, the Zapotec center at Monte Albán, and the Classic Vera Cruz culture were the dominant civilizations of the Classic era.

Teotihuacán. Some 48 km (some 30 mi) northeast of Mexico City is the site of Teotihuacán ("place of the gods"). Here the first truly urban Mesoamerican civilization developed, and its influence was predominant through the first half of the 1st millennium AD. A classic aesthetic evolved, emphasizing order and refinement. Austerely elegant, stylized design resulted in the creation of a monumental art, the effect of which is serene simplicity and noble grandeur. Buildings, for example, were designed using the *talud-tablero* (slope-and-panel) system. With this type of design the contrasting horizontal and vertical elements were all rigidly controlled and unified, as were the projecting and recessive structural areas, the light and dark effects, and the illustrative and geometric ornamentation.

The monumentality of Teotihuacán architecture is evident in the Pyramid of Quetzalcoatl at Cholula, the largest single pre-Columbian structure, and the Pyramid of the Sun at Teotihuacán, which is second in size. In area covered and in volume, both structures are larger than any ancient Egyptian pyramid. Palace complexes organized around plazas are among the most impressive examples of pre-Columbian residences. All Teotihuacán architecture was thickly covered with stucco, which was usually painted with murals. The best remaining examples of these frescoes decorate the interior walls of palaces at Teotihuacán. Three styles of murals have been categorized: decorative designs with symbolic meaning; stylized conceptual images of deities and mythological creatures; and narrative scenes that are more perceptual or realistic than abstract and schematic.

Few monumental examples of stone sculpture survive. The most famous is an architectonic monolith of the water goddess Chalchiuhtlicue. The most characteristic examples of Teotihuacán stone carving are stylized human masks originally attached to mummy bundles.

Two distinct types of ceramics were produced. Delicately shaped, thin orange-ware was widely traded throughout Mesoamerica, but the most prized pottery consisted of ceremonial objects thinly coated with plaster that was incised and then painted in a manner resembling ceremonial murals. The tripod—a straight-sided bowl supported by three flat legs—was the vessel shape initiated and most used by Teotihuacán potters. Clay figurines were produced, many being repre sentations of people of the time and of dancin spirits of the dead.

Maya. Maya civilization dominated Mesoameric in the second half of the first millennium AD. Al though originating in the Pre-Classic period an continuing until the time of the Spanish con quest, Maya culture achieved its most significan artistic and intellectual achievements during th epoch from about 600 to about 900, or the Clas sic phase.

In variety and quality of architecture, the May are unexcelled by any other pre-Columbian civilization. Primarily found in lowland tropica areas, Classic Maya sites are all believed to b ceremonial centers, rather than true cities lik Teotihuacán. The majority of Mayan ruins are i Mexico; they include Palenque, Yaxchilán, an Bonampak and, in the Yucatán Peninsula, Chichén Itzá, Coba, Dzilbilchaltun, Edzna, Hochob, Kabah, Labná, Sayil, Uxmal, and Xpuhil. Othe major sites are Copán in Honduras and, in Guatemala, Piedras Negras, Quirique, and Tikal, the largest of all Maya ceremonial centers. Maya architecture is characterized by an exquisite sense of proportion and design and by structural

This polychrome pottery vessel from the Mayan site at Maxcanu, Yucatán, Mexico (late part of the Classic period, c. 600–900) is decorated with an all-over design of religious significance. Sotheby Parke-Bernet–Editorial Photocolor Archives

The ruins of the Temple of the Warriors at Chichén Itzá, Yucatán, Mexico. Chichén Itzá, the most important center of the Post-Classic phase of Maya culture, was at its peak between 1000 and 1200. **Editorial Photocolor Archives**

refinement and subtle detailing. The Maya used sculpture more extensively for architectural decoration than any other pre-Columbian civilization. The corbel arch was employed not only to vault interior spaces, but also to construct triumphal arches. Despite the lack of carts and domesticated beasts of burden, the Maya were the first to build an extensive network of paved roadways. These connected major religious and administrative centers and seem to have been used for ceremonial processions, as well as for commercial traffic.

Maya art is the most highly refined and elegant in technique and design of any pre-Columbian civilization. Dignity and majesty were stressed in figurative art, as well as the representation of both physical and psychological reality. Rather than stasis and economy of form, the Maya seem to have sought exuberant, sensual movement and lavish ornamentation. Although Maya artists adhered to the basic precepts of their aesthetic tradition and iconography, innovation and individuality were encouraged.

Stelae with figurative carving and inscriptions are the most characteristic examples of the monumental freestanding stone sculpture of the Maya. The most elaborate examples are found at Copán, where the softness of the stone made possible baroque flamboyance of ornament. Most major sites have well-developed traditions of architectural relief panels in stone, and at Palenque stucco was effectively used for reliefs.

The Maya mastered all known pre-Columbian art forms except metalworking. Although no Maya textiles remain, their character and decoration can be discerned from representations in painting, figurines, and sculptures. Jade was skillfully carved, as were wood, bone, and shell; in clay, however, the Maya excelled. Realistic figurines (especially those from the islands of Jaina) and polychromed pottery with mythological or genre scenes (produced at Chama) are among the finest accomplishments of pre-Columbian sculpture and painting.

Fresco painting was practiced. Particularly fine examples have been found at Bonampak, Palenque, and Tikal. The Maya also had libraries of codices with pictographs. Of the three remaining codices the Dresden Codex (Sachsische Landesbibliothek, Dresden, Germany) best illustrates the Maya's descriptive and formally dynamic use of line.

Zapotec. In the Valley of Oaxaca the Zapotec culture (sometimes referred to as Monte Albán culture) had been developing since the Pre-Classic period, but it reached its height between about AD 300 and 900. Monte Albán, the major Zapotec urban complex, indicates that this civilization was early influenced by the Olmec, then Teotihuacán, and finally the Maya. An elitist theocratic society, the Zapotec were obsessed with death. Much of their art, therefore, was created for funerary rites. Tombs at Monte Albán and throughout the Oaxaca area have yielded elaborate burial urns depicting various Zapotec deities, especially Cocijo, the god of rain.

The temples of Monte Albán show the influence of the *talud-tablero* design of Teotihuacán architecture, as do the spacious plazas surrounded by monumental stairways leading to platform temples. Stelae with mythological reliefs and glyph inscriptions are scattered around the site. Tombs were often multichambered and adorned with frescoes that reflect the influence of Teotihuacán murals.

Classic Vera Cruz. Along the Gulf of Mexico coast another culture developed; once erroneously called Totonac, it is now referred to as Classic Vera Cruz (after the modern Mexican state in which its activity was concentrated). El Tajín was the culture's principal ceremonial center. Its seven ball courts indicate the importance of the Mesoamerican ritual ball game *tlachtli* to this culture's ritual observances. Many of the most significant reliefs decorate the ball courts, and some indicate human sacrifice of the players.

The major artifacts of the Classic Vera Cruz culture are associated with the ball game. *Hachas* ("axes"), *yugos* ("yokes"), and *palmas* ("palms") are all made of stone and resemble in shape the objects for which they are named. Their actual use remains a much debated subject; however, most scholars now believe they were awarded to leading ballplayers and were worn not during play but for ceremonial processions and celebrations. The *hachas* may also have been ball-court markers.

Clay figurines of outstanding quality were also widely produced, especially in the Remojadas region, which is famous for its broad-faced laughing figurines. Highly naturalistic hollow figurines, produced wholly or partly by molds, are among the most significant large-scale pre-Columbian clay sculptures. Their detailed features and ornamental detail were characteristically emphasized by applying black pitch or asphalt after firing.

Because of its central location and accessibility, the Classic Vera Cruz culture was eclectic. Its art and architecture, especially at the site of Cerro de las Mesas, show Olmec, Teotihuacán, Zapotec, and Maya influence.

Post-Classic Period. During the Post-Classic period important cultures developed among the Toltec, the Tarascan, the Huastec and Totonac, the Mixtec, and the Aztecs.

Toltec and Maya-Toltec. About 72 km (about 45 mi) north of Mexico City is Tula, the capital of the militaristic Toltec, whose early Post-Classic empire extended as far as the Yucatán Peninsula. An austere society of pragmatic warriors, the Toltec were concerned more with function than form, and they produced few luxury objects. Their most valued pottery, for example, was plumbate ware imported from non-Toltec artisans who lived on the Pacific coast near the Mexico-Guatemala border. (The only glazed pottery developed in ancient America, plumbate ware had a metallic, usually greenish-gray surface that resulted when a clay coating melted to form glaze.)

Toltec architecture and sculpture were diminished reflections of the ruins of nearby Teotihuacán. The psychology of Toltec aesthetics, however, was to inspire temporal fear rather than the spiritual aspiration and harmony sought by the Teotihuacán civilization. The temple atop of the pyramid of Tlahuizcalpantecuhtli at Tula has columns 4.6 m (15 ft) high, fashioned as fearsome warriors rigidly guarding the sacred precinct. Around the base of this pyramid are palaces and ceremonial halls, probably for the military elite. At the north foot of the pyramid is an architectural feature developed by the Toltec; called the *coatepantli,* or serpent wall, it may have enclosed a secret ceremonial space. Another Toltec innovation to inspire dread was the *tzompantli,* a low platform near the main pyramid on which racks were erected to display the severed heads and skulls of human beings that had been sacrificed.

In 987 the Toltec invaded the Yucatán Peninsula and made the Puuc Maya city of Chichén Itzá their colonial capital. Most of this site now reflects the juxtaposition of Late Maya and Early Toltec taste and iconography. In addition to Tula architectural innovations, serpentine columns shaped like the god Quetzalcoatl (the Plumed Serpent) and Chacmools—recumbent figures holding offering bowls—are also found. Realistic frescoes depict the Toltec invasion and conquest. The quality of design and artistry at Chichén Itzá, however, is superior to that at Tula, reflecting the more advanced artistic traditions and abilities of the conquered Maya architects and artisans.

After 200 years, Toltec power waned in the Yucatán, and a new Maya capital was established at Mayapán, a walled city rather than the open ceremonial center built by the Classic Maya. Tulum is another Post-Classic Maya walled city. Located on the Caribbean coast, this was the first Mesoamerican city described by the Spanish.

Polychrome ceramic vessel in anthropomorphic shape (c. 1300–1400, Anthropological Museum, Mexico City) from the Mixtec culture, great pottery makers of the Post-Classic period in Mexico.
Editorial Photocolor Archives

Tarascan. The Tarascan flourished in western Mexico from the beginning of the Post-Classic period until the Spanish conquest. Their capital at Tzintzuntzan on Lake Pátzcuaro had yacatas—characteristic stepped circular temples arranged in a line and connected by a single rectangular platform. The earliest metalwork in Mesoamerica probably was done by the Tarascan, who may have learned the technique through Pacific Ocean trade with Central American or Andean Indians. Tarascan copper ornaments were as sought after as their feather work and textiles.

Huastec and Totonac. At the time of the Spanish conquest the Huastec culture was located on the northern coast of the Gulf of Mexico, while the central coast was occupied by the Totonac, whose major city was Cempoala. Excellent stone sculptors, the Huastec were also known for carving seashells with intricate cutout designs.

Mixtec. By the 10th century the Zapotec of the Valley of Oaxaca had been conquered by the Mixtec. Occupying Monte Albán as a necropolis, or city of the dead, they built fortified cities such as Yagul, as well as the important religious center of Mitla. Mixtec architecture is characterized by geometric ornamental reliefs called stone mosaics and by elaborate cross-shaped tombs.

Mixtec codices, murals, and painted pottery attest to this people's accomplishments at drawing and painting. They were the finest metalworkers of Mesoamerica, and the pottery produced in the Mixtec-Puebla style at Cholula was the most highly valued ceramic ware in 14th- and 15th-century Mexico. The Mixtec also excelled in decorating masks, sacrificial knives, and other objects with mosaic inlays of coral, shell, turquoise, and other stones, as well as obsidian. Woodcarving was also a highly developed craft, used particularly for making intricately decorated atlatls (spear-throwers) and for carving teponaztli, (slit-drums, or hollow horizontal, cylindrical percussion instruments) for ceremonial use.

Aztec. The last major Mesoamerican civilization was that of the Aztecs, who were also called Mexica (from which the name Mexico is derived). Between 1428 and 1521 the Aztecs produced and collected as tribute some of the finest remaining examples of pre-Columbian art.

The Aztec capital of Tenochtitlán, the present site of Mexico City, was possibly the largest and one of the most beautiful cities in the world at the time of the Spanish conquest. Built in Lake Texcoco on natural islands and artificial islands called chinampas, Tenochtitlán was similar in concept to Venice, Italy. The streets were primarily canals, and boats were the major form of transportation. Today, on the Zócalo, or great central plaza of Mexico City, the National Palace and the National Cathedral occupy the site of the main temples and palaces of the Aztecs.

Unlike the Mixtec, the Aztecs produced monumental freestanding stone sculpture. Its design and artistry are among the most impressive manifestations of pre-Columbian artistic genius. In their scuplture the Aztecs were capable of abstraction, as well as a realism that reveals both the internal and external character of the deity, person, or animal portrayed. Much Aztec stone sculpture was used for architectural decoration and representations of deities; it was also employed for human sacrificial altars, *cuauhxicalli* (containers for human hearts and blood), calendar stones, and other major ceremonial objects.

In execution and conception the codices produced by the Aztecs are of extremely high quality. Only about 30 survived the wanton destruction of Aztec libraries by zealous Christian conquerors.

CENTRAL ANDEAN AREA

Unlike those in Mesoamerica, major urban ruins in the Central Andean Area date from before the discovery of pottery.

Pre-Ceramic Period. In the Chicama Valley of the northern Peruvian coast at Huaca Prieta, monumental ceremonial mounds of refuse were built about 2500 BC. Highly skilled cotton weaving has been found at this site as well as gourds carved with stylized geometric motifs. Another Pre-Ceramic site on the northern coast is Las Haldas, where perhaps the first true pyramids and platform temples in the Americas were constructed of earth about 1800 BC. El Paraido, or Chuquintana, on the central Peruvian coast, is the region's largest excavated Pre-Ceramic site. Various residential complexes of clay and stone were built by piling rooms and terraces onto one another, as in the Pueblo towns in the southwestern U.S. The fourth important Pre-Ceramic site is Kotosh in the northern highlands of Peru. At Kotosh, terraced temples were made of fieldstone set in earth and decorated with clay reliefs of crossed hands.

Pre-Classic Period. Two important cultures developed in Peru in the Pre-Classic period, Chavín de Huantar and Paracas.

Chavín. Between about 1200 and 200 BC, in the northern Peruvian highland ceremonial center of Chavín de Huantar, a civilization flourished that in many ways paralleled the contemporary Olmec civilization of Mesoamerica. Both were the first major civilizations in their archaeological areas, and both were centered on the worship of a feline deity. It appears that Chavín artistic influence was spread not by military but by religious and intellectual conquest. From Ecuador to southern coastal Peru, evidence remains of Chavín artistic and iconographic influence.

Chavín de Huantar is composed of a series of platforms and hillside temples with corbel vaults in some of the corridors. The finest stone sculpture in the Central Andean Area is found at Chavín de Huantar or at Chavín-related sites such as Cerro Blanco and Cerro Sechin. Unlike the Olmec and other Mesoamericans, however, the Chavín and later Peruvian civilizations created very little freestanding stone sculpture or even clay figurines. Chavín shallow-relief carving achieved its expressive height in the stylized rectilinear design of the stela called the Raimondi Stone.

Probably originating in northern Peru, the stirrup-spout vessel—a closed pot having a hollow U-shaped handle surmounted by a tubular spout—was the most characteristic Chavín ceramic shape. Resembling Olmec ceramics, fine Chavín pottery was produced at colonial outposts rather than at the principal ceremonial center. In northern Peruvian coastal valleys at Cupisnique, Chongoyape, and Tembladera, highly accomplished effigy pots were made with abstract and realistic designs.

Metalworking developed during the Classic period, and the Chavín excelled at making hammered gold, or repoussé, body ornaments. Characteristic of the metalwork of the Chavín are cutout decorative plaques that were attached to garments, and high cylindrical crowns with mythological reliefs, which were worn by the Chavín nobility.

Paracas. Another civilization developed from about 1100 to 200 BC at Paracas on the southern Peruvian coast. Because of the area's extreme aridity, Paracas textiles have been perfectly preserved. Buried in desert tombs, mummies were bundled with layers of cloth that was woven or painted with complex designs or elaborately embroidered. Effigy pots were also found in the Paracas necropolis. Many of these show distinct Chavín influence, especially in the use of feline-cult iconography.

Peruvian southern coastal art has always been more influenced by schematized textile designs, rather than by the clay and metal sculpture that promoted the realism of northern Peruvian art. The decoration of Paracas ceramics, therefore, was highly stylized, frequently incised, and brightly polychromed. The vessels themselves were often double spouted and round bottomed, rather than stirrup spouted and flat based like northern coastal pots.

Classic Period. Dominating the Classic period were the Moche and Nazca cultures and the later Tiahuanacu and related Huari cultures.

Moche. Between about 200 BC and AD 700 a militaristic society flourished on the northern Peruvian coast. Formerly named after its language, Mochica, this civilization is now referred to by the name of its major ceremonial administrative site, Moche.

Centered on two large terraced platform pyramids of sun-baked brick, Moche is one of Peru's most monumental sites. Although a warrior society, the Moche displayed none of the spartan taste or disdain for luxury that characterized the Mesoamerican Toltec. Moche tombs were filled with some of the most proficient pottery and metalwork of the Central Andean Area.

Moche ceramics, the best known of ancient Peruvian artifacts, are among the finest pre-Columbian accomplishments of sculptural realism and narrative drawing. So-called portrait-head effigy pots are especially notable for realistically depicting human features and portraying emotion. On other Moche pottery the curved vessel walls are decorated with dynamic scenes drawn with delicate stylized lines and showing this people's religious and military life. The Moche also produced more erotic pottery than any other pre-Columbian civilization. These artifacts are now interpreted as having ceremonial rather than pornographic meaning.

Moche metalwork was more ornate and technologically advanced than that of earlier civilizations. Body ornaments of gold, silver, copper, and alloys were frequently inlaid with turquoise and lapis lazuli. Geometric patterns and mytho-

Stirrup-spout jar decorated with a spirited representation of a mythological being, from the Moche culture of Peru (c. 200–700, Castello d'Albertis Ethnographic Museum, Genoa, Italy). Scala–Editorial Photocolor Archives

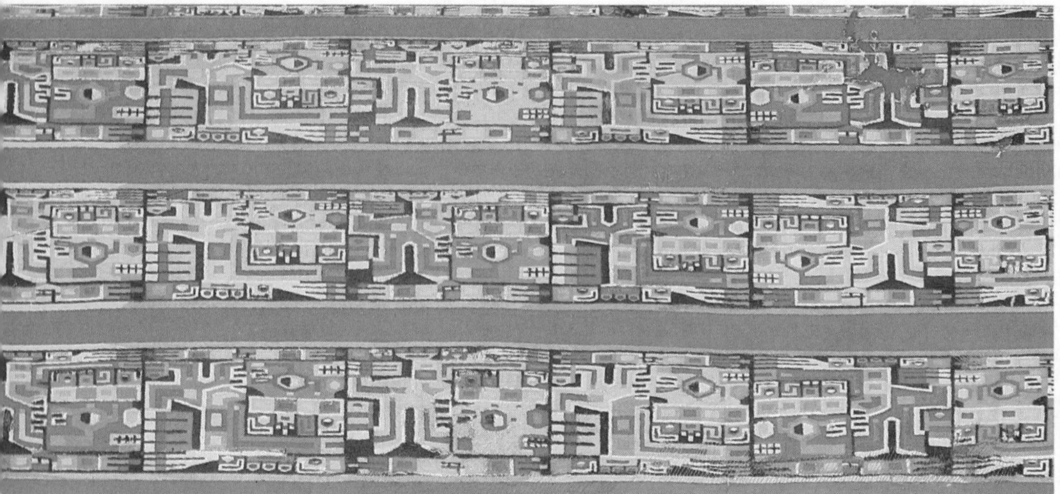

Coastal Huari woven panel, perhaps for a poncho (about AD *700). The controlled, abstract patterns of the fine textiles produced by this culture were based on motifs on Tiahuanacu pottery.* Sotheby Parke-Bernet–Editorial Photocolor Archives

logical motifs, especially the feline deity, were used.

Nazca. The Nazca of Peru's southern coastal region were roughly contemporary with the Moche. Like their Paracas predecessors, the Nazca produced little architecture and excelled at making textiles and pottery with colorful stylized designs that contrast sharply to the realism and restrained color of northern Peruvian ceramics. Nazca pottery is as exuberantly polychromed as it is boldly designed and drawn. Paracas incising was no longer used, and color was applied before (instead of after) firing. Although both the Moche and the Nazca made pots that combined modeled elements and drawings, the Moche preferred sculptural pottery, and the Nazca, painted.

Among the most enigmatic of all pre-Columbian remains are the Nazca lines. These are drawings in the earth of geometric shapes, animals, birds, and fish that can be fully recognized only from the air. Certainly ceremonial in use, the images recall those painted on Nazca pottery. They were made by removing dark upper-surface stones to reveal a lighter substratum.

Tiahuanacu. Tiahuanacu is a Bolivian site in the southern Central Andean highlands near Lake Titicaca. Although Tiahuanacu was settled as early as about 200 BC, it was between about AD 200 and 600 that this urban complex became the center of another major Classic period civilization.

In Tiahuanacu art and architecture the emphasis is on austerity, control, and permanence. Decorative motifs and religious imagery are rigidly stylized. Both buildings and sculpture are characterized by a monumental effect and monolithic appearance. The Gateway of the Sun at Tiahuanacu is cut from a single stone and ornamented with finely executed relief decoration; only 3.7 m (12 ft) high, it appears more monumental because of its design. Scattered throughout the Tiahuanacu area are pillarlike monolithic statues that reach heights of more than 6 m (more than 20 ft) and are decorated with low-relief detailing. The Tiahuanacu culture was one of the few in the Central Andean Area committed to an extensive use of stone for architecture, sculpture, and ceremonial objects.

Huari. The Huari (Wari) shared a religion and iconography with the Tiahuanacu, but were socioeconomically separate. Between about 750 and 1000 the Huari Empire put an end to Peruvian regionalism, thereby preparing for the cultural unification of the Inca period.

Like the Moche, the Huari were a warrior society that appreciated fine artistry and design. Coastal Huari cultures (formerly referred to as Coastal Tiahuanacu) produced textiles of the highest quality. Many of the patterns, especially for ponchos, were abstractions of motifs painted on Tiahuanacu pottery. Although less refined than Tiahuanacu ceramics, Huari pottery stressed solid construction, bold design, and a rich use of polychromy.

Post-Classic Period. The Inca were preeminent during the Post-Classic period, rivaled only by the Chimu.

Chimu. Northern Peru was dominated by the Chimu from about 1000 until 1470. Their imperial capital of Chan Chan was constructed of large walled adobe compounds reflecting those of earlier Huari settlements. The largest Andean urban site and a true city, Chan Chan consists of ten major quadrangles, each containing small pyramids, residences, markets, workshops, reservoirs, storehouses, gardens, and cemeteries. The buildings are decorated with geometrically patterned mosaics of adobe bricks or bas-reliefs, molded in clay plaster, of stylized animals, birds, and mythological figures.

Although Chan Chan was not fortified, the Chimu defended their empire by building fortresses on the frontiers. Paramonga, which defended the southern border, is considered a masterpiece of military engineering, as is the later Inca fortress of Saccasihuamán above Cuzco.

Chimu pottery was primarily mass-produced through the use of molds. Its characteristic black color was achieved through almost smothering the flame, drastically reducing the oxygen in the kiln, during firing. Decoration was usually molded relief, and the surface was polished after firing to give the pot a silverlike sheen.

Metalworkers also mass-produced objects by using molds. Compared with Chimu pottery, however, the metalwork is more distinctive in design and individual in artistic execution.

Textiles were made with the same quality and quantity as other Chimu arts. The featherwork was especially outstanding, and their feathered ponchos were among the most luxurious garments made in the Post-Classic period.

Inca. The Inca, who called themselves Tawantinsuyu, ruled from Cuzco an empire extending between Ecuador and Chile. A highland warrior people, the Inca preferred an aesthetic that was formally simple, decoratively sparse, and functional. Because the Inca were the Indians that the Spanish conquered, their culture is the Central Andean Area civilization of which most is known; however, as happened with the treasures of their Mesoamerican contemporaries, the Aztecs, many Inca artifacts were destroyed by the Spanish, out of greed for gold and silver or out of Christian militancy.

Highland Inca cities such as Machupicchu were carefully planned to harmonize with the landscape, both through the use of indigenous materials and through the architectural repetition

Post-Classic metalwork from northern Peru, although largely mass-produced from molds, was highly sophisticated in design. Left: Chimu silver beaker in the shape of a human head. The three rows of beading indicate hair. The tall cylindrical vessel measures 23 cm (9 in) in height. Below: Lambayeque-Chimu gold band, embossed with figures of standing warriors holding pointed clubs and wearing plumed helmets and short shirts. Both objects date from about 900–1400.

Sotheby Parke-Bernet–Editorial Photocolor Archives

View of the remains of the Inca city of Machupicchu, near Cuzco, Peru. The granite building blocks of the walls were cut to shape with bronze tools and fit tightly together without mortar. Marcus S. Dubin–Editorial Photocolor Archives

of surrounding natural forms. Structurally among the most accomplished in the pre-Columbian period, Inca buildings were constructed with carefully shaped, precisely fitted stone masonry that was left undecorated. Trapezoidal doors and windows were characteristic.

The Inca produced neither large-scale freestanding statues nor architectural sculpture. Metal figurines and small stone ceremonial bowls in the shape of llamas and alpacas are among the finest examples of their sculpture.

Inca pottery, like that of the Chimu, was mass-produced, but it was less distinguished. The most characteristic shape was that of the aryballos, a polychromed container for carrying liquids. In both textiles and metalwork, the Inca continued the Central Andean tradition of high-quality design and execution.

INTERMEDIATE AREA

In lower Central America, Colombia, and Ecuador notable artistic and architectural styles also developed.

Lower Central America. Well-executed, large-scale stone sculpture was carved in Nicaragua and Costa Rica. In addition to statues of deities reflecting Mesoamerican influence, the Central American cultures made elaborately conceived ceremonial stone metates, or surfaces for grinding corn. Jade was made into celts, or ceremonial axes.

Metalwork, which was widely practiced, indicates the influence of northern South America. Among the finest examples are body ornaments made by the Veraguas culture of Panama and the Chiriqui culture of Costa Rica.

The boldly drawn and colored pottery of the Panamanian Coclé is strikingly similar in its dynamic rhythmic patterns to the modern *molas,* or reverse appliqués, sewn by the Cuna Indians of San Blas. On the Nicoya Peninsula of Costa Rica the Chorotega culture made the best examples of Central American polychromed effigy pots.

Colombia. Few major architectural sites have been discovered in Colombia. The earliest and largest archaeological zone is San Augustín, an area covered with freestanding stone sculptures, many related to a feline cult. Underground tombs and temples were also built. At Tierradentro, deep richly painted shaft tombs were cut into the rock. The Caribbean site of Tairona has stone streets and stone foundations for circular houses.

Goldwork was the major Colombian art. The Calima, Quimbaya, Tairona, Tolima, Sinu, Darién, and Chibcha, or Muisca, all produced different regional styles of metalworking and developed particular shapes and iconographies. Reflecting the influence of Central Andean metallurgy, Colombian metalwork is, however, often more innovative in form and technique.

Pottery seldom reached the aesthetic level of metalworking except among cultures such as the Quimbaya, whose robust clay figurines and pots were the equal of their goldwork.

Ecuador. Although fine metalwork was produced in Ecuador, high-quality ceramics were more commonly produced there than in Colombia. Scholars argue whether the earliest pottery in the western hemisphere was made at the Ecuadorian site of Valdivia (c. 3000 BC), or whether it was being produced at the Colombian north coast site of Puerto Hormiga at approximately the same time. Figurines and effigy pots were made by such cultures as the Chorrera, Guangala, Bahia, Jama-Coaque, La Tolita, Mantano, and Carchi.

Architectural and freestanding stone sculpture was rarely carved. The Mantano low reliefs at Cerro Jaboncillo are among the finest examples. Also from the Mantano period (AD 850–1500) are Manabi carved stools; these U-shaped seats borne by sculpted humans or animals are the most characteristic Ecuadorian stone artifacts.

PERIPHERAL AREA

Several archaeological sites in the Amazonian Basin have preserved pottery artifacts, and in the Caribbean, the Arawak, or Taino, developed a distinctive culture and art.

Amazonian Basin. Most Amazonian art was and continues to be made of perishable materials such as wood, feathers, and plant fibers. The most important pre-Columbian ceramic remains from this region have been found in the Amazon River delta in Brazil. At Santarem (c. AD 1250–1500) vessels with elaborate figurative modeling have been excavated. On Marajo Island, earth mounds dating from 1000 to 1250 have yielded intricately patterned, incised, and painted pottery, including enormous burial urns. Effigy pots of seated men were produced on Maraca Island.

Caribbean Area. Pre-Columbian artifacts of the Caribbean area mostly come from the Greater Antilles islands of Puerto Rico, Jamaica, and Hispaniola (Haiti and the Dominican Republic). The principal people to inhabit this area were the Arawak, who migrated from Venezuela's Orinoco River delta. Their arts, therefore, are closely related to those of northern South America. Settling in Puerto Rico about AD 200, the Arawak were known as the Taino, and their culture continued until the Spanish conquest. The most characteristic Taino objects are made of bone, wood, and stone. They include spatulas for inducing vomiting for religious purification; *dujos,* or carved wooden stools for chiefs or priests; and *zemi,* or triangular stones carved with human or animal features representing major natural spirits and deities. Pottery included incised pots with geometric designs and effigy vessels in human shapes.

The most monumental Taino architectural complex is at Utuado, Puerto Rico. Ten squares are surrounded by incised stones. The site indicates that the Mesoamerican ceremonial ball game *tlachtli* had been introduced from the Mexican mainland. R.J.Lo.

For further information on this topic, see the Bibliography in volume 28, section 645.

PREDESTINATION, in Christian theology, the teaching that the eternal destiny of a person is predetermined by God's unchangeable decree. Predestination does not necessarily imply a denial of free will, however. Most exponents of the doctrine have maintained that it is only the individual's final destiny that is predetermined, not the individual's actions, which remain free. The doctrine customarily takes one of two forms: single predestination or double predestination.

Single Predestination. Single predestination is the less severe form of the teaching. It is based on the experience of the presence of God and his love, and on the concurrent understanding that God grants the gift of his presence as an act of sheer grace. In order to emphasize that God's gift is independently willed by him and is in no sense a response to some human act, some Christians have asserted that their relation to God depends only on God and on God's eternal decree established before the foundation of the world.

This point of view is implied only twice in the New Testament, in Rom. 8 and Eph. 1. "For those whom he foreknew he also predestined to be conformed to the image of his Son. . . . And those whom he predestined he also called; and those whom he called he also justified; and those whom he justified he also glorified" (Rom. 8:29–30). These verses imply single predestination, because they concern only predestination to life with God.

Double Predestination. Double predestination is a conclusion deduced from single predestination. If some are to enjoy God's presence by his eternal decree, others must then be eternally separated from God, also by his decree. Because salvation and glory are predestined, it follows that condemnation and destruction must also be predestined. The first theologian to enunciate a doctrine of double predestination was St. Augustine in the 5th century. He has not, however, had many successors. The best-known exponent of double predestination was the Swiss reformer John Calvin: "We call predestination God's eternal decree, by which he determined within himself what he willed to become of each man. For all are not created in equal condition; rather, eternal life is foreordained for some, eternal damnation for others" (*Institutes* 3. 21. 5).

After Augustine, Roman Catholic theologians rejected double predestination, insisting that no predestination to evil exists and that those who suffer damnation bear full responsibility for it. Anglicans have also adhered to a doctrine of single predestination. In the 17th century, the Dutch Protestant theologian Arminius, whose teachings inspired the movement called Arminianism, criticized the injustice of Calvin's doctrine of predestination and formulated a modified version of it that allowed for human free will. Liberal Protestant theologians have tended to ignore or deny predestination in either the single or double form. The most influential restatement of the doctrine of single predestination was made by the 20th-century Swiss theologian Karl Barth, who claimed that God's will is revealed in Jesus Christ, and all are elect through him. In this form the doctrine of predestination is virtually universalist—that is, all are promised salvation. C.P.P.

PREFERRED STOCK. *See* FINANCE; STOCK.

PREGNANCY AND CHILDBIRTH, terms for the gestation period of the human reproductive cycle (*see* REPRODUCTION).

Pregnancy. Pregnancy starts when a male's sperm fertilizes a female's ovum (egg), and the fertilized ovum implants in the lining of the uterus (*see* FERTILIZATION; REPRODUCTIVE SYSTEM). Because pregnancy changes a woman's normal hormone patterns, one of the first signs of pregnancy is a missed menstrual period (*see* MENSTRUATION). Other symptoms include breast tenderness and swelling, fatigue, nausea or sensitivity to smells, increased frequency of urination, mood swings, and weight gain. Some women also experience cravings for unusual substances such as ice, clay, or cornstarch; this condition, called pica, can indicate a dietary deficiency in iron or other nutrients. By the 12th week of pregnancy many of these symptoms have subsided, but others appear. For example, a woman's breasts usually increase in size, and her nipples darken. The most obvious symptom is weight gain; most physicians now recommend a gain of about 9 to 12 kg (about 22 to 26 lb) by the end of pregnanc

The first few months of pregnancy are the mos critical for the developing infant, because durin this period the infant's brain, arms, legs, an internal organs are formed. For this reason pregnant woman should be especially carefu about taking any kind of medication except o the advice of a physician who knows that she i pregnant. X rays should also be avoided, an pregnant women should avoid smoking and al cohol consumption.

Complications. Most women worry about th health of their unborn child, especially mother over the age of 35, when genetic problems ar more common. Safe, effective tests are availabl that can detect genetic disorders which caus mental retardation and other problems. The mos common test is amniocentesis (q.v.), and in abou 95 percent of the cases tested the baby is foun to be normal. Some doctors recommend that a pregnant women over the age of 35 have a amniocentesis test.

Although most pregnancies proceed normall certain complications can develop. One rare bu life-threatening complication is ectopic preg nancy, in which the fertilized egg implants ou side the uterus, in the abdomen, or in a Fallo pian tube. Symptoms include sudden, intens pain in the lower abdomen about the sevent or eight week of pregnancy. If not promptl treated by surgical means, ectopic pregnanc can result in massive internal bleeding and pos sibly death.

About 15 percent of all pregnancies end i miscarriage, most of which occur between th 4th and 12th weeks of pregnancy. A physicia should be contacted immediately if a woma suspects that she is pregnant and then experi ences severe abdominal cramping or vagina bleeding.

Toxemia (q.v.) is another potentially seriou complication of late pregnancy. Symptoms in clude high blood pressure; rapid, large weigh gain, due to edema (swelling), of as much as 1 to 13 kg (25 to 30 lb) in a month; and protein i the urine. If untreated, toxemia can lead to sei zures and coma and death of the infant. Onc severe toxemia is diagnosed, the infant is usuall delivered as soon as possible to protect bot mother and child. The condition disappears wit birth.

Labor and Childbirth. A normal pregnancy las about 39 weeks, or 280 days, after the beginnin of the last menstrual period. Occasionally wom en go into labor before the expected date c birth, resulting in a premature infant. About percent of all infants are premature—that is, bor before the 37th week of pregnancy. Babies born just a few weeks early usually develop normally. Recent advances in the care of premature infants now allow many babies who are born after only 25 to 26 weeks of pregnancy to survive.

Delivery, the process by which the baby is expelled from the uterus through the birth canal and into the world, begins with irregular contractions of the uterus that occur every 20 to 30 minutes. As labor progresses, the contractions increase in frequency and severity. The usual length of labor for a first-time mother is about 13 to 14 hours, and about 8 or 9 hours in a woman who has given birth previously. Wide variations exist, however, in the duration of labor.

Most women prefer some kind of anesthesia to alleviate the pain associated with childbirth. Natural (unmedicated) childbirth, however, is becoming more popular, in part because many women are aware and concerned that the anesthesia and medication given to them is rapidly transported across the placenta to the unborn baby. Heavy doses of anesthesia can make the newborn baby less alert after birth.

Other options available regarding childbirth include regional (local) anesthesia, in which only those areas of the mother that are affected by the pain of childbirth are numbed. Such anesthesias include a lower spinal block and epidural anesthesia, in which the pelvic region is anesthetized. Another option is cesarean section (q.v.), in which the baby is surgically removed from the uterus. Cesarean section is usually performed only for a specific medical reason. M.R. & P.A.Co.

For further information on this topic, see the Bibliography in volume 28, sections 521–24.

PREJUDICE, strictly defined, a preformed and unsubstantiated judgment or opinion about an individual or a group, either favorable or unfavorable in nature. In modern usage, however, the term most often denotes an irrationally unfavorable or hostile attitude toward the members of another racial or ethnic group. The distinguishing characteristic of a prejudice, as opposed to an ordinary opinion or belief, is that it reflects only the feelings within an individual, without regard to facts. This willful disregard of reality usually leads to the use of stereotypes, or oversimplified generalizations, about the group against which the prejudice is directed.

Examples of prejudice abound in history. In most cases, a prejudiced attitude held by a dominant ethnic group against a minority or disadvantaged group within the same society results in various forms of discrimination (q.v.). The most elaborate kind of discrimination is segregation—the isolation of ethnic groups enforced by law or custom or both. Examples of segregation include the strict confinement of Jews to the ghettos of medieval European cities and the rigid race-separation laws of modern-day South Africa. Integration (q.v.), the mixing of ethnic groups, might be expected to lead to the rapid disappearance of prejudice, on the theory that prolonged contact between people should destroy stereotypes. In practice, however, prejudiced attitudes often have proved extremely difficult to eradicate, even when integration is enforced by law.

See also CIVIL RIGHTS AND CIVIL LIBERTIES; MINORITIES.

For further information on this topic, see the Bibliography in volume 28, section 162.

PREMINGER, Otto Ludwig (1906–86), American stage and film producer, director, and actor born in Vienna. He received a law degree in 1928, but had by that time become an actor, director, and producer at Max Reinhardt's theater. He immigrated to the U.S. in 1935. On Broadway he directed such hits as *Outward Bound* (1938) and *Margin for Error* (1939). He played German roles in many films during World War II. He is best known, however, as a film director, specializing in screenplays with sensitive social themes. His many films include *Laura* (1944), *The Moon Is Blue* (1953), *Anatomy of a Murder* (1959), *Exodus* (1960), *Such Good Friends* (1971), and *The Human Factor* (1980). *Preminger: An Autobiography* appeared in 1977.

PRENDERGAST, Maurice Brazil (1859–1924), American painter, born in Boston, and trained in art as a painter of advertising placards in Boston and later in France and Italy. He returned to Boston in 1900. In 1914 he moved to New York City, where he spent the remainder of his life. His work is characterized by rich, powerful color applied in dots and in short brushstrokes. Many of his subjects are landscapes with figures, as for example, *Central Park* (1901, Whitney Museum, New York City). A number are of the seashore. Others include Boston street scenes and sketches of Neapolitan and Venetian life.

PREPOSITION. *See* PARTS OF SPEECH.

PRE-RAPHAELITES, a group of 19th-century English painters, poets, and critics who reacted against Victorian materialism and the outworn neoclassical conventions of academic art by producing earnest quasi-religious works inspired by medieval and early Renaissance painters up to the time of the Italian painter and architect Raphael. They were also influenced by the Nazarenes, young German artists who formed a brotherhood in Rome in 1810 to restore Christian art to its medieval purity.

The Pre-Raphaelite Brotherhood was established in 1848, and its central figure was the painter and poet Dante Gabriel Rossetti. Other members were his brother, William Michael Rossetti (1829–1919), an art critic; painters John Everett Millais and William Holman Hunt; art critic Frederick George Stephens (1828–1907); painter James Collinson (1825?–81); and sculptor and poet Thomas Woolner (1825–92).

Essentially Christian in outlook, the brotherhood deplored the imitative historic and genre painting of their day. Together they sought to revitalize art through a simpler, more positive vision. In portrait painting, for example, the group eschewed the somber colors and formal structure preferred by the Royal Academy. They found their inspiration in the comparatively sincere and religious, and scrupulously detailed, art of the Middle Ages. Pre-Raphaelite art became distinctive for its blend of archaic, romantic, and moralistic qualities, but much of it has been criticized as superficial and sentimental, if not artificial. Millais eventually left the group, but other English artists joined it, including the painter and designer Edward Coley Burne-Jones and the poet and artist William Morris. The eminent English art critic John Ruskin was an ardent supporter of the movement. Examples of Pre-Raphaelite painting include Millais's *The Carpenter Shop* (1850, Tate Gallery, London) and D. G. Rossetti's *The Wedding of St. George and the Princess Sabra* (1857, Tate Gallery).

In literature, the Pre-Raphaelites may be considered a recurrent phase of the romantic movement. In looking back to the Middle Ages, the school paralleled both the Oxford movement in the Anglican church and a Gothic revival led by the English architect Augustus Welby Northmore Pugin. For a time in 1850 the members published a periodical called *The Germ,* in which some of Rossetti's earliest literary work appeared.

PRESBYOPIA, form of hyperopia, or farsightedness, resulting from advanced age. *See* VISION.

PRESBYTERIANISM, a form of church government and a particular theological tradition found in the Presbyterian and Reformed denominations. The churches in this tradition constitute one of the four major groups that issued from the Protestant Reformation (q.v.) of the 16th century—Lutheran, Anabaptist, Anglican, and Presbyterian and Reformed.

CHURCH ORGANIZATION

The term Presbyterian is from the Greek *presbyteros* ("elder"), and church government by elders characterizes the organization of Presbyterian and Reformed churches. Both clergy and laity may be elders, and in most Presbyterian churches today, both men and women are elders.

Presbyterian church government is often called a "mixed" system of democratic and hierarchical elements, because the power is balanced between clergy and laity and between congregations and larger governing bodies of the church. Although the structure of Presbyterian church government varies, it usually consists of ascending church bodies, or courts. Each congregation is governed by a ruling body called a session, or consistory, composed of the pastor and the elders, who are elected representatives of the congregation. Congregations belong to a presbytery, or classis, which coordinates and governs the activities of congregations within a particular geographic area. The members of a presbytery include all the pastors and elected representative elders from each of the congregations.

The power to ordain ministers lies in the presbytery, in contrast to episcopal forms of church government, in which this is done by a bishop, and congregational church government, in which the congregation retains the power of ordination. In a larger sense, the presbytery serves as a communal bishop, exercising both pastoral and judicial responsibilities for its churches.

Presbyteries belong to synods, which are larger geographic units of the church, and a general assembly, or general synod, unites the entire church. At these levels as well, the church is governed by its elders—clergy and laity elected as representatives of the people.

HISTORY

The roots of Presbyterianism can be traced to the theology of John Calvin, the leader of the Protestant Reformation in Geneva (*see* CALVINISM). Calvin sought to establish a church government based on the New Testament concept of the office of elder, but Calvin and the early reformed theologians did not finally insist on presbyterianism as the only form of church government sanctioned by the Bible. This has allowed some variation in the forms of Calvinist government and the potential for toleration of other ecclesiastical polities. For example, many Congregational and Baptist churches consider themselves Calvinist in theology but do not have a presbyterian form of church government.

From its earliest days, the Reformed tradition was the most international of all branches of Protestantism. It quickly spread from Geneva through France, Germany, and Holland into eastern Europe, the British Isles, and North America. When Calvinists organized churches with a presbyterian form of government on the European continent, they called them Reformed; in the British Isles and North America, these churches were known as Presbyterian.

Simple meetinghouse architecture and the unostentatious gown of the preacher are marks of Presbyterianism. Joseph M. Elkins–Presbyterian Board of Missions

Until the 19th century, Presbyterianism's greatest strength was in Great Britain, Holland, and North America, but with the rapid expansion of missionary actvity after 1800, Presbyterian or Reformed churches were established on every continent. Currently, English-speaking members of the Presbyterian and Reformed churches are a minority, and large Presbyterian and Reformed churches can be found in Asia, Africa, Latin America, and elsewhere throughout the world.

Theology. Although the theology of Presbyterianism is characterized by diversity today, Calvin's theology serves as a central source. His most important and influential work is *Institutes of the Christian Religion* (1536), which he revised throughout his life (*see* CALVIN, JOHN). The last edition (1559) has been the most widely used.

Like the German religious reformer Martin Luther, Calvin emphasized the two central doctrines of the Protestant Reformation: the authority of Scripture and justification (q.v.) by grace (q.v.) through faith. Also, like Luther, Calvin reduced the number of Christian sacraments to two—baptism (q.v.) of both infants and adults, and the Lord's Supper (*see* EUCHARIST). Calvin differed from Luther and other Protestant reformers in his understanding of the nature of the Lord's Supper, church government, and the role of the law in Christian life. His theology is characterized by its reliance on the Bible as interpreted through the aid of the Holy Spirit and by his stress on the sovereignty of God and the inability of people to achieve salvation through their own works.

Confessions. Although Presbyterian and Reformed churches regard the Bible as the supreme authority for the church and the individual believer, they are also known as "confessional" churches because of their effort to write confessions that define and guide the theology and practice of the church. Many Reformed confessions have been written in different countries at different times, from the 16th to the 20th century. The most important early confessions were the First Helvetic Confession (1536), the Scots Confession (1560), the Belgic Confession (1561), the Heidelberg Catechism (1563), the Second Helvetic Confession (1566), the Canons of the Synod of Dort (1619), and the Westminster Confession and Shorter Catechism (1647). Two examples of recent confessional statements are the Theological Declaration of Barmen, issued by the German Evangelical Church in 1934, and the Confession of 1967, adopted by the United Presbyterian Church in the U.S.A. The most influential of all these confessions, particularly for Anglo-American Presbyterian churches, has been the Westminster Confession.

Forms of Worship. Presbyterian worship has always allowed for considerable flexibility in forms and practices, but it is based on Calvin's definition of the essential characteristics of the church being the faithful proclamation of the gospel and the celebration of the sacraments. In the U.S., the influence of Puritanism (q.v.) and revivalism (*see* REVIVALS, RELIGIOUS) contributed to a growing emphasis on the sermon as the center of worship; liturgy was practically absent, and the Lord's Supper was celebrated only occasionally. During the late 19th and early 20th centuries, however, a renewal of the Reformed understanding of worship and the ecumenical movement (q.v.) brought greater richness to Presbyterian worship. The sermon is still important, but services are also characterized by a greater use of liturgy and a more regular celebration of the Lord's Supper.

Ecumenism. The churches in the Presbyterian tradition have usually been organized according to national boundaries, although within each country they have often suffered divisions. As a group, however, they have been known for their ecumenical spirit. They are associated within their own tradition in the World Alliance of Reformed Churches, and they provided leadership in the founding of the World Council of Churches. In the U.S. they cooperate with other denominations in the work of the National Council of Churches and the Consultation on Church Union. Similar ecumenism within Presbyterianism has been shown in the establishment of the United Church of Canada, the Church of South India, and united churches in other countries.

Presbyterianism in the U.S. Presbyterian churches in the U.S. draw their members from many different ethnic groups, but their early history was heavily influenced by English and Scotch-Irish Presbyterians. The First American Presbyterian churches were founded by English colonists on Long Island, N.Y., and in New England during the 1640s; a later wave of Scottish and Scotch-Irish immigrants established churches as they settled along the eastern shore of Maryland, Virginia, and Delaware, as well as in the middle colonies of New York, New Jersey, and Pennsylvania. Some interpreters point to an English current in American Presbyterianism emphasizing piety, experience, and experimentation, and a Scotch-Irish influence of rationalism, order, and clearly defined authority. These two impulses have characterized much of American Presbyterian history.

Francis Makemie, a Scottish Presbyterian minister who came to the colonies in 1683, is generally considered the father of American Presbyterianism. Under his leadership, the first presbytery was organized in 1706. The first synod was established in 1716, and the first general assembl met in 1789.

Divisions. Four major divisions have occurred i American Presbyterianism. The first arose durin the 1740s over the revivalism of the first Grea Awakening (q.v.); the second occurred during th 1830s due to slavery, theological issues, and th conduct of missionary work; the third took plac in 1861 because of the American Civil War; an the fourth was during the 1920s and '30s at th peak of the controversy between Fundamentalisr (q.v.) and modernism (q.v.).

The division that occurred during the Civil Wa produced the United Presbyterian Church in th U.S.A. (2.5 million members in 1980), popularl known as the "northern" Presbyterian church and the Presbyterian Church in the United State (860,000 members in 1980), commonly called th "southern" Presbyterians. In 1983 these two bod ies were formally reunited as the Presbyteria Church (U.S.A.); it had nearly 3 million member in the late 1980s.

Other Presbyterian churches include the Pres byterian Church in America, merged in 1982 wit the Reformed Presbyterian Church, Evangelica Synod; the Associate Presbyterian Church o North America; the Associate Reformed Presby terian Church; the Bible Presbyterian Church; th Cumberland Presbyterian Church; the Secon Cumberland Presbyterian Church in the Unite States; the Orthodox Presbyterian Church; th Reformed Presbyterian Church; the Reforme Presbyterian Church of North America; and th Evangelical Presbyterian Church.

The American Reformed churches with pres byterian government are the Reformed Church i America, the Christian Reformed Church, th Hungarian Reformed Church in America, th Netherlands Reformed Congregations, the Prot estant Reformed Churches of America, and th Reformed Church in the United States.

Influence. Presbyterians in the U.S. have had a impact on many areas of society. In politics the have been inspired by Calvin's affirmation of lav as a potential structure of God's grace and b the doctrines of election and vocation as theo logical bases for participation in political affairs Presbyterian clergy and laity were nearly unan imous in supporting the American Revolution and John Witherspoon, the Presbyterian presiden of what later became Princeton University (q.v.) was the only clergyman to sign the Declaratio of Independence. Calvinist ideas are also credite with playing a role in shaping the American po litical structure, with its system of checks an balances, separation of powers, and constitution al limits to authority.

In education, Presbyterians have traditionally emphasized the need for a highly trained clergy and a literate laity who can understand the Bible. Presbyterians were instrumental in founding Princeton University in 1746, and the first Presbyterian seminary was established in Princeton in 1812. They were also instrumental in establishing scores of other educational institutions. Education has been a strong component of Presbyterian missionary work, along with medical aid and economic development.

See also CHRISTIANITY; PROTESTANTISM. J.M.Mu.

For further information on this topic, see the Bibliography in volume 28, section 95.

PRESCHOOL EDUCATION, term applied universally to educational group experience for children who have not yet entered the first grade. It usually refers to the education of boys and girls from ages three to six or seven, depending on the admission requirements of schools in the area.

Many educators have found that children who have been enrolled in preschool centers develop positive self-concepts and basic understandings and skills that make them better able to apply their efforts to intellectual tasks when they enter school. Preschool education may be provided in day-care centers, nursery schools, or kindergartens in elementary schools. *See also* KINDERGARTEN.

Day Nurseries. The day-nursery movement began in Europe in the early 19th century as a response to the increasing employment of women in industry. The absence of large numbers of mothers from their homes during the day led to child neglect, which, in turn, stimulated a variety of charitable agencies to seek ways of caring for the children of working parents.

The early leader of this movement was French philanthropist Jean Baptiste Firmin Marbeau (1798–1875), who in 1846 founded the Crèche (Fr., "cradle") Society of France, with the aim of fostering child care. Within a relatively short period, day nurseries were established in many parts of France and in several other European countries. Many were wholly or partly supported by local and national governments. A large number of nurseries were set up in factories, enabling mothers to take brief periods from their work to tend to their young children.

In the U.S. the first day nursery was opened in 1854 by the Nursery and Child's Hospital of New York City. Most of the nurseries established in the latter half of the 19th century were supported by charitable organizations. Both in Europe and in the U.S., the day-nursery movement received great impetus during World War I, when unprecedented numbers of women replaced men in industry. In Great Britain, France, Germany, and Italy, nurseries were established even in munitions plants, under direct government sponsorship. The number of nurseries in the U.S. also rose, but without government aid of any kind. During the years following World War I, federal, state, and local governments in the U.S. gradually began to exercise some control over preschool education through licensing, inspection, and regulation of conditions within the facilities.

Nursery Schools. As studies of children revealed the importance of the early years in physical, social, emotional, and intellectual development, the nursery school movement spread rapidly in Great Britain and other European countries. The first nursery schools in the U.S. were started under the auspices of colleges and universities and served as laboratories for child study, teacher education, and parent education. For many years, day nurseries were mainly charitable institutions operated for custodial care, whereas nursery schools were generally commercial ventures offering educational programs. Now, in most instances, both day-care centers and nursery schools employ trained personnel and offer various educational activities; day-care centers, however, are open for longer hours to accommodate working parents.

Modern Developments. With the outbreak of World War II, the number of day nurseries increased rapidly as women were again called on to work in industry. This time the U.S. government immediately came to the support of facilities for young children, allocating $6 million in July 1942 for a program for the children of working mothers. Many states and local communities supplemented this federal aid. By 1945, more than 100,000 children were being cared for in centers receiving federal subsidies. After the war, the government abandoned the subsidies, causing a sharp drop in the number of centers. The expectation that most employed mothers would leave their jobs at the end of the war was only partially fulfilled, and during the postwar years a widespread movement developed, headed by sociologists, social workers, teachers, and other groups, which sought renewed government aid to meet the need for a comprehensive day-care program.

Beginning in the 1960s, more and more women with children joined the work force, and the popularity of preschool educational programs has steadily increased. The quality of preschool programs, however, varies. Some schools are more child-minding centers than educational institutions. Other schools provide solid educational programs that stimulate the development of skills in communication; a growing awareness of size, shape, and color; manipulative skills; and physical development.

Head Start. In 1965, the U.S. instituted a federally sponsored program, known as Head Start, intended to provide preschool education for children from culturally and economically disadvantaged backgrounds. Within the framework of the Head Start program, children receive educational, psychological, medical, nutritional, and social services.

Head Start is administered by the U.S. Department of Health and Human Services. In 1987, Head Start centers throughout the nation served some 446,000 children. Many of the centers operate more than six hours a day, serving as day-care facilities. Head Start programs actively seek the direct participation of parents, whom they assist in developing child-rearing skills. Beginning in 1973, Head Start was required by law to accept severely handicapped children. Ten percent of the children in a center may come from nonpoverty families. L.L.

For further information on this topic, see the Bibliography in volume 28, sections 317–18.

PRESCOTT, city, seat of Yavapai Co., central Arizona; inc. 1881. Situated at an altitude of about 1630 m (about 5350 ft), it is a mining, ranching, and resort center, with some manufacturing industries. Products include firearms, plastic goods, and aerospace equipment. In the city are Prescott College (1975), a school of aeronautics, a large junior college, and the headquarters of Prescott National Forest. Tourist attractions in the city include Sharlot Hall Museum, featuring displays on Arizona history; the Smoki Museum, containing Indian artifacts; and the annual Prescott Frontier Days Rodeo (first held 1888). The community was founded in 1864, shortly after the discovery of gold in the region, and is named for the historian William Hickling Prescott. The community was the capital of the Arizona Territory from 1864 to 1867 and again from 1877 to 1889, when it was replaced by Phoenix. Pop. (1980) 20,055; (1990) 26,455.

PRESCOTT, town, SE Ontario, located above the former rapids on the St. Lawrence R.; inc. as a town 1851. The International Bridge connects Prescott with Ogdensburg, N.Y. Industries include electronics, paper products, clothing, plastics, and sporting goods. Fort Wellington National Historic Site is located here. Nearby is a stone windmill, scene of an early-19th-century battle. The community, founded in 1810, was named after Gen. Robert Prescott (1726–1815), Canadian governor in chief from 1797 to 1807. Pop. (198 4583; (1991) 4512.

PRESCOTT, William Hickling (1796–1859 American historian, born in Salem, Mass., an educated at Harvard University. He was th grandson of Col. William Prescott (1726–95), wh led the American troops in the Battle of Bunk Hill. Nearly blind during his adult life, he devote himself to research and writing on Spanish, Mex ican, and Peruvian history. His works, with the skillful narrative and lucid style, became ver popular; some have been published in more tha ten languages, and many are still in print. A though some of the information he include about American Indian civilizations, which h obtained entirely from Spanish sources, was suc cessfully challenged by later historians, Prescott historical narrative still appears to be basicall sound.

His writings include *History of the Reign Ferdinand and Isabella the Catholic* (3 vol., 1838 *History of the Conquest of Mexico* (3 vol., 1843 *History of the Conquest of Peru* (2 vol., 1847 and an unfinished *History of the Reign of Phil the Second* (3 vol., 1855–58).

PRESIDENTIAL MEDAL OF FREEDOM, meda awarded annually by the president of the U.S. t individuals selected by him or recommended t him by the Distinguished Civilian Service Award Board. Recipients of the medal are those wh have made outstanding contributions to the se curity or national interest of the U.S. or to worl peace, or those who have made a significan public or private accomplishment. In 1963 President John F. Kennedy ordered the former Meda of Freedom renamed and the recommendin board altered by adding five members from out side the executive branch of the government t the five members from within it. Recipients hav included educators, diplomats, authors, scien tists, and business executives.

PRESIDENTIAL RANGE, mountain range, N New Hampshire, in the White Mts. A scenic, foreste region, it contains Mt. Washington (1917 m/628 ft), the highest peak in the northeastern U.S. A number of the mountains in the range are name for early U.S. presidents.

PRESIDENTIAL SUCCESSION. *See* CONSTITUTION OF THE UNITED STATES; PRESIDENT OF THE UNITED STATES.

PRESIDENT OF THE UNITED STATES, chief executive officer of the federal government, administrative head of the executive department (q.v.) o the government, and commander in chief of th armed forces of the nation. Authority providin for the office of president is derived from th U.S. Constitution, which, in Article II, Section states that "the Executive power shall be vested in a President of the United States of America." The duties and qualifications of the president, term of office, mode of selection and remuneration, grounds and procedure for removal from office, and methods for replacement should the president not complete the term of office are described in Article II of the Constitution, as well as in the 12th, 22d, and 25th Amendments. A number of presidential powers are either explicitly stated in or are inferred from other articles of the Constitution. Still other powers are vested in the president by congressional measures based on constitutional provisions for such enactments. For the text of the U.S. Constitution, see CONSTITUTION OF THE UNITED STATES.

RESPONSIBILITIES AND POWERS

On assuming office the president takes an oath, as prescribed by the Constitution, faithfully to discharge the duties of office and to "preserve, protect and defend the Constitution of the United States." The president is charged by the Constitution with executing the laws of the U.S. In discharging this responsibility the president is assisted by the vast network of agencies constituting the executive branch of the government and administered by the members of the cabinet (q.v.) and the heads of the independent federal agencies. Also in the discharge of this responsibility, the president may, at the request of a state government, employ the National Guard or federal troops to quell disorder, suppress insurrection, or repel invasion. Or, the president may declare martial law in times of overwhelming public danger, when the courts are not open or cannot function freely. In such situations, the president may, with congressional authorization, suspend the right of the writ of habeas corpus (q.v.; *see* MARTIAL LAW). The president may grant reprieves and pardons for offenses against the U.S., "except in cases of impeachment" (*see* IMPEACHMENT).

Pursuant to the intention of the framers of the Constitution of creating a government of checks and balances in which each of three coordinate branches of the national government could restrain either of the other two, the president may veto legislation enacted by Congress. The Congress may then override such a veto by a two-thirds vote of each house. The president also advises Congress "from time to time," in formal addresses communicated in writing or in person, on "the state of the Union"; recommends the enactment of legislation, including, since 1921, an annual executive budget; may convene either or both houses of Congress in special session; and, under certain circumstances described in the Constitution, may adjourn Congress (*see* CONGRESS OF THE UNITED STATES).

Legislative and Judicial Functions. The president exercises important legislative functions by issuing executive orders that have the force of law and by authorizing administrative agencies to "promulgate rules in conformity with law." Important judicial functions are also discharged by the executive department of the government through such agencies as the Immigration and Naturalization Service (q.v.), which holds hearings in connection with the deportation of aliens illegally in the U.S., and the National Labor Relations Board (q.v.), which adjudicates disputes between management and labor. Such hearings and adjudications have been held by the courts not to be subject to judicial review as to fact, and the agencies holding and making them are quasi-judicial bodies.

Economic Functions. The president exerts a decisive influence on the economic life of the U.S. through the exercise of discretionary powers vested in the chief executive by congressional enactments. In addition, as head of the executive department, the president is, in effect, the largest single employer in the U.S. The number of federal civil employees fluctuates with the contraction and expansion of the executive departments and agencies. During World War II it was approximately 3,750,000; after the war it declined by more than 1,500,000 (*see* CIVIL SERVICE).

Foreign Policy. The president directs U.S. foreign policy in its political, diplomatic, financial, and commercial aspects. By provision of the Constitution the president may negotiate treaties only "by and with the advice and consent of the Senate"; but by precedent and custom the president may negotiate executive agreements with foreign countries that have the force and effect of law and that do not require congressional approval. The president receives the ambassadors and "other public ministers" of foreign nations and has the power of recognition.

Military Functions. As commander-in-chief of the armed forces the president has the power to formulate and direct the military strategy of the nation in war and is the nominal head of the military government of foreign territory occupied and administered by the U.S., as in Germany after World War II. In the view of many constitutional analysts and political scientists, the president, as director of foreign policy and as commander-in-chief, has the power to create situations that can result in war, reducing to a formality the constitutional provision vesting Congress with exclusive power to declare war. Since World War II, conflicts in Korea and South-

PORTRAITS OF THE PRESIDENTS OF

George Washington
1789–93, 1793–97

John Adams
1797–1801

Thomas Jefferson
1801–05, 1805–09

James Madiso
1809–13, 1813–

James Monroe
1817–21, 1821–25

John Quincy Adams
1825–29

Andrew Jackson
1829–33, 1833–37

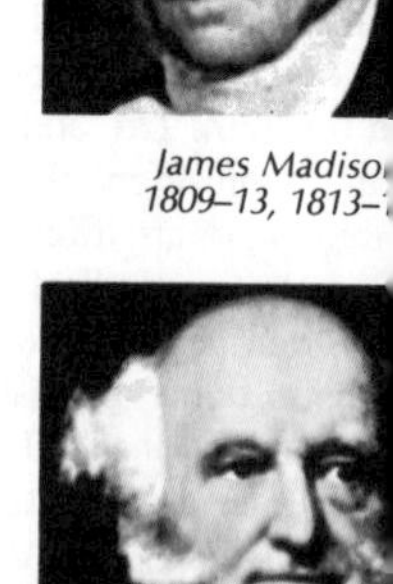
Martin Van Bur
1837–41

William H. Harrison
1841 (d. in office)

John Tyler
1841–45

James Knox Polk
1845–49

Zachary Taylor
1849–50 (d. in off

Millard Fillmore
1850–53

Franklin Pierce
1853–57

James Buchanan
1857–61

Abraham Lincol
1861–65, 1865 (d. in c

Andrew Johnson
1865–69

Ulysses Simpson Grant
1869–73, 1873–77

Rutherford B. Hayes
1877–81

James Abram Garfi
1881 (d. in office

THE UNITED STATES OF AMERICA

ester Alan Arthur
1881–85

Grover Cleveland
1885–89, 1893–97

Benjamin Harrison
1889–93

William McKinley
1897–1901, 1901 (d. in office)

eodore Roosevelt
1901–05, 1905–09

William Howard Taft
1909–13

Woodrow Wilson
1913–17, 1917–21

Warren G. Harding
1921–23 (d. in office)

Calvin Coolidge
1923–25, 1925–29

Herbert Clark Hoover
1929–33

Franklin D. Roosevelt
1933–45 (d. in office)

Harry S. Truman
1945–49, 1949–53

vight D. Eisenhower
1953–57, 1957–61

John F. Kennedy
1961–63 (d. in office)

Lyndon B. Johnson
1963–65, 1965–69

Richard M. Nixon
1969–73, 1973–74

Gerald R. Ford
1974–77

Jimmy Carter
1977–81

Ronald W. Reagan
1981–85, 1985–89

George H. Bush
1989–93

William J. Clinton
1993–

east Asia have been conducted by the U.S. without congressional declaration. The policy of President James K. Polk, which resulted in war with Mexico in 1846, is frequently cited as an example of the presidential power to bring about a state of armed hostilities with other nations.

Appointive Powers. Subject to confirmation by a majority of the Senate, the president appoints the members of the cabinet and the heads of the independent federal agencies; a large part of the administrative personnel of the federal executive departments and agencies; federal judges, including the justices of the U.S. Supreme Court; many federal employees; and the diplomatic representatives of the U.S. The president also commissions, subject to congressional confirmation, all officers of the armed forces.

Federal judges are beyond the reach of the president's power of removal and may be removed from office only by impeachment. In a 1926 decision of the Supreme Court, the president was declared to have the power to remove those officers who are under presidential authority. A later decision, in 1935, held that officers in quasi-judicial and quasi-legislative posts, as those in the Federal Trade Commission (q.v.), can be removed only for causes established by law. In connection with official duties, the president disburses large sums of money; during World War II Congress placed hundreds of millions of dollars at the disposal of President Franklin D. Roosevelt, to be expended solely at his discretion within the general limits of presidential powers.

ELECTION AND SUCCESSION

Originally, the Constitution provided for the election of the president and vice-president by a body of electors, to be chosen in such manner as the state legislatures might direct, and subsequently known as the electoral college (q.v.). The electors were to vote for two persons, the one receiving the higher vote becoming president and the other, vice-president. A tie vote in the election of 1800 between Thomas Jefferson and Aaron Burr led to the enactment in 1804 of the 12th Amendment to the Constitution, providing for the separate election by the electors of the president and vice-president. The method of choosing the electors varied and gradually evolved into its present form, wherein the designation of the president and vice-president by the electoral college is only a nominal function reflecting the outcome of national elections. George Washington was elected unanimously. All other presidents, with the exception of Thomas Jefferson in 1800, were elected by majorities in the electoral college. In accordance with the original constitutional provision, the president and vice-president were inaugurated on March 4 of the year following their election; in 1933, when the 20th Amendment went into effect, the inauguration date was changed to January 20 of the year following their election (*see* LAME DUCK AMENDMENT). Pursuant to a congressional enactment of 1845, presidential elections are held in each quadrennial year on the Tuesday following the first Monday in November.

Term of Office. Article II of the Constitution specifies 4-year terms for both the president and the vice-president. Following the precedent established by George Washington, and until the precedent was broken in 1940, no president served more than two terms. During World War II, Franklin D. Roosevelt was elected for a third term in 1940 and a fourth term in 1944. The 22d Amendment to the Constitution (1951) provides that "no person shall be elected . . . President more than twice."

Presidential Succession. Once inaugurated, the president and vice-president, like all other civil officers of the U.S., may be removed from office only "on impeachment for, and conviction of, treason, bribery, or high crimes and misdemeanors." In 1868 Andrew Johnson was impeached but not convicted. In 1974 articles of impeachment against Richard M. Nixon were drafted by the Judiciary Committee of the House of Representatives; Nixon then resigned from office. No vice-president has ever been impeached. Should the president die in office, resign, or be unable to discharge the duties of the office, the vice-president succeeds. The eight presidents who died in office and their vice-presidential successors were William Henry Harrison (1841, John Tyler), Zachary Taylor (1850, Millard Fillmore), Abraham Lincoln (assassinated 1865, Andrew Johnson), James A. Garfield (assassinated 1881, Chester A. Arthur), William McKinley (assassinated 1901, Theodore Roosevelt), Warren G. Harding (1923, Calvin Coolidge), Franklin D. Roosevelt (1945, Harry S. Truman), and John F. Kennedy (assassinated 1963, Lyndon B. Johnson).

When Nixon resigned, he was succeeded by his vice-president (1974, Gerald R. Ford).

On four occasions Congress has enacted legislation in accordance with the constitutional provision empowering it to determine the order of succession to the presidency in the event of the "removal, death, resignation, or inability, both of the president and vice-president." A measure passed in 1792 provided for the succession of the president pro tempore of the Senate and the Speaker of the House, in that order, but only for the purpose of "ordering a new election." A law enacted in 1886 superseded the earlier measure and provided that should the presidency and vice-presidency both be vacant, first the secretary of state and then the other cabinet members, in the order of their seniority, should succeed to the presidency. In 1947 Congress changed the order of succession to Speaker of the House of Representatives, followed by the president pro tempore of the Senate, secretary of state, and then the other members of the cabinet, in the event of the removal, death, resignation, or disability of the president and vice-president. In 1967 the 25th Amendment was passed, providing that the vice-president shall become acting president during any period that the president has declared himself, or has been declared, unable to discharge the powers and duties of the office.

Presidential Qualifications and Salary. The following qualifications for the presidency are established by the Constitution: The president must be a natural-born citizen of the U.S., 35 years of age or older, and "fourteen years a resident within the United States." Also by constitutional provision, the president receives "a compensation which shall neither be increased nor diminished during the period for which he shall have been elected, and he shall not receive within that period any other emolument from the United States or any of them." Originally, the salary of the president was established by Congress as $25,000 annually; it was doubled in 1873; and in 1907 annual tax-exempt allowances of $25,000 for expenses in connection with the discharge of his duties was voted the president by Congress. In 1909 the salary of the president was increased to $75,000 annually; in 1949 it was increased to $100,000, and allowances to $90,000; in 1969 the salary was increased to $200,000. As a public official, the president is enjoined by the Constitution from accepting "without the consent of the Congress . . . any present, emolument, office, or title, of any kind whatever, from any king, prince, or foreign state." The official residence of the president is the White House (q.v.) in Washington, D.C.

THE EXECUTIVE DEPARTMENT

An idea of the vast responsibilities of the president and the magnitude of the administrative task may be had from a consideration of the organization of the executive department.

Administrative Organization. Under the direction of the president are 14 executive departments. In order of original inception, they are the Departments of State, Treasury, Defense, Justice, Interior, Agriculture, Commerce, Labor, Health and Human Services, Housing and Urban Development, Transportation, Energy, Education, and Veterans Affairs. See separate articles on each of these departments, listed under their key word, for example, Agriculture, Department of. Independent agencies under the direction of the president include the Environmental Protection Agency, Export-Import Bank of the U.S., Farm Credit Administration, Federal Communications Commission, Federal Deposit Insurance Corporation, Federal Maritime Commission, Federal Mediation and Conciliation Service, Federal Reserve System, Federal Trade Commission, General Services Administration, Interstate Commerce Commission, National Aeronautics and Space Administration, National Foundation on the Arts and the Humanities, National Labor Relations Board, National Science Foundation, Securities and Exchange Commision, Small Business Administration, and Tennessee Valley Authority (qq.v.), Office of Personnel Management (*see* PERSONNEL MANAGEMENT, OFFICE OF), U.S. Information Agency (*see* INTERNATIONAL COMMUNICATION AGENCY), and U.S. Postal Service (*see* POSTAL SERVICE, UNITED STATES).

Executive Supervision. Under the immediate supervision of the president is the Executive Office of the President, comprising the White House Office, Office of Management and Budget, Council of Economic Advisers, National Security Council, Office of Policy Development, Council on Environmental Quality, Office of Science and Technology Policy, Office of the U.S. Trade Representative, Office of National Drug Control Policy, and a number of other agencies. Through the personnel of the White House Office, often called the White House staff, the president maintains communication and contact with Congress, individual senators and representatives, heads of the executive departments and agencies, the press, radio and television, important citizens, and the public generally. The Office of Management and Budget was established in 1970 (replacing the Bureau of the Budget) to assist the president in bringing about more efficient and economical government service. It aids the chief executive in preparing the governmental budget; supervises and controls the administration of the budget; and keeps the president informed of the progress of various executive department agencies so that their activities and finances may be coordinated. The Council of Economic Advisers, created by Congress in 1946 and made up of three members, assists the president in preparing the Economic Report that is submitted periodically to Congress and makes studies and recommendations. Other duties are analyzing the national economy and appraising federal economic policies. The Office of Science and Technology Policy, created in 1976, serves as a source of scientific analysis with respect to major federal policies and programs.

Party Responsibilities. In addition to the powers conferred by the Constitution and legislative enactment, the president possesses immense authority as a political leader. As the head of a major political party, he exercises powers not contemplated by the Constitution, but, as experience has demonstrated, not in conflict with it. In the view of many political scientists, the president is more powerful as a political executive than in the constitutional capacity as the chief executive of the federal government. Of equal or greater consequence has been the president's influence on legislation when his party was in the majority in Congress, through its domination of the apparatus of control, especially the House of Representatives, but also the Senate.

HISTORY OF PRESIDENTIAL LEADERSHIP

Presidential political leadership began with Thomas Jefferson who created and, until his death, led the first effective political party, and who, through its domination of the then newly instituted congressional caucus (*see* CAUCUS), controlled the national legislature as no other president has ever done. Jefferson determined the memberships of the committees of both houses of Congress, and the leaders of these committees served as his lieutenants in supervising the enactment of legislation he desired. Beginning with Jefferson, the crucial problem of presidential political leadership has been the relationship between the president and Congress, and has pivoted on control of legislation. During the terms of Jefferson's successors, James Madison, James Monroe, and John Quincy Adams, Congress recovered its independence of the president; and through the use of the congressional caucus to nominate presidential candidates, the tendency of development was toward the subordination of the presidency to Congress.

Jackson's Administration. A new era in the relationship between the presidency and Congress took place during the administration of Andrew Jackson. Jackson's administration marked the end of the old methods of selecting presidents by congressional control of the designation of candidates and the emergence of direct popular participation in the process of choosing the chief executive. Jackson, moreover, aggressively asserted the independence of the presidency, not only of congressional control but also of judicial restraint by the Supreme Court (for a discussion of the relations between the presidency and the judicial branch of government, *see* SUPREME COURT OF THE UNITED STATES). Jackson has been called the first true presidential political executive.

The Civil War. During the American Civil War, in Abraham Lincoln's administration, the powers of the president were further strengthened. Without congressional authorization, Lincoln increased the armed forces beyond the limits established by law, expended millions of dollars for which no appropriations had been made, emancipated the slaves in the rebellious, southern states, established the political basis for the reconstruction of those states by presidential proclamation, and suspended the right of habeas corpus. He justified many of his actions as a legitimate exercise of his powers as commander-in-chief of the armed forces, and declared that he was motivated by the necessity of preserving the Constitution he had sworn to uphold. He said: "I felt that measures, otherwise unconstitutional, might become lawful by becoming indispensable to the preservation of the Constitution through the preservation of the nation." Following Lincoln's assassination, Andrew Johnson attempted to continue presidential leadership over Congress but was defeated and impeached, although not removed from office. Under Ulysses S. Grant, the presidency was subjected to congressional control. Presidential leadership was partly restored in the administrations of Rutherford B. Hayes, James A. Garfield, and Chester A. Arthur, but was not again established until the administration of Theodore Roosevelt.

20th Century. Roosevelt's conception of the presidency was essentially that of Lincoln and Jackson. In *An Autobiography* (1913), Roosevelt said: "My view was that every executive officer . . . in high position was steward of the people bound actively and affirmatively to do all he could for the people . . . I declined to adopt the view that what was imperatively necessary for the nation could not be done by the President unless he could find some specific authorization to do it . . . Under this interpretation of executive power I did and caused to be done many things not previously done by the President and the heads of departments. I did not usurp power but did greatly broaden the use of executive power." Guided by this theory, Roosevelt encouraged the secession of Panama from Colombia and afterward began construction of the Panama Canal without consulting Congress. By close cooperation with Joseph Gurney Cannon, the most powerful Speaker of the House in the history of Congress, Roosevelt exercised great control over Congress. When Congress, disturbed by his bold and independent course, passed a resolution establishing a commission of distinguished attorneys to investigate the legality of his executive acts and asked him for copies of his executive orders, he ignored the resolution.

As a political scientist before becoming president, Woodrow Wilson expressed his conception of the presidency in the following words: "The President is at liberty, both in law and conscience, to be as big a man as he can. His capacity will set the limit." Later, as president, he said: "It is . . . becoming more and more true, as the business of government becomes more and more complex and extended, that the President is becoming more and more a political and less and less an executive officer." In accordance with the precedent established by Grover Cleveland almost a quarter of a century before, Wilson regarded his cabinet officers primarily as administrators, rather than as political advisers, and delegated to them many of his duties as a constitutional executive in order to take a leading role in realizing his legislative program of reform, which he called the New Freedom. He held that the principal weapon of the president in establishing his leadership over Congress, which he felt to be essential for the best interests of the nation, was public opinion. On two occasions when Congress refused to enact measures recommended by him, Wilson threatened to resign and to carry the issue directly to the people in a series of electoral contests; Congress refused to accept the challenge. Wilson secured enactment of legislation establishing the Federal Reserve System, the Federal Trade Commission, and the Federal Power Commission, but he failed to win congressional endorsement of his most cherished project, the League of Nations.

Wilson's Republican successors, Warren Harding, Calvin Coolidge, and Herbert Hoover, all believed that a strong executive was dangerous to the liberty of the people. Harding opposed "personal government, individual, dictatorial, autocratic, or what not." Coolidge said: "I have never felt that it was my duty to attempt to coerce Senators or Representatives . . . I felt I had discharged my duty when I had done the best I could with them." Hoover saw "the militant safeguard to liberty . . . [in] legislative independence." He conceived it to be the prerogative of Congress to initiate and formulate legislation.

The New Deal. An entirely different view of presidential powers and responsibilities was taken by Franklin Delano Roosevelt, who believed in the Jacksonian theory of the presidency. In his first inaugural address, in the midst of the deepening economic depression, Roosevelt declared: "I am prepared under my constitutional duty to recommend the measures that a stricken nation in the midst of a stricken world may require. These measures or such other measures as Congress may build out of its experience and wisdom, I shall seek with my constitutional authority to bring to speedy adoption. But in the event that Congress shall fail to take these courses and in the event that the national emergency is still critical I shall not evade the clear course or duty that will then confront me. I shall ask the Congress for the one remaining instrument to meet the crisis—broad executive power to wage a war against the emergency, as great as the power that would be given to me if we were in fact to be invaded by a foreign foe."

Congress proved itself enthusiastically amenable to the course of the president, and in 100 days of harmonious labor enacted his legislative program. By the adroit use of radio appeals to the people Roosevelt established an unparalleled body of favorable public opinion which was skillfully utilized in later years, when Congress was not as acquiescent to the president's wishes. The measures sponsored by the president and passed by Congress affected virtually every phase of the life of the country and the life of every member of the population. The result was an unprecedented expansion of governmental responsibilities, especially of social responsibilities (*see* NEW DEAL), and of governmental regulation of economic activity. A further consequence was a great increase in the size and scope of the executive department of the government and of the power of the presidency. Roosevelt almost doubled the administrative apparatus of the federal government. He issued several thousand executive orders, many more than any other president, and from 125 to 150 administrative agencies issued legislation in the form of rules, known collectively since 1938 as the Federal Code of Regulation. During his administration, the quasi-judicial functions of the executive branch also were expanded. In 1936 the Treasury Department, for example, disposed of more than 600,000 separate cases involving controversies and problems in connection with matters within its jurisdiction; in the same year all the federal courts, both constitutional and legislative (*see* COURTS IN THE UNITED STATES), decided only approximately 20,600 cases. During World War II the power of the executive was still further increased by the legislative enactment of presidential war powers. Roosevelt became the political and military leader of the country and a symbol of national unity.

The Presidency Since Roosevelt. After Roosevelt's death the power of the presidency decreased as the wartime powers voted by Congress lapsed, and as Congress began to exercise a greater initiative in formulating legislation than it had done under Roosevelt. Nonetheless, the executive branch of the government retained enormous powers, which accrued significantly under Roosevelt's successor Harry S. Truman. Many were authorized by Congress; others were initiated as executive orders. Truman's views on the scope of presidential prerogative were best exemplified, perhaps, by his seizure in 1952 of the steel mills to avert an impending strike. The U.S. Supreme Court ruled this move unconstitutional.

Dwight D. Eisenhower, a Republican who served as president from 1953 to 1961, was a decidely less aggressive leader than either Roosevelt or Truman. The next president, John F. Kennedy, a Democrat, was more forceful in shaping national policies than was his predecessor.

Kennedy was assassinated in 1963, and he was succeeded by Lyndon B. Johnson, who in 1964 was elected to a full term in office. Richard M. Nixon, a Republican, was elected president in 1968; he was reelected by a larger margin in 1972. Both Johnson and Nixon concentrated power in their hands and those of a few advisers. Critics spoke of the development of the "imperial presidency," well removed from the influence and control of the American people. It was said that Johnson involved the U.S. in large-scale warfare in Indochina without properly informing or consulting either the U.S. Congress or the country at large. During his second term Nixon became increasingly withdrawn as revelations arising from the Watergate (q.v.) scandal indicated that some of his closest associates, and perhaps he himself, had engaged in criminal misconduct. Under public pressure Nixon resigned on Aug. 9, 1974, the first president to do so. He was succeeded by Gerald R. Ford. In 1977 the Democratic candidate Jimmy Carter became president, pledging to maintain a more accessible administration. Carter helped to bring about a peace treaty (1979) between Israel and Egypt. His success was overshadowed, however, by his inability to secure the release of American hostages, who had been seized during the 1979 Iranian takeover of the U.S. embassy in Tehran. This failure, along with rising inflation, which weakened the U.S. economy, led to his defeat in the 1980 election by Republican candidate Ronald Reagan. During Reagan's two terms a strong economic recovery took place, but at the same time, the national debt soared. Reagan remained a popular president and he was succeeded in 1989 by his vice-president, George Bush. For much of his presidency Bush was preoccupied with foreign affairs, including the 1991 Persian Gulf War (q.v.). During his administration, the Communist governments in eastern Europe began to collapse, culminating in the disintegration of the Soviet Union in 1991. With the downfall of Communism, U.S. attention shifted to domestic concerns. Bush was perceived by many people as having few solutions to serious economic problems and his popularity eroded. He was defeated in the 1992 election by the Democratic candidate, Bill Clinton.

For further information on U.S. presidents, see their biographies. For a list of U.S. presidential election returns from 1789 to the present, *see* UNITED STATES OF AMERICA: *Government.*

For further information on this topic, see the section Biographies in the Bibliography in volume 28, and sections 183, 263.

PRESLEY, Elvis Aron (1935–77), American singer and actor, who helped create the first nationwide sweep of rock-and-roll music. Born Jan. 8, 1935, in Tupelo, Miss., he was recognized as a talented singer at church services and revival meetings. In his teens he taught himself to play guitar and gained a strong following on the local touring circuit for country-and-western music. His fusion of the country sound with black rhythm-and-blues influences and the new rock-and-roll style led to his discovery in Nashville, Tenn., and his subsequent recording and film career. His romantic, suggestive ballads were matched by his erotic gyrations on stage, characteristics that made him one of the first mass idols of U.S. adolescent culture. His many hit songs include "Love Me Tender," "All Shook Up," and "Don't Be Cruel." He died Aug. 16, 1977, in Memphis, Tenn., possibly of drug and alcohol abuse.

PRESQUE ISLE, city, Aroostook Co., NE Maine, near the Aroostook R.; inc. as a city 1940. It is a summer resort and a commercial and distribution hub for the agricultural Aroostook valley. The University of Maine at Presque Isle (1903), a junior college, and a regional airport are here. Settled in the late 1820s, it grew as a shipping and processing point for potatoes after the railroad arrived (1895). Pop. (1980) 11,172; (1990) 10,550.

PRESS, FREEDOM OF THE, immunity of the communications media—including newspapers, books, magazines, radio, and television—from government control or censorship (q.v.). It is regarded as fundamental to individual rights, human dignity, self-respect, and personal responsibility. Without free media, a free society and democratic self-government would not be possible. By recognizing the right to dissent, the governments of the U.S., Canada, Western Europe, and other emerging democracies encourage peaceful and orderly social and political change.

When the first U.S. Congress met in 1789, its priority was the adoption of ten amendments to the U.S. Constitution, which became known as the Bill of Rights (q.v.). The 1st Amendment provides that "Congress shall make no law . . . abridging the freedom of speech, or the press" (*see* SPEECH, FREEDOM OF). Although intended as a guarantee limiting the federal government, its reach was extended by the 14th Amendment (1868) to protect the press from abridgment by the states. In its constitutional sense, the term *press* has been interpreted by the U.S. Supreme Court to encompass not only newspapers, but also books, magazines, and other printed matter, as well as motion pictures. (Other broadcasting media, regulated by the Federal Communications Commission since 1934, are moving toward 1st Amendment parity with the print media.)

Limitations. Freedom of the press, however, is not absolute. The principle has long been established that the press may not be used in circumstances that would create a "clear and present danger" of bringing about serious consequences to some significant interest that the government has a right or duty to protect. During World War I, for example, restrictions were placed on the direct advocacy of treason and on criticism of the government, conscription, or the American flag.

Another limit on the free press is the law of libel (q.v.), involving the defamation of a person, false accusations, or exposure of someone to hatred, ridicule, or pecuniary loss. In 1964 the Supreme Court weighed the libel law against the interests protected by the 1st Amendment. It held that a public figure who sues a newspaper for libel can recover damages only if the person can prove that the statement printed was made with actual malice, that is, "with knowledge that it was false or with reckless disregard of whether it was false or not." Subsequent court cases have extended this for the further protection of a free press.

Until about the mid-20th century, the law of obscenity (q.v.) was also a substantial limitation on freedom of the press. Today this exception, like the law of libel, has been narrowed so as to exclude from the constitutional guarantee only so-called hard-core pornography (q.v.).

Protection of the Press. In the 18th century the British Parliament imposed a tax on printed matter. Since the tax raised the cost of newspapers, it became known as a tax on knowledge. In 1936 the U.S. Supreme Court held that the 1st Amendment will not tolerate any "taxes on knowledge."

During the era of unrest caused by U.S. participation in the Vietnam War, prosecutors sometimes subpoenaed journalists' notes or publications' files and government agents made unannounced newsroom searches. Under the Privacy Protection Act of 1980, however, law-enforcement officers seeking evidence of crime must afford reporters notice and opportunity to contest the subpoena in court.

Occasionally the courts have tried to compel journalists to disclose their sources of information. Reporters have gone to jail, charged with contempt of court, for refusing to comply. Many states have enacted shield laws giving journalists the right to refuse to disclose confidential sources. Under many laws, however, journalists are still required to disclose this information.

Although some problems involving freedom of the press have not been fully resolved in the U.S. or in other democracies, in the Communist nations and many Third World countries a free press remains an unattained ideal. The primary function of the press in totalitarian countries has been to promote the aims of the government. By the late 1980s, however, a few Communist governments were allowing the press some measure of freedom to report national and international news.

See also BOOK TRADE; BROADCASTING, RADIO AND TELEVISION; CIVIL RIGHTS AND CIVIL LIBERTIES; NEWSPAPERS. M.R.K.

For further information on this topic, see the Bibliography in volume 28, sections 256–57.

PRESS ASSOCIATIONS AND PRESS AGENCIES, organizations for the collection, transmission, and distribution of news to newspapers, periodicals, television, radio and other journalistic and mass communications media. These news-gathering organizations originated in a general need for faster transmission of news. The invention of telegraphy in the mid-19th century provided the means for this as well as the impetus for the modern development and extension of wire services.

Present-day press agencies and associations vary in form. The best known operate as worldwide news-reporting services, providing general news coverage. Others provide national or regional coverage of routine or special news (stock market quotations are an example of the latter). Still others offer specialized services, reporting news of particular interest to persons of a specific religion or profession. Large newspapers, such as the *New York Times*, usually have their own news-gathering networks and syndicate stories filed by their reporters; however, these papers rely on the international services for broader coverage. Straight news reports are still the mainstay of most modern press agencies and associations, but service in some cases now also includes transmission of news photographs and production of films for television news programs.

The oldest press association in the U.S., the Associated Press (AP), was formed in 1848 by six New York dailies to finance cooperatively the cost of gathering national news. From this modest beginning, it has since become the largest worldwide news service. United Press International (UPI), another giant U.S. agency offering international news coverage, was formed in 1958 by a merger of United Press and International News Service; the former had been founded in 1907 by the American newspaper publisher Edward Wyllis Scripps and the latter in 1909 by his counterpart William Randolph Hearst. UPI was acquired by Middle East Broadcasting Center Ltd. in 1992.

Baron Paul Julius von Reuter established the pioneer British news agency, Reuters. Reuter set up his chief office in 1851 in London; beginning in 1865, cables were laid between England and Germany and between France and the U.S. Today Reuters is one of the largest European agencies, with subscribers in such countries as Australia and New Zealand. Another pioneer British press group, the Press Association, was established in 1868 for speedier transmission of domestic news. Besides Reuters, the most important press agencies in continental Europe currently are Agence France-Press, set up in 1944 as successor to the Havas Agency (founded in 1835), and ITAR-Tass, the Russian news agency, successor to Tass, the news agency of the Soviet Union.

An important international wire service in Asia is the Kyodo News Agency of Japan. The largest press association in Canada is Canadian Press, a cooperative with headquarters in Toronto, Ont.

PRESSURE, in mechanics, the force per unit area exerted by a liquid or gas on a body or surface, with the force acting at right angles to the surface uniformly in all directions. In the British system, pressure is usually measured in pounds per square inch (psi); in international usage, in kilograms per square centimeters, or in atmospheres; and in the international metric system (SI), in newtons per square meter (*see* INTERNATIONAL SYSTEM OF UNITS). The unit atmosphere (atm) is defined as a pressure of 1.03323 kg/sq cm (14.696 lb/sq in), which, in terms of the conventional mercury barometer, corresponds to 760 mm (29.921 in) of mercury. The unit kilopascal (kPa) is defined as a pressure of 0.0102 kg/sq cm (0.145 lb/sq in).

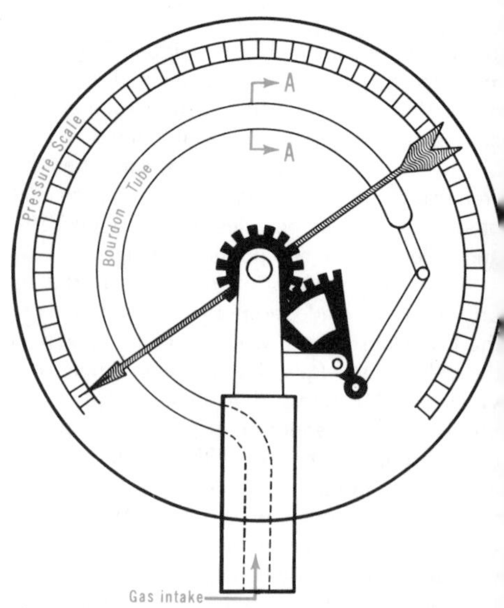

The straightening of the Bourdon tube is proportionate to the pressure of the gas admitted into the tube. A system of levers moves the indicator along the scale.

Pressure Gauges. Most gauges record the difference between the fluid pressure and local atmospheric pressure. For small pressure differences, a **U**-tube manometer is used. It consists of a **U**-shaped tube with one end connected to the container and the other open to the atmosphere. Filled with a liquid, such as water, oil, or mercury, the difference in the liquid surface levels in the two manometer legs indicates the pressure difference from local atmospheric conditions. For higher pressure differences, a Bourdon gauge, named after the French inventor Eugène Bourdon (1808–84), is used. This consists of a hollow metal tube with an oval cross section, bent in the shape of a hook. One end of the tube is closed, the other open and connected to the measurement region. If pressure (above local atmospheric pressure) is applied, the oval cross section will become circular, and at the same time the tube will straighten out slightly. The resulting motion of the closed end, proportional to the pressure, can then be measured via a pointer or needle connected to the end through a suitable linkage. Gauges used for recording rapidly fluctuating pressures commonly employ piezoelectric or electrostatic sensing elements that can provide an instantaneous response.

As most pressure gauges measure the difference between the fluid and the local atmospheric pressure, the atmospheric pressure must be added to the gauge pressure to arrive at the true absolute pressure. A negative gauge-pressure reading corresponds to a partial vacuum (q.v.).

Low gas pressure (down to about 10^{-6} mm

mercury absolute) can be measured by the so-called McLeod gauge, in which a measured volume of gas at the unknown low pressure is compressed at constant temperature to a much smaller volume, and then the pressure is measured directly with a manometer. The unknown pressure is then calculated from Boyle's law (*see* GASES). For still lower pressures, various gauges depending on radiation, ionization, or molecular effects are used (*see* VACUUM TECHNOLOGY).

Range. Depending on the use, pressures may range from 10^{-8} to 10^{-2} mm of mercury (absolute) for high-vacuum work to thousands of kilograms per square centimeter for hydraulic presses and controls. Pressures in the range of millions of kilograms per square centimeter have been obtained for experimental purposes and for the manufacture of artificial diamonds, where pressures of about 70,000 kg/sq cm (about 1 million lb/sq in), together with temperatures in excess of 2770° C (5000° F), are required.

In the atmosphere the decreasing weight of the air column with altitude leads to a reduction in local atmospheric pressure. Thus the pressure decreases from its sea-level value to 0.85 kg/sq cm (12.1 lb/sq in) at 1.6 km (1 mi), the elevation of Denver, Colo.; and to about 0.24 kg/sq cm (3.4 lb/sq in) at 10,700 m (35,000 ft) elevation, a normal jet flight altitude.

Partial pressure is the term applied to the effective pressure a single constituent exerts in a mixture of gases. In the atmosphere the total pressure (atmospheric pressure) is equal to the sum of the partial pressures of its constituents (oxygen, nitrogen, carbon dioxide, and rare gases). F.La.

PRESSURE GAUGE. *See* PRESSURE.

PRESTER JOHN, legendary Christian king and priest, whose vast territory was believed during the Middle Ages to lie either in Asia or in Africa. The first record of Prester (Priest, or Presbyter) John appears in the chronicle of the German bishop and historian Otto of Freising (1114?–58). It was believed that the Nestorian Christians had built up a rich monarchy ruled by a priest-king named John. Letters from this mysterious personage addressed to the Byzantine emperor or the pope were circulated, describing the size and wealth of the territory. In the 14th and 15th centuries the home of Prester John was generally believed to be located in Africa, where it was frequently identified with the Christian kingdom of Abyssinia.

PRESTON, borough, administrative center of Lancashire, NW England, on the Ribble R., near the Irish Sea. Preston is an important port, handling a large trade with Ireland. It is also a market center for the surrounding agricultural area. Among the many manufactures here are textiles, aircraft parts, machinery, and electrical equipment. Preston is the seat of Lancashire College of Agriculture and Horticulture (1894), a polytechnic college, and a grammar school (1550). Preston received its first charter in the 12th century and grew in the Middle Ages as an important market center. In 1648, during the English Revolution, the Parliamentarian forces of Oliver Cromwell defeated the Royalists here. Pop. (1991 prelim.) 126,200.

PRETORIA, city, NE South Africa, administrative capital of the country and capital of Transvaal Province, on the Apies R. It is a major commercial, manufacturing, transportation, and cultural center. Principal products include iron and steel, processed food, ceramics, and chemicals.

The modern city is well planned and contains large parks and a number of landmarks commemorating its history. Pretoria is the site of the University of South Africa (1873), the University of Pretoria (1908), a technical college, the State Library, and government archives. Points of interest include the home of Paul Kruger, president of the South African Republic (the Transvaal) from 1883 to 1900; the Transvaal Museum, containing natural history displays; the Municipal Art Gallery, featuring South African art; the Pretoria Art Museum, with a collection of 17th-century Dutch art; the National Cultural History and Open-Air Museum, with a variety of collections; the Military Museum, which is located in Fort Schanskop (built 1867); and the National Zoological Gardens.

The settlement was established by Marthinus W. Pretorius (1819–1901) in 1855 and named in honor of his father, Andries W. J. Pretorius (1798–1853), the Boer soldier and statesman. It became the capital of the South African Republic in 1860. The Peace of Vereeniging, ending the Boer War, was signed here in 1902. When the Union of South Africa was organized in 1910, Pretoria was designated the seat of its administration, a position it retained after the Republic of South Africa was formed in 1961. (Cape Town is the country's legislative capital.) Pop. (1985, greater city) 822,925.

PREVENTIVE MEDICINE, medical specialty that promotes health and prevents illness. In the late 20th century this specialty gained importance as U.S. public health (q.v.) officials became concerned about the increasing cost of health care. Preventive medicine strategies can focus on the population or on individuals.

Population-based Programs. Historically, the first preventive strategies were based on the finding that many diseases are transmitted by organisms, and that transmission can be stopped by public hygiene measures such as quarantining ill persons, removing the dead, and providing sewage systems. A major advance was the discovery that immunization (q.v.) protects most people against many infectious diseases.

Preventive medicine is also concerned with chronic disease and has developed such measures as screening programs to identify individuals with high blood pressure and those who have breast or cervical cancer. Unfortunately, screening for lung cancer has not been as successful.

Governments have attempted to prevent disease by requiring greater purity of air and water and by prohibiting the use of food additives that cause cancer in animals. U.S. federal regulations also promote safety in the workplace, for example, by requiring the removal of accident hazards and by limiting employees' exposure to chemicals and radiation (*see* OCCUPATIONAL AND ENVIRONMENTAL DISEASES).

Individual Action. Researchers in human health problems also uncover actions that people can take individually to improve their health. Primary among these are maintaining a nutritious and balanced diet with a low fat content, getting sufficient sleep and regular exercise, and having periodic medical and dental examinations. Many physicians recommend reducing the intake of cholesterol and salt in the diet to cut down heart disease, although evidence is not conclusive. Dentists have introduced the application of fluoride to children's teeth to prevent tooth decay. Public health officials also stress the use of automobile seat belts, especially for children. Physicians and health officials encourage people to stop smoking (q.v.) as the most effective way to combat the increasing occurrence of lung cancer. Some scientists advocate the massive use of vitamin C to prevent colds and the use of vitamins A and E to prevent some cancers, but these measures remain controversial (*see* VITAMIN).

See also MEDICINE.

For further information on this topic, see the Bibliography in volume 28, sections 487, 499, 508.

PRÉVOST (d'Exiles, Antoine François) Abbé (1697–1763), French novelist, born in Hesdin, and educated there at a Jesuit school. He was ordained a priest in the Benedictine Order in 1726 but abandoned the order two years later and lived several years in England and Holland. He is best known as the author of *Mémoires et aventures d'un homme de qualité* (Memoirs and Adventures of a Man of Quality, 7 vol., 1728–31), the seventh volume of which is *Histoire du chevalier des Grieux et de Manon Lescaut* (1731), popularly known as *Manon Lescaut.* This novel chronicles with sympathy and honesty the tragic romance of a young aristocrat and a luckless courtesan; it inspired two popular operas, *Manon* (1884), by the French composer Jules Massenet, and *Manon Lescaut* (1893), by the Italian composer Giacomo Puccini. His several books with English themes and his translations of the novels of the British novelist Samuel Richardson, including *Pamela* (1742) and *Clarissa* (1751), stimulated French interest in English literature.

PRIAM, in Greek mythology, king of Troy. He was the father of 50 sons, notably the great warrior Hector, and 50 daughters, including the prophet Cassandra. As a young man Priam fought with the Phrygians against the Amazons, but by the time of the Trojan War he was too old to fight. The conflict had begun when the Greeks set out to recapture Helen of Troy, who had been abducted by Priam's son Paris. During the ten years of fighting, Priam anxiously watched the course of battle from the walls of Troy with his wife, Queen Hecuba. After his son Hector was slain by the Greek hero Achilles, Priam went to the Greek camp to beg for his body. Achilles spared Priam's life and gave him Hector's body for burial, but during the sack of Troy, Priam was killed by Achilles' son Neoptolemus.

PRIAPUS, in Greek mythology, god of fertility, protector of gardens and herds. He was the son of Aphrodite, goddess of love, and of Dionysus, god of wine, or, according to some accounts, of Hermes, messenger of the gods. He was usually represented as a grotesque individual with a huge phallus. The Romans set up crude images of Priapus in their gardens as scarecrows.

PRIBILOF ISLANDS, also Fur Seal Islands, group of islands, SW Alaska, in the Bering Sea. Saint Paul, Saint George, Otter, and Walrus islands are the largest of the group; the remainder are islets. All are hilly and of volcanic origin. The native inhabitants are Aleuts. St. Paul (pop., 1990, 763) and St. George (pop., 1990, 138) are famous as mating places for most of the fur-bearing seals of the world. Otter, polar bear, blue and white fox, and many species of birds inhabit the islands during all or part of the year.

In 1786 the Pribilof Islands were discovered and claimed for his country by the Russian navigator Gerasim Pribilof (fl. late 18th cent.), for whom the group is named. After the U.S. purchased Alaska from Russia in 1867, the islands were leased by the federal government to sealing companies. The rapid depletion of the seal herd resulted in the signing of a treaty in 1911 to control sealing, with supervision of the seal herd by the U.S. Fish and Wildlife Service. The herd is now controlled by the U.S. Department of the Interior. Under this protection the seal herd has greatly increased in size. Area, about 161 sq km (62 sq mi); pop. (1990 est.) 901.

PRICE, (Mary) Leontyne (1927–), American operatic soprano, born in Laurel, Miss., and trained at the Juilliard School, New York City. She first appeared professionally in 1952 in *Four Saints in Three Acts* by Virgil Thomson; later that year she sang Bess in George Gershwin's *Porgy and Bess.* She has sung with the San Francisco Opera Company, the Vienna State Opera, La Scala in Milan, Covent Garden in London, and the Metropolitan Opera Company in New York City. She retired from opera in 1985.

PRICES. *See* BUSINESS CYCLE; COST OF LIVING; FINANCE; INFLATION AND DEFLATION; MONEY; SUPPLY AND DEMAND.

PRICHARD, city, Mobile Co., SW Alabama, an industrial community near Mobile; inc. 1925. Major manufactures are plastics, paper products, and chemicals. The area was settled by the French in the early 18th century. The site was reached by railroad in 1848 and grew as a shipping point with large railroad shops. The city is named for Cleveland Prichard (1840–99), a local developer. Pop. (1980) 39,541; (1990) 34,311.

PRICKLY PEAR, common name for plants of the genus *Opuntia,* of the family Cactaceae (*see* CACTUS). The plants are characterized by flat-jointed stems covered with small clusters of stiff hairs (glochids) and usually also spines. The flowers are commonly yellow and develop into warty, pear-shaped edible fruits. The most important species are the tuna, *O. tuna,* and the Indian fig, *O. ficus-indica.* These species originated in American subtropical and tropical areas, and they have been naturalized in tropical regions throughout the world. As forage for cattle, prickly pears are cultivated in arid lands of the western U.S.

PRIDI PHANOMYONG (1900–83), Thai statesman, who, along with Phibun Songgram (1897–1964), led the coup that changed Thailand from an absolute to a constitutional monarchy in 1932. After the coup he held several cabinet posts (interior, foreign affairs, finance) until 1941, when he resigned in protest against Phibun's pro-Japanese policies. Pridi's faction, however, gained power in 1944, and in 1946 he became prime minister, only to be forced from office after young King Ananda Mahidol (1925–46) was mysteriously shot. Although no evidence linked Pridi to the death, he was compelled to flee the country in 1947, after which he lived in obscurity in China and, from 1970 until his death, in France.

PRIEST, one especially consecrated to the service of a divinity and through whom worship, prayer, sacrifice, or other service is offered to the object of worship, and pardon, blessing, or deliverance is obtained by the worshiper. In earliest history the functions of priest were discharged by the head of the family; later the office became a public one, in many instances associated with that of the sovereign.

Under Jewish law, priests especially consecrated to the service of the Temple and the altar were selected from the tribe of Levi. The actual priesthood of Israel, however, was reserved for the male descendants of Aaron, who were authorized to offer sacrifice, supervise hygiene, and instruct the people in the Law of Moses. With the destruction of Jerusalem in AD 70, the concept of a priesthood disappeared from Judaism.

In the Roman Catholic and Eastern Orthodox churches and in the Church of England and other Anglican churches, the priest is a member of the sacerdotal ministry. The priest has the power to celebrate Mass and to administer the sacraments, except holy orders (reserved for the bishop), matrimony (administered to one another by the couple and witnessed by the priest), and, in the Roman Catholic church and the Church of England, confirmation (usually performed by a bishop). The Mormons recognize both a high priesthood and a lower one. Most Protestant churches acknowledge no specific priesthood. They believe in the universal priesthood of all believers and do not recognize the need for a mediator betweem themselves and God. The priesthood has traditionally been restricted to men, but in recent years women have been ordained as priests within the Anglican Communion.

Religions outside the Judeo-Christian tradition have often had a priesthood. A priestly class was recognized by the ancient civilizations of Egypt, Greece, and Rome and by the Celtic tribes of Ireland, Britain, and Gaul. The priestly function continues to be important in modern-day Shinto, Buddhism, and Hinduism.

For further information on this topic, see the Bibliography in volume 28, section 75.

PRIESTLEY, J(ohn) B(oynton) (1894–1984), English writer, born in Bradford. He served in the infantry during World War I, after which he attended the University of Cambridge. A newspaper essayist and critic, he wrote on a variety of subjects and often revealed his opposition to materialism and mechanization in society. The publication of *The Good Companions* (1929) and *Angel Pavement* (1930) established him as a successful popular novelist. Whereas his novels were traditional in form, his plays, beginning with *Dangerous Corner* (1932), were experimental, particularly in their treatment of time and of past and future events. Priestley's major plays include *An Inspector Calls* (1946) and *Dragon's Mouth* (1952); on the latter, he collaborated with his wife, Jacquetta Hawkes (1910–), the English archaeologist and writer. Later books include the autobiographical *Margin Released* (1962); *Man and Time* (1964); *Essays of Two Decades* (1968); *The Edwardians* (1970); and *The English* (1973). Priestley was director of the influential journal *New Statesman and Nation* and, after declining a knighthood and a peerage, accepted the Order of Merit from Queen Elizabeth II in 1977. He died in Stratford-on-Avon on Aug. 14, 1984.

PRIESTLEY, Joseph (1733–1804), British chemist, who isolated and described several gases, including oxygen, and who is considered one of the founders of modern chemistry because of his experimental methods.

Priestley was born on March 13, 1733, in Fieldhead, Yorkshire, the son of a Calvinist minister, and was himself trained as a minister of the Dissenting church, which comprised various churches that had separated from the Church of England. He was educated at Daventry Academy, where he became interested in physical science. His first ministry was at Needham Market, Suffolk, in 1755, and he was minister at Nantwich from 1758 to 1761. While there he opened a day school and later became a tutor at Warrington Academy in Lancashire, where he was noted for his development of practical courses for students planning to enter industry and commerce. He also wrote a text, *Rudiments of English Grammar* (1761), which broke with older, classical approaches. He was ordained in 1762.

Priestley was encouraged to conduct experiments in the new science of electricity by the American statesman and scientist Benjamin Franklin, whom he met in London in 1766, and he wrote *The History of Electricity* the following year; he also discovered that charcoal can conduct electricity. In 1767 he became minister at Leeds, where he grew interested in research on gases. His innovative experimental work resulted in his election to the French Academy of Sciences in 1772, the same year in which he was employed by William Petty, 2d earl of Shelburne, as librarian and literary companion.

During Priestley's experiments in 1774, he discovered oxygen and its role in combustion and in respiration. An advocate of the phlogiston (q.v.) theory, however, he termed the new gas dephlogisticated air and was unaware of the further importance of his discovery. (Actually, the Swedish chemist Carl Wilhelm Scheele may have discovered oxygen two years earlier but did not make his work known in time to be credited with its discovery.) Priestley also isolated and described the properties of several other gases, including ammonia, nitrous oxide, sulfur dioxide, and carbon monoxide.

Joseph Priestley

In 1780 Priestley left Petty's employ because of religious differences and became a minister in Birmingham. By this time he had become still more radical in religion and had turned to Unitarian thinking; his *History of the Corruptions of Christianity* (1782) was officially burned in 1785. Because of his open sympathy with the French Revolution, his house and effects were burned by a mob in 1791. He went to live in London, and in 1794 he emigrated to the U.S., where he spent the remainder of his life in writing. He died in Northumberland, Pa., on Feb. 6, 1804. His posthumously collected *Theological and Miscellaneous Works* (25 vol., 1817–32) and *Memoirs and Correspondence* (2 vol., 1831–32) cover a multitude of subjects in science, politics, and religion.

PRIMARY ELECTION. *See* ELECTION.

PRIMATE, any member of the mammal order Primates. Two divisions of primates exist; suborder Prosimii, including the lemur, loris, and, sometimes, the tree shrew (qq.v.), and suborder Anthropoidea, comprising monkeys, apes, and humans (*see* APE; MONKEY).

In the evolution of the tree-dwelling prosimians, the eyes of the animals moved to the front of the head, permitting binocular vision. They also developed hands with separate fingers and opposing thumbs that could grasp and hold onto branches. Some prosimians, such as the ring-tailed lemur, *Lemur catta,* of Madagascar, spend much of their time on the ground, where they travel on all fours. Other lemurs stay mostly in the trees. In Asia are found the big-eyed loris (*Loris*) and the tarsier (*Tarsius*). Their large eyes are set in a fixed position so that the animals must turn their heads to look to the side; their heads can rotate 180°.

About 30 million years ago a more advanced type of primate, the monkey, appeared in Africa and began to replace the lemur, with whom it competed for living space and food. (Since Madagascar had become an island, the lemurs there went unchallenged.) A monkey's most important sense is its vision, which is better than that of the prosimians; it has three-dimensional perception, and its color vision is excellent. All monkeys make a variety of sounds. The howlers (*Alouatta villosa*) roar in chorus morning and night, producing the loudest noise made by animals of any kind.

Throughout primate evolution, a trend toward size increase is evident. The more primitive New World monkeys generally are smaller than those in Africa and Asia, and many have the advantage of a prehensile tail as a useful fifth limb. In the Old World, on the other hand, some monkeys, such as the baboon (q.v.), have become almost completely terrestrial. When the apes became too large to walk along a branch safely, they began swinging under it on their arms. The most acrobatic is the gibbon (q.v.). Among the great apes (family Pongidae), however, the orangutan (q.v.) stays mostly in the trees, except for the very big older males that travel on the ground.

As the higher primates became larger, so did their brains. The first hominids (prehuman apes) appeared about 3 million years ago; fossils discovered in Africa indicate that they walked erect and had bipedal stride even before the great increase in their brain size.

A wide range of social patterns can be found among primates. Many of them exchange multiple signals that are subtle and sophisticated, using voice, facial expression, gesture, posture, and behavior. The care of the young varies from 90 days in the tree shrew to about 7 years in the great apes and 14 years in humans. Some live in family groups, as the gibbons do. The howler monkeys form large, mixed troops; chimpanzees also live in a large, loosely organized group.

For further information on this topic, see the Bibliography in volume 28, sections 475, 482.

PRIMATICCIO, Francesco (1504–70), Italian painter, decorator, and architect, active mainly in France. There he supervised the decoration of the Château de Fontainebleau under Francis I and was supervisor of buildings under the succeeding monarchs, Henry II and Charles IX. Working with his countryman, the Mannerist painter Rosso Fiorentino, Primaticcio exercised a decisive influence over contemporary French art. They moderated the violent distortions of Italian Mannerism (q.v.) and created a more elegant, indigenous variant of the style. Few of Primaticcio's works remain, but his drawings for the project and the surviving stucco reliefs at Fontainebleau—sinuous nude figures of mythological beings—indicate his refined sensuality.

PRIME MERIDIAN, the meridian, or line of longitude, that is designated 0° longitude and from which the longitude of all points on the surface of the earth are measured. The meridian passing through the original site of the Royal Greenwich Observatory in Greenwich, England, has been recognized by international agreement since 1884 as the prime meridian. It is sometimes called the Greenwich meridian. *See* LATITUDE AND LONGITUDE.

PRIME MINISTER *or* **PREMIER,** in government, the highest ranking minister and in practice often the chief executive, even though a nation's constitution might provide for a king (monarchy) or a president (republic) as head of state. In most instances the prime minister is the chief formulator of governmental policy. The office of prime minister is particularly associated with the parliamentary system of government, and it is commonly held by the leader of the majority party or of a coalition of political parties. He or she is assisted by a cabinet and is responsible to the legislature. The legislature either elects or approves the prime minister and, when a majority of its members oppose government policies, may force him or her out of office.

In Canada the designation *prime minister* has traditionally been reserved for the leader of the Canadian government, and the term *premier* has been used to describe a leader of one of the ten provincial governments. The leader of the Québec Province government is called prime minister, however, as was the Ontario leader until 1972. In France today the powers of the premier are secondary to those of the president of the republic. In West Germany the prime minister is known as chancellor. In the U.S. the office of president is a combination of prime minister and head of state.

For further information on this topic, see the Bibliography in volume 28, section 261, Collective Biographies.

PRIME NUMBER. *See* NUMBER THEORY.

PRIMITIVE ART, term conventionally used to designate the art of the indigenous peoples of sub-Saharan Africa, the islands of the Pacific Ocean, and the Americas. *See* AFRICAN ART AND ARCHITECTURE; AMERICAN INDIANS; ART; INUIT; CRAFTS; OCEANIAN ART AND ARCHITECTURE.

PRIMITIVE MUSIC AND DANCE, term sometimes used for the music and dance of preliterate or tribal cultures. Most anthropologists consider the term *primitive* to be inaccurate, even misleading, and prefer to speak of specific cultures. Aspects of the music and dance of tribal cultures are discussed in DANCE and MUSIC. *See also* AFRICAN MUSIC AND DANCE; AMERICAN INDIANS.

PRIMITIVE RELIGION. *See* RELIGION.

PRIMO DE RIVERA Y ORBANEJA, Miguel, Marqués de Estella (1870–1930), Spanish soldier and dictator, born in the province of Cádiz. During the Spanish-American War he served in Cuba and in the Philippines. He fought in Morocco from 1909 to 1913 and was military governor of Cádiz from 1915 to 1917. In 1922 he became military governor of Barcelona. At the request of King Alfonso XIII, he established a military dictatorship in Spain. When the military directorate was abolished in 1925, Primo de Rivera became prime minister of the new civil government. Despite the successful suppression of a Moroccan revolt (1926) and the launching of a public works program, his administration aroused much opposition, particularly among liberals. Forced to resign in 1930, he went into voluntary exile in Paris.

His son José Antonio (1903–36), founder of the Fascist-oriented Falange party (1933), was executed by the Republicans during the Spanish civil war (1936–39) and was revered as a martyr by the regime of Gen. Francisco Franco.

PRIMOGENITURE, term formerly applied in England, and in most continental European countries, to the right of the firstborn son to the real property of a deceased ancestor. According to the feudal system of the Middle Ages, primogeniture determined the disposition of property held as a reward for military service. Land of the father passed to the son best able to defend it—the eldest. Under primogeniture, the eldest son or his issue, or, if no lineal descendants (male or female) existed, the eldest male in the next degree of consanguinity succeeded to all the real estate of which his ancestor died intestate, to the exclusion of all female and of junior male descendants of equal degree of relationship. When female descendants alone survived, they divided the estate of the ancestor equally. Following adoption of the Statute of Wills (1540), under which the eldest son could be completely bypassed, primogeniture applied only in cases in which the deceased left no will. This rule of descent was introduced into the American colonies with the rest of the common law system, but was soon abandoned. Primogeniture was completely abolished in England in 1925 and no longer exists in most European countries.

The term *primogeniture* has also been applied to the right of an eldest son of a king or other hereditary ruler to succeed to the sovereign power.

PRIMROSE, also primula, common name for the family Primulaceae, a medium-size group of flowering plants of wide distribution, and for its representative genus, *Primula*. The family, comprising about 800 species placed in 22 genera, is made up of annual and perennial herbs and is most abundant in the North Temperate Zone. Many species produce showy flowers on erect, leafless stalks. The family contains many popular ornamentals, such as the cowslip (q.v.). Members of the genus *Primula,* in particular, such as the common primrose, *P. vulgaris,* are useful in rock gardens and are also grown as houseplants. Primroses are among the earliest-blooming spring flowers. Cyclamens, genus *Cyclamen,* are grown both outdoors and indoors for their interestingly shaped, early-appearing flowers. Loosestrife (q.v.), *Lysimachia,* and shooting star, *Dodecatheon,* are also often cultivated. A few members of the family yield medicinally useful chemicals, and others produce dyes.

The family Primulaceae is placed in the order Primulales with two other families. The family

This species of primrose, Primula allionii, *is one of more than 800 known species, many of which are cultivated for the beauty and variety of their flowers.* Jane Latta

Myrsinaceae, with about 1250 species placed in 37 genera, is a group of mostly tropical Old and New World trees and shrubs of little economic value, except for a few genera that are grown as ornamentals in tropical and subtropical areas. The family Theophrastaceae contains about 90 species of tropical American trees and shrubs placed in 5 genera.

Plants in the order Primulales are members of the class Magnoliopsida (*see* DICOTS) in the division Magnoliophyta (*see* ANGIOSPERM). M.R.C.

For further information on this topic, see the Bibliography in volume 28, sections 452, 592.

PRIMUS, Pearl (1919–), Trinidadian-American choreographer and anthropologist. Her extensive research into African and Caribbean dance influenced her choreography in works such as *Fanga* (1941) and *Congolese Wedding* (1974). She also examined racial problems in *Strange Fruit* (1943), the story of a lynching. Primus often worked in collaboration with her husband, Percival Borde (1923?–79). Her dances have been performed in Broadway musicals, by the Alvin Ailey Dance Theater, and by her own company.

PRINCE ALBERT, city, central Saskatchewan, on the North Saskatchewan R.; inc. 1904. It is a manufacturing and distribution center situated in an agricultural, lumbering, and fur-trapping area. Major manufactures include processed food, beverages, paper, wood and petroleum products, and building materials. Tourism is also important to the city's economy. An art gallery and a provincial heritage museum are here, and Prince Albert National Park and a number of lakes are nearby. The settlement, named for the prince consort of Queen Victoria of Great Britain, was established in 1866, when a Presbyterian Indian mission was founded here. Pop. (1986) 33,686; (1991) 34,181.

PRINCE ALBERT NATIONAL PARK, central Saskatchewan, established 1927. The park encompasses a portion of the transition zone between the prairie grasslands of S central Canada and the evergreen forests to the N. Diverse wildlife is found here, including moose, black bear, woodland caribou, and many species of birds. Area, 3875 sq km (1496 sq mi).

PRINCE EDWARD ISLAND, one of the three Maritime and one of the four Atlantic provinces of Canada, bounded on the N, E, and W by the Gulf of Saint Lawrence and on the S by Northumberland Strait (which separates it from Nova Scotia and New Brunswick).

Prince Edward Island became part of the Canadian Confederation on July 1, 1873, as the seventh province. Farming is the island's chief economic activity. The province is named for Edward Augustus, duke of Kent and Strathern (1767–1820), a son of George III of England. The province is also known as P.E.I. or The Island.

Stacks of lobster pots (traps) at dockside at North Lake, in Prince Edward Island. Lobstering is a major industry of the province. Canadian Government Office of Tourism

LAND AND RESOURCES

Prince Edward Island, with an area of 5660 sq km (2185 sq mi), is the smallest province of Canada. Its extreme length is about 195 km (about 120 mi), and its extreme width is about 65 km (about 40 mi). The province has a coastline of some 1260 km (some 783 mi), which is indented by many bodies of water, such as Bedeque, Egmont, Hillsborough, and Malpeque bays. Several inlets on the N coast have been largely closed off by sandbars. Some small islands, including Boughton, Lennox, and Saint Peters islands, are part of the province. Elevations range from sea level to 142 m (465 ft), near the community of Hunter River.

Physical Geography. All of Prince Edward Island is part of the Maritime Plain, which also covers parts of nearby New Brunswick and Nova Scotia. The island is situated almost entirely at a low elevation, and the landscape is generally level to gently undulating, with few steep hills. The province is covered with a thick, mostly stone-free mantle of glacial deposits. Iron in the underlying rock has given much of the fertile surface soil a reddish color. Nearly all the rivers of Prince Edward Island are tidal; the tidal Hillsborough R. almost bisects the province. No freshwater lakes of significant size occur.

Climate. Prince Edward Island has a cool, changeable climate. The average July temperature at Charlottetown is about 18.4° C (about 65° F), and the average January temperature in the city is about –6.7° C (about 20° F). The recorded temperature has ranged from a low of –37.2° C (–35° F) in 1884, at Kilmahumaig in the NW, to a

Charlottetown, the capital of Prince Edward Island, the site in 1864 of the Canadian Confederation conference that led to the birth of the modern nation of Canada.
G. Zimbel–Monkmeyer Press

high of 36.7° C (98.1° F) in 1935, at Charlottetown. Northumberland Strait and its arms usually freeze over in winter, and the island is normally icebound for a few months each year. Spring is late; often snow is on the ground in the latter part of April. The growing season, however, extends into October and averages some 150 days, which is longer than in other parts of the Maritime provinces. The average annual precipitation of about 1120 mm (about 44 in) is fairly evenly distributed throughout the year; about one-fourth of the precipitation is in the form of snow.

Plants and Animals. About one-half of Prince Edward Island is covered with forest, usually in the form of relatively small lots. The forest is mostly a mixture of deciduous and coniferous trees such as sugar maple, yellow birch, red spruce, balsam fir, hemlock, and white pine. The wildlife of the province is limited. Small numbers of white-tailed deer and black bear are among the few large mammals; furbearing animals such as beaver, muskrat, mink, otter, and red fox also inhabit the island. Many marine animals, notably lobster, oysters, clams, scallops, cod, and hake, live in coastal waters. A commercially valuable alga called Irish moss is harvested along the shoreline.

Mineral Resources. Prince Edward Island has few known mineral resources aside from such basic materials as sand and gravel. Significant petroleum and natural-gas deposits may lie underneath coastal waters, however. W.F.S.

POPULATION

According to the 1991 census, Prince Edward Island had 129,765 inhabitants, an increase of 2.5% over 1986. The overall population density in 1991 was 23 persons per sq km (59 per sq mi). English was the sole native language of about 94% of the people; about 4% had French as their lone first language. Approximately 1100 American Indians lived in the province. The largest religious groups included Roman Catholics, members of the United Church of Canada, and Presbyterians. Prince Edward Island is the least urbanized of Canada's provinces; only 40% of the people lived in areas defined as urban and the rest lived in rural areas. Charlottetown was the capital and largest city in the province. Other major communities included Summerside, Sherwood, Saint Eleanors, West Royalty, and Parkdale.

EDUCATION AND CULTURAL ACTIVITY

Prince Edward Island has notable cultural and educational institutions as well as several points of historical interest.

Education. The first schools in Prince Edward Island were established in the early 19th century, and a provincial board of education was formed in the 1870s. In 1972, school boards were consolidated into five regional divisions. In the early 1990s the province had 73 elementary and secondary schools with a combined annual enrollment of about 25,000 students. The only university in the province, the University of Prince Edward Island, situated in Charlottetown, was formed in 1969 by the merger of Wales College (1834) and Saint Dunstan's University (1855). It is attended by about 2300 students each year. Holland College (1969), with branches in Charlottetown, Elmsdale, Montague, Souris, Summerside, and West Royalty, also offers postsecondary instruction. A nursing school is in Charlottetown.

Cultural Institutions. The most important cultural institution in Prince Edward Island is the Confederation Centre of the Arts, opened in 1964 in Charlottetown, which contains a museum, theaters, the city's major library, and art galleries. Other museums in the province include the Musée Acadien, in Miscouche; the House of International Dolls, in DeSable; the Woodleigh Replicas, near Kensington, with large-scale models of famous buildings such as the York Minster of England; and the Basin Head Fisheries Museum, near Souris.

Historical Sites. Fort Amherst National Historic Site, near Charlottetown, encompasses the sites of French and English fortifications of the 18th century. Some ruins are still visible. Province House (1847), in Charlottetown, is the meeting place of the provincial Legislative Assembly and contains the Confederation Room, used in 1864 for discussions that helped prepare the way for Canadian confederation in 1867. Also of historical interest are the birthplace, in New London, of the author Lucy Maud Montgomery (1874–1942), who wrote the popular novel *Anne of Green Gables* (1908), and the Micmac Indian Village, near Rocky Point, a re-creation of an 18th-century Indian community.

Sports and Recreation. Prince Edward Island's national park, its provincial parks, and its many beaches offer ideal conditions for swimming, fishing, boating, camping, and golfing. The island also has facilities for skiing. Horse racing is a popular spectator sport, with tracks in Charlottetown, O'Leary, Pinette, Saint Peters, Souris, and Summerside. The Prince Edward Island Sports Hall of Fame is in Summerside.

Communications. In the late 1980s Prince Edward Island was served by four commercial radio stations, three AM and one FM. The province had three daily newspapers—the *Guardian* and the *Patriot,* published in Charlottetown, and the *Journal-Pioneer,* published in Summerside—with a total daily circulation of about 35,200.

GOVERNMENT AND POLITICS

Prince Edward Island has a parliamentary form of government.

Executive. The nominal chief executive of Prince Edward Island is a lieutenant governor, who is appointed by the Canadian governor-general in council to a term of five years. The lieutenant governor represents the British sovereign and holds a position that is largely honorary. The premier, most often the leader of the majority party in the provincial legislature, is the actual head of the provincial government and presides over the executive council (cabinet). In addition to the premier, the executive council is made up of about ten ministers who head such government departments as finance, health and social services, agriculture, environment, and justice.

Legislature. The unicameral Prince Edward Island Legislative Assembly is made up of 32 members, including the premier and the rest of the executive council. Members of the legislature are popularly elected to terms of no more than five years.

Judiciary. Prince Edward Island's highest tribunal, the supreme court, consists of three divisions: appellate, trial, and bankruptcy. Lesser matters are handled in the provincial courts. Judges of the supreme court are federally appointed; provincial court judges are appointed by the executive council.

Local Government. Prince Edward Island is divided into three counties, which are mainly geographical divisions and have no government structure. The province has one city (Charlottetown) and eight towns; most of the towns employ the mayor-council form of government.

National Representation. Prince Edward Island is represented in the Canadian Parliament by four senators appointed by the Canadian governor-general in council and by four members of the House of Commons popularly elected to terms of up to five years.

Politics. The Liberal party controlled the Prince Edward Island Legislative Assembly for most of the years from the mid-1930s through the late 1970s. The Progressive Conservative party was in power in the province during 1959–66 and again from 1979 to 1986, when the Liberals regained a majority.

ECONOMY

Prince Edward Island has a mixed economy in which manufacturing, farming, and service industries all play a major role. Fishing and tourism are also significant sources of income.

Agriculture. Prince Edward Island has much fertile soil, and more than one-quarter of its land area is used for crops. The province has about 2360 farms, which have the relatively small average size of 110 ha (271 acres). The annual value of farm production in the early 1990s was approximately $216 million. Table and seed potatoes are the most valuable crop; considerable quantities of barley, hay, peas, beans, broccoli, brussels sprouts, tobacco, and such fruit as strawberries, raspberries, and blueberries also are produced. Cattle, poultry, and hogs are raised widely, and dairy products are an important source of income. More than one commodity is produced on almost all farms in the province.

Forestry, Fishing, and Mining. Compared with the other Canadian provinces, Prince Edward Island has a very small forest-products industry. Its total annual production in the late 1980s was only about 460,000 cu m (about 16.2 million cu ft).

Little commercial mining activity takes place on the island; annual mineral output (virtually all sand and gravel) was worth about Can.$2 million in the early 1990s.

The yearly value of the Prince Edward Island fish catch in the early 1990s was some Can. $60 million, with lobster accounting for most of the total. Other major sources of income were landings of cod, crab, bluefin tuna, and redfish. Irish moss, an alga used in food processing, is harvested along the shoreline.

Manufacturing. Prince Edward Island has a small manufacturing sector compared with other Canadian provinces. The yearly value of shipments was approximately Can.$449 million in the early 1990s. Fish and agricultural products are the most important manufactures. Chemical products, printed materials, machinery, and wood products also are produced on the island. Most enterprises are small scale.

Tourism. The tourist industry is important to Prince Edward Island's economy. Annually the province attracts about 560,000 visitors, who spend more than Can. $80 million. Major attractions include the lovely countryside, the opportunities for fishing and swimming, and Prince Edward Island National Park. The province maintains a system of about 30 parks, recreation areas, campgrounds, and roadside rest sites.

Transportation. Prince Edward Island has about 5240 km (about 3255 mi) of highways and roads. The province has no mainline railroad service. Charlottetown is the main seaport of the island. It is connected to New Brunswick by year-round ferry and to Nova Scotia by ferries that operate when coastal waters are not ice covered. The principal airport serves Charlottetown.

INDEX TO MAP OF PRINCE EDWARD ISLAND

Cities and Towns

Other Features

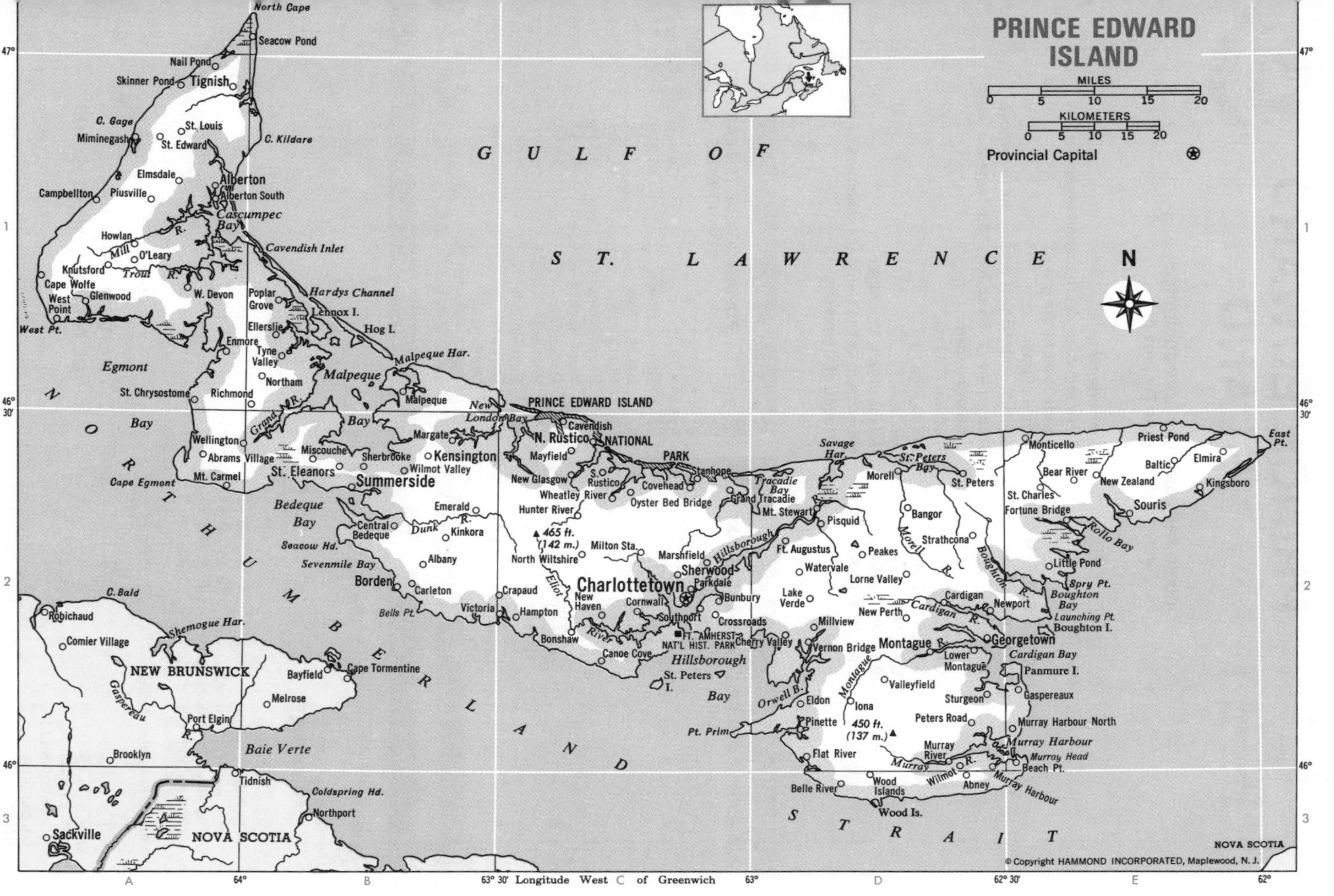
PRINCE EDWARD ISLAND
MILES
0 5 10 15 20
KILOMETERS
0 5 10 15 20
Provincial Capital
N
GULF OF ST. LAWRENCE
NORTHUMBERLAND STRAIT
North Cape
Seacow Pond
Nail Pond
Skinner Pond
Tignish
C. Gage
Miminegash
St. Louis
St. Edward
C. Kildare
Elmsdale
Alberton
Alberton South
Campbellton
Piusville
Cascumpec Bay
Cavendish Inlet
Howlan
Mill R.
O'Leary
Trout R.
Knutsford
Cape Wolfe
Glenwood
West Point
West Pt.
W. Devon
Poplar Grove
Hardys Channel
Lennox I.
Hog I.
Ellerslie
Enmore
Tyne Valley
Northam
Malpeque Har.
Malpeque
Egmont Bay
St. Chrysostome
Richmond
Grand R.
Wellington
Abrams Village
Mt. Carmel
Cape Egmont
Miscouche
St. Eleanors
Sherbrooke
Margate
Kensington
Wilmot Valley
Summerside
New London Bay
PRINCE EDWARD ISLAND NATIONAL PARK
Cavendish
N. Rustico
Mayfield
S. Rustico
New Glasgow
Wheatley River
Covehead
Oyster Bed Bridge
Stanhope
Hunter River
Bedeque Bay
Central Bedeque
Emerald
Dunk R.
Kinkora
465 ft. (142 m.)
Milton Sta.
North Wiltshire
Seacow Hd.
Sevenmile Bay
Albany
Borden
Carleton
Bells Pt.
Crapaud
Victoria
Hampton
Eliot River
New Haven
Bonshaw
Cornwall
Canoe Cove
Charlottetown
Southport
Marshfield
Sherwood
Parkdale
Bunbury
Crossroads
FT. AMHERST NAT'L HIST. PARK
Hillsborough Bay
St. Peters I.
Pt. Prim
Tracadie Bay
Grand Tracadie
Mt. Stewart
Hillsborough R.
Ft. Augustus
Pisquid
Watervale
Lake Verde
Cherry Valley
Vernon Bridge
Millview
Orwell B.
Eldon
Pinette
Flat River
Belle River
Savage Har.
Morell
St. Peters Bay
St. Peters
Bangor
Morell R.
Strathcona
Peakes
Lorne Valley
New Perth
Cardigan R.
Cardigan
Montague
Montague R.
Georgetown
Valleyfield
Iona
450 ft. (137 m.)
Wood Islands
Wood Is.
Lower Montague
Sturgeon
Peters Road
Murray River
Murray R.
Wilmot R.
Abney
Murray Harbour
Murray Head
Beach Pt.
Murray Harbour North
Gaspereaux
Panmure I.
Cardigan Bay
Boughton I.
Launching Pt.
Boughton Bay
Spry Pt.
Newport
Boughton R.
Little Pond
Rollo Bay
Fortune Bridge
St. Charles
Monticello
Bear River
New Zealand
Souris
Priest Pond
Baltic
Elmira
Kingsboro
East Pt.
C. Bald
Robichaud
Comier Village
Shemogue Har.
NEW BRUNSWICK
Gaspereau R.
Cape Tormentine
Bayfield
Melrose
Port Elgin
Brooklyn
Baie Verte
Tidnish
Coldspring Hd.
Northport
Sackville
NOVA SCOTIA
47°
46° 30′
46°
64°
63° 30′ Longitude West of Greenwich
63°
62° 30′
62°
A B C D E
1 2 3
© Copyright HAMMOND INCORPORATED, Maplewood, N. J.

PRINCE EDWARD ISLAND

JOINED THE CANADIAN CONFEDERATION:
July 1, 1873, as the 7th province

CAPITAL:	**Charlottetown**
MOTTO:	***Parva sub ingenti*** **(The small under the protection of the great)**
FLORAL EMBLEM:	**Lady's slipper**
POPULATION (1991):	**129,765; 10th largest among the provinces**
AREA:	**5660 sq km (2185 sq mi); 10th largest among the provinces**
COASTLINE:	**1260 km (783 mi)**
HIGHEST POINT:	**142 m (465 ft)**
LOWEST POINT:	**Sea level**
PRINCIPAL RIVERS:	**Hillsborough, Montague**
CANADIAN PARLIAMENT:	**4 members of the Senate; 4 members of the House of Commons**

POPULATION OF PRINCE EDWARD ISLAND SINCE 1861

Year of Census	Population	Percentage of Total Can. Pop.
1861	80,857	2.5%
1881	108,891	2.5%
1901	103,259	1.9%
1911	93,728	1.3%
1921	88,615	1.0%
1961	104,629	0.6%
1971	111,641	0.5%
1981	122,506	0.5%
1986	126,646	0.5%
1991	129,765	0.5%

POPULATION OF TEN LARGEST COMMUNITIES

	1991 Census	1986 Census
Charlottetown	15,396	15,776
Summerside	7,474	8,020
Sherwood	6,006	5,769
Saint Eleanors	3,514	3,757
West Royalty	3,142	2,070
Parkdale	2,198	2,065
Wilmot	2,176	1,734
East Royalty	2,052	2,039
Cornwall	2,038	1,894
Montague	1,901	2,038

CLIMATE CHARLOTTETOWN

Average January temperature range	–11.7° to –3.3° C (11° to 26° F)
Average July temperature range	15° to 23.3° C (59° to 74° F)
Average annual temperature	5.6° C (42° F)
Average annual precipitation	1128 mm (44 in)
Average annual snowfall	3051 mm (120 in)
Average number of days per year with appreciable precipitation	169
Average dates of freezing temperatures (0° C/32° F or less):	
Last in spring	May 17
First in autumn	Oct. 15

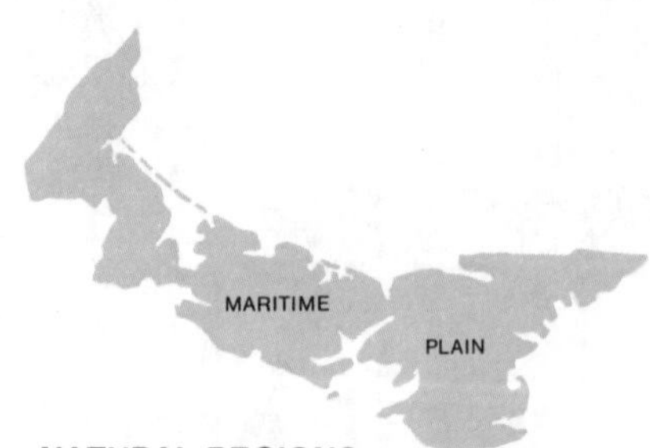

NATURAL REGIONS OF PRINCE EDWARD ISLAND

PRINCIPAL PRODUCTS OF PRINCE EDWARD ISLAND

ECONOMY

Province budget		revenue $714 million
		expenditure $625 million
Provincial gross domestic product		$2.0 billion
Personal disposable income, per capita		$13,208
Labor force		64,000
Employed in services		36%
Employed in manufacturing and construction		16%
Employed in commerce		16%
Employed in public administration		9%
Employed in agriculture		8%
	Quantity Produced	Value
FARM PRODUCTS		**$216 million**
Crops		**$118 million**
Potatoes	820,000 metric tons	$97 million
Tobacco	1700 metric tons	$8 million
Vegetables		$5 million
Barley	97,000 metric tons	$3 million
Fruits		$2 million
Livestock and Livestock Products		**$98 million**
Dairy products	96,000 kiloliters	$39 million
Cattle, calves	35,000	$29 million
Hogs	175,000	$22 million
Poultry	2300 metric tons	$4 million
Eggs	33 million	$3 million
MINERALS		**$2 million**
Sand, gravel	1.1 million metric tons	$2 million
FISHING	**34,000 metric tons**	**$60 million**
FORESTRY	**460,000 cu m**	**$2 million**
		Value of Shipments
MANUFACTURING		**$449 million**
Food and beverage products		$345 million
Chemical products		$27 million
Printing and publishing		$15 million
Machinery		$13 million
Wood products		$10 million
		Wages and Salaries
SERVICE-PRODUCING INDUSTRIES		**$819 million**

ANNUAL GROSS DOMESTIC PRODUCT

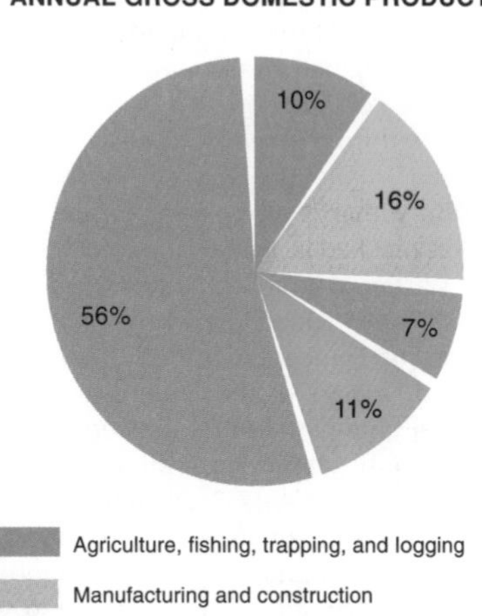

- Agriculture, fishing, trapping, and logging
- Manufacturing and construction
- Transportation and other utilities
- Wholesale and retail trade
- Government and other services

Sources: Canadian government publications
All figures are in Canadian dollars

The historic room in Province House, Charlottetown, where the "Fathers of Confederation" first met (1864) to explore unification of the Canadian colonies. PEI Tourism

Energy. Unlike the other Maritime provinces, Prince Edward Island has no hydroelectric installations. Installed electricity-generating capacity is only 122,100 kw, of which 58% derives from conventional steam-powered generators, 33% from gas-powered turbines, and 9% from internal combustion engines. In the early 1990s, however, virtually all of Prince Edward Island's electricity was imported from other provinces. A.H.

HISTORY

The territory that is now called Prince Edward Island was reached in 1534 by the French explorer Jacques Cartier, who found Micmac Indians living here. In 1603 Samuel de Champlain claimed the island for France and called it Îsle-St-Jean. The island, a part of the French province of Acadia, held little interest for the Europeans and supported only temporary fishing villages for nearly 200 years. After 1713, when the British acquired possession of mainland Acadia from France, French authorities encouraged the Acadians and new arrivals from France to settle on the island. The British won control of Île-St-Jean in 1745; France regained sovereignty in 1748. British troops occupied the island in 1758, during the French and Indian War; the island was finally ceded to Great Britain by the Treaty of Paris in 1763, when it was renamed Saint John's Island and became part of Nova Scotia. Most of the French settlers were expelled between 1753 and 1763.

In 1767 the land was divided into 67 large lots, which were granted to British citizens to whom the government of Great Britain was indebted. Settlers were thus forced to become tenant farmers. Settlement was slow and the colony isolated; the establishment of responsible government and a prosperous economy was delayed by strife between tenant farmers and the absentee landlords. The island was separated from Nova Scotia in 1769 and an independent administration established. In 1799 the island was renamed to honor the son of King George III, Edward Augustus, duke of Kent and Strathern, the commander in chief of royal forces in North America.

Responsible government was granted in 1851. A brief period of prosperity ensued in the 1850s and '60s, when native-built wooden ships carried island products all over the world. Although Charlottetown was the scene of the Canadian Confederation conference in 1864, Prince Edward Island refused to join the Confederation of Canada when it was established in 1867. The islanders finally were led to do so in 1873 after an attempt by the colonial government to build a railroad left the colony bankrupt. The terms under which the island became a province provided that the federal government take over the railroad, provide and maintain year-round ferry service, establish telegraph communications, and buy out the absentee landlords and permit former tenants to buy the land cheaply. In addition to complying with these requirements, the Canadian government initiated a policy of providing annual subsidies and per capita grants to the province and remission of some federal taxes.

Canada's smallest province has enjoyed a quiet history since Confederation. The island's economy, based on fishing and farming, changed little until the mid-20th century. The population actually declined from 109,000 in 1891 to 88,000 in 1931 as islanders went to the mainland in search of employment. (During the last half century, the population has grown to more than 125,000.) After 1950 agriculture was slowly modernized; the number of farms decreased, while their size increased. A similar process brought specialization and lower employment to the fisheries. Since the mid-1960s tourism has become a major source of income. Federal transfer payments and social policies have been especially important in bringing educational and health benefits to islanders. In the late 1970s completion of the maritime power grid made available to the province additional and cheaper sources of energy.

Political power in the province has alternated between the Liberal party and the Progressive Conservative party. The Liberals won the parliamentary elections of 1986 and increased their majorities in 1989 and 1993. REV. BY P.R.

For further information on this topic, see the Bibliography in volume 28, section 1116.

PRINCE EDWARD ISLAND NATIONAL PARK, N shore of Prince Edward Island, established 1937. The park, a coastal strip (40 km/25 mi long) on the Gulf of Saint Lawrence, contains a varied landscape of beaches, dunes, bays, and cliffs. Spruce forests are present inland. Area, 26 sq km (10 sq mi).

PRINCE GEORGE, city, central British Columbia, at the confluence of the Fraser and Nechako rivers; inc. 1915. Prince George is a summer resort and a manufacturing and distribution center for an agricultural and lumbering region. Major manufactures include pulp, paper, lumber, and other forest products; refined petroleum; processed food; and chemicals. In the city are Prince George College (1962) and the Prince George Art Gallery. In 1807 the Canadian explorer Simon Fraser (1776–1862) built a fur-trading post here for the North West Co. and named it after George III of England. Settlement of the site was slow, however, until 1913–14, when a railroad was constructed linking the community with the seaport of Prince Rupert. Pop. (1986) 67,621; (1991) 69,653.

PRINCETON, borough and township, Mercer Co., W central New Jersey, near Trenton. The borough (inc. 1813) is surrounded by the township (inc. 1838); each has a separate municipal government. They are residential and educational centers, being the site of Princeton University (1756; originally founded as the College of New Jersey, 1746), Princeton Theological Seminary (1812), Westminister Choir College (1926), and the Institute for Advanced Study (1930). In the township are many research industries, corporate headquarters, and arboreal nurseries.

The site of Princeton was settled in 1696 by Quakers. Originally called Stony Brook, the community was renamed about 1724 for William III of England, also prince of Orange. A battle of the American Revolution (1777) took place in the area, in which Americans under Gen. George Washington surprised and defeated a superior British force. The first New Jersey state legislature convened (mid-1777) here, and the Continental Congress met from June to November 1783 in Princeton's Nassau Hall (1756). Also of note is Morven (1701), until 1982 the official residence of New Jersey's governor, and Drumthwacket, the present official residence. Borough pop. (1980) 12,035; (1990) 12,016; township pop. (1980) 13,683; (1990) 13,198.

PRINCETON, BATTLE OF, battle of the American Revolution, fought at Princeton, N.J., on Jan. 3, 1777. The forces of Gen. George Washington defeated Hessian troops, German mercenaries allied with the British, in Trenton, N.J., on Dec. 26, 1776. One week later British forces under Gen. Charles Cornwallis advanced along the Delaware River to attack Washington's troops. To thwart British plans, on the night of Jan. 2, 1777, Washington's army moved quickly and quietly around the enemy, leaving the American campfires burning. The next morning Washington advanced toward Princeton, where, joined by reinforcements, he defeated a British regiment that was marching to join Cornwallis. Because he was outmaneuvered, Cornwallis withdrew the British forces to New Brunswick, N.J., and thus was prevented from entering Philadelphia. Washington and his men spent the rest of the winter in Morristown, N.J.

PRINCETON UNIVERSITY, institution of higher learning, in Princeton, N.J.

History. Founded in 1746 as the College of New Jersey, the school was established by the Presbyterian Synod of Philadelphia. Classes were originally conducted in Elizabeth and Newark before the college was moved to Princeton in 1756. The present name was adopted in 1896 after the school became nondenominational. The former U.S. president Woodrow Wilson, a graduate of the university, taught political science there and served as university president from 1902 to 1910. Other noted alumni were the novelist F. Scott Fitzgerald and the critics and literary scholars Edmund Wilson and Christian Gauss (1878–1951).

Undergraduate Activities. Princeton's undergraduate school offers courses leading to the B.A. degree in the liberal arts, natural and social sciences, and engineering. Senior degree candidates are required to write a thesis. Accelerated course programs are available to students who wish to earn degrees in three instead of the usual four years. Since 1905 Princeton has used the preceptorial system, in which formal lectures are supplemented by meetings between professors and small groups of students. All senior faculty members must teach or lecture on the undergraduate level.

A distinctive feature of Princeton undergraduate life is the eating-club system, to which about half of all undergraduate students belong.

Princeton is among the most selective of U.S. colleges. Ninety percent of the entering class were in the top quarter of their high school classes. Women have been admitted to the undergraduate school since 1969.

Graduate and Professional Schools. Princeton offers advanced degrees in the humanities and the social and natural sciences. Among its well-known graduate schools are the School of Architecture and Urban Planning and the Woodrow Wilson School of Public and International Affairs. The renowned Institute for Advanced Study (q.v.), located also in Princeton, shares facilities on a reciprocal basis with the university.

Facilities and Publications. Nassau Hall, one of the original university structures, is the administrative center and campus symbol; when, in 1783, Princeton was the nation's capital, Nassau Hall functioned as the capitol building. The Princeton University Art Museum (1882) houses a full range of Western paintings, ethnographic and Far Eastern art objects, and prints and drawings. Also on campus is the Museum of Natural History (1805). Princeton's library, one of the foremost university collections in the U.S., has more than 3 million volumes. Princeton University Press, founded in 1905, publishes such books as the prestigious Bollingen series of scholarly works on psychology and art. S.D.P.

For further information on this topic, see the Bibliography in volume 28, section 322.

PRINCE OF WALES ISLAND, island, SE Alaska, the largest island of the Alexander Archipelago, in the Pacific Ocean. The island, 5778 sq km (2231 sq mi) in area, is mountainous and heavily forested. The chief settlements on the island are Craig, Klawock, and Hydaburg. Principal industries on Prince of Wales include lumbering, fishing, and canning.

PRINCE OF WALES ISLAND, island, N Australia, in Queensland, the largest of the Torres Strait Islands, off the Cape York Peninsula. The island, about 180 sq km (about 70 sq mi) in area, is rugged and wooded with little fertile soil.

PRINCE OF WALES ISLAND, island, N Canada, in the Northwest Territories, between Victoria and Somerset islands, in the Arctic Ocean. The mostly low-lying island, 33,338 sq km (12,872 sq mi) in area, was discovered in 1851. Its irregular coastline is deeply indented by Browne and Ommanney bays. No permanent settlement has been established.

PRINCE WILLIAM SOUND, inlet of the Gulf of Alaska, S Alaska, bordered on the W by the Kenai Peninsula. Montague Island and Hinchinbrook Island lie at the entrance to the sound, and the chief ports on the Alaskan mainland are Valdez and Cordova. Fishing is a major coastal industry.

PRINCIPAL AND AGENT, in law, voluntary relationship between two parties whereby one, the agent, is authorized by express or implied consent to act on behalf of the other, called the principal. The designated agent can thus affect or conduct the legal affairs of the principal with others, as in the case, for example, of the agreement known as power of attorney. The authorized acts of the agent are thus considered to be the acts of the principal, who is entitled to the benefits, if any, from these actions. The relationship differs from that of master and servant in that the agent is the representative, as well as the employee, of the principal.

Any person who has legal capacity to make contracts can appoint an agent, who in turn must be of legal age and of sound mind. A corporation or a partnership, as well as an individual, can be either principal or agent. The agent may be appointed by actual agreement, or may be acknowledged as such by actions on his or her and a principal's part indicating such a mutual agreement. Obligations of the agent vary according to the particular agreement with the principal, who is generally required to act by specific instructions and is held responsible for wrongful acts of the agent only when they fall within the scope of the legal contract. The agent, besides being paid for services, is entitled to reimbursement for particular expenses.

PRÍNCIPE ISLAND. *See* SÃO TOMÉ AND PRÍNCIPE.

PRINTED CIRCUIT, electrical circuit made by depositing conductive material on the surface of an insulating base. In such circuits a network of fine conductive lines, printed and bonded on a thin ceramic or plastic sheet, replaces the wiring used in conventional circuits. In addition other electrical elements, such as transistors, resistors, condensers, and inductors, that serve to modify the flow of current may be introduced into the circuit by printing or mounting those elements on the same base as the printed wiring. *See* ELECTRICITY; ELECTRONICS; INSULATION; MICROPROCESSOR; TRANSISTOR.

Printed circuits were developed during World War II by the National Bureau of Standards for use in the proximity fuze for artillery shells. Subsequently, the printed circuit found wide use in communication equipment, such as television and radio receivers, radar, and hearing aids, computers, and in instrumentation for guided missiles and airplanes.

PRINTING, name used for several processes by which words, pictures, or designs are reproduced on paper, fabrics, metal, or other suitable materials. These processes, sometimes called the graphic arts (q.v.), consist essentially of making numerous identical reproductions of an original by mechanical means, and the printed book has thus been called the first mass product.

The history of printing, which by its very nature is the most thoroughly documented of any history, is practically identical with that of relief, or letterpress, printing (printing from a raised surface). Historically, the bulk of all printing has been produced by this entirely mechanical method. Modern printing, however, increasingly relies on photomechanical and chemical processes.

Ancient Techniques. The application of signet stones is possibly the earliest known form of printing. Used in ancient times in Babylonia and elsewhere, apparently both as substitutes for signatures and as religious symbols, the devices consisted of seals and stamps for making impressions in clay, or of stones with designs cut or scratched on the surface. The stone, often set in a ring, was dabbed with pigment or mud and pressed against a smooth, resilient surface in order to make an impression.

The elaboration of printing from the simple stamping or signet-stone method to the process of printing on a printing press apparently occurred independently at different times in different parts of the world. Books copied by hand in ink applied with pen or brush were a significant feature of the Egyptian, Greek, and Roman civilizations. Such handwritten books were also produced in medieval monasteries and were greatly valued (*see* ILLUMINATED MANUSCRIPTS). In ancient Rome, commercial book publishers issued editions comprising as many as 5000 copies of such works as the epigrams of the Roman poet Martial. This copying work was done by literate slaves.

Printing in the East. By the 2d century AD the Chinese had developed and put into fairly widespread use the art of printing texts. Like most inventions, it was not entirely new, because the printing of designs and pictures on textiles had preceded the printing of words in China by at least a century.

Two important influences that favored the development of printing by the Chinese were their invention of paper (q.v.) in AD 105 and the spread of the Buddhist religion in China. The common writing materials of the ancient Western world, papyrus (q.v.) and vellum, were not suited to printing. Papyrus is too fragile to be used as a printing surface, and vellum, a thin tissue taken from inside the hides of newly skinned animals, is an expensive material. Paper, on the other hand, is relatively strong and inexpensive. The Buddhist practice of making many copies of prayers and sacred texts encouraged mechanical means of reproduction.

The earliest surviving examples of Chinese printing, produced before AD 200, were printed from letters and pictures cut in relief on wood blocks. In 972 the Tripitaka, the sacred Buddhist scriptures comprising more than 130,000 pages, was printed entirely from wood blocks. A Chinese inventor of this period progressed beyond wood blocks to the concept of printing entirely from movable type, that is, from individual characters arranged in sequence as in present-day printing. Because the Chinese language requires between 2000 and 40,000 separate characters, however, movable type did not seem practical to the early Chinese, and the invention was abandoned. Movable type made from molds was invented separately by the Koreans in the 14th century, but they also found it less practical than the traditional block printing.

Printing in the West. Movable metal type was first cast in Europe and printed with a printing press on paper by the middle of the 15th century. The invention appears to have been unrelated to earlier developments in the Far East, and the techniques differed considerably in detail. Whereas Eastern printers had used water-soluble inks, Western printers used oil-based inks from the beginning (*see* INK). In the East, printers made impressions simply by pressing the paper against the wood block with a flat piece of wood. The earliest Western printers in the Rhine River valley used mechanical presses derived in design from winepresses, and made of wood. The Eastern printers who had used movable type held the letters together with clay or with rods pushed between the types. Western printers developed a technique of casting types with such precision that the letters could be held together by pressure applied to the edges of the tray containing the type for the page. In this system, a single letter a fraction of a millimeter too big could cause the letters surrounding it to fall out of the page. The development of a method of casting letters to precise dimensions was the essential contribution of the Western invention.

The principles involved in printing had been used by European textile workers, in printing designs on cloth, for at least a century before printing on paper was invented. The art of papermaking, introduced into the West in the 12th century, spread throughout Europe in the 13th and 14th centuries. By the mid-15th century paper was available in abundance. During the Renaissance, the rise of a prosperous and literate middle class increased the demand for quantities of reading matter. The rise of Martin Luther and of the Reformation and the subsequent religious wars were heavily dependent on the printing press and on the steady stream of printed pamphlets.

Johann Gutenberg, of the German city of Mainz, is traditionally considered the inventor of Western printing. The date associated with the invention is 1450. Both Dutch and French historians of printing have attributed the invention to people in their own countries and have produced considerable supporting evidence. The books of the first Mainz printer, however, particularly the book known as the Gutenberg Bible, far surpass in beauty and artisanship all the books that reputedly preceded them. Gutenberg's great accomplishment undoubtedly contributed decisively to the immediate acceptance of the printed book as a substitute for the handwritten or manuscript book. Books printed before 1501 are said to belong to the incunabula (q.v.) era of printing.

In the period between 1450 and 1500, more than 6000 separate works were printed. The number of printers increased rapidly during the same period. In Italy, for example, the first press was established in Venice in 1469, and the city had 417 printers by 1500. In 1476 a Greek grammar was printed wholly in Greek type in Milan, and a Hebrew Bible was printed at Soncino in 1488. Also in 1476 printing was brought to England by William Caxton; in 1539 Juan Pablos (d. 1561?) set up a press in Mexico City, bringing printing to the New World. Stephen Day, a locksmith by profession, came to Massachusetts Bay in 1628 and helped established the Cambridge Press. He is often considered the earliest printer in the New England region. In 1639 *The Freeman's Oath,* a broadside, was issued from this press, followed in 1640 by the *Whole Book of Psalmes* or *Bay Psalm Book* and an almanac.

A print shop, 16th-century illustration in the Book of Trades, *by Jost Amman.* **Metropolitan Museum of Art–Rogers Fund**

The printers of northern Europe produced mostly religious books, such as Bibles, Psalters, and missals. Italian printers, on the other hand, printed chiefly secular works, for example, the newly revived Greek and Roman classics, the stories of secular Italian writers, and the scientific works of Renaissance scholars. An important early use of printing was in pamphleteering: in the religious and political controversies of the 16th and 17th centuries propaganda pamphlets were widely circulated. The production of these pamphlets made considerable work for the printers of those days.

Printing Presses. The machine used to transmit the ink from a printing plate (q.v.) to the printed page is called a press. The first printing presses, such as those of the 16th century and earlier, were screw-type presses designed primarily to bring pressure on the printing form, which was placed face up in a flat bed. The paper, generally dampened, was pressed against the type by the movable surface, or platen. The upperparts of the osts of the press often were braced against the eiling, and after the form was inked the platen vas screwed down against the form. The press vas equipped with rails on which the form could e slid out of the press and then back onto the ed, so that the platen did not have to be raised ar. Nevertheless, the operation was slow and umbersome; such a press produced only about 50 impressions an hour, printing only one side f the paper at a single impression.

In the 17th century springs were added to the ress to aid in lifting the platen rapidly. Presses nade of iron were introduced about 1800, and bout that time levers were substituted for the crews that brought the platen down onto the ed. These levers were of necessity rather comlex; the first portion of travel on the lever bar ad to bring the platen down most of the way, nd the last portion of travel of the bar had to nove the platen the remainder of the distance nd apply great pressure. Although the best andpresses of this period produced only about 00 impressions an hour, much larger forms ould be used with metal presses than with vooden ones, and therefore the press operator roduced many more pages at each impression. or a discussion of folio, quarto, octavo, and the arger multiple-page production processes, *see* BOOK.

During the 19th century improvements included the development of the steam-powered press; the cylinder press, which uses a revolving cylinder to press the paper against a flat printing form; the rotary press, in which both the paper and a curved printing plate are carried on cylinders; and a practical perfecting press, which prints on both sides of a sheet of paper simultaneously. Large-circulation daily newspapers require a number of these presses side by side printing identical material simultaneously. In 1863 the American inventor William A. Bullock (1813–67) patented the first web-fed newspaper press, which printed from paper in rolls rather than sheets. In 1871 the American printer Richard March Hoe (1812–86) perfected the continuous roll press; his device produced as many as 18,000 newspapers in an hour.

Book Illustration. Painters had hand-illustrated manuscript books for centuries; with the advent of printing, artists cut their designs in wood and metal, enabling Renaissance printers to reproduce pictures as well as text on their presses. Among the notable Renaissance artists who made book illustrations were the Italian Andrea Mantegna and the Germans Albrecht Dürer and Hans Holbein the Younger. The widespread reproduction of their works markedly influenced the development of Renaissance art.

Typefaces, Steel Presses, and Typesetting Machines. Up to the 19th century many beautiful typefaces were created and presswork was perfected. (For a more complete account of the de-

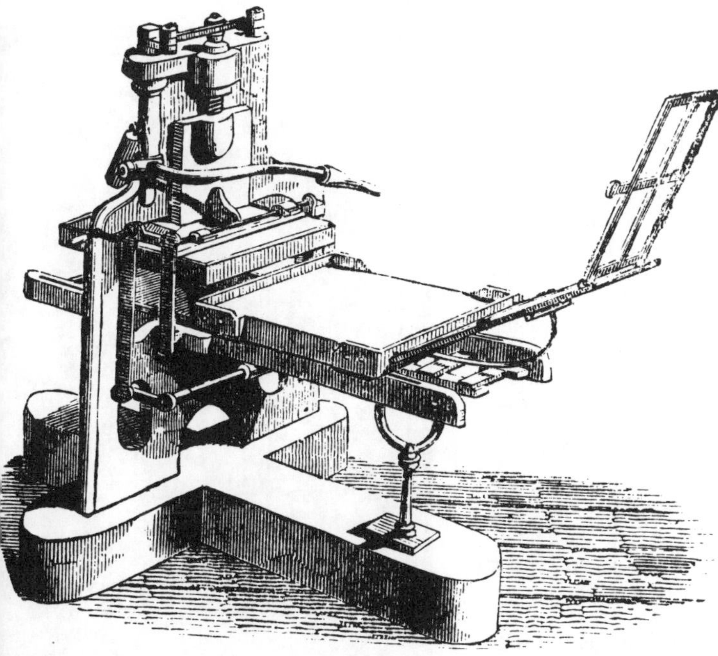

The Stanhope press, invented in the 18th century by Charles Stanhope. Bettmann Archive

The perfecting printing press, developed in the 19th century by Richard March Hoe, was the first to print from rolls of paper rather than from sheets. Bettmann Archive

velopment of typefaces, *see* TYPE.) Around 1800, however, developments in printing began to emphasize increased speed. Charles, 3d earl of Stanhope (1753–1816), introduced the first printing press made entirely of steel. In 1803, in London, the brothers Henry Fourdrinier (1766–1854) and Sealy Fourdrinier (d. 1847) installed their first papermaking machine; they produced a continuous roll of paper, satisfying a steadily increasing demand. Then, in 1814 the steam-driven printing press was invented by Friedrich König (1774–1833), and the whole printing industry was revolutionized. The large editions that now became possible were further extended in 1829 by the introduction of practical stereotypes, by which duplicate printing plates of type that has been set can be made. In 1886 typesetting machines were perfected that cut the time needed to set a text to a fraction of that required to set it by hand. (For a discussion of the various methods of setting type developed during and since the 19th century, *see* TYPESETTING EQUIPMENT.) Finally, photography contributed to the development of modern photomechanical processes.

In the 1950s, the first phototypesetting machines appeared. They produced photographic images of type instead of casting them in metal. These images are photographed with a graphic-arts camera to produce film negatives that are then used to make lithographic plates. Improvements in plate technology in the 1950s and '60s combined with phototypesetting to end the 500-year reign of letterpress as the premier printing process. Hot-metal typesetting has all but disappeared, but relief processes are still widely used. Most relief printing plates are now made by direct photomechanical means. *See* PHOTOENGRAVING; PRINTING TECHNIQUES.

Computers today can generate images for printing, reducing the time and expense required to produce printing surfaces for all the major processes. Computers are now routinely used to create artwork, set type, scan and retouch photographs, and merge all of these elements together on a single piece of film or directly on the printing plate. *See* OFFICE SYSTEMS. E.R

For further information on this topic, see the Bibliography in volume 28, sections 23–24.

PRINTING PLATE, surface from which printing is done. Three configurations are possible. Relief

Photopolymer printing plates, made in both rigid and flexible types, have a sensitive composition and reduce exposure time. E. I. du Pont de Nemours & Company

plates have raised image areas to which ink is applied by rollers and then transferred either directly or indirectly (offset) to paper or other material. Hard metal or plastic relief plates are used in the letterpress process; soft rubber or plastic, in the flexographic process. Planographic plates have image areas on the same plane as the nonimage areas and therefore require that the nonimage areas be treated to repel ink. Intaglio plates have image areas recessed below the nonimage areas. Ink is applied to the entire plate and then wiped from the smooth nonimage surface with a steel blade. The ink remaining in the recesses is transferred to the paper during printing. *See also* LITHOGRAPHY; PHOTOENGRAVING; PRINTING TECHNIQUES. F.C.

PRINTING TECHNIQUES, several different ways in which printing (q.v.) may be accomplished, such as lithography, letterpress, flexography, gravure, and screen printing. All of these printing techniques use simple mechanisms for rapidly applying colorants to substrates such as paper or plastic to form multiple reproductions of original images for mass distribution.

Multiple colors can be printed in one pass through the press. Spot color printing uses custom mixed inks to reproduce specific colors and is widely used in package printing, where large areas of uniform color are common. Process color printing uses four transparent inks—cyan (blue-green), magenta (red), yellow, and black—printed one on top of another in varying amounts. Color photographs and other artwork can be faithfully reproduced by this method.

Most modern printing presses transfer ink from a cylindrical printing surface to moving sheets or rolls of substrate. Presses that print on rolls, or webs, can achieve speeds of 600–900 m (2000–3000 ft) per minute. Presses that print on sheets are generally slower than web presses but can print on thicker substrates, such as bristol board and sheet metal.

Since the 1960s, advancements in photography and electronics have had a profound effect on the manufacture of printing surfaces. Light-sensitive materials such as diazonium resins and photopolymers make it possible to produce durable printing surfaces photographically rather than mechanically. Computer-based systems allow the rapid production of the films used to transfer images to printing surfaces. Some printing surfaces can even be prepared directly by machines employing computer-controlled laser beams or diamond styluses. Images generated on computer systems and stored in databases can now be transferred directly to printing surfaces without any intermediate steps. Taken as a whole, these changes have been called the prepress revolution. *See* PHOTOENGRAVING.

LITHOGRAPHY

By far the most important and versatile printing process today is offset lithography. The underlying principles were established at the end of the 18th century by a German map inspector, Aloys Senefelder (1771–1834), who was experimenting with methods of producing limestone relief printing surfaces using an acid etching process. Senefelder found that a wet limestone surface would repel an oil-based printing ink, and that an image drawn on the surface with a grease pencil would repel water and attract ink. Any drawing on the stone surface could be reproduced by bringing a damp sheet of paper into contact with the freshly inked image. This cycle could be repeated several hundred times before the drawing could no longer be faithfully reproduced.

The process, called chemical printing by Senefelder, quickly became a popular art medium because it enabled artists to produce multiple copies of freehand drawings. By the late 19th century, multiple stones were being used to transfer as many as 30 separate colors to a single sheet of paper to produce exquisite color lithographs that resembled fine watercolor paintings. Modern color lithography uses only four inks for a wide range of natural colors.

The Offset Principle. In the early part of the 20th century, it was discovered that ink could be transferred from the lithographic surface to an intermediate rubber surface and then to paper. The rubber intermediate, called a blanket, can transfer ink to paper and to a wide variety of materials that cannot be printed directly, including plastics and metals. Because the soft blanket conforms to the texture of the surface to be printed, lithographic image quality is unrivaled.

Offset Lithography Today. The function of the original stone printing surface is now served by thin aluminum plates, although other materials, such as stainless steel and plastic, can also be used. The plates are wrapped around the circumference of the printing cylinder and make direct contact with the rubber blanket cylinder. Rubber rollers carry ink and water to the plate surface. The ink is transferred first to the blanket cylinder and then to the paper.

Lithographic plates are the least expensive printing surfaces available today, and this fact has contributed greatly to the success of the process. Aluminum plate materials have a thin surface coating of light-sensitive material, such as a photopolymer, that undergoes a solubility change when exposed to an intense source of

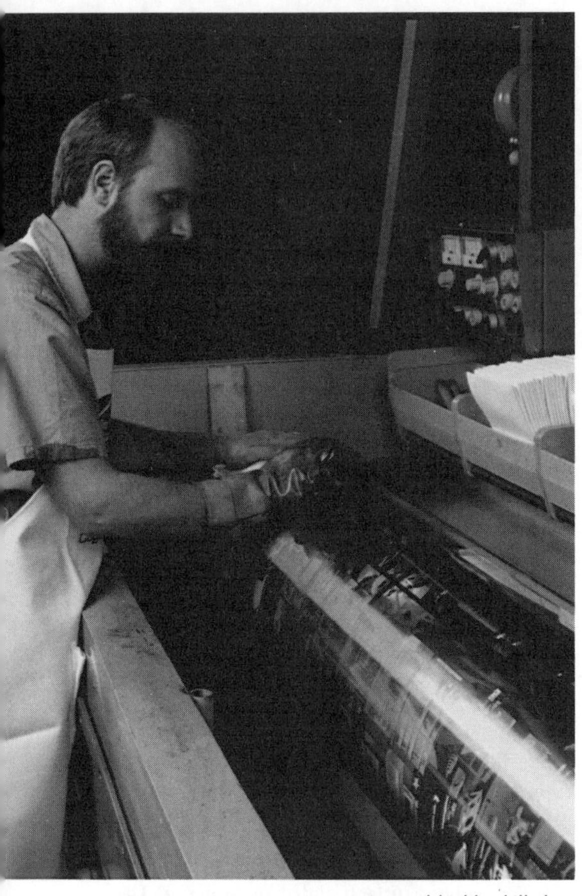

Gravure printing is an expensive and highly skilled process but is widely used in long-run products, such as magazines, catalogs, and advertising sections for newspapers. Left: A prepress technician prepares a cylinder for the press. Right: Results can be checked with a proof press. Courtesy of R. R. Donnelley & Sons Company

blue and ultraviolet light. Images are transferred to the surface by exposing the plate through a film positive or negative (*see* PHOTOGRAPHY). Some materials can be exposed directly, as in a graphic-arts camera or by a computer-controlled laser beam, thereby eliminating the expense of film and speeding up the platemaking process.

Modern offset lithographic presses range in size from small sheet-fed duplicators—used for small, single-color jobs such as brochures and newsletters—to massive web presses capable of printing millions of copies of magazines, catalogs, mailing pieces, and packaging materials in full color. No other process has such a broad range of applications.

See also LITHOGRAPHY.

RELIEF PRINTING

Relief printing processes work on the same principle as a rubber stamp. Ink is applied to the raised portions of the printing surface, and is then transferred by pressure to paper or some other substrate. Two forms of relief printing—letterpress and flexography—are currently in use, distinguished by the physical characteristics of their printing surfaces and inks. Letterpress printing is accomplished using a hard metal or plastic printing surface and a highly viscous ink. Flexography employs a soft rubber or plastic printing surface and a fluid ink.

Letterpress Printing. Letterpress, the oldest form of printing, originated with the invention of movable metal type (*see* TYPE) in the middle of the 15th century and was for five centuries the only viable mass printing process. In the mid-20th century, letterpress printing, despite its superiority in the clarity of impression and in the density of ink, lost its predominance to lithography, a much faster process.

Originally, letterpress printing surfaces were prepared by assembling thousands of pieces of metal type on which individual letters or letter combinations were cast in relief to create pages of text called type forms. Ink was applied to the raised areas of the form and then transferred under pressure to paper or vellum. Woodcuts and engravings could be combined with type to produce composite pages containing both text and graphics.

Duplicate Plates. The first letterpress printing plate was created by making a plaster mold of a type form and then casting a metal duplicate of the original, called a stereotype. Stereotyping became an extremely important technology during the Industrial Revolution because it yielded a one-piece printing surface that could be used in place of the original type form on a variety of automated printing presses. Curved stereotypes cast from papier-mâché molds were used on rotary letterpresses for printing daily newspapers until the early 1970s, when hot-metal machine typesetting was largely replaced by computer typesetting. *See* TYPESETTING EQUIPMENT.

Another important duplicate plate, called an electrotype, was made by electroplating a thin layer of copper onto a wax impression of the original type form and then filling the resulting copper shell with type metal. Electrotypes retained more detail from the original relief surface than stereotypes and were therefore preferred to stereotypes for higher-quality letterpress printing.

Photopolymer plates. In the late 1950s a radical new way of making relief printing surfaces was introduced; it employed a soluble plastic that hardened upon exposure to ultraviolet radiation. Since then a large number of photopolymer plate materials have been created. A thick coating of photopolymer on a metal or plastic support can be exposed to ultraviolet light through a piece of film that allows the light to pass through only those areas that will transfer ink. The photopolymer hardens, or polymerizes, in these areas, and the remaining unexposed coating is washed away with water or some other solvent. The result is a relief printing surface that can be mounted directly on a printing press.

In a variation of this process, a liquid photopolymer that solidifies when exposed to ultraviolet radiation is spread on a paper or plastic support. After exposure the unexposed liquid is blown away with air. These plates can be made rapidly and are therefore most suitable for newspaper printing, where deadlines are critical.

High-speed rotary web presses and photopolymer plates have allowed letterpress to remain competitive in some areas, such as in newspaper printing, despite the fact that lithography is now the uncontested leader among printing processes.

Flexographic Printing. The soft plates and highly fluid inks used in flexography make the process ideal for printing on nonporous materials such as foil laminates and polyethylene. Originally, all flexographic plates were made of molded rubber, which is still the preferred material when multiple copies of the same image are needed on a single printing cylinder. Rubber plate molds are impressions of original relief surfaces, such as type forms or engravings, and are normally used to make several duplicate rubber plates. The preparation of a printing cylinder using molded rubber plates is a time-consuming process because many rubber plates are mounted on a single cylinder and each plate must be carefully positioned in relation to the others.

In the 1970s photopolymer plate materials were introduced, and the time required to manufacture and mount a set of plates was reduced significantly. This has allowed the process to enter new markets, most notably newspaper printing. In addition, water-based inks can be used in flexography, eliminating the need for toxic solvents.

Flexographic printing presses are simple in design because the fluid ink is easily distributed to the printing surface without an elaborate inking system. Printing is usually done on rolls or webs of substrate rather than on cut sheets, and the printed rolls are then converted into finished products in a separate manufacturing process.

GRAVURE

Gravure, also called rotogravure, is a high-volume printing process employing an ink transfer mechanism that is fundamentally different from that of relief printing. The printing surface is a polished metal cylinder covered with an array of tiny recesses, or cells (as many as 50,000 per sq in), that constitute the images to be printed. The cylinder, which can be 2.5 m (8 ft) or more in length, is partially immersed in a reservoir of solvent-based fluid ink. As the cylinder rotates, it is bathed in ink. A steel blade called a doctor blade running the entire length of the cylinder wipes the ink from the polished surface, leaving ink only in the cells. The ink is then transferred immediately to a moving web of paper forced against the cylinder under great pressure.

Gravure cylinders are constructed of steel with a thin surface layer of electroplated copper. The copper can be either chemically etched or electronically engraved to form the cells that will transfer ink. Once the cells have been created, the cylinder is electroplated with a thin layer of chromium to produce a hard surface for the

Web presses are large rotary presses in which the operations may be completely automatic. The mini-web offset press shown here is used mainly for short-run book production. Courtesy of R. R. Donnelley & Sons Company

doctor blade. Each cell transfers a tiny spot of ink to the paper. The cells can be made to vary in depth from one part of a cylinder to another, causing the darkness of the resulting ink spots to vary also. This enables gravure to print a wide range of gray tones and thus to render excellent reproductions of photographic originals.

Color printing is accomplished by using separate printing cylinders for the cyan, magenta, yellow, and black inks. Each cylinder is housed in a separate printing unit. The web is transported by rollers from unit to unit and can reach speeds of close to 900 m (3000 ft) per minute. After each color is printed, the web passes through a dryer, where the solvent base of the ink is evaporated. The solvent is either reclaimed or burned to produce energy. Some gravure printers have begun to use water-based inks. This trend is likely to continue because of health and environmental threats posed by the use of hydrocarbon-based solvents.

The expense of manufacturing a set of gravure cylinders has restricted its use to long-run jobs (millions of reproductions). Mass-circulation monthly magazines, mail-order catalogs, and packaging are natural markets for the process. Gravure is also used to reproduce a variety of textures and patterns on decorative materials. Most of the simulated wood grains on inexpensive furniture, for example, are printed by gravure. New methods of manufacturing gravure cylinders using computer-controlled electronic engraving machines have reduced the time required to prepare a set of cylinders, but they are still far more expensive than lithographic printing surfaces.

Intaglio printing is a specialized process related to gravure that employs engraved rotary printing surfaces of steel to print currency, bonds, stock certificates, and high-quality business stationery. Ink is transferred from engraved recesses on the printing surface directly to sheets of paper transported through the press. Intaglio printing excels at reproducing artwork that consists of fine lines and small solid areas. It cannot be used to reproduce photographic images or to print large unbroken solids. The use of paste ink and deeply recessed printing surfaces gives intaglio printing a distinctive raised texture. (Powdered resins can be heat-fused to freshly printed wet lithographic or letterpress inks to simulate this effect at far less expense, which is why "engraved" business cards and stationery are usually produced in this manner.)

SCREEN PRINTING

Originally called silk-screen printing because of its silk-based stencils, screen printing has become important in the production of a wide array of manufactured items, including decorative panels, printed circuit boards, touch-sensitive switches, plastic containers, and printed garments. Stencils for commercial screen printing are usually produced by photomechanical means. A fine synthetic fabric or metal mesh is stretched over a rectangular frame, and a photopolymer coating is applied to the entire surface. Exposure of the photopolymer through a film positive causes it to harden in the areas not intended to print. The unexposed material is then washed away to create the open areas of the stencil. In the printing press, this screen is pressed against the surface to be printed, and ink is forced through the open areas of the stencil with a rubber squeegee.

Presses for screen printing range from simple manual devices for the small-scale printing of T-shirts and banners to large sheet-fed presses for multicolor, high-volume commercial applications. The process is distinguished by its ability to print finely detailed images on practically any surface, including paper, plastics, metals, and three-dimensional surfaces. It is also the only major printing process that is routinely used to produce images that are not meant to be viewed. The circuit patterns in touch-sensitive switch panels, for example, are screen-printed with special conductive inks.

ELECTRONIC PRINTING PROCESSES

All the processes previously discussed employ a fixed printing surface that transfers the same pattern of ink during each cycle of the press. Simple physical ink-transfer mechanisms allow these processes to operate at high speed. Because of the high cost of making a set of plates, mounting them on the press, and running the press until the printing is in register (properly aligned) and colors are correct, these processes require fairly long press runs to be economically feasible. For short-run printing—especially of highly variable information, electronic processes are more economical. These processes do not use printing plates, and they produce good reproductions without wasting paper.

Electrophotographic Printing. Modern electrostatic office copiers have a printing surface that can be instantaneously formed by photographing or scanning an original. The surface is coated with a photoconductive material such as selenium or cadmium sulfide. In the dark, a photoconductor acts as an insulator, retaining a charge of static electricity. Areas of the surface illuminated in a camera or by a laser beam become conductive and lose their charge. The remaining areas retain their charge, attracting oppositely charged particles of colorant called toner. The toner is then transferred to a piece of paper or plastic using electrostatic forces rather than pressure. This cycle is repeated for each copy, making the process far too slow and complicated for mass printing applications. For small quantities, however, some color electrophotographic printers can reproduce color originals with image quality that approaches that of offset lithography. *See also* OFFICE SYSTEMS.

Ink-jet Printing. A computer-controlled array of ink nozzles can produce images on a moving

Types of early American rotogravure presses.

The increasing demand for full-color printing has been met through the development of ultrasophisticated color separation scanners such as the one seen here. The machines separate colors for printing by a combination of laser and computer technology. HCM Graphic Systems, Inc.

sheet or a web of paper. Simple ink-jet printers are used routinely to print variable information such as the expiration dates on food packages or address labels on direct mail pieces, and are sometimes installed on the end of a conventional printing press. Sophisticated color ink-jet printers are able to produce lithographic-quality reproductions in extremely short runs.

Microcapsule Printing. This technology uses paper impregnated with billions of microscopic capsules of liquid photopolymer-based dye. The paper is exposed to light reflected from an original image, and the dyes inside the capsules harden in proportion to the amount of light they receive. The exposed paper is then pressed through steel rollers against a receiver paper, and varying amounts of unhardened dye are deposited on the receiver to form an image. The process can be used to make high-quality color reproductions in small quantities.

Thermal Sublimation and Wax-Transfer Printing. Computer-controlled arrays of heating elements can transfer dyes or wax layers from a plastic ribbon to a piece of receiver paper. The high cost of materials and the slowness of thermal processes have restricted their use to applications in which only a few copies are required.

The emerging relationship between traditional printing and electronic printing is more complementary than competitive. Digital color printing processes are increasingly used to predict the appearance of images before they are processed into films and plates for lithography, gravure, or relief printing, thus reducing the likelihood that changes will be necessary after the job has reached the press.

See also PRINTING PLATE. F.C.

For further information on this topic, see the Bibliography in volume 28, section 23.

PRINTS AND PRINTMAKING, pictorial images that can be inked onto paper, and the art of creating and reproducing them. The two basic categories of prints are those that are made photomechanically, such as newspaper and magazine illustrations or reproductions of original art sold in museum shops and other stores, and those created by hand for limited reproduction by any of several techniques that require artistic skills and special materials.

TECHNIQUES OF PRINTMAKING

The graphic artist can use any of several hand-printing methods: relief, intaglio, planographic, monotype, or stencil. The terms *fine print* or *original print* are used to describe the finished work.

Relief Printing. In relief printing, the artist carves the image into a block of wood, either as a woodcut or as a wood engraving.

Woodcut. This is the oldest method of printmaking. For centuries the basic technique of relief printing has been the cutting away of a portion of the surface of a wood block so that the desired image remains as a printing surface. The most popular wood is pine; fruitwoods such as cherry and pear can also be used, but the surfaces of maple and oak are too hard for cutting. The surface, first smoothed, may be hardened by treating it with a shellac, which makes it more durable under the pressure of a press and facilitates the carving of strong, bold images. The artist may paint or draw the image on the surface; the wood is cut away between the drawn lines, and only the drawn image is left standing on the surface of the block. In essence, this is a relief image.

A roller holding a film of oil-based ink is rolled completely over the block. A sheet of paper—ideally a highly absorbent type such as rice paper—is placed over the block, and the artist may then print the image by hand rubbing the surface with the bowl of a spoon or with any other burnishing instrument. The block and paper may also be run through a press; under the pressure of the press the image is transferred to the paper. The impression is pulled by carefully lifting a corner of the paper and peeling it off the block. Separate blocks are used for color woodcuts, with one block for each color.

Wood engraving. Historically, the wood engraving was chiefly used for illustrations in magazines and books. It is similar to the woodcut, but in the wood engraving, the artist uses a graver to incise the image directly into an end-grain block (or cross section) of wood. Boxwood is commonly used, but cherry and pearwood are also suitable. These woods have naturally hard surfaces that allow the artist to create extremely detailed images with fine lines. By varying the spaces between the engraved lines, the artist can build subtle tonal effects and can create the highly illustrative quality associated with this medium. A printer's ink of stiff consistency is cautiously applied to the surface, so that the ink does not fill the engraved lines. A sheet of thin, smooth paper is placed on the block and printed, either by hand or by running it through a press.

Intaglio Printing. Intaglio printing is the opposite of relief printing, in that the image is cut or incised into a metal plate with various tools or with acids. The wide variety of methods used gives this medium its enormous range. The two basic types of intaglio printing are engraving the image into the plate with finely ground tools called needles, burnishers, scrapers, and rockers; and etching the image with acids.

Engraving. In an engraving, the artist, by the placement and thickness of the line, determines either a dense and detailed image, or an image with a sketchy or feathery quality. After the image is cut into the plate, soft ink is applied with a roller across the entire plate, making certain that all the incised lines are filled with ink.

Engraver's Tools *(1974), copper engraving by Armin Landeck. Included in this semiabstract design are representations of an engraver's protective goggles, as well as burins (or gravers), punches, burnishers, scrapers, hammers, and the copper plates on which all these instruments are used.*
Associated American Artists

Then the surface of the plate is carefully wiped clean, leaving behind only the ink held in the drawn lines or crevices. The plate is then placed on the bed of the press; dampened paper is placed over the plate, and felt blankets or padding are laid on top of the paper. Under the pressure of the rollers from the press, the paper and padding draw the ink up from the incised lines onto the paper.

Etching. To make an etching, a metal plate is coated with an acid-resistant wax-base substance called a ground. An etching needle, which has an extremely fine point, is used to draw the image on the plate. The surface ground is removed wherever the point of the needle makes contact with the plate. The plate is immersed in a tray containing an acid bath. The acid bites into the plate in the lines exposed by the etching tool; the length of time the plate is exposed to the acid determines the strength of the line.

Aquatint. Aquatint, an intaglio process similar to etching, produces a print of an entirely different appearance. Large segments of the plate are exposed to the acid bath, creating tonal areas rather than lines. Aquatint prints date from the 18th century, when artists endeavored to recreate the effect of water-color and wash drawings in prints. To create an aquatint, certain areas of the plate are sprinkled with resin, then heated to make the resin adhere to the plate surface. The plate is then immersed in a mild acid, which bites the areas of the plate not covered with resin. If the artist wishes some areas to be darker than others, those areas are exposed to the acid somewhat longer. The plate surfaces exposed to acid become pitted and thus retain the ink more readily. The aquatint method is often difficult to control and is usually used in combination with etching and drypoint techniques.

Drypoint. Drypoint technique is similar to line engraving. A pencillike tool, usually with a diamond point, is used to draw an image on an untreated copper or zinc plate. Each movement of the tool makes a furrow with a soft metal ridge on either side called a burr, pushed up from the plate by the tool. The artist endeavors to retain the fragile burr throughout printing, because the burr holds the ink and results in a print with rich, velvety lines. The delicacy of the burr and the continuous pressure of the press seldom allow more than 20 to 30 impressions to be printed before the burr is lost. As in the aquatint process, the drypoint print is produced by inking the plate, wiping it clean, placing dampened paper over the plate, and putting the plate through the press.

The art of Francisco José de Goya y Lucientes. With or Without Reason, *one of the series of etchings entitled The Disasters of War.*

Raphael Soyer's lithograph Bowery Nocturne *(1933) derives immediacy and strength from its dramatic contrasts between light and dark.* Associated American Artists

Mezzotint. Another technique used in intaglio printing is the mezzotint. The primary tools are various scrapers and the mezzotint rocker, a heavy instrument with a semicircular serrated edge. When the tool is rocked over a copper plate, the edge leaves serrated "teeth" marks. Each movement of the rocker, in effect, leaves the surface covered with burr. In this long and tedious process, the artist completely covers the surface, first working the rocker in one direction, then at right angles to the first direction, then in diagonal directions, and finally once more between the diagonals. If the plate were inked and printed at this stage, the image would be a solid velvety black. The artist creates the image by working a scraper over the surface of the plate, reducing or in some cases completely eliminating the teeth created by the rocker. When the burnishing is complete, the plate is inked and printed. The gradation of tone from solid black areas to pure white gives the mezzotint the striking contrasts for which this medium is best known.

Planographic Printing—Lithography. In planographic printing the image is created directly on the surface of a stone or a metal plate without cutting or incising it. The most common method is called lithography, a process based on the incompatibility of grease and water. Traditionally, the material used for lithography is a special limestone, usually from Bavaria, that is quite heavy and often expensive. Limestone is sensitive to water, particularly in the open areas of the surface left untouched. Zinc or aluminum plates, however, are also often used.

The artist first draws the image on a freshly ground surface with a grease crayon or with a pen or brush loaded with thin greasy ink. A mixture of nitric acid and gum arabic is then applied to the entire surface to increase the stone's ability to hold water in a thin film all over. Next, water is poured or wiped over the entire surface; the water is repelled by the grease of the crayon marks but is absorbed elsewhere. When a roller impregnated with greasy ink is passed over the surface, the ink adheres to the greasy drawn areas but is rejected by the wet part of the surface. After the stone is placed on a press and paper is applied, the pressure of the press transfers the image to paper.

Monotype Printing. The monotype is a unique print; only one good impression can be pulled from a plate. The artist draws an image with oils or watercolors, or inks, on virtually any smooth surface. Glass is most often used, but a polished copper plate or porcelain can also be employed. The image can be created either by painting it on the surface directly or by the reverse process: first covering the plate completely with an even coat of pigments and then carefully rubbing this away with the fingers or with a brush to form the image. Paper is then applied to the plate and the image is transferred either by rubbing the back of the paper or with the use of an etching press.

Stencil Printing. Although the stencil process was used in ancient Rome, its greatest popularity began in the U.S. during the 1960s, when many artists expressed themselves with blocks of pure color and hard-edged imagery. A stencil is a cutout with open and closed areas. The easiest way to create a stencil is to cut the desired image into paper; the design appears as an open space with solid areas around it. The completed stencil is then placed over a piece of paper, and paint is brushed over the surface. Only the cutout portion will allow the paint to pass through and reproduce the image below.

In producing a silk screen—also called serigraph or screenprint—a piece of silk or comparable porous material is stretched tightly across a wooden frame. The artist creates the image by painting the surface of the silk with glue. The entire surface is then sealed with a lacquer. When dry, the underside of the screen is rubbed with water along the drawn areas; the glue dissolves and is peeled away, leaving the areas of the design exposed. Paper is then placed beneath the screen. Ink is pushed across the entire surface of the screen with a squeegee, and as the squeegee passes over the exposed areas (from which the glue has been removed), the ink is deposited below and the design is transferred to the paper.

PRINT AND PRINTMAKING TERMS

Printmakers, print dealers, and print collectors use six terms that are necessary for the comprehension of prints.

Edition. The number of images printed from the plate, stone, block, or the like is called an edition. These identical images are pulled either by the artist or, under the artist's supervision, by the printer. The body of the edition is numbered—as, for example, 1/100 through 100/100—directly on the print, usually in pencil. Additional proofs, such as artist's proofs, are also part of the edition.

Numbering. Numbering indicates the size of the edition and the number of each particular print. Therefore, 25/75 means that the print is the 25th impression from an edition of 75.

Artist's Proofs. Artist's proofs are those impressions from an edition (see above) that are specifically intended for the artist's own use. These impressions are in addition to the numbered edition and are so noted in pencil as *artist proof* or *A/P.*

Restrike. A subsequent printing from an original plate, stone, or block is called a restrike. Restrikes are usually printed posthumously or without the artist's authorization.

States. Once the artist has drawn an image, he or she may pull several prints. If the artist subsequently changes the image, the first prints are called *first state,* and the subsequent prints with the change, *second state.* The artist can continue to make changes, with the number of states going as high as ten or more.

Catalogue Raisonné. A scholarly reference text in which each print known to have been executed by a particular artist is completely documented and described is a catalogue raisonné. The information given may include title, alternate titles, date, medium, size of the edition, image size, paper used, and other pertinent facts. The term is also used for similar catalogs of paintings, sculptures, drawings, watercolors, or other works by a single artist or workshop.

HISTORY OF PRINTMAKING

Printmaking originated in China after paper was invented (about AD 105). Relief printing first flourished in Europe in the 15th century, when the process of papermaking was imported from the East. Since that time, relief printing has been augmented by the various techniques described earlier, and printmaking has continued to be practiced as one of the fine arts.

Chinese Stone Rubbings and Woodcuts. Stone rubbing actually predates any form of woodcut. To enable Chinese scholars to study their scriptures, the classic texts and accompanying holy images were carved onto huge, flat stone slabs. After the lines were incised, damp paper was pressed and molded on the surface, so that the paper was held in the incised lines. Ink was applied, and the paper was then carefully removed. The resulting image appeared as white lines on a black background. In this technique lies the very conception of printing. The development of printing continued with the spread of Buddhism from India to China; images and text were printed on paper from a single block. This method of combining text and image is called block-book printing.

The earliest known Chinese woodcut with text and image combined is a famous Buddhist scroll, about 5 m (about 17 ft) long, of the Diamond Sutra (AD 868, British Museum, London). These early devotional prints were reproduced from drawings by anonymous artisans whose skill varied greatly. The crudeness of the images indicates that they were reproduced without any thought of artistic interpretation, but as was to be true in Europe during the 1400s, such early works of folk art were important in the development of the print.

Toward the end of the Ming dynasty in the 1640s, there appeared a text called *Painting Manual of the Mustard-Seed Garden.* This was actually an encyclopedia of painting, intended for the

Two Geishas Out Walking, *woodcut by Kitae Shigemasa. This print shows the long, flowing lines and elegant, elongated forms characteristic of early prints of the Ukiyo-e ("pictures of the floating world") school. The multicolor printing technique, invented in 1765, allowed subtle and delicate color effects.*

Metropolitan Museum of Art–The Henry L. Phillips Collection. Bequest of Henry L. Phillips, 1940

instruction and inspiration of artists. Many of its beautiful instructive woodcuts were in color as well as in black and white. A reprint edition of the *Painting Manual* was brought to Japan, and with it came the basic woodcut technique, which Japanese artists gradually developed.

Japanese Prints. The history of Japanese prints is inextricably linked with the art history of China and the relief technique invented there.

Early Japanese woodcuts—Ukiyo-e. The style of Japanese graphic art that emerged in the middle of the 18th century is known as the Ukiyo-e (q.v.), or "pictures of the floating world," school. Early Ukiyo-e prints were black and white. Created for a popular audience, they were the ephemera of the day, akin to postcards. Certain prints were made for home decoration; others often set the style of the day for fashion and behavior. Color printing from multiple blocks was soon introduced. Flat, solid shapes and dramatic color, design, and composition characterize these later Ukiyo-e prints. The popular theater of Japan, kabuki, helped the Ukiyo-e print to flourish; portraits of the most famous actors in dramatic roles were particular favorites. The artist most associated with this period is Tōshūsai Sharaku (fl. 1790–95). His prints are highly melodramatic, emphasizing exaggerated facial lines and beautiful costumes.

Another popular Ukiyo-e subject was the genre scene. Harunobu concentrated on the beauty of young women, depicting them with grace and poetic charm. Perhaps the most outstanding artist to concentrate on the female figure was the inventive Utamaro, who created imagery that is often intimate and candid in na-

The Milkmaid *(1510), an engraving by Lucas van Leyden.*
Art Institute of Chicago–Clearence Buckingham Collection

ture, with a lyrical quality of line, delicate compositional detail, and assured draftsmanship.

19th-Century Japanese prints. In the 19th century the emphasis shifted from figurative to landscape subjects. The unsurpassed masters of landscape imagery were Hokusai and Hiroshige.

An artist who frequently signed his work "The Man Mad About Painting," Hokusai was preoccupied with landscape. His fascination with every aspect of nature led him to detail seasonal changes; studies of birds, waterfalls, waves, insects, fish, trees, and mountains culminated in a famous 13-volume sketchbook called *Hokusai manga* (begun 1814).

Hiroshige stressed the quality of line and also achieved extraordinary effects with color against color. The gradation from intense coloration to the merest hint of color, along with a highly stylized form, characterize Hiroshige's astonishing prints. Among his most notable works are several sets of prints depicting travelers on the Tokaido Highway (1804) and the *Sixty-nine Stations on the Kiso Highway.*

By 1856 Hokusai prints had been discovered in Paris, and many others soon surfaced. The enthusiasm they stirred created a wave of *japonisme* that was to last in Paris for the next 40 years and to become a significant influence on modern art.

Gothic Prints. With the establishment of paper mills in several areas of Germany, France, and Italy in the 15th century, the first woodcuts were made in the Western world. The earliest Gothic images were crudely cut from blocks of wood, inked, and printed. The first prints were made to be used as playing cards, then a popular means of entertainment; they were sold for pennies and could be produced in large quantity. Because much of Gothic life centered around the church, the clergy used prints for devotional purposes and distributed them among the people. The images consisted mostly of saints and depictions of the life of Christ and of the Virgin Mary; they also illustrated numerous Bible stories. With the development of movable type, block books became popular, and illustrations could be combined with text. Once a good and inexpensive paper was manufactured, the quality of printing improved, and many editions of illustrated books were published.

Renaissance Prints. The most illustrious artist of the Renaissance in northern Europe was Albrecht Dürer. Born in Nuremberg and trained as a goldsmith, he became the first great graphic master. His phenomenal versatility with the graver and woodcut knife, along with his keen observation of nature and his devotion to prints, brought him uccess and the admiration of his contemporaries. Of particular note are his numerous series of religious prints and such magnificent single prints as *Knight, Death, and the Devil* (1513).

The Dutch engraver Lucas van Leyden (1494–1533), greatly influenced by Dürer and by the classical style of his Italian contemporaries, gently depicted Dutch landscape and interior scenes. They are important as the foundation of the Dutch school of painting in the following century. The Italian graphic masters Andrea Mantegna—better known for his paintings—and Marcantonio Raimondi created classical images with a distinctive sense of composition, detail, and sensitivity. Engraving in France and Spain during this time was negligible.

By the mid-16th century, prints had become very popular. They were used for all manner of illustrations, including topographical survey, and for portraiture.

Baroque Prints. Baroque artists of the 17th century felt that an image could be more than just the depiction of reality; it could have a powerful emotional impact. Gesture could become highly characterized, exaggerated even to a point of being grotesque.

Virgin Seated by a Tree *(1513), wood engraving by Albrecht Dürer.*
Parke-Bernet Galleries

Seventeenth-century French engraving and etching are most notably represented by the work of two artists from vastly different schools. Robert Nanteuil (1625?-78) produced distinguished court portraits; these highly popular engravings brought greater attention to the sculptural, molded quality and delicate strokes that could be produced in this medium.

Quite different was Jacques Callot, from the province of Lorraine, who was the first major artist to develop the potential of the etching medium. He discovered that various additional bitings of a plate could create perspective in a print, giving the image a foreground, middleground, and background. His experimentation in special grounds made it possible for work of intense detail to be etched into a tiny plate. With this technical proficiency, Callot created extraordinary imagery in a wide variety of subjects. Kings of France and Spain commissioned Callot to document various historical events. From his wartime etchings Callot issued his own bitter and devastating series of prints, *Miseries of War* (1633).

For a time Callot joined a band of gypsies, resulting in his *Commedia dell' arte* (1618) and *Gobbi* (1622) series of prints. Here he captured the grotesque, often humorous images of dwarfs and beggars in a variety of costumes and poses. Many print connoisseurs consider Callot's views of cities and country fairs to be among his best work. Among these is the print *Fair at Impruneta* (1620); in this one large-scale image, Callot captured more than 1000 figures.

Callot did much for the advancement of the medium, but Rembrandt stands out as the baroque graphic master. Accomplished in rendering a wide range of subjects from portraits and religious scenes to landscapes, Rembrandt produced prints of both power and subtlety, such as *Self-Portrait of the Artist Leaning on a Stone Sill* (1639).

The Dutch school of graphic artists flourished with portraits, landscapes, interior studies, and scenes of daily life. Ferdinand Bol (1616-80), Adriaen van Ostade (1610-85), and Anthony Waterloo (1609?-76?) pictured Dutch life in etchings. Bol made many fine portraits; van Ostade was noted for his depictions of Dutch peasant life; and Waterloo created beautiful landscapes.

The Antwerp workshop of the Flemish master Peter Paul Rubens was very active. From the pages of the master's sketchbooks and drawings, various artists produced a veritable flood of prints. Anthony van Dyck, Rubens's most talented pupil, settled (1632) in England as the court painter to Charles I. Van Dyck undertook, with artist collaborators, to etch 128 portraits of the most famous men of his day. The *Iconography* (c. 1634-41), as it is called, is marked by sparseness of line and technical excellence.

18th-Century European Prints. At the turn of the 18th century, Paris was the artistic center of Europe. Such artists as François Boucher and Jean Honoré Fragonard documented court life in drawings and sketches; influential publishers then had these made into engravings, which proved extremely popular.

Until the 18th century England had not developed great strength in the graphic arts. Academic paintings of the nobility and aristocracy were popular, and these images were reproduced beautifully through the mezzotint medium. While the portraitist Sir Joshua Reynolds continued to dignify academic tradition, a triumvirate of English satirists headed by William Hogarth worked against this tradition. James Gillray, Thomas Rowlandson, and Hogarth used engraving to satirize almost every aspect of 18th-century England. In tone, they ranged from gentle moralizing to savage commentary and occasional bawdiness.

During the 18th century the graphic arts once again flourished in Italy, as exemplified in the work of Giovanni Battista Tiepolo, Antonio Canale, known as Canaletto, and Giovanni Battista Piranesi. Tiepolo is noted for his delicacy of line and the spacious quality achieved through economy of line and detail. Canaletto's solid draftsmanship, coupled with a lightness of line, enabled him to capture the courtyards, canals, and beautiful architecture of 18th-century Venice. With an architect's background and his expertise with the graver, Piranesi found a channel for interpreting his passion for Roman antiquities. He created several thousand prints, but of particular note is the series *Carceri d'Invenzione* (1745; 2d ed. 1760). These are large-scale views of imaginary prisons in spectacular architectural detail, combining the eeriness of a dungeon with huge vaulted ceilings, endless staircases, and massive interior bridges.

19th-Century European Prints. In the 19th century, leading artists produced an extraordinary range of prints. Spain's Francisco de Goya, for example, combined aquatint with etching to produce bluntly truthful visions of the follies of humankind and the heinous acts of war. Goya's highly individualistic style comes across most characteristically in the print series *Los Caprichos* (The Caprices, 1797-99), in which he is almost ferocious in his attacks on the clergy and on the government for its wealth, corruption, and hypocrisy. During the French occupation of Spain

Scene of Paris, Le Petit Pont, *by the 19th-century French artist Charles Méryons.* Metropolitan Museum of Art

in the Peninsular War (1808–14), Goya created his second most famous series of prints, *Desastres de la guerra* (Disasters of War, 1810), horrifying images of the hideous fate of people caught in war.

In Paris, lithography provided the inexpensive means to reproduce images on a large scale in the form of prints, periodicals, and book illustrations. Honoré Daumier was the true voice of the middle class; his particular gift was for political satire and social commentary, and the corrupt reign of Charles X was perfect fuel for his powerful wit. Periodicals such as *Le Charivari* carried his acute, biting observations on government, the legal profession, and the upper classes and their many foibles.

A strong school of romantic landscape painting developed in England during the early decades of the century, with Joseph Turner and John Constable as its most notable artists. In this milieu, William Blake produced several books of mystical verse with his own unique and strange illustrations. Blake's masterpieces are his illustrations for the Book of Job (1826).

Prominent among mid-19th century French artists was the melancholic figure of Charles Méryon. More important than Méryon's technical acumen in etching was the manner in which he saw his adored city of Paris, in particular the oldest sections slated for demolition. He portrayed the charm and elegance of these old buildings in a highly dramatic manner.

From the 1860s to the end of the century, the Japanese print exerted an enormous influence on the art and artists of the time. According to tradition, the Parisian artist Félix Braquemond (1833-1914) received a set of porcelain from Japan, and found that the plates had been wrapped with the prints of Hokusai. Braquemond enthusiastically showed the prints to his impressionist artist friends, who were intrigued by their flat, bold, asymmetrical composition. Edgar Degas' lithographic scenes of women bathing and dressing are reminiscent of the Japanese style. Henri de Toulouse-Lautrec was perhaps the most striking and original exponent of *japonisme*. Employing the subtle to brilliant coloration and the cropping of images characteristic of Japanese prints, he designed posters that capture the essence of charm and elegance.

Through the influence of the poster artist Jules Chéret (1836-1932), color lithography grew in popularity. The beautiful color lithographs of Pierre Bonnard and Édouard Vuillard portray Parisian scenes as well as the intimacies of family life. Along with Chéret's work, that of Théophile Steinlen (1859-1923) and Toulouse-Lautrec made posters (q.v.) powerful mediums for advertising.

Elles *(1896), a lithographic poster by Henri de Toulouse-Lautrec. French printmakers of this period were widely influenced by the asymmetrical graphic techniques of Japanese printmakers, such as the sweeping lines and quick, sharp strokes of the lithographic crayon shown here.* Joseph Martin–Scala–Editorial Photocolor Archives

The Czech artist Alphonse Mucha, in his stylish posters, emphasized the sensuous line and the decorative quality that was characteristic of the turn-of-the-century Art Nouveau (q.v.) movement.

The passionate and masterly Norwegian artist Edvard Munch created woodcuts and lithographs marked by powerful, highly personal imagery. His women are often lush and sensuous, while other images, including his men, are fraught with anxieties and inner tension.

20th-Century European Prints. The many art movements that have coursed through this century are unusual in their diversity and number, and also in their rapid development. They include Fauvism, cubism, expressionism, surrealism, abstract expressionism, op art, pop art, and superrealism; printmakers have played a part in all these movements.

At the turn of this century Paris still reigned as the center of Western art and printmaking. A group of postimpressionists exhibited their paintings at the 1905 Salon d'Automne, among them Henri Matisse, Georges Rouault, and André Derain. Critics called them Fauves (*see* FAUVISM), literally "wild beasts." These youthful artists sought to use color in a totally unrestrained fashion, which, with the exception of Matisse's graphic works, carried over into their prints. Matisse's most important prints, however, are black-and-white lithographs. In his many odalisques (models posed as harem beauties), Matisse chose a highly decorative background filled with a patterned design, while his model was dressed in an exotic Persian-style costume. This rich, opulent atmosphere suggests, in black and white, the intensity of vivid color.

Fairy with a Splendid Headdress *(1935), drypoint by Henri Matisse.* Associated American Artists

Model and Large Sculptured Head *(1933), etching by Pablo Picasso.* Sotheby Parke Bernet–Editorial Photocolor Archives

Cubism (q.v.), which translated the realistic image into abstract form by dissolving it into cubic elements and by crisscrossing shapes and planes, was the joint achievement of the French artist Georges Braque and the Spaniard Pablo Picasso, who worked together beginning in 1909. Founded on the qualities of superb draftsmanship, Picasso's earliest prints (1904) speak of directness and compassion, and evoke a somber and sentimental nature. In 1930 he was commissioned by the publisher Ambroise Vollard (1865–1939) to issue a series of 100 prints, the famous *Vollard Suite* (pub. 1937), one of the artist's greatest graphic achievements. The subject matter of these etchings and aquatints ranges from the artist's studio and model to sensuous and emotional depictions of minotaurs, and to portraits of Vollard himself. Other artists who produced important cubist prints were Braque, Jacques Villon (1875–1963), Juan Gris, and Louis Marcoussis (1883–1941). Each worked to achieve a warm and harmonious relationship between the etched line and overall tonal quality.

Surrealism (q.v.), which sought imagery that welled up from the unconscious and from dreams, produced a number of famous printmakers, exemplified in the work of the Spaniard Joan Miró, whose color lithographs have a delightfully whimsical quality. A similar whimsicality, with bizarre overtones, is found in works by André Masson (1896–1987) and Yves Tanguy. In 1910 Marc Chagall came to Paris from Russia. Throughout a long career Chagall distinguished himself as a painter and printmaker, combining a folkloric, naive charm with rich, dreamlike imagery. Chagall's major graphic achievements are the early series *My Life* (1922), the 105 etchings illustrating the Bible (1956), and the 100 etchings (1948) for the novel *Dead Souls* by the Russian writer Nikolay Gogol.

At the turn of the century, German artists developed expressionism (q.v.)—a style emphasizing subjective emotions and responses to the external world—in reaction against French impressionism and postimpressionism. As in the Gothic tradition, the immediacy and boldness of the woodcut made it a perfect medium. One group of Dresden-based artists was called Die Brücke ("The Bridge"), which consisted of Ernst Ludwig Kirchner, Karl Schmidt-Rottluff, Erich Heckel (1883–1970), and Otto Mueller (1874–1930). Their styles varied from striking contrasts of sections of roughly gouged wood, in Schmidt-Rottluff's cartoonlike prints and Heckel's harsh portraits, to Mueller's lyrical composition of female figures. *See* BRÜCKE, DIE.

In Munich another group, Der Blaue Reiter ("The Blue Rider"), emerged, led by the Russian-born Wassily Kandinsky. Together with the Swiss artist Paul Klee, Der Blaue Reiter artists developed a refined abstraction, in which rhythm of line and a dramatic sense of color dominated, with an absence of representational objects. Klee, a unique genius, soon chose to work alone in Switzerland; he used images with seemingly childlike, naive qualities to create highly sophisticated personal statements with universal implications in the guise of fantasy. *See* BLAUE REITER, DER.

Early American Prints. In colonial America the decorative arts rather than the graphic arts flourished. There was, however, an interest in portraiture; the first mezzotint in America, dated 1728, is a portrait of the noted clergyman Cotton Mather by Peter Pelham (1697–1751).

After the American Revolution, more diversified subject matter developed. Engravings were made to commemorate famous battles, to depict historical events, and to honor generals and noted statesmen. Perhaps the best-known American historical print of this period is the silversmith Paul Revere's *Boston Massacre* (1770). Most early American prints were made by professional engravers who almost always relied on paintings for their subject matter. Prints also became a vehicle for the spread of political and social ideas.

19th-Century American Prints. By the 1800s the first truly American printmaking movement had come into being. Topographical imagery was popular, as were genre scenes of American farm and city life. The most outstanding prints created during the 1820s and '30s were the remarkable engravings by Robert Havell, Jr. (1793–1878), for John James Audubon's folios of American birds (pub. 1827–38).

Because they were less costly to produce, lithographs soon became more popular than engravings.The first private American concern to sell prints was founded by Nathaniel Currier (1813–88). He and his partner, James Ives (1824–95), became "printmakers to the American people" (*see* CURRIER & IVES).

Winslow Homer began his career as a magazine illustrator for *Harper's Weekly.* He eventually created two masterful engravings, *Eight Bells* (1887) and *Perils of the Sea* (1888), based on two of his best-known canvases. The most important American printmaker of the last half of the 19th century was James Abbott McNeill Whistler. He learned etching technique at the U.S. Coastal Survey in Washington, D.C. About 1860 Whistler moved to England, where he soon began creating his famous series of prints of London, Paris, and Venice. His experimentation with technique and refinement of compositional details earned Whistler a high position in printmaking.

Mary Cassatt, an artist from Philadelphia, went to study in Paris and settled there. An early impressionist, she developed expert technique in drypoint, etching, and aquatint. She further expanded her oeuvre by endeavoring to re-create the quality of the Japanese woodblock print in a series of color aquatints in which areas of soft color are combined with decorative patterning; these rank among her most famous prints.

Childe Hassam and Maurice Prendergast were America's important impressionists. Hassam concentrated on etching, using short staccato strokes within a firm design. Predergast for a short time produced monotypes. His subtle and refined palette was well suited to this spontaneous and demanding method of printmaking.

20th-Century American Prints. The Ashcan school was America's first art movement to break away from European styles. The etchings of John Sloan and Edward Hopper and the lithographs of George Bellows were the first American prints to catch the vitality of urban life in all its aspects, from squalor to grandeur.

Rockwell Kent's wood engraving Sea and Sky *(1931) is a powerful linear design.* Associated American Artists

The Armory Show (q.v.) exhibition of 1913 brought modernism to American printmakers; the repercussions of the show influenced American artists for many years to follow. John Marin's *Brooklyn Bridge Swaying* (1913) is one of the earliest American prints to break away from traditionalism. In this work, the vibrancy and swerving energy of the etched line and the semidistortion express the artist's moods and the emotions aroused during the work's creation. Lyonel Feininger, through the boldness of the woodcut medium, also created abstract patterns that convey his intense personal involvement.

During the depression of the 1930s, evocations of the American scene came into vogue. The Midwest regionalists Thomas Hart Benton, John Steuart Curry, and Grant Wood epitomized rural America in stylized detail in their prints. Reginald Marsh, Isabel Bishop, and their teacher Kenneth Hayes Miller (1876–1952) were the best-known members of the so-called Fourteenth Street school of New York City's Greenwich Village. This street, during the 1930s, was a lively commercial area; its office girls, shoppers, and panhandlers were vividly captured by all three artists in their prints. Miller was an influential teacher at the Art Students League; his students—Marsh, Bishop, Bellows, and others—each developed a highly personal view of New York. Raphael Soyer (1899–1987) continued to make prints in the realistic tradition, with many lithographs and etchings of young women—dancers and models.

Recent Trends. The English artist Stanley William Hayter (1901–88) established and ran, from 1927 to 1940, a Paris workshop called Atelier 17 to teach etching and engraving. Atelier 17 was transferred to New York in 1940 and remained in operation for 15 more years, becoming the mecca for creative intaglio printmaking. The technical innovations that later came from such artists as Mauricio Lasansky (1914–), Antonio Frasconi (1919–), and Gabor Peterdi (1915–) were a direct result of Hayter's inspiration.

In the 1960s the specialized workshop for the graphic artist became important. The most influential was the studio run by Tatyana Grosman (1904–82) on Long Island, where major artists gathered to make prints. This arrangement was so successful that a close working relationship between master printer and artist developed in several other studios. The Tamarind Lithography Workshop, founded in California by June Wayne (1918–) and now located in New Mexico, became an important creative center for graphic artists. Many of the best contemporary artists have been drawn to such centers, including Larry Rivers, Josef Albers, and such abstract expressionists (*see* ABSTRACT EXPRESSIONISM) as Robert Motherwell, Robert Rauschenberg, Jasper Johns, and Jim Dine (1935–). Printmaking workshops are now spread across the country, mostly located at major colleges and universities.

Drawing away from the vision of the abstract

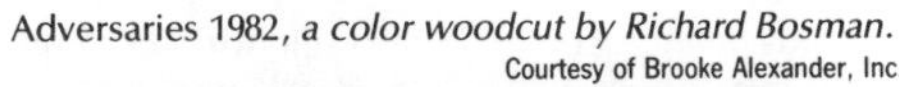

Adversaries 1982, *a color woodcut by Richard Bosman.* Courtesy of Brooke Alexander, Inc.

expressionists were young artists of the pop culture (*see* POP ART). Here material from the mass media—magazines, newspapers, films, and photographs—were combined impersonally and repetitively, often resulting in imaginative imagery. Through the use of advertisements and other mundane images, artists such as Andy Warhol, Roy Lichtenstein, and Robert Indiana (1928–) set out to challenge graphic tradition.

See also BOOK; ILLUSTRATION; LITHOGRAPHY; PHOTOGRAPHY; PRINTING; PRINTING TECHNIQUES; XEROGRAPHY. For additional information on individual artists, see biographies of those whose names are not followed by dates. S.Co.

For further information on this topic, see the Bibliography in volume 28, sections 643, 671, 715.

PRION, type of tiny particle, consisting solely of protein, that was identified and named by the American neurologist Stanley B. Prusiner (1942–). Prusiner and his colleagues found the particles in the brains of sheep that had died of the disease called scrapie. The particles occurred in protein plaques that had formed in the sheep's brains. Similar plaque formation is observed in a number of animal diseases, such as bovine spongiform encephalopathy, and in human diseases such as kuru and Creutzfeldt-Jakob disease. The possibility therefore exists that prions are implicated in such diseases. Prusiner proposed that prions themselves are infectious agents, although how they might reproduce inside an organism remains unexplained. The concept of prions as infectious particles has generally not been accepted by the scientific community, and the causative agents of the diseases concerned are more widely considered to be "slow viruses" not yet identified.

PRIOR, Matthew (1664–1721), English poet and diplomat, born in Wimborne, Dorset, and educated at the University of Cambridge. In 1687 he collaborated with the English statesman and poet Charles Montagu in writing a highly successful parody of the allegorical poem *The Hind and the Panther* by the English poet John Dryden. The work made Prior famous. He entered diplomatic service in 1690, sat in Parliament in 1701, returned to diplomacy in 1710. After the fall of the Tory party in 1714 he was impeached as a result of political dissatisfaction over diplomatic negotiations with France. During two years of semi-imprisonment he continued his writing. Prior is known for the elegance and wit of his light, amorous verse. A humorous long poem, "Alma; or, The Progress of the Mind," was written during his imprisonment and published in 1718, together with an earlier serious work, "Solomon on the Vanity of the World."

PRIPYAT, river, E Europe, rising in the Pripet Marshes, near Kovel, in NW Ukraine. About 805 km (about 500 mi) long, it flows E into S Belarus, then SE, entering the Dnepr R. near Kiev, Ukraine. The river is navigable for about 483 km (about 300 mi); it is connected to the Bug, Vistula, and

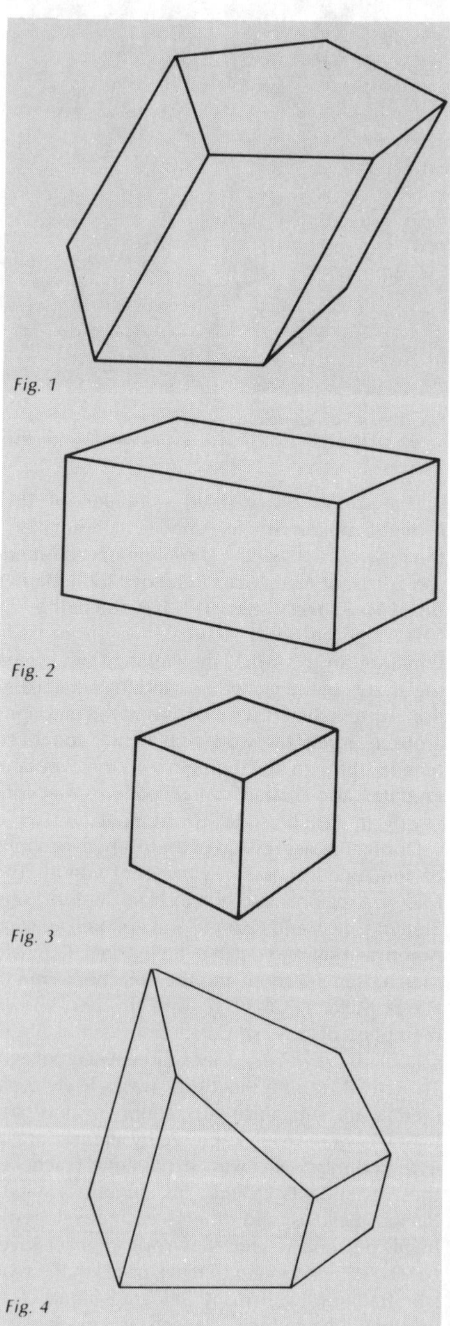

iemen rivers by canals. Large parts of the basin f the river were reclaimed for agriculture.

RISCIAN, full name PRISCIANUS CAESARIENSIS (fl. about AD 500), Roman grammarian, born in Caesaria, Mauretania (now Cherchell, Algeria). He taught Latin in Constantinople. His great work is a Latin grammar entitled *Institutiones Grammaticae,* the first 16 books of which treat ounds, word formation, and inflections; the last wo, constituting nearly one-third of the whole work, deal with syntax. The grammar, written in atin, contains quotations from Greek and Roman authors whose writings have not otherwise urvived. The work became the standard text for eaching grammar in medieval schools.

RISM, in geometry, three-dimensional solid, of which the bases are two parallel planes. The aces of the prism in these planes are congruent polygons. The lateral faces of the prism are parallelograms (see Fig. 1). The intersections of the ateral faces, called the lateral edges, are parallel o each other. A prism is called a right prism if the ateral edges are perpendicular to the bases; if hey are not, it is called an oblique prism. A prism s triangular, square, and so on, according to whether its bases are triangles, squares, or some other geometrical figure. A parallelopiped is a prism that has parallelograms as the bases; a rectangular parallelopiped, or box, is one in which all six faces (four lateral faces and two bases) are rectangles (see Fig. 2); in a cube (q.v.) the six faces are squares (see Fig. 3).

The altitude of a prism is the perpendicular distance between the planes of the bases. A truncated prism is that portion of a prism between a base and a section formed by a plane not parallel to the base but cutting all lateral edges (see Fig. 4). The volume, V, of a prism is given by the area, B, of a base multiplied by the altitude, h; in symbols, $V = Bh$. If a, b, c are the lengths of three edges of a rectangular parallelopiped that meet at one vertex, the volume is given by $V = abc$. In particular, if a is the length of one of the twelve equal edges of a cube, the volume of the cube is $V = a^3$ and its total surface area, S, is $S = 6a^2$.

See also CYLINDER; GEOMETRY; SOLID GEOMETRY.

J.Si.

PRISON, institution for the confinement of persons convicted of crimes. *See* CRIME; CRIMINOLOGY.

Throughout history, most societies have built places in which to hold persons accused of criminal acts pending some form of trial. The idea, however, of confining persons after trial, as punishment for their crimes, is relatively new. In ancient times, and indeed through approximately the 15th century in Europe, the penalties for crime were generally some type of corporal punishment, ranging from whipping or periods in the stocks (q.v.), for less serious crimes, to execution or enslavement, for serious offenses. Some few persons, charged with or convicted of crimes against the state, were incarcerated for life in recognition of their high rank and as a "reduction" of the death penalty.

Early History. In 16th-century England, vagrants and petty offenders were committed to correctional institutions known as workhouses. During the reign of Queen Elizabeth I, the government began transporting convicted felons to the English colonies, a practice that continued for some 200 years. The punishment was initially thought of as the hard labor to which the prisoners were consigned; the housing provided for them was merely incidental. The idea, however, that persons convicted of crime could be punished (and confined), and then released after a relatively long period of time, was a new concept. Jails in England first served as collection points for criminals awaiting transportation.

Beginning in the 17th century, England and other European countries—including Italy, Germany, and the Netherlands—began imprisoning debtors, delinquent juveniles, minor misdemeanants, and felons. Early jails were mostly dark, overcrowded, and filthy. Prisoners were herded together indiscriminately, with no separation of men and women, the young and the old, the convicted and the unconvicted, or the sane and the insane. Agitation for more humanitarian treatment of prisoners arose gradually during the 18th century. In Great Britain the social reformer John Howard led the movement for prison reform that culminated in the passage of

An inmate of the Seagoville (Tex.) Correctional Institution, on a work-release assignment, mills pistons in a Dallas aircraft plant. Dehnel–Bureau of Prisons

The Stateville Correctional Center, a state prison in Joliet, Ill., is the largest walled prison in the U.S. and the only one with round cell houses. Illinois Dept. of Corrections

legislation providing for improvement of prison sanitation and separate confinement of the sexes.

Early American Prisons. In America, the concept of imprisonment came to fruition. Spurred by deep religious beliefs, the English Quaker William Penn, founder of the colony of Pennsylvania, abolished the death penalty for most crimes in the late 1600s, substituting imprisonment as a punishment. The colonists, however, were compelled by the British government in 1718 to reinstate the death penalty. In 1789, shortly after independence, the Pennsylvania legislature replaced capital punishment (q.v.) with incarceration as the primary punishment for felons; the Walnut Street Gaol, in Philadelphia, became the first prison in the U.S. By the mid-19th century, most states had followed suit.

Two models soon emerged in the states. The first system began in Auburn State Prison in New York in 1817. Prisoners worked together in total silence during the day, but were housed separately at night. Strict discipline was enforced, and violators were subjected to severe reprisals. The second model, the Pennsylvania system, begun in 1829 in the Eastern State Penitentiary at Cherry Hill, was based on solitary confinement for convicts by day and night.

Vigorous debate erupted between proponents of the two systems. Those favoring the Pennsylvania model focused on its hope of rehabilitation, the theory being that a felon, alone in a cell with only the Bible to read, would soon become penitent (hence the term *penitentiary*). The Auburn system was criticized as being virtual slavery, because prisoners there were often put to work for private entrepreneurs who had contracted with the state for their labor. Furthermore, prisoners were never paid, thus leaving handsome profits for the business owners and the state. Advocates of the Auburn system, however, alleged that the idleness of the prisoners in the Cherry Hill penitentiary sometimes caused madness. Proponents of the Auburn system stressed the activity of the prisoners and the profits from their labor, which meant the state did not have to finance the prison.

Most states found the argument based on profit irresistible and adopted the Auburn approach. European countries, however, emulated the Pennsylvania model, primarily as a result of a report by the French writer Alexis de Tocqueville, who went to the U.S. to investigate the two systems so as to inform the French government of their respective merits.

The Goal of Rehabilitation. The primary objective of both the Auburn and Pennsylvania systems was the confinement of prisoners for the duration of their sentences. Thus, the facilities themselves were usually massive institutions, with high stone walls, substantial perimeter security, and restriction of prisoner movement; some of those prisons are still in use. By the mid-19th century, however, penologists began to argue that prisoners could and should be rehabilitated while incarcerated.

In 1870 the National Congress on Penitentiary and Reformatory Discipline (now known as the American Correctional Association) met for the first time in Cincinnati, Ohio. The congress adopted a set of principles for corrections, chief of which was the primacy of the goal of rehabilitation. This led to the establishment for juvenile offenders of so-called reformatories, championed by the American penologists E. C. Wines (1806-79) and Zebulon Brockway (1827-1920). Although their attempts to rehabilitate were relatively unsuccessful, the goal of rehabilitation changed the criminal justice system in the following decades. Probation and parole (qq.v.), work release, community corrections, and even a separate system of procedures and courts for dealing with juvenile offenders can all be traced to the ideals first enunciated in 1870. *See* JUVENILE COURT; JUVENILE CRIME.

Restrictions on prison labor. Concomitantly, the industrial prison of the Auburn model was coming under increasingly severe attacks. It had always been opposed by private business, which considered the unpaid prison labor unfair competition. Early trade unions in the North also challenged the idea, but with little effect. As labor influence grew in the late 19th and early 20th centuries, however, dramatic changes occurred. By the 1920s, labor critics, joined by the humanitarian critics, achieved their aim of severely restricting prison labor. The U.S. Congress enacted the Hawes-Cooper Act (1929), which divested prison-made goods of the protection afforded by the Interstate Commerce Act and made such goods subject to state punitive laws. During the depression of the 1930s, Congress completed the task by prohibiting transport companies from accepting prison-made products for transportation into any state in violation of the laws of that state. This legislation, the Ashurst-Sumners Act (1935), effectively closed the market to goods made by prisoners, and most states then terminated prison industry.

Changes in the prison system. Confronted with thousands of prisoners who would otherwise be idle, American prison systems rapidly reembraced the idea of rehabilitation as the principal goal of incarceration. Social scientists, moreover, sought to provide methods by which prisoners could be classified according to their likelihood of rehabilitation, so that their specific needs could be articulated. The fortresslike prison was recognized as being unsuitable for prisoners who could truly be reformed, and a wide variety of institutions, including reformatories, work camps, and minimum-security prisons were established. By the 1960s this general trend was augmented by the concept of community corrections, in which prisoners would work in the communities by day, but return to an institution (sometimes only a private home leased by the state) at night. Work-release centers, community

A prisoner in the Nassau Co., N.Y., jail writes letters during free time. UPI

correctional centers, and halfway houses, all with minimal security, were established.

Rehabilitation programs. Programs such as vocational training, guidance counseling, and psychotherapy were begun within the prison system to achieve the major goal of rehabilitation. In 1975, however, a study of more than 240 such programs essentially concluded that none was truly successful in reducing the recidivism rate (that is, the rate of repeat offenders). Although this study was immediately criticized by some, many penologists have agreed with its basic conclusion that participation in these programs was often not really voluntary, because prisoners hoped parole boards would look favorably on those who enrolled. Most penologists also now agree that rehabilitation is not a proper reason for imprisoning someone. Concomitant with these changing views, a movement was begun to preclude parole boards from knowing whether or not a prisoner has participated in such a program. Thus, rehabilitation is no longer the only, or even the main, objective of corrections agencies.

Prison Population and Housing. In theory, the U.S. prison system today consists of a variety of institutions, each adapted to the characteristics and risks posed by its population. In fact, however, that is not the case. A recent survey showed that more than 50 percent of all prisoners continued to be housed in maximum-security facilities, even though penologists agree that no more than 15 percent of the population requires such secure housing. Similarly, only 11 percent of the prison population is housed in minimum-security institutions, even though correctional-systems personnel are virtually unanimous in their belief that at least one-third of all prisoners could safely be housed in such facilities. Pronounced differences exist between these two kinds of prisons.

Maximum-security institutions are massive buildings, with high masonry walls or electrified fences, in which the primary concern is security. Prisoners are under constant surveillance; their movements are severely restricted, and many are required to remain in their cells almost the entire day. Outdoor recreation is minimal, and visits, when allowed, are often conducted by telephone, with a glass partition between the prisoner and the visitor.

Minimum-security prisons, on the other hand, are often built on a campuslike arrangement, which allows prisoners autonomy and freedom within broad bounds. Prisoners may have rooms with opaque doors rather than cells that are under constant surveillance. Visits are usually private and rarely monitored; close contact with visitors is encouraged in order to enhance the prisoner's ties with family and community. Some prisons have even experimented with conjugal visitation, allowing the prisoner to spend up to 72 hours with a spouse and other family members in separate housing, such as a trailer. Such visitation programs are common in the Scandinavian countries.

In the U.S., a major impediment to modernizing the prison housing system is the burgeoning American prison population. In 1945 approximately 133,000 persons were confined in state and federal prisons and reformatories. This figure rose slowly to about 180,000 in 1971; in the following years the prison population escalated sharply to more than 500,000 by mid-1986. In view of these increases, prison personnel have been concerned with the immediate problems of overcrowding and the tensions this causes, rather than with the long-range issues of establishing a new housing pattern for convicted criminals.

Prison Organization. All American prison systems today are highly centralized, in contrast to the situation in the last century, when each prison was managed as a separate institution, without regard to other facilities in the same state. This centralization has generally led to increased professionalism among wardens and other prison staff members. In earlier days, wardens were selected on the basis of political favoritism, often without any qualifications, training, or experience in corrections.

The jails that are used to hold persons pending trial, or those serving sentences of less than one year, are typically not part of the state prison system. They are managed individually by the districts or counties in which they are located. Only a few states have an integrated prison and jail system, which allows for much greater flexibility in placing short-term prisoners in locations near their homes. Most local jail systems still reflect the same kind of political patronage that until recently characterized the prison systems: The county sheriff or other person assigned to manage the jail often has little experience in or concern about corrections. This system has been severely criticized by many penologists, who have stated that the jails are the worst part of the U.S. penal organization.

Efforts are currently being made to increase both the qualifications for correctional jobs and the training of those who are hired. In 1967, for example, few states required that wardens, or correctional administrators, have even a high school diploma; today that requirement is much more widespread. Training courses are now generally operated by the state for both its own per-

This model prison in Oak Park Heights, Minn., opened in 1982. The interior cell block is in sharp contrast to the numerous highly criticized, overcrowded, unsanitary U.S. prisons. J.P. Laffont–Sygma

sonnel and those of county jails; such training, however, is still below the level offered in many other countries. The relatively low level of training may be dictated by the need to place prison personnel quickly into the system; not only is turnover among prison guards exceptionally high, but also the number of U.S. prison cells almost doubled from 1980 to 1990.

Racial relations are an important concern in U.S. prisons. Although about half the prison population is black and about 5 percent is Hispanic, only about 15 percent of the staff nationwide is of minority background. Some penologists believe that this makes communication between prisoners and officials difficult, exacerbating tensions. As a result, employment programs are being encouraged to seek more minority personnel.

The recent changes in American correctional organization, in which a highly bureaucratized and effective central administration controls prisons throughout the state, emulate those found in many European countries, where only persons with great experience in correctional work are appointed to manage the most secure prisons. In other respects, however, U.S. prisons continue to lag behind those of other countries. The Scandinavian nations, for example, employ prisoners at meaningful labor, with substantial wages and other work benefits, including in some cases vacations from prison. Only a handful of American prisons are now experimenting with such ideas. The U.S. incarceration rate is the highest in the world, partly because of the high crime rate, partly because of mandatory sentencing policies.

In recent decades, most state prison systems in the U.S. have come under legal scrutiny, and the courts have found them severely wanting. Many have been declared unconstitutional in the sense that the conditions—including idleness, overcrowding, poor medical care, substantial violence, and lack of rights accorded prisoners—render confinement in these institutions "cruel and unusual" punishment and hence in violation of the 8th Amendment to the U.S. Constitution (*see* BILL OF RIGHTS). Such judicial decisions have increased the pressure on state prison authorities to replace their antiquated prison facilities with more modern and humane institutions, in keeping with the ideals set forth by penologists a century ago. *See also* PENOLOGY. R.G.Si.

For further information on this topic, see the Bibliography in volume 28, section 303.

PRISONERS OF WAR, in international law, term used to designate incarcerated members of the armed forces of an enemy, or noncombatants who render them direct service and who have been captured during wartime. Surgeons, chaplains, news correspondents, and hospital attendants of the International Red Cross are not included in this category, nor are civilians who are detained and interned in belligerent countries. Throughout the 19th and 20th centuries the Red Cross has brought comfort, legal aid, and attention to the plight of interned soldiers.

Prisoners of war have no protection from the law of the nation that captures them and no civil remedy. By the customs, treaties, and conventions of international law, however, prisoners of war are supposed to be granted humane treatment by the enemy.

History. In ancient times prisoners of war were usually treated without mercy. Among the Greeks, for example, it was common practice to put to death the whole adult male population of a conquered state. The ancient Britons also killed their prisoners in a most barbarous fashion. The Ottoman Turks executed 30,000 Christian prisoners during the War of Candia (1667–68).

In western Europe, however, as chivalry spread in late medieval times, generosity to a fallen foe asserted itself, and the practice of sparing and ransoming prisoners was introduced.

In modern times, the Hague Conferences, the Geneva Convention in 1906, and the more detailed convention of 1929 provided international rules for the humane treatment of prisoners. A prisoner of war may not be treated as a criminal but may be employed in nonmilitary paid work. The prisoner has a right to adequate food, clothing, and quarters and to the transmission of letters and parcels. A member of the armed forces is bound to supply name, rank, and serial number but cannot legally be compelled to give further information to the enemy. The provisions of the Geneva Convention of 1906 and 1929 were largely disregarded by totalitarian regimes, particularly those of Germany and Japan during World War II.

After the experiences of World War II, another Geneva Convention was convened in August 1949 to deal with the treatment of prisoners of war. The rules that were put forth there are binding on most of the countries of the world. These rules have not always been strictly observed.

Korean War. At the beginning of the Korean War the belligerents promised to honor the principles of the 1949 convention. In spite of this, the Communist forces were responsible for numerous violations; prisoners received inadequate food, clothing, and shelter and poor medical treatment, often resulting in loss of lives.

In the course of truce negotiations during the war, a new problem arose regarding repatriation of prisoners. Because of the apparent unwillingness of Communist soldiers made prisoners of war to return to their homelands, the UN Command posited the principle of "voluntary repatriation," stating that prisoners of war should not be returned against their will. Although the Geneva Convention does not specifically authorize voluntary repatriation, the UN Command held that the humanitarian spirit of the convention would be violated if the prisoners were forcibly repatriated. The new principle was finally incorporated in the armistice agreement (July 26, 1953) following a yearlong deadlock; the agreement granted the belligerents the right to speak with prisoners opposed to repatriation. The Korean War was distinctive among wars throughout history for the extensive and effective use of psychological warfare, or brainwashing of prisoners, by North Korea.

War in Vietnam. Further violations of the Geneva Convention occurred in the Vietnam War. Ill treatment of prisoners was brought to light by the Red Cross throughout the war. In September 1969 the North Vietnamese Red Cross declared that U.S. pilots, guilty of "crimes against humanity," would not be given the protections afforded by the Geneva Convention. South Vietnamese mistreatment of prisoners of war was alleged in 1970 in reports that so-called tiger cages were used to confine North Vietnamese prisoners.

In the Vietnamese conflict, a major concern in negotiations between the U.S. and North Vietnam was the release of hundreds of American prisoners of war and the repatriation of both North and South Vietnamese prisoners. By 1971 the prospects of U.S. withdrawal from Vietnam depended largely on a solution of the prisoner-of-war problem, which had been employed as a bargaining point by North Vietnam. On Feb. 12, 1973, after the signing of the cease-fire in January, the first contingent of 143 American military and civilian prisoners of war arrived in the Philippines. During the following weeks, 444 prisoners were released. More than a decade later, some U.S. soldiers are still unaccounted for and are listed as missing in action. *See* VIETNAM WAR.

For further information on this topic, see the Bibliography in volume 28, section 248.

PRIŠTINA, city, S Yugoslavia, capital of Kosovo Autonomous Province, in Serbia. It is primarily a commercial and transportation center for the surrounding mining region. Major manufactures include processed food, jewelry, textiles, metal and wooden goods, and pharmaceuticals. The University of Kosovo (1970) is here. In the 14th century, the community became the capital of the Serbian Empire. Pop. (1981) 210,040.

PRIVATEER, in international law, term applied to a privately owned armed vessel whose owners are commissioned by a belligerent nation to carry on naval warfare. Such naval commissions or authorizations are called letters of marque. Privateering is distinguished from piracy, which is carried out without enlistment by a government. Privateering was abolished by the Declaration of Paris of 1856, but the declaration was not supported by the U.S., Spain, Mexico, and Venezuela. The Hague Conference of 1907 prescribed the conditions under which a private merchant vessel converted to war purposes has the status of a warship. Under the U.S. Constitution, Congress has the power to issue letters of marque and therefore to make use of privateers.

The practice of privateering anteceded the creation of national navies. During the Middle Ages, European states having few or no warships hired merchant vessels for hostile purposes. The issuing of letters of marque to shipowners or procurers, authorizing them to prey on the commerce of the enemy, eventually came into general use. By way of compensation, privateers were allowed to share any booty captured.

Privateering was carried on during the American Revolution and the War of 1812. Congress authorized the president to commission privateering in 1863 during the American Civil War, but the power was not exercised; the Confederacy, however, engaged in privateering during this period. Privateering was expressly renounced by the U.S. during the Spanish-American War of 1898. At the Hague Conference of 1922–23, called to formulate the regulation of the use of aircraft and radio in time of war, the countries then present issued a joint declaration against the use of privateers in aerial warfare. The report stated that because belligerent rights at sea could be exercised only by units under the direct authority, immediate control, and responsibility of the warring nation, belligerent rights in the air should also be exercised only by military aircraft.

PRIVET, common name applied to plants of the genus *Ligustrum,* of the family Oleaceae (*see* OLIVE). Privets are shrubs or small trees with opposite leaves, which are simple and entire at the margin. The flowers are small, white, and in terminal panicles.

PRIVY COUNCIL. *See* CABINET; GREAT BRITAIN.

PRIZEFIGHTING. *See* BOXING.

PROBABILITY, also theory of probability, branch of mathematics that deals with measuring or determining quantitatively the likelihood that an event or experiment will have a particular outcome. Probability is based on the study of permutations and combinations (q.v.) and is the necessary foundation for statistics (q.v.).

The foundation of probability is usually ascribed to the 17th-century French mathematicians Blaise Pascal and Pierre de Fermat, but mathematicians as early as Gerolamo Cardano (1501–76) had made important contributions to its development. Mathematical probability began in an attempt to answer certain questions arising in games of chance, such as how many times a pair of dice must be thrown before the chance that a six will appear is 50–50. Or, in another example, if two players of equal ability, in a match to be won by the first to win ten games, are obliged to suspend play when one player has won five games, and the other seven, how should the stakes be divided?

The probability of an outcome is represented by a number between 0 and 1, inclusive, with "probability 0" indicating certainty that an event will not occur and "probability 1" indicating certainty that it will occur. The simplest problems are concerned with the probability of a specified "favorable" result of an event that has a finite number of equally likely outcomes. If an event has n equally likely outcomes and f of them are termed favorable, the probability, p, of a favorable outcome is f/n. For example, a fair die can be cast in six equally likely ways; therefore, the probability of throwing a 5 or a 6 is 2/6. More involved problems are concerned with events in which the various possible outcomes are not equally likely. For example, in finding the probability of throwing a 5 or 6 with a pair of dice, the various outcomes (2, 3, . . . , 12) are not all equally likely. Some events may have infinitely many outcomes, such as the probability that a chord drawn at random in a circle will be longer than the radius.

Problems involving repeated trials form one of the connections between probability and statistics. To illustrate, what is the probability that exactly five 3s and at least four 6s will occur in 50 tosses of a fair die? Or, a person, tossing a fair coin twice, takes a step to the north, east, south, or west, according to whether the coin falls head,

Privet, genus Ligustrum

head; head, tail; tail, head; or tail, tail. What is the probability that at the end of 50 steps the person will be within 10 steps of the starting point?

In probability problems, two outcomes of an event are mutually exclusive if the probability of their joint occurrence is zero; two outcomes are independent if the probability of their joint occurrence is given as the product of the probability of their separate occurrences. Two outcomes are mutually exclusive if the occurrence of one precludes the occurrence of the other; two outcomes are independent if the occurrence or nonoccurrence of one does not alter the probability that the other will or will not occur. Compound probability is the probability of all outcomes of a certain set occurring jointly; total probability is the probability that at least one of a certain set of outcomes will occur. Conditional probability is the probability of an outcome when it is known that some other outcome has occurred or will occur.

If the probability that an outcome will occur is p, the probability that it will not occur is $q = 1 - p$. The odds in favor of the occurrence are given by the ratio $p:q$, and the odds against the occurrence are given by the ratio $q:p$. If the probabilities of two mutually exclusive outcomes X and Y are p and P, respectively, the odds in favor of X and against Y are p to P. If an event must result in one of the mutually exclusive outcomes $O_1, O_2, \ldots, O_n$, with probabilities $p_1, p_2, \ldots, p_n$, respectively, and if $v_1, v_2, \ldots, v_n$ are numerical values attached to the respective outcomes, the expectation of the event is $E = p_1v_1 + p_2v_2 + \ldots\ p_nv_n$. For example, a person throws a die and wins 40 cents if it falls 1, 2, or 3; 30 cents for 4 or 5; but loses \$1.20 if it falls 6. The expectation on a single throw is $3/6 \times .40 + 2/6 \times .30 - 1/6 \times 1.20 = .10$.

The most common interpretation of probability is used in statistical analysis. For example, the probability of throwing a 7 in one throw of two dice is 1/6, and this answer is interpreted to mean that if two fair dice are randomly thrown a very large number of times, about one-sixth of the throws will be 7s. This concept is frequently used to statistically determine the probability of an outcome that cannot readily be tested or is impossible to obtain. Thus, if long-range statistics show that out of every 100 people between 20 and 30 years of age, 42 will be alive at age 70, the assumption is that a person between those ages has a 42 percent probability of surviving to the age of 70.

Mathematical probability is widely used in the physical, biological, and social sciences and in industry and commerce. It is applied in such diverse areas as genetics, quantum mechanics, an insurance. It also involves deep and importar theoretical problems in pure mathematics an has strong connections with the theory, know as mathematical analysis, that developed out c calculus. J.Si.; REV. BY J.Le.E

For further information on this topic, see th Bibliography in volume 28, sections 374–75.

PROBATE. *See* EXECUTOR; SURROGATE'S COUR WILL.

PROBATION, in U.S. criminal law, a method c substituting supervision by a court-appointe agent in lieu of imprisonment. As a general rule probation is used mostly in instances of misde meanors committed by youthful offenders an first offenders. A probation officer is usually em ployed to supervise the offender for the proba tion period, which is fixed by the state, the cour and sometimes by statute. During this perioc the offender must not commit criminal offense and must report to the probation officer at regu lar intervals to give an account of his or her activ ities, including employment and leisure time. A the end of the probation period, the probatione is discharged.

For further information on this topic, see th Bibliography in volume 28, section 303.

PROBOSCIS MONKEY, large, long-tailed pri mate, *Nasalis larvatus,* of the family Cercopitheci dae, found on the island of Borneo. The adu male has a flat, fleshy nose that droops down ward over the chin and is probably a sexual fea ture. Males measure about 76 cm (about 30 in) i head and body length; the females are shorte Proboscis monkeys are chiefly arboreal and ea leaves and fruit, but they are also capable swim mers, taking to waters of mangrove swamps an delta regions, where they are commonly found They are chestnut red on the back, shading int cinnamon and white on the face and belly.

PROCAINE, a regional anesthetic, commonly re ferred to by its trademark Novocaine, used i dentistry and surgery. Procaine hydrochloride, a this alkaloid (*see* ALKALOIDS) is properly called was first synthesized in 1905. It quickly replace cocaine, because it is easier to synthesize an sterilize, has a shorter duration of action, is non addictive, and is four to six times less toxic. Pro caine, like other local anesthetics such as tetra cain, acts as a nerve block, halting the generatio and conduction of nerve impulses that signa pain. In dentistry it permits painless tooth extrac tion. In minor surgery it is commonly used to gether with a vasoconstrictor drug that restrict blood flow. It is also used in obstetrics and some times for relief of pain in the lower back Some individuals are hypersensitive to procain and develop hives when the drug is injected beneath the skin. Procaine's chemical formula is $C_{13}H_{20}O_2N_2HCl$.

PROCESS PHILOSOPHY, a speculative world view which asserts that basic reality is constantly in a process of flux and change. Indeed, reality is identified with pure process. Concepts such as creativity, freedom, novelty, emergence, and growth are fundamental explanatory categories for process philosophy. This metaphysical perspective is to be contrasted with a philosophy of substance, the view that a fixed and permanent reality underlies the changing or fluctuating world of ordinary experience. Whereas substance philosophy emphasizes static being, process philosophy emphasizes dynamic becoming.

Although process philosophy is as old as the 6th-century BC Greek philosopher Heraclitus, renewed interest in it was stimulated in the 19th century by the theory of evolution. Key figures in the development of modern process philosophy were the British philosophers Herbert Spencer, Samuel Alexander, and Alfred North Whitehead, the American philosophers Charles S. Peirce and William James, and the French philosophers Henri Bergson and Pierre Teilhard de Chardin. Whitehead's *Process and Reality: An Essay in Cosmology* (1929) is generally considered the most important systematic expression of process philosophy.

Proboscis monkey, Nasalis larvatus
R. Van Nostrand–National Audubon Society

Contemporary theology has been strongly influenced by process philosophy. The American theologian Charles Hartshorne, for instance, rather than interpreting God as an unchanging absolute, emphasizes God's sensitive and caring relationship with the world. A personal God enters into relationships in such a way that he is affected by the relationships, and to be affected by relationships is to change. So God too is in the process of growth and development. Important contributions to process theology have also been made by such theologians as William Temple (1881–1944), Daniel Day Williams (1910–73), Schubert Ogden (1928–), and John Cobb, Jr. (1925–). R.M.B.

PROCLUS (410?–85), the last important ancient Greek philosopher and the most influential representative of the Athenian school of Neoplatonism (q.v.). Born in Constantinople, he studied in Alexandria, Egypt, with the Greek philosopher Olympiodorus (fl. 5th cent. AD) and later joined the Academy in Athens, eventually becoming director, or *diadochus* ("successor" to Plato, who founded the academy in 387 BC). Under the influence of the philosopher Iamblichus, the Athenian school was characterized by elaborate metaphysical speculation and a belief in paganism and magic. Proclus gave systematic form to this tradition. Despite his opposition to Christianity, he made an important contribution to both Eastern and Western medieval Christian theology through his influence on the 6th-century theologian known as the Pseudo-Dionysius.

Like the great 3d-century Neoplatonist philosopher Plotinus, Proclus taught the existence of an ultimate, indescribable reality, the One, from which lesser realities, including humanity and the material universe, are produced by a process of emanation (q.v.). According to this tradition, the task of philosophy is to transcend the limitations of the human senses and intellect and thus to point the way to a mystical reunion of the individual with the One. This "negative theology" is, in essence, a religious interpretation of Plato's thought.

Aside from his commentaries on Plato's works, the most important of Proclus's surviving works are *Elements of Theology* (trans. 1789) and *Platonic Theology.*

PROCOPIUS (500?-65?), Byzantine historian, whose writings are the chief source of information about the reign of the emperor Justinian I.

Born in Caesarea, Procopius studied law and then practiced in Constantinople. There, in 527, he was appointed secretary to Belisarius, Justinian's general, whom he accompanied on his campaigns in the first Persian war (527-31), against the Vandals in Africa (533-34) and against the Ostrogoths in Italy (536-40?). In 542 he was probably back in Constantinople, for he wrote in considerable detail about the plague that struck the city that year. In 562-63 he may have held the post of prefect of Constantinople.

Procopius wrote in Greek. His major work is *The Books About the Wars.* The first two books cover the Persian wars waged by Justin I (452-527) and his nephew Justinian I (to c. 550); the next two describe the wars in Africa (532-46); the next three the war with the Ostrogoths (536-52); and the last book covers events up to 554. Although mainly concerned with military affairs, the work contains valuable information on other subjects. Other writings are the *Secret History,* a highly critical, scandal-mongering commentary on the lives of Justinian I, his wife, Theodora, and the Byzantine court; and *On the Buildings* (written c. 553-55), a flattering work about the elaborate building program undertaken by Justinian in and around the Byzantine imperial capital.

PROCOPIUS THE GREAT (c. 1380-1434), Bohemian priest and military leader, who led the Hussites (q.v.) in the Hussite Wars (q.v.). Born in Prague, he became a follower of the Bohemian religious reformer John Huss (Jan Hus) at an early age. At first he was associated with the moderate (Utraquist, or Calixtine) faction of the Hussites, and he tried to reconcile the feuding factions within the movement. After the death of John Zizka (1376-1424), Procopius took his place as commander of the armies defending Bohemia against the invading forces sent by the pope and the Holy Roman emperor Sigismund to reimpose orthodox Catholicism. Procopius carried no arms but was a brilliant tactician, and he won important defensive victories (1426, 1427, 1431) and then took the offensive by invading Catholic strongholds in Lusatia, Silesia, and Austria. His victories over Catholic forces compelled the convening of the Council of Basel (*see* BASEL, COUNCIL OF) in 1431, which attempted unsuccessfully to resolve the dispute. Procopius led the Bohemian delegation there in 1433.

After the failure of the council, Procopius affiliated himself with the radical faction of Hussites, the Taborites. When fighting resumed, he led his troops in an attack on Pilsen, Bohemia, but after suffering reverses they rebelled and he retired to Prague. When Utraquist and Catholic nobles joined together in 1434 in support of Sigismund's claims to Bohemia, Procopius returned to lead the antifeudal Taborite forces at the Battle of Lipany, but they were defeated and he was killed on the battlefield. L.B.W.

PROCRUSTES, in Greek mythology, a robber who lived near Eleusis in Attica. Originally named Damastes or Polypemon, he acquired the name Procrustes ("The Stretcher") because he tortured his victims by cutting them down to fit his bed if they were too tall, or hammering and stretching them if they were too short. He was captured by the Greek hero Theseus, who inflicted upon Procrustes the same kind of torture that he had imposed upon his victims.

PRODUCER GAS. *See* GASES, FUEL.

PRODUCTION, in economics, manufacture and processing of goods or merchandise, including their design, treatment at various stages, and financial services contributed by bankers. Various economic laws, price data, and available resources are among the factors in production that must be considered by both private and governmental producers.

PROFIT, in business, the monetary difference between the cost of producing and marketing goods or services and the price subsequently received for those goods or services. Profit is an essential competitive feature of buying and selling in the economic system. The opposite of profit is loss, whereby the cost of producing certain goods or services is higher than the price a buyer is willing to pay for them. In free enterprise, the will to make and function by profits is termed the *profit motive.*

PROGESTERONE, hormone formed by the granulosa cells of the corpus luteum of the ovary. The corpus luteum is a structure in the ovary that develops at the site where a mature egg was released at ovulation. Therefore the level of progesterone rises in the second half of the menstrual cycle (*see* MENSTRUATION). If the released ovum is not fertilized, production of progesterone falls just before the onset of the next menstrual cycle and the corpus luteum degenerates. Progesterone was isolated and crystallized by three independent groups of investigators in 1934. It is a steroid hormone, a compound possessing the same chemical nucleus as the female estrogenic hormones and the male androgenic hormones, as well as cholesterol and adrenal steroid hormones. The principal function of progesterone is the preparation of the mucous membrane of the uterus for the reception of the ovum. The hormone also stimulates the formation of saclike structures in the lacteal glands in preparation for their function of producing milk, and inhibits the release in the pituitary of prolactin hormone.

PROGRAMMED INSTRUCTION, technique of teaching in a sequence of controlled steps. Sometimes referred to as programmed learning, it is the product of a careful development process resulting in a reproducible sequence of instructional events, which has been demonstrated to produce measurable and consistent learning by students.

History. Programmed instruction received its major impetus from the work of the American psychologist B. F. Skinner, who, in 1954, described how programs could be developed scientifically. By the late 1950s programs had been developed for use in all levels of teaching, from grade school to graduate school, as well as in the armed services and industry. Most early programs presented information in small steps. Students read a sentence or two and then responded to a question by filling in a blank or choosing from a set of alternative answers. Then they viewed the correct answer and checked the accuracy of their own responses. Such formats, which seem impoverished in comparison to the variety of programs now available, usually addressed only trivial instructional goals. Intellectual skills, such as problem solving, the formulation and expression of new ideas, and the exploration of new fields, can now be taught with carefully designed programs.

Reinforcement. Early programs were based on experimental studies that showed that voluntary acts of behavior tend to recur when such acts are immediately followed by favorable consequences. If, for example, a child says "please" when asking for something and gains immediate attention, the child will be likely to repeat the voluntary "please" in the future. Such consequences, which are favorable to an individual, are referred to as reinforcing events. Each step in the early programs provided students with an opportunity to respond and to be reinforced when the response was appropriate. Although more advanced students benefit from relatively large steps, the concept of reinforcing events continues to be important in programming.

Grades, diplomas, prizes, and educational rewards are not especially effective as reinforcing events because they seldom occur at the right time. While tangible reinforcers (such as money or candy) and praise sometimes are used, people seem to be reinforced by successfully manipulating the environment. It is often highly reinforcing to a student to work out the right answer to a question if the question is perceived as challenging. A good instructional program is designed in such a way that students are required to respond to challenging situations and are frequently reinforced by success in giving correct responses. As a result, motivation may be quite different from that of traditional instruction, in which students typically study to avoid the unpleasant consequences of not studying.

Validity. Instructional programs, to be valid, also must achieve a purpose; students must attain the goals of instruction to which the program is directed. Such validity imposes two requirements.

First, the broad goals of instruction must be defined so that their attainment can be measured. The question that confronts all educators is: What must students be able to do as a result of instruction? In answering this question, instructional programmers should be as explicit as possible, employing modern techniques of task and content analysis in order to specify the broadest, most worthwhile educational goals. This analysis also will indicate how the attainment of goals can be measured—either by direct observation of student capability (as in learning to drive an automobile) or by evaluating student performance on a broad set of tasks (as in determining mathematical knowledge).

Second, the requirement for consistent attainment by students means that programmed instruction must be available in a format that is sufficiently reusable to assure such consistency. Early programs appeared in textual form or were presented with the help of mechanical devices called teaching machines. This term was unfortunate because the program, not its method of presentation, accomplished the instruction. Current programs are available in a variety of additional formats, involving computers, special training simulators, multimedia devices such as videocassettes, and even sophisticated instructional systems that include elaborate instructor manuals to specify the precise role recommended for teachers and other support personnel.

Constructing a Program. The first step in constructing a program is to define the instructional goals in terms of the measurable capabilities to be acquired by the student. A task analysis provides the basis for the design of mastery tests; each test is a representative sampling of the competencies to be achieved. The tests are first tried out with a small group of students and revised on the basis of student performance. Once

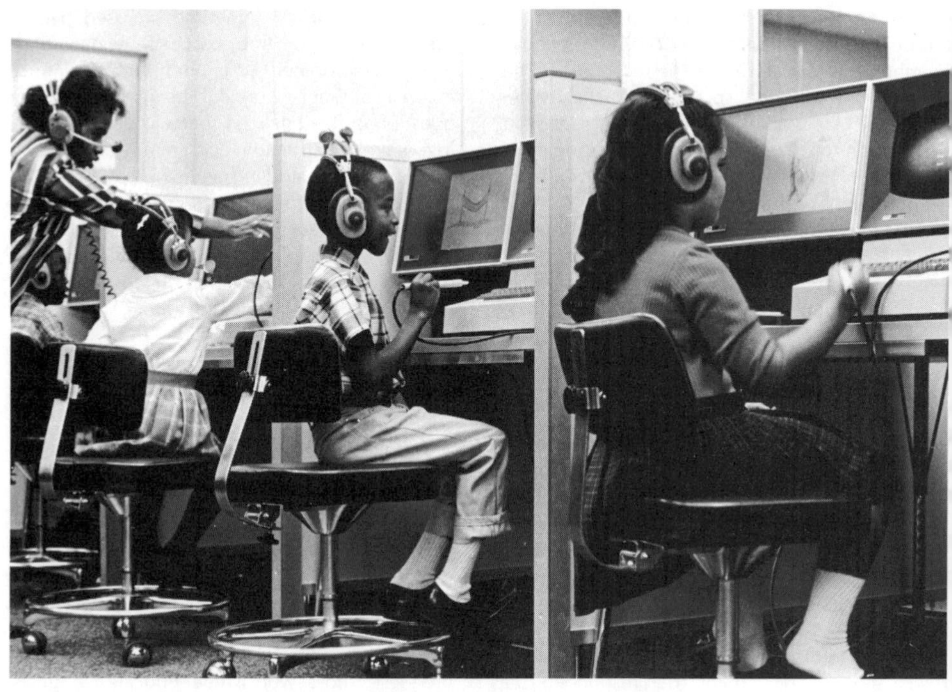

Youngsters at the Brentwood School, Stanford University, receive programmed instruction in a computer-assisted education project. Through such instruction, students can learn at a pace that is continuous and consistent with their individual abilities. Stanford University

goals are analyzed and associated tests are developed, the first drafts of instructional sequences are prepared. These are also based on the task analysis, with early steps in the program designed to prepare the students for subsequent steps. Hints and suggestions are used to increase the chances that students will respond correctly, but gradually all such assistance is withdrawn. Like the tests, drafts of instruction are tried out on a few students and revised to make them work better.

The final stage of program development requires the administration of the instructional materials in actual schools by teachers who have received some special in-service training. This step provides evidence that the instructional program works, that it enables students to attain those capabilities for which the program was designed.

Merits of Programmed Instruction. One advantage often claimed for programmed instruction is that most programs are self-paced. Students who can work rapidly are not held back, and those who need to work more slowly have a chance to master each stage of a program before moving on to the next stage. Under such conditions, individual progress can be continuous and the overall efficiency of the system, quite high.

Another significant effect on educational systems worldwide has been a consistent improvement in the ability to define and measure student attainment of educational goals. Thus, attention to the outcomes of formal education has increased. In the U.S. this has been reflected, for example, in the growing interest in educational accountability and in legislation, in several states, directed to providing evidence of the quality of instructional materials. S.M.M. & P.W.T.

For further information on this topic, see the Bibliography in volume 28, section 314.

PROGRAMMING, COMPUTER. *See* COMPUTER.

PROGRAM MUSIC, music that describes a nonmusical subject, such as a story, object, or scene, through the use of musical effects. Attempts to use music for descriptive purposes are probably as old as music itself. The question of whether music alone is capable of describing anything is an old one that has never really been answered. It is questionable whether listeners would recognize what is being described in music without the aid of titles, synopses or program notes, literary quotations, or quotations of well-known melodies that have special associations, such as military marches, hymns, traditional love songs, hunting songs, or patriotic songs. Obvious imitations of actual sounds, such as thunder effects on the kettledrums or approximations of birdsong on the flute, are possible and have been used by composers for centuries. Listeners probably recognized without being told the meaning of the keyboard piece *La poule* (The Hen, 1706) by the French composer Jean Philippe Rameau. The virtuoso Italian violinist Nicolò Paganini could reproduce on his instrument sounds that his listeners immediately recognized as those of a barnyard or the ringing of church bells. Except for such literal or stuntlike possibilities of musical description, however, the element of imagination is essential to the listener, even if the composer has provided extramusical explanations. In some cases, such as the so-called fate theme that begins the Fifth Symphony of Ludwig van Beethoven, the public has provided meanings for music that the composer did not announce, at least in words.

Preromantic Works. Early composers for keyboard and string instruments often created descriptive pieces such as, in the 16th century, *Mr. Byrd's Battell,* a keyboard piece depicting a battle, by the English composer William Byrd. Such depictions continued to be written throughout the 17th and 18th centuries. Some notable examples are *Musical Representations of Various Biblical Stories,* a set of six harpsichord sonatas by the German organist-composer Johann Kuhnau (1660–1722), and *The Four Seasons,* a set of four concerti grossi by the Italian composer Antonio Vivaldi. During the classical era in music (c. 1750–c. 1820) the aesthetic goals of music did not encourage the description of extramusical subjects; instead, these goals stressed the coordination of musical elements according to purely musical laws. If instrumental works of the time contained descriptions, the nonmusical elements were usually made to fit within a purely musical scheme of relationships. An example of this approach is the *Pastoral* Symphony (1808) by Beethoven. True program music followed later in the 19th century, when composers allowed the program to determine the overall form of a composition as well as its internal relationships.

19th Century. Early in the 19th century, music was greatly influenced by the literary movement known as romanticism. The French composer Hector Berlioz and the Hungarian composer Franz Liszt were leaders in the development of program music, as it then became known. They created works based on or inspired by literary, pictorial, and other subjects, such as Berlioz's *Symphonie fantastique* (Fantastic Symphony, completed in 1831), in which a recurring melodic idea represents the woman who haunts a musician's dreams. Berlioz composed some of his finest works on subjects taken from William Shakespeare and Vergil. The cult of the romantic hero, prevalent in these times, inspired highly charged symphonic works full of atmosphere, such as Berlioz's symphony *Harold in Italy* (1834), based on an epic poem by the British poet George Gordon, Lord Byron. Franz Liszt based his *Faust* Symphony (1857) and the *Dante* Symphony (1857) on great works of literature. In these symphonies and in works such as *Les préludes* (1854), for which he devised the term *symphonic poem* (q.v.), Liszt employed the leitmotiv, using specific melodic phrases to identify characters, actions, or symbols, an innovation developed by Liszt's son-in-law, the German composer Richard Wagner, in his music dramas.

During the course of the 19th century, the rise of nationalism was reflected in such works as *Má vlast* (My Country, 1874–79), a cycle of symphonic poems describing aspects of his native country, by the Czech composer Bedřich Smetana, and *Finlandia* (1900), a passionate symphonic poem in praise of his country, by the Finnish composer Jean Sibelius. Program music probably reached its most complex form in the symphonic poems of the German composer Richard Strauss, who employed all the resources of the modern orchestra for the depiction of romantic heroes and events, such as in his *Don Quixote* (1898), based on the novel by the Spanish writer Miguel de Cervantes Saavedra. In this work a solo cello is used to represent the hero and a solo viola represents the hero's faithful servant, while the full orchestra comments on and illustrates their adventures.

Other Developments. Other kinds of program music are exemplified by *La danse macabre* (1874), a study in the grotesque, by the French composer Camille Saint-Saëns; the *Enigma* Variations (1899), which paint tonal portraits of a group of friends, by the British composer Sir Edward Elgar; *The Afternoon of a Faun* (1894), a musical evocation of the poem of the same name by the French poet Stéphane Mallarmé, composed by the Frenchman Claude Debussy; and *Music for a Great City* (1964), an orchestral work describing the life of New York City, by the American composer Aaron Copland.

Program music also has been used as political propaganda, as in the Third (*May Day*) Symphony (1931) by the Soviet composer Dmitry Shostakovich.

More recent composers, particularly those employing the twelve-tone system, have tended to emphasize the abstract nature of music and, if they used titles at all, to choose them for their general rather than specific connotations, as in *Differences* (1959) by the Italian composer Luciano Berio and *Moments* (1965) by the German composer Karlheinz Stockhausen. Music produced by synthesizer or electronic tape can be said to reverse the traditional procedure in musical description, because it works with recognizable extramusical sounds from many sources and, by blending, mixing, and distorting them, takes what was specific into the realm of the abstract. Much music of this kind has been used to describe the fantastic or antic aspects of life, as in *Silver Apples of the Moon* (1967) by Morton Subotnick (1933–).

PROGRESSION, in mathematics. *See* ARITHMETIC PROGRESSION; GEOMETRIC PROGRESSION.

PROGRESSIVE-CONSERVATIVE PARTY, one of Canada's two main political parties; its members are called either Tories or Conservatives. The party originated in a coalition of conservative- and liberal-minded politicians in 1854, although the present name was not taken until 1942. The party, like its Liberal rival, lacks a distinct ideology, but it normally occupies the right of center position in the political spectrum and historically has tended to favor close ties with Great Britain.

The Conservatives were the dominant party in the nation during the late 19th century, when their leader, John A. Macdonald, fashioned an appealing strategy of economic development and pan-Canadian nationalism. In the 20th century, however, the party's inability to win much support among the French-Canadians in Québec has usually kept it from power on the national level, although Conservatives have often won office in the provinces of English-speaking Canada. The party did control the national government during World War I, when it angered French-Canadians by instituting military conscription, and again during the early 1930s, when its failure to ameliorate the Great Depression and its reputation as a friend of big business led to a considerable loss of support in English-speaking Canada as well. Thereafter, except for brief periods in office under Prime Ministers John Diefenbaker and Joseph Clark (1957–63 and 1979–80, respectively), the Conservatives existed as a weak alternative to successive Liberal governments. In 1984, under Brian Mulroney, the Conservatives swept back to power. Mulroney's government sponsored some important initiatives, including the Meech Lake accord, aimed at conciliating Quebec, and a 1988 free-trade agreement with the U.S. The latter led to the North American Free Trade Agreement, signed by Mulroney and the U.S. and Mexican presidents in December 1992. Politically, Mulroney won reelection in 1988, though with a reduced majority. His position was weakened further in 1990, when the Meech Lake accord failed to secure the unanimous approval of the provinces, and in 1992, when a revised accord reached at a conference in Charlottetown, P.E.I., failed in a national referendum. In February 1993 Mulroney announced his resignation; in June the party elected Kim Campbell (1947–) to succeed him.

PROGRESSIVE EDUCATION. *See* DEWEY, JOHN; EDUCATION, HISTORY OF.

PROGRESSIVE PARTY, name of three distinct political parties in U.S. history.

The Bull Moose Party. The first Progressive party, known colloquially as the Bull Moose party, was founded after a bitter fight for the Republican presidential nomination among the incumbent president William H. Taft, the Wisconsin senator Robert M. La Follette (leader of the Republican party's progressive "insurgents"), and the former president Theodore Roosevelt. At the Republican convention in June 1912, most La Follette supporters switched to Roosevelt, but the nomination went to Taft. Roosevelt, incensed at Taft's conservative bent, then formed the Progressive party. Many liberal Republicans bolted to the new party, which in August 1912 nominated Roosevelt for president and the California governor Hiram W. Johnson (1866–1945) for vice-president. Condemning Taft as unduly responsive to big business, the Progressives advocated primary elections, prohibition of child labor, woman suffrage, national social insurance, and restrictions on the use of injunctions in labor disputes. Although the Progressives greatly outpolled the Republicans in the election, the net result was a victory for the Democratic candidate, Woodrow Wilson. Most Progressives soon rejoined the Republican party, and the Progressive party died out in 1917.

League for Progressive Political Action. In 1924 a liberal coalition, frustrated by conservative domination of both major parties, formed the League for Progressive Political Action, popularly called the Progressive party. Nominating Senator La Follette for president and Montana Democratic Senator Burton K. Wheeler for vice-president, the party, which also drew support from the Socialists, advocated government ownership of public utilities and labor reforms such as the right to collective bargaining. Although he was overwhelmingly defeated by the Republican candidate, the incumbent president Calvin Coolidge, La Follette polled more than 4.8 million votes, about 16.5 percent of the total ballots cast, and 13 electoral votes.

For the 1948 presidential elections, the Progressive party nominated as its candidate Henry A. Wallace (right, with wife) for president and Glen H. Taylor (center, with wife and children) for vice-president. UPI

The Election of 1948. A third Progressive party was formed in 1948 by dissident Democrats, most of whom had been prominent in developing the New Deal program of President Franklin D. Roosevelt. With the former vice-president Henry A. Wallace and the former undersecretary of agriculture Rexford G. Tugwell among their leaders, the Progressives nominated Wallace for president and Idaho Democratic senator Glen H. Taylor (1904–84) for vice-president. Charging that both major parties advocated policies that would lead to economic crisis at home and war with the USSR abroad, the party favored high-level international conferences to lessen tension with the USSR. At home they advocated full constitutional rights for all minority and political groups, federal curbs on monopolies, anti-inflation measures such as price and rent controls, and repeal of the Taft-Hartley Act. When the U.S. Communist party supported the Progressives, the Democrats and Republicans attacked them as Communist-dominated. The Progressives maintained their right to support from any group backing them. Defeated by the Democrats under the incumbent president Harry S. Truman, the Progressives received more than 1 million popular votes, but after 1948 they no longer played a role in national politics.

See also POLITICAL PARTIES IN THE UNITED STATES.

For further information on this topic, see the Bibliography in volume 28, section 204.

PROHIBITION, legal ban on the manufacture and sale of intoxicating drink; by extension, the term also denotes those periods in history when such bans have been in force, as well as the political and social movements advocating them. Such movements (also called temperance movements) have occurred whenever significant numbers of people have believed that the consumption of alcoholic beverages presented a serious threat to the integrity of their most vital institutions, especially the institution of the family. Drunkenness is considered an evil in most of the world's major religious traditions, and Islam has for centuries forbidden even the moderate use of fermented drink. In the West, however, efforts to ban the consumption of alcohol have been a relatively recent phenomenon. Their origin can be traced to the apparently rapid spread of the technology of distillation and of alcohol abuse in 18th-century Europe, which alarmed those concerned with public health and morals.

The Early Prohibition Movement in the U.S. In England and the American colonies, governments after 1750 made repeated and futile efforts to discourage the excessive use of distilled spirits. In the U.S., as the annual per capita consumption of alcohol from all spiritous beverages during the 1830s rose to about 15 liters (this is computed as absolute, or 200 proof, spirits and would be the equivalent of 37.5—about 10 gal—of the usually 80 proof whiskey, rum, or gin), many religious and political leaders were beginning to see drunkenness as a national curse. Abraham Lincoln said of this period that intoxicating liquor was "used by everybody, repudiated by nobody" and that it came forth in society "like the Egyptian angel of death, commissioned to slay if not the first, the fairest born in every family."

Many people believed a close relationship existed between drunkenness and the rising incidence of crime, poverty, and violence, concluding that the only way to protect society from this threat was to abolish the "drunkard-making business." The first state prohibition law, passed in Maine in 1851, prohibited the manufacture and sale of "spiritous or intoxicating liquors" not intended for medical or mechanical purposes, and 13 of the 31 states had such laws by 1855. By that time the annual per capita consumption of absolute alcohol had fallen to about 4 liters (about 1 gal).

The political crisis that preceded the American Civil War distracted attention from Prohibition. Many of the early state laws were modified, repealed, or ignored, and for years few restraints were placed on manufacturing or selling anything alcoholic. The population increased rapidly after the Civil War, and soon there were more than 100,000 saloons in the country (about 1 for every 400 men, women, and children in 1870); these saloons became increasingly competitive for the drinkers' wages. Thus, many of them permitted gambling, prostitution, sales to minors, public drunkenness, and violence.

The Anti-Saloon League. In reaction to this, the extraordinary "Women's War" broke out across the nation in 1873. Thousands of women marched from church meetings to saloons, where with prayer and song they demanded—with transitory results—that saloonkeepers give up their businesses. By 1900, millions of men and women were beginning to share this hostility toward the saloon and to regard it as the most dangerous social institution then threatening the family. The Anti-Saloon League of America (ASL), organized in Ohio, effectively marshaled such people into political action. State chapters of the ASL endorsed candidates for public office and demanded of their state governments that the people be allowed to vote yes or no on the question of continuing to license the saloons.

By 1916, no less than 23 of the 48 states had adopted antisaloon laws, which in those states closed the saloons and prohibited the manufacture of any alcoholic beverages. Even more significant, the national elections of that year returned a U.S. Congress in which the ASL-supported dry members (those who supported Prohibition) outnumbered the wet members (those who were against Prohibition) by more than two to one. On Dec. 22, 1917, with majorities well in excess of the two-thirds requirement, Congress submitted to the states the 18th Amendment to the Constitution, which prohibited "the manufacture, sale, or transportation of intoxicating liquors." By January 1919 ratification was complete, with 80 percent of the members of 46 state legislatures recorded in approval.

Prohibition in Other Countries. At this point in history, most Protestant nations had come to regard drinking as a social evil, and the Prohibition movement was being accelerated by the circumstances of World War I. While rallying British workers to increase their productivity in support of the war effort, Prime Minister David Lloyd George stated that "we are fighting Germany, Austria, and drink; and, as far as I can see, the greatest of these three deadly foes is drink." Soon the British government limited the sale of alcoholic drink to a few early evening hours. In Scotland, the citizens of towns and villages had the right (local option) to vote out drinking establishments after 1920. In Sweden, where the movement had been strong since the 1830s, the government abolished both the profit motive and the competition from the liquor traffic after 1922 by nationalizing it. An even harsher measure there restricted sales to 1 liter (about 1 qt) per family per week. In Norway, voters outlawed the sale of drinks with an alcoholic content of more than 12 percent by referendum in 1919. That same year the Finnish government banned the sale of any drink of more than 2 percent alcohol. Canada was then dry in all provinces.

National Prohibition in the U.S. To enforce the 18th Amendment, Congress passed the National Prohibition Act, usually called the Volstead Act because Congressman Andrew Volstead (1860–1947) of Minnesota introduced it in 1919. This law defined the prohibited "intoxicating liquors" as those with an alcoholic content of more than 0.5 percent, although it made concessions for liquors sold for medicinal, sacramental, and industrial purposes, and for fruit or grape beverages prepared for personal use in homes. Because the Congress and the state legislatures, however, were reluctant to appropriate enough money for

A federal agent destroys kegs of contraband alcohol during the Prohibition era. Granger Collection

more than token enforcement—and because the opportunities for disregarding the law through smuggling, distilling, fermenting, and brewing were legion—Prohibition always represented more of an ideal than a reality. On this basis the Prohibition era began at midnight on Jan. 16, 1920.

The effects of Prohibition. The era inspired an extensive body of colorful literature, most of it alleging that the period was one of moral decay and social disorder precisely because of "Volsteadism," which came to mean the intolerable searches, seizures, and shootings by police who, with their token enforcement, seemed to threaten intrusion into the private lives of law-respecting persons. It also alleged that Prohibition distorted the role of alcohol in American life, causing people to drink more rather than less; that it promoted disrespect for the law; that it generated a wave of organized criminal activity, during which the bootlegger (one who sold liquor illegally), the "speakeasy" (an illegal saloon), and the gangster became popular institutions; and that the profits available to criminals from illegal alcohol corrupted almost every level of government. Historians, however, believe that in the beginning of the era, and at least until the middle of the decade, most Americans respected the law, hoped that it would endure, and regarded its passage as directly responsible for the reduced incidence of public drunkenness and of alcohol-related crime, imprisonments, and hospitalizations. Statistics show that Prohibition reduced the annual per capita consumption from 9.8 liters (2.6 gal) of absolute alcohol during the period before state laws were effective (1906–1910) to 3.7 liters (0.97 gal) after Prohibition (1934). Moreover, no striking statistical evidence of a crime wave during the 1920s exists, although the crime rate did rise.

Movement toward repeal. In the late 1920s, however, more and more Americans found the idea of repeal increasingly attractive. The reasons for this were numerous and complex, the government's failure to enforce the law being only one of them. Most Americans were happy that the old-time saloon had been abolished, but they felt that a new society was emerging in the 1920s—a primarily urban and industrial society of great geographic and social mobility and great ethnic and religious diversities, in which the protection of the family from alcohol was perhaps less socially urgent than the expansion and protection of individual freedom.

This disillusionment with Prohibition occurred in every country that had earlier attempted it. In Canada, the dry laws of 1919 were soon repealed because of economic pressures, not the least of which were the opportunities to sell liquor to citizens of the dry U.S. Provincial laws after repeal did, however, provide for government-owned stores and for local option. In Norway, a referendum in 1926 abolished the earlier restriction, but strict regulation of the times and places liquor could be sold preserved a tight rein on drunkenness. Sweden held to state monopoly and severe rationing. Finland repealed its prohibition law by referendum in 1932.

The End of Prohibition. In the U.S., a major shift in public opinion occurred during the early years of the Great Depression, when opponents could argue persuasively that Prohibition deprived people of jobs and governments of revenue and generally contributed to economic stagnation. The actual political campaign for repeal was largely the work of the Association Against the Prohibition Amendment (AAPA), a nonpartisan organization of wealthy and influential citizens in all states who were "wet" in principle and who feared that through Prohibition the federal government might permanently compromise the tradition of individual freedom. Like the ASL, the AAPA actively endorsed and opposed candidates for state and federal offices. Its goal was that Congress should submit to the states the 21st Amendment to the Constitution, which would repeal the 18th, and submit it in such a way as to circumvent the various state legislatures in which, it feared, dry legislators from rural districts, in opposition to majority sentiment, might present a serious challenge to ratification. To avoid this, Congress—for the first time since the Constitution itself was ratified and for much the same reason—called for ratifying conventions in each of the states: Delegates would be elected by the people for the specific purpose of voting yes or no regarding the question of the 21st Amendment. The elections for convention delegates in 1933 produced a repeal vote running almost 73 percent. In a remarkably coordinated effort by the states and the Congress, ratification was complete in December of that year.

Following repeal, liquor control again became a state rather than a federal problem. The annual per capita consumption of absolute alcohol in the country rose after the repeal from 4.2 liters (1.1. gal) in 1935 to 7.6 liters (2.0 gal) in 1975, but most states still retain restrictions on the sale and consumption of alcohol. N.H.C.

For further information on this topic, see the Bibliography in volume 28, section 1159.

PROHIBITION PARTY, political organization in the U.S. It was founded by delegates from 20 states in Chicago in September 1869 to advocate the enactment of legislation outlawing the manufacture and sale of intoxicating liquor; it is one of the oldest so-called third parties of the nation. Candidates initially were entered in a number of state electoral contests. In 1872 the Prohibition party participated for the first time in a presidential election, receiving only about 5600 votes. Thereafter it nominated candidates in each presidential election. The party polled its highest vote, 264,133, in the presidential election of 1892; John Bidwell (1819–1900), a former congressman, was the candidate.

The party scored a moral victory on Jan. 16, 1919, when the 18th Amendment to the U.S. Constitution was ratified. The amendment banned the manufacture, sale, and transportation of intoxicating beverages in interstate commerce. Conversely, the party suffered a defeat in 1933, when the 18th Amendment was repealed by ratification of the 21st Amendment.

The Prohibition party continues to run candidates for the presidency, but it no longer attracts any significant support.

See PROHIBITION; TEMPERANCE.

For further information on this topic, see the Bibliography in volume 28, section 204.

PROJECTILE, in military terminology, a missile discharged from small arms (q.v.) or from artillery weapons (*see* ARTILLERY); or a self-propelled weapon such as a rocket or a torpedo (qq.v.), or guided missiles (q.v.). The terms *projectile, shell,* and *missile* are loosely interchangeable, but in modern military usage projectile is preferable as a more precise term. In physics and ballistics, a projectile is any body projected through space.

PROKOFIEV, Sergey Sergeyevich (1891–1953), influential Russian composer, a major figure in 20th-century music. Born April 23, 1891, in Sontzovka, near Ekaterinoslav (now Dnepropetrovsk, Ukraine), he studied with the Russian composers Reinhold Glière and Nikolay Rimsky-Korsakov. From 1918 to 1933 he lived in Europe, touring internationally as a pianist. He returned to his homeland in 1934.

Prokofiev's early works, such as the Piano Concerto No. 1 (1914) and the *Scythian* Suite for orchestra (1914), gained him a reputation as a musical iconoclast. During his expatriate years he composed for the Russian-born ballet impresario Sergey Diaghilev the ballets *Chout* (The Buffoon,

1921) and *Le Pas d'Acier* (The Age of Steel, 1927), an apotheosis of the industrialization then occurring in Russia. Also from this period are the operas *The Love of Three Oranges* (1921) and *The Flaming Angel* (1919; staged, 1955). His most important work from this period is the Classical Symphony (1918), which helped establish the neoclassical style that dominated much 20th-century music; it is a concise, irreverent work using modern harmonies and rhythms in the traditional 18th-century format.

After his return to Russia, Prokofiev maintained his musical idiom, and his works show extraordinary integrity under the pressure of the Soviet artistic dogma of "socialist realism." They include *Peter and the Wolf* (1934), for narrator and orchestra; the ballet *Romeo and Juliet* (1936; performed 1940); the opera *War and Peace* (1946; rev. 1952); the powerful Symphony No. 5 (1945); and, for film, the suite *Lieutenant Kije* (1933) and the cantata *Alexander Nevsky* (1938, for the film by the Soviet director Sergey Eisenstein). In 1948, although he had thus far been honored, he was officially censured for "excessive formalism" and cacophonous harmony. He promised more lyricism, but his opera *Tale of a Real Man* (1948) was again censured. He regained favor with his Symphony No. 7 (1952; Stalin Prize). He died March 5, 1953, in Moscow, as rehearsals began for his ballet *Tale of the Stone Flower* (1950; staged 1954).

PROKOPYEVSK, city, S Siberian Russia. Located on a branch of the Trans-Siberian Railroad, Prokopyevsk is a leading coal-mining center of the Kuznetsk Basin. Manufactures include mining equipment and food products. The city was created (1931) by a fusion of smaller mining settlements. Pop. (1987 est.) 278,000.

PROMETHEUS, in Greek mythology, one of the Titans, known as the friend and benefactor of humanity, the son of the Titan Iapetus by the sea nymph Clymene or the Titaness Themis. Prometheus and his brother Epimetheus were given the task of creating humanity and providing humans and all the animals on earth with the endowments they would need to survive. Epimetheus (whose name means afterthought) accordingly proceeded to bestow on the various animals gifts of courage, strength, swiftness, and feathers, fur, and other protective coverings. When it came

This bronze sculptural representation of Prometheus, completed in 1934 by the American artist Paul Manship, is the center of a fountain at Rockefeller Center, New York City. National Sculpture Society

time to create a being who was to be superior to all other living creatures, Epimetheus found he had been so reckless with his resources that he had nothing left to bestow. He was forced to ask his brother's help, and Prometheus (whose name means forethought) took over the task of creation. To make humans superior to the animals, he fashioned them in nobler form and enabled them to walk upright. He then went up to heaven and lit a torch with fire from the sun. The gift of fire that Prometheus bestowed upon humanity was more valuable than any of the gifts the animals had received.

Because of his actions Prometheus incurred the wrath of the god Zeus. Not only did he steal the fire he gave to humans, but he also tricked the gods so that they should get the worst parts of any animal sacrificed to them, and human beings the best. In one pile, Prometheus arranged the edible parts of an ox in a hide and disguised them with a covering of entrails. In the other, he placed the bones, which he covered with fat. Zeus, asked to choose between the two, took the fat and was very angry when he discovered that it covered a pile of bones. Thereafter, only fat and bones were sacrificed to the gods; the good meat was kept for mortals. For Prometheus's transgressions, Zeus had him chained to a rock in the Caucasus, where he was constantly preyed upon by an eagle. Finally he was freed by the hero Hercules, who slew the eagle.

PROMETHIUM, radioactive metallic element, symbol Pm, one of the rare earth elements (q.v.) in the lanthanide series (q.v.) of the periodic table (*see* PERIODIC LAW); at.no. 61, at.wt. (most stable isotope) 147. Promethium melts at about 1042° C (about 1908° F), boils at about 3000° C (about 5432° F), and has a sp.gr. of 7.26. Promethium was one of the last elements to be identified. In 1926 evidence from spectroscopic analysis indicated the existence of the element in various minerals, and the names *illinium* and *florentium* were proposed for the element. The fission of uranium is known to produce several radioactive isotopes with at.no. 61. These isotopes were investigated and isolated in 1945 by scientists at the nuclear-research laboratory at Oak Ridge, Tenn.; among them were the Americans Charles DuBois Coryell (1912–71), Jacob A. Marinsky (1918–), and Lawrence E. Glendenin (1918–), who proposed the name *promethium.* Isotopes with mass numbers from 134 to 155 have been investigated, and visible amounts of the isotope of mass 147, having a half-life of 2.6 years, have been prepared. The metal has been used in atomic batteries and as a beta-particle source in thickness gauges. *See* BETA PARTICLE; RADIOACTIVITY.

PROMISSORY NOTE, in the law of negotiable instruments (q.v.), written instrument containing an unconditional promise by a party, called the maker, who signs the instrument, to pay to another, called the payee, a definite sum of money either on demand or at a specified or ascertainable future date. The note may be made payable to the bearer, to a party named in the note, or to the order of the party named in the note. The following is an example of a promissory note.

> December 1, 19—
>
> Thirty days after date I promise to pay to the order of John Doe Five Hundred and 00/100 Dollars. Payable at Bank of Gotham, New York City. Value received with interest at 12%.
>
> James Roe

A promissory note differs from an IOU in that the former is a promise to pay and the latter is a mere acknowledgment of a debt. A promissory note is negotiable by endorsement if it is specifically made payable to the order of a person.

PRONGHORN, only extant member, *Antilocapra americana,* of the mammal family, Antilocapridae, order Artiodactyla, related to the antelope and found in North America. Both sexes carry erect, hollow horns that are shed yearly. Horns of the male have two prongs; the female's are short spikes. The animal is reddish brown with a dark brown mane, white underparts, two white bands on its neck, and a large white patch on its rump. When alarmed, the animal can make this hair stand straight out, producing a white flash.

Considered the fastest animals in North America, with an average maximum speed of 80 km/hr (50 mph), they inhabit open plains and semidesert, where they eat grass, forb, sagebrush, and cactus. They live alone or in small groups in summer; some males join groups of females with offspring. In these mixed groups, a female leader and a dominant male are found. Other males form unisexual herds. The number of pronghorns was 26,000 in 1925, but control of hunting and good wildlife management have brought the population to several hundred thousand.

For further information on this topic, see the Bibliography in volume 28, sections 461, 475, 478.

PRONOUN. *See* PARTS OF SPEECH.

PRONUNCIATION. *See* DIALECT; PHONETICS.

PROOF, in law, the process of establishing in a trial or legal action, through evidence (q.v.) and argument, the actual facts of a disputed issue. Evidence and arguments are generally presented by counsels for the defendant and the plaintiff (the instigating party in a case) in such a manner, and under the rules governing judicial procedure, that a judge or jury may be convinced of its truth. The submission of evidence may be by witnesses or by documents; arguments usually concern the inference that may properly be drawn from facts admitted or established. In an action at law, the plaintiff or party seeking relief is said to have the burden of proof—that is, the burden of sustaining the case until the trial is ended. Unless the plaintiff can present sufficient proof to overbalance that of the defendant, he or she is not considered to have sustained the burden of proof, and the case is dismissed.

In insurance law, the term *proof of loss* is applied to the statement of particulars of the nature, amount, and cause of damages sustained by an insured party; this statement must be filed with the insurer as a condition of reimbursement for the loss.

PROPAGANDA, dissemination of ideas and information for the purpose of inducing or intensifying specific attitudes and actions. Because propaganda is frequently accompanied by distortions of fact and by appeals to passion and prejudice, it is often thought to be invariably false or misleading. This view is relative, however. Although some propagandists may intentionally distort fact, others may present it as faithfully as objective observers. A lawyer's brief is as much propaganda as a billboard advertisement. Education, whatever its objective, is a form of propaganda. The essential distinction lies in the intentions of the propagandist to persuade an audience to adopt the attitude or action he or she espouses.

Propaganda may be disseminated by or for individuals, businesses, ethnic associations, religious organizations, political organizations, and governments at every level. Thousands of special-interest groups disseminate propaganda. Among such groups are patriotic and temperance societies, fire-prevention and traffic-safety committees, leagues promoting conservation or the prevention of cruelty to animals, labor unions, and chambers of commerce. No matter what its objective, propaganda attempts to persuade through rational or emotional appeal or through the organization of personal opinion. Efficient use of the communication media is central to these efforts.

Religious Propaganda. One of the earliest uses of the word *propaganda* was in connection with religious missionary activity. A notable propagandist was St. Paul, who established the first Christian churches in Asia Minor, Greece, and Italy. Christianity was spread beyond the Roman world by such evangelists as St. Augustine, the first archbishop of Canterbury, who introduced it into Britain, and by St. Boniface, who converted Germanic tribes. In modern times Roman Catholic missionary activity has been conducted by several well-known religious orders, notably the Society of Jesus. By skillful propaganda the Jesuits were able in the 17th century to reclaim for the church large areas of central Europe that had

Pronghorn, Antilocapra americana
Alfred M. Bailey–National Audubon Society

been lost to Protestantism during the Reformation. In 1622 Pope Gregory XV (1554–1623) established the Congregation of Propaganda to direct these activities of the Roman Catholic church. Protestants have been equally zealous in spreading their doctrines. The Protestant reformers of the 16th century were effective propagandists, and missionaries have carried the Protestant faith to every part of the world. *See also* MISSIONARY MOVEMENTS.

Political Propaganda. Propaganda for distinctly political ends is as old as history. The Bible, for example, relates that the Assyrian king Sennacherib attempted to terrify the Kingdom of Judah into surrendering by the use of threatening propaganda (see 2 Kings 18–19). Julius Caesar wrote the *Gallic Wars* to enhance his reputation in Rome and to speed his rise to power.

The quality of the propaganda literature of the American Revolution is outstanding. Before the Revolution the letters circulated by the patriot Samuel Adams and such pamphlets as *Letters from a Farmer in Pennsylvania* by John Dickinson sought to inform and unify American opinion in the quarrel with Great Britain. The Declaration of Independence, written by Thomas Jefferson, was a masterpiece of rational propaganda intended to crystallize public opinion at home and justify the controversial American cause abroad. During the period when that cause seemed closest to military defeat, the radical writer Thomas Paine wrote a series of pamphlets titled *The Crisis,* which rallied and sustained American morale for the long struggle. After the war, when controversy raged over the adoption of the federal Constitution, the articles written by Alexander Hamilton, James Madison, and John Jay, and known collectively as *The Federalist* (*see* FEDERALIST, THE), explained the new constitution and persuaded Americans to ratify it (*see* CONSTITUTION OF THE UNITED STATES). *The Federalist* was also an effective propaganda instrument among the citizens of the new American nation.

Literary Propaganda. Propaganda by individuals has sometimes taken literary forms. Many classics of philosophy, history, religion, and economics, as well as novels, poems, and plays, have been written in part with propagandist intent. The histories of the French author Voltaire, the pamphlets of Martin Luther, and the works of Karl Marx are examples. Propaganda for social justice was carried on by the British statistician Charles Booth and by the American social-settlement worker Jane Addams. In American literature, an outstanding novel of propaganda is *Uncle Tom's Cabin* (1852) by Harriet Beecher Stowe. By her depiction of black slavery in the South, Stowe contributed to the growth of the abolitionis movement before the American Civil War (*se* ABOLITIONISTS).

Wartime Propaganda. Massive modern propa ganda techniques began with World War I. From the beginning of the war, both German and British propagandists worked hard to win sympathy and support in the U.S. German propagandists appealed to the many Americans of German descen and to those of Irish descent who were traditionally hostile to Great Britain. Soon, however, Germany was virtually cut off from direct access to the U.S. Thereafter British propaganda had little competition in the U.S., and it was conducted more skillfully than that of the Germans. Once engaged in the war, the U.S. organized the Committee on Public Information, an official propaganda agency, to mobilize American public opinion. This committee proved highly successful, particularly in the sale of Liberty Bonds. The exploitation by the Allies of President Woodrow Wilson's Fourteen Points (q.v.), which seemed to promise a just peace for both the victors and the vanquished, contributed greatly toward crystallizing opposition within the Central Powers to continuation of the war.

After World War I propaganda achieved great importance as an instrument of national policy in the totalitarian state. Germany, Italy, Japan, and the Soviet Union deliberately molded public opinion through government propaganda agencies. In Germany, Adolf Hitler established the extremely powerful ministry of propaganda headed by Paul Joseph Goebbels. Completely dominating all public utterances in Germany, this agency instigated the so-called war of nerves. Before each new aggressive move by Germany, as, for example, against Czechoslovakia in 1938, the German press and radio publicized alleged evidence of persecution of German minorities in the victim country. Incidents were manufactured and exploited to justify German intervention, and the German war machine was depicted as invincible. The technique proved effective in dividing populations, weakening the power of the victim to resist, and causing its allies to hesitate. As the European crisis intensified, German agents in France spread propaganda of defeatism. Through books, pamphlets, and venal newspapers and in the legislature and the army, they encouraged dissatisfaction with the government, distrust of allies, and fear of German military power. These divisive efforts hastened the collapse of French resistance when the German army finally struck in May 1940.

The propaganda aspects of World War II were similar to those of World War I, except that the

Motion picture stars Douglas Fairbanks, Mary Pickford, and Charlie Chaplin support a Liberty loan drive during World War I. UPI

war was greater in scope. Radio played a major role, and propaganda activities overseas were more intense. Both Germany and Great Britain again sought to sway American opinion. German propagandists played on anti-British sentiment, represented the war as a struggle against communism, and pictured Germany as the invincible champion of a new order in world affairs. German agents also gave their support to movements in the U.S. that supported isolationism. German propaganda efforts again proved ineffective, especially after the Japanese attack on Pearl Harbor; the evidence of German aggression was too clear, and American sympathies were increasingly on the side of Great Britain. After the U.S. entered the war, the Axis powers sought to weaken the morale of the Allied armed forces and civilian populations by radio propaganda. The British traitor William Joyce (1906–executed 1946) broadcast from Germany under the sardonic name "Lord Haw Haw"; the American poet Ezra Pound broadcast for the Fascist cause from Italy; U.S. forces in the South Pacific became familiar with the voice of Iva Ikuko Toguri D'Aquino (1916–), a native Californian of Japanese descent, who broadcast from Japan as "Tokyo Rose."

Allied propaganda efforts were aimed at separating the peoples of the Axis nations from their governments, which were solely blamed for the war. Radio broadcasts and leaflets dropped from the air carried Allied propaganda to the enemy. The official U.S. propaganda agencies during World War II were the Office of War Information (OWI), charged with disseminating information at home and abroad, and the Office of Strategic Service (OSS), charged with conducting psychological warfare against the enemy. At Supreme Headquarters in the European theater of operations, the OWI and OSS were coordinated with military activities by the Psychological Warfare Division.

Cold-War Propaganda. In the period of the cold war, a marked conflict of interests between the U.S. and the Soviet Union following World War II, propaganda continued to be a significant instrument of national policy. Both the democratic and Communist blocs of states attempted by sustained campaigns to win to their side the great masses of uncommitted peoples and

Posters and billboards such as the one shown here in Guilin (Kuei-lin), China, are used to announce both important news items and government-sponsored propaganda slogans.
Eric Kroll–Taurus Photos

thereby achieve their objectives without resorting to armed conflict. Every aspect of national life and policy was exploited for purposes of propaganda. The cold war was also marked by the use of defectors, trials, and confessions for propaganda purposes.

In this propaganda war the Communist nations seemed initially to have a distinct advantage. Because their governments controlled all media, they could largely seal off their peoples from Western propaganda. At the same time, the highly centralized governments could plan elaborate propaganda campaigns and mobilize resources to carry out their plans. They could also count on aid from Communist parties and sympathizers in other countries. Democratic states, on the other hand, could neither prevent their peoples from being exposed to Communist propaganda nor mobilize all their resources to counter it. This apparent advantage for Communist governments eroded during the 1980s, as communications technology advanced. Inability to control the spread of information was a major factor in the disintegration of many Communist regimes in Eastern Europe at the end of the decade.

The U.S. Information Agency (USIA), established in 1953 to conduct propaganda and cultural activities abroad, operates the Voice of America, a radio network that carries news and information about the U.S. in more than 40 languages to all parts of the world. In 1978 USIA functions were taken over by the International Communication Agency (q.v.); its name was changed back to the U.S. Information Agency in 1982. In 1967 it was revealed that the Central Intelligence Agency (CIA) had for many years covertly supported numerous American and foreign labor, student, and political organizations, such as Radio Free Europe, the efforts of which benefited U.S. foreign policies.

Other Propaganda. In recent years the growing sophistication of propaganda techniques has been evident in election campaigns; these include the propaganda of the deed (influencing public opinion by actions rather than words), the use of television, the manufacture of news by staged events, the skillful recruitment and use of opinion leaders, and the adjustment of appeals to group interest. The civil rights struggles of the 1950s and '60s benefited from the propaganda effects of protest marches, assemblies, picketing, sit-ins, and "freedom rides." Large business corporations and commercial interests, such as railroads and oil companies, have also carried on extensive propaganda campaigns through advertising and other techniques in attempts to develop public support for legislation favorable to their interests.

In the 1970s and '80s, various kinds of propaganda became tools for such diverse special interests as antinuclear-energy groups, women's rights activists, pro-abortion and antiabortion forces, gun-control lobbies, adherents of capital punishment, senior citizen groups, and the Moral Majority. The technological advances of the mass media, especially those of the electronic media, are expanding the outlets available to propagandists and are likely to have a significant impact on propaganda efforts in the future.

See also ADVERTISING; PUBLIC OPINION; PUBLIC RELATIONS. For additional information on historical figures, see biographies of those whose names are not followed by dates. H.L.C.

For further information on this topic, see the Bibliography in volume 28, sections 157–58.

A large crowd with slogan-covered banners assembles in Washington, D.C., to protest the use of nuclear reactors. Philip Jon Bailey–Taurus Photos

PROPANE, colorless, odorless gas of the alkane series of hydrocarbons, of formula C_3H_8. It occurs in crude oil, in natural gas, and as a by-product of petroleum refining. Propane does not react strongly at room temperature. It does react, however, with chlorine at room temperature if the mixture is exposed to light. At higher temperatures, propane burns in air, producing carbon dioxide and water as final products, and is valuable as a fuel.

About half the propane produced annually in the U.S. is used as a domestic and industrial fuel. When it is used as a fuel, propane is not separated from the related compounds, butane, ethane, and propylene. Butane, with b.p. −0.5° C (31.1° F), however, reduces somewhat the rate of evaporation of the liquid mixture. Propane forms a solid hydrate at low temperatures, and this causes great inconvenience when a blockage occurs in a natural-gas line. Propane is used also as so-called bottled gas, as a motor fuel, as a refrigerant, as a low-temperature solvent, and as a source of propylene and ethylene.

Propane melts at −189.9° C (−309.8° F) and boils at −42.1° C (−43.8° F).

PROPELLER, mechanical device that produces a force, or thrust, along the axis of rotation when rotated in a fluid, gas or liquid. Propellers may operate in either air or water, although a propeller designed for efficient operation in one of these media would be extremely inefficient in the other. Virtually all ships are equipped with propellers, and until the development of jet propulsion (q.v.), virtually all aircraft, except gliders, were also propelled in the same way. A propeller, mounted on a high-speed wheel geared to a generator, acts as a windmill (q.v.) when placed in a wind current.

The propeller is essentially a screw that, when turned, pulls itself through the air or water in the same way that a bolt pulls itself through a nut. Marine propellers are frequently termed *screws,* and aircraft propellers are termed *airscrews* in Great Britain. Typical propellers consist of two, three, or four blades, each of which is a section of a helix, which is the geometric form of a screw thread. The distance that a propeller or propeller blade will move forward when the propeller shaft is given one complete rotation, if there is no slippage, is called the geometric pitch; this corresponds to the pitch, or the distance between adjacent threads, of a simple screw. The distance that the propeller actually moves through the air or water in one rotation is called the effective pitch, and the difference between effective and geometric pitch is called slip. In general, an efficient propeller slips little, and the

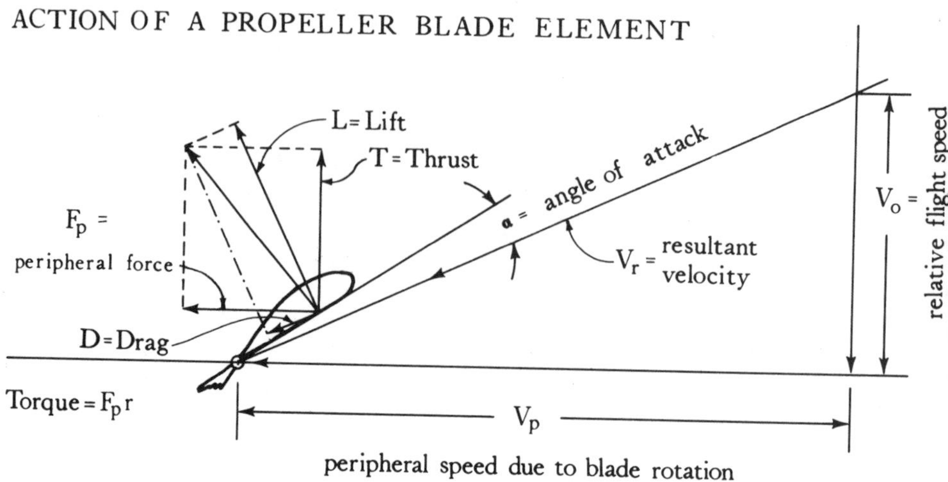

effective pitch is almost equal to the geometric pitch; the criterion of propeller efficiency is not slip, however, but the ratio of propulsive energy produced to energy consumed in rotating the propeller shaft. Aircraft propellers are often operated at efficiencies as high as 86 percent, but marine propellers operate at lower efficiencies.

Aircraft Propellers. An aircraft propeller blade is aerodynamically similar to a wing, which, when driven through the air, creates lift and drag, perpendicular and parallel to the air velocity relative to a section of the blade (*see* AERODYNAMICS; AIRPLANE). The forces created by the motion of the propeller are resolved into a component, thrust in the direction of the flight, when all the blade elements and the number of blades are accounted for. The other component in the plane of rotation represents the force that must be overcome by the torque, or the turning force, of the driving engine. The complete motion of a blade element involves a combination of the forward velocity represented by the flight speed, and the peripheral velocity due to the rotation of the blade. This simple concept of propeller action has been extensively refined by aerodynamicists in recent years. Another method of analysis of propeller action is based on the changes in momentum of the flow as it passes through the propeller disk. This approach was originally used by the British engineer and naval architect William Froude (1810–79) but, in general, it is not as comprehensive as the blade-element theory. The diagram shows the lift and drag on a blade section are resolved into the thrust and torque force, and also indicates how the flight speed and the rotational speed are combined.

For a given rotational speed, the resultant velocity at a blade element increases in magnitude as the forward speed is increased, while at the same time the angle of the resultant velocity vector (q.v.) with the plane of rotation is also increased. Thus, if the blade has a fixed pitch, a condition will eventually be reached at which the blade will produce little or no thrust. On the other hand, as the forward speed is decreased, the angle between the velocity vector and the blade will become so large as to cause the blade to stall, with a severe corresponding drop in the blade's efficiency.

In order to adapt a given propeller to aircraft with different flight characteristics, adjustable-pitch propellers are sometimes used, in which the blade can be rotated in the hub so as to alter the effective pitch. This operation must be accomplished on the ground with the propeller removed from the aircraft. A more effective procedure is to use a variable-pitch propeller with the pitch or blade angle controllable in flight so as to maintain operating conditions very close to the optimum. Propellers of this type are usually operated at a constant rotational speed by means of either a hydraulic or electrical governing mechanism. Controllable-pitch propellers are usually capable of being feathered, that is, the blade angle can be set parallel to the flight direction, so as to prevent windmilling that could otherwise occur in the event of an engine failure. The capability of setting the blade in a negative pitch condition may also be included in the design so as to provide negative thrust and aerodynamic braking action in landing.

Modern propeller blades are usually made either of solid aluminum alloy or of hollow steel. The propellers are equipped with deicing equipment. The propeller must be very precisely balanced, both statically and dynamically. If, for example, a 57-g (2-oz) weight were attached to the middle of one blade of a two-bladed propeller, and a 28.5-g (1-oz) weight were attached to the tip of the other blade, the propeller would be in static balance, that is, it would not rotate if the propeller shaft were placed on knife edges with the blades in any position; it would not, however, be in dynamic balance, and would vibrate if rotated at high speed.

The rotor of an autogiro or helicopter (qq.v.) is essentially similar to an ordinary aircraft propeller in that it consists of several blades, each shaped like an airfoil in cross section, and produces lift. The blades are not twisted, but, like ordinary aircraft propeller blades, their pitch may be varied.

Ship Propellers. A ship propeller operates in much the same way as the airplane propeller. In the ship propeller, however, each blade is very broad (from leading to trailing edge) and very thin. The blades are usually built of copper alloys to resist corrosion. The speed of sound in water is much higher than the speed in air, and because of the high frictional resistance of water, the top speed never approaches the speed of sound. Although efficiencies as high as 77 percent have been achieved with experimental propellers, most ship propellers operate at efficiencies of about 56 percent. Clearance is also less of a problem on ship propellers, although the diameter and position of the propeller are limited by the loss in efficiency if the propeller blades come anywhere near the surface of the water. The principal problem of ship-propeller design and operation is cavitation, the formation of a vacuum along parts of the propeller blade, which leads to excessive slip, loss of efficiency, and pitting of the blades. It also causes excessive underwater noise, a serious disadvantage on submarines.

See also FLUID MECHANICS.

PROPERTIUS, Sextus (50?–15? BC), Roman poet, born in Assisi. After studying law at Rome, he devoted himself to the writing of elegies, primarily on sensual love. The source of his inspiration was his mistress Hostia (fl. 29–24 BC), whom he called Cynthia. Propertius composed four books of elegies. The first, published about 25 BC, deals almost entirely with his love for Cynthia. It brought the author instant recognition and the patronage and friendship of the statesman Maecenas. Of the remaining three books, two are devoted to love lyrics, but the last is diversified in subject matter.

PROPERTY, any object or right that can be owned. Ownership involves, first and foremost, possession; in simple societies to possess something is to own it. Beyond possession, ownership in modern societies implies the right to use, prevent others from using, and dispose of property, and it implies the protection of such rights by the government.

Property is usually obtained by purchase, inheritance, or gift. Ownership may be public or private. Public ownership is by the government. Private ownership is by an individual, a group of individuals, a corporation, or some other form of organization.

Types of Property. The two kinds of property are real and personal. Real property, according to English legal tradition, is the land and anything firmly attached to it, such as buildings and the permanent fixtures of those buildings, and the minerals beneath the surface of the land. Personal property is anything that can be owned other than real property. Personal property can be divided into tangible and intangible property. Tangible property exists physically; an example is a book. Intangible personal property has no physical existence but nevertheless can be legally owned; an example is patent rights. Certain items, such as the atmosphere and the high seas, are viewed as neither real nor personal property.

History. The concept of property originated in ancient times. Societies apparently held most property rights—such as the right to hunt or fish in a given area—in common. Although some private ownership of personal property, such as weapons and cooking utensils, existed, real property seems to have been publicly owned. Land was not privately owned until the demise of the Middle Ages. Under feudalism, land could be held, not owned, and such holdings involved numerous obligations. In the modern sense of ownership, only the monarch and the church owned land.

The rise of a mercantile class in late feudal times gradually affected the relative importance of real and personal property. Personal property had historically been of only minor importance in comparison to the land itself. Thus, little regulation of the ownership, transfer, and inheritance of personal property existed. The rising middle class could amass wealth and transmit it at will, with comparative ease. With the Industrial Revolution, the consequent shift away from agriculture, and the establishment of revenue-producing stocks and bonds, personal property became as important as real property. Land then became a commodity that could be bought and sold like anything else.

Property and Political Philosophies. The concept of private property has been challenged by political philosophies such as communism and socialism. According to Communist doctrine, for example, ownership of real property and most personal property should be public; that is, the state should own the means of industrial production, as well as all wealth-generating personal property (*see* MARX, KARL). Actual Communist societies have, in fact, retained some private property, just as capitalist governments own some property publicly. Socialist societies do not generally hold that all property must be owned by the state; much of it is privately held.

PROPHECY, religious phenomenon in which a message is sent by God (or by a god) to human beings through an intermediary, or prophet. The message may contain a reference to future events, but it is often simply a warning, encouragement, or piece of information. Prophecy in its fullest sense thus includes augury, divination (q.v.), and oracles (*see* ORACLE), which are techniques by which, it is believed, the will of the gods can be learned. Prophets have often spoken in ecstasy, a state that may be induced by various methods, including dance or music. The emphasis of the prophetic message has varied, some prophets stressing the cultic, others the moral, and still others the missionary aspect of religious life. Prophets have appeared throughout history and in virtually all societies.

Eastern Religions. The scriptures of Hinduism (q.v.) contain several prophetic messages. The Buddha's advent on earth is said to have been predicted long before his birth (*see* BUDDHISM). In China, prophecy, particularly the use of divination, was a common religious practice. The use of the *I Ching* (q.v.), or *Book of Changes,* remained popular among all classes of Chinese society, even though the classical Confucian state religion (*see* CONFUCIANISM) stressed the superiority of reason to inspiration and divination.

Judaism and Christianity. Prophecy was elevated to an unprecedented religious significance in Judaism and Christianity. According to Judaism (q.v.), the prophet is an individual chosen by God, often against his will, to reveal God's intentions and plans to the people. As a bearer of divine revelation, he often experiences God's overwhelming presence and receives the strength to communicate to others what God has said, even though this may lead to persecution, suffering, and death.

Christianity (q.v.) inherited the idea of prophecy from Judaism, and Christians interpret Hebrew writings in light of the teachings of Christ, who is considered the prophet promised in Deuteronomy. Indeed, in many respects Jesus was a typical Judaic prophet. Prophecy was recognized as a gift in apostolic times, but it gradually disappeared as the hierarchical structure of the church began to develop toward the end of the 1st century, discouraging individual inspiration. Christian visionaries throughout the ages have often been called prophetic, but they never achieved the status of the great prophets.

Islam. Islam (q.v.) accepts in principle the prophetic tradition of Judaism and regards Muhammad as the final prophet, the seal, or culmination, of a line of prophets running from Adam through Christ. Despite this belief, followers of the Islamic mystical movement called Sufism (q.v.) have at times assumed a prophetic role.

Explanations of Prophecy. Prophecy has been the subject of much debate among scholars, whose discussion has often centered on the question of whether or not prophecy derives from some force external to the prophet. One tendency is to view prophecy as an essentially subconscious psychological phenomenon, involving hallucination, wishful thinking, guesswork, and sometimes forgery. Another theory also relates prophecy to the subconscious mind, but ultimately traces it to the workings of God. Some historians of religion regard the true prophet as one who, like the mystic, is raised to a supranormal psychological state by divine intervention.

See also OCCULTISM. J.A.Sa.

PROPHET. *See* PROPHECY.

PROPORTION, in arithmetic and geometry, particular kind of relation between groups of numbers or quantities. According to the arithmetical definition, proportion is the equality of ratios; ratio is in turn defined as the relation of two numbers to each other, shown by a division of the one by the other. Thus, the ratio of 12 to 3, expressed by 12/3, or 4, denotes that 12 contains 3 four times. The ratio of 8 to 2 is also 4, and therefore, according to the definition of proportion, the four numbers, 12, 3, 8, and 2, are in proportion, or 12:3::8:2, read 12 is to 3 as 8 is to 2. In every true proportion "the product of the first and last terms (the extremes) is equal to the product of the second and third term (the means)"; upon this property directly depends the arithmetical rule called proportion. The object of this rule is to find a fourth number that is proportional to three given numbers; the number is found by multiplying together the second and third terms and dividing the product by the first. Continued proportion is a property of every three consecutive or equidistant terms in a geometric progression (q.v.), for instance, in the series 2, 4, 8, 16, 32 . . ., 2:4::4:8 and 4:8::8:16.

In ancient Greece the theory of numbers was not adequate to give an arithmetical account of geometrical magnitudes. Eudoxus of Cnidus therefore proposed a separate theory of geometrical proportion in the early 4th century BC. An account of this theory is found in books five and six of Euclid's *Elements*. J.Si.; REV. BY J.Le.B.

PROPORTIONAL REPRESENTATION, electoral system designed to produce legislative bodies in which the number of seats held by any group or party is proportional to the number of votes cast for members of that group during the most recent election. The purpose of proportional representation has usually been to reduce the power of a dominant political party and to provide minority groups with a degree of representation that has been denied them previously.

History. Modern systems of proportional representation probably originated during the French Revolution. The principle was favored by the British philosopher John Stuart Mill, who believed that in several of the new national states it might protect the interests of ethnic and linguistic minorities that were then seriously threatened by the domination of the majority. The technique was first used in Denmark in 1855, and subsequently in such multinational countries as Switzerland (1891), Belgium (1899), and Finland (1906). By 1920, some form of proportional representation was being used by almost all the countries of continental Europe. A variant of proportional representation used in the Weimar Republic in Germany in the 1920s is thought to have been instrumental in allowing the National Socialist party to gain legislative representation.

During the past 50 years, the practices of proportional representation have been subject to several modifications and refinements. The "list system" used by most European democracies for legislative elections allows the voter to select a party, which is then allotted representation proportional to the number of votes it has received. The Hare System, first proposed by the British barrister Thomas Hare (1806–91), is used primarily in Anglo-Saxon countries, in an effort to make every voter equally influential in the electoral process. This system, as used frequently in local elections, allows each voter to submit a schedule of preferences; candidates are marked in numerical order according to the number of representatives to be chosen; the totaling of these preferences determines the election.

Application in the U.S. The Hare System and the principles of proportional representation were advocated by municipal reformers in the U.S. during the early 20th century. The movement for proportional representation finally brought the system to 23 towns and cities, where reformers said that it would give each vote its maximum influence. They hoped to prevent "boss" and "machine" politics and to assure honest representation of minority groups. In Cincinnati, Ohio, the reformers of the 1920s used proportional representation to break the power of the local Republican party, which had dictated civic affairs for more than a generation. In New York City, where the system was used from 1937 to 1948, it was directed against the domination of the Democratic party. In both cities the proportional system permitted the representation of groups normally excluded by majority politics, such as blacks, socialists, and Communists. Opponents argued that the system was too complicated and that it offered an undesirable attraction to extremists. It was subsequently abandoned in New York and Cincinnati and in other cities that had adopted it. In the 1970s, the Democratic party began using proportional representation in selecting delegates to its national political convention.

PROSERPINE. *See* PERSEPHONE.

PROSODY, general term for the art of writing poetry, involving the study of the laws of metrical structure, or versification (q.v.).

PROSSER, Gabriel (c. 1776–1800), American leader of an aborted slave uprising, whose intention was to create a free black state in Virginia. Born near Richmond, he was the son of an African mother who instilled in him the love of freedom. Inspired perhaps by the success of the black revolutionaries of Haiti, he plotted with other slaves, notably Jack Bowler (d. 1800), in the spring of 1800 to seize the arsenal at Richmond and kill whites. On August 30 as many as 1000 armed slaves gathered outside Richmond ready for action. A torrential downpour and thunderstorm, however, washed away a bridge vital to the insurrectionists' march; at the same time Gov. James Monroe, the future president, was informed of the plot and dispatched the state militia against them. Prosser and some 35 of his young comrades were captured and hanged.

PROSTAGLANDINS, in biochemistry and medicine, family of hormonelike chemicals occurring naturally in all mammals (*see* BIOCHEMISTRY; HORMONE). Prostaglandins, fatty-acid derivatives, are found in almost all tissues in the human body. More than a dozen biologically important forms of prostaglandins occur, affecting many essential physiological functions.

Although they were first identified in 1935 by the Swedish physiologist Ulf von Euler (1905–83), research into their actual composition, structure, functions, and medical uses began in the late 1960s. The British pharmacologist John Robert Vane (1927–) showed in 1971 that the many medical uses of aspirin (q.v.) stem from its ability to block the production of certain prostaglandins.

The first uses of prostaglandins were in obstetrics (q.v.). By constricting blood vessels in the uterus, some prostaglandins stimulate contractions, making them useful in delivery or therapeutic abortion. In the late 1970s this same action was shown to cause the pain and cramping, called dysmenorrhea, that many women experience during the menstrual period. Administration of drugs that inhibit prostaglandin synthesis, such as ibuprofen and naproxen, relieves dysmenorrhea in most cases. The effects of prostaglandins on blood vessels are also thought to cause some migraine headaches.

The two prostaglandins discovered in the 1970s, thromboxane and prostacyclin, were found to affect the clotting ability of blood: one of them (thromboxane) promoting and the other (prostacyclin) inhibiting the clumping of platelets (thrombocytes), the small corpuscles in the blood (q.v.) that aid in wound healing. Because aggregation of platelets is thought to contribute to stroke and heart attacks, prostaglandin-synthesis inhibitors such as aspirin are now being tested for the ability to prevent these events. Prostaglandins also promote inflammation (q.v.); thus drugs that block prostaglandin synthesis are effective against arthritis (q.v.) and similar diseases.

Prostaglandins block production of gastric acid, and work is progressing on the development of drugs that may prove useful for treatment of peptic ulcer and other conditions caused by gastric hyperactivity.

For further information on this topic, see the Bibliography in volume 28, sections 493–94.

PROSTATE GLAND, glandular structure surrounding the male urethra immediately in front of and beneath the neck of the bladder. Its function is to produce a fluid that is admixed with sperm from the testes and fluid from the seminal vesicles to form semen. The prostate gland is often the site of acute or chronic inflammation that causes discomfort and a urethral discharge. The most frequent disorder to which it is subject—chronic enlargement, or hypertrophy—occurs in later life and is the most common cause of difficulty in urinating and retention of urine. In severe cases it may have to be removed surgically, an operation known as prostatectomy. Cancer of the prostate is a frequent form of cancer in men. *See* REPRODUCTIVE SYSTEM.

PROSTHETICS, mechanical contrivances adapted to reproduce the form, and as far as possible, the function, of a lost or absent member. The replacement of a missing body part by an artificial substitute is called prosthesis; the branch of surgery dealing with prosthesis is prosthetics.

History. Artificial limbs, in one form or other, have been in use from ancient times. In 1885 a specimen was discovered in a tomb at Capua, Italy, along with other relics dating from 300 BC. The celebrated artificial hand built in 1509 for the German knight Gőtz von Berlichingen (1480–1562), who was called Gőtz of the Iron Hand, weighed about 1.4 kg (3 lb) and had articulated fingers so constructed as to be able to grasp a sword or lance. The hand is in the Nuremberg Museum and is still in working order. Early in the 19th century a German prosthetist built a hand with fingers that could be flexed or extended without assistance and yet could still close to hold light objects, such as a pen, a handkerchief, or a hat. In 1851 a French prosthetist invented an artificial arm fitted with a wooden hand and attached to a leather socket that fitted the stump firmly. The fingers were half-closed, the thumb pivoted on a pin and could press firmly against the fingertips by a concealed, strong rubber band; the grasp of the thumb could be operated by a mechanism attached to the opposite shoulder. The same inventor devised a leg that reproduced a natural gait and lengthened the stride.

Development. Before World War I, wood was universally considered the best substance for making artificial legs. Prosthetic devices made of leather reinforced with metal bands tended to lose their shape and were therefore unsatisfactory. Finally, the use of an aluminum alloy called Duraluminum, and later of fiber materials, made possible the manufacture of an artificial limb that was both lightweight and strong. Synthetic polymers now being introduced provide a skinlike covering for some forms of prosthesis.

Only in recent years, as a result of the needs arising out of the two world wars, has the manufacture of prosthetic devices developed into a science. Artificial legs with joints at knee and ankle can simulate a natural gait. The arm presents many more difficulties to the maker than the leg, and intricate mechanical devices make the use of metal imperative. Artificial arms are fitted with elbow joints and wrists capable of rotation. With the aid of springs controlled by shoulder movements, the hand can be manipulated, assuring a positive grip. Hip joint prostheses can provide virtually normal mobility for persons with damaged hip joints (*see* HIP).

Application. To ensure maximum comfort for the wearer some prosthetic devices are now fitted immediately following amputation of the natural limb. A rigid plaster dressing is applied to the site, serving as a socket for the attachment of a temporary prosthetic device. More recently, use of a removable plaster dressing has reduced pain and infections while the prosthesis is being fitted. In certain severe cases permanent artificial arms are equipped with small battery-powered motors, which facilitate movement at the joints.

The design and development of prosthetic devices are coordinated by the Committee on Prosthetics Research and Development of the National Research Council. Special prosthetic training schools have been set up at several universities for the teaching of modern prosthetic concepts to physicians, surgeons, prosthetists, and physical and rehabilitation counselors. H.R.L.

PROSTITUTION, the performance of sexual acts solely for the purpose of material gain. Persons prostitute themselves when they grant sexual favors to others in exchange for money, gifts, or other payment and in so doing use their bodies as commodities. In legal terms, the word *prostitute* refers only to those who engage overtly in such sexual-economic transactions, usually for a specified sum of money. Prostitutes may be of either sex, but throughout history the majority have been women, reflecting both the traditional socioeconomic dependence of women and the tendency to exploit female sexuality. Although prostitution has often been characterized as the "world's oldest profession," the concept of women as property, which prevailed in most cultures until the end of the 19th century, meant that the profits of the profession most often accrued to the men who controlled it. Men have traditionally been characterized as procurers and customers, but they are increasingly being identified as prostitutes. They generally serve male customers and sometimes impersonate women.

Prostitution in various forms has existed from earliest times. It is dependent on the economic, social, and sexual values of a society. It has been secular or under the guise of religion. In some societies prostitution was believed to ensure the preservation of the family. Women have usually entered prostitution through coercion or under economic stress. In most societies prostitutes have had low social status and a restricted future, because their sexual service was disapproved and considered degrading. A few female prostitutes, however, have acquired wealth and power through marriage; one example is the Byzantine empress Theodora, wife of Justinian I.

Preindustrial Societies. Prostitution was widespread in preindustrial societies. The exchange of wives by their husbands was a practice among many primitive peoples. In the ancient Middle East and India temples maintained large numbers of prostitutes. Sexual intercourse with them was believed to facilitate communion with the gods.

In this early 17th-century engraving by the Dutch engraver Crispin Van De Passe, an apparently affluent prostitute leads a client into her bedchamber while her servant exits discreetly.
New York Public Library Picture Collection

In ancient Greece prostitution flourished on all levels of society. Prostitutes of the lowest level worked in licensed brothels and were required to wear distinctive clothing as a badge of their vocation. Prostitutes of a higher level usually were skilled dancers and singers. Those of the highest level, the hetaerae, kept salons where politicians met, and they often attained power and influence.

In ancient Rome prostitution was common despite severe legal restrictions. Female slaves, captured abroad by the Roman legions, were impressed into urban brothels or exploited by owners in the households they served. The Roman authorities attempted to limit the spread of slave prostitution and often resorted to harsh measures. Brothel inmates, called *meretrices,* were forced to register with the government for life, to wear garish blond wigs and other distinctive raiment, to forfeit all civil rights, and to pay a heavy tax.

In the Middle Ages the Christian church, which valued chastity, attempted to convert or rehabilitate individual prostitutes but refrained from campaigning against the institution itself. In so doing the church followed the teaching of St. Augustine, who held that the elimination of prostitution would breed even worse forms of immorality and perversion, because men would continue to seek sexual contact outside marriage. By the late Middle Ages, prostitution had reached a high point in Western history. Licensed brothels flourished throughout Europe, yielding enormous revenues to government officials and corrupt churchmen. In Asia, where women were held in low esteem and no religious deterrent existed, prostitution was accepted as natural.

During the 16th century prostitution declined sharply in Europe, largely as the result of stern reprisals by Protestants and Roman Catholics. They condemned the immorality of brothels and their inmates, but they were also motivated by the perception of a connection between prostitution and an outbreak of syphilis, a previously unknown disease. Brothels in many cities were closed by the authorities. Under a typical ordinance, enacted in Paris in 1635, prostitutes were flogged, shaved bald, and exiled for life without formal trial.

Industrial Societies. These harsh strictures did not, however, eradicate prostitution and venereal disease. Gradually it became obvious that these ills were increasing, especially in the large, crowded cities that accompanied the industrialization of the West in the 18th and 19th centuries. Beginning with Prussia in 1700, most continental European governments shifted their tactics from suppression of prostitution and venereal disease to control through a system of compulsory registration, licensed brothels, and medical inspection of prostitutes. Great Britain, although it did not license brothels, passed Contagious Disease Prevention acts in the 1860s providing for medical inspection of prostitutes in certain naval and military districts. In Britain and the U.S. prostitution flourished openly in urban red-light districts. City officials, viewing prostitutes as a "necessary evil," allowed prostitutes to ply their trade as long as they refrained from annoying any "respectable" person who happened into the area. A lucrative white-slave trade developed, in which women and girls were shipped across international borders for immoral purposes.

In time the ineffectuality and corruption of licensed prostitution stirred protests throughout Europe. Britain repealed the Contagious Disease Prevention acts, which were not proving to be a deterrent to venereal disease and were, moreover, regarded as a threat to the civil liberties of their subjects. Many governments sought to check prostitution by attacking the international traffic in women and children. Britain passed the Criminal Amendment Act (1885) forbidding such traffic, and 13 major powers signed a treaty (1904) outlawing it and providing for an international exchange of data on the subject.

Prostitution in the U.S. Beginning about 1910, religious and civic organizations in the U.S. developed a nationwide campaign against both the immorality of prostitution and its relationship to venereal disease. On the federal level, Congress passed the White Slave Traffic Act (Mann Act, 1910) forbidding the interstate transport of women and girls for immoral purposes. On the local level, many antiprostitution laws were passed. Some laws reflected the belief that prostitutes were misguided, coerced unfortunates who needed rehabilitation and protection from procurers. Others represented the view that prostitutes were morally or mentally inferior human beings. Although both kinds of laws still exist, the latter type is enforced today.

Prostitution in the U.S. in the late 20th century takes various forms. Some prostitutes, or "call girls," operate out of their own apartments and maintain a list of regular customers. Some follow convention circuits or work in certain resort areas, such as Las Vegas, Nev., where demand for their services is high. Others work in so-called massage parlors, a newer version of the old-time brothel. The majority are "streetwalkers," soliciting, or being solicited by, customers on city streets. Increasing numbers are young runaways to the city who turn to the streets for survival. Because the statutes are enforced in such a way as to punish overtness and visibility rather than any specific act, almost all of the prostitutes arrested each year are streetwalkers. Customers, although legally culpable, are rarely arrested.

Many prostitutes are managed by men known as pimps, who occasionally act as procurers and who usually take much of the money earned by the women in their "stables." For the prostitute, the pimp often takes the place of a husband or father figure. He provides some measure of protection, arranges for bail when necessary, and often forms emotional attachments with the women who work for him.

Current U.S. Attitudes. Until the 1960s, attitudes toward prostitution were based on the Judeo-Christian view of immorality. Researchers have recently attempted to separate moral issues from the reality of prostitution. The rationale for its continued illegal status in the U.S. rests on three assumptions: prostitution is linked to organized crime; prostitution is responsible for much ancillary crime; and prostitution is the cause of an increase in venereal disease. These assumptions are now in question.

Recognized experts have pointed out that prostitution is no longer an attractive investment for organized crime because it is difficult to control, is too visible, and affords too small a return compared to the severe penalties for procuring. It is obvious that ancillary crime—larceny, robbery, assault, and misuse of narcotics—does occur in conjunction with prostitution, especially when a streetwalker is involved. Whether it is rational to make one activity criminal in order to reduce or control another merits serious inquiry. Finally, public-health officials indicate that prostitutes account for only a small percentage of the venereal disease cases in the U.S. Greater sexual freedom has made young people the major source of such cases.

Furthermore, strong arguments have been made in support of legalizing prostitution. Decriminalization would free the courts and police from handling victimless crime, allowing these forces more time to deal with serious and violent crimes. The constitutional question of violation of equal protection has also been raised, since the law penalizes prostitutes but not their customers.

In the U.S. today, prostitution is legal only in the state of Nevada (at the option of each county government). Polls have shown that approximately half of the U.S. population would favor decriminalization of prostitution throughout the country.

A Worldwide Social Problem. Prostitution exists almost everywhere; in 1985 a revival of the practice was even noted in China, where emphasis on equality between the sexes combined with government repression seemed to have eliminated the profession. The issue of prostitution has been partially resolved through decriminalization and tolerance. The U.S. remains one of the few countries with laws against prostitution. In other nations criminal laws seek instead to deal with the social problems of prostitution through control of public solicitation and restriction of those who would exploit prostitutes. The prevalence of the AIDS virus among prostitutes, however, caused renewed concern about the problem of prostitution in the 1980s. J.J.

For further information on this topic, see the Bibliography in volume 28, section 155.

PROTACTINIUM, formerly protoactinium, radioactive metallic element, symbol Pa, member of the actinide series (q.v.) of the periodic table (*see* PERIODIC LAW); at.no. 91, at.wt. (most stable isotope) 231. Protactinium melts at about 1552° C (about 2826° F), boils at about 4227° C (about 7641° F), and has a sp.gr. of 15.37. It was discovered in 1918 by the Austrian-Swedish physicist Lise Meitner and the German physical chemist Otto Hahn. Protactinium is a member of the uranium-actinium radioactive-decay series and is found in uranium ores. Isotopes of protactinium ranging in mass number from 215 to 238 are known. Protactinium-233 has a half-life of 27 days. Protactinium-231 has a half-life of more than 32,000 years; by emission of an alpha particle it decays to actinium. *See* RADIOACTIVITY.

PROTAGORAS (480?–411? BC), Greek philosopher, born in Abdera, Thrace. About 445 BC he went to Athens, where he befriended the statesman Pericles and won great fame as a teacher and philosopher. Protagoras was the first thinker to call himself a Sophist and to teach for pay, receiving large sums from his pupils. He gave instruction in grammar, rhetoric, and the interpretation of poetry. His chief works, of which only a few fragments have survived, were entitled *Truth* and *On the Gods.* The basis of his speculation was the doctrine that nothing is absolutely good or bad, true or false, and that each individual is his or her own final authority; this belief is summed up in his saying: "Man is the measure of all things." Charged with impiety, he fled into exile; he drowned on his way to Sicily. Two dialogues by Plato, the *Theaetetus* and the *Protagoras,* refuted the doctrines of Protagoras. G.E.D.

PROTECTORATE, in international law, relationship between two states in which the stronger state guarantees to protect the weaker one from external aggression or internal disturbance in return for full or partial control over its foreign and domestic affairs. This relationship is established by treaty between the states concerned; usually the extent and character of the protectorate are outlined in the treaty. No matter how great the right of interference—and in some cases it may be tantamount to virtual control—the protected state retains its nominal sovereignty, thus differing from a colony (*see* COLONIES AND COLONIALISM) or a mandated territory (*see* MANDATE).

With the growth of modern nation-states, many small, autonomous political units placed themselves under the protection of a more powerful state, as Trieste did with Austria in 1382. Particularly during the 19th century many European powers used the protectorate to control territories that, for diplomatic reasons such as fear of war with other powers, they were unwilling or unable to incorporate bodily into their growing colonial empires. *See* IMPERIALISM; INTERNATIONAL LAW.

PROTEIN, any of a large number of organic compounds that make up living organisms and are essential to their functioning. First discovered in 1838, proteins are now recognized as the predominant ingredients of cells, making up more than 50 percent of the dry weight of animals. The word *protein* is coined from the Greek *proteios*, or "primary."

Protein molecules range from the long, insoluble fibers that make up connective tissue and hair to the compact, soluble globules that can pass through cell membranes and set off metabolic reactions. They are all large molecules, ranging in molecular weight from a few thousand to more than a million, and they are specific for each species and for each organ of each species. Humans have an estimated 30,000 different proteins, of which only about 2 percent have been adequately described. Proteins in the diet serve primarily to build and maintain cells, but their chemical breakdown also provides energy, yielding close to the same 4 calories per gram as do carbohydrates (*see* METABOLISM).

Besides their function in growth and cell maintenance, proteins are also responsible for muscle contraction. The digestive enzymes are proteins, as are insulin and most other hormones. The antibodies of the immune system (q.v.) are proteins, and proteins such as hemoglobin carry vital substances throughout the body. Proteins also transmit all hereditary characteristics in the form of genes (*see* GENE).

Nutrition. Whether found in humans or in single-celled bacteria, proteins are composed of units of about 20 different amino acids (q.v.), which, in turn, are composed of carbon, hydrogen, oxygen, nitrogen, and sometimes sulfur. In a protein molecule these acids form peptide bonds—bonds between amino and carboxyl (COOH) groups—in long strands (polypeptide chains). The almost numberless combinations in which the acids line up, and the helical and globular shapes into which the strands coil, help to explain the great diversity of tasks that proteins perform in living matter.

To synthesize its life-essential proteins, each species needs given proportions of the 20 main amino acids. Although plants can manufacture all their amino acids from nitrogen, carbon dioxide, and other chemicals through photosynthesis (q.v.), most other organisms can manufacture only some of them. The remaining ones, called essential amino acids, must be derived from food. Eight essential amino acids are needed to maintain health in humans: leucine, isoleucine, lysine, methionine, phenylalanine, theonine, tryptophan, and valine. All of these are available in proteins produced in the seeds of plants, but because plant sources are often weak in lysine and tryptophan, nutrition experts advise supplementing the diet with animal protein from meat, eggs, and milk, which contain all the essential acids.

Most diets—especially in the United States, where animal protein is eaten to excess—contain all the essential amino acids. (Kwashiorkor, a wasting disease among children in tropical Africa, is due to an amino acid deficiency.) For adults, the Recommended Dietary Allowance (RDA) for protein is 0.79 g per kg (0.36 g per lb) of body weight each day. For children and infants this RDA is doubled and tripled, respectively, because of their rapid growth (*see* NUTRITION, HUMAN).

Structure of Proteins. The simplest protein, called a primary structure, is a linear sequence of amino acids. Different sequences of the acids along a chain, however, affect the structure of a protein molecule in different ways. Forces such as hydrogen bonds, disulfied bridges, attractions between positive and negative charges, and hydrophobic ("water-fearing") and hydrophilic ("water-loving") linkages cause a protein molecule to coil or fold into a secondary structure, examples of which are the so-called alpha helix and the beta pleated sheet. When forces cause the molecule to become even more compact, as in globular proteins, a protein of a tertiary structure is formed. When a protein is made up of more than one polypeptide chain, as in hemoglobin (q.v.) and some enzymes, it is called a quaternary structure.

Interaction with Other Proteins. Polypeptide chains are sequenced and coiled in such a way that the hydrophobic amino acids usually face inward, giving the molecule stability, and the hydrophilic amino acids face outward, where they are free to interact with other compounds and especially other proteins. Globular proteins, in particular, can join with a specific compound such as a vitamin derivative and form a coenzyme (*see* ENZYME), or join with a specific protein and form an assembly of proteins needed for cell chemistry or structure.

Fibrous Proteins. The major fibrous proteins, described below, are collagen, keratin, fibrinogen, and muscle proteins.

Collagen. Collagen, which makes up bone, skin, tendons, and cartilage, is the most abundant protein found in vertebrates. The molecule usually contains three very long polypeptide chains, each with about 1000 amino acids, that twist into a regularly repeating triple helix and give tendons and skin their great tensile strength. When long collagen fibrils are denatured by boiling, their chains are shortened to form gelatin (q.v.).

Keratin. Keratin, which makes up the outermost layer of skin and the hair, scales, hooves, nails, and feathers of animals, twists into a regularly repeating coil called an alpha helix. Serving to protect the body against the environment, keratin is completely insoluble in water. Its many disulfide bonds make it an extremely stable protein, able to resist the action of proteolytic (protein-hydrolyzing) enzymes. In beauty treatments, human hair is set under a reducing agent, such as thioglycol, to reduce the number of disulfide bonds, which are then restored when the hair is exposed to oxygen.

Fibrinogen. Fibrinogen is a blood plasma protein responsible for blood clotting. With the catalytic action of thrombin, fibrinogen is converted into molecules of the insoluble protein fibrin, which link together to form clots.

Muscle proteins. Myosin, the protein chiefly responsible for muscle contraction, combines with actin, another muscle protein, forming actomyosin, the different filaments of which shorten, causing the contracting action.

Globular Proteins. Unlike fibrous proteins, globular proteins are spherical and highly soluble. They play a dynamic role in body metabolism. Examples are albumin, globulin, casein, hemoglobin, all of the enzymes, and protein hormones. The albumins and globulins are classes of soluble proteins abundant in animal cells, blood serum, milk, and eggs. Hemoglobin is a respiratory protein that carries oxygen throughout the body and is responsible for the bright red color of red blood cells. More than 100 different human hemoglobins have been discovered, among which is hemoglobin S, the cause of sickle-cell anemia (q.v.), a hereditary disease suffered mainly by blacks.

Enzymes. All of the enzymes are globular proteins that combine rapidly with other substances, called substrate, to catalyze the numerous chemical reactions in the body. Chiefly responsible for metabolism and its regulation, these molecules have catalytic sites on which substrate fits in a lock-and-key manner to trigger and control metabolism throughout the body.

Protein hormones. These proteins, which come from the endocrine glands, do not act as enzymes. Instead they stimulate target organs that in turn initiate and control important activities—for example, the rate of metabolism and the production of digestive enzymes and milk. Insulin (q.v.), secreted by the islands of Langerhans, regulates carbohydrate metabolism by controlling blood glucose levels. Thyroglobulin, from the thyroid gland, regulates overall metabolism; calcitonin, also from the thyroid, lowers blood calcium levels. Angiogenin, a protein structurally determined in the mid-1980s, directly induces the growth of blood vessels in tissues.

Antibodies. Also called immunoglobulins, antibodies (*see* ANTIBODY) make up the thousands of different proteins that are generated in the blood serum in reaction to antigens (body-invading substances or organisms). A single antigen may elicit the production of many antibodies, which combine with different sites on the antigen molecule, neutralize it, and cause it to precipitate from the blood.

Microtubules. Globular proteins can also assemble into minute, hollow tubes that serve both to structure cells and to conduct substances from one part of a cell to another. Each of these microtubules, as they are called, is made up of two types of nearly spherical protein molecules that pair and join onto the growing end of the microtubule, adding on length as required. Microtubules also make up the inner structure of cilia, the hairlike appendages by which some microorganisms propel themselves. M.L.H.

For further information on this topic, see the Bibliography in volume 28, sections 439, 608.

PROTESILAUS, in Greek mythology, king of Phylace in Thessaly, who was killed in the Trojan War. An oracle had proclaimed that the first Greek to touch the Trojan soil would be the first to die. Aware of it, Protesilaus bravely leaped ashore and was slain. His wife, Laodamia, grieved so that the gods permitted him to visit her for three hours.

PROTESTANT EPISCOPAL CHURCH. *See* EPISCOPAL CHURCH.

PROTESTANTISM, one of the three major divisions of Christianity (q.v.), the others being Roman Catholicism and Orthodoxy. Protestantism began as a movement to reform the Western Christian church in the 16th century, resulting in the Protestant Reformation (q.v.), which severed the reformed churches from the Roman Catholic church. The declared aim of the original reformers was to restore the Christian faith as it had been at its beginning, while keeping what they thought valuable from the Roman Catholic tradition that had developed during the intervening centuries.

The four main Protestant traditions that emerged from the Reformation were the Lutheran (known in continental Europe as Evangelical), the Calvinist (Reformed), the Anabaptist, and the Anglican. Despite the considerable differences among them in doctrine and practice, they agreed in rejecting the authority of the pope and in emphasizing instead the authority of the Bible and the importance of individual faith.

The term Protestantism was given to the movement after the second Diet of Speyer (1529), an imperial assembly at which the Roman Catholic majority withdrew the tolerance granted to Lutherans at the first diet three years earlier. A protest was signed by six Lutheran princes and the leaders of 14 free cities of Germany, and Lutherans in general became known as Protestants. The term Protestant has gradually been attached to all Christian churches that are not Roman Catholic or part of the Orthodox or other Eastern Christian traditions. As the 1990s began, the world had about 436 million Protestants (including some 73 million Anglicans), constituting at least one-fourth of all Christians.

HISTORY

The Protestant movement actually preceded the 16th-century Reformation. Several dissident movements in the late medieval church anticipated the Reformation by protesting the pervasive corruption in the church and by criticizing fundamental Catholic teachings.

Precursors. Beginning in the 12th century, the Waldensians, followers of the merchant Peter Waldo (c. 1140–1217) of Lyons, France, practiced what they believed to be the simple, uncorrupted Christianity of the primitive church. The movement, concentrated in France and Italy, survived violent official persecution, and during the Reformation many Waldensians adopted Calvinism.

In the 1380s the Lollards (q.v.) arose in England, inspired by the teachings of the theologian John Wycliffe. Wycliffe denied the authority of morally corrupted church prelates, rejected transubstantiation (q.v.) and other traditional teachings, and advocated biblical faith. The Lollards suffered persecution but survived to play a role in the English Reformation.

Wycliffe's teachings strongly influenced the Bohemian reformer John Huss (Jan Hus), whose followers, called Hussites (q.v.), reformed the Bohemian church and achieved virtual independence after Huss's martyrdom in 1415. Many converted to Lutheranism in the 16th century.

The Reformation. A number of conditions in 16th-century Europe account for the success of Martin Luther and the other reformers as compared to their predecessors. Both the Holy Roman emperor and the pope were declining in power and were preoccupied with the threat posed by the Turks. The invention of printing in the 15th century made possible the rapid dissemination of the reformers' ideas. Finally, the growth of secular learning, the rise of nationalism, and the increasing resentment of the pope's authority among both rulers and ordinary citizens made people, especially in northern Europe, more receptive to Protestant teachings.

Luther. The event usually considered the beginning of the Reformation is Martin Luther's publication, in 1517, of his Ninety-five Theses attacking the indiscriminate sale of indulgences to finance the construction of Saint Peter's Basilica in Rome (*see* INDULGENCE). Luther, an Augustinian monk and professor of theology at the University of Wittenberg, had been unable to find assurance of salvation in traditional Catholic teachings. He came to believe that such assurance was to be found in the doctrine of justification by divine grace through faith (see Doctrines and Practices below), which he thought Catholic theology had obscured by giving equal weight to the efficacy of good works. The sale of indulgences, he believed, was an abuse that originated in the mistaken emphasis on works.

Luther at first intended only to bring about reform within the church, but he met with firm opposition. In refusing to recant his views and demanding to be proven wrong by Scripture, he denied the authority of the church, and he was excommunicated. Protected by Frederick the Wise of Saxony (1463–1525), he wrote a series of books and pamphlets, and his ideas spread rapidly throughout the states of Germany and elsewhere in Europe. In Scandinavia, national Lutheran churches were quickly established.

Zwingli. Within a few years of Luther's rebellion an independent and more radical reform movement emerged in Zürich, Switzerland, under the leadership of the Swiss pastor Huldreich Zwingli.

Zwingli's biblical studies led him to the conclusion that only what was specifically authorized by the Scriptures should be retained in church practice and doctrine. Lutheranism had kept many elements of the medieval liturgy, but Zwingli devised a very simple service, and, in opposition to both Roman Catholicism and Lutheranism, he interpreted the Eucharist (q.v.) as a purely symbolic ceremony. Zwingli's reforms, adopted peacefully through votes of the Zürich town council, soon spread to other Swiss cities.

Calvin. The dominant reformer in the generation after Luther and Zwingli was John Calvin, a French theologian who settled in Geneva in 1536. Calvin's reforms were not as radical as those of Zwingli, but they were accompanied by a severe regime that in effect combined church and state in order to enforce moral and doctrinal conformity. Calvin wrote the first systematic exposition of Protestant theology, set up a democratic presbyterian church government, and founded influential educational institutions that trained men such as John Knox, who introduced Calvinism into Scotland, where it became the established Presbyterian church. Calvinism also spread to France, where its adherents were known as Huguenots (q.v.), and to Holland, where it reinforced the Dutch determination to achieve independence from Catholic Spain.

England. The Anglican church became the established church in England when Henry VIII assumed (1534) the ecclesiastical authority over the English church that had previously been exercised by the pope. Henry's motive was to annul his marriage to Catherine of Aragón rather than to reform church doctrine, and he imposed severe laws upholding the major tenets of medieval Catholicism. Under King Edward VI and Queen Elizabeth, however, the Anglican church developed a distinctly Protestant creed that was set forth in the Thirty-nine Articles. Anglican ritual and church organization nevertheless retained many of the forms of Roman Catholicism, which were protested by Calvinist-influenced dissenters known as Puritans (*see* PURITANISM).

Radical Sects. As the Lutherans, Calvinists, and Anglicans formed established churches, a number of more radical Protestant groups emerged. All of them maintained that the established Protestants had not gone far enough in the direction of a simplified, biblical Christianity. They therefore attacked the established Protestant churches and the Roman Catholic church with equal vehemence and in turn were violently persecuted by both. Some of these groups led political rebellions or invaded churches, destroying stained-glass windows, statues, and organs. Others renounced all use of force. Most of them rejected ties between church and state. The most prominent of these sects were the Anabaptists (q.v.), who were concentrated in Germany and the Netherlands and who played a major role in the Peasants' War (q.v.). They rejected infant baptism, advocating baptism only of adult believers. The Mennonites (q.v.), an Anabaptist sect that originated in Holland and Switzerland, were pacifists who tried to form separate cooperative communities based on the principles of the New Testament. In England, a movement led by Robert Browne rejected church government by either presbyters or bishops and developed into the Separatists, or Independents. These earlier groups greatly influenced the Quakers, who began in the 1640s as followers of George Fox and who professed pacifism and the "inner light" (*see* FRIENDS, SOCIETY OF).

The American Colonies. Many of these smaller, more radical sects fled persecution by immigrating to America, beginning with the Puritans. They were followed to New England by Congregationalists and Baptists. The middle colonies were settled by a diversity of sects, particularly Lutherans, Mennonites, and Anabaptists. In the southern colonies the Church of England was made the established church.

Wars and Orthodoxy. The early history of Protestantism was marked by warfare in which political motives were entwined with religious ones. In Germany, the religious wars of the 16th century and the Thirty Years' War (q.v.) in the 17th century were bitter and devastating. In France the Calvinist Huguenots fought a bloody civil war with the Roman Catholics, culminating in the Massacre of Saint Bartholomew's Day (*see* SAINT BARTHOLOMEW'S DAY, MASSACRE OF) in 1572, in which many Huguenot leaders were killed. The Huguenots were granted toleration by the Edict of Nantes (1598), but most of them were forced to emigrate when it was revoked by Louis XIV in 1685. In England, the civil war between Parliament and monarchy largely corresponded to the division between the Puritans and the Anglicans. After the Peace of Westphalia (1648), Protestantism entered into a period of consolidation. On the Continent the 17th century was a period in which Protestant orthodoxy was carefully defined and systematically expounded. This tendency has subsequently been called Protestant Scholasticism, by analogy with the systematic Catholic theology of the Middle Ages. Its emphasis was on the authority of the Bible and on rigorous logic.

Pietism. By the 1670s in Germany a movement called Pietism (q.v.) developed in reaction to the intellectualism of orthodoxy. Under the leadership of the German pastor Philipp Jakob Spener, people began to meet in small groups in private homes to study the Bible and pray. Pietism stressed individual conversion and a simple, active piety rather than the acceptance of correct theological propositions. It spread throughout Germany and to Scandinavia and America.

Rationalism. The influence of scientific thought and the Enlightenment (*see* ENLIGHTENMENT, AGE OF) on Protestant theology was reflected in rationalism, a tendency that appeared in the late 17th and 18th centuries. It was anticipated by several earlier movements, including Arminianism (q.v.), which denied the Calvinist doctrine of unconditional predestination (q.v.), and Latitudinarianism, a tolerant, antidogmatic tendency that arose within the Church of England during the 17th century. Rationalism introduced a critical spirit into theology by insisting that traditional beliefs be examined in the light of reason and science. By stressing broad agreement on the major tenets of religion rather than the fine points of theology, it tended to undermine the rigid orthodoxies that had developed earlier in the 17th century. The purest expression of the rationalist tendency was Deism (q.v.), a philosophical religion that rejected revelation, miracles, and the specific dogmatic teachings of any church.

Another form of Protestant rationalism that became influential in the 18th century was Unitarianism (q.v.). It had originated in the 16th century on the Continent, where it was called Socinianism, after its founder, the Italian reformer Fausto Socinus. After the Toleration Act of 1689, Unitarianism was openly professed in England, and during the 18th century it began to gain adherents in New England as well. Unitarians denied the doctrines of the Trinity and the divinity of Jesus Christ, stressing instead his ethical teachings and example.

Methodism and Revivalism. The reaction against intellectual and formalistic tendencies in Protestantism that had produced Pietism continued in the 18th century, with the emergence of several popular movements that made a direct appeal to emotional religious experience. In England, the reaction took the form of Methodism (q.v.), founded by John and Charles Wesley, who were influenced by both Pietism and Arminianism. Stressing conversion and a concern for the poor, they preached to large outdoor meetings throughout Britain and brought about a revival of religious fervor among the British working classes, who had been alienated by the prevailing formalism and rationalism of the Church of England. Because of official disapproval, the movement eventually separated from the Anglican church and became one of the nonconformist denominations.

In the American colonies, the English evangelist George Whitefield and other itinerant ministers preached at large open-air religious revivals and inspired the first Great Awakening (q.v.), a general revival of religious enthusiasm.

The 19th Century. During the 19th century Protestantism became a worldwide movement as a result of intensive missionary activity. It also became increasingly varied, as new sects and theological tendencies appeared. The most influential Protestant theologian of the century was the German Friedrich Schleiermacher. Schleiermacher understood religion as an intuitive feeling of dependence on the Infinite, or God, which he believed to be a universal experience of humanity. This emphasis on religious experience rather than dogma was taken up by the theological school of liberalism. Liberal theologians tried to reconcile religion with science and modern society, and they made use of the new historical and critical techniques of biblical scholarship (q.v.) in an effort to distinguish the historical Jesus and his teachings from what they regarded as mythological and dogmatic embellishments.

The Oxford movement. Conservative trends were also present, notably the Oxford movement (q.v.) in the Church of England, which strongly affirmed the catholic and apostolic traditions of the church. Although some of its leaders, such as John Henry Newman, eventually entered the Roman Catholic church, the Anglo-Catholics, as the adherents of the Oxford movement came to be called, continued to exercise an important influence in the Anglican church, where they revived fasting and confessions and founded religious sisterhoods.

Revivalism. Revivalism continued to be important throughout the Protestant world, especially in the U.S., under the inspiration of such preachers as Dwight L. Moody. Many new revivalistic sects appeared, such as the Adventists and the Holiness churches (qq.v.).

Social concerns. Protestants played important roles in many humanitarian and reform movements during the century. In England evangelical Protestants were leaders of the agitation that led to the abolition by Parliament of slavery in British dominions. In the U.S. evangelical Protestants also actively campaigned against slavery (leading to schisms in some churches) and against intemperance, prostitution, and other social disorders. Responding to the probems of the Industrial Revolution, other movements, such as Christian Socialism and the Social Gospel (qq.v.), tried to employ Christian principles to bring about fundamental social changes.

The 20th Century. The 20th century produced two reactions against theological liberalism. One was Fundamentalism (q.v.), an American movement that was rooted in revivalism and insisted on the inerrancy of the Bible. The other was crisis theology, or neoorthodoxy, which developed in response to the suffering caused by World War I and which is particularly associated with the Swiss theologian Karl Barth. Barth reaffirmed the sinfulness of humanity, the absolute transcendence of God, and the essential human dependence on God, doctrines that had been central to the Reformation. Unlike the Fundamentalists, however, Barth accepted the results of modern biblical scholarship.

After World War II, Evangelicalism (q.v.), a more moderate outgrowth of Fundamentalism, became a major force in Protestantism. Concern with social and political issues also increased, as many Protestants participated in antiwar movements and the American civil rights movement led by the Baptist minister Martin Luther King, Jr.

Another important development was the ecumenical movement (q.v.), which brought about the mergers of many Protestant denominations throughout the world and led to the formation (1948) of the World Council of Churches. Protestants entered into dialogues with the Roman Catholic and Orthodox churches, as well as with non-Christian faiths.

BELIEFS AND PRACTICES

Most Protestant churches retained the central doctrines of the Roman Catholic and Orthodox traditions, such as the Trinity (q.v.), the atonement and resurrection of Christ, the authority of the Bible, and the sacramental character of bap-

The Union Baptist Church in Mystic, Conn. Most Protestant churches are characterized by sober, relatively severe interior architecture. Shown here is a usual arrangement of the sanctuary, with communion table, lectern, choir, and organ.
Dan Budnik–Woodfin Camp & Associates

tism (q.v.) and the Eucharist, or Lord's Supper. Certain doctrines and practices, however, distinguish the Protestant tradition from the two older Christian traditions.

Justification by Grace Through Faith. Luther believed that salvation depends not on human effort or merit but only on the freely given grace of God, which is accepted in faith. Good works are not disdained but are regarded as the result of God's grace working in the life of the believer. This doctrine of justification (q.v.) by grace through faith became a fundamental tenet of Protestant churches. Luther and other reformers believed that Catholicism had put too much emphasis on the need for believers to gain merits, to work their way into God's favor by performing good deeds, by fasting, by making pilgrimages, and, in the popular view of Luther's time, by buying indulgences. To Protestants this seemed to make the redemptive sacrifice of Christ unnecessary and to leave human beings, all of whom are necessarily sinners, in doubt as to their salvation. The reformers intended to stress the mercy of God, who bestows grace on undeserving sinners through the saving activity of Jesus Christ.

Authority of the Bible. Protestants affirm the authority of the Bible, which is considered the sole source and standard for their teachings; they reject the Roman Catholic position giving ultimate authority to the pope in matters of faith and morals. Luther and other reformers therefore made translations of the Bible to enable the laity to study it and use their own judgment in matters of doctrine. Despite this general agreement on the primacy of the Bible, however, Protestants disagree on questions of biblical interpretation and scholarship. Those who accept the results of the "higher criticism," the historical and critical study of the Bible that was developed during the 19th and 20th centuries, are willing to consider some biblical passages inauthentic and to interpret certain other passages in a symbolic or allegorical sense. Conservative Protestants, such as Fundamentalists and most Evangelicals, insist on the absolute inerrancy of the Bible, not only in questions of faith but also in relevant areas of history, geography, and science. Furthermore, some Protestants believe that individual judgment should decide all questions of biblical interpretation, while others defer to the confessions formulated by some churches to guide members in their faith.

Priesthood of All Believers. The leaders of the Reformation reacted against the Catholic institution of the priesthood by affirming the "priesthood of all believers." Furthermore, as Luther argued, the vocation of any Christian, by contributing to society and thus serving one's neighbor,

David Read of the Madison Avenue Presbyterian Church in New York City became known in many parts of the U.S. through his radio sermons. He is shown here at the pulpit of St. Giles (Presbyterian) Cathedral in Edinburgh. Julian Calder

s as fulfilling before God as any specifically religious vocation. Nevertheless, most Protestant denominations have an ordained ministry. Whereas the Roman Catholic priest is seen as a mediator of God's grace through his administration of the sacraments, the Protestant minister is regarded as one of the laity who has been trained to perform certain church functions (such as preaching and administering the sacraments). As a result of this belief in the essential equality of all church members, Protestant church government has been democratic in tendency, although there are wide variations. The major forms of church government are episcopal polity (in which bishops exercise authority), which is found in the Anglican, Episcopal, and Methodist churches; presbyterianism (in which presbyters, or elders, are elected to governing bodies as representatives of congregations), found in the Presbyterian and Reformed churches; and congregationalism (in which the congregation itself is the highest authority), found in Congregational, Baptist, and many other churches.

Worship. In comparison with the Roman Catholic mass and the Orthodox liturgy, Protestant liturgies are simpler and place greater emphasis on preaching. The reformers established services in the vernacular languages and introduced the singing of hymns by the congregation. Some Protestant services (for instance, the Pentecostal) are almost completely unstructured and spontaneous, are centered on congregational participation, and emphasize spiritual gifts, such as speaking in tongues. All the Protestant traditions reduced the number of sacraments from the seven in Roman Catholicism to two, baptism and the Eucharist (*see* SACRAMENT).

Recent Tendencies. Protestantism has continued to be dynamic in character, and change has accelerated since the 1960s. Some denominations have adopted very informal varieties of worship services in an effort to attract young members. Some congregations and denominations have divided over such questions as the ordination of women as ministers, the modernization of liturgical language, and mergers with other churches, as well as the perennial question of biblical interpretation and its relation to scientific truth. Protestants as individuals and as churches continue to be conspicuously involved in controversial political and social issues, some on the conservative side, some on liberal or radical sides. The characteristic that distinguished the first Protestants—a willingness to question received opinions, to protest abuses, and to defy established authorities—has been retained by 20th-century Protestantism, which continues to expand and to exercise a profound influence on contemporary culture and society.

See also CHRISTIANITY; THEOLOGY.

For further information on this topic, see the Bibliography in volume 28, sections 85, 92–109.

PROTEUS, in Greek mythology, son of Poseidon, god of the sea, or his attendant and the keeper of his seals. Proteus knew all things past, present, and future but was able to change his shape at will to avoid the necessity of prophesying. Each day at noon Proteus would rise from the sea and sleep in the shade of the rocks on the island of Pharos in Egypt with his seals lying around him. Persons wishing to learn the future had to catch hold of him at that time and hold on as he assumed dreadful shapes, including those of wild animals and terrible monsters. If all his ruses proved unavailing, Proteus resumed his usual form and told the truth. Among those who fought with Proteus to learn the truth was Menelaus, king of Sparta.

PROTISTA, kingdom of lower and mostly unicellular organisms with eucaryotic cells. The kingdom Protista was first proposed by the German biologist Ernst Haeckel because of the difficulty of separating one-celled organisms into plants and animals.

Eucaryotic cells have nuclei consisting of several or many chromosomes separated from the rest of the cell (the cytoplasm) by a nuclear membrane. They are also characterized by the presence of organelles, specialized cell structures such as mitochondria, chloroplasts, and advanced flagella. In these respects they represent a major evolutionary step from the more primitive procaryotic cells of bacteria and blue-green algae, which form the kingdom Monera. The procaryotes lack a membrane-enclosed nucleus and have no organelles. It has been theorized that eucaryotic cells may have evolved from symbiotic associations of procaryotes. Mitochondria, for example, could have derived from bacteria that were taken into other cells. Similarly, chloroplasts could have derived from procaryotes resembling blue-green algae. Eucaryotic cells probably evolved several times and in various symbiotic combinations, eventually giving rise to the great diversity of organisms that constitute the kingdom Protista.

The protists thus represent many evolutionary lines, the limits of which are difficult to define. Most protists, for example, are microscopic one-celled organisms, but some, such as the Foraminifera, form colonies that contain many cells and may be visible to the naked eye. Such colonies represent a complexity of organization more typical of higher organisms; and, indeed, it is

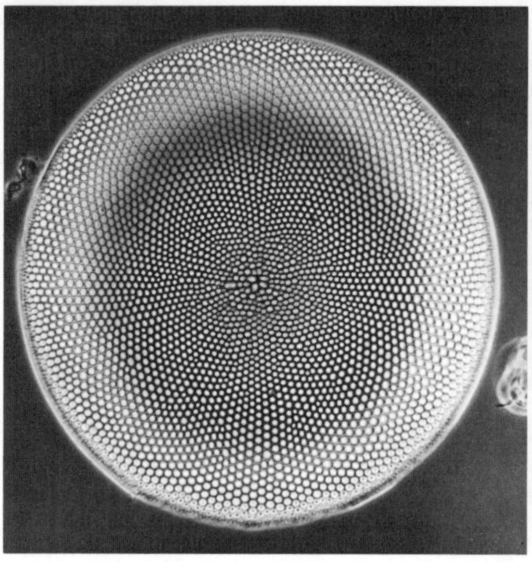
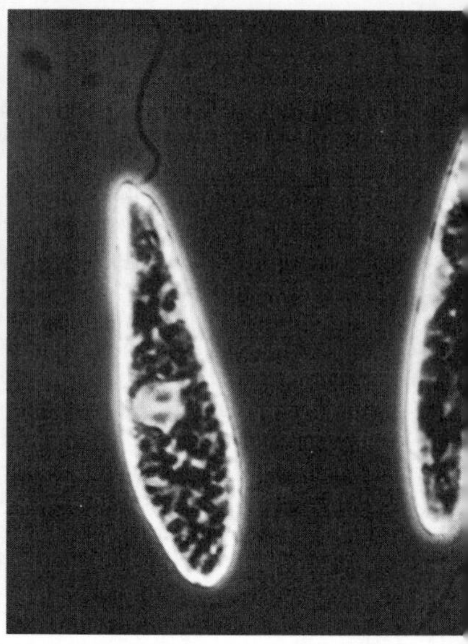

Organisms of the kingdom Protista: (left) the golden alga Coscinodiscus; *(right) the euglenoid* Euglena gracilis.
Walter Dawn—Photo Researchers, Inc.

now believed that multicellular organisms evolved numerous times from protistan ancestors (*see* CLASSIFICATION).

Protista can therefore be called a middle kingdom. Its boundaries may be narrowly defined, including only single eucaryotic cells and simple colonies of these, or broadly defined to take in some of the higher algae and other so-called transitional groups. The latter consist of organisms that are multicellular but lack the complex tissue organization of plants, animals, and fungi. These forms include the plantlike green, red, and brown algae (*see* ALGAE); the animallike mesozoans, placozoans, and sponges; and the funguslike slime molds and chytrids.

Thus, the limits of the kingdom Protista have not been definitively established. Many groups are quite distantly related insofar as their nutritional modes are concerned. Some resemble plants in that they are capable of photosynthesis; others ingest their food like animals; still others absorb their nutrients in the manner of fungi. Such great diversity makes a description of a typical protist difficult. Perhaps the most representative member of the kingdom, however, would be a flagellate (*see* FLAGELLATES), a single-celled organism with one or more advanced flagella (as distinguished from the simple flagella of bacteria) and sometimes with one or more chloroplasts.

The classification followed in this encyclopedia, which excludes most of the transitional forms mentioned above, recognizes the following major groups. The plantlike protists include golden algae, or Chrysophyta (*see* DIATOM); dinoflagellates (q.v.), or Pyrrophyta; cryptomonads, or Cryptophyta; and euglenoids (q.v.), or Euglenophyta. The animallike protists, which are also called protozoa (q.v.), include animal flagellates, or Zoomastigina; amoeboid forms, or Sarcodina (*see* FORAMINIFERA); ciliates and suctorians of the phylum Ciliophora (q.v.), and the parasitic, spore-producing Sporozoa. Funguslike forms include the hyphochytrids (Hyphochytridiomycota) and the plasmodiophores (Plasmodiophoromycota). The slime molds (q.v.), constituting several disputed phyla here treated as belonging to the Protista, have characteristics of both fungi and protozoans. R.H.W.

For further information on this topic, see the Bibliography in volume 28, sections 438, 448.

PROTON, nuclear particle having a positive charge identical in magnitude to the negative charge of an electron and, together with the neutron (q.v.), a constituent of all atomic nuclei. The proton is also called a nucleon, as is the neutron. The proton forms, by itself, the nucleus of the hydrogen atom (*see* NUCLEUS). The mass of a proton is approximately 1836 times that of an electron, or 1.6726×10^{-24} g. Consequently, the mass of an atom is contained almost entirely in the nucleus. The proton has an intrinsic angular momentum, or spin (q.v.), and thus a magnetic moment (*see* MAGNETISM). In addition, the proton obeys the exclusion principle (q.v.). The number of protons in the nucleus of an atom determines what element it is; the atomic number of an element denotes the number of protons in the nucleus. In nuclear physics the proton is used as a projectile in large accelerators to bombard nuclei to produce fundamental particles (*see* PARTICLE ACCELERATORS). As the hydrogen ion, the proton plays an important role in chemistry (*see* CHEMICAL REACTION; ION).

The antiproton, the antiparticle of the proton, is also called a negative proton. It differs from the proton in having a negative charge and not being a constituent of atomic nuclei. The antiproton is stable in a vacuum and does not decay spontaneously. When an antiproton collides with a proton or a neutron, however, the two particles are transformed into mesons, which have an extremely short half-life (*see* RADIOACTIVITY). Although physicists had postulated the existence of this elementary particle since the 1930s, the antiproton was positively identified for the first time in 1955 at the University of California Radiation Laboratory.

Because protons are essential parts of ordinary matter, they are obviously stable. Particle physicists are nevertheless interested in learning whether protons eventually decay after all, on a time scale of many billions of billions of years. This interest derives from current attempts at grand unification theories that would combine all four fundamental interactions of matter in a single scheme (*see* UNIFIED FIELD THEORY). Many of these attempts call for the ultimate instability of the proton, so research groups at a number of accelerator facilities are conducting tests to detect such decays. By the end of the 1980s no clear evidence had yet been found; possible results thus far can also be interpreted in other ways.

For further information on this topic, see the Bibliography in volume 28, section 402.

PROTOPLASM, term once used to describe the ground substance—the living material—of cells. This material would include the complex colloidal organization of substances making up a cell's nucleus, cytoplasm, plastids, and mitochondria. The term *protoplasm* has to a great extent been replaced by the term *cytoplasm* (*see* CELL); the latter, however, does not include the cell nucleus. Protoplasm is also used to describe the contents of the tubelike structures (hyphae) of which fungi (q.v.) are composed.

PROTOZOA, collective name for animallike, single-celled organisms, some of which may form colonies. In the classification followed in this encyclopedia the protozoa are placed in the kingdom Protista with other single-celled organisms that have membrane-enclosed nuclei. Protozoa have little or no differentiation into tissue systems. Several phyla are commonly recognized. They include flagellated Zoomastigina, many species of which live as parasites in plants and animals; the amoeboid Sarcodina, which includes the Foraminifera and Radiolaria—both important components of the plankton; ciliated Ciliophora, many with specialized structures suggesting the mouth and anus of higher organisms; Cnidosporidia, parasites of invertebrates, fish, and a few reptiles and amphibians; and Sporozoa, many species of which are parasites of animals (including humans). More than 20,000 species are known, including such familiar forms as paramecium and amoeba.

Most species are found in such aquatic habitats as oceans, lakes, rivers, and ponds. They vary in length from 2 to 70 micrometers. Protozoa obtain their food by ingesting bacteria, waste products of other organisms, algae, or other protozoa. Most species are motile, either by whiplike structures called flagella, hairlike structures called cilia, or amoeboid motion, a streaming type of movement involving the formation of pseudopods (footlike extensions).

For further information on this topic, see the Bibliography in volume 28, sections 438, 448.

PROUDHON, Pierre Joseph (1809–65), French writer and political theorist, sometimes referred to as the father of modern anarchism.

Proudhon was born in Besançon on Jan. 15, 1809. Belonging to a poor family, he received scholarships that enabled him to study and to write. In his pamphlet *What Is Property?* (1840; trans. 1876), Proudhon condemned the abuses of concentrated economic power and private property. His radical theories made him popular as an anarchist thinker, and he was elected to the constituent assembly after the Revolution of 1848. In the assembly, his proposal to levy antiproperty tax on rent and interest was defeated. He also attempted to found a people's bank at which credit would be provided to borrowers without interest.

Proudhon opposed the view of the French utopian socialists François Fourier and Claude Rouvroy, comte de Saint-Simon, on the ground that society could not be transformed in accordance with a preconceived plan. He envisioned a society in which people's ethical nature and sense of moral responsibility would be so highly developed that government would be unnecessary to regulate and protect society. Proudhon rejected the use of force to impose any system on people. In the ideal state of society, what he called "order in anarchy," people would act in a responsible, ethical manner of their own free will.

Proudhon was imprisoned from 1849 to 1852 for criticizing Louis Napoleon (Napoleon III). After his release he lived in exile in Belgium. After being pardoned (1862), he returned to France in broken health and died on Jan. 19, 1865.

Proudhon's greatest work is generally considered his *System of Economic Contradictions;* or, *The Philosophy of Misery* (1846; trans., vol. 1, 1888). Other major works are *Les idées révolutionnaires* (Revolutionary Ideas, 1849), *De la justice dans la révolution et dans l'église* (Of Justice in the Revolution and in the Church, 3 vol., 1858), and *De la capacité politique des classes ouvrières* (Of the Political Capacity of the Working Classes, 1863).

See also ANARCHISM.

PROUST, Joseph Louis (1754–1826), French chemist, born in Angers, and educated in Paris. He is best known for establishing the chemical law of definite proportions, sometimes called Proust's law, which states that in a compound, the elements are all present in a fixed proportion by weight, regardless of the method of preparation. Proust also discovered grape sugar, or what is now called glucose (q.v.). In 1816 he was elected to the French Academy of Sciences. *See* CHEMICAL REACTION.

PROUST, Marcel (1871–1922), French writer, creator of the 16-volume *À la recherche du temps perdu* (1913–27), the awesome cyclic novel known in English as *Remembrance of Things Past* (1922–32) and regarded as one of the greatest achievements in world literature.

Proust was born July 10, 1871, in Paris, of a well-to-do family and educated at the Lycée Condorcet. As a young man he studied law, but gave it up after a brief time to mingle with Parisian fashionable society and to write. His first work, a collection of essays and stories titled *Pleasures and Regrets* (1896; trans. 1948), was not notable, but the impressions he gathered in salons provided the material for this book and were used to greater effect in his later work. At the age of 35, Proust, a victim of asthma since childhood, became a chronic invalid. He spent the rest of his life as a recluse, almost never leaving his cork-lined room, and worked on his masterpiece, the vast *À la recherche du temps perdu.* Proust died Nov. 18, 1922, before the final three volumes of the novel, which comprises seven related books, had been published. In Proust's novel the physical life and, more particularly, the life of the mind of a man of leisure moving in elegant society are described in minute detail. The entire work is written as an interior monologue in the first person and is in many respects autobiographical. The first part, *Swann's Way* (1913; trans. 1928), published initially at Proust's own expense, failed to attract attention. Five years later the second part, *Within a Budding Grove* (1919; trans. 1922), was a great success and won the prestigious Prix Goncourt. The third and

Marcel Proust Bettmann Archive

fourth parts, *The Guermantes Way* (2 vol., 1920–21; trans. 1925) and *Cities of the Plain* (2 vol., 1921–22; trans. 1927), were also well received. The three final parts, left in manuscript form at Proust's death, were published posthumously: *The Captive* (1923; trans. 1929), *The Sweet Cheat Gone* (2 vol., 1925; trans. 1930), and *Time Regained* (2 vol., 1927; trans. 1932).

The importance of Proust's novel lies not so much in his descriptions of changing French society as in the psychological development of characters and in his philosophical preoccupation with time. As Proust traced the path of his hero from happy childhood through romantic attachment to self-awareness as a writer, he was also concerned with seeking eternal truths in the changing world. He treated time both as a destroyer and as a positive element that can be grasped only by intuitive memory. The sequence of time is perceived in the light of the theories of the French philosopher Henri Bergson, whom Proust admired. Time is in constant flux, moments of the past and the present having equal reality. Proust also boldly explored the depths of the human psyche, subconscious motivations, and the irrationality of human behavior, particularly in relation to love. The work, translated into many languages, established Proust's reputation throughout the world, and his method of writing, which entailed analyzing his characters' development in minute detail, had an important influence on 20th-century literature. Another Proust novel, discovered and published after his death, is *Jean Santeuil* (3 vol., 1952; trans. 1956).

PROVENÇAL LANGUAGE, also Occitan or Languedoc, Romance language spoken in the southern third of France, used by about one-fourth of the French population. Provençal developed an eminent literature in the 11th to 15th centuries, including the poems of the troubadours. It extended significantly north of its present speech region, and its standard literary dialect bridged many local dialects. This literary language began to wane after France established dominion over the south in the 14th century. In the 19th century the poet Frédéric Mistral led a movement to establish a modern standard literary Provençal.

Provençal dialect groups include Limousin and Auvergnat in south-central France, Languedoc and Provençal proper in the Mediterranean area, and Gascon (sometimes considered a separate language) in southwest France. These regions were settled by the Romans earlier than the rest of France, and their Latin-derived speech was less influenced than northern French by Frankish and other Germanic languages. Although Provençal has been increasingly influenced by French, its structure is closer to that of Spanish and Catalan.

The term Franco-Provençal refers to a distinctive group of dialects spoken northeast of the Provençal area, extending slightly into Switzerland and Italy.

PROVENÇAL LITERATURE, vernacular Latin literature written in southern France from about the 9th to the 15th century.

The earliest attempts at composition in the Provençal language probably were made by priests and monks in the 9th century. In order to arouse the religious sympathies of the people, they composed, or translated from the Latin into the vulgar idiom, prayers, hymns, pious tales, allegories, and legends of saints. Toward the close of the 11th century Provençal poetry was greatly stimulated as a result of the religious wars of the Crusades and the introduction of the institution of chivalry.

Provençal literature was essentially poetic. Its prose works are of little importance; later, in the 14th and 15th centuries, prose works became more numerous and included scientific, juridical, philological, and other works. Drama was not cultivated. The only productions that might come under drama are pieces on pious subjects in dramatized form, such as the *Mystery of the Passion* and the *Marriage of the Virgin*.

Poetry of the Provençal troubadours began appearing in the early 12th century and reached its fullest expression in three poets writing at the end of the century: Bertran de Born, Arnaud Daniel, and Guiraut de Bornelh (1150?–1220). Within just a few generations this poetry developed into a complicated art form so perfect technically that in the 13th century Provençal was considered by some experts to be the most suitable language for lyric poetry.

In this poetry the lady, married and belonging to the aristocracy, is separated from her lover (the poet) for various reasons, social or geographical or even psychic; and the poet, in singing of his love, attempts to reach an overwhelming sentiment, which he calls *joie* ("joy, happiness"). On the whole, Provençal poetry is the expression of a sensuous love and is quite opposed to the traditional Christian concept of love.

The two distinguishing characteristics of Provençal versification are the rhyme and the syllabic accent. The great number of final syllables of the same sound existing in the declensions and conjugations of the language offered great ease of rhyming. With the war against the Albigenses in the 13th century and the establishment of French domination in the south, Provençal poetry began to decline rapidly. During the following centuries there are almost no Provençal works worthy of notice. In the 19th century, however, a new poetic activity began to manifest itself, commencing with the poet Jacques Jasmin (1798–1864), and after him Frédéric Mistral, a poet of great genius and one of the founders of the Félibrige, a society dedicated to reviving the use of Provençal; Théodore Aubanel (1829–86); and others. Poetic festivals have also been introduced to aid the movement. W.F.

PROVENCE, region, SE France, comprising the departments of Basses-Alpes, Var, and Bouches-du-Rhône and parts of the departments of Vaucluse and Alpes-Maritimes. Provence is bordered on the E by Italy, on the S by the Mediterranean Sea, and on the W by the Rhône R. The area abounds with flower fields, vineyards, orchards, and olive and mulberry groves. Along the seacoast is the French Riviera and the ports of Marseille and Toulon. The modern inhabitants of Provence preserve a distinct regional character, as well as their own language (*see* PROVENÇAL LANGUAGE; PROVENÇAL LITERATURE).

The region originally formed part of a Roman province, Provincia Romana, constituted about 120 BC. It passed successively into the possession of several ancient Germanic peoples, the Visigoths, the Ostrogoths, and the Frankish kings. In

AD 879 the area was incorporated into the kingdom of Provence, sometimes call Cisjurane Burgundy, and in the 10th century into the kingdom of Arles. After being ruled by the house of Anjou from about 1245 to 1482, the region came into the possession of King Louis XI of France, and in 1486 it was annexed to the French Kingdom. Provence was a province of France until the French Revolution, after which the area was distributed among several departments.

PROVERB, concise statement, in general use, expressing a shrewd perception about everyday life or a universally recognized truth. Most proverbs are rooted in folklore and have been preserved by oral tradition. An example of such commonplace wisdom is "A rolling stone gathers no moss." The Bible has provided a large number of proverbs, for example, "An eye for an eye and a tooth for a tooth." Some proverbs have literary origins, as in the case of Benjamin Franklin's adaptation of Aesop's proverb "The gods help them that help themselves." Franklin himself originated the proverb "Early to bed and early to rise, makes a man healthy, wealthy, and wise." Proverbs are appealing because they are succinct and because they use simple rhyme ("A friend in need is a friend indeed"), irony ("Physician, heal thyself"), metaphor ("Still waters run deep"), and comparison or contrast ("Feed a cold and starve a fever").

PROVERBS, book of the Old Testament filled with expressions of wisdom and experience. It is one of the books comprising the third part, the Writings, of the Hebrew canon. Commentators and scholars have long regarded it as a prime example of the wisdom literature of the Old Testament. Tradition has ascribed the entire work to the Hebrew king Solomon, whose wisdom reputedly "surpassed the wisdom of all the people of the east, and all the wisdom of Egypt" (1 Kings 4:30). This tradition is now recognized, however, as an example of an ancient custom of paying tribute to famous figures and of lending new works the prestige attached to great names. Proverbs is a collection of short moral sayings composed or compiled by a number of unknown persons. The most commonly accepted view is that these persons were professional sages who offered moral and religious instruction to young, upper-class Jewish men. Although some of the material in Proverbs may date from Solomonic, and perhaps even pre-Solomonic times, the whole collection most likely was given its present form during the 5th or 4th century BC.

According to the textual headings, Proverbs consists of the following eight sections: 1:1–9:18, "proverbs of Solomon, son of David, king of Israel"; 10:1–22:16, "proverbs of Solomon"; 22:17–24:22, "the words of the wise"; 24:23–34, words that "are also sayings of the wise"; 25:1–29:27, "proverbs of Solomon which the men of Hezekiah king of Judah copied"; chapter 30, "words of Agur son of Jakeh"; 31:1–9, "words of king Lemuel"; and 31:10–31, words in praise of a "good wife."

The first section includes a brief introduction (1:1–6) stating the title and the purpose of the whole work. This section, regarded by many scholars as the latest material in the book, is believed by some to be the work of a 4th-century teacher, who may have also compiled the entire book for instructional use. Its two personifications of wisdom (1:20–33, 8:1–36) have been proposed as one source of the doctrine of the Logos, or Word, in the Gospel of John.

The second and fifth sections consist of proverbial sayings attributed to Solomon. With few exceptions, each saying is a separate poetic line, the two halves of which balance. The proverbs are concerned with various virtues and vices and their consequences. The second section is thought to include the oldest material in the book. The third section is patterned largely after the Egyptian Wisdom of Amenemope, dated variously from 1000 to 600 BC. The section contains some 30 maxims and counsels concerned chiefly with personal behavior. This, too, is written in balanced poetic lines. The fourth section, of indeterminate date, is similar to the third in both content and form.

The sixth and seventh sections were probably written by two persons who are unidentified but may have belonged to neighboring Canaanite peoples. The sixth section consists of a dialogue rather reminiscent of the longer skeptical dialogues in the book of Job and of a collection of numerical sayings. An example of this type of proverb is 30:29–31. The seventh section contains a mother's advice to her son, a king, on women and wine. The eighth section is a poetic portrait of the ideal wife. In Hebrew this last section is an acrostic poem of 22 lines, each line beginning with a successive letter of the Hebrew alphabet.

PROVIDENCE, city, capital of Rhode Island, and seat of Providence Co., at the head of Narragansett Bay on the Providence R., in the N part of the state; inc. 1831. In addition to being the seat of the state government, it is a busy seaport and a commercial, manufacturing, and financial center. The city is noted for the production of jewelry and silverware; other major manufactures include electronics, machinery, metal goods, telecommunications equipment, textiles, and processed food.

The skyline of Providence. In the foreground, pleasure boats are tied up at a marina on the Providence River. Kenneth Martin–Amstock

Among Providence's many historic buildings, some dating back to colonial times, are the Old State House (1762); the present State House (1895–1900), with a large marble dome; the First Unitarian Church (1816), with a bell cast by Paul Revere; the John Brown House (1786), now housing the Rhode Island Historical Society; the Cathedral of Saint John (completed 1811); and the First Baptist Church (1775), the meeting house of the oldest Baptist congregation in the U.S. Also of note are the Roger Williams National Memorial; Providence Athenaeum (1753), one of the oldest libraries in the U.S.; and the Museum of Art. The city is the seat of Brown University, Johnson & Wales University (1914), Providence College (1917), Rhode Island College (1854), the Rhode Island School of Design, a branch of Roger Williams College (1948), and a branch of the New England Institute of Technology (1940).

In 1636, Roger Williams, who had been banished from Plymouth Colony mainly because of his religious beliefs, established Providence as a haven for those who shared his beliefs. He secured the land from the Narragansett Indians and named the community in gratitude for God's "providence." The settlement soon attracted other dissenters, and in 1638 a plan for local government was adopted. In 1644 the British granted a charter that joined Providence and nearby settlements in the Colony of Providence Plantations. During King Philip's War (1675–76), Indians destroyed much of Providence, but by the early 18th century the community was thriving as a port for trade with the West Indies.

In 1772 Providence residents burned the British ship HMS *Gaspée,* which had been sent to police British navigation laws. They also protested English taxation by burning tea in the public square. Two months before the signing of the U.S. Declaration of Independence, the Rhode Island Independence Act was signed (May 4, 1776) in Providence. Later, during the American Revolution, Providence was an important base for American and French troops, who were quartered in University Hall (1770) at Brown University. The community's growth after the Revolution was slow, but by the mid-19th century it was a manufacturing center noted for jewelry and textiles. Many European immigrants settled here later in the century. In 1900 Providence became the sole capital of Rhode Island (Newport had been the joint capital since 1854). The city was badly damaged by a hurricane in 1938. Pop. (1980) 156,804; (1990) 160,728.

PROVINCETOWN, town, Barnstable Co., E Massachusetts, on Cape Cod Bay at the N end of Cape Cod; inc. 1727. It is a noted artists' colony, a fishing port, and a tourist center, situated adjacent to Cape Cod National Seashore.

The Pilgrims first set foot on American soil here

in 1620 before venturing on and establishing a permanent settlement at Plymouth. A community developed on the site about 1700, and by the 19th century the town had grown into an active salt-processing center and whaling port. The Provincetown Players, a noted theatrical group, was founded here in 1915.

Provincetown is the site of the tall granite Pilgrim Monument (1907–10), which commemorates the Pilgrims' landing and the signing in the harbor of the Mayflower Compact; the Provincetown Historical Museum, which has displays of colonial art and artifacts; the Provincetown Art Association museum, with a collection of works by Provincetown artists; and the Provincetown Heritage Museum, containing historical items. Pop. (1980) 3536; (1990) 3561.

PROVINCETOWN PLAYERS, experimental theater group of actors, playwrights, and stage designers, organized in 1915 in Provincetown, Mass. Their noncommercial theater, controlled by artists rather than businesspeople, presented plays by new writers in highly experimental productions. The company's Massachusetts productions, staged in the Wharf Theater, a remodeled fishing boat, included *Bound East for Cardiff* (1916), the first work by Eugene O'Neill ever to be produced. Later in 1916 they moved to New York City; they remained active until 1929. Led by O'Neill and by the producer Kenneth Macgowan (1888–1962), the group had a profound influence on the development of the American theater. They produced some 90 new American plays in a small Greenwich Village theater. These included works by E. E. Cummings, Paul Green (1894–1981), Edna Ferber (1887–1968), and Edna St. Vincent Millay, as well as O'Neill.

PROVO, city, seat of Utah Co., N Utah, on the Provo R., situated between the Wasatch Mts. on the E and Utah Lake on the W; inc. 1851. It is a regional educational, recreational, and industrial center. Manufactures include computer hardware and software, clothing, electronic equipment, and processed food; a large integrated steel plant is nearby in Orem. The city is the seat of Brigham Young University and two junior colleges. Provo is the gateway to nearby ski resorts, Timpanogos Cave National Monument, and other scenic attractions. The site was settled as Fort Utah by Mormon colonists in 1849. In 1850 it was named for Étienne Provost (or Provot, c. 1782–1850), an early French-Canadian trapper who arrived in the region in 1825. The city grew rapidly after it was reached by rail in the 1870s. Pop. (1980) 74,108; (1990) 86,835.

PRUDHOE BAY, bay, N Alaska, an arm of the Beaufort Sea. Since the discovery in 1968 of vast petroleum deposits in the region, the bay has been a center of oil-drilling activities. A pipeline to transport petroleum to the S was built in the mid-1970s between the bay and the city of Valdez on Prince William Sound.

PRUD'HON, Pierre Paul (1758–1823), French painter, born in Cluny, and trained in Dijon, Paris, and Rome. He was greatly influenced by the soft style of the Renaissance painters Leonardo da Vinci, Raphael, and Correggio and by the graceful neoclassical sculpture of his con-

Andromache and Astyanax *(1814–17), by Pierre Paul Prud'hon.*
Metropolitan Museum of Art–Bequest of Collis P. Huntington

temporary, Antonio Canova, who became his friend in Rome.

Prud'hon gained public recognition through his illustrations for books issued by the French publisher Didot and for his designs for French government stationery. Napoleon then employed him as court painter and decorator. Prud'hon was widely acclaimed for his portrait *Empress Josephine* (1805, Louvre, Paris). He executed a number of allegorical paintings, of which the best known are *Justice and Divine Vengeance Pursuing Crime* (1808, Louvre) and *Venus and Adonis* (1812, Wallace Collection, London). In 1816 Prud'hon became a member of the Académie des Beaux-Arts. In the era of French neoclassical painting dominated by the stern, sculptural style of Jacques Louis David, Prud'hon was distinctive for his delicate treatment of the figure and his use of chiaroscuro. His expression of emotion foreshadows the romantic style.

PRUNE. *See* PLUM.

PRUNING, removal of parts of woody plants, usually branches or branch tips, to relieve the burden on the remaining parts of the plant, to cut out diseased or broken parts, to increase the quantity and quality of flowers or fruits, to train individual parts to positions structurally favorable to the health of the plant, or to shape the plant into some artificial form. Natural pruning is effected by the action of wind, excessive fruit loads, and ice or snow. Such natural pruning frequently leaves stubs or slowly healing wounds that are susceptible to decay and disease. The hollows that result provide feeding areas, nesting sites, and shelter for arboreal animals. Artificial pruning prevents decay and promotes quick healing of wounds.

Plants that produce spring-blooming buds in the fall are pruned in the summer. In the eastern U.S., pruning may be done during the winter months, but in the Midwest winter pruning may result in sufficient loss of water through evaporation to kill the plants. In dry, hot areas, excessive pruning of trees frequently results in sunscald of the branches and trunks. Summer pruning of trees usually stimulates flower and fruit production, whereas winter pruning increases the production of leaves and branches. When the branches of trees and shrubs are pruned, wood or stem production is encouraged; the pruning of roots reduces wood production but increases fruit bearing.

PRUSSIA (Ger. *Preussen*), former kingdom and state of Germany. At the height of its expansion, in the late 19th century, Prussia extended along the coasts of the Baltic and North seas, from Belgium, the Netherlands, France, and Luxembourg on the west to the Russian Empire on the east, to Austria-Hungary on the east, southeast, and south, and to Switzerland on the south.

Modern Prussia was successively, with geographical modifications, an independent kingdom (1701–1871); the largest constituent kingdom of the German Empire (1871–1918); a constituent state, or land, of the Weimar Republic (1918–34); and an administrative division, comprising 13 provinces, of the centralized German Third Reich (1934–45). After World War I, West Prussia was lost to Poland, and East Prussia was separated from the rest of German Prussia in 1919, under the terms of the Treaty of Versailles, by a strip of formerly Prussian territory known as the Polish Corridor, designed to give Poland an outlet on the Baltic Sea. The other provinces of Prussia between the two World Wars were Rhine, Brandenburg, Pomerania, Berlin, Saxony, Schleswig-Holstein, Hannover, Westphalia, Grenzmark Posen-Westpreussen (now in Poland), Hesse-Nassau, Hohenzollern, and Silesia (now parts of Poland, the Czech Republic, and Germany). In 1947, after World War II, Prussia was abolished as a political unit and, with the exception of East Prussia, partitioned into various parts of the four zones of occupation in Germany, administered by France, Great Britain, the U.S., and the Soviet Union. The northeastern part of East Prussia was annexed by the USSR, and the remainder was put under Polish administration. Berlin was the capital, and the principal cities included Frankfurt-am-Main, Cologne, Essen, Dortmund, Düsseldorf, Magdeburg, Stettin (now Szczecin, Poland), and Königsberg (now Kaliningrad, Russia).

Early History The people from whom the name Prussia is derived were usually called Prussi, or Borussi, in the earliest sources. They were related to the Lithuanians and inhabited the region between the Vistula and lower Niemen rivers. The Saxons, a Teutonic people, entered eastern Europe in the 10th century and failed in their attempts to convert the Prussians to Christianity. In 997 the Bohemian bishop and saint Adalbert was martyred as a missionary in Prussia. The Christian faith was not established until about the middle of the 13th century, when the Teutonic Knights subdued the country and brought German and Dutch settlers into the conquered territory. By the end of the century the region was completely subjugated. Thereafter it was ruled by the Teutonic Knights as a papal fief.

During the second half of the 14th century, strong opposition to the Germans developed in eastern Europe. In 1386 Poland and Lithuania entered into a dynastic union, and in 1410 a Polish

King Frederick II, the Great, of Prussia reviewing his troops in Potsdam, near Berlin (from an 18th-century engraving by Daniel N. Chodowiecki). Bettmann Archive

and Lithuanian army defeated the Teutonic Knights in the Battle of Tannenberg. After a further period of warfare, the terms of the second Peace of Thorn, in 1466, left the Knights in possession of the eastern part of Prussia, which it held as a fief of the Polish crown. Western Prussia was ceded to Poland, becoming known as Polish Royal Prussia. Eastern Prussia became a secular duchy, known as East Prussia or Ducal Prussia, under the last grand master of the Teutonic Knights, Albert of Hohenzollern (1490–1568), a Lutheran, who created himself 1st duke of Prussia in 1525. In 1618 the duchy, still a vassal state of Poland, passed to John Sigismund (1572–1619), a Hohenzollern; his grandson, Frederick William, elector of Brandenburg, secured ducal Prussia's independence of Poland at the Peace of Oliva in 1660. Frederick William centralized the administration of the duchy and assumed governing powers that were formerly exercised by the nobility and the town oligarchies.

Kingdom of Prussia. Frederick William's son, Frederick I, became king of Prussia in 1701, receiving royal recognition in exchange for a promise of military aid to Holy Roman Emperor Leopold I. Frederick's son, Frederick William I, greatly increased the size of the Prussian army and rebuilt the organization of the state around the military establishment. To his son, Frederick II, the Great, he left enormous financial reserves and the best army in Europe. Through the military genius of Frederick the Great, Prussia became a major power in Europe. In 1740 he invaded the Austrian province of Silesia and precipitated the War of the Austrian Succession.

By the end of the Seven Years' War, in 1763, Prussian territory included Silesia, and in 1772 Frederick annexed Polish Royal Prussia, thus linking his kingdom of Prussia in the east with Brandenburg and the main body of his German possessions in the west. Frederick's regime was noted as a model of "enlightened despotism." Frederick William III succeeded to the throne in 1797 and with the aid of his ministers, Baron vom und zum Stein and Prince Karl August von Hardenberg, instituted a series of liberal reforms within the kingdom. From 1801 to 1805, during the Napoleonic Wars, Prussia was dominated by Napoleon. In 1806, however, Frederick William joined a coalition against Napoleon. Frederick William was defeated, and much of his territory was lost. Prussian fortunes rose after the Battle of Waterloo in 1815 that resulted in the fall of the French Empire.

Prussian Dominance in Germany. After the negotiations at the Congress of Vienna, Prussia emerged as the major German power of Western Europe. By 1844 almost all German states were economically linked with Prussia. Under King William I and his prime minister and imperial chancellor, Prince Otto von Bismarck, Prussia became the largest kingdom of the German Empire, containing two-thirds of the German population.

For further information on this topic, see the Bibliography in volume 28, sections 938–39.

PRUSSIAN BLUE. *See* IRON.

PRUSSIC ACID. *See* HYDROGEN CYANIDE.

PRUT, also Pruth or Prutul, river, SE Europe, a major tributary of the Danube R. It rises in the Carpathian Mts. in SW Ukraine and flows generally in a SE direction for some 965 km (some 600 mi). It enters the Danube near Galaţi, Romania. Along its course, the river forms much of the boundary between Romania and Ukraine, and between Romania and Moldova. It is navigable for approximately 320 km (about 200 mi) above the Danube.

PRZHEVALSKI'S HORSE. *See* HORSE.

PSALMS (Gr., "song"), book of the Old Testament, a collection of 150 hymns or poems known also as the Psalter. The book is divided into five sections (each one marked at the end by a doxology: Pss. 41:13, 72:18–20, 89:52, 106:48, 150), perhaps in imitation of the Pentateuch, the first five books of the Old Testament. The Hebrew title of the book is Tehillim (Praises or Songs of Praise). Psalms is the first book in the Writings, the third part of the Hebrew canon. It is found between the books of Job and Proverbs in Christian versions of the Bible.

Some of the Psalms appear to have been written for individual recital, others for recital by the congregation. Many of them were written by professional musicians and include musical directions for instrumental performers. A few directions, such as the congregational response "Praise the Lord," or "Hallelujah," are still understood and used liturgically.

A partial classification of the individual psalms would include the following: hymns of praise acclaiming God as creator of the world (19, 65), as ruler of history (107), and as king of Jerusalem (47, 135); supplications and laments recited by individuals seeking deliverance in times of personal crisis (3, 77), and by the whole people in times of national peril or woe (137); royal psalms (72, 110); songs of faith and trust in God (23); wisdom teachings and meditations (1, 101); and maledictions (59). Numerous literary forms appear in the Book of Psalms, many of them pat-

David playing the harp (from a 13th-cent. Latin manuscript).

terned after 14th- and 13th-century BC Ugaritic poetry (from the Canaanite city of Ugarit, now Ras Shamra in northern Syria).

The text attributes 74 psalms to the Hebrew king David, 12 psalms to his son and successor Solomon, and 1 to Moses; 32 psalms are identified with other individuals, but the rest are anonymous. Some bear descriptive titles such as "A Psalm of Ascents" (120–134) and "Psalm for the Thank Offering" (100). Ancient Jewish and Christian ecclesiastical traditions both held David to be the author of the book (and final editor of those psalms ascribed by the text to others), but modern biblical scholars agree that the book was compiled from older independent collections. Some have suggested that Pss. 42–83, which use Elohim, a name for God not found in the other psalms (where Yahweh is used), may have been a separate anthology belonging to the northern kingdom, Israel. The most widely accepted view of their date of composition holds that the collection reflects a long period, from the Exodus about 1300 BC to the immediate postexilic period after 538 BC.

Jesus Christ often quoted or referred to Psalms; for instance, at his temptation (Matt. 4:6), in the Sermon on the Mount (Matt 5:7, 35, 7:23), and at the crucifixion (Luke 23:34; Matt. 27:46). It is likely that the first Christian congregations used selections from the book in their public services. The 5th-century church scholar St. Augustine called the book the "language of devotion," and Martin Luther regarded Psalms as "a Bible in miniature."

PSALTERY, musical instrument consisting of a set of strings, one for each note, stretched over a horizontal soundboard; its shape is basically trapezoidal, often with one or two incurved sides. The strings are plucked with the fingers or with a plectrum. The name is from the ancient Greek *psalterion,* probably denoting a harp. The psaltery originated in the Middle East and was popular in Europe during the Middle Ages. During the 14th and 15th centuries, keyboards were linked to psalteries, giving rise to the harpsichord. Modern psalteries include the Arabic *qanun* and the Finnish *kantele.* The psaltery is classified as a subtype of the zither family.

PSAMTIK I, in Greek, Psammetichos, king of Egypt (r. 664–610 BC), founder of the 26th or Saite dynasty. He ruled first as regent for the Assyrian king Ashurbanipal, who had subjugated Egypt about 670 BC. About 660 BC Psamtik renounced his allegiance to Assyria and unified Lower Egypt under his independent rule. He established his capital city of Sais, from which the name of the dynasty was taken. During his reign Egypt entered into friendly relations with Greece, and Greek merchants and soldiers were encouraged to settle in Egypt. Psamtik extended his rule by capturing the Egyptian city of Thebes from the Assyrians in 654 BC. He also protected the independence of Egypt by strengthening the frontiers and reforming his army. His reign was notable for a flourishing of commerce and the arts.

PSEUDEPIGRAPHA (from Gr. *pseudepigraphos,* "falsely ascribed"), Jewish and Christian writings that appeared in the latter days of the Old Testament and continued well into Christian times; they were attributed by their authors to great religious figures and authorities of the past.

Pseudepigrapha exist in the canon of the Old Testament, for example, Ecclesiastes (associated with Solomon), the Song of Solomon, and Daniel. Protestants and Jews, however, customarily use the term Pseudepigrapha to describe those writings that Roman Catholics would term Apocrypha—that is, late Jewish writings that all scholars consider extracanonical. Among such works are the Book of Jubilees, the Psalms of Solomon, the Fourth Book of Maccabees, the Book of Enoch, the Fourth Book of Ezra, the Apocalypse of Baruch, and the Testaments of the Twelve Patriarchs, all of which are ascribed to canonical worthies of the Old Testament, date from intertestamental times, and have not been preserved in their original Hebrew or Aramaic. Fragments of other, hitherto unknown Pseudepigrapha, preserved in Hebrew or Aramaic, have turned up among the Qumran material (*see* DEAD SEA SCROLLS).

See also APOCRYPHA; BIBLE; BIBLICAL SCHOLARSHIP. B.V.

PSITTACOSIS (Lat. *psittacus,* "parrot"), also parrot fever, disease of birds that primarily affects the respiratory system and which is caused by a strain of the parasitic bacterium *Chlamydia psittaci.* Transmissible to humans, psittacosis is often considered an occupational disease among pigeon breeders, farmers, flock owners, and employees of poultry-processing plants.

Poultry infected with psittacosis may have diarrhea, respiratory symptoms, and weakness, or they may show no outward signs of the disease. Treatment with chlortetracycline and the other tetracyclines in the feed or water is effective.

Psittacosis is transmitted to humans through dust particles, handling of infected birds or their carcasses, and bite wounds. No instances of human beings becoming infected by simply eating poultry are known; apparently the causative agent is destroyed during cooking. In humans the disease causes chills and fever, sore throat, headache, loss of appetite, nausea, and vomiting.

PSKOV, city, W European Russia, capital of Pskov Oblast, on the Velikaya R. The city is an important rail junction and the trade center of a flax-growing region. Principal manufactures produced here include machinery, linen, and building materials. Notable historic structures include a kremlin (13th cent.) and churches of the 14th and 15th centuries. Pskov was a dependency of Novgorod from 903 to 1348, when it became the seat of an independent and democratically governed state. An important trade and craft center, it was annexed by Moscow in 1510. During World War II the city was occupied (1941–44) by the German army and suffered extensive damage. Pop. (1987 est.) 202,000.

PSORIASIS, chronic recurring disease of the skin, characterized by the appearance of plaques, patches, or papules on the skin surface. The lesions are usually slightly elevated above the normal skin surface, sharply distinguishable from normal skin, and red to reddish-brown in color. They are usually covered with small whitish-silver scales that adhere to the underlying eruption and, if scraped off, leave bleeding points. The extent of the disease may vary from a few tiny lesions to generalized involvement of most of the skin. Characteristically the elbows, knees, scalp, and chest are involved.

The cause of the disease is unknown. It almost never occurs in persons of naturally dark skin pigment, and the affliction is often seen in families. A variety of preparations applied locally may be helpful, and the rash often subsides on exposure to sunlight. In 1979 a successful treatment for severe, chronic psoriasis was introduced. It consists of first coating the skin with a dye that absorbs ultraviolet light and then shining ultraviolet light on the painted area. Because this technique causes an increased incidence of mild skin cancers, it is reserved for severe cases of psoriasis.

PSYCHE, in Roman mythology, beautiful princess loved by Cupid, god of love. Jealous of Psyche's beauty, Venus, goddess of love, ordered her son, Cupid, to make Psyche fall in love with the ugliest man in the world. Fortunately for Psyche, Cupid instead fell in love with her and carried her off to a secluded palace where he visited her only by night, unseen and unrecognized by her. Although Cupid had forbidden her ever to look upon his face, one night Psyche lit a lamp and looked upon him while he slept. Because she had disobeyed him, Cupid abandoned her, and Psyche was left to wander desolately throughout the world in search of him. Finally, after many trials she was reunited with Cupid and was made immortal by Jupiter, king of the gods.

PSYCHEDELIC DRUG, term used during the 1960s to denote drugs that produce changes in perception or mood. *See* BARBITURATE; ERGOT; HALLUCINATION; LYSERGIC ACID DIETHYLAMIDE; MARIJUANA; PEYOTE; PSYCHOACTIVE DRUGS; STIMULANT.

PSYCHIATRY, branch of medicine specializing in mental disorders (q.v.). Psychiatrists not only diagnose and treat these disorders but also conduct research directed at understanding and preventing them.

A psychiatrist is a doctor of medicine who has had four years of postgraduate training in psychiatry. Many psychiatrists take further training in psychoanalysis, child psychiatry, or other subspecialties. Psychiatrists treat patients in private practice, in general hospitals, or in specialized facilities for the mentally ill (psychiatric hospitals, outpatient clinics, or community mental health centers). Some spend part or all of their time doing research or administering mental health programs. By contrast, psychologists, who often work closely with psychiatrists and treat many of the same kinds of patients, are not trained in medicine; consequently, they neither diagnose physical illness nor administer drugs.

The province of psychiatry is unusually broad for a medical specialty. Mental disorders may affect most aspects of a patient's life, including physical functioning, behavior, emotions, thought, perception, interpersonal relationships, sexuality, work, and play. These disorders are caused by a poorly understood combination of biological, psychological, and social determinants. Psychiatry's task is to account for the diverse sources and manifestations of mental illness.

Historical Development. Physicians in the Western world began specializing in the treatment of the mentally ill in the 19th century. Known as alienists, psychiatrists of that era worked in large asylums, practicing what was then called moral treatment, a humane approach aimed at quieting mental turmoil and restoring reason. During the second half of the century, psychiatrists abandoned this mode of treatment and, with it, the tacit recognition that mental illness is caused by both psychological and social influences. Their attention focused almost exclusively, for a while, on biological factors. Drugs and other forms of somatic treatment were common. The German psychiatrist Emil Kraepelin identified and classified mental disorders into a system that is the foundation for modern diagnostic practices. Another important figure was the Swiss psychiatrist Eugen Bleuler, who coined the word *schizophrenia* (q.v.) and described its characteristics.

The discovery of unconscious sources of behavior—an insight dominated by the psychoanalytic writings of Sigmund Freud in the early 20th century—enriched psychiatric thought and changed the direction of its practice (*see* PSYCHOANALYSIS). Attention shifted to processes within the individual psyche, and psychoanalysis came to be regarded as the preferred mode of treatment for most mental disorders. In the 1940s and '50s emphasis shifted again: this time to the social and physical environment. Many psychiatrists had all but ignored biological influences, but others were studying those involved in mental illness and were using somatic forms of treatment such as electroconvulsive therapy (electric shock) and psychosurgery.

Dramatic changes in the treatment of the mentally ill in the U.S. began in the mid-1950s with the introduction of the first effective drugs for treating psychotic symptoms. Along with drug treatment, new, more liberal and humane policies and treatment strategies were introduced into mental hospitals. More and more patients were treated in community settings in the 1960s and '70s. Support for mental health research led to significant new discoveries, especially in the understanding of genetic and biochemical determinants in mental illness and the functioning of the brain. Thus, by the 1980s, psychiatry had once again shifted in emphasis to the biological, to the relative neglect of psychosocial influences in mental health and illness. *See* PSYCHOTHERAPY.

Diagnosis. Psychiatrists use a variety of methods to detect specific disorders in their patients. The most fundamental is the psychiatric interview, during which the patient's psychiatric history is taken and mental status is evaluated. The psychiatric history is a picture of the patient's personality characteristics, relationships with others, and past and present experience with psychiatric problems—all told in the patient's words (sometimes supplemented by comments from other family members). Psychiatrists use mental-status examinations much as internists use physical examinations. They elicit and classify aspects of the patient's mental functioning.

Some diagnostic methods rely on testing by other specialists. Psychologists administer intelligence and personality tests, as well as tests designed to detect damage to the brain or other parts of the central nervous system. Neurologists also test psychiatric patients for evidence of impairment of the nervous system. Other physicians sometimes examine patients who complain of physical symptoms. Psychiatric social workers explore family and community problems. The psychiatrist integrates all this information in making a diagnosis according to criteria established by the psychiatric profession.

Treatment. Psychiatric treatments fall into two classes: organic and nonorganic forms. Organic treatments, such as drugs, are those that affect the body directly. Nonorganic types of treatment improve the patient's functioning by psychological means, such as psychotherapy, or by altering the social environment.

Drugs. Psychotropic drugs (*see* PSYCHOACTIVE DRUGS) are by far the most commonly used organic treatment. The first to be discovered were the antipsychotics, used primarily to treat schizophrenia. The phenothiazines are the most frequently prescribed class of antipsychotic drugs. Others are the thioxanthenes, butyrophenones, and indoles. All antipsychotic drugs diminish such symptoms as delusions, hallucinations, and thought disorder. Because they can reduce agitation, they are sometimes used to control manic excitement in manic-depressive patients and to calm geriatric patients. Some childhood behavior disorders respond to these drugs.

Despite their value, the antipsychotic drugs have drawbacks. The most serious is the neurological condition tardive dyskinesia, which occurs in patients who have taken the drugs over extended periods. The condition is characterized by abnormal movements of the tongue, mouth, and body. It is especially serious because its symptoms do not always disappear when the drug is stopped, and no known treatment for it has been developed.

Most psychotropic drugs are chemically synthesized. Lithium carbonate, however, is a naturally occuring element used to prevent, or at least reduce, the severity of shifts of mood in manic-depression (*see* DEPRESSION). It is especially effective in controlling mania. Psychiatrists must monitor lithium dosages carefully, because only a small margin exists between an effective dose and a toxic one.

Two major classes of antidepressant drugs are used. The tricyclic and tetracyclic antidepressants, the most frequently prescribed, are used for the most common form of serious depression. Monoamine oxidase (MAO) inhibitors are used for so-called atypical depressions. Although both classes are quite effective in relieving depression in correctly matched patients, both also have disadvantages. The tricyclics and tetracyclics can take two to five weeks to become effective and can cause such side effects as oversedation and cardiac problems. MAO inhibitors can cause severe hypertension in patients who ingest certain types of food (such as cheese, beer, and wine) or drugs (such as cold medicines).

In the free-association method of analytic psychotherapy, the patient verbalizes uncensored thoughts and feelings while the psychiatrist listens. Lee Lockwood–Black Star

Anxiety (q.v.), tension (*see* STRESS-RELATED DISORDERS), and insomnia (q.v.) are often treated with drugs that are commonly called minor tranquilizers. Barbiturates have been used for the longest time, but they produce more severe side effects and are more often abused than the newer classes of antianxiety drugs (*see* DRUG DEPENDENCE). Of the new drugs, the benzodiazepines are the most frequently prescribed, very often in nonpsychiatric settings.

The stimulant drugs, such as amphetamine—a drug that is often abused—have legitimate uses in psychiatry. They help to control overactivity and lack of concentration in hyperactive children (*see* HYPERACTIVITY) and to stimulate the victims of narcolepsy, a disorder characterized by sudden, uncontrollable attacks of sleep.

Other organic treatments. Another organic treatment is electroconvulsive therapy (q.v.), or ECT, in which seizures similar to those of epilepsy are produced by a current of electricity passed through the forehead. ECT is most commonly used to treat severe depressions that have not responded to drug treatment. It is also sometimes used to treat schizophrenia. Other forms of organic treatment are much less frequently used than drugs and ECT. They include the controversial technique psychosurgery, in which fibers in the brain are severed; this technique is now used very rarely (*see* LOBOTOMY).

Psychotherapy. The most common nonorganic treatment is psychotherapy. Most psychotherapies conducted by psychiatrists are psychodynamic in orientation, that is, they focus on internal psychic conflict and its resolution as a means of restoring mental health. The prototypical psychodynamic therapy is psychoanalysis, which is aimed at untangling the sources of unconscious conflict in the past and restructuring the patient's personality. Psychoanalysis is the treatment in which the patient lies on a couch, with the psychoanalyst out of sight, and says whatever comes to mind. The patient relates dreams, fantasies, and memories, along with thoughts and feelings associated with them. The analyst helps the patient interpret these associations and the meaning of the patient's relationship to the analyst. Because it is lengthy and expensive, often several years in duration, classical psychoanalysis is now infrequently used.

More common are shorter forms of psychotherapy that supplement psychoanalytic principles with other theoretical ideas and scientifically derived information. In these types of therapy, psychiatrists are more likely to give the patient advice and try to influence behavior. Some use techniques derived from behavior therapy, which is based on learning theory (although these methods are more commonly used by psychologists).

Besides psychotherapy, the other major form of nonorganic treatment used in psychiatry is milieu therapy. Usually carried out in psychiatric wards, milieu therapy directs social relations among patients and staff toward therapeutic ends. Ward activities, too, are planned to serve specific therapeutic goals.

In general, psychotherapy is relied on more heavily for the treatment of neuroses and other nonpsychotic conditions than it is for psychoses. In psychotic patients, who usually receive psychoactive drugs, psychotherapy is used to improve social and vocational functioning. Milieu therapy is limited to hospitalized patients. Increasingly, psychiatrists use a combination of organic and nonorganic techniques for all patients, depending on their diagnosis and response to treatment. P.L.E.

For further information on this topic, see the Bibliography in volume 28, sections 526, 528–29.

PSYCHICAL RESEARCH, also parapsychology, scientific investigation of alleged phenomena and events that appear to be unaccounted for by conventional physical, biological, or psychological theories. Parapsychologists study two kinds of so-called psi phenomena: extrasensory perception (ESP), or the acquiring of information through nonsensory means; and psychokinesis (PK), or the ability to affect objects at a distance by means other than known physical forces. Psychical research also investigates the survival of personality after death and deals with related topics such as trance mediumship, hauntings, apparitions, poltergeists (involuntary PK), and out-of-body experiences. The name of this field of investigation is taken from the Society of Psychical Research, founded in England in 1882 and in the U.S. in 1884; both groups continue to publish their findings today.

Historical Development. Among the early achievements of the British group was the investigation of hypnotism (*see* HYPNOSIS), a field later claimed by medicine and psychology. The society also investigated phenomena produced at spiritualistic séances and the claims of spiritualism (q.v.). Psi phenomena to be investigated were classified as either physical or mental. The physical effects, or PK, include the movement of physical objects or an influence upon material processes by the apparent direct action of mind over matter. The mental manifestations, or ESP, include telepathy, which is the direct transmission of messages, emotions, or other subjective states from one person to another without the use of any sensory channel of communication; clairvoyance, meaning direct responses to a physical object or event without any sensory contact; and precognition, or a noninferential response to a future event.

One of the first specific investigations in the field was the examination, by the British chemist and physicist Sir William Crookes, of the phenomena produced at séances held by the Scottish medium Daniel Dunglas Home (1833–86). Home, a physical medium, held his séances in full light, and the validity of the paranormal phenomena he produced has never been successfully impugned. The contents of verbal utterances by mental mediums were also studied. Significant early research involved the American medium Leonore E. Piper (1859–1950), whose apparent psychical gifts were discovered by the American philosopher and psychologist William James. Other lines of investigation dealt with psychic experiences that seemed to occur spontaneously in everyday life, and involved the controlled testing of persons with apparently outstanding ESP abilities.

Rhine's Laboratory. In the U.S., one of the earliest groups to become active in parapsychology was the Parapsychology Laboratory of North Carolina's Duke University, which began publishing literature in the 1930s. There, under the direction of the American psychologist Joseph Banks Rhine, methods were developed that advanced psychical investigations from the correlations of isolated and often vague anecdotal reports to a mathematical study based on statistics and the laws of probability.

In the experiments dealing with ESP, Rhine and his associates used mainly a deck of 25 cards, somewhat similar to ordinary playing cards but bearing on their faces only five designs: star, circle, cross, square, and wavy lines. If a subject correctly named 5 out of the shuffled deck of 25 concealed cards, that was considered pure chance. Certain subjects, however, consistently named 6 out of 10 cards correctly; so Rhine and his associates concluded that this demonstrated the existence of ESP. In their experiments on PK, the group used ordinary dice that were thrown from a cup against a wall or tumbled in mechanically driven cages. In these tests, an apparent relationship was found between the mental effort of subjects to "will" particular faces of the dice to appear upward and the percentage of times the faces actually did so. The results obtained in many individual experiments and in the research as a whole, Rhine and his workers decided, could not reasonably be attributed to the fluctuations of chance.

Rhine retired from Duke University in 1965 and transferred his research to a privately endowed organization, the Foundation for Research on the Nature of Man. Since that time parapsychology has become better established in other universities, as illustrated by the offering of credit courses in the subject in increasing numbers. In addition, independent research centers continue to be founded, among them the American Society for Psychical Research, with headquarters in New York City. The Parapsychological Association, an international group of scholars actively working in the field, was formed in 1957 and was granted affiliation status by the American Association for the Advancement of Science in 1969.

Criticisms. Although parapsychologists are increasingly employing and refining scientific methodologies for their observations, one of the chief criticisms of their work is that experiments in psi phenomena can rarely be duplicated. Under the most rigorous laboratory controls, for example, experiments on phenomena such as out-of-body experiences—in which individuals demonstrate an apparent ability to locate their center of perception outside their bodies—indicate that even reputable psychics are rarely able to duplicate earlier, high-scoring performances. The scores of such individuals, in fact, tend to drop to the level of probability the more the experiment is repeated. Nonparapsychologists find psi experiments even more difficult to repeat, and a majority of conventional scientists dismiss parapsychology findings as unscientific or at best inconclusive.

A similar criticism is based on the claim by most parapsychologists that psi phenomena occur beyond the law of causality, which is one of the fundamental premises of any scientific investigation. Indeed, results of psi experiments often turn out to be far from or even contradictory to the original predictions. Parapsychologists admit that psi phenomena fall so far outside ordinary comprehension that they are often unsure whether an ESP event or a PK event has occurred; Rhine himself stated that one kind of event could not occur without the other. Because these phenomena are difficult to define or isolate when they appear to happen—and, further, because the phenomena occur only for a select group of observers—most scientists think that psi investigations fall far short of the rules of objectivity required by the scientific method. As a result, many parapsychologists, rather than trying to demonstrate the reality of psi phenomena to a skeptical scientific community, have turned to exploring how such phenomena might actually work; they even have drawn on quantum physics for empirical support. Some workers in the field object to the very notion of repeatability of experiments as foreign to the nature of psi phenomena; they consider the scientific method, as currently understood, too restrictive a formulation for exploring the unknown.

For further information on this topic, see the Bibliography in volume 28, section 146.

PSYCHOACTIVE DRUGS, chemical substances that alter mood, behavior, perception, or mental functioning. Throughout history, many cultures have found ways to alter consciousness through the ingestion of substances. In current professional practice, psychoactive substances known as psychotropic drugs have been developed to treat patients with severe mental illness.

Psychoactive substances exert their effects by modifying biochemical or physiological processes in the brain. The message system of nerve cells, or neurons, relies on both electrical and chemical transmission. Neurons rarely touch each other; the microscopic gap between one neuron and the next, called the synapse, is bridged by chemicals called neuroregulators, or neurotransmitters. Psychoactive drugs act by altering neurotransmitter function. The drugs can be divided into six major pharmacological classes based on their desired behavioral or psychological effect: alcohol, sedative-hypnotics, narcotic analgesics, stimulant-euphoriants, hallucinogens, and psychotropic agents.

Alcohol has always been the most widely used psychoactive substance. In most countries it is the only psychoactive drug legally available without prescription. Pleasant relaxation is commonly the desired effect, but intoxication impairs judgment and motor performance. When used chronically, alcohol can be toxic to liver and brain cells and can be physiologically addicting, producing dangerous withdrawal syndromes. *See* ALCOHOLISM.

Sedative-hypnotics, such as the barbiturates and diazepam (widely known under the brand name Valium), include brain depressants, which are used medically to help people sleep (sleeping pills), and antianxiety agents, which are used to calm people without inducing sleep. Sedative-hypnotics are used illegally to produce relaxation, tranquillity, and euphoria. Overdoses of sedative-hypnotics can be fatal; all can be physiologically addicting, and some can cause a life-threatening withdrawal syndrome.

Narcotic analgesics—opiates (*see* OPIUM) such as morphine and heroin—are prescribed to produce analgesia. Because the relief of pain is one of the primary tasks of medical treatment, opiates have been among the most important and valuable drugs in medicine. Illegal use of narcotic analgesics involves injecting these substances, particularly heroin, into the veins to produce euphoria. Opiates are physiologically addicting and can produce a quite unpleasant withdrawal syndrome.

Stimulant-euphoriants, such as amphetamines, are prescribed by physicians to suppress the appetite and to treat children often diagnosed as hyperactive (*see* HYPERACTIVITY). Although amphetamines stimulate adults, they have a paradoxically calming effect on certain children who have short attention spans and are hyperactive. Cocaine (q.v.) is used medically as a local anesthetic. Amphetamines and cocaine are used illegally to produce alertness and euphoria, to prevent drowsiness, and to improve performance in physical and mental tasks such as athletic events and college examinations.

Hallucinogens—psychedelic drugs such as LSD (*see* LYSERGIC ACID DIETHYLAMIDE), mescaline, and PCP (*see* PHENCYCLIDINE)—thus far have little medical use. They are taken illegally to alter perception and thinking patterns. Marijuana (q.v.) is a weak hallucinogen that may be medically useful in suppressing the nausea caused by cancer treatments and possibly in reducing eye pressure in certain severe glaucomas.

Psychotropic drugs have been in use since the early 1950s. Antipsychotic drugs decrease the symptoms of schizophrenia, allowing many schizophrenic patients to leave the hospital and rejoin community life. Antidepressant drugs help the majority of patients with severe depression (q.v.) recover from their disorder. Lithium salts eliminate or diminish the episodes of mania and depression experienced by manic-depressive patients (*see* LITHIUM).

See also CONSCIOUSNESS, STATES OF; DRUG DEPENDENCE. P.A.B.

For further information on this topic, see the Bibliography in volume 28, sections 145, 503–4.

PSYCHOANALYSIS, name applied to a specific method of investigating unconscious mental processes and to a form of psychotherapy (q.v.). The term refers, as well, to the systematic structure of psychoanalytic theory, which is based on the relation of conscious and unconscious psychological processes.

THEORY OF PSYCHOANALYSIS

The technique of psychoanalysis and much of the psychoanalytic theory based on its application were developed by Sigmund Freud. His work concerning the structure and the functioning of the human mind had far-reaching significance, both practically and scientifically, and it continues to influence contemporary thought.

The Unconscious. The first of Freud's innovations was his recognition of unconscious psychiatric processes that follow laws different from those

Sigmund Freud and his daughter, Mathilde Hollitscher. UPI

that govern conscious experience. Under the influence of the unconscious, thoughts and feelings that belong together may be shifted or displaced out of context; two disparate ideas or images may be condensed into one; thoughts may be dramatized in the form of images rather than expressed as abstract concepts; and certain objects may be represented symbolically by images of other objects, although the resemblance between the symbol and the original object may be vague or farfetched. The laws of logic, indispensable for conscious thinking, do not apply to these unconscious mental productions.

Recognition of these modes of operation in unconscious mental processes made possible the understanding of such previously incomprehensible psychological phenomena as dreaming (q.v.). Through analysis of unconscious processes, Freud saw dreams as serving to protect sleep (q.v.) against disturbing impulses arising from within and related to early life experiences. Thus, unacceptable impulses and thoughts, called the latent dream content, are transformed into a conscious, although no longer immediately comprehensible, experience called the manifest dream. Knowledge of these unconscious mechanisms permits the analyst to reverse the so-called dream work, that is, the process by which the latent dream is transformed into the manifest dream, and through dream interpretation, to recognize its underlying meaning.

Instinctual Drives. A basic assumption of Freudian theory is that the unconscious conflicts involve instinctual impulses, or drives, that originate in childhood. As these unconscious conflicts are recognized by the patient through analysis, his or her adult mind can find solutions that were unattainable to the immature mind of the child. This depiction of the role of instinctual drives in human life is a unique feature of Freudian theory.

According to Freud's doctrine of infantile sexuality, adult sexuality is an end product of a complex process of development, beginning in childhood, involving a variety of body functions or areas (oral, anal, and genital zones), and corresponding to various stages in the relation of the child to adults, especially to parents. Of crucial importance is the so-called Oedipal period, occurring at about four to six years of age, because at this stage of development the child for the first time becomes capable of an emotional attachment to the parent of the opposite sex that is similar to the adult's relationship to a mate; the child simultaneously reacts as a rival to the parent of the same sex. Physical immaturity dooms the child's desires to frustration and his or her first step toward adulthood to failure. Intellectual immaturity further complicates the situation because it makes children afraid of their own fantasies. The extent to which the child overcomes these emotional upheavals and to which these attachments, fears, and fantasies continue to live on in the unconscious greatly influences later life, especially love relationships.

The conflicts occurring in the earlier developmental stages are no less significant as a formative influence, because these problems represent the earliest prototypes of such basic human situations as dependency on others and relationship to authority. Also basic in molding the personality of the individual is the behavior of the parents toward the child during these stages of development. The fact that the child reacts, not only to objective reality, but also to fantasy distortions of reality, however, greatly complicates even the best-intentioned educational efforts.

Id, Ego, and Superego. The effort to clarify the bewildering number of interrelated observations uncovered by psychoanalytic exploration led to the development of a model of the structure of the psychic system. Three functional systems are distinguished that are conveniently designated as the id, ego, and superego (qq.v.).

The first system refers to the sexual and aggressive tendencies that arise from the body, as distinguished from the mind. Freud called these tendencies *Triebe,* which literally means "drives," but which is often inaccurately translated as "instincts" to indicate their innate character. These inherent drives claim immediate satisfaction, which is experienced as pleasurable; the id thus is dominated by the pleasure principle. In his later writings, Freud tended more toward psychological rather than biological conceptualization of the drives.

How the conditions for satisfaction are to be brought about is the task of the second system, the ego, which is the domain of such functions as perception, thinking, and motor control that can accurately assess environmental conditions. In order to fulfill its function of adaptation, or reality testing, the ego must be capable of enforcing the postponement of satisfaction of the instinctual impulses originating in the id. To defend itself against unacceptable impulses, the ego develops specific psychic means, known as defense mechanisms. These include repression, the exclusion of impulses from conscious awareness; projection, the process of ascribing to others one's own unacknowledged desires; and reaction formation, the establishment of a pattern of behavior directly opposed to a strong unconscious need. Such defense mechanisms are put into operation whenever anxiety signals a danger that the original unacceptable impulses may reemerge.

An id impulse becomes unacceptable, not only as a result of a temporary need for postponing its satisfaction until suitable reality conditions can be found, but more often because of a prohibition imposed on the individual by others, originally the parents. The totality of these demands and prohibitions constitutes the major content of the third system, the superego, the function of which is to control the ego in accordance with the internalized standards of parental figures. If the demands of the superego are not fulfilled, the person may feel shame or guilt. Because the superego, in Freudian theory, originates in the struggle to overcome the Oedipal conflict, it has a power akin to an instinctual drive, is in part unconscious, and can give rise to feelings of guilt not justified by any conscious transgression. The ego, having to mediate among the demands of the id, the superego, and the outside world, may not be strong enough to reconcile these conflicting forces. The more the ego is impeded in its development because of being enmeshed in its earlier conflicts, called fixations or complexes, or the more it reverts to earlier satisfactions and archaic modes of functioning, known as regression, the greater is the likelihood of succumbing to these pressures. Unable to function normally, it can maintain its limited control and integrity only at the price of symptom formation, in which the tensions are expressed in neurotic symptoms.

Anxiety. A cornerstone of modern psychoanalytic theory and practice is the concept of anxiety (q.v.), which institutes appropriate mechanisms of defense against certain danger situations. These danger situations, as described by Freud, are the fear of abandonment by or the loss of the loved one (the object), the risk of losing the object's love, the danger of retaliation and punishment, and, finally, the hazard of reproach by the superego. Thus, symptom formation, character and impulse disorders, and perversions, as well as sublimations, represent compromise formations—different forms of an adaptive integration that the ego tries to achieve through more or less successfully reconciling the different conflicting forces in the mind.

PSYCHOANALYTIC SCHOOLS

Various psychoanalytic schools have adopted other names for their doctrines to indicate deviations from Freudian theory.

Carl Jung. Carl Gustav Jung, one of the earliest pupils of Freud, eventually created a school that he preferred to call analytical psychology. Like Freud, Jung used the concept of the libido (q.v.); however, to him it meant not only sexual drives, but a composite of all creative instincts and impulses and the entire motivating force of human conduct. According to his theories, the unconscious is composed of two parts; the personal unconscious, which contains the results of the individual's entire experience, and the collective

Carl Gustav Jung Gamma Agency, Inc.

Alfred Adler UPI

unconscious, the reservoir of the experience of the human race. In the collective unconscious exist a number of primordial images, or archetypes, common to all individuals of a given country or historical era. Archetypes take the form of bits of intuitive knowledge or apprehension and normally exist only in the collective unconscious of the individual. When the conscious mind contains no images, however, as in sleep, or when the consciousness is caught off guard, the archetypes commence to function. Archetypes are primitive modes of thought and tend to personify natural processes in terms of such mythological concepts as good and evil spirits, fairies, and dragons. The mother and the father also serve as prominent archetypes.

An important concept in Jung's theory is the existence of two basically different types of personality, mental attitude, and function. When the libido and the individual's general interest are turned outward toward people and objects of the external world, he or she is said to be extraverted. When the reverse is true, and libido and interest are centered on the individual, he or she is said to be introverted. In a completely normal individual these two tendencies alternate, neither dominating, but usually the libido is directed mainly in one direction or the other; as a result, two personality types are recognizable.

Jung rejected Freud's distinction between the ego and superego and recognized a portion of the personality, somewhat similar to the superego, that he called the persona. The persona consists of what a person appears to be to others, in contrast to what he or she actually is. The persona is the role the individual chooses to play in life, the total impression he or she wishes to make on the outside world.

Alfred Adler. Alfred Adler, another of Freud's pupils, differed from both Freud and Jung in stressing that the motivating force in human life is the sense of inferiority, which begins as soon as an infant is able to comprehend the existence of other people who are better able to care for themselves and cope with their environment. From the moment the feeling of inferiority is established, the child strives to overcome it. Because inferiority is intolerable, the compensatory mechanisms set up by the mind may get out of hand, resulting in self-centered neurotic attitudes, overcompensations, and a retreat from the real world and its problems.

Adler laid particular stress on inferiority feelings arising from what he regarded as the three most important relationships: those between the individual and work, friends, and loved ones. The avoidance of inferiority feelings in these relationships leads the individual to adopt a life goal that is often not realistic and frequently is expressed as an unreasoning will to power and dominance, leading to every type of antisocial behavior from bullying and boasting to political tyranny. Adler believed that analysis can foster a sane and rational "community feeling" that is constructive rather than destructive.

Karen Horney UPI

Otto Rank Alfred A. Knopf, Inc.

Otto Rank. Another student of Freud, Otto Rank, introduced a new theory of neurosis, attributing all neurotic disturbances to the primary trauma of birth. In his later writings he described individual development as a progression from complete dependence on the mother and family, to a physical independence coupled with intellectual dependence on society, and finally to complete intellectual and psychological emancipation. Rank also laid great importance on the will, defined as "a positive guiding organization and integration of self, which utilizes creatively as well as inhibits and controls the instinctual drives."

Other Psychoanalytic Schools. Later noteworthy modifications of psychoanalytic theory include those of the American psychoanalysts Erich Fromm, Karen Horney, and Harry Stack Sullivan. The theories of Fromm lay particular emphasis on the concept that society and the individual are not separate and opposing forces, that the nature of society is determined by its historic background, and that the needs and desires of individuals are largely formed by their society. As a result, Fromm believed, the fundamental problem of psychoanalysis and psychology is not to resolve conflicts between fixed and unchanging instinctive drives in the individual and the fixed demands and laws of society, but to bring about harmony and an understanding of the relationship between the individual and society. Fromm also stressed the importance to the individual of developing the ability to fully use his or her mental, emotional, and sensory powers.

Horney worked primarily in the field of therapy and the nature of neuroses, which she defined as of two types: situation neuroses and character neuroses. Situation neuroses arise from the anxiety attendant on a single conflict, such as being faced with a difficult decision. Although they may paralyze the individual temporarily, making it impossible to think or act efficiently, such neuroses are not deeply rooted. Character neuroses are characterized by a basic anxiety and a basic hostility resulting from a lack of love and affection in childhood.

Sullivan believed that all development can be described exclusively in terms of interpersonal relations. Character types as well as neurotic symptoms are explained as results of the struggle against anxiety arising from the individual's relations with others and are a security system, maintained for the purpose of allaying anxiety.

Melanie Klein. An important school of thought is based on the teachings of the British psychoanalyst Melanie Klein. Because most of Klein's followers worked with her in England, this has come to be known as the English school. Its influence, nevertheless, is very strong throughout the European continent and in South America. Its principal theories were derived from observations made in the psychoanalysis of children. Klein posited the existence of complex unconscious fantasies in children under the age of six months. The principal source of anxiety arises from the threat to existence posed by the death instinct. Depending on how concrete representations of the destructive forces are dealt with in the unconscious fantasy life of the child, two basic early mental attitudes result that Klein characterized as a "depressive position" and a "paranoid position." In the paranoid position, the ego's defense consists of projecting the dangerous internal object onto some external representative, which is treated as a genuine threat emanating from the external world. In the depressive position, the threatening object is introjected and treated in fantasy as concretely retained within the person. Depressive and hypochondriacal symptoms result. Although considerable doubt exists that such complex unconscious fantasies operate in the minds of infants, these observations have been of the utmost importance to the psychology of unconscious fantasies, paranoid delusions, and theory concerning early object relations.

See also PSYCHIATRY. J.L.H. & J.A.A.

For further information on this topic, see the Bibliography in volume 28, section 528.

PSYCHOLOGICAL TESTING, measurement of some aspect of human behavior by procedures consisting of carefully prescribed content, methods of administration, and interpretation. Test content may be addressed to almost any aspect of intellectual or emotional functioning, including personality traits, attitudes, intelligence, or emotional concerns. Tests usually are administered by a qualified clinical, school, or industrial psychologist, according to professional and ethical principles. Interpretation is based on a comparison of the individual's responses with those previously obtained to establish appropriate standards for the test scores. The usefulness of psychological tests depends on their accuracy in predicting behavior. By providing information about the probability of a person's responses or performance, tests aid in making a variety of decisions.

History of Testing. The primary impetus for the development of the major tests used today was the need for practical guidelines for solving social problems. The first useful intelligence test was prepared in 1905 by the French psychologists Alfred Binet and Théodore Simon (1873–1961). The two developed a 30-item scale to ensure that no child could be denied instruction in the Paris school system without formal examination. In 1916 the American psychologist Lewis Terman produced the first Stanford Revision of the Binet-Simon scale to provide comparison standards for Americans from age three to adulthood. The test was further revised in 1937 and 1960, and today the Stanford-Binet remains one of the most widely used intelligence tests.

The need to classify soldiers during World War I resulted in the development of two group intelligence tests—Army Alpha and Army Beta. To help detect soldiers who might break down in combat, the American psychologist Robert Woodworth (1869–1962) designed the Personal Data Sheet, a forerunner of the modern personality inventory.

During the 1930s controversies over the nature of intelligence led to the development of the Wechsler-Bellevue Intelligence Scale, which not only provided an index of general mental ability but also revealed patterns of intellectual strengths and weaknesses. The Wechsler tests now extend from the preschool through the adult age range and are at least as prominent as the Stanford-Binet.

As interest in the newly emerging field of psychoanalysis grew in the 1930s, two important projective techniques introduced systematic ways to study unconscious motivation: the Rorschach or inkblot test—developed by the Swiss psychiatrist Hermann Rorschach (1884–1922)—using a series of inkblots on cards, and a storytelling procedure called the Thematic Apperception Test—developed by the American psychologists Henry A. Murray (1893–1988) and C. D. Morgan. Both of these tests are frequently included in contemporary personality assessment.

During World War II the need for improved methods of personnel selection led to the expansion of large-scale programs involving multiple methods of personality assessment. Following the war, training programs in clinical psychology were systematically supported by U.S. government funding, to ensure availability of mental-health services to returning war veterans. As part of these services, psychological testing flourished, reaching an estimated several million Americans each year. Since the late 1960s increased awareness and criticism from both the public and professional sectors have led to greater efforts to establish legal controls and more explicit safeguards against misuse of testing materials.

Uses of Tests. In educational settings, intelligence and achievement tests are administered routinely to assess individual accomplishment and to improve instruction and curriculum planning. Elementary schools use kindergarten and first-grade screening procedures to determine readiness for reading and writing programs. Screening tests also identify developmental, visual, and auditory problems for which the child may need special assistance. If the child's progress in school is unusually slow, or if he or she shows signs of a learning disability or behavior disorder, testing may clarify whether the difficulty is neurologically or emotionally based. Many high schools administer interest inventories and aptitude tests to assist in the students' educational or vocational planning.

In clinics or hospitals, psychological tests may be administered for purposes of diagnosis and treatment planning. Clinical tests can provide information about overall personality functioning and the need for psychotherapy; testing also may focus on some specific question, such as the presence or absence of organically based brain disorder. Clinical testing usually involves a battery of tests, interpreted as a whole, to describe intellectual and emotional states. Decisions about treatment do not depend exclusively on psychological test results but are based on the judgment of relevant staff members with whom the psychologist collaborates.

Tests are also used in industrial and organizational settings, primarily for selection and classification. Selection procedures provide guidelines for accepting or rejecting candidates for jobs. Classification procedures, which are more complex, aim to specify the types of positions for which an individual seems best suited. Intelligence testing is usually supplemented by methods devised expressly to meet the needs of the organization.

Types of Tests. Currently, a wide range of testing procedures is used in the U.S. and elsewhere. Each type of procedure is designed to carry out specific functions.

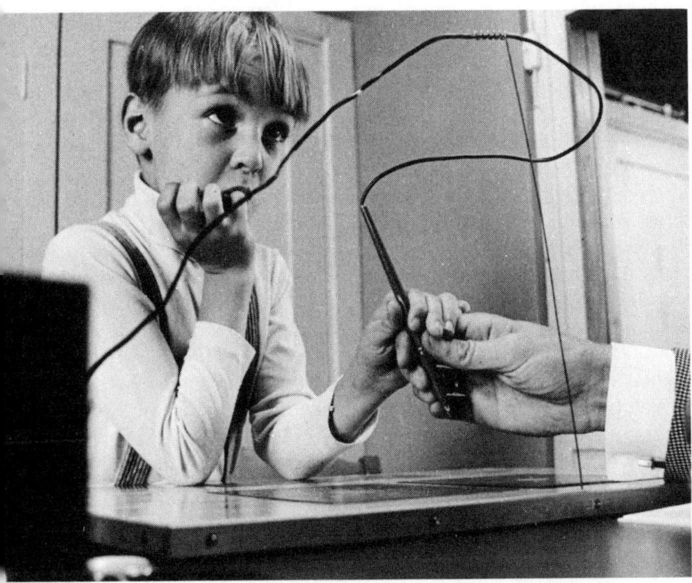

A child is tested to determine which hand has the better motor coordination.
E. Mandelmann–WHO

Achievement tests. These tests are designed to assess current performance in an academic area. Because achievement is viewed as an indicator of previous learning, it is often used to predict future academic success. An achievement test administered in a public school setting would typically include separate measures of vocabulary, language skills and reading comprehension, arithmetic computation and problem solving, science, and social studies. Individual achievement is determined by comparison of results with average scores derived from large representative national or local samples. Scores may be expressed in terms of "grade-level equivalents"; for example, an advanced third-grade pupil may be reading on a level equivalent to that of the average fourth-grade student.

Aptitude tests. These tests predict future performance in an area in which the individual is not currently trained. Schools, businesses, and government agencies often use aptitude tests when assigning individuals to specific positions. Vocational guidance counseling may involve aptitude testing to help clarify individual career goals. If a person's score is similar to scores of others already working in a given occupation, likelihood of success in that field is predicted. Some aptitude tests cover a broad range of skills pertinent to many different occupations. The General Aptitude Test Battery, for example, not only measures general reasoning ability but also includes form perception, clerical perception, motor coordination, and finger and manual dexterity. Other tests may focus on a single area, such as art, engineering, or modern languages.

Intelligence tests. In contrast to tests of specific proficiencies or aptitudes, intelligence tests measure the global capacity of an individual to cope with the environment. Test scores are generally known as intelligence quotients, or IQs, although the various tests are constructed quite differently. The Stanford-Binet is heavily weighted with items involving verbal abilities; the Wechsler scales consist of two separate verbal and performance subscales, each with its own IQ. There are also specialized infant intelligence tests, tests that do not require the use of language, and tests that are designed for group administration.

The early intelligence scales yielded a mental-age score, expressing the child's ability to do as well as average children who were older, younger, or equivalent in chronological age. The deviation IQ used today expresses the individual's position in comparison to a representative group of people of the same age. The average IQ is set at 100; about half of those who take the test achieve scores between 90 and 110. IQ scores may vary according to testing conditions, and, thus, it is advisable to understand results of the tests as falling within a certain range, such as average or superior.

Interest inventories. Self-report questionnaires on which the subject indicates personal preferences among activities are called interest inventories. Because interests may predict satisfaction with some area of employment or education, these inventories are used primarily in guidance counseling. They are not intended to predict success, but only to offer a framework for narrowing career possibilities. For example, one frequently used interest inventory, the Kudor Preference Record, includes ten clusters of occupational interests: outdoors, mechanical, computational, scientific, persuasive, artistic, literary, musical, social service, and clerical. For each item, the subject indicates which of three activities is best or least liked. The total score indicates the occupational clusters that include preferred activities.

Objective personality tests. These tests measure social and emotional adjustment and are used to identify the need for psychological counseling. Items that briefly describe feelings, attitudes, and behaviors are grouped into subscales, each representing a separate personality or style, such as social extroversion or depression. Taken together, the subscales provide a profile of the personality as a whole. One of the most popular psychological tests is the Minnesota Multiphasic Personality Inventory (MMPI), constructed to aid in diagnosing psychiatric patients. Research has shown that the MMPI may also be used to describe differences among normal personality types.

Projective techniques. Some personality tests are based on the phenomenon of projection, a mental process described by Sigmund Freud as the tendency to attribute to others personal feelings or characteristics that are too painful to acknowledge. Because projective techniques are relatively unstructured and offer minimal cues to aid in defining responses, they tend to elicit concerns that are highly personal and significant. The best-known projective tests are the Rorschach test, popularly known as the inkblot test, and the Thematic Apperception Test; others in clude word-association techniques, sentence-completion tests, and various drawing procedures. The psychologist's past experience provides the framework for evaluating individual responses. Although the subjective nature of interpretation makes these tests particularly vulnerable to criticism, in clinical settings they are part of the standard battery of psychological tests.

A 79-year-old volunteer is tested on his ability to solve a mental problem. He is one of 500 elderly persons who are tested periodically by the Gerontology Branch of the National Institutes of Health, Bethesda, Md., to study their capacities and condition as they grow older. J. Mohr–WHO

Interpretation of Results. The most important aspect of psychological testing involves the interpretation of test results.

Scoring. The raw score is the simple numerical count of responses, such as the number of correct answers on an intelligence test. The usefulness of the raw score is limited, however, because it does not convey how well someone does in comparison with others taking the same test. Percentile scores, standard scores, and norms are all devices for making this comparison.

Percentile scoring expresses the rank order of the scores in percentages. The percentile level of a person's score indicates the proportion of the group that scored above and below that individual. When a score falls at the 50th percentile, for example, half of the group scored higher and half scored lower; a score at the 80th percentile indicates that 20 percent scored higher and 80 percent scored lower than the person being evaluated.

Standard scores are derived from a comparison of the individual raw score with the mean and standard deviation of the group scores. The mean, or arithmetic average, is determined by adding the scores and dividing by the total number of scores obtained. The standard deviation measures the variation of the scores around the mean. Standard scores are obtained by subtracting the mean from the raw score and then dividing by the standard deviation.

Tables of norms are included in test manuals to indicate the expected range of raw scores. Normative data are derived from studies in which the test has been administered to a large, representative group of people. The test manual should include a description of the sample of people used to establish norms, including age, sex, geographical location, and occupation. Norms based on a group of people whose major characteristics are markedly dissimilar from those of the person being tested do not provide a fair standard of comparison.

Validity. Interpretation of test scores ultimately involves predictions about a subject's behavior in a specified situation. If a test is an accurate predictor, it is said to have good validity. Before validity can be demonstrated, a test must first yield consistent, reliable measurements. In addition to reliability, psychologists recognize three main types of validity.

A test has content validity if the sample of items in the test is representative of all the relevant items that might have been used. Words included in a spelling test, for example, should cover a wide range of difficulty.

Criterion-related validity refers to a test's accuracy in specifying a future or concurrent outcome. For example, an art-aptitude test has predictive validity if high scores are achieved by those who later do well in art school. The concurrent validity of a new intelligence test may be demonstrated if its scores correlate closely with those of an already well-established test.

Construct validity is generally determined by investigating what psychological traits or qualities a test measures; that is, by demonstrating that certain patterns of human behavior account to some degree for performance on the test. A test measuring the trait "need for achievement," for instance, might be shown to predict that high scorers work more independently, persist longer on problem-solving tasks, and do better in competitive situations than low scorers.

Controversies. The major psychological testing controversies stem from two interrelated issues: technical shortcomings in test design and ethical problems in interpretation and application of results. Some technical weaknesses exist in all tests. Because of this, it is crucial that results be viewed as only one kind of information about any individual. Most criticisms of testing arise from the overvaluation of and inappropriate reliance on test results in making major life decisions. These criticisms have been particularly relevant in the case of intelligence testing. Psychologists generally agree that using tests to bar youngsters from educational opportunities, without careful consideration of past and present resources or motivation, is unethical. Because tests tend to draw on those skills associated with white, middle-class functioning, they may discriminate against disadvantaged and minority groups. As long as unequal learning opportunities exist, they will continue to be reflected in test results. In the U.S., therefore, some states have established laws that carefully define the use of tests in public schools and agencies. The American Psychological Association, meanwhile, continues to work actively to monitor and refine ethical standards and public policy recommendations regarding the use of psychological testing.

See also PSYCHOLOGY. P.K.S.

For further information on this topic, see the Bibliography in volume 28, section 144.

PSYCHOLOGICAL WARFARE. *See* WARFARE.

PSYCHOLOGY, scientific study of behavior and experience—that is, the study of how human beings and animals sense, think, learn, and know. Modern psychology is devoted to collecting facts about behavior and experience and systematically organizing such facts into psychological theories. These theories aid in understanding and explaining people's behavior and sometimes in predicting and influencing their future behavior.

Psychology, historically, has been divided into many subfields of study; these fields, however, are interrelated and frequently overlap. Physiological psychologists, for instance, study the functioning of the brain and the nervous system, and experimental psychologists devise tests and conduct research to discover how people learn and remember. Subfields of psychology may also be described in terms of areas of application. Social psychologists, for example, are interested in the ways in which people influence one another and the way they act in groups. Industrial psychologists study the behavior of people at work and the effects of the work environment. School psychologists help students make educational and career decisions. Clinical psychologists assist those who have problems in daily life or who are mentally ill.

HISTORY

The science of psychology developed from many diverse sources, but its origins as a science may be traced to ancient Greece.

Philosophical Beginnings. Plato and Aristotle, as well as other Greek philosophers, took up some of the basic questions of psychology that are still under study: Are people born with certain skills, abilities, and personality, or do all these develop as a result of experience? How do people come to know the world? Are certain ideas and feelings innate, or are they all learned?

Such questions were debated for many centuries, but the roots of modern psychological theory are found in the 17th century in the works of the French philosopher René Descartes and the British philosophers Thomas Hobbes and John Locke. Descartes argued that the bodies of people are like clockwork machines, but that their minds (or souls) are separate and unique. He maintained that minds have certain inborn, or innate, ideas and that these ideas are crucial in organizing people's experiencing of the world. Hobbes and Locke, on the other hand, stressed the role of experience as the source of human knowledge. Locke believed that all information about the physical world comes through the senses and that all correct ideas can be traced to the sensory information on which they are based.

Most modern psychology developed along the lines of Locke's view. Some European psychologists who studied perception (q.v.), however, held onto Descartes's idea that some mental organization is innate, and the concept still plays a role in theories of perception and cognition.

Scientific Developments. Against this philosophical background, the field that contributed most to the development of scientific psychology was physiology—the study of the functions of the various organ systems of the body. The German physiologist Johannes Müller (1801–58) tried to relate sensory experience both to events in the nervous system and to events in the organism's physical environment. The first true experimental psychologists were the German physicist Gustav Theodor Fechner (1801–87) and

Wilhelm Wundt Culver Pictures

the German physiologist Wilhelm Wundt. Fechner developed experimental methods for measuring sensations in terms of the physical magnitude of the stimuli producing them. Wundt, who in 1879 founded the first laboratory of experimental psychology in Leipzig, Germany, trained students from around the world in this new science. *See* PSYCHOLOGY, EXPERIMENTAL.

Physicians who became concerned with mental illness also contributed to the development of modern psychological theories. Thus, the systematic classification of mental disorders developed by the German psychiatric pioneer Emil Kraepelin remains the basis for methods of classification that are now in use. Far better known, however, is the work of Sigmund Freud, who devised the system of investigation and treatment known as psychoanalysis (q.v.). In his work, Freud called attention to instinctual drives and unconscious motivational processes that determine people's behavior. This stress on the contents of thought, on the dynamics of motivation rather than the nature of cognition in itself, exerted a strong influence on the course of modern psychology.

20th-Century Psychology. In the U.S., psychology was influenced greatly, as well, by a strong practical orientation. American practitioners tried to apply psychology in school and business settings. Partly as a result of these practical goals, and partly because of disputes about methods of doing research on mental or "inner" life, American psychologists from about 1920 to 1960 showed little concern with mental processes, focusing their attention instead on behavior itself. This movement, known as behaviorism (q.v.), was led by the American psychologist John B. Watson.

Modern psychology still retains many aspects of the fields and kinds of speculation from which it grew. Some psychologists, for example, are primarily interested in physiological research, others are medically oriented, and a few try to develop a more encompassing, philosophical understanding of psychology as a whole. Although some practitioners still insist that psychology should be concerned only with behavior—and may even deny the meaningfulness of an inner, mental life—more and more psychologists would now agree that mental life or experience is a valid psychological concern.

MAJOR AREAS OF RESEARCH

The areas of modern psychology range from the biological sciences to the social sciences.

Physiological Psychology. The study of underlying physiological bases of psychological functions is known as physiological psychology. The two major communication systems of the body—the nervous system and the circulatory

John B. Watson Culver Pictures

system—are the focus of most research in this area.

The nervous system consists of the central nervous system (the brain and the spinal cord) and its outlying neural network, the peripheral nervous system; the latter communicates with the glands and muscles and includes the sensory receptors for seeing, hearing, smelling, tasting, touching, feeling pain, and sensing stimuli within the body. The circulatory system circulates the blood and also carries the important chemical agents known as hormones from the glands to all parts of the body. Both these communication systems are very important in overall human behavior.

The smallest unit of the nervous system is the single nerve cell, or neuron. When a neuron is properly stimulated, it transmits electrochemical signals from one place in the system to another. The nervous system has 12.5 billion neurons, of which about 10 billion are in the brain itself.

One part of the peripheral nervous system, the somatic system, transmits sensations into the central nervous system and carries commands from the central system to the muscles involved in movement. Another part of the peripheral nervous system, the autonomic system, consists of two divisions that have opposing functions. The sympathetic division arouses the body by speeding the heartbeat, dilating the pupils of the eye, and releasing adrenaline into the blood. The parasympathetic division operates to calm the body by reversing these processes.

A simple example of communication within the nervous system is the spinal arc, which is seen in the knee-jerk reflex. A tap on the patellar tendon, just below the kneecap, sends a signal to the spinal cord via sensory neurons. This signal activates motor neurons that trigger a contraction of the muscle attached to the tendon; the contraction, in turn, causes the leg to jerk. Thus, a stimulus can lead to a response without involving the brain, via a connection through the spinal cord. *See* REFLEX.

Circulatory communication is ordinarily slower than nervous-system communication. The hormones secreted by the body's endocrine glands circulate through the body, influencing both structural and behavioral changes (*see* ENDOCRINE SYSTEM). The sex hormones, for example, that are released during adolescence effect many changes in body growth and development as well as changes in behavior, such as the emergence of specific sexual activity and the increase of interest in the opposite sex. Other hormones may have more direct, short-term effects; for instance, adrenaline, which is secreted when a person faces an emergency, prepares the body for a quick response—whether fighting or flight.

Conditioning and Learning. A central area of study in psychology is how organisms change as a result of experience, that is, how they learn. Much research in learning has been performed using such animals as rats, pigeons, and dogs. Two major kinds of learning are usually distinguished: classical conditioning and instrumental learning.

Classical conditioning is also called Pavlovian conditioning after its discoverer, the Russian physiologist Ivan Pavlov. He showed that if some arbitrary event, such as ringing a bell, regularly precedes a biologically important event, such as presenting food to an animal subject, the bell will become a signal for the food, and the animal will salivate and "get ready to eat" when the bell rings. The animal's behavior, then, is a conditioned response to the bell. In Pavlov's terms, the pairing of a conditioned stimulus (the bell) with an unconditioned stimulus (the food) results in learning. Eventually, some parts of the unconditioned response (getting ready to eat the food) are elicited by the conditioned stimulus alone. The number and consistency of pairings of the stimuli (the bell and the food) are responsible for the learning. If, however, one discontinues the food but keeps presenting the bell, the animal eventually stops responding to it. In other words, the response is extinguished.

In instrumental learning, emphasis is placed on what the animal does and what kinds of outcomes follow its actions. In general, if some action is followed by a reward, the action will be repeated the next time the animal is in the same situation. For example, if a hungry animal is rewarded with food for turning right in a simple maze, the animal will tend to turn right the next time it is in the maze. If the rewards cease, then other behaviors will appear.

Both of these kinds of animal research concern the elementary aspects of the learning experience. In classical conditioning, emphasis is placed on the importance of the pairing of the conditioned and the unconditioned stimuli; in instrumental learning, emphasis is placed on the importance of the pairing of response and reward. That is, the former is concerned with what kinds of events go together in the learning experience, whereas the latter is concerned with the consequences of actions. Most learning situations involve some elements of both kinds of conditioning.

Cognitive Studies. Studies of human learning, however, tend to be more complex than animal studies and cannot readily be categorized as either classical conditioning or instrumental learning. Human learning and memory have been studied mostly with verbal materials (such as word lists and stories) or with tasks requiring motor skills (such as learning to type or to play an instrument). Such studies have emphasized the negatively accelerated learning curve (showing large gains at first, and then slower and slower learning) and the corresponding negatively accelerated curve of forgetting (large losses immediately after learning, then small losses).

In more recent decades, psychological research has drawn increasing attention to the role of cognition (q.v.) in human learning, freeing itself from the more restrictive aspects of behavioral studies. Such research has come to stress the roles of attention, memory, perception, pattern recognition, and language use (psycholinguistics) in learning processes, and this approach has been increasingly extended beyond the laboratory to therapeutic uses.

Higher mental processes such as concept formation and problem solving are difficult to study. The most popular way to investigate them is through an information-processing approach. This method—using metaphors from computer technology—asks how information is encoded, transformed, stored, retrieved, and transmitted (output) by humans. Thus, this method considers people as if they were designed along the same functional lines as computers. Although the information-processing approach has been fruitful in suggesting models of human thinking and problem solving that can be tested in narrow, limited situations, it has also been shown that general models of human thinking will be difficult to achieve in these terms. *See also* CYBERNETICS; INFORMATION THEORY.

Tests and Measurements. Many fields of psychology use tests and measurement devices. The best-known psychological tool is intelligence testing. Since the early 1900s psychologists have been measuring intelligence—or, more accurately, the ability to succeed in schoolwork. Such tests have proved useful in classifying students, assigning people to training programs, and predicting success in many kinds of schooling. Special tests have been developed to predict success in different occupations and to assess how much knowledge people have about different kinds of specialties. In addition, psychologists have constructed tests for measuring aspects of personality, interests, and attitudes. Thousands of tests have been devised for measuring different human traits. *See* PSYCHOLOGICAL TESTING.

A key problem in test construction, however, is the development of a criterion—that is, some standard to which the test is to be related. For intelligence tests, for example, the usual criterion has been success in school, but intelligence tests have frequently been attacked on the basis of cultural bias (that is, the test results may reflect a child's background as much as it does learning ability). For vocational-interest tests, the standard generally has been persistence in an occupation. One general difficulty with personality tests is the lack of agreement among psychologists as to what standards should be used. Many criteria have been proposed, but most are only indirectly related to the aspect of personality that is being measured.

Very sophisticated statistical models have been developed for tests, and a detailed technology underlies most successful testing. Many psychologists have become adept at constructing testing devices for special purposes and at devising measurements, once agreement is reached as to what should be measured.

Social Psychology. A number of theories in social psychology (q.v.) can be roughly classified as balance theories. These relate to the problem, of both practical and theoretical importance, of how and why people change their attitudes. If, for example, people hear a speech from someone whom they regard highly, they usually expect to hear ideas with which they agree. If that is not the case, then either the listeners will like the speaker less, or else they will change their attitudes and like the ideas more. Thus, the listeners will bring their attitudes toward the speaker and toward the ideas into balance. Similarly, people tend to try to balance, or reconcile, their own ideas with their actions. Social psychology also deals with mass behavior.

Abnormal Psychology. Abnormal psychology—perhaps the best-known subdivision in the field—is what most people usually think of when they hear the word *psychology.* Because the abnormal is a distortion or magnification of the traits and behaviors of the average, or normal, person, the case histories and symptoms of patients who exhibit abnormal psychological behavior strike responsive chords in many people. For example, to have some fears is normal, but to be afraid all the time with no rational cause is abnormal. Because of the strong medical orientation of study in this area, stress is laid on the dynamics—the causes and results—of such behavior, but the cognitive aspects of abnormal experiences can also be examined.

Systems for classifying abnormal behavior change as knowledge grows and customs change. The following classification draws from the commonly accepted terms of the past but groups them in terms of current practice. The three major groups of disorders are psychotic disorders, or psychoses, which involve a loss of contact with reality (schizophrenia, manic-depression, and organic psychoses); nonpsychotic disorders, or neuroses, which do not usually involve a break with reality but make life painful, unhappy, or ineffective (such as anxiety disorder, phobias, obsessive-compulsive disorder, and hysteria, as well as amnesia and multiple personality); and personality disorders, which include the antisocial personalities known as psychopaths or sociopaths, among other exaggerated or deviant behaviors. These classifications are discussed at length in MENTAL DISORDERS and under their separate headings in this encyclopedia.

APPLICATIONS OF PSYCHOLOGY

Psychology can be applied to problems in every area of society. Thus, psychologists consult with organizations as different as courts of law and large business firms. The following are three of the most important areas of applied psychology.

Industrial Psychology. Psychologists in industry serve many roles. In the personnel office, they assist in hiring through testing and interviewing, in developing training programs, in evaluating employees, and in maintaining good employee relations and communications. Some psychologists do research for marketing and advertising departments. Others work in the field of human engineering, which involves designing machines and workplaces to make them more suitable for people. *See* INDUSTRIAL PSYCHOLOGY.

School Psychology. Psychologists in the educational system give most of their attention to counseling and guidance. They help students plan their school and work careers. Educational psychologists deal with the processes of teaching and learning; for example, they may investigate new methods of teaching children how to read or to do mathematics, in order to make classroom learning more effective. *See* EDUCATIONAL PSYCHOLOGY.

Clinical Psychology. Many applied psychologists work in hospitals, clinics, and private practice, providing therapy to people who need psychological help. By testing and interviewing, they classify their patients and engage in all forms of treatment that are not exclusively medical, such as drug therapy and surgery. *See* PSYCHOTHERAPY.

A special contribution of clinical psychology is behavior therapy, which is based on principles of learning and conditioning. Through behavior therapy, clinical psychologists try to change the behavior of the patient and to remove unpleasant or undesirable symptoms by arranging the proper conditioning experiences or the proper

Psychologist Gene Gauron (seated, left) leads the University of Iowa swimming team in a series of mental-conditioning drills designed to improve concentration and facilitate relaxation. Wide World Photos

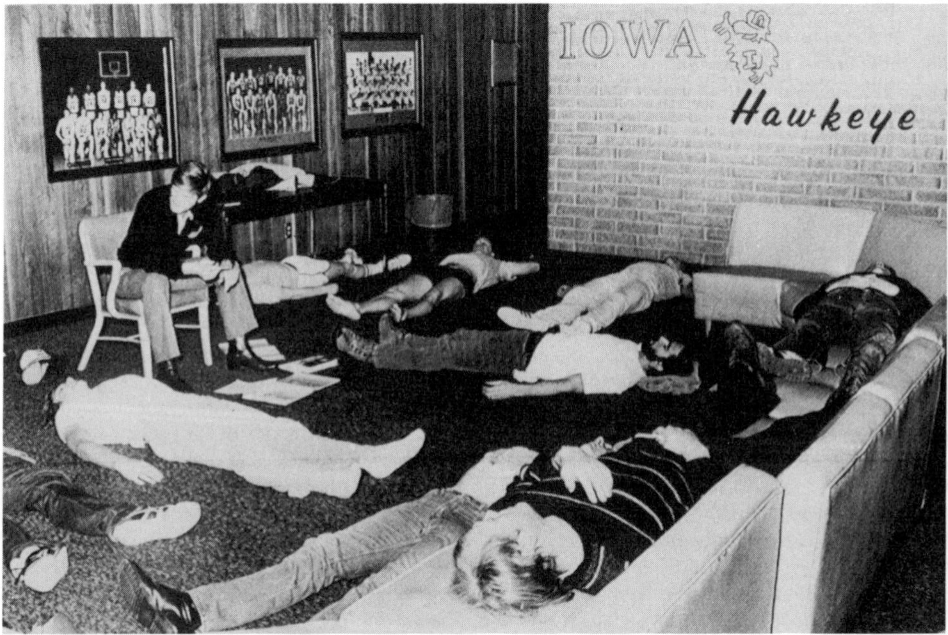

rewards for desired behavior. A patient with a phobia about dogs, for example, might be "desensitized" by a series of rewards given for closer and closer contact with dogs in nonthreatening situations. In other forms of therapy, the psychologist may try to help patients better understand their problems and find new ways of dealing with them.

TRENDS AND DEVELOPMENTS

Psychology today is an increasingly specialized field, a result of growing awareness of the need for such specialization and of new influences on the field as a whole. Child psychologists, for example, have been greatly influenced by the naturalistic observations and "clinical experiments" of the Swiss psychologist Jean Piaget. Psychologists interested in language and communication have been strongly affected by the revolution in linguistic thought led by the American linguist Noam Chomsky. The ethological work of the Austrian zoologist Konrad Lorenz and the Dutch zoologist Nikolaas Tinbergen, who studied animals in their natural habitats rather than in the laboratory, has called attention to the uniqueness of species and their behavioral development (*see* ANIMAL BEHAVIOR; SOCIOBIOLOGY). These and other influences have helped to broaden greatly the interests and research techniques of the field of psychology.

Another change in modern psychology has resulted from the invention of the digital computer. Computers have provided not only an important new way of thinking about cognitive functions but also the means for testing complex theories about these processes. Computers are symbol manipulators—that is, the machines take in information in symbolic form, transform it, and use it according to their programmed purposes. Computer scientists are now working to develop machines that perform those complex tasks that seem to require judgment and decision making.

At the same time, some psychologists, using the computer as a model, are trying to look at human beings as "information processors." In pursuing these activities, computer scientists have learned that often they must understand how a person performs a difficult task in order to duplicate it on a computer. Psychologists, in turn, have learned that their theories must be precise and explicit if they want to program them for the computer. Even complicated psychological theories can give specific predictions when they are prepared as computer programs. As a result, more people are now studying complex behavior, and better theories are being proposed and tested. *See* COMPUTER.

See also BEHAVIORAL MEDICINE; PSYCHIATRY. For additional information on individuals mentioned, see biographies of those whose names are not followed by dates. J.J.J.

For further information on this topic, see the Bibliography in volume 28, sections 141–51, 313.

PSYCHOLOGY, ABNORMAL. *See* MENTAL DISORDERS.

PSYCHOLOGY, DEVELOPMENTAL. *See* DEVELOPMENTAL PSYCHOLOGY.

PSYCHOLOGY, EDUCATIONAL. *See* EDUCATIONAL PSYCHOLOGY.

PSYCHOLOGY, EXPERIMENTAL, application of laboratory techniques to investigations of mind and behavior, including such subjects as perception, memory, thinking, learning, and problem solving.

Experimental psychology as a defined field of science began with the German physicist Gustav Theodor Fechner (1801–87), whose *Elements of Psychophysics* (1860; trans. 1966) presented experimental evidence for relating magnitudes of sensation in the person being tested to objective magnitudes of stimulation. Then, in 1879, the German psychologist Wilhelm Max Wundt established the first research laboratory for psychological experimentation. Wundt trained people to describe in detail sensations evoked by systematically controlled stimuli. The psychologist also measured reaction times in tests of varied complexity and tried to catalog the components of consciousness and to work out the laws of their combination.

Wundt and his conception of psychology dominated the field until the turn of the 20th century but then lost authority as introspective methods proved incapable of deciding such controversial issues as whether imageless thoughts are possible. Rivals in the field rebelled against Wundt's rules. For example, the German psychologist Hermann Ebbinghaus conducted a monumental investigation of memory that involved rote learning of strings of nonsense syllables, thus setting a pattern for succeeding generations of psychologists in search of laws of learning. The same goal was pursued by scientists who began to use laboratory animals for psychological experiments; the American psychologist Edward Lee Thorndike gave both methodological and conceptual direction to this trend. Thereafter in behaviorism (q.v.), as promulgated by the American psychologist John Broadus Watson, psychology was defined as the science of behavior, as opposed to the science of mental life. This development meant the rejection of previous mentalistic concepts and introspective methods.

Introspection continued to be used, however, in Gestalt psychology (q.v.), which began as an approach to perception and was later extended to problem solving, learning, creativity, and even social dynamics. Gestalt psychology emphasized configuration, relationship, and active organization, in contrast to behaviorist conceptions.

Experimental psychology thus encompasses a considerable diversity of methods, interests, and viewpoints, and it has found practical applications in industry, education, and therapy, among other areas. Traditional concerns with psychophysics, perception, memory, and learning persist, but they are complemented by physiological approaches and the use of statistical procedures in experiment design and data analysis; computer technology has also had an impact on both method and theory. The powerful influence of behaviorist doctrine has been mitigated by the revival of cognitive conceptions and a renewed alliance with biology. As yet, however, no one theory unifies experimental psychology; its practice crosses the boundaries of many fields of psychological interest and schools of psychological thought. *See also* PSYCHOLOGY. C.G.B.

PSYCHOPHARMACOLOGY, study of the relationship between drugs and brain function, including mood, perceptions, and behavior. Psychopharmacology is a branch of pharmacology (q.v.), the study of the action of drugs on living organisms. Psychopharmacology is employed in psychiatry, psychology, neurology, and in medical specialties concerned with brain function.

Throughout history, almost every culture has sought ways to alter consciousness by experimenting with plant substances that yield many of the psychoactive drugs (q.v.) of today. Important developments in ancient psychopharmacology include the discovery and use of alcohol, cannabis, and opium (qq.v.) in Europe and Asia and of caffeine, nicotine, cocaine (qq.v.), and hallucinogenic plants such as peyote (q.v.) and psilocybin in the pre-Columbian Americas. Developments in the 19th century include the isolation of the potent analgesic morphine from opium; the introduction of the anesthetics nitrous oxide, ether, and chloroform (q.v.); and the early use of cocaine as a stimulant. The first sedative hypnotics, the barbiturates (*see* BARBITURATE), were introduced in the early 20th century, followed by the discovery and use of amphetamines (*see* EPINEPHRINE) as psychostimulants in the 1930s; the discovery of the hallucinogenic properties of lysergic acid diethylamide (q.v.) in 1943; the discovery of lithium carbonate as a treatment for manic-depression (*see* DEPRESSION) in 1948; the discovery of the antipsychotic, antischizophrenic activity of chlorpromazine in 1952; and the discovery, in 1957, of two treatments for depression: tricyclic antidepressants and monoamine oxidase (MAO) inhibitors. In the latter 20th century many drugs continue to be found that fall within these major groupings. Also included among the psychoactive agents are the so-called minor tranquilizers, the benzodiazepines. P.A.B.

PSYCHOSIS. *See* MENTAL DISORDERS.

PSYCHOSOMATIC MEDICINE. *See* BEHAVIORAL MEDICINE.

PSYCHOTHERAPY, treatment of psychological distress with techniques that rely heavily on verbal and emotional communication and other symbolic behavior. Psychotherapy differs in two ways from the informal help one person gives another. First, it is conducted by a psychotherapist who is specially trained and licensed or otherwise culturally sanctioned. Second, psychotherapy is guided by theories about the sources of distress and the methods needed to alleviate it. Because communication is the primary means of healing in most forms of psychotherapy, the relationship between the therapist and patient, or client, is much more important than in other medical treatments. The therapist's personality influences the patient and may be used quite deliberately to achieve therapeutic ends.

Attempts to ameliorate emotional and mental disorders through psychological means date from ancient times. Throughout most of history these efforts have been grounded in religious and magical beliefs. Attempts to base psychotherapeutic practices on scientific principles date from the mid-18th century, when the Austrian physician Franz Anton Mesmer used a form of suggestion called animal magnetism. Neuroses were treated in the 19th century with such physical agents as water or painful electrical currents, both of which also depended for effectiveness on the use of suggestion. Hypnotism as a method of suggestion for alleviating certain psychological disturbances reached its height late in the 19th century, as practiced by the French neurologist Jean Martin Charcot and his associates at the Salpêtrière Hospital in Paris.

PSYCHOANALYTIC PSYCHOTHERAPY

Stimulated by Charcot's demonstrations of the therapeutic value of hypnosis, the Austrian physician and founder of psychoanalysis, Sigmund Freud, used the hypnotic state, not for the purpose of suggestion, but to uncover painful and forgotten memories in his neurotic patients. By this technique, he not only attempted to help his patients but also collected the data from which he formulated psychoanalytic theory. Freud believed that during the course of a person's devel-

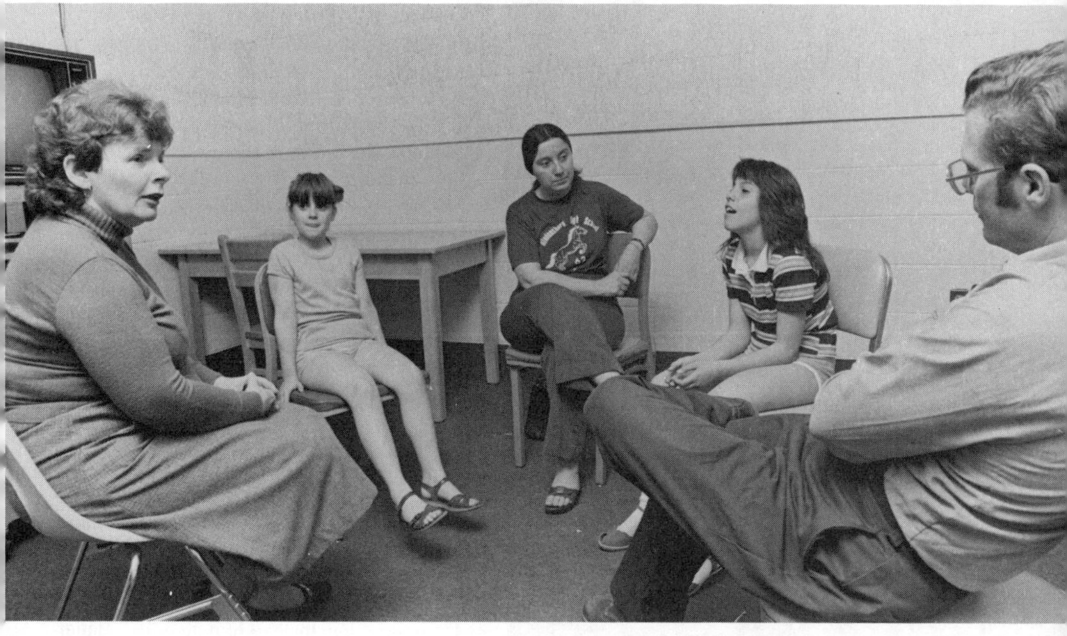

A family therapy session with Dr. Elizabeth Brown at the University of Maryland. APA

opment unacceptable sexual and aggressive drives are forced out of consciousness. These repressed urges, constantly striving for release, are sometimes expressed as neurotic symptoms. *See* PSYCHOANALYSIS.

Freud thought that such symptoms could be eliminated by bringing the repressed fantasies and emotions into consciousness. He first used hypnosis as the means of gaining access to the unconscious. He soon abandoned the technique, however, in favor of free association, a method in which patients were asked to report whatever thoughts came to their minds about dreams, fantasies, and memories. By interpreting these associations Freud helped his patients gain the insight into their unconscious that he believed to be curative. Later he placed great value on what could be learned from so-called transference, that is, the patient's emotional response to therapists, which in Freud's view reflected earlier feelings toward the patient's family members. Free association and transference reactions are still central features of Freudian psychoanalysis. Patients lie on a couch during the sessions, which take place from three to five times a week.

DIVERGENT PSYCHOANALYTIC SCHOOLS

Some of Freud's most gifted followers disagreed with him on important aspects of theory and therapeutic technique and subsequently founded schools of their own.

Jung. Perhaps the most influential was Carl Gustav Jung, a Swiss psychiatrist, who believed that Freud overemphasized sexual instincts as a source of behavior. Jung thought that nonsexual potentials within the person must be realized, or neuroses will develop. Jungian therapists attempt to help patients recognize their own inner resources for growth and for dealing with conflict. They see patients frequently at first, then weekly for a period of months or years. Techniques for solving immediate problems are varied and pragmatic. Dreams and art are used to draw out the patient's associations to the unconscious images that Jung believed are shared by all.

Adler. Another of Freud's students to break with him was the Austrian psychologist Alfred Adler. Adler, too, minimized the importance of instinctual sexual drives in behavior. He believed that the smallness and helplessness of children lead to feelings of inferiority. In reaction to these feelings, many people strive for superiority. Countering this search for power and significance is the quality of what he called social interest, that is, empathy and identification with other people. According to Adler, psychological disorders result from a faulty way of living, including mistaken opinions and goals and underdeveloped social interest. The therapist's job is to reeducate patients—to convince them of their errors and to encourage them to develop more social interest.

Erik Erikson New York Public Library Picture Collection

Fromm, Horney, and Erikson. Several of Freud's followers elaborated theories of neuroses that emphasized the role of social and cultural influences in the formation of personality. These so-called neo-Freudians include Erich Fromm, Karen Horney, and Erik Erikson. All three emigrated from Germany to the U.S. in the 1930s. Fromm believed that the fundamental problem confronted by everyone is a sense of isolation deriving from the individual's separateness. The goal of life and of therapy, according to Fromm, is to orient oneself, establish roots, and find security by uniting with other people while remaining a separate individual. Horney believed that neurotic behavior blocks a person's inherent capacity for healthy growth and change. The job of therapy, in her view, is to disillusion the patient of such defense blockages, that is, to identify and clarify them, and then to help the patient mobilize innate constructive forces for change. Erikson, like Horney, was convinced that human beings are capable of growth throughout their lives. Guiding such change is the person's ego, which can develop in a healthy way when given the right environment. Failing that, a person can acquire through therapy the basic trust and confidence needed for a healthy ego. Unlike traditional psychoanalysts, Erikson, who began practice as a child analyst, typically worked with a patient's family while treating the patient.

HUMANISTIC PSYCHOTHERAPY

Begun as reaction against psychoanalytic psychotherapy, humanistic therapies are based on views of human nature that emphasize the human potential for goodness.

Rogers. The oldest of the humanistic therapies is the client-centered psychotherapy of Carl Rogers, an American psychologist. Rogers believed that people, like other living organisms, are driven by an innate tendency to maintain and enhance themselves, which in turn moves them toward growth, maturity, and life enrichment. Within each person, Rogers believed, is the capacity for self-understanding and constructive change. In therapy this capacity can be realized with the help of a therapist who has certain essential qualities.

Rogers attached more importance to the therapist's attitudes than to his or her technical training or skills. Accurate and sensitive understanding of the client's experiences and feelings is paramount, because it helps the client focus on the experience of the moment. (Rogers used the word *client* instead of patient to indicate that the treatment is neither manipulative nor medically prescriptive.) A second important quality in a therapist is unconditional positive regard, that is, a nonjudgmental caring for the patient. Genuineness, or an absence of sham, is a third quality that Rogers felt was essential in a therapist.

Carl Rogers American Psychological Association

Rogers described the treatment process itself as the client's reciprocation of the therapist's attitudes. Because the therapist listens, the client learns to listen to ever more frightening thoughts and feelings until he or she reaches a stage of self-acceptance where change and growth are possible.

Gestalt Therapy. Another humanist approach, Gestalt therapy, was developed by Frederick S. (Fritz) Perls (1893–1970), a German-born former psychoanalyst who immigrated to the U.S. Perls believed that modern civilization inevitably produces neurosis, because it forces people to repress natural desires and consequently frustrates an inherent human tendency to adjust biologically and psychologically to the environment. Neurotic anxiety results; in order for a person to be cured, unmet needs must be brought back to awareness. Perls, disavowing the psychoanalytic tradition, believed that intellectual insight is powerless to change people. Instead he devised exercises designed to enhance the person's awareness of his or her emotions, physical state, and repressed needs, as well as physical and psychological stimuli in the environment. Gestalt therapy is conducted with both individuals and groups, typically in once-a-week sessions lasting up to two years.

BEHAVIOR THERAPY

In contrast to most other forms of psychological therapy, behavior therapy is not based on a theory of neurosis. Rather, it is the application of the methods of experimental psychology to the problems of an individual who comes for treatment. Behavior therapists, who are usually psychologists, are not directly concerned with underlying psychological forces. Instead they focus on the behavior that is causing distress for their clients. They believe that behavior of all kinds, normal and maladaptive, is learned according to specifiable principles. These principles have been studied extensively—in Russia, for example, by the psychologist Ivan Pavlov and in the U.S. by psychologists such as B. F. Skinner. Behavior therapists believe that these same learning principles can be used to correct troublesome behavior.

Regardless of the specific technique they later use, behavior therapists begin treatment by finding out as much as they can about the client's problem and the circumstances surrounding it. They do not infer causes or look for hidden meanings; rather, they concentrate on observable and measurable phenomena. On the basis of this behavioral analysis, they formulate hypotheses about the circumstances creating and maintaining the problem. They then set out to alter the circumstances, one by one, and observe whether the client's behavior changes as a result.

Desensitization. Of the many techniques used by behavior therapists, one of the oldest and most common is systematic desensitization, a procedure developed by the South African psychiatrist Joseph Wolpe (1915–). Used for treating symptoms caused by excessive anxiety, this method calls for helping the client to relax and then, gradually, to approach the situations or objects that are feared.

Cognitive Approaches. Recently, behavior therapists have begun to give more attention to the influence of thought on behavior, spurred by such thinkers as the American psychologist Albert Bandura (1925–). Cognitive behavior therapy uses the behavioral approach to change

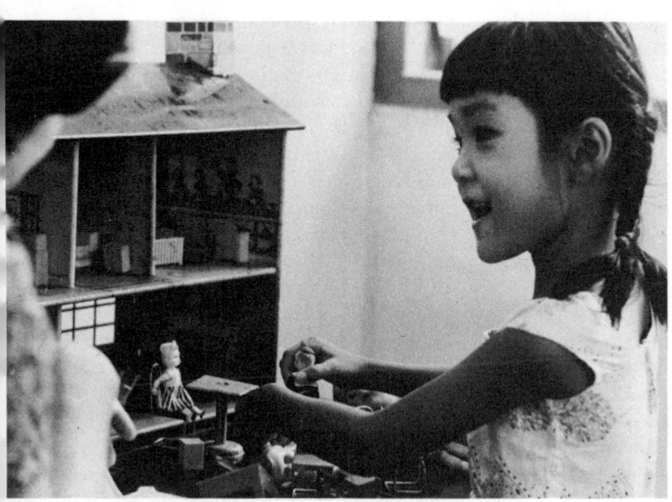

The language of toys is universal and full of significance for the psychiatrist. Here, a child in Thailand plays with a dollhouse as the psychiatrist listens for clues that may reveal her difficulties in getting along with people among whom she lives. Pierre A. Pittet–WHO

beliefs and habits of thought that appear to be the source of the client's distress.

Similar cognitive approaches have been devised by therapists who were trained in psychoanalysis but who become disenchanted with its theories and techniques. The oldest is the rational-emotive therapy of the American psychologist Albert Ellis (1913-), who believes that irrational beliefs and illogical thinking are the cause of emotional disturbances. In his treatment he confronts patients with their irrationality and encourages them to work vigilantly at replacing it with more reasonable thoughts and emotions.

A related technique, which has shown promise in the treatment of depression (q.v.), was developed by the American psychologist Aaron T. Beck (1921-). Beck believes that depressed people tend to have negative conceptions of themselves, to interpret their experiences negatively, and to view the future with hopelessness. He sees these tendencies as basically a problem of faulty thinking. His treatment techniques, like strictly behaviorist approaches, are aimed at correcting the problem directly rather than understanding its possible origins in the past.

GROUP THERAPY

Because it requires fewer therapists, group psychotherapy is less expensive than individual therapy. It may offer other advantages as well, such as demonstrating to patients that their problems are not unique. In group treatment, interactions among group members are considered the main source of change and cure; the therapist's job is to encourage and control these interactions.

Origins. Group therapy originated in the U.S. and Europe in the early part of the 20th century. In the U.S. it began in tuberculosis clinics, where patients were lectured in classrooms; early groups conducted with mental patients also took the form of lectures. In Europe group psychotherapy was first used by Jacob L. Moreno (1898–1974), a psychiatrist who had his patients act out their problems as a means of heightening their awareness of them. Moreno brought his "psychodrama" to the U.S. in 1925, and its use spread to other parts of the world as well. It is used for treating both neurotic and psychotic patients and also for training mental health professionals.

Many forms of group psychotherapy are practiced today, and most of the theoretical orientations found in individual psychotherapy are also represented in group work. In addition, group therapy is conducted at the psychological growth centers that are part of the human potential movement. Many therapists see their patients both individually and in groups.

Family Therapy. One special type of group treatment is family therapy. Adler had worked with whole families in the 1930s, but not until the early 1950s did several therapists in different locales independently begin treating families instead of individuals. They and their successors work from the rationale that current family relationships profoundly affect, and are affected by, an individual family member's psychological problems. Rather than explore the inner conflicts of individuals, family therapists try to promote interactions among family members, thereby enhancing the well-being of each.

NEW APPROACHES TO PSYCHOTHERAPY

In the late 1960s and the '70s, a large number of new psychotherapeutic methods were devised and promoted. Many, like the earlier humanistic therapies, were born out of dissatisfaction with psychoanalytically oriented psychotherapy, which was considered too costly, too time consuming, and elitist. Some critics also believed that psychoanalytic practices were too intellectualized and rational, overly preoccupied with the past, and unnecessarily committed to preserving the Western values of individualism, achievement, and productivity. In reaction, they developed methods that emphasize emotion over reason and the present over the past and future. Others who became dissatisfied with psychoanalysis, such as Ellis and Beck, turned in a different direction and placed even more emphasis on the power of reason to overcome emotional disturbance.

Among the recent methods to have attracted a great deal of public interest are primal therapy, which was devised by the American psychologist Arthur Janov (1924-), and transactional analysis, based on the work of Eric Berne (1910–70). In primal therapy, patients are encouraged to relive early experiences with an intensity of feeling that had been suppressed at the time. Janov believes that such cathartic reactions free the patient from compulsively neurotic behavior. Transactional analysis is based on the theory that a person, when interacting with others, functions as either parent, adult, or child. In therapy, usually conducted in groups, patients are taught to recognize when they are assuming one of these roles and to understand when being an authoritarian parent or an impulsive child is appropriate and to act as an adult as much of the time as possible.

BRIEF PSYCHOTHERAPY AND CRISIS INTERVENTION

Another recent trend in psychotherapy is the use of brief methods, often to help people deal with crises. These brief psychotherapies were developed partly as a result of dissatisfaction with the length of psychoanalytic therapies, which sometimes continue for many years, and partly in light of a growing understanding of the human response to crises. At critical times in life, such as after the death of a loved one, people are more susceptible to change, for better or worse. Intervening at these times not only can help them overcome the crises but may also help them to become stronger psychologically than they were before the crises.

Two major types of brief psychotherapy are practiced. One type, directed at suppressing anxiety, uses supportive techniques such as reassurance, suggestion, manipulation of the environment, and medications. The other type, which uses techniques that provoke anxiety, is directed at disrupting a patient's usual neurotic defenses so that change can occur. Psychoanalysis is itself an example of such an anxiety-provoking technique; as conducted by Freud, psychoanalysis was much shorter (less than a year) than is usual today.

CHILD PSYCHOTHERAPY

Psychotherapy with children is guided by the same frames of reference used in adult psychotherapy, with the important difference that child therapists must constantly keep in mind the developmental stage of their patients. Techniques also differ. What talk is to adult therapy, play is to child therapy. Whether the therapist's orientation is psychoanalytic or behaviorist or focuses on the family as a system, the actual technique used is likely to involve play with clay, dolls, and other toys. The use of play as a means of communicating with a child in therapy was first developed by the psychoanalysts Anna Freud and Melanie Klein.

THE THERAPIST

Psychotherapists come principally from the fields of medicine, psychology, social work, and psychiatric nursing. Their training is remarkably different, considering that their actual clinical practice may be quite similar.

Psychiatrists are physicians. They attend medical school for four years, then typically do a 1-year internship, and are trained in psychiatry during a 3-year residency. Psychoanalysts undergo further training of three years or more at a psychoanalytic institute. They are also required to undergo a personal analysis themselves.

Psychologists usually earn a Ph.D. degree in clinical psychology and undergo a year of supervised therapeutic practice before they are considered fully trained. Social workers follow a specialty in mental health and earn master's or doctoral degrees before practicing. Some psychologists and social workers, like psychoana-

A psychologist administering the Rorschach test, a projective technique for personality measurement in which the patient interprets the shapes of a series of bisymmetrical ink blots. Mark Loete

lysts, take further training in an institute devoted to a particular psychotherapeutic school, and many undergo therapy as well. Psychiatric nurses usually hold master's degrees and practice primarily in hospitals and mental health centers.

In most states, psychotherapists from the four major professions must be licensed to practice. They are accountable primarily to their peers, that is, other members of their profession. Nothing—except public wariness—prohibits an untrained or poorly trained person from practicing as a psychotherapist.

EVALUATION

The various types of psychotherapy have different goals, ranging from the psychoanalyst's ambition to alter basic personality structure and deal with existential dilemmas to the behavior therapist's contention that the job of therapy is to relieve distressing symptoms. For that reason, each method of treatment must be judged against its own goal. Yet, because psychotherapy is sometimes covered by public and private health insurance, enormous pressure is not being placed on psychotherapists to prove the effectiveness of their methods.

It is easier to measure whether a symptom has disappeared than it is to measure more global psychotherapeutic goals. Not surprisingly, behavior therapy and other more directive, limited types of therapy are supported by evidence that is considered more scientifically valid than that used to defend psychoanalysis and related methods. The trend is now to move away from the case histories that were once used as testimonials for a particular method and to judge treatments instead by criteria that would be applied to the evaluation of a new drug. Typically, large samples of patients receiving a standardized version of a treatment are compared with other patients who receive another treatment or no therapy at all. The goal of these investigations is to pinpoint which type of treatment is best suited for a given type of patient. This degree of specificity has so far eluded researchers, with one exception: Behavior therapy seems most effective in the treatment of phobias (*see* PHOBIA). More generally, the majority of people who undergo psychotherapy of any type have been demonstrated to benefit from it. B.E.Wo.

For further information on this topic, see the Bibliography in volume 28, section 529.

PTAH, in ancient Egyptian mythology, one of the greatest of gods. Ancient inscriptions describe him as "creator of the earth, father of the gods and all the being of this earth, father of beginnings." He was regarded as the patron of metalworkers and artisans and as a mighty healer. He is usually represented as a mummy bearing the symbols of life, power, and stability. The main center of his worship was in Memphis.

PTARMIGAN, common name for three species constituting the genus *Lagopus* of the grouse (q.v.) subfamily Tetraoninae, family Phasianidae, found in mountain and tundra areas around the northern hemisphere. One bird, the white-tailed ptarmigan, *L. leucurus,* is confined to high mountains of western North America. The willow ptarmigan, *L. lagopus,* and the rock ptarmigan, *L. mutus,* are circumpolar, and are among the very few nonmigratory birds of the Arctic. Ptarmigan are notable for having a molting cycle unique among birds, in that they assume a white plumage in winter, in addition to the usual spring and fall plumages. Their toes, at best sparsely feathered at other times, become heavily feathered in winter, creating efficient "snowshoes". One population of willow ptarmigan, the red grouse of the British Isles, *L. l. scoticus,* differs in lacking the white winter plumage.

Male willow ptarmigan during the breeding season have chestnut heads and breasts, white bellies, and mottled backs. Females are buffier, heavily barred with black on the underparts. In the fall males assume a more femalelike plumage before attaining the winter white. The corresponding spring and fall plumages of male rock and white-tailed ptarmigan are grayer.

For further information on this topic, see the Bibliography in volume 28, sections 472–73, 814.

PT BOAT, high-speed military attack craft, armed with two to four torpedoes, 20-mm and 40-mm guns, and several depth charges. PT boats (patrol torpedo boats) averaged about 18 m (about 60 ft) in length and had a maximum speed of about 40 knots. Speed and maneuverability were their

White-tailed ptarmigan, Lagopus leucurus
© Alan G. Nelson–Animals Animals

An artist's conception—based on skeletal remains—of the probable appearance of the great flying reptiles known as pterosaurs. Popularly called pterodactyls, these huge creatures became extinct more than 70 million years ago.

American Museum of Natural History

chief assets. Because of their short cruising range and inability to operate in rough seas, however, they were phased out of the U.S. Navy after World War II.

During the American Civil War ordinary boats were first used to plant explosives under cover of darkness, on enemy ships at anchor. In 1935 Great Britain began building what is known as the motor torpedo boat, and in 1938 the craft was introduced into the U.S. Navy. During World War II, PT boats played an important role in combat around the Philippine Islands.

PTERODACTYL. *See* PTEROSAUR.

PTEROSAUR (Gr. *ptero,* "feather, wing"; *sauros,* "lizard"), term applied to any flying reptile of the order Pterosauria, which existed during the Mesozoic era from the Late Triassic period nearly to the end of the Cretaceous period. Many fossil remains of pterosaurs, which are often popularly referred to as pterodactyls, have been found in all continents except Antarctica; about 60 genera have been discovered. Pterosaurs did not have feathers. The wings were thin membranes of skin, similar to the wings of a bat, which extended along the sides of the body, and were attached to the extraordinarily long fourth digit of each arm. The bones were hollow and had openings at each end. Unlike typical reptiles, pterosaurs had a breastbone that was well developed for the attachment of flight muscles and a brain that was also more developed.

In early pterosaurs of the Late Triassic period, the best-known form of which is *Rhamphorhynchus,* the skull was about 9 cm (about 3.5 in) long and the body was about 10 cm (about 4 in) long. The flexible tail, which was about 38 cm (about 15 in) long, had a diamond-shaped terminal appendage, used as a rudder in controlling flight. Later pterosaurs of the Upper Cretaceous period, the best known of which is *Pteranodon,* had a wingspread of more than 6 m (more than 20 ft). The skull was long and slender and the jaws were toothless. Although later pterosaur forms were fairly adept fliers, these creatures are not more ancestral to birds than are other reptiles.

Early in 1975 scientists announced that partial skeletons of three huge, long-necked pterosaurs had been discovered in the Late Cretaceous nonmarine rock at Big Bend National Park in Texas. With an estimated wingspan of approximately 11–12 m (approximately 36–39 ft), the Big Bend pterosaur is the largest flying creature known to have existed.

For further information on this topic, see the Bibliography in volume 28, section 436.

PTOLEMAIC DYNASTY, Macedonian family that ruled Egypt during the Hellenistic period, from the death of Alexander the Great in 323 BC until Egypt became a Roman province in 30 BC. At various times the Ptolemies also controlled Cyrenaica (now northeastern Libya), Palestine, and Cyprus.

The dynasty was founded by Alexander's general, Ptolemy. Named governor of Egypt by Alexander, he established himself as an independent ruler in 305 BC, adopting the name Ptolemy I Soter. The kingdom prospered under him and his successors, Ptolemy II Philadelphus and Ptolemy III Euergetes, who vied with another Macedonian dynasty, the Seleucids of Syria, for supremacy in the eastern Mediterranean.

The capital of the Ptolemaic state was Alexandria—a cosmopolitan city with a large Greek and Jewish population—which became one of the great commercial and intellectual centers of the ancient world. Although not of Egyptian origin, the Ptolemies observed many of the country's traditional customs. Like Alexander, they had themselves portrayed on public monuments in Egyptian style and dress, and they participated in Egyptian religious rituals. They preserved Egypt's ancient architectural traditions, erecting temples to the Egyptian gods at Edfu, Dandarah,and other places. Nevertheless, their government, dominated by Greek and Macedonian officials, was not popular. Egyptian nationalism remained strong among the people, manifesting itself in frequent rebellions.

The power of the dynasty declined under a succession of weak kings in the 2d and 1st centuries BC, when Rome began to intervene increasingly in Egyptian affairs. The last and probably the most famous Ptolemaic ruler was Cleopatra, who ruled independently first through the support of Julius Caesar and later that of Mark Antony. With her death and that of her son, Ptolemy XIV, called Caesarion (b. 47 BC), in 30 BC, the dynasty came to an end.

For further information on individual members of the dynasty, see biographies of those whose names are not followed by dates. D.P.S.

PTOLEMAIC SYSTEM, in astronomy, theory of the order and action of the heavenly bodies, advanced in the 2d century AD by the Greek astronomer Ptolemy. The Ptolemaic theory held that Earth is stationary and at the center of the universe; closest to Earth is the Moon, and beyond it, extending outward, are Mercury, Venus, and the Sun in a straight line, followed successively by Mars, Jupiter, Saturn, and the so-called fixed stars. Later, astronomers supplemented this system with a ninth sphere, the motion of which supposedly produced the precession of equinoxes (*see* ECLIPTIC). A tenth sphere or primum mobile, which was thought to motivate the other heavenly bodies, was also added. To explain the various observed motions of the planets, the Ptolemaic system described them as having small circular orbits called epicycles; the centers of the epicycles, on circular orbits around Earth, were called deferents. The motion of all spheres is from west to east. After the decline of classical Greek culture, Arabian astronomers attempted to perfect the system by adding new epicycles to explain unpredicted variations in the motions and positions of the planets. These efforts failed, however, to resolve the many inconsistencies in the Ptolemaic system, which was finally superseded in the 16th century by the Copernican system (q.v.). *See* ASTRONOMY; SOLAR SYSTEM.

Ptolemaic system of planetary motions.

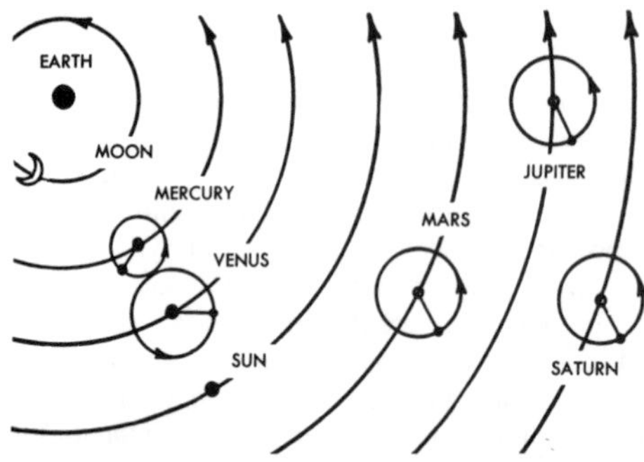

PTOLEMY (about AD 100–70), astronomer and mathematician, whose synthesis of the geocentric theory—that the earth is the center of the universe—dominated astronomical thought until the 17th century (*see* PTOLEMAIC SYSTEM). He is also remembered for his contributions to the fields of mathematics, optics, and geography. Ptolemy was probably born in Greece, but his actual name, Claudius Ptolemaeus, reflects all that is really known of him: "Ptolemaeus" indicates that he was a resident of Egypt, and "Claudius" signifies Roman citizenship. In fact, ancient sources report that he lived and worked in Alexandria, Egypt, for the greater part of his life.

The Almagest. Ptolemy's earliest and most famous treatise, originally written in Greek, was translated into Arabic as *al-Majisti* (Great Work). In Europe, medieval Latin translations reproduced the title as *Almagesti,* and it has since become known simple as the *Almagest.* In this work, Ptolemy proposed a geometric theory to account mathematically for the apparent motions and positions of the planets, sun, and moon against the background of fixed stars. He began by accepting the generally held theory that the earth did not move but was at the center of the system. The planets and stars, moving eternally, were considered (for philosophical reasons) to move in perfectly circular orbits. He then elaborated on the theory in an attempt to account for such astronomical puzzles as the periodically retrograde (backward) motions of the planets and periodic variations in size or brightness of the moon and planets.

Ptolemy's abilities as an observational astronomer have been questioned, but his complex system seemed to account for celestial motions. Anomalies in a planet's motion were accounted for by the use of the epicycle, a circle centered on the circumference of a larger circle called the deferent. The planets, sun, and moon were regarded as located on the rims of rotating epicycles, and the earth itself was placed eccentrically to the center of the deferent. By adjusting the

Ptolemy Bettmann Archive

radii of the circles and their speeds of rotation, Ptolemy made the system fit most of the observed facts.

Ptolemy also had to introduce, however, another mathematical device known as the equant: an imaginary point halfway between the center of the deferent and the eccentric point representing the earth's position. Rather than maintain the constant, uniform motion of all circles in the system (deferents and epicycles), as had been required in all previous models of ancient astronomy, he assumed that the deferent moved uniformly with respect to the equant. (Thus the deferent's motion would not be uniform with respect to its own center.) This major departure from traditional assumptions was one reason the Polish astronomer Nicolaus Copernicus rejected Ptolemy's system in the 16th century and developed his own heliocentric world view of a sun-centered system. (*see* COPERNICAN SYSTEM). Even so, Copernicus retained an elaborate system of epicycles.

Other Works. Ptolemy also contributed substantially to mathematics by advancing the study of trigonometry, and he applied his theories to the construction of astrolabes and sundials. In his *Tetrabiblios,* he applied astronomy to astrology and the casting of horoscopes. Of considerable historical importance, despite considerable factual inaccuracies, is Ptolemy's *Geography,* which charts the then-known world. This work, which employs a system of longitude and latitude, influenced mapmakers of the Renaissance, but it suffered from a lack of reliable information. Ptolemy also devoted a treatise, *Harmonica,* to music theory, and in *Optics* he explored the properties of light, especially refraction and reflection. This latter work, known only from an Arabic version, is of special interest for its combination of experiment and the construction of apparatus to promote the study of light and to develop a mathematical theory of its properties. J.W.D

PTOLEMY I (367?–283 BC), called Ptolemy Soter ("preserver"), king of Egypt (323–285 BC), founder of the Ptolemaic dynasty. The son of Lagus, a Macedonian of common birth, Ptolemy was a general in the army of Alexander the Great and took a leading part in Alexander's later campaigns in Asia. On the death of Alexander in 323 BC, his empire was divided among the Diadochi (successors) by the imperial regent Perdiccas (365–321 BC) and Ptolemy was appointed satrap of Egypt and Libya. He was from the first an independent ruler, engaging in long wars with other Macedonian chiefs in order to secure and extend his rule. Ptolemy was prevented from holding Cyprus and parts of Greece, but he resisted invasions of Egypt and Rhodes and occupied Palestine and Cyrenaica. In 305 BC he assumed the title of king. Alexandria was his capital, and he founded the famous Alexandrian library (*see* ALEXANDRIA, LIBRARY OF). He was the author of a lost history of the campaigns of Alexander. In 285 BC Ptolemy I abdicated in favor of one of his younger sons.

PTOLEMY II (309–246 BC), called Ptolemy Philadelphus ("brotherly"), king of Egypt (285–246 BC), the son of Ptolemy I by Berenice I (d. before 283 BC). His wars with the Seleucid king Antiochus I established Ptolemaic Egypt as the dominant maritime power in the eastern Mediterranean Sea. The economy of the country was brought under government control and the cultural life at the Alexandrian court flourished under Ptolemy II; the Greek poets Callimachus and Theocritus were among the literary figures connected with the court. Ptolemy increased the number of books in the Alexandrian library (*see* ALEXANDRIA, LIBRARY OF) and was an active patron of literature and scholarship.

PTOLEMY III (282?–221 BC), called Ptolemy Euergetes ("benefactor"), king of Egypt (246–221 BC), the son of Ptolemy II. He reunited Cyrenaica and Egypt, invaded the Seleucid Kingdom of Syria to avenge the murder of his sister and her infant son, the heir to the Seleucid throne, and established Egyptian naval predominance in the Aegean Sea. Ptolemy III was a liberal patron of the arts and added to the collection of the Alexandrian library (*see* ALEXANDRIA, LIBRARY OF). His rule marked the height of Egyptian power, prosperity, and wealth under the Ptolemies.

PTOLEMY V (210?–181 BC), called Ptolemy Epiphanes ("illustrious"), king of Egypt (205–181 BC), grandson of Ptolemy II Euergetes. At the beginning of his reign, Antiochus III of Syria and Philip V of Macedonia agreed to divide the foreign possessions of Egypt between them, and Egypt was greatly weakened. The official coronation of Ptolemy V was held in 197 BC; it was the occasion on which the Egyptian priesthood published the decree that forms the trilingual inscription on the Rosetta Stone. In 193 BC Ptolemy married the Seleucid princess Cleopatra I.

PTOLEMY VI (186?–145 BC), called Ptolemy Philometor ("loving his mother"), king of Egypt (181–145 BC), the son of Ptolemy V and Cleopatra I. During his reign, Egypt was invaded by the Seleucid king Antiochus IV, and Ptolemy was made a prisoner. The throne was then given by the Alexandrians to his brother, Ptolemy VII. After Antiochus withdrew, the brothers ruled as joint kings. Conflicts between them arose, and through Roman arbitration, Cyrenaica was given to Ptolemy VII to rule. After the death of the Seleucid king Demetrius I in 150 BC, Ptolemy VI was offered the Seleucid crown by the people of Antioch, but he declined in favor of the legitimate heir, Demetrius II. In 145 BC Ptolemy VI died of wounds received in a battle, which resulted in the final defeat of Demetrius II's rival, Alexander Balas (d. 145 BC).

PTOLEMY VII (184?–116 BC), called Ptolemy Euergetes ("benefactor") II, king of Egypt (145–116 BC), the son of Ptolemy V and the brother of Ptolemy VI. He was portrayed by Greek writers as a cruel despot, but Egyptian writings credit him with administrative reforms and the liberal endowment of religious institutions. The Ptolemaic Empire became permanently disunited after his death. His will bequeathed Cyrenaica to his illegitimate son Ptolemy Apion (d. 96 BC) and Egypt and Cyprus to his second wife Cleopatra III, who was instructed to choose one of her sons as joint ruler.

PTOMAINES, class of organic nitrogenous compounds formed by the action of putrefactive bacteria on nitrogenous matter. The ptomaines are similar in chemical, physical, and physiological properties to the alkaloids, which are nitrogenous plant bases; to the leucomaines, produced normally within the animal body; and to certain toxins, which are specific secretion products of animals or bacteria. Most ptomaines are amino compounds, containing the radical NH_2; and some, such as putrescine, $NH_2(CH_2)_4NH_2$, and cadaverine, $NH_2(CH_2)_5NH_2$, which are common in rotting meat, are diamines. A few ptomaines are poisonous; most are harmless. The term *ptomaine* was formerly applied to all nitrogenous poisons, including alkaloids and toxins, and the term *ptomaine poisoning* is often erroneously used to indicate a disorder now known to be caused by bacterial toxins. *See* BOTULISM; SALMONELLA. S.Z.L.

PUBERTY, period in the human life span during which the organs of sexual reproduction mature. This maturation is evidenced in females by the onset of menstruation (q.v.), in males by the production of semen, and in both by the enlargement of the external genitalia. Rapid growth marks a range of physiological changes. Various secondary sexual characteristics also appear for the first time during puberty; in males, production of body hair increases markedly, particularly in the pubic, axillary, and facial regions, and the voice usually changes and becomes deeper in tone; in females, hair also appears in the pubic and axillary regions, and the breasts become enlarged. Accelerated development of the sweat glands in both sexes may trigger acne (q.v.).

Puberty usually occurs in males between the ages of 13 and 16, and in females between the ages of 11 and 14. Among the pathological conditions related to puberty are amenorrhea and pubertas praecox. The former is characterized by an absence or cessation of menstrual flow not caused by pregnancy. The latter is the premature appearance in the male or female of the typical physiological characteristics of puberty and is caused by disturbances of secretion in the anterior pituitary, in the adrenals, or in the gonads. *See* ADOLESCENCE.

PUBLIC DEFENDER, lawyer appointed by a local government to represent indigent persons who are accused of crime. Although the right to counsel varies from country to country, most have now recognized the need for defense counsel in criminal cases. Some form of assigned counsel is usually provided to the needy. The U.S. Supreme Court has upheld the right to counsel of all persons accused of felonies, regardless of their ability to pay. For any case that involves the possibility of imprisonment, the poor are guaranteed a publicly provided defense lawyer during the police questioning, pretrial hearing, trial, and appeal.

PUBLIC HEALTH, the protection and improvement of the health of the public through community action, primarily by governmental agencies. Public health includes four major areas: (1) the promotion of positive health and vitality; (2) the prevention of infectious and noninfectious disease as well as injury; (3) the organiza-

An inspector for the New York City Department of Health checks food shipments at a food market. Daily inspections are made to assure the cleanliness and wholesomeness of the food supply. Homer Page–WHO

tion and provision of services for diagnosis and treatment of illness; and (4) the rehabilitation of sick and disabled persons to their highest possible level of function. Inclusion of these four major areas among the concerns of public health agencies was expressed on a worldwide scale in 1948, when health was defined by the World Health Organization (q.v.), or WHO, to include physical, mental, and social well-being and not merely the absence of disease or infirmity.

Promotion of Health. This broad area of public health represents, in a sense, a rediscovery of ancient concepts. As long ago as 3000 BC, cities on the Indian subcontinent had developed environmental sanitation programs such as the provision of underground drains and public baths. Essential aspects of health were woven into daily activities, including personal hygiene, health education, exercise, codes of conduct and self-discipline, dietary practices, food and environmental sanitation, and treatment of minor ailments and injuries. By 1400 BC, this society's so-called science of life, or Ayurveda, mainly featured total health care through health promotion and education, although advances were also made in curative medicine and surgery.

This tradition was also highly developed in ancient Greece and Rome and has persisted to the present, but it has been overshadowed in the 20th century by the great advances in the prevention and treatment of disease. Only in recent decades has a resurgence of interest in positive health occurred. This is evidenced by the important research conducted on the effect of malnutrition in pregnant women on the physical and mental development of their children, and research on the effects of diet supplementation in improving the health and vitality of undernourished populations; by the studies of optimal levels of temperature and other environmental conditions affecting human comfort and ability to function; and by the widespread recognition of the value of physical exercise in achieving positive health and well-being.

Disease Prevention. Humanity remained largely powerless to prevent disease until the conclusive proof of the germ theory in the last quarter of the 19th century by Louis Pasteur in France and Robert Koch in Germany. Their bacteriological findings led to the first epidemiological revolution: the conquest of infectious disease. Environmental sanitation—safe water supplies, improved sewage disposal systems, pasteurization of milk, and sanitary control of food supplies—resulted in the virtual disappearance of cholera and typhoid fever and the marked reduction in diarrhea and infant mortality in industrial countries. The discovery of effective vaccines, based on the growth of the science of immunology (*see* IMMUNE SYSTEM), led not only to the recent worldwide eradication of smallpox but also to the marked decline in such diseases as diptheria, tetanus, whooping cough, poliomyelitis, and measles. Lack of adequate sanitation facilities, however, still impedes the developing countries in their efforts to reduce the toll of diarrhea in infants and children—the main cause of death in the world today. Malaria, tuberculosis, influenza, and other infectious diseases also remain as major health problems in many countries.

The world now stands on the threshold of the second epidemiological revolution: the conquest of noninfectious diseases. These are not only the leading causes of mortality in the industrial nations but have become increasingly important in the developing nations as well. Epidemiologists have developed effective methods for the prevention of heart disease, certain kinds of cancer, stroke, accidents, chronic obstructive lung disease, and cirrhosis of the liver; and application of these methods has already resulted in dramatic reductions in death rates. In the U.S. from 1968 to 1978, for example, the age-adjusted death rate for coronary heart disease declined by 25 percent, and the age-adjusted death rate for stroke showed an even more dramatic decline of 38 percent. These advances were achieved largely through public health programs for the control of high blood pressure and through health education of the public on the hazards of saturated fats and cigarette smoking.

Provision of Medical Care. Three basic systems of medical care exist in the world today: public assistance, health insurance, and national health service. The first is dominant in 108 countries constituting 49 percent of the world's population; the countries are located in Asia, Africa, and Latin America. For the great majority of the people in these countries, whatever medical care is available is provided through a public assistance system for the poor. This includes government hospitals and health centers financed by general taxation. The system and its facilities are generally underfinanced, overcrowded, and insufficiently staffed. In addition to such systems administered by health departments, programs may exist that are operated by social security agencies for industrial or white-collar workers. Where they exist, these programs usually cover only a small part of the population. In all these countries a small stratum of landowners, businesspeople, officials, and professionals use private physicians and hospitals for their care.

The health insurance system is dominant in 23 countries constituting 18 percent of the world's population. These industrialized nations with a capitalist economy are located in Western Europe and North America but also include Australia, New Zealand, Japan, and Israel. In most of them a mix of governmental and nongovernmental insurance exists. In some, however—Canada, Denmark, Finland, Iceland, New Zealand, and Norway—the entire population is covered by governmental medical care insurance. Although most of the countries finance their programs through social security taxes on employees and employers, a considerable portion of the cost is borne by general governmental funds. In Canada, Denmark, Iceland, Ireland, Italy, and New Zealand the program is funded entirely, or almost entirely, by general taxation. Most national health insurance programs in the industrial nations are based on fee-for-service private practice. Physicians and other practitioners contract with the government or with authorized sick funds to provide care.

Safe drinking water is a primary goal of public health programs. A health worker in Iran explains to villagers how to protect their well. D. Deriaz–World Health Organization

The system of national health service is dominant in 14 countries constituting 33 percent of the world's population. They include nine socialist nations in Europe, four in Asia, and Cuba; all are either industrialized or undergoing rapid industrialization. National health services cover the entire population. Financing is almost always through general governmental funds, and services are provided by salaried physicians and other health personnel who work in government hospitals and health centers. Practically all services are included and provided free of charge, and administration is unified by health departments. Regional integration of facilities, which is almost impossible to realize under the health insurance program, is one of the important achievements of the national health service.

The worldwide trend is toward a national health service. Among the industrial capitalist nations, for example, Great Britain in 1948 was the first to establish such a service. The entire population is covered; hospital specialists are government employees, but the general practitioners are still not salaried physicians working in community health centers. Instead they work as solo physicians or in small partnerships, usually in their own offices, and have the same kind of contractual relationship with the government that they had under the former system of national health insurance. In the developing countries, transition toward a national health service is facilitated by the fact that both the public assistance and the social security health systems in these countries generally have developed on the basis of government hospitals and clinics employing salaried physicians. Costa Rica, for example, is now moving toward merging the two systems to form a complete national health service. *See* HEALTH INSURANCE; MEDICARE AND MEDICAID; PUBLIC HEALTH SERVICE; SOCIALIZED MEDICINE.

Rehabilitation. During the past several decades, a great many rehabilitation programs and services have been developed to mitigate the functional disability resulting from disease and injury and to restore individuals to their maximum possible function in society. Not only physical restoration but also vocational and social rehabilitation are being given increasing emphasis as a major aspect of public health services. This is consistent with the focus on health rather than disease adopted by WHO. Today health is considered a state of physical, mental, and social well-being, rather than merely the absence of illness or infirmity. In the Alma-Ata Declaration of 1978, the member countries of WHO committed themselves to "Health for All." The guiding principle of all health departments—local, state, provincial, regional, and national—is to achieve this goal as fully and rapidly as possible. M.T.

For further information on this topic, see the Bibliography in volume 28, sections 505, 568–69.

PUBLIC HEALTH SERVICE, agency of the U.S. Department of Health and Human Services, established in July 1798 under the terms of congressional legislation authorizing marine hospitals for seamen in the merchant marine. Subsequent legislation vastly increased the scope of the agency's activities. Today it is the principal health agency of the federal government. The Public Health Service is charged with promoting the highest level of health attainable for every American and cooperating with foreign governments in health projects. It provides financial assistance for the development and delivery of local health services, for education in the health professions, and for research in medical sciences. Among its other functions are protecting the population against unsafe food and drugs and preventing or controlling communicable diseases.

The service, administered by an assistant secretary for health, includes the following major units: Agency for Toxic Substances and Disease Registry; Alcohol, Drug Abuse, and Mental Health Administration; Centers for Disease Control (q.v.); Food and Drug Administration (q.v.); Health Resources and Services Administration (q.v.); Indian Health Service; and the National Institutes of Health (q.v.).

PUBLIC LANDS, in U.S. law, term designating largely vacant and unappropriated lands administered by the Bureau of Land Management (BLM) of the U.S. Department of the Interior. The U.S. has approximately 110 million ha (272 million acres) of public land exclusive of its national parks, national forests, national wildlife refuges, and other land set aside for particular uses (*see* NATIONAL PARK SERVICE). Most of this BLM-administered land has never been privately owned.

Acquisition of the Public Domain. The developing nation acquired its first public domain following the end of the American Revolution. At that time certain of the original states ceded their claims to lands beyond the Allegheny Mountains to the federal government. These claims, based on colonial charters, had been a source of contention and bloodshed between the colonies long before the American Revolution. After the war, New Jersey, Delaware, and Maryland, having no claim to western land, proposed that the landed states cede their western lands to the federal government (*see* NORTHWEST TERRITORY). Maryland refused to ratify the Articles of Confederation until it was assured that this would be

Much public land had been devoted to wildlife refuges. Here sandhill cranes, Grus canadensis, *feed on their wintering grounds at the Bosque del Apache National Wildlife Reserve, New Mexico.* © Thomas D. Mangelsen–Peter Arnold, Inc.

done. New York renounced its claim to western lands in 1780, and eventually other states followed its example. With the cession by Georgia in 1802, state cessions to the federal government reached a total of more than 96 million ha (236 million acres). The Louisiana Purchase of 1803 added some 215 million ha (530 million acres). Other acquisitions include the following: Red River Basin (1808), Spanish Cession (1819), Oregon Compromise (1846), Mexican Cession (1848), lands purchased from Texas (1850), Gadsden Purchase (1853), and Alaska Purchase (1867). Through the course of the nation's history 729 million ha (1.8 billion acres) of land have at some time been a part of the public domain.

Disposal of the Public Domain. The first significant legislation pertaining to the disposal and use of public land came in 1776, when the Continental Congress offered land grants to induce soldiers to desert from the British army. Later in the same year, Congress promised land bounties to its own soldiers as partial payment for military service. Military land grants were continued through the Mexican War. Only a small part of the land conveyed by military warrants, however, was ever occupied by the returning veterans. Land warrants were purchased for a mere fraction of their face value by speculators. It was not until 1969 that the last of the outstanding warrants were cleared from the public land records of the nation.

In the early years of the American republic, many national leaders saw public lands as a source of government revenue, and public policy was directed toward the sale of land. At the same time, many private citizens believed that vacant land belonged to the person who occupied and cleared it. So-called squatting, or unlawful occupation of land, was a common practice of the day, and conflicts often arose between those who held legal claim to land and those who occupied it. The policy of selling public land was never highly successful and failed to raise the revenue expected. Grants of public lands were awarded by Congress to encourage the construction of canals, wagon roads, and railroads, and to reclaim swamplands. The Land Ordinance of 1785 provided for the reservation of one section in each township for future use or support of public elementary schools. Other grants were made to colleges to promote the teaching of agriculture and the mechanical arts (*see* LAND-GRANT COLLEGES). Beginning with the creation of Yellowstone National Park in 1872, many of the national parks, forests, and wildlife refuges were carved from the public domain.

A general change in the policy of public land disposal came with the passage of the Homestead Act in 1862 (*see* HOMESTEAD LAWS). Designed to encourage agricultural development, the law allowed the head of a household to claim up to 64 ha (160 acres) of public land for an initial fee of $30. In return, the homesteader was required to meet residency and cultivation requirements before a patent to the land was granted. By 1932 more than 1 million settlers were drawn to the public land in search of farms, and more than 109 million ha (more than 270 million acres) passed from public to private ownership. By 1962 all agricultural land had passed from public ownership, and in 1976 the Homestead Laws were repealed by Congress.

Rules for Administering the Public Lands. Article IV, Section 3, of the U.S. Constitution authorized Congress to dispose of and make all needful rules and regulations respecting the territory or other properties belonging to the U.S. The Land Ordinance of 1785 provided for the survey of the public lands. The administration of public lands was later charged to the U.S. Department of the Treasury, created in 1789. In 1812 Congress established the General Land Office within the Treasury Department to oversee public-land disposal. The General Land Office was transferred to the Department of the Interior on its establishment in 1849.

In 1934 Congress passed the Taylor Grazing Act to provide for the leasing of public land for livestock grazing and established the Grazing Service as an agency of the Department of the Interior to administer the act. The Grazing Service was combined with the General Land Office to form the Bureau of Land Management in 1946. With the enactment of the Federal Land Policy and Management Act of 1976, Congress established for the first time a comprehensive legislative mandate for retaining public lands in federal ownership and managing those lands for the public.

Public Lands Today. With the exception of a number of scattered fragments of public land in other states, BLM-administered lands are located primarily in the Far West and Alaska.

BLM is responsible for the balanced management of the public lands and resources and their various values so that they are considered in a combination that will best serve the needs of the American people. Management is based on the principles of multiple use and sustained yield—a combination of uses that takes into account the long-term needs of future generations for renewable and nonrenewable resources. These resources include recreation, range, timber, minerals, watershed, fish and wildlife, wilderness, and natural scenic and scientific values.

Under the Recreation and Public Purposes Act of 1926, local units of government or nonprofit organizations may buy or lease public land for recreational use or for other public purposes. BLM also sells parcels of public land that are surplus to public needs. All public land is sold at fair market value, as determined by public auction.

BLM administers the leasing of public land to state and local government agencies and to certain nonprofit organizations. It manages grazing lands to produce maximum forage. The BLM manages, develops, and protects commercial forest land, and supervises the sale of timber from this land. The bureau also administers the public mineral resources of the U.S., including those on the continental shelf. In a recent year, gross receipts from BLM-administered lands amounted to more than $1.5 billion.

The public land supports a variety of fish and wildlife, and although the BLM develops habitat to support these populations, the management of wildlife is the responsibility of individual states. The agency has developed the recreational potential of the public lands because of their increasing use by the public.

See also CONSERVATION; FOREST.

For further information on this topic, see the Bibliography in volume 28, section 223.

PUBLIC OPINION, attitudes, perspectives, and preferences of a population toward events, circumstances, and issues of mutual interest. It is characteristically measured by the sample survey or public opinion poll.

Opinion Formation. Public opinion is shaped both by relatively permanent circumstances and by temporary influences. Among the former are the ideas that characterize the popular culture of a given place at a given time. In the U.S., for example, the youth-oriented culture of the late 20th century affects the attitudes of many people toward aging and the elderly. Other fairly permanent circumstances such as race, religion, geographical location, economic status, and educational level can strongly influence the opinions of an individual or a particular group about many subjects. Certain temporary factors also affect the public's attitudes. Among these are the impact of current events; the opinions of influential or authoritative persons; the effect of the mass communications media; and the concerted campaigns of public relations professionals (*see* PUBLIC RELATIONS).

History. The systematic measurement of public attitudes is a 20th-century development. Although occasionally opinion polls were conducted before the 1930s, they were generally neither systematic nor scientific. They dealt with unrepresentative samples or used methods that made certain people far more likely to be included in the poll than others. For example, in "straw polls" the only people counted were those who volunteered to take part.

Public opinion polling improved vastly in the 1930s when business and educational organizations began to develop methods that allowed the relatively unbiased selection of respondents and the systematic gathering of data from a wide cross section of the public. By present-day standards these polls were crude, but their results were in some ways useful. Among the pioneers were George H. Gallup, Elmo Roper (1900–71), and Archibald M. Crossley (1896–1985).

Two events encouraged polling agencies to further refine their methods. In 1936 a poll conducted by the *Literary Digest* incorrectly determined that the Republican candidate, Alf Landon, would win the U.S. presidential election. The error arose largely because of biases that caused wealthy people to be overrepresented in the poll. In the 1948 election, most polls mistakenly predicted a victory for the Republican candidate, Thomas E. Dewey, over President Harry S. Truman, again because poor people were underrepresented and also because the polling agencies missed last-minute changes of attitude among the voting public. Since 1948 techniques of public opinion research and polling have improved considerably. Efforts are now made to select respondents without bias, to improve the quality of questionnaires, and to train able and reliable interviewers.

Uses. Opinion polls are generally accepted as useful tools by business, political organizations, the mass media, and government as well as in academic research. Hundreds of public opinion polling firms operate around the world. Best known in the U.S. are the organizations, such as the Gallup Poll and Harris Poll, the findings of which regularly appear in major newspapers.

In business, polls are used to test consumers' preferences and to discover what it is about a product that gives it appeal. Response to commercial polls aid in planning marketing and advertising strategies and in making changes in a product to increase its sales (*see* MARKETING).

In politics, polls are used to obtain information about voters' attitudes toward issues and candidates, to put forward candidates with winning potential, and to plan campaigns. Polling organizations have also been successful in predicting the outcome of elections. In addition, by polling voters on election day, it is often possible to determine the probable winner even before the voting booths close.

Newspapers, magazines, radio, and television are heavy users of public opinion polling information, especially political information that helps to predict elections or gauge the popularity of government officials and candidates. The public's attitude toward various social, economic, and international issues is also considered newsworthy.

Governments use opinion polls to tap public sentiment about issues of interest. In addition, government agencies use polling methodology to determine unemployment rates, crime rates, and other social and economic indicators.

Polls have been employed extensively in academic research, particularly in the social sciences, where they have proven valuable in studying delinquency, socialization, political attitudes, and economic behavior. Among the prominent organizations that primarily serve academic research purposes are the Survey Research Center at the University of Michigan and the National Opinion Research Center at the University of Chicago.

Methods and Techniques. Public opinion polling involves procedures to draw a representative sample of the population under study. If, for example, one is studying the attitudes of all adults in the U.S., the survey organization would seek to draw up a list of the entire adult population of the country and then select at random a sample to be surveyed. When proper techniques are used and the sample is large enough—1000 to 1500 people—the results obtained are likely to be very close to the results one would get if the entire population were surveyed. Thus, if 60 percent of the sample says it approves of the president's policies, statistical theory shows that if the entire population were surveyed, the probability is 95 percent that between 58 to 62 percent of the people would express the same approval as the sample. The criterion of excellence in a sample is representativeness, not size.

Sampling is vital to the validity of an opinion poll. In practice, however, sampling can be a complicated procedure involving a great deal of estimation and guesswork. The population to be surveyed usually cannot be precisely enumerated. Efforts must be made to break down the population into sampling units of approximately equal size. A certain amount of interviewer discretion is necessary, and complications arise when a proposed respondent is not at home, has moved, or is unwilling to be interviewed. Often only about two-thirds of the intended respondents are actually interviewed and give valid responses. When mail questionnaires are used, problems of nonresponse are higher.

Great care must be used when fashioning the questionnaire or interview schedule, and testing the questions before using them in the field is always advisable. Ideally, questions should be short, clear, direct, and easily comprehended. Apart from such an obvious necessity as trying to avoid bias, many subtle problems arise in framing a question. A word or phrase, for example, may mean different things to different people. In making a question simple enough to be understood by everyone, the issue may be so oversimplified that it has no meaning to the more sophisticated respondent. Sometimes the order in which questions are asked can affect the response. In addition, the tone of the question may alter the measured response: A study once found that the percentage of the public in favor of "forbidding" speeches against democracy was 16 points lower than the percentage in favor of "not allowing" such speeches.

Other problems can be traced to interviewer effects. Age, sex, class, or racial differences between the respondent and the interviewer can sometimes affect the respondent's answer.

Once the opinion data have been gathered, the analyst must seek to find meaning in the results, keeping in mind the problems of sampling variability, question-wording biases, and interviewer effects. The results are tabulated and analyzed using various statistical techniques to determine patterns. Much successful analysis involves comparison: comparing subgroups of the population as they react to the same question; comparing the results of surveys conducted at different times to discover opinion trends; and comparing the responses to different questions. Because of comparison-based analysis, the survey may be divided into small subgroups for comparison—for instance, educated, politically active women with educated, politically active men.

Criticisms of the Research. Criticisms of public opinion research come from a variety of sources. Many people simply are not convinced that the opinions of a small sample of the population are a viable representation of the opinions of the whole. On this matter, however, the polling agencies can point to the science of statistics (q.v.) and also to decades of experience from which it can be shown, for example, that the same question asked on two different sample surveys at the same time will almost always generate similar results. Other criticisms deal with sample procedures that, for reasons of economy or expediency, sometimes use outdated population data or make compromises with rigorous statistical requirements.

Even assuming that the basic poll data are valid, analyses of the data may be casual and superficial. In some cases, the raw data are simply presented as the public's "opinion" on an issue without deep and careful analysis to probe nuance and possible bias. The subtle influence of variations in question wording on the measured response is often ignored.

In the political area, criticism sometimes focuses on the appropriateness of opinion polling, rather than on its validity. It is argued that elected officials may be too willing to act on what a poll says their constituents think rather than deciding the issues on their merits. Some experts believe that polls may influence voters to favor certain political candidates who seem to be enjoying a notable popularity at the moment. The information that a certain candidate is far ahead in the polls may discourage people from voting at all or encourage them to vote for that candidate and thus may affect the results of the election. J.E.Mu.

For further information on this topic, see the Bibliography in volume 28, section 158.

PUBLIC RELATIONS, management function that creates, develops, and carries out policies and programs to influence public opinion (q.v.) or public reaction about an idea, a product, or an organization. The field of public relations has become an important part of the economic, social, and political pattern of life in many nations. That field includes advertising (q.v.), publicity, promotional activities, and press contact. Public relations also coexists in business with marketing (q.v.) and merchandising to create the climate in which all selling functions occur.

History. In the U.S, the tremendous growth of industry from the end of the American Civil War to the early 20th century took place with little regard for public welfare. When a group of reformers and activists known as muckrakers waged a campaign to expose the excesses of big business, some industrialists realized the need to improve their public image. From this impetus, the profession of public relations slowly evolved as a major force in business, politics, entertainment, and society in general. One of the first effective public relations practitioners was Ivy L. Lee (1877–1934), who worked for the American industrialist John D. Rockefeller. The pioneer work of Edward L. Bernays (1891–) linked public relations to research, psychology, and the social sciences.

During World War I, both the Allies and the Germans made extensive efforts to influence opinion through the dissemination of propaganda (q.v.). When the U.S. entered the conflict,

Congress set up the Committee on Public Information to help mold American opinion in favor of the war effort. By the end of the war, the profession of public relations had grown into an important tool for government and business.

Activities and Methods. Public relations activities in the modern world help institutions to cope successfully with many problems, to build prestige for an individual or a group, to promote products, and to win elections or legislative battles. The majority of public relations workers are staff employees working within a corporate or institutional framework. Others operate in public relations counseling firms. In the U.S. today, approximately 120,000 people are employed full time in the public relations field.

In industry, public relations personnel keep management informed of changes in the opinions of various publics (that is, the groups of people whose support is needed): employees, stockholders, customers, suppliers, dealers, the community, and government. These professionals counsel management as to the impact of any action—or lack of action—on the behavior of the target audiences. Once an organizational decision has been made, the public relations person has the task of communicating this information to the public using methods that foster understanding, consent, and desired behavior. For example, a hospital merger, an industrial plant closing, or the introduction of a new product all require public relations planning and skill.

Public relations activities are a major part of the political process in the U.S. and many other nations. Politicians seeking office, government agencies seeking acceptance and cooperation, officials seeking support for their policies, and foreign governments seeking aid and allies abroad all make extensive use of counseling services provided by public relations specialists.

Public relations also plays an important role in the entertainment industry. The theater, motion pictures, sports, restaurants, and individuals all use public relations services to increase their business or enhance their image. Other public relations clients are educational, social service, and charitable institutions, trade unions, religious groups, and professional societies such as the American Medical Association.

The successful public relations practitioner is a specialist in communication arts and persuasion. The work involves various functions including the following: (1) programming—that is, analyzing problems and opportunities, defining goals, determining the public to be reached, and recommending and planning activities; (2) writing and editing materials such as press releases, speeches, stockholder reports, product information, and employee publications; (3) placing information in the most advantageous way; (4) organizing special events such as press functions, award programs, exhibits, and displays; (5) setting up face-to-face communication, including the preparation and delivery of speeches; (6) providing research and evaluation using interviews, reference materials, and various survey techniques; and (7) managing resources by planning, budgeting, and recruiting and training staff to attain these objectives. Specialized skills are required to handle public opinion research, media relations, direct mail activities, institutional advertising, publications, film and video production, and special events.

Although its activities, goals, and effects have been subject at times to severe criticism, public relations is a significant force in the U.S. and Western Europe. To avoid misuse of professional skills, several public relations organizations have developed a code of ethics for members. In totalitarian countries, the state has a monopoly on communications, and any public relations activities are government controlled. Public relations services are so far virtually unused in many developing nations, but they are likely to be a future government concern. A.Sc.

For further information on this topic, see the Bibliography in volume 28, section 621.

PUBLIC SCHOOL, in the U.S., an elementary or secondary school controlled and maintained by civil authority, acting through an official board expending public money, and open to all local children. Public schools include grade or grammar schools, junior and senior high schools, and vocational schools; they are distinguished from private or independently financed schools. The meanings of these terms are reversed in England, where public schools are relatively exclusive schools and state schools are other primary and secondary schools.

PUBLIC SPEAKING. *See* RHETORIC.

PUBLIC TRANSPORTATION, also called mass transit, urban passenger transportation service usually available on payment of a prescribed fare and operated on established schedules along designated routes with specific stops. Cities as small as Lausanne, Switzerland (pop. 125,004), have constructed rapid rail transit systems. All larger cities, and of course many smaller towns, rely on buses for transporting their citizens.

History. Although a few reports exist of horse-drawn carriage services as early as the 1500s, the first modern omnibus was not introduced until 1829, when George Shillibeer (1797–1866), an enterprising coach builder, established a service in

A horse-drawn streetcar in New York City about 1855.

London; this was followed in New York City by a line along Broadway in 1831. The omnibus was short-lived. In the U.S. the first horse-drawn streetcar line was begun in 1831 on the Fourth Avenue Street Railroad in New York City. By the 1860s most U.S. cities had horse- or mule-powered street railways franchised by the city.

With the Industrial Revolution and the consequent growth of cities, an urban circulation system to transport people—to work; to social, cultural, and sporting events; and for shopping, medical, and other personal trips—became increasingly important. The cable car, made possible by the invention in 1869 by Andrew Hallidie (1836–1900) of a grip that can grasp a continuously running cable, was introduced in 1873 in San Francisco. A rapid revolution in urban public transportation occurred following the completion in 1888 of the first electrified portion of a horsecar line in Richmond, Va., by Frank J. Sprague (1857–1934). Because of its speed, versatility, and suitability to train cars, the electric street railway (streetcar, tram, or trolley) became popular throughout the country and provided the basic transportation in U.S. cities. The first underground rapid transit service, or subway, opened in New York City in 1904.

When the private automobile became available in the 1910s and '20s, many street railway companies went bankrupt. In the 1930s an effort for revitalization of street railways was made with the development (by the Electric Railway President's Conference Committee) of the PCC car. Most cities, however, utilized instead the gasoline- and diesel-powered bus, because it allowed route selection flexibility and freedom from overhead wires.

Transit ridership grew rapidly in the U.S. until 1920, but declined sharply following World War I and during the depression. Because of gas rationing and lack of automobile production, ridership again rose sharply in the 1940s—reaching almost 24 billion passengers per year by the end of World War II. This was a short-lived peak: With the enormous increase in private automobile ownership and the government's massive highway construction program, the use of transit rapidly decreased. By the mid-1960s yearly patronage had decreased to about 7 billion passengers; it has since remained roughly constant. Although the annual number of passengers has changed little, the share of transit travel has been declining—from about 35 percent in the mid-1940s to a mere 3 percent of all urban travel during the 1980s. Nonetheless, public transportation serves a critical function in many large metropolitan areas, where more than 50 percent of workers may depend on mass transit for travel to and from the central employment area. European cities have not experienced the drastic reduction in mass transit use that American cities have.

Types of Service. Public transportation can be classified into modes that have the following distinct characteristics: right-of-way separation, guidance control, propulsion, and the type of service provided.

Subways. Rail rapid transit (subway or metro) uses high-speed passenger rail cars that operate in tunnels, on elevated structures, or in exclusive rights-of-way that are grade-separated to avoid interference with traffic. It uses high-performance trains with running speeds of up to 120 to 130 km/hr (up to 75 to 80 mph) and can carry as many as 40,000 passengers per hour in one direction. Except for the French-developed rubber-tired systems, which are also used in Mexico City and Montréal, most rapid transit systems use steel wheels on rails. Trains can be operated by one person with various forms of automatic train con-

Buses are by far the most common form of public transit. Shown here is a 1980 model New York City bus, made by General Motors. Courtesy of New York City Transit Authority

trols and can run at 90-second intervals. Stations have high platforms to allow level and quick exit and entrance. Station spacing is between 1200 and 4500 m (4000 and 15,000 ft), requiring a secondary feeder system of buses and ample parking facilities at suburban locations.

Light rail transit (LRT), also called streetcar or tram, is a metropolitan electric railway system characterized by its ability to operate single cars or short trains propelled by motors with power pickup from overhead catenaries. The distinguishing feature of LRT is its diversity of options for alignment, configuration, and design. In dense downtown areas it can be placed in tunnels or on the surface in pedestrian malls. Outside center cities, cars can run on the medians or reserved lanes of arterial highways or on abandoned railroad beds or utility corridors. Depending on the degree of separation from road traffic, average speeds range from 16 to 40 km/hr (10 to 25 mph). The capacity of a moderate-sized system is about 12,000 people per hour.

There has been a steady growth of North American LRT systems. From 1977 to 1987 the combined length of all systems increased 47 percent to 547 km (336 mi) from 368 km (229 mi). By the late 1980s at least 19 U.S. cities had plans for new LRT systems or extensions of existing systems.

Buses. Bus transit systems use self-propelled rubber-tired vehicles that are not confined to fixed guideways. Motor buses operate along fixed routes and on fixed schedules, but they can operate over exclusive freeway bus lanes, freeways, arterials, or local streets. The standard bus is either 11 m (36 ft) or 12 m (39 ft) long and, depending on the seating arrangements, can carry up to 53 seated passengers. A few electric trolley bus lines remain in use in U.S. cities. Buses operate on downtown streets at average speeds of 13 km/hr (8 mph) or less but at a higher speed on suburban streets or freeways. On average, a bus will travel about 48,000 km (about 30,000 mi) per year, but this can vary significantly depending on city size and age of bus (average bus life is about 15 years). During the 1980s U.S. transit agencies annually bought about 4000 standard buses manufactured in the U.S. and abroad.

Paratransit. Paratransit is a form of transportation service that is more flexible and personalized than conventional fixed-route, fixed-schedule service. Vehicles are usually available to the public on demand by subscription or on a shared-ride basis and operate over the highway and street system. Paratransit is a transportation service that falls somewhere between the private automobile and fixed-route public transit. It includes hail or phone services provided by taxicabs, jitneys, buses, and vans; hire-and-drive services offered by rental car and limousine agencies; and prearranged ride-sharing services of van pools and car pools. Paratransit modes are generally named in terms of the service characteristics rather than by the vehicle used or type of labor employed in providing the service. Paratransit is characterized by its provision of point-to-point service, for its flexibility in meeting changing demands and conditions, and for the generally free and unrestricted marketplace in which it operates. Many elderly and handicapped people are users of this specialized transit service.

Problems Since World War II. Since about 1950 public transportation in the U.S. has had to struggle to survive. The growth of private automobile ownership, the change in cities with accelerated urban sprawl, the dispersal of employment away from the central city, and the immense highway construction program have added to transit problems. Moreover, changes in life-style have contributed to reduced transit use, which has resulted in lower revenues from fares at a time when costs for operations have increased greatly.

As private transit systems were taken over by local government and the cost of operations continued to increase, pressure was exerted for federal participation in urban public transportation. The 1964 Urban Mass Transportation Act established this commitment. The legislation limited federal assistance to 80 percent of the capital expenditure for buses, rail cars, and fixed facilities. In 1974 the federal government added operating assistance to its program. Because passenger fares account for only about one-third of the average system's operating funds, demand for federal subsidies escalated rapidly. In the early 1980s a change in federal transportation policy resulted in relaxation of the rigid standards governing the way federal aid is used, imposing requirements for private sector participation and increased state, regional, and local funding. By the end of the 1980s state and local operating assistance amounted to about 52 percent of the funds needed to operate U.S. transit systems; fare box and other revenue accounted for 43 percent, and federal assistance, 5 percent.

Private sector initiatives in public transportation include transit services provided by private operators under competitively bid contracts, and innovative public-private projects such as joint development of transit stations.

It is estimated that 8 million people in the U.S. (5 percent of the urban population) have physical handicaps that prevent them from using conventional transportation services. With the aging of the population, more than one-fifth of the people living in the U.S. will be over 65 in the year 2030. Many of the people in these groups are dependent on public transportation. In 1990 Congress passed the Americans with Disabilities Act, which will virtually require all transit services to be accessible to the disabled.

Future Trends. In the short run, existing transit modes with proven technologies will be im-

Mexico City, like Moscow and some other large metropolitan areas, has made its subway system an architectural showpiece. The cars in this system run on rubber wheels. Marc & Evelyne Bernheim–Woodfin Camp & Associates

Despite the city's size and relative age, Washington, D.C., did not begin operating a subway-elevated railroad as part of its mass transit system until 1976. Plans for the facility were approved in 1969. Tom Tracy–The Stock Shop

proved. Cities with such systems will extend their lines, while others will plan and construct new ones, including rapid transit, buses, and light rail transit. The lower-cost alternatives will have a better chance of adoption. There is also a strong interest in commuter rail. Part of the appeal of this mode of transportation is that many cities have unused and underused rail corridors that can provide rights-of-way at low cost.

Because of major environmental concerns, electric trolley buses and methanol-powered and other alternative fuel-powered buses will replace diesel engine buses.

An enormous range of new technology exists in the area of intelligent vehicle systems. For example, a commuter will be able to get real-time information on home computers as to when the next bus will arrive at the nearest bus stop. Information for trip planning will be available as well. Transit agencies will use advanced technologies for traffic and fleet management of their vehicles. Vehicle control systems that will guide buses along prescribed corridors and routes are being researched to reduce vehicle delay, increase capacity, and improve safety.

Automation through new technology can provide a means for reducing labor while providing performance and safety. A number of automated guideway transit systems operate in airports, shopping centers, college campuses, and amusement parks. Their applicability to a more diverse use is continually evaluated. Research is under way on magnetically levitated and air-supported vehicles. Longitudinal control, spacing, switching, and lateral control are among the many problems needing more development before such systems can be widely accepted. Other promising developments include the moving walkway, designed for short distance, which will accelerate a pedestrian from three to five times walking speed.

Unique structural systems have been designed to support advanced transit concepts. Suspended monorails with widely spaced columns or pretensioned cable systems are examples of lower-cost systems under development. *See* MONORAIL.

W.C.G.

For further information on this topic, see the Bibliography in volume 28, section 334.

PUBLIC UTILITIES, business enterprise set up to provide essential services to the public, for example, electricity, gas, water, sewerage, telephone, and telegraph.

Ownership. Because public utilities are so vital, they were usually operated as a natural monopoly (q.v.) and were subjected to a high degree of governmental control. The monopoly status of many utilities, however, has eroded during the 1980s, largely due to government deregulation. There is now competition in such areas as long-distance telephone service, natural gas pipelines, interstate railroads, and intercity bus service.

Some public utilities are publicly, or municipally, owned—for example, water-supply systems and sewerage systems. The proper scope of municipal ownership remains a subject of debate. The relative cheapness and efficiency of service coupled with local conditions are the chief factors to be considered in deciding between public and private ownership. Sufficient methods of financing municipally owned undertakings must also be planned so as not to increase municipal debt beyond prudent limits. In addition, recent changes in federal tax laws have made it more difficult for municipalities to raise capital for the acquisition of utility property through tax-exempt financing.

The vast majority of public utilities in the U.S. are owned by private corporations. These private firms differ from other businesses in that utility companies are obligated to serve all who ask for their services and in that they must usually make a very large capital investment in relation to the revenues they receive.

Regulation. Control of most public utilities lies with public service commissions, agencies formed to protect the safety of the people and property under their jurisdiction. These commissions operate at the federal, state, and local levels, sharing the responsibility for determining rates and supervising the service provided. The grant by a governmental authority to a privately owned utility company giving the company the right to use public streets for placement of poles, wires, mains, tracks, and the like is called a franchise. Franchises are now extended to public utilities for a limited number of years, in contrast to the previous practice of unlimited franchises. Present franchises usually allow for governmental review of revenues, expenses, and income; provide for arbitrations of disagreements; and explain the conditions that must be met by the utility in order for it to retain the franchise. The purpose of granting a franchise is to protect the public interest and to allow the utility the right to use public property.

At the federal level, commissions that control utility operations are the Interstate Commerce Commission (q.v.), which regulates most public utilities classified as common carriers; and the Federal Communications Commission (q.v.), which regulates telephone, telegraph, and broadcasting companies. Until its abolition, the Federal Power Commission (q.v.) regulated interstate transmission of electricity and gas and set pipeline rates charged to local utility companies. In 1978 most of its functions were transferred to the Federal Energy Regulatory Commission in the Department of Energy.

At the state level, utility companies are regulated under the constitutional power of the state to enact laws exercising control of private interests for the protection of its people and property; this power is known as the police power. State commissions generally are responsible for regulating the standards of service and safety, and fix rates and charges.

States also may delegate regulatory authority to the cities in which the public utilities are located. City control over utilities usually concerns street uses and safety standards for installations. In return for granting the privilege of operating a utility in a municipality, some cities receive payments as part of the franchise or levy utility taxes against the gross receipts of a public utility.

Impact on the Environment. Since most utilities affect the appearance of the landscape, many municipalities and states now require that public-utility power lines for telephone, telegraph, and electricity be placed below ground. Much attention has been focused on the destructive effect that some public utilities have had on the environment. Certain utilities, such as sewage-disposal systems, are directly connected to the rapidly increasing pollution of air, land, and water throughout the world. In the U.S. in the 1960s and '70s, federal funds and legislation were channeled toward control and upgrading of these utilities.

In the 1980s growing concern over the potential dangers of nuclear power plants led to conflicts in many nations between advocates and opponents of nuclear energy. In the U.S. several nuclear power plants remain incomplete or unopened. Currently, it is unclear as to whether adequate safeguards will ever be developed to satisfy public and government doubts about the safety of nuclear facilities.

See also AIR POLLUTION; SEWAGE DISPOSAL; WATER POLLUTION; WATER SUPPLY AND WATERWORKS.

PUBLIC WORKS ADMINISTRATION (PWA), former U.S. government agency established by Congress as the Federal Emergency Administration under the National Industrial Recovery Act of 1933. Organized under the New Deal, the PWA was responsible for the construction of roads, buildings, dams, and other projects and loaned money to states and municipalities for similar projects. The agency's goal was to increase employment and business activity. In its 10-year existence, the PWA spent more than $4 billion on public projects. In 1943 the functions of the agency were transferred to the Federal Works Agency, which in turn was abolished in 1949 when its functions were assumed by the General Services Administration.

PUBLISHING. *See* BOOK TRADE.

PUCCINI, Giacomo (1858–1924), Italian composer, whose operas blend intense emotion and theatricality with tender lyricism, colorful orchestration, and a rich vocal line.

Giacomo Puccini Bettmann Archive

Puccini was born Dec. 22, 1858, in Lucca, the descendant of a long line of local church musicians. In 1880 he wrote a mass, *Messa di Gloria,* that encouraged his great-uncle to help underwrite his musical education. After studying (1880–83) music at the Milan Conservatory, Puccini wrote his first opera, *Le Villi* (1884); this brought him a commission to write a second, *Edgar* (1889), and a lifelong connection with Ricordi, a major music publisher. His third opera, *Manon Lescaut* (1893), was hailed as the work of a genius. *La Bohème* (1896), although containing some of the most popular arias in the repertoire today, displeased the audience at its Turin premiere, even with Arturo Toscanini conducting. Subsequent productions, however, won the composer worldwide acclaim.

Puccini's other operas include *Tosca* (1900), a standard repertory piece; *Madama Butterfly* (1904), which drew hisses at La Scala in Milan on opening night but scored a success after Puccini revised it; *The Girl of the Golden West* (1910), an opera on an American theme; the high-spirited *La Rondine* (1917); and *Il Trittico,* a trilogy of one-act operas comprising *Il Tabarro, Suor Angelica,* and the comic *Gianni Schicchi* (1918). Puccini was working on *Turandot* when he died, Nov. 29, 1924, in Brussels. The opera, his most exotic, was completed by Franco Alfano (1876–1954) and had its premiere in 1926.

Although his work lacks the grandeur of Giuseppe Verdi's, many consider him second only to Verdi among Italian composers who lived after Gioacchino Rossini.

PUDELPOINTER, breed of dog, developed in Germany in the 19th century for use in hunting. The dog, which somewhat resembles the German wirehaired pointer (*see* GERMAN POINTER), stands about 60 cm (about 24 in) at the shoulder and weighs about 27 kg (about 60 lb). It has a thick, wiry outer coat and a softer inner coat, with bushy growths on the forehead and chin. The color is usually brownish. The ears hang and the tail is docked to a length of about 17 cm (about 7 in).

PUDOVKIN, Vsevolod Ilarionovich (1893–1953), Soviet motion picture director and actor. He trained at the State Film School in Moscow under the influential Soviet director Lev Kushelov (1899–1970). Pudovkin is known for his ability to convey emotions through the juxtaposition of different images, achieved by skilled film editing. His major early films, *Mother* (1926) and *The End of St. Petersburg* (1927), were followed by the internationally successful *Storm over Asia* (1928). His films with sound include *Deserter* (1933) and *Admiral Nakhimov* (1947).

PUEBLA, in full Puebla de Zaragoza, city, central Mexico, capital of Puebla State. It is an agricultural, commercial, manufacturing, and tourist center located in Mexico's central plateau at an altitude of about 2163 m (about 7095 ft). Major products include textiles, glass, pottery, tiles, and processed food. In the city are the Autonomous University of Puebla (1937), the University of the Americas (1940), and the Popular Autonomous University of Puebla State (1973); the José Luis Bello y González Museum of Art (1938); a 16th-century cathedral; and an 18th-century theater, believed to be the oldest in North America. The community, established in 1532, is one of the oldest European settlements in Mexico. In 1847, during the Mexican War, Puebla was occupied by U.S. troops, and it was held by the French from 1863 to 1867. Pop. (1980) 835,759.

PUEBLO, city, seat of Pueblo Co., central Colorado, on the Arkansas R., at the E foothills of the Rocky Mts.; inc. as a city 1885. It is an industrial and transportation center in an irrigated farming region. Manufactures include steel, computer components, aerospace equipment, and plastic. Pueblo is the location of several federal offices, including a branch of the Government Printing Office. The University of Southern Colorado (1933), the state fairgrounds, and a U.S. Army depot are also here. The community is named for Fort El Pueblo, built here by fur traders in 1842 and abandoned in 1854. A new settlement, founded in 1858, was reached by rail in 1872. Flooding in 1921 led to the construction of a flood-control project on the Arkansas R. Pop. (1980) 101,686; (1990) 98,640.

PUEBLO INDIANS (Span. *pueblo,* "village"), American Indians living in compact, apartment-like villages of stone or adobe in northwestern New Mexico and northeastern Arizona. The Pueblo people are small in stature, with straight black hair, stocky build, and skin that is light tan to reddish-brown. They belong to four distinct linguistic groups, but the cultures of the different villages are closely related.

The eastern villages, located along the upper Rio Grande near Santa Fe and Albuquerque, include Isleta (q.v.), Jemez, Nambe, Picuris, San Ildefonso, San Juan, Santa Clara, and Taos (q.v.), whose inhabitants speak Tanoan languages, and Cochiti, Santa Ana, Santo Domingo, San Felipe, and Zia, where Keresan languages are spoken. Two slightly westward Keresan pueblos, Acoma and Laguna (qq.v.), along with the Zuñi and Hopi pueblos, make up the western villages. Since about 1700 the Zuñi have been concentrated in one large village in westernmost New Mexico. Their language shows no certain relation to any other language. The Hopi live on or near three mesas in northeastern Arizona. Their language is part of the Uto-Aztecan language family. The Hopi pueblos include Mishongnovi, Shongopovi, Shupapulovi, Sichomavi, and Oraibi and the Tewa-Hopi village of Hano, founded about 1700 by Tewa-speaking refugees. *See also* AMERICAN INDIAN LANGUAGES; HOPI; ZUÑI INDIANS.

Archaeology and Prehistory Archaeologists relate the Pueblo to an older Southwest culture known by the term *Basket Maker.* The entire cultural sequence is called the Anasazi (Navajo, "ancient ones") culture. During the early Basket Maker phase (c. 100 BC–AD 500) prehistoric settlements were established in the northern part of the Southwest. The Indians practiced weaving; they lived in caves or built shelters of poles and adobe mud. Pumpkins and corn were grown as a supplement to hunting and gathering. Food was stored in underground pits, often lined with stone slabs. With the addition of a bean crop and the domestication of the turkey, agriculture became more important than hunting and gathering during the Modified Basket Maker period (500–700). Pottery was introduced. The food storage pits developed into semisubterranean houses and ceremonial chambers, and buildings began to take their present connected form.

The transition from the Basket Maker to the Pueblo culture occurred about 700. Stone construction was adopted, and the connected, now-aboveground houses became larger. The ceremonial chamber developed into the kiva, an underground chamber used for rituals and as a male lodge. Several kinds of corn were grown, and the cultivation of cotton may have been introduced. Pottery was produced in a diversity of shapes and styles. During this period the Anasazi made their greatest territorial expansion, reaching as far as central Utah, southern Colorado, and a large part of northern Mexico.

During the Classic Pueblo period (1050–1300) the northernmost regions were no longer occupied, and the population became concentrated in large multistoried, terraced pueblos and in similar villages built in recesses in cliffs. Notable advances occurred in pottery and weaving. At the end of this period many large centers of Pueblo life were abandoned, possibly because of drought or because of invading bands of Navajo and Apache. During the Regressive Pueblo period (1300–1700) many villages inhabited today were founded. Houses became less elaborate, but pottery and weaving continued to develop. *See* CASA GRANDE NATIONAL MONUMENT; CHACO CULTURE NATIONAL HISTORICAL PARK; CLIFF DWELLER; MESA VERDE NATIONAL PARK.

Historic Period. During the Modern Pueblo period (1700–present), cattle, goats, horses, and sheep were introduced by the Spanish, and wool replaced cotton as the principal textile.

The Pueblos, probably the Zuñi, were first encountered by the Spanish in 1539, when the Franciscan missionary Marcos de Niza (1495–1558) arrived. A year later the Spanish explorer Francisco Vásquez de Coronado, searching for the legendary Seven Cities of Cíbola, led an expedition among the Hopi; failing to find any treasure, he withdrew. In 1598 the Spanish occupied the Pueblo country, and by 1630 Spanish missions were established in almost every village. A mass Pueblo revolt in 1680 drove the Spanish from the territory, and the Pueblo were not reconquered until 1692. Few of the missions were reestablished, and most of the villages continued their ancient religion. The number of villages during this time was reduced from about 80 to about 30. The Pueblo remained under Spanish, and then Mexican, domination until the close of the Mexican War in 1848, when they came under U.S. jurisdiction. Throughout this time, they faithfully preserved their traditional culture, often adopting superficial religious or governmental changes but maintaining the old ways in secrecy. The western villages, in particular, resisted Spanish influence; in the eastern villages, some Spanish elements were assimilated.

Present-Day Life. The communal building of a present-day pueblo is a solid structure of adobe bricks or stone set in clay and mortar. The rooms are square, with thick flat roofs; they are built in terraced stories, and the roof of one level is

Three children of Laguna Pueblo sit in the sun before an adobe mission church. New Mexico Tourism and Travel

reached by a movable ladder from the level below. Traditionally, access to the interiors is by ladders to trapdoors in the roofs, and the outer walls have neither windows nor doors (originally a precaution against attackers). Modern buildings, however, often have glass windows and hinged doors. Rooms are added to the original structure as needed, and a whole village often lives in a single complex building. Each village has at least two, and usually several, kivas.

Social organization is in clans and lineages. Descent is matrilineal, and women own the houses. Marriage is monogamous and must be to someone outside the clan or group of related clans; divorce can occur at will. Although nominally Christianized, all Pueblo maintain—some to a great extent—their ancient beliefs. The principal ceremonies, arranged by the secret societies that use the kivas, are held between crop seasons and consist of prayers and thanksgivings for rain and good crops. Particularly among the western Pueblo, ancestral and other benevolent spirits called *kachinas* are revered as bringers of rain and social good. Their spirits are believed to possess the masked dancers who impersonate them in rituals, and dolls depicting them are given to children. Some of the eastern Pueblos divide their villages into Summer and Winter People, who alternate responsibility for rituals. *See* SNAKE DANCE.

The Pueblo economy is based on agriculture, supplemented by raising livestock and, often, by the sale of handicrafts. Each village cultivates fields in common. The crops include corn, beans, cotton, melon, squash, and chili peppers. Men generally work the fields, weave, build houses, and conduct ceremonies; women prepare food, care for children, make baskets and pottery, and transport water. They often help with gardening (as they did in ancient times when hunting was important) and in building the houses.

Each community has an individual style and technique of basketry. Pueblo pottery is characterized by a beauty of decoration and shape that is unmatched among modern North American Indians; the work of Pueblo potters such as Maria Martinez (1887–1980) is prized by Indian art collectors. Pueblo men continue to be skilled weavers, producing cotton and woolen clothing and fine woolen blankets.

In the 20th century, low incomes, poor health care, poor schooling, and in some pueblos, unemployment, together with a clash of values with the dominant white culture, have led to significant anger and social distress. Most Pueblo who have left their villages return from time to time to regain contact with the social and religious values of their tradition.

For further information on this topic, see the Bibliography in volume 28, sections 117, 665, 727, 1105–8.

At San Ildefonso Pueblo, in northern New Mexico, the famed potter Maria Martinez fashions one of her prized blackware pots. New Mexico Tourism and Travel

PUERPERAL FEVER, infection, once prevalent in women after childbirth. In most cases puerperal fever occurred because aseptic techniques during delivery and occasionally during abortion and miscarriage were not used. Also called childbed fever, the infection in most instances was due to streptococci that entered the body during delivery. The efforts of the physicians Ignaz Philipp Semmelweis and Oliver Wendell Holmes brought about the adoption of rigid cleanliness and asepsis in maternal delivery procedures, and the mortality from puerperal fever was reduced more than 90 percent after their adoption.

In addition to the use of strict asepsis in obstetrical procedures, the availability of modern antiseptics has made puerperal fever a rarity.

PUERTO BARRIOS, city, E Guatemala, capital of Izabal Department, on the Bay of Amatique (an arm of the Caribbean Sea). The leading port of Guatemala and the N terminus of the railroad from the capital, Puerto Barrios lies near an area of extensive banana plantations, and bananas, coffee, chicle, fruits, and tropical woods are exported. It has bathing and fishing facilities. The city developed in the early 1900s and became departmental capital in 1920. Pop. (1981 prelim.) 46,782.

PUERTO CABELLO, city, N Venezuela, in Carabobo State, a port on the Caribbean Sea. The principal industries are meat packing, cotton and flour milling, and fishing; exports include coffee, cacao, and copra. Pop. (1980 est.) 94,000.

PUERTO CORTÉS, town, NW Honduras, Cortés Department, on the Gulf of Honduras. It is the country's busiest Caribbean port and serves as a manufacturing and distribution center for the surrounding agricultural region. Bananas, coffee, and wood are shipped from here. Major manufactures include processed food, beverages, soap, leather items, and refined petroleum. The community was established nearby in 1525 as Puerto Caballos and was moved to its present site and renamed in 1869. Pop. (1987 est.) 42,100.

PUERTO PLATA, also San Felipe de Puerto Plata, city, N Dominican Republic, capital of Puerto Plata Province, on the Atlantic Ocean near Santiago. Chocolates and matches are manufactured here. Puerto Plata is one of the country's leading ports; exports include tobacco, coffee, and sugarcane. Pop. (1981) 45,348.

PUERTO RICO, officially Commonwealth of Puerto Rico (Span. *Estado Libre Asociado de Puerto Rico*), freely associated commonwealth of the U.S. Composed of one large island and several small islands, Puerto Rico is bordered on the N by the Atlantic Ocean, on the E by the Virgin Passage (which separates it from the Virgin Islands), on the S by the Caribbean Sea, and on the W by the Mona Passage (which separates it from the Dominican Republic).

Puerto Rico became a U.S. commonwealth on July 25, 1952. It was claimed by Christopher Columbus in 1493 and was subsequently a Spanish possession before the U.S. gained control in 1898. Its name, Spanish for "rich port,"was first applied to its capital, known as San Juan Bautista de Puerto Rico in the 16th century. Gradually, the city came to be called San Juan and the island Puerto Rico. The name formerly was spelled Porto Rico. Puerto Rico is sometimes called the Island of Enchantment.

LAND AND RESOURCES

Puerto Rico is one of the larger islands of the West Indies, and the commonwealth also includes several small islands, such as Culebra, Mona, and Vieques. It is located about 1610 km (about 1000 mi) SE of Florida and is almost twice as far from the mainland of North America as it is from South America. Puerto Rico is roughly rectangular in shape; its greatest E to W distance is about 180 km (about 110 mi), and its extreme N to S distance is about 65 km (about 40 mi). The highest point is 1338 m (4389 ft), atop Cerro de Punta. Puerto Rico has an area of 9104 sq km (3515 sq mi), which makes it larger than Delaware or Rhode Island. Its coastline measures some 501 km (some 311 mi).

Physical Geography. Puerto Rico is mountainous. The Central Mountains form an E to W backbone that extends almost the entire length of the island. The average elevation of these mountains, which include the Cordillera Central and the Sierra de Luquillo, is about 915 m (about 3000 ft). Although the mountains and adjacent foothills cover most of Puerto Rico, on the N side of the island lies a coastal plain up to about 19 km (about 12 mi) wide, and a narrower coastal plain up to about 13 km (about 8 mi) wide extends along the S coast. For most of its length the mountain system is nearer the S coast than the N coast, and the slopes are generally steeper on the S side. At the E end of the island, however, the mountains curve toward the NE corner.

Rivers and Lakes. Puerto Rico has many relatively short rivers and streams. Some of the rivers are dammed for hydroelectric power and thus have small lakes along their courses. One such body of water is Lago de Yauco, on the Yauco R. The longest river is the Grand de Arecibo, which flows to the N coast. Other rivers include the Grand de Añasco, Bayamón, Cibuco, Culebrinas, and La Plata. None of the rivers is navigable by large vessels.

Climate. Puerto Rico is a mountainous, tropical island directly in the path of the trade winds.

A view of El Yunque rain forest in the mountains of eastern Puerto Rico; it is the natural habitat of many rare tropical trees, vines, and flowering plants. Freda Leinwand

These conditions account for its tropical rain forest and tropical wet and dry climates. Except at night, in the highest areas, the air is always warm. There is little difference from season to season in the energy received from the sun, and the length of the day remains fairly constant throughout the year. In addition, the average termperature of the seawater surrounding the island is about 27° C (about 81° F), with little variation during the course of the year. Trade winds reaching Puerto Rico from the E blow over this warm water and carry the warmth over the land. This air also contains much water vapor, and as the air is forced to rise over the mountains, it becomes cooler, and part of its water vapor condenses and falls as rain. The mountain areas receive more rain than almost any other part of the U.S. The SW coastal area generally receives the least rain in Puerto Rico and has a distinct dry season. The mean annual temperature at San Juan, in the N, is about 26° C (about 79° F), and the city receives some 1500 mm (some 59 in) of precipitation each year. The recorded temperature in the commonwealth has ranged from 4.4° C (40° F) in 1911 at Aibonito to 39.4° C (103° F) in 1906 at San Lorenzo. Puerto Rico is sometimes struck by damaging hurricanes traveling from the E, especially from August to October.

Plants and Animals. Several thousand varieties of tropical plants grow in Puerto Rico, including the kapok tree with its thick trunk, the poinciana with its brilliant reddish blossoms, the breadfruit, and the coconut palm. A tropical rain forest in the NE section of the island has tree ferns, orchids, and mahogany trees; part of this tropical area is included in the Caribbean National Forest. In the dry SW corner of Puerto Rico are cactus and bunch grass.

Puerto Rico has no large wild mammals. The mongoose was brought in to control rats on sugarcane plantations. Iguanas and many small lizards abound, and bats are present. The island has one animal found almost nowhere else in the world—the coquí, a small tree frog that produces a loud, clear "song" from the branches of trees at night. Barracuda, kingfish, mullet, Spanish mackerel, tuna, lobster, and oysters are among the many fish inhabiting coastal waters.

Mineral Resources. Puerto Rico's mineral deposits include limestone, glass sand, clay, copper,

POPULATION OF PUERTO RICO SINCE 1899

Census	Population	% growth from previous census
1899	953,243	–
1910	1,118,012	17.3%
1920	1,299,809	16.3%
1930	1,543,913	18.8%
1940	1,869,255	21.1%
1950	2,210,703	18.3%
1960	2,349,544	6.3%
1980	3,196,520	17.9%
1990	3,522,037	10.2%

POPULATION OF TEN LARGEST COMMUNITIES

	1990 Census	1980 Census
San Juan	426,832	424,600
Bayamón	202,103	185,087
Carolina	162,404	147,835
Ponce	159,151	161,739
Caguas	92,429	87,214
Mayagüez	83,010	82,968
Guaynabo	73,385	65,075
Arecibo	49,545	48,779
Trujillo Alto	44,336	41,141
Cataño	34,587	26,243

cobalt, chromium, nickel, iron ore, and peat. Great deposits of copper are in the central region near Adjuntas and Utuado. D.J.P.

POPULATION

According to the 1990 census, Puerto Rico had 3,522,037 inhabitants, an increase of about 10.2% over 1980. The average population density in 1990 was 387 persons per sq km (1002 per sq mi), a much higher density than for any U.S. state except New Jersey and Rhode Island. The great majority of Puerto Rico's inhabitants are of Hispanic background; Spanish is the official language of the commonwealth. About 80% of the people are Roman Catholic. In 1990 approximately 71% of the island's inhabitants lived in areas defined as urban and the rest lived in rural areas. The largest communities in Puerto Rico included San Juan, the capital; Bayamón; Carolina; Ponce; Caguas; and Mayagüez.

EDUCATION AND CULTURAL ACTIVITY

In the 20th century Puerto Rico greatly improved its educational institutions, and by the early 1980s nearly 90% of the adult population was literate, compared with some 67% in 1940. The commonwealth also contains a number of notable cultural institutions and historical sites.

Education. Puerto Rico's first free primary school was founded in the early 19th century in San Juan. By the late 1980s the commonwealth's public schools annually enrolled about 486,200

The Ponce Art Museum, in Ponce, Puerto Rico.
Puerto Rico Information Service

elementary pupils and about 165,000 secondary students.

The University of Puerto Rico, founded in 1903, is the oldest institution of higher education in Puerto Rico; it has branches in Arecibo, Bayamón, Cayey, Humacao, Mayagüez, Ponce, Río Piedras, and San Juan. In the late 1980s the commonwealth had a total of 55 institutions of higher education with a combined enrollment of about 153,000 students. Besides the University of Puerto Rico, these institutions included Bayamón Central University (1970), in Bayamón; Inter-American University of Puerto Rico (1912), with major campuses in Hato Rey and San Germán; Catholic University of Puerto Rico (1948), in Ponce; and the University of the Sacred Heart (1935), in Santurce.

Cultural Institutions. A number of Puerto Rico's major cultural institutions are in San Juan. These include the Museum of Puerto Rican Art, housing works from pre-Columbian times to the present; the Museum of Military and Naval History; and the Museum of Natural History. In addition, metropolitan San Juan is the home of the Symphony Orchestra of Puerto Rico, the Conservatory of Music of Puerto Rico (1959), and ballet and dance companies. It also is the site of the annual Festival Casals, which includes programs of orchestra and chamber music. Of note, too, is the Ponce Art Museum, which has exhibits of paintings by European and Puerto Rican artists.

Historical Sites. Puerto Rico's Spanish heritage is preserved in many sites in San Juan, especially in the insular part of the city known as Old San Juan. Among these sites are El Morro and San Cristóbal fortresses, both part of San Juan National Historic Site; La Fortaleza, once a fortress and now the governor's palace, its oldest section completed in 1540; Old Santo Domingo Convent, built between 1523 and 1528; and Fort San Geronimo (completed late 18th cent.).

Sports and Recreation. Puerto Rico's mild climate and sandy beaches make it a popular recreation area, especially for swimming, fishing, boating, tennis, and golf. Both horse racing and cockfighting attract many spectators. Baseball, basketball, and boxing also are popular sports in Puerto Rico.

Communications. In the early 1990s Puerto Rico had 62 AM and 37 FM radiobroadcasting stations and 34 television stations. The commonwealth's first radio station, WKAQ in San Juan, began operations in 1922. WKAQ-TV in San Juan, Puerto Rico's initial television station, first went on the air in 1954. *La Gaceta de Puerto Rico,* the island's first newspaper, was initially published in 1807. Influential newspapers in Puerto

Rico now include the Spanish-language *El Nuevo Día* and *El Vocero de Puerto Rico* and the English-language *San Juan Star,* all published in San Juan.

GOVERNMENT AND POLITICS

The Commonwealth of Puerto Rico is governed under a constitution of 1952, as amended. An amendment to the constitution may be proposed by the commonwealth's legislature or by a constitutional convention. To become effective an amendment must be approved by a majority of persons voting on an issue in an election. Puerto Ricans share most rights and obligations of other U.S. citizens; residents of the commonwealth may not vote in U.S. presidential elections, however, and, except for federal employees and members of the U.S. armed forces, are not required to pay federal income taxes.

Executive. The chief executive of Puerto Rico is a governor, who is popularly elected to a 4-year term and who may be reelected any number of times. The secretary of state succeeds the governor should the latter resign, die, or be removed from office. The governor, with the consent of the legislature, appoints the heads of the commonwealth's executive departments.

Legislature. The bicameral Puerto Rico Legislative Assembly is made up of a senate and a house of representatives. In the early 1990s the senate had 27 members, and the house had 53 members. Legislators are popularly elected to 4-year terms.

Judiciary. Puerto Rico's highest tribunal, the supreme court, is composed of a chief justice and six associate justices, who serve until the age

INDEX TO MAP OF PUERTO RICO

Communities

Adjuntas . . . . B 2
Aguada . . . . A 2
Aguadilla . . . . A 2
Aguas Buenas . . . . C 2
Aibonito . . . . C 2
Añasco . . . . A 2
Angeles . . . . B 2
Arecibo . . . . B 2
Arroyo . . . . C 3
Arus . . . . B 2
Bahomamey . . . . A 2
Bajadero . . . . B 2
Barceloneta . . . . B 2
Barranquitas . . . . C 2
Bayamón . . . . C 2
Boquerón . . . . A 2
Cabo Rojo . . . . A 2
Caguas . . . . C 2
Camuy . . . . B 2
Carolina . . . . D 2
Cataño . . . . C 2
Cayey . . . . C 2
Ceiba . . . . D 2
Central Aguirre . . . . C 3
Ciales . . . . C 2
Cidra . . . . C 2
Coamo . . . . C 2
Comerío . . . . C 2
Coquí . . . . C 3
Corozal . . . . C 2
Corral Viejo . . . . B 2
Coto Laurel . . . . B 2
Culebra . . . . E 2
Dewey (Culebra) . . . . . . E 2
Dorado . . . . C 2
Ensenada . . . . B 3
Esperanza . . . . E 2
Fajardo . . . . D 2
Florida . . . . B 2
Guánica . . . . B 3
Guayama . . . . C 3
Guayanilla . . . . B 2
Guaynabo . . . . C 2
Gurabo . . . . D 2
Hatillo . . . . B 2
Hato Rey . . . . C 2
Hormigüeros . . . . A 2
Humacao . . . . D 2
Isabela . . . . A 1
Isabel Segunda . . . . E 2
Jayuya . . . . B 2
Jobos . . . . C 3
Juana Díaz . . . . C 2
Juncos . . . . D 2
Lajas . . . . A 2
Lares . . . . B 2
Las Marías . . . . B 2
Las Piedras . . . . D 2
Levittown . . . . C 2
Loíza . . . . D 2
Loíza Aldea . . . . D 2
Luquillo . . . . D 2
Manatí . . . . C 2
Maricao . . . . B 2
Maunabo . . . . D 2
Mayagüez . . . . A 2
Moca . . . . A 2
Morovis . . . . C 2
Naguabo . . . . D 2
Naranjito . . . . C 2
Orocovis . . . . C 2
Palmer . . . . D 2
Palo Seco . . . . C 2
Parguera . . . . A 3
Patillas . . . . D 2
Peñuelas . . . . B 2
Playa de Fajardo . . . . . D 2
Playa de Humacao . . . . D 2
Playa de Ponce . . . . B 3
Ponce . . . . B 2
Puerto Nuevo . . . . C 2
Puerto Real . . . . A 2
Puerto Real (Playa de Fajardo) . . . . D 2
Punta Santiago (Playa de Humacao) . . . . D 2
Quebradillas . . . . B 2
Rincón . . . . A 2
Río Blanco . . . . D 2
Río Grande . . . . D 2
Río Piedras . . . . C 2
Rosario . . . . A 2
Sabana Grande . . . . B 2
Sabana Seca . . . . C 2
Salinas . . . . C 3
San Antonio . . . . A 2
San Germán . . . . A 2
San Juan (cap.) . . . . C 1
San Lorenzo . . . . D 2
San Sebastián . . . . B 2
Santa Isabel . . . . C 3
Santurce . . . . C 2
Tallaboa . . . . B 2
Toa Alta . . . . C 2
Toa Baja . . . . C 2
Trujillo Alto . . . . C 2
Utuado . . . . B 2
Vega Alta . . . . C 2
Vega Baja . . . . C 2
Vieques (Isabel Segunda) . . . . E 2
Villalba . . . . C 2
Yabucoa . . . . D 2
Yauco . . . . B 2

Other Features

Aguadilla (bay) . . . . A 2
Arenas (point) . . . . D 2
Bauta (river) . . . . C 2
Bayamón (river) . . . . . . C 2
Boquerón (bay) . . . . A 2
Borinquen (point) . . . . . A 2
Cabullones (point) . . . . . B 3
Caja de Muertos (island) . . . . B 3
Canovanas (river) . . . . . D 2
Caonillas (lake) . . . . B 2
Carite (lake) . . . . C 2
Carraízo (lake) . . . . C 2
Cayey, Sierra de (mts.) . C 2
Central, Cordillera (range) . . . . B 2
Coamo (river) . . . . C 3
Culebra (island) . . . . . . E 2
Culebrinas (river) . . . . . A 2
Culebrita (island) . . . . . E 2
El Toro (mt.) . . . . D 2
El Yunque (mt.) . . . . . . D 2
Este (point) . . . . E 2
Figuras (point) . . . . C 3
Fosforescente (bay) . . . . A 3
Grande de Añasco (river) . . . . A 2
Grande de Arecibo (river) . . . . B 2
Grande de Loíza (river) . . . . D 2
Grande de Manatí (river) . . . . C 2
Guajataca (lake) . . . . . . B 2
Guanajibo (river) . . . . . . A 2
Guaniquilla (point) . . . . . A 2
Guayabal (lake) . . . . C 2
Guayanés (river) . . . . . . D 2
Guayanilla (bay) . . . . . . B 3
Guayo (lake) . . . . B 2
Guilarte (mt.) . . . . B 2
Honda (bay) . . . . D 2
Humacao (river) . . . . . . D 2
Jacaguas (river) . . . . . . B 2
Jaicoa (mts.) . . . . B 2
Jiguero (point) . . . . A 2
Jobos (bay) . . . . C 3
Lima (point) . . . . D 2
Luquillo, Sierra de (mts.) . . . . D 2
Manglillo (point) . . . . . . B 3
Mayagüez (bay) . . . . . . A 2
Miquillo (point) . . . . D 2
Molinos (point) . . . . E 2
Mona (passg.) . . . . A 2
Nigua (river) . . . . C 2
Ola Grande (point) . . . . . C 3
Petrona (point) . . . . C 3
Pirata (mt.) . . . . D 2
Plata (river) . . . . C 2
Puerca (point) . . . . D 2
Puerto Medio Mundo (bay) . . . . D 2
Punta, Cerro de (mt.) . . . B 2
Ramey AFB . . . . A 1
Rincón (bay) . . . . C 3
Rojo (cape) . . . . A 3
Roosevelt Roads Nav. Res. . . . . D 2
Salinas (point) . . . . C 1
San José (lake) . . . . D 2
San Juan, Cabezas de (prom.) . . . . D 2
San Juan National Hist. Site . . . . C 1
Sardina (point) . . . . A 1
Soldado (point) . . . . E 2
Sucia (bay) . . . . A 3
Tanamá (river) . . . . B 2
Torrecilla (lagoon) . . . . . D 2
Tortuguero (lake) . . . . . . C 2
Vacía Talega (point) . . . . D 2
Vieques (island) . . . . . . E 2
Vieques (passg.) . . . . . . D 2
Vieques (sound) . . . . . . E 2
Yagüez (river) . . . . A 2
Yeguas (point) . . . . D 2

Luxury resort hotels dominate this beach scene near the city of Fajardo on the eastern coast of Puerto Rico. Tourism is one of the island's largest revenue sources.
Bob Glander–Shostal Associates

of 70. The major trial court of the commonwealth is the superior court, made up of 108 judges who serve 12-year terms. Judges of both courts are appointed by the governor, with the consent of the senate.

Local Government. Puerto Rico is not divided into counties but has 78 *municipios* (municipalities). Each is governed by a popularly elected mayor and municipal assembly. The mayor appoints a secretary-auditor and a treasurer.

National Representation. Puerto Rico is represented by a nonvoting resident delegate in the U.S. Congress. The delegate is elected by Puerto Ricans to a 4-year term.

Politics. In the early 1990s Puerto Rico's leading political parties were the Popular Democratic party (founded 1938), which advocates the maintenance of commonwealth status, and the New Progressive party (1967), which advocates Puerto Rico's becoming a U.S. state. The small Puerto Rico Independence party (1946) favors independence for the island.

ECONOMY

Economic development in Puerto Rico has historically lagged well behind that of most mainland states of the U.S. Significant improvements have been made in economic conditions since the late 1940s, however, after the development program known as Operation Bootstrap was begun by the government. Growth has occurred largely through stimulation of the manufacturing sector. Much development has been concentrated in the San Juan metropolitan area. In the early 1990s manufacturing was the leading economic activity, and government, commerce, and tourism also were important sources of income.

Agriculture. Puerto Rico has two substantially different agricultural systems: one of very small farms mainly producing subsistence commodities, and another of much larger farms principally producing goods for export. Nearly half the commonwealth's approximately 20,000 farms encompass less than 4 ha (10 acres) each. Only about 1700 farms exceed 40 ha (100 acres) in size, but they account for the dominant share of the annual value of agricultural products sold. Coffee is the most valuable crop, followed by vegetables, sugarcane, bananas, pineapples, and rice. Dairy products, poultry, and beef cattle and calves are also important sources of income.

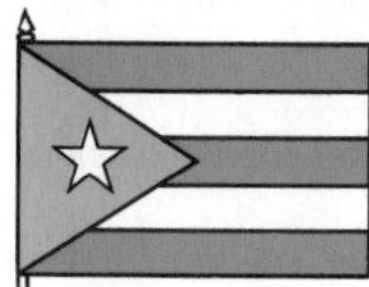

PUERTO RICO

BECAME A COMMONWEALTH: July 25, 1952

CAPITAL:	**San Juan**
MOTTO:	***Joannes est nomen ejus (John is thy name)***
ANTHEM:	**"La Borinqueña" (music by Felix Astol y Artés)**
POPULATION (1990):	**3,522,037**
AREA:	**9104 sq km (3515 sq mi), includes 145 sq km (56 sq mi) of inland water**
COASTLINE:	**501 km (311 mi)**
HIGHEST POINT:	**Cerro de Punta, 1338 m (4389 ft)**
LOWEST POINT:	**Sea level**
COMMONWEALTH LEGISLATURE:	**27 members of the senate; 53 members of the house of representatives**

ECONOMY

Commonwealth budget	general revenue $5.7 billion
	general expenditure $5.6 billion
	accumulated debt $12.6 billion
Gross domestic product	$32.5 billion
Manufacturing	39%
Commercial, financial, and professional services	38%
Government	11%
Agriculture	1%
Merchandise trade	imports $15.0 billion
	exports $17.5 billion
Personal income, per capita	$5653
Assets, insured commercial banks (15)	$15.1 billion
Labor force (civilian nonfarm)	1,063,000
Employed in government	20%
Employed in trade	17%
Employed in manufacturing	15%
Employed in agriculture	3%

	Annual Payroll
MANUFACTURING	**$2.2 billion**
Chemicals and allied products	$555 million
Food and kindred products	$287 million
Electronic equipment	$285 million
Apparel and textile mill products	$273 million
Instruments and related products	$142 million
Industrial machinery and equipment	$121 million
Rubber and plastics products	$101 million
Stone, clay, and glass products	$56 million
Leather and leather products	$55 million
Fabricated metal products	$54 million
Printing and publishing	$51 million

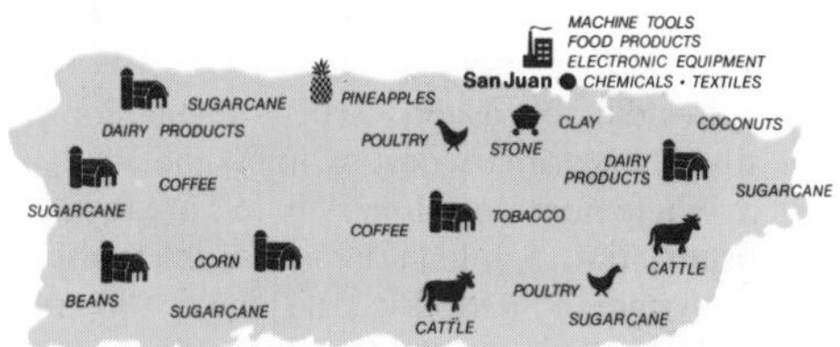

PRINCIPAL PRODUCTS OF PUERTO RICO

CLIMATE	SAN JUAN	SANTA ISABEL
Average January temperature range	20.6° to 27.8° C (69° to 82° F)	18.3° to 28.3° C (65° to 83° F)
Average July temperature range	23.9° to 30.6° C (75° to 87° F)	22.2° to 30.6° C (72° to 87° F)
Average annual temperature	26.1° C (79° F)	25° C (77° F)
Average annual precipitation	1499 mm (59 in)	838 mm (33 in)
Average number of days per year with appreciable precipitation	200	99
Mean number of clear days	58	105

COASTAL PLAIN

CENTRAL MOUNTAINS

NATURAL REGIONS OF PUERTO RICO

Forestry and Fishing. Much of Puerto Rico's forest cover had been cut by about 1900, and despite concerted efforts after 1935 to replant trees, the forestry industry remains small. Commercial fishing plays a relatively minor role in Puerto Rico's economy. Tuna species caught include yellowfin, skipjack, and bluefin. Small-scale freshwater fish farming is a growing economic activity; fish raised include bass, bluegill, and catfish.

Mining. The value of the minerals extracted in Puerto Rico exceeds $160 million annually. Almost all of Puerto Rico's mineral production consists of construction materials, notably cement, sand, gravel, and stone. Other minerals are clay, graphite, lime, and salt.

Manufacturing. Manufacturing activity in Puerto Rico has been encouraged by government incentives such as tax exemptions, loans, and research assistance. The island has benefited from importing capital, technology, and entrepreneurship from the conterminous U.S. Apparel making is Puerto Rico's leading manufacturing industry in terms of employment, followed by the production of electronic goods, processed foods, and chemicals. The modern apparel industry evolved from a small-scale labor-intensive needlework industry of the 1940s, and most apparel plants are branches of mainland U.S. firms. San Juan and Mayagüez are the leading centers for making clothing. Other major manufactures include pharmaceuticals, industrial machinery, printed materials, rubber and plastics, metal items, precision instruments, timepieces, footwear, and alcoholic beverages.

Tourism. The warm year-round climate in Puerto Rico and its abundant sunshine and coastal beaches attract about 3.5 million tourists each year; spending by visitors exceeds $1.4 billion annually. Their primary destination is the San Juan area, where numerous luxury hotels are located.

Transportation. San Juan dominates the transportation system of Puerto Rico. It is the leading port and also has the busiest airport, Puerto Rico International Airport. Transportation facilities in the rest of the island are generally much poorer than on the mainland of the U.S. Altogether, Puerto Rico is served by about 19,340 km (about 12,020 mi) of roads, the great majority of which are paved. The island's limited railroad trackage is used to haul sugarcane, especially in the Ponce area of the S.

Energy. Puerto Rico's installed electricity generating capacity is about 4.2 million kw, and yearly production in the mid-1980s was approximately 12.3 billion kwh. Approximately 98% of the commonwealth's electricity was generated in thermal plants, most of which burned refined petroleum. Most of the rest was produced in hydroelectric installations. J.D.Lo.

HISTORY

Christopher Columbus reached the island and claimed it for Spain on Nov. 19, 1493. He named it San Juan Bautista. It became known as Puerto Rico after 1521, when the city of San Juan had been founded and given the island's original name.

Spanish Conquest and Settlement. Puerto Rico was conquered for Spain in 1509 by Juan Ponce de León, who became the first governor. The island was originally peopled by the Borinqueno Indians, an agricultural people who were enslaved and largely exterminated as the result of harsh treatment. As the Indians were decimated, they were replaced by black African slaves who worked the plantations and sugar mills.

Privateers and pirates harassed the island's residents during the early colonial years. The Spanish constructed strong fortifications and in 1595 defeated the English navigators Sir Francis Drake and Sir John Hawkins when they attempted to capture Puerto Rico; Hawkins was mortally wounded. Raids, however, continued for a long time. San Juan was burned during a Dutch attack in 1625, and the English sacked Arecibo in 1702.

Puerto Rico was opened to foreign trade in 1804, and in 1808 it was accorded representation in the Spanish Parliament. Short-lived uprisings against Spanish rule occurred a few times during the 19th century (the most serious uprising, known as El Grito de Lares, took place in 1868), but all were quickly suppressed. Slavery was abolished in 1873. The island was granted autonomy in 1897.

Spanish-American War and U.S. Control. As a result of the Spanish-American War, Puerto Rico was ceded to the U.S. by the Treaty of Paris, Dec. 10, 1898. In 1900 the U.S. Congress established a civil government on the island. U.S. citizenship was granted to Puerto Ricans in 1917, and the U.S. instituted measures designed to solve various economic and social problems of the overpopulated island. From 1940 to 1948 a hydroelectric-power expansion program was instituted to attract U.S. industry and to provide more employment for Puerto Ricans. Irrigation projects were also initiated. During World War II the island became a key U.S. military base. Naval bases were constructed in San Juan harbor and on Culebra.

Under the leadership of Luis Muñoz Marín, head of the Popular Democratic party, a development program known as Operation Bootstrap was launched in 1942, resulting in greatly in-

The Castle of El Morro, built between 1539 and 1584, made San Juan the strongest Spanish fortress in the New World. Puerto Rico Tourism Dev. Co.

creased manufacturing and a large rise in the general living standard. In 1948, Muñoz became the first elected governor of the island.

Commonwealth Status. On June 4, 1951, Puerto Rican voters approved in a referendum a U.S. law that granted them the right to draft their own constitution. The constituent assembly began its deliberations in the following September. In March 1952 the electorate approved the new constitution, and on July 25 Gov. Muñoz proclaimed the Commonwealth of Puerto Rico. The commonwealth held its first general election under the new statute on November 4; Muñoz and the Popular Democratic party received an overwhelming majority. The Nationalist party, which advocated independence, did not participate.

The attainment of commonwealth status did not halt agitation for total independence. Pro-independence sentiment, which had led to an attempt on the life of U.S. President Harry S. Truman in 1950, again erupted violently in March 1954, when four nationalists fired shots into the chamber of the U.S. House of Representatives, wounding five members.

Gov. Muñoz was reelected in 1956 and 1960, and his victory was regarded as a popular endorsement not only of his economic and social policies but also of commonwealth status. In a referendum held in July 1967, Puerto Ricans once more voted to remain a commonwealth.

The Statehood Question. In the election of 1968, Luis Alberto Ferré (1904–), candidate of the New Progressive party, was elected governor. He favored statehood for Puerto Rico but believed that its economy would not be ready for it before 1980. In 1972, in an upset, the Popular Democratic party returned to power when Rafael Hernández Colón (1936–), who was a supporter of commonwealth status, defeated Ferré for the governorship. The New Progressive party regained control of the legislature in 1976, and its candidate for the governorship, Carlos Romero Barceló (1932–), was also a winner.

Romero, a firm advocate of statehood, chose to play down the issue after the 1980 elections, in which he retained his office by only a narrow margin, and the Popular Democratic party scored impressive victories in legislative and mayoral contests. Meanwhile, extreme nationalist groups such as the U.S.-based Armed Forces of National Liberation (Fuerzas Armadas de Liberación Nacional, or FALN) used terrorist tactics in the late 1970s and early '80s to press the cause of independence for Puerto Rico. In 1984, Hernández Colón won the governorship from Romero, and the Popular Democratic party established commanding majorities in both legislative houses; he was reelected in 1988. The legislature voted to make Spanish Puerto Rico's official language. After losing a symbolic plebiscite on the commonwealth question in 1991, Hernández Colón decided not to run for another term. In 1992 Pedro Rosselló (1944–) of the New Progressive party was elected governor on a pro-statehood platform.

For further information on this topic, see the Bibliography in volume 28, section 1135.

PUFFBALL, any of about 270 species of globular fungi (q.v.), order Lycoperdales, that proliferate in moist humus or on decaying tree stumps. The mature fruiting body becomes leathery and dry and, when disturbed, emits puffs of powdery spores through an opening at the top. The giant puffball, *Calvatia gigantea,* one of the many species that are edible when immature, grows as large as 1.2 m (4 ft) across. Earthstars, the leathery covers of which peel back in the form of stars, are also puffballs.

PUFFER, any of about 120 species of fish constituting the family Tetraodontidae. Most live in tropical seas, but a few occur in fresh or brackish waters. The teeth of the upper and lower jaws are separately fused with a vertical gap in front—hence the family name, which means "four-toothed." Like the related porcupine fish (q.v.), the puffer uses its beaklike teeth for feeding on corals or hardshelled animals. Puffers are usually about 45 cm (about 18 in) long, although some species are larger. Also called blowfish and globefish, they are named for their habit of inflating themselves with water or air when threatened. They are used as food fish, but some species are poisonous unless prepared properly.

PUFFIN, common name for the three species of birds of the genus *Fratercula,* of the family Alcidae (*see* AUK), characterized by large, triangular, laterally flattened bills, of which the outer layers are shed after the breeding season. The Atlantic puffin, *F. arctica,* is black above and white below, with the bill patterned in red, yellow, and bluish gray. The horned puffin, *F. corniculata,* of the northern Pacific coast, is similar in body color but with a yellow, red-tipped bill. Also from the Pacific but breeding south to California is the tufted puffin, *F. cirrhata,* with an all-black body, white face, and long, straw-colored plumes curving behind the eye.

PUG, breed of toy dog, believed to have originated in China, from which it may have been imported into England in the 17th century; the modern pug is descended from dogs subsequently developed by English breeders. The dog has a short, compact body; a large, round, and massive head; a short, square, and blunt muzzle; large, bold, dark eyes; straight legs; and a tightly curled tail. The coat is close-haired, soft, and glossy; the color is silver or apricot-fawn, in either case with a black trace from midskull to tail; or it is solid black. About 30 cm (about 12 in) high at the shoulder, weighing 6 to 8 kg (14 to 18 lb), the pug is a popular pet.

PUGET SOUND, arm of the Pacific Ocean, W Washington State, extending about 130 km (about 80 mi) from Admiralty Inlet to Olympia, Wash. It is divided into several branches and is navigable by large vessels. The principal ports of the sound are Seattle and Tacoma on the E shore, Bremerton on the W shore, and Port Townsend at the entrance. Puget Sound is named for Peter Puget (1762–1822), a British naval officer who accompanied the British explorer George Vancouver to the Pacific Northwest (1792–95).

PUGIN, Augustus Welby Northmore (1812–52), English architect and furniture designer, who championed the 19th-century Gothic Revival (q.v.) in England. His first and most influential work was his quasi-ecclesiastical interior and exterior decoration and furniture for the new Houses of Parliament (begun 1836) in London, designed by the British architect Sir Charles Barry. This work, along with his 1836 treatise *Contrasts* on the Gothic style, earned him many commissions; he executed many churches, town and country houses, and municipal and collegiate buildings. Pugin's devotion to the Gothic manner was based more on his reactionary, somewhat fanatical, religious convictions than on any inherent understanding of Gothic architecture; his executed designs tended to be stiff and two-dimensional. His influence on Victorian English architecture and interior design was derived mainly from his books and published drawings.

PUKASKWA NATIONAL PARK, S Ontario, administered by the Canadian government since 1978. Situated on the N shore of Lake Superior, the park encompasses islets in the lake and, inland, a hilly wilderness region with many rivers and streams. It has a great variety of wildlife. Area, 1878 sq km (725 sq mi).

PULASKI, Casimir (1748–79), Polish nobleman and army officer, born in Podolia (now in Ukraine). In 1768 Pulaski took part in the Confederation of Bar, a patriotic Polish revolt against Russian control of Poland, and became a leader of the patriots. The revolt was unsuccessful and he escaped to Turkey. In 1775 he was in France, where the representative of the American colonies, Benjamin Franklin, induced him to join the colonists' fight against Great Britain. He arrived in Philadelphia and entered the Continental army in 1777. For distinguished service at the Battle of the Brandywine, he was appointed chief of dragoons with the rank of brigadier general.

In 1778, with a commission from the Continental Congress, Pulaski organized an independent corps of cavalry and light infantry, known as the Pulaski Legion. Pulaski and the corps were ordered to South Carolina in 1779 to support the American general Benjamin Lincoln (1733–1810). They reached Charleston, S.C., in May and helped to defend the city against a British attack. Later that year Pulaski joined forces with Gen.

The puli has a long, dense coat that falls naturally into heavy corded belts. H. Reinhard–Bruce Coleman, Inc.

Lincoln, who, assisted by a French force, was planning to besiege Savannah, Ga. The Polish general commanded the French and American cavalry during the siege, but in an attack on Oct. 9, 1779, he was wounded and died two days later.

PULI (pl. pulik), breed of working dog, used as a sheepdog in Hungary for more than 1000 years. Brought in by the Magyars, it may have orginated from the Tibetan terrier. This small, dark haired dog worked sheep during the day; the lighter colored, larger komondor and kuvasz were used to guard the sheep at night. The puli's coat is its distinctive feature and acts as a natural protector. It is dull black with tinges of bronze or gray or gray and white. The dense, woolly undercoat tangles with the profuse topcoat to form long matted cords over the length of the body and the head when not groomed. Intelligent and vigorous, the puli makes an ideal watchdog and companion. It averages 43 cm (17 in) in height and about 13 kg (about 30 lb) in weight.

PULITZER, Joseph (1847–1911), American journalist, born in Makó, Hungary. Pulitzer immigrated to the U.S. in 1864 and served in the First New York Cavalry during the American Civil War. He became an American citizen in 1867, a reporter on a German daily, the *Westliche Post,* in Saint Louis, Mo., the same year, and managing editor and part owner of the newspaper in 1871. Two years later he left the paper. After receiving a law degree and working as a correspondent for the *New York Sun,* in 1878 he bought the *St. Louis Evening Dispatch* and *Evening Post,* combining them into the *Post-Dispatch.* In 1883 he acquired the *New York World.* Under his management, it became a major paper, famous for sensationalism, exposés, careful and extensive reportage, crusades against corruption, and a strong prolabor stance. In 1887 he broke down from overwork, but although invalid, blind, and often absent, he continued his supervision. In 1903 he provided for the Pulitzer Prizes in literature and journalism and donated $1 million to Columbia University for the founding of a school of journalism.

PULITZER PRIZES, series of awards for outstanding achievements in letters and journalism, established by the will of Joseph Pulitzer, publisher of the *New York World.* They have been presented annually since 1917 by Columbia University on recommendation of the advisory board of the school of journalism.

A newspaper photography award was made for the first time in 1942 and an award for a musical composition for the first time in 1943. Between 1970 and 1985, prizes for commentary, criticism, and feature writing were added; categories for news reporting have been revised several times. The value of the prizes for journalism and the arts is $3000 (originally $500); for meritorious public service, a gold medal is awarded instead. Dates following a prize title indicate the period during which an award in that category was given. No awards were given for years omitted.

For further information on this topic, see the Bibliography in volume 28, section 2.

PULITZER PRIZE WINNERS

BIOGRAPHY OR AUTOBIOGRAPHY

1917 *Julia Ward Howe,* Laura E. Richards and Maude Howe Elliott assisted by Florence Howe Hall
1918 *Benjamin Franklin, Self-Revealed,* William Cabell Bruce
1919 *The Education of Henry Adams,* Henry Adams
1920 *The Life of John Marshall,* Albert J. Beveridge
1921 *The Americanization of Edward Bok,* Edward Bok
1922 *A Daughter of the Middle Border,* Hamlin Garland
1923 *The Life and Letters of Walter H. Page,* Burton J. Hendrick
1924 *From Immigrant to Inventor,* Michael Idvorsky Pupin
1925 *Barrett Wendell and His Letters,* M. A. DeWolfe Howe
1926 *The Life of Sir William Osler,* Harvey Cushing
1927 *Whitman,* Emory Holloway
1928 *The American Orchestra and Theodore Thomas,* Charles Edward Russell
1929 *The Training of an American: The Earlier Life and Letters of Walter H. Page,* Burton J. Hendrick
1930 *The Raven,* Marquis James
1931 *Charles W. Eliot,* Henry James
1932 *Theodore Roosevelt,* Henry F. Pringle
1933 *Grover Cleveland,* Allan Nevins
1934 *John Hay,* Tyler Dennett
1935 *R. E. Lee,* Douglas S. Freeman
1936 *The Thought and Character of William James,* Ralph Barton Perry
1937 *Hamilton Fish,* Allan Nevins
1938 *Pedlar's Progress,* Odell Shepard; *Andrew Jackson,* Marquis James
1939 *Benjamin Franklin,* Carl Van Doren
1940 *Woodrow Wilson, Life and Letters,* Vol. VII and VIII, Ray Stannard Baker
1941 *Jonathan Edwards,* Ola Elizabeth Winslow
1942 *Crusader in Crinoline,* Forrest Wilson
1943 *Admiral of the Ocean Sea,* Samuel Eliot Morison
1944 *The American Leonardo: The Life of Samuel F. B. Morse,* Carlton Mabee
1945 *George Bancroft: Brahmin Rebel,* Russell Blaine Nye
1946 *Son of the Wilderness,* Linnie Marsh Wolfe
1947 *The Autobiography of William Allen White*
1948 *Forgotten First Citizen: John Bigelow,* Margaret Clapp
1949 *Roosevelt and Hopkins,* Robert E. Sherwood
1950 *John Quincy Adams and the Foundations of American Foreign Policy,* Samuel Flagg Bemis

1951 *John C. Calhoun: American Portrait,* Margaret Louis Coit
1952 *Charles Evans Hughes,* Merlo J. Pusey
1953 *Edmund Pendleton, 1721–1803,* David J. Mays
1954 *The Spirit of St. Louis,* Charles A. Lindbergh
1955 *The Taft Story,* William S. White
1956 *Benjamin Henry Latrobe,* Talbot F. Hamlin
1957 *Profiles in Courage,* John F. Kennedy
1958 *George Washington,* Douglas S. Freeman (Vol. 1–6) and John Alexander Carroll and Mary Wells Ashworth (Vol. 7)
1959 *Woodrow Wilson, American Prophet,* Arthur Walworth
1960 *John Paul Jones,* Samuel Eliot Morison
1961 *Charles Sumner and the Coming of the Civil War,* David Donald
1963 *Henry James:* Vol. II, *The Conquest of London,* and Vol. III, *The Middle Years,* Leon Edel
1964 *John Keats,* Walter Jackson Bate
1965 *Henry Adams,* Ernest Samuels
1966 *A Thousand Days: John F. Kennedy in the White House,* Arthur M. Schlesinger, Jr.
1967 *Mr. Clemens and Mark Twain,* Justin Kaplan
1968 *Memoirs (1925–1950),* George F. Kennan
1969 *The Man from New York: John Quinn and His Friends,* Benjamin Lawrence Reid
1970 *Huey Long,* T. Harry Williams
1971 *Robert Frost: The Years of Triumph, 1915–1938,* Lawrence R. Thompson
1972 *Eleanor and Franklin,* Joseph P. Lash
1973 *Luce and His Empire,* W. A. Swanberg
1974 *O'Neill, Son and Artist,* Louis Sheaffer
1975 *The Power Broker: Robert Moses and the Fall of New York,* Robert A. Caro
1976 *Edith Wharton,* R. W. B. Lewis
1977 *A Prince of Our Disorder: The Life of T. E. Lawrence,* John E. Mack
1978 *Samuel Johnson,* Walter Jackson Bate
1979 *Days of Sorrow and Pain: Leo Baeck and the Berlin Jews,* Leonard Baker
1980 *The Rise of Theodore Roosevelt,* Edmund Morris
1981 *Peter the Great: His Life and World,* Robert K. Massie
1982 *Grant: A Biography,* William S. McFeely
1983 *Growing Up,* Russell Baker
1984 *Booker T. Washington,* Louis R. Harlan
1985 *The Life and Times of Cotton Mather,* Kenneth Silverman
1986 *Louise Bogan: A Portrait,* Elizabeth Frank
1987 *Bearing the Cross: Martin Luther King Jr. and the Southern Christian Leadership Congress,* David J. Garrow
1988 *Look Homeward: A Life of Thomas Wolfe,* David Herbert Donald
1989 *Oscar Wilde,* Richard Ellmann
1990 *Machiavelli in Hell,* Sebastian de Grazia
1991 *Jackson Pollock: An American Saga,* Steven Naifeh and Gregory White Smith
1992 *Fortunate Son: The Healing of a Vietnam Vet,* Lewis B. Puller, Jr.
1993 *Truman,* David McCullough

CARTOONS

1922 Rollin Kirby (*New York World*)
1924 Jay Norwood Darling (*New York Tribune*)
1925 Rollin Kirby (*New York World*)
1926 D. R. Fitzpatrick (*St. Louis* [Mo.] *Post-Dispatch*)
1927 Nelson Harding (*Brooklyn* [N.Y.] *Daily Eagle*)
1928 Nelson Harding (*Brooklyn* [N.Y.] *Daily Eagle*)
1929 Rollin Kirby (*New York World*)
1930 Charles R. Macauley (*Brooklyn* [N.Y.] *Daily Eagle*)
1931 Edmund Duffy (*Baltimore* [Md.] *Sun*)
1932 John T. McCutcheon (*Chicago Tribune*)
1933 Harold Morton Talburt (*Washington* [D.C.] *Daily News*)
1934 Edmund Duffy (*Baltimore* [Md.] *Sun*)
1935 Ross A. Lewis (*Milwaukee* [Wis.] *Journal*)
1937 Clarence Daniel Batchelor (*New York Daily News*)
1938 Vaughn Shoemaker (*Chicago Daily News*)
1939 Charles G. Werner (*Oklahoma City* [Okla.] *Daily-Oklahoman*)
1940 Edmund Duffy (*Baltimore* [Md.] *Sun*)
1941 Jacob Burck (*Chicago Times*)
1942 Herbert L. Block (Newspaper Enterprise Association Service)
1943 Jay Norwood Darling (*New York Herald Tribune*)
1944 Clifford K. Berryman (*Washington* [D.C.] *Evening Star*)
1945 Bill Mauldin (United Feature Syndicate)
1946 Bruce Alexander Russell (*Los Angeles Times*)
1947 Vaughn Shoemaker (*Chicago Daily News*)
1948 Reuben O. (Rube) Goldberg (*New York Sun*)
1949 Lute Pease (*Newark* [N.J.] *Evening News*)
1950 James T. Berryman (*Washington* [D.C.] *Evening Star*)
1951 Reginald W. Manning (*Phoenix Arizona Republic*)
1952 Fred L. Packer (*New York Mirror*)
1953 Edward D. Kuekes (*Cleveland* [Ohio] *Plain Dealer*)
1954 Herbert L. Block (*Washington* [D.C.] *Post* and *Times Herald*)
1955 Daniel R. Fitzpatrick (*St. Louis* [Mo.] *Post-Dispatch*)
1956 Robert York (*Louisville* [Ky.] *Times*)
1957 Tom Little (*Nashville Tennessean*)
1958 Bruce M. Shanks (*Buffalo* [N.Y.] *Evening News*)
1959 Bill Mauldin (*St. Louis* [Mo.] *Post-Dispatch*)
1961 Carey Orr (*Chicago Tribune*)
1962 Edmund S. Valtman (*Hartford* [Conn.] *Times*)
1963 Frank Miller (*Des Moines* [Iowa] *Register*)
1964 Paul Conrad (*Denver* [Colo.] *Post*)
1966 Don Wright (*Miami* [Fla.] *News*)
1967 Patrick B. Oliphant (*Denver* [Colo.] *Post*)
1968 Eugene Gray Payne (*Charlotte* [N.C.] *Observer*)
1969 John Fischetti (*Chicago Daily News*)
1970 Thomas F. Darcy (*Newsday,* Garden City, N.Y.)
1971 Paul Conrad (*Los Angeles Times*)
1972 Jeff MacNelly (*Richmond* [Va.] *News Leader*)
1974 Paul Michael Szep (*Boston Globe*)
1975 Garry Trudeau (*Doonesbury,* Universal Press Syndicate)
1976 Tony Auth (*Philadelphia Inquirer*)
1977 Paul Szep (*Boston Globe*)
1978 Jeff MacNelly (*Richmond* [Va.] *News Leader*)
1979 Herbert L. Block (*Washington* [D.C.] *Post*)
1980 Don Wright (*Miami* [Fla.] *News*)
1981 Mike Peters (*Dayton* [Ohio] *Daily News*)
1982 Ben Sargent (*Austin* [Tex.] *American-Statesman*)
1983 Richard Locher (*Chicago Tribune*)
1984 Paul Conrad (*Los Angeles Times*)
1985 Jeff MacNelly (*Chicago Tribune*)
1986 Jules Feiffer (*Village Voice,* New York, N.Y.)
1987 Berke Breathed (*Bloom County,* The Washington Post Writers Group)
1988 Doug Marlette (*Atlanta* [Ga.] *Constitution* and *Charlotte* [N.C.] *Observer*)
1989 Jack Higgins (*Chicago Sun-Times*)
1990 Tom Toles (*Buffalo* [N.Y.] *News*)
1991 Jim Borgman (*Cincinnati* [Ohio] *Enquirer*)
1992 Signe Wilkinson (*Philadelphia Daily News*)
1993 Stephen R. Benson (*Arizona Republic*)

COMMENTARY

1970 Marquis Childs (*St. Louis* [Mo.] *Post-Dispatch*)
1971 William A. Caldwell (*Record,* Hackensack, N.J.)
1972 Mike Royko (*Chicago Daily News*)
1973 Davis S. Broder (*Washington* [D.C.] *Post*)
1974 Edwin A. Roberts, Jr. (*National Observer*)
1975 Mary McGrory (*Washington* [D.C.] *Star-News*)
1976 Walter (Red) Smith (*New York Times*)
1977 George F. Will (*Washington* [D.C.] *Post*)
1978 William Safire (*New York Times*)
1979 Russell Baker (*New York Times*)
1980 Ellen Goodman (*Boston Globe*)
1981 Dave Anderson (*New York Times*)
1982 Art Buchwald (Los Angeles Times Syndicate)
1983 Claude Sitton (*Raleigh* [N.C.] *News & Observer*)
1984 Vermont Royster (*Wall Street Journal*)
1985 Murray Kempton (*Newsday*)
1986 Jimmy Breslin (*New York Daily News*)
1987 Charles Krauthammer (The Washington Post Writers Group)
1988 Dave Barry (*Miami* [Fla.] *Herald*)
1989 Clarence Page (*Chicago Tribune*)
1990 Jim Murray (*Los Angeles Times*)
1991 Jim Hoagland (*Washington* [D.C.] *Post*)
1992 Anna Quindlen (*New York Times*)
1993 Liz Balmaseda (*Miami* [Fla.] *Herald*)

CRITICISM

1970 Ada Louise Huxtable (*New York Times*)
1971 Harold C. Schonberg (*New York Times*)
1972 Frank Peters, Jr. (*St. Louis* [Mo.] *Post-Dispatch*)
1973 Ronald Powers (*Chicago Sun-Times*)
1974 Emily Genauer (Newsday Syndicate, Garden City, N.Y.)
1975 Roger Ebert (*Chicago Sun-Times*)
1976 Alan M. Kriegsman (*Washington* [D.C.] *Post*)
1977 William McPherson (*Washington* [D.C.] *Post*)
1978 Walter Kerr (*New York Times*)
1979 Paul Gapp (*Chicago Tribune*)
1980 William A. Henry III (*Boston Globe*)
1981 Jonathan Yardley (*Washington* [D.C.] *Star*)
1982 Martin Bernheimer (*Los Angeles Times*)
1983 Manuela Hoelterhoff (*Wall Street Journal*)
1984 Paul Goldberger (*New York Times*)
1985 Howard Rosenberg (*Los Angeles Times*)
1986 Donal Henahan (*New York Times*)
1987 Richard Eder (*Los Angeles Times*)
1988 Tom Shales (*Washington* [D.C.] *Post*)
1989 Michael Skube (*Raleigh* [N.C.] *News & Observer*)
1990 Allan Temko (*San Francisco Chronicle*)
1991 David Shaw (*Los Angeles Times*)
1993 Michael Dirda (*Washington* [D.C.] *Post*)

DRAMA

1918 *Why Marry?* Jesse Lynch Williams
1920 *Beyond the Horizon*, Eugene O'Neill
1921 *Miss Lulu Bett*, Zona Gale
1922 *Anna Christie*, Eugene O'Neill
1923 *Icebound*, Owen Davis
1924 *Hell-Bent for Heaven*, Hatcher Hughes
1925 *They Knew What They Wanted*, Sidney Howard
1926 *Craig's Wife*, George Kelly
1927 *In Abraham's Bosom*, Paul Green
1928 *Strange Interlude*, Eugene O'Neill
1929 *Street Scene*, Elmer L. Rice
1930 *The Green Pastures*, Marc Connelly
1931 *Alison's House*, Susan Glaspell
1932 *Of Thee I Sing*, George S. Kaufman, Morrie Ryskind, and Ira Gershwin
1933 *Both Your Houses*, Maxwell Anderson
1934 *Men in White*, Sidney Kingsley
1935 *The Old Maid*, Zoe Akins
1936 *Idiot's Delight*, Robert E. Sherwood
1937 *You Can't Take It with You*, Moss Hart and George S. Kaufman
1938 *Our Town*, Thornton Wilder
1939 *Abe Lincoln in Illinois*, Robert E. Sherwood
1940 *The Time of Your Life*, William Saroyan (award declined)
1941 *There Shall Be No Night*, Robert E. Sherwood
1943 *The Skin of Our Teeth*, Thornton Wilder
1945 *Harvey*, Mary Chase
1946 *State of the Union*, Russel Crouse and Howard Lindsay
1948 *A Streetcar Named Desire*, Tennessee Williams
1949 *Death of a Salesman*, Arthur Miller
1950 *South Pacific*, Richard Rodgers, Oscar Hammerstein II, and Joshua Logan
1952 *The Shrike*, Joseph Kramm
1953 *Picnic*, William Inge
1954 *The Teahouse of the August Moon*, John Patrick
1955 *Cat on a Hot Tin Roof*, Tennessee Williams
1956 *The Diary of Anne Frank*, Frances Goodrich and Albert Hackett
1957 *Long Day's Journey into Night*, Eugene O'Neill
1958 *Look Homeward Angel*, Ketti Frings
1959 *J.B.*, Archibald MacLeish
1960 *Fiorello!*, Geroge Abbott, Jerome Weidman, Sheldon Harnick, and Jerry Bock
1961 *All the Way Home*, Tad Mosel
1962 *How to Succeed in Business Without Really Trying*, Abe Burrows and Frank Loesser
1965 *The Subject was Roses*, Frank D. Gilroy
1967 *A Delicate Balance*, Edward Albee
1969 *The Great White Hope*, Howard Sackler
1970 *No Place to Be Somebody*, Charles Gordone
1971 *The Effect of Gamma Rays on Man-in-the-Moon Marigolds*, Paul Zindel
1973 *That Championship Season*, Jason Miller
1975 *Seascape*, Edward Albee
1976 *A Chorus Line*, Michael Bennett, James Kirkwood, Nicholas Dante, and Edward Kleban
1977 *The Shadow Box*, Michael Cristofer
1978 *The Gin Game*, Donald L. Coburn
1979 *Buried Child*, Sam Shepard
1980 *Talley's Folly*, Lanford Wilson
1981 *Crimes of the Heart*, Beth Henley
1982 *A Soldier's Play*, Charles Fuller
1983 *'night, Mother*, Marsha Norman
1984 *Glengarry Glen Ross*, David Mamet
1985 *Sunday in the Park with George*, Stephen Sondheim and James Lapine
1987 *Fences*, August Wilson
1988 *Driving Miss Daisy*, Alfred Uhry
1989 *The Heidi Chronicles*, Wendy Wasserstein
1990 *The Piano Lesson*, August Wilson
1991 *Lost in Yonkers*, Neil Simon
1992 *The Kentucky Cycle*, Robert Schenkkan
1993 *Angels in America: Millennium Approaches*, Tony Kushner

EDITORIAL WRITING

1917 *New York Tribune*
1918 *Louisville* (Ky.) *Courier-Journal*
1920 Harvey E. Newbranch (*Omaha* [Nebr.] *Evening World-Herald*)
1922 Frank M. O'Brien (*New York Herald*)
1923 William Allen White (*Emporia* [Kans.] *Gazette*)
1924 *Boston Herald;* special prize to Frank I. Cobb (*New York World*)
1925 *Charleston* (S.C.) *News and Courier*
1926 Edward M. Kingsbury (*New York Times*)
1927 F. Laurison Bullard (*Boston Herald*)
1928 Grover Cleveland Hall (*Montgomery* [Ala.] *Advertiser*)
1929 Louis Isaac Jaffe (*Norfolk Virginian-Pilot*)
1931 Charles S. Ryckman (*Fremont* [Nebr.] *Tribune*)
1933 *Kansas City* (Mo.) *Star*
1934 E.P. Chase (*Atlantic* [Iowa] *News Telegraph*)
1936 Felix Morley (*Washington* [D.C.] *Post*); George B. Parker (Scripps-Howard Newspapers)
1937 John W. Owens (*Baltimore* [Md.] *Sun*)
1938 W. W. Waymack (*Des Moines* [Iowa] *Register and Tribune*)
1939 Ronald G. Callvert (*Portland Oregonian*)
1940 Bart Howard (*St. Louis* [Mo.] *Post-Dispatch*)
1941 Reuben Maury (*New York Daily News*)
1942 Geoffrey Parsons (*New York Herald Tribune*)
1943 Forrest W. Seymour (*Des Moines* [Iowa] *Register and Tribune*)
1944 Henry J. Haskell (*Kansas City* [Mo.] *Star*)
1945 George W. Potter (*Providence* [R.I.] *Journal-Bulletin*)
1946 Hodding Carter (*Greenville* [Miss.] *Delta Democrat-Times*)
1947 William H. Grimes (*Wall Street Journal*)
1948 Virginius Dabney (*Richmond* [Va.] *Times-Dispatch*)
1949 John H. Crider (*Boston Herald*) and Herbert Elliston (*Washington* [D.C.] *Post*)
1950 Carl M. Saunders (*Jackson* [Mich.] *Citizen Patriot*)
1951 William H. Fitzpatrick (*New Orleans* [La.] *States*)
1952 Louis LaCoss (*St. Louis* [Mo.] *Globe-Democrat*)
1953 Vermont C. Royster (*Wall Street Journal*)
1954 Don Murray (*Boston Herald*)
1955 Royce Howes (*Detroit Free Press*)
1956 Loren Soth (*Des Moines* [Iowa] *Register and Tribune*)
1957 Buford Boone (*Tuscaloosa* [Ala.] *News*)
1958 Harry S. Ashmore (*Little Rock Arkansas Gazette*)
1959 Ralph McGill (*Atlanta* [Ga.] *Constitution*)
1960 Lenoir Chambers (*Norfolk Virginian-Pilot*)
1961 William J. Dorvillier (*San Juan* [Puerto Rico] *Star*)
1962 Thomas M. Storke (*Santa Barbara* [Calif.] *News-Press*)
1963 Ira B. Harkey, Jr. (*Pascagoula* [Miss.] *Chronicle*)
1964 Hazel Brannon Smith (*Lexington* [Miss.] *Advertiser*)
1965 John R. Harrison (*Gainesville* [Fla.] *Sun*)
1966 Robert Lasch (*St. Louis* [Mo.] *Post-Dispatch*)
1967 Eugene C. Patterson (*Atlanta* [Ga.] *Constitution*)
1968 John S. Knight (Knight Newspapers)
1969 Paul Greenberg (*Pine Bluff* [Ark.] *Commercial*)
1970 Philip L. Geyelin (*Washington* [D.C.] *Post*)
1971 Horance G. Davis, Jr. (*Gainesville* [Fla.] *Sun*)
1972 John Strohmeyer (*Bethlehem* [Pa.] *Globe-Times*)
1973 Roger B. Linscott (*Berkshire Eagle*, Pittsfield, Mass.)
1974 F. Gilman Spencer (*Trenton* [N.J.] *Trentonian*)
1975 John Daniell Maurice (*Charleston* [W.Va.] *Daily Mail*)
1976 Philip K. Kerby (*Los Angeles Times*)
1977 Warren L. Lerude, Foster Church, and Norman F. Cardoza (*Reno* [Nev.] *Evening Gazette* and *Nevada State Journal*)
1978 Meg Greenfield (*Washington* [D.C.] *Post*)
1979 Edwin M. Yoder, Jr. (*Washington* [D.C.] *Star*)
1980 Robert L. Bartley (*Wall Street Journal*)
1982 Jack Rosenthal (*New York Times*)
1983 *Miami* (Fla.) *Herald*
1984 Albert Scardino (*Georgia Gazette*)
1985 Richard Aregood (*Philadelphia Daily News*)
1986 Jack Fuller (*Chicago Tribune*)
1987 Jonathan Freedman (*San Diego* [Calif.] *Tribune*)
1988 Jane E. Healy (*Orlando* [Fla.] *Sentinel*)
1989 Lois Wille (*Chicago Tribune*)
1990 Thomas J. Hylton (*Pottstown* [Pa.] *Mercury*)
1991 Ron Casey, Harold Jackson, and Joey Kennedy (*Birmingham* [Ala.] *News*)
1992 Maria Henson (*Lexington* [Ky.] *Herald-Leader*)

FICTION

1918 *His Family*, Ernest Poole
1919 *The Magnificent Ambersons*, Booth Tarkington
1921 *The Age of Innocence*, Edith Wharton
1922 *Alice Adams*, Booth Tarkington
1923 *One of Ours*, Willa Cather
1924 *The Able McLaughlins*, Margaret Wilson
1925 *So Big*, Edna Ferber
1926 *Arrowsmith*, Sinclair Lewis (award declined)
1927 *Early Autumn*, Louis Bromfield
1928 *The Bridge of San Luis Rey*, Thornton Wilder
1929 *Scarlet Sister Mary*, Julia Peterkin
1930 *Laughing Boy*, Oliver La Farge
1931 *Years of Grace*, Margaret Ayer Barnes
1932 *The Good Earth*, Pearl S. Buck
1933 *The Store*, T. S. Stribling
1934 *Lamb in His Bosom*, Caroline Miller
1935 *Now in November*, Josephine Winslow Johnson
1936 *Honey in the Horn*, Harold L. Davis
1937 *Gone with the Wind*, Margaret Mitchell
1938 *The Late George Apley*, John P. Marquand
1939 *The Yearling*, Marjorie Kinnan Rawlings
1940 *The Grapes of Wrath*, John Steinbeck
1942 *In This Our Life*, Ellen Glasgow
1943 *Dragon's Teeth*, Upton Sinclair
1944 *Journey in the Dark*, Martin Flavin
1945 *A Bell for Adano*, John Hersey

1947 *All the King's Men*, Robert Penn Warren
1948 *Tales of the South Pacific*, James A. Michener
1949 *Guard of Honor*, James Gould Cozzens
1950 *The Way West*, A. B. Guthrie, Jr.
1951 *The Town*, Conrad Richter
1952 *The Caine Mutiny*, Herman Wouk
1953 *The Old Man and the Sea*, Ernest Hemingway
1955 *A Fable*, William Faulkner
1956 *Andersonville*, MacKinlay Kantor
1958 *A Death in the Family*, James Agee
1959 *The Travels of Jamie McPheeters*, Robert Lewis Taylor
1960 *Advise and Consent*, Allen Drury
1961 *To Kill a Mockingbird*, Harper Lee
1962 *The Edge of Sadness*, Edwin O'Connor
1963 *The Reivers*, William Faulkner
1965 *The Keepers of the House*, Shirley Ann Grau
1966 *The Collected Stories of Katherine Anne Porter*, Katherine Anne Porter
1967 *The Fixer*, Bernard Malamud
1968 *The Confessions of Nat Turner*, William Styron
1969 *House Made of Dawn*, N. Scott Momaday
1970 *Collected Stories*, Jean Stafford
1972 *Angle of Repose*, Wallace Stegner
1973 *The Optimist's Daughter*, Eudora Welty
1975 *The Killer Angels*, Michael Shaara
1976 *Humboldt's Gift*, Saul Bellow
1978 *Elbow Room*, James Alan McPherson
1979 *The Stories of John Cheever*, John Cheever
1980 *The Executioner's Song*, Norman Mailer
1981 *A Confederacy of Dunces*, John Kennedy Toole
1982 *Rabbit Is Rich*, John Updike
1983 *The Color Purple*, Alice Walker
1984 *Ironweed*, William Kennedy
1985 *Foreign Affairs*, Alison Lurie
1986 *Lonesome Dove*, Larry McMurtry
1987 *A Summons to Memphis*, Peter Taylor
1988 *Beloved*, Toni Morrison
1989 *Breathing Lessons*, Anne Tyler
1990 *The Mambo Kings Play Songs of Love*, Oscar Hijuelos
1991 *Rabbit at Rest*, John Updike
1992 *A Thousand Acres*, Jane Smiley
1993 *A Good Scent From a Strange Mountain*, Robert Olen Butler

GENERAL NONFICTION

1962 *The Making of the President 1960*, Theodore H. White
1963 *The Guns of August*, Barbara W. Tuchman
1964 *Anti-Intellectualism in American Life*, Richard Hofstadter
1965 *O Strange New World*, Howard Mumford Jones
1966 *Wandering Through Winter*, Edwin Way Teale
1967 *The Problem of Slavery in Western Culture*, David Brion Davis
1968 *The Story of Civilization* (Vol. X), Will and Ariel Durant
1969 *So Human an Animal*, René Jules Dubos, and *The Armies of the Night*, Norman Mailer
1970 *Gandhi's Truth*, Erik H. Erikson
1971 *The Rising Sun*, John Toland
1972 *Stilwell and the American Experience in China, 1911–1945*, Barbara W. Tuchman
1973 *Fire in the Lake*, Frances FitzGerald, and *Children of Crisis* (Vol. II and III), Robert Coles
1974 *The Denial of Death*, Ernest Becker
1975 *Pilgrim at Tinker Creek*, Annie Dillard
1976 *Why Survive? Being Old in America*, Robert N. Butler
1977 *Beautiful Swimmers: Watermen, Crabs, and the Chesapeake Bay*, William W. Warner
1978 *The Dragons of Eden*, Carl Sagan
1979 *On Human Nature*, Edward O. Wilson
1980 *Gödel, Escher, Bach: An Eternal Golden Braid*, Douglas R. Hofstadter
1981 *Fin-de-Siècle Vienna: Politics and Culture*, Carl E. Schorske
1982 *The Soul of a New Machine*, Tracy Kidder
1983 *Is There No Place on Earth for Me?* Susan Sheehan
1984 *The Social Transformation of American Medicine*, Paul Starr
1985 *The Good War: An Oral History of World War II*, Studs Terkel
1986 *Move Your Shadow: South Africa, Black and White*, Joseph Lelyveld, and *Common Ground: A Turbulent Decade in the Lives of Three American Families*, J. Anthony Lukas
1987 *Arab and Jew: Wounded Spirits in a Promised Land*, David K. Shipler
1988 *The Making of the Atomic Bomb*, Richard Rhodes
1989 *A Bright Shining Lie: John Paul Vann and America in Vietnam*, Neil Sheehan
1990 *And Their Children After Them*, Dale Maharidge and Michael Williamson
1991 *The Ants*, Bert Holldobler and Edward O. Wilson
1992 *The Prize: The Epic Quest for Oil, Money, and Power*, Daniel Yergin
1993 *Lincoln at Gettysburg: The Words That Remade America*, Garry Wills

HISTORY

1917 *With Americans of Past and Present Days*, J. J. Jusserand
1918 *A History of the Civil War, 1861–1865*, James Ford Rhodes
1920 *The War with Mexico*, Justin H. Smith
1921 *The Victory at Sea*, William Sowden Sims in collaboration with Burton J. Hendrik
1922 *The Founding of New England*, James Truslow Adams
1923 *The Supreme Court in United States History*, Charles Warren
1924 *The American Revolution—A Constitutional Interpretation*, Charles Howard McIlwain
1925 *A History of the American Frontier*, Frederick L. Paxson
1926 *The History of the United States*, Edward Channing
1927 *Pickney's Treaty*, Samuel Flagg Bemis
1928 *Main Currents in American Thought*, Vernon Louis Parrington
1929 *The Organization and Administration of the Union Army, 1861–1865*, Fred Albert Shannon
1930 *The War of Independence*, Claude H. Van Tyne
1931 *The Coming of the War: 1914*, Bernadotte E. Schmitt
1932 *My Experiences in the World War*, John J. Pershing
1933 *The Significance of Sections in American History*, Frederick J. Turner
1934 *The People's Choice*, Herbert Agar
1935 *The Colonial Period of American History*, Charles McLean Andrews
1936 *The Constitutional History of the U.S.*, Andrew C. McLaughlin
1937 *The Flowering of New England*, Van Wyck Brooks
1938 *The Road to Reunion, 1865–1900*, Paul Herman Buck
1939 *A History of American Magazines*, Frank Luther Mott
1940 *Abraham Lincoln: The War Years*, Carl Sandburg
1941 *The Atlantic Migration, 1607–1860*, Marcus Lee Hansen
1942 *Reveille in Washington*, Margaret Leech
1943 *Paul Revere and the World He Lived In*, Esther Forbes
1944 *The Growth of American Thought*, Merle Curti
1945 *Unfinished Business*, Stephen Bonsal
1946 *The Age of Jackson*, Arthur M. Schlesinger, Jr.
1947 *Scientists Against Time*, James Phinney Baxter III
1948 *Across the Wide Missouri*, Bernard DeVoto
1949 *The Disruption of American Democracy*, Roy Franklin Nichols
1950 *Art and Life in America*, Oliver W. Larkin
1951 *The Old Northwest, Pioneer Period 1815–1840*, R. Carlyle Buley
1952 *The Uprooted*, Oscar Handlin
1953 *The Era of Good Feelings*, George Dangerfield
1954 *A Stillness at Appomattox*, Bruce Catton
1955 *Great River: the Rio Grande in North American History*, Paul Horgan
1956 *The Age of Reform: From Bryan to F.D.R.*, Richard Hofstadter
1957 *Russia Leaves the War*, George F. Kennan
1958 *Banks and Politics in America—From the Revolution to the Civil War*, Bray Hammond
1959 *The Republican Era: 1869–1901*, Leonard D. White
1960 *In The Days of McKinley*, Margaret Leech
1961 *Between War and Peace: the Potsdam Conference*, Herbert Feis
1962 *The Triumphant Empire, Thunder-Clouds Gather in the West*, Lawrence H. Gipson
1963 *Washington Village and Capital, 1800–1878*, Constance McLaughlin Green
1964 *Puritan Village: The Formation of a New England Town*, Sumner Chilton Powell
1965 *The Greenback Era*, Irwin Unger
1966 *The Life of the Mind in America*, Perry Miller
1967 *Exploration and Empire*, William H. Goetzmann
1968 *The Ideological Origins of the American Revolution*, Bernard Bailyn
1969 *Origins of the Fifth Amendment*, Leonard W. Levy
1970 *Present at the Creation: My Years in the State Department*, Dean Gooderham Acheson
1971 *Roosevelt: The Soldier of Freedom*, James MacGregor Burns
1972 *Neither Black nor White*, Carl M. Degler
1973 *People of Paradox*, Michael Kannen
1974 *The Americans: The Democratic Experience*, Daniel J. Boorstin
1975 *Jefferson and His Time*, Vol. I–V, Dumas Malone
1976 *Lamy of Santa Fe*, Paul Horgan
1977 *The Impending Crisis*, David M. Potter
1978 *The Visible Hand: The Managerial Revolution in American Business*, Alfred D. Chandler, Jr.
1979 *The Dred Scott Case*, Don E. Fehrenbacher
1980 *Been in the Storm So Long*, Leon F. Litwack
1981 *American Education: The National Experience, 1783–1876*, Lawrence A. Cremin

1982 *Mary Chesnut's Civil War*, C. Vann Woodward
1983 *The Transformation of Virginia, 1740–1790*, Rhys L. Isaac
1985 *The Prophets of Regulation*, Thomas K. McCraw
1986 *. . . the Heavens and the Earth: A Political History of the Space Age*, Walter A. McDougall
1987 *Voyagers to the West: A Passage in the Peopling of America on the Eve of the Revolution*, Bernard Bailyn
1988 *The Launching of Modern American Science 1846–1876*, Robert V. Bruce
1989 *Parting the Waters: America in the King Years, 1954–63*, Taylor Branch, and *Battle Cry of Freedom: The Civil War Era*, James M. McPherson
1990 *In Our Image: America's Empire in the Philippines*, Stanley Karnow
1991 *A Midwife's Tale—The Life of Martha Ballard, Based on Her Diary, 1785–1812*, Laurel Thatcher Ulrich
1992 *The Fate of Liberty—Abraham Lincoln and Civil Liberties*, Mark E. Neely, Jr.
1993 *The Radicalism of the American Revolution*, Gordon S. Wood

MERITORIOUS PUBLIC SERVICE

1918 *New York Times*
1919 *Milwaukee Journal*
1921 *Boston Post*
1922 *New York World*
1923 *Memphis Commercial Appeal*
1924 *New York World*
1926 *Columbus* (Ga.) *Enquirer Sun*
1927 *Canton* (Ohio) *Daily News*
1928 *Indianapolis Times*
1929 *New York Evening World*
1931 *Atlanta Constitution*
1932 *Indianapolis News*
1933 *New York World-Telegram*
1934 *Medford* (Oreg.) *Mail Tribune*
1935 *Sacramento* (Calif.) *Bee*
1936 *Cedar Rapids* (Iowa) *Gazette*
1937 *St. Louis* (Mo.) *Post-Dispatch*
1938 *Bismarck* (N.D.) *Tribune*
1939 *Miami* (Fla.) *Daily News*
1940 *Waterbury* (Conn.) *Republican and American*
1941 *St. Louis* (Mo.) *Post-Dispatch*
1942 *Los Angeles Times*
1943 *Omaha World-Herald*
1944 *New York Times*
1945 *Detroit Free Press*
1946 *Scranton* (Pa.) *Times*
1947 *Baltimore* (Md.) *Sun*
1948 *St. Louis* (Mo.) *Post-Dispatch*
1949 *Lincoln Nebraska State Journal*
1950 *Chicago Daily News and St. Louis* (Mo.) *Post-Dispatch*
1951 *Miami* (Fla.) *Herald* and *Brooklyn Eagle*
1952 *St. Louis* (Mo.) *Post-Dispatch*
1953 *Whiteville* (N.C.) *News Reporter* and *Tabor City* (N.C.) *Tribune*
1954 *Newsday* (Garden City, N.Y.)
1955 *Columbus* (Ga.) *Ledger & Sunday Ledger-Enquirer*
1956 *Watsonville* (Calif.) *Register-Pajaronian*
1957 *Chicago Daily News*
1958 *Little Rock Arkansas Gazette*
1959 *Utica* (N.Y.) *Observer-Dispatch* and *Utica* (N.Y.) *Daily Press*
1960 *Los Angeles Times*
1961 *Amarillo* (Tex.) *Globe-Times*
1962 *Panama City* (Fla.) *News-Herald*
1963 *Chicago Daily News*
1964 *Saint Petersburg* (Fla.) *Times*
1965 *Hutchinson* (Kans.) *News*
1966 *Boston Globe*
1967 *Louisville Courier-Journal* and *Milwaukee Journal*
1968 *Riverside* (Calif.) *Press-Enterprise*
1969 *Los Angeles Times*
1970 *Newsday* (Garden City, N.Y.)
1971 *Winston-Salem* (N.C.) *Journal and Sentinel*
1972 *New York Times*
1973 *Washington* (D.C.) *Post*
1974 *Newsday* (Garden City, N.Y.)
1975 *Boston Globe*
1976 *Anchorage* (Alaska) *Daily News*
1977 *Lufkin* (Tex.) *News*
1978 William K. Marimow and Jonathan Neumann (*Philadelphia Inquirer*)
1979 *Point Reyes* (Calif.) *Light*
1980 Gannett News Service
1981 *Charlotte* (N.C.) *Observer*
1982 *Detroit News*
1983 *Jackson* (Miss.) *Clarion-Ledger*
1984 *Los Angeles Times*
1985 *Fort Worth* (Tex.) *Star-Telegram*
1986 *Denver Post*
1987 Andrew Schneider and Matthew Brelis (*Pittsburgh Press*)
1988 *The Charlotte Observer*
1989 *Anchorage* (Alaska) *Daily News*
1990 *Philadelphia Inquirer* and *Washington* [D.C.] *Daily News*
1991 Jane Schorer (*Des Moines* [Iowa] *Register*)
1992 Tom Knudson (*Sacramento* [Calif.] *Bee*)
1993 *Miami* (Fla.) *Herald*

MUSIC

1943 *Secular Cantata No. 2, A Free Song*, William Schuman
1944 *Symphony No. 4 (Op. 34)*, Howard Hanson
1945 *Appalachian Spring*, Aaron Copland
1946 *The Canticle of the Sun*, Leo Sowerby
1947 *Symphony No. 3*, Charles Ives
1948 *Symphony No. 3*, Walter Piston
1949 *Louisiana Story*, Virgil Thomson
1950 *The Consul*, Gian-Carlo Menotti
1951 *Giants in the Earth*, Douglas Stuart Moore
1952 *Symphony Concertante*, Gail Kubik
1954 *Concerto for Two Pianos and Orchestra*, Quincy Porter
1955 *The Saint of Bleecker Street*, Gian-Carlo Menotti
1956 *Symphony No. 3*, Ernst Toch
1957 *Meditations on Ecclesiastes*, Norman Dello Joio
1958 *Vanessa*, Samuel Barber
1959 *Piano Concerto*, John La Montaine
1960 *Second String Quartet*, Elliott Carter
1961 *Symphony No. 7*, Walter Piston
1962 *The Crucible*, Robert Ward
1963 *Piano Concerto No. 1*, Samuel Barber
1966 *Variations for Orchestra*, Leslie Bassett
1967 *Quartet No. 3*, Leon Kirchner
1968 *Echoes of Time and the River*, George Crumb
1969 *String Quartet No. 3*, Karel Husa
1970 *Time's Encomium*, Charles W. Wuorinen
1971 *Synchronisms No. 6 for Piano and Electronic Sound*, Mario Davidowsky
1972 *Windows*, Jacob Druckman
1973 *String Quartet No. 3*, Elliott Carter
1974 *Notturno*, Donald Martino
1975 *From the Diary of Virginia Woolf*, Dominick Argento
1976 *Air Music*, Ned Rorem
1977 *Visions of Terror and Wonder*, Richard Wernick
1978 *Déjà Vu for Percussion Quartet and Orchestra*, Michael Colgrass
1979 *Aftertones of Infinity*, Joseph Schwantner
1980 *In Memory of a Summer Day*, David Del Tredici
1982 *Concerto for Orchestra*, Roger Sessions
1983 *Three Movements for Orchestra*, Ellen T. Zwilich
1984 *Canti del Sole*, Bernard Rands
1985 *Symphony, RiverRun*, Stephen Albert
1986 *Wind Quintet IV*, George Perle
1987 *The Flight Into Egypt*, John Harbison
1988 *12 New Etudes for Piano*, William Bolcom
1989 *Whispers Out of Time*, Roger Reynolds
1990 *Duplicates*, Mel Powell
1991 *Symphony*, Shulamit Ran
1992 *The Face of the Night, the Heart of the Dark*, Wayne Peterson
1993 *Trombone Concerto*, Christopher Rouse

PHOTOGRAPHY

News Photography (1942–67)
(Discontinued category)

1942 Milton Brooks (*Detroit News*)
1943 Frank Noel (Associated Press)
1944 Frank Filan (Associated Press); Earle L. Bunker (*Omaha* [Neb.] *World-Herald*)
1945 Joe Rosenthal (Associated Press)
1947 Arnold Hardy (amateur)
1948 Frank Cushing (*Boston Traveler*)
1949 Nathaniel Fein (*New York Herald Tribune*)
1950 Bill Crouch (*Oakland* [Calif.] *Tribune*)
1951 Max Desfor (Associated Press)
1952 John Robinson and Don Ultang (*Des Moines* [Iowa] *Register & Tribune*)
1953 William M. Gallagher (*Flint* [Mich.] *Journal*)
1954 Mrs. Walter M. Schau (amateur)
1955 John L. Grant, Jr. (*Los Angeles Times*)
1956 *New York Daily News*
1957 Harry A. Trask (*Boston Traveler*)
1958 William C. Beall (*Washington* [D.C.] *Daily News*)
1959 William Seaman (*Minneapolis* [Minn.] *Star*)
1960 Andrew Lopez (United Press International)
1961 Yasushi Nagao (Tokyo [Japan] Mainichi Newspapers)
1962 Paul Vathis (Associated Press)
1963 Héctor Rondón (Caracas [Venezuela] *La Republica*)
1964 Robert H. Jackson (*Dallas* [Tex.] *Times-Herald*)
1965 Horst Faas (Associated Press)
1966 Kyoichi Sawada (United Press International)
1967 Jack R. Thornell (Associated Press)

Feature Photography

1968 Toshio Sakai (United Press International)
1969 Moneta Sleet, Jr. (*Ebony*)
1970 Dallas Kinney (*Palm Beach* [Fla.] *Post*)
1971 Jack Dykinga (*Chicago Sun-Times*)
1972 Dave Kennerly (United Press International)
1973 Brian Lanker (*Topeka* [Kans.] *Capital-Journal*)
1974 Slava Veder (Associated Press)
1975 Matthew Lewis (*Washington* [D.C.] *Post*)
1976 *Louisville* (Ky.) *Courier-Journal and Times*
1977 Robin Hood (*Chattanooga News-Free Press*)
1978 J. Ross Baughman (Associated Press)
1979 *Boston Herald American*
1980 Erwin H. Hagler (*Dallas Times-Herald*)
1981 Taro M. Yamasaki (*Detroit Free Press*)
1982 John H. White (*Chicago Sun-Times*)
1983 James B. Dickman (*Dallas Times-Herald*)
1984 Anthony Suau (*Denver* [Colo.] *Post*)
1985 Stan Grossfeld (*Boston Globe*) and Larry C. Price (*Philadelphia Inquirer*)
1986 Tom Gralish (*Philadelphia Inquirer*)
1987 David Peterson (*Des Moines* [Iowa] *Register*)
1988 Michel duCille (*Miami* [Fla.] *Herald*)
1989 Manny Crisostomo (*Detroit Free Press*)
1990 David C. Turnley (*Detroit Free Press*)
1991 William Snyder (*Dallas Morning News*)
1992 John Kaplan (Block Newspapers)
1993 Associated Press staff

Spot News Photography

1968 Rocco Morabito (*Jacksonville* [Fla.] *Journal*)
1969 Edward T. Adams (Associated Press)
1970 Steve Starr (Associated Press)
1971 John Paul Filo (amateur)
1972 Horst Faas and Michael Laurent (Associated Press)
1973 Huynh Cong Ut (Associated Press)
1974 Anthony K. Roberts (Free-lance)
1975 Gerald H. Gay (*Seattle* [Wash.] *Times*)
1976 Stanley Forman (*Boston Herald American*)
1977 Neal Ulevich (Associated Press) and Stanley Forman (*Boston Herald-American*)
1978 John W. Blair (Free-lance)
1979 Thomas J. Kelly, 3d (*Pottstown* [Pa.] *Mercury*)
1980 United Press International
1981 Larry C. Price (*Fort Worth* [Tex.] *Star-Telegram*)
1982 Ron Edmonds (Associated Press)
1983 Bill Foley (Associated Press)
1984 Stan Grossfeld (*Boston Globe*)
1985 *Santa Ana* (Calif.) *Register*
1986 Michel duCille and Carol Guzy (*Miami* [Fla.] *Herald*)
1987 Kim Komenich (*San Francisco Examiner*)
1988 Scott Shaw (*Odessa* [Tex.] *American*)
1989 Ron Olshwanger (*St. Louis* [Mo.] *Post-Dispatch*)
1990 *Oakland* [Calif.] *Tribune*
1991 Greg Marinovich (Associated Press)
1992 Associated Press staff
1993 Ken Geiger and William Snyder (*Dallas Morning News*)

POETRY

(Established in 1922. The prizes in 1918 and 1919 were made from gifts provided by the Poetry Society.)

1918 *Love Songs*, Sara Teasdale
1919 *Old Road to Paradise*, Margaret Widdemer; *Corn Huskers*, Carl Sandburg
1922 *Collected Poems*, Edwin Arlington Robinson
1923 *The Ballad of the Harp-Weaver; A Few Figs from Thistles; Eight Sonnets in American Poetry, 1922, A Miscellany*, Edna St. Vincent Millay
1924 *New Hampshire: A Poem with Notes and Grace Notes*, Robert Frost
1925 *The Man Who Died Twice*, Edwin Arlington Robinson
1926 *What's O'Clock*, Amy Lowell
1927 *Fiddler's Farewell*, Leonora Speyer
1928 *Tristram*, Edwin Arlington Robinson
1929 *John Brown's Body*, Stephen Vincent Benét
1930 *Selected Poems*, Conrad Aiken
1931 *Collected Poems*, Robert Frost
1932 *The Flowering Stone*, George Dillon
1933 *Conquistador*, Archibald MacLeish
1934 *Collected Verse*, Robert Hillyer
1935 *Bright Ambush*, Audrey Wurdemann
1936 *Strange Holiness*, Robert P. Tristram Coffin
1937 *A Further Range*, Robert Frost
1938 *Cold Morning Sky*, Marya Zaturenska
1939 *Selected Poems*, John Gould Fletcher
1940 *Collected Poems*, Mark Van Doren
1941 *Sunderland Capture*, Leonard Bacon
1942 *The Dust Which Is God*, William Rose Benét
1943 *A Witness Tree*, Robert Frost
1944 *Western Star*, Stephen Vincent Benét
1945 *V-Letter and Other Poems*, Karl Shapiro
1947 *Lord Weary's Castle*, Robert Lowell
1948 *The Age of Anxiety*, W. H. Auden
1949 *Terror and Decorum*, Peter Viereck
1950 *Annie Allen*, Gwendolyn Brooks
1951 *Complete Poems*, Carl Sandburg
1952 *Collected Poems*, Marianne Moore
1953 *Collected Poems, 1917–52*, Archibald Macleish
1954 *The Waking: Poems (1933–1953)*, Theodore Roethke
1955 *Collected Poems*, Wallace Stevens
1956 *Poems: North and South—A Cold Spring*, Elizabeth Bish
1957 *Things of This World*, Richard Wilbur
1958 *Promises: Poems 1954–56*, Robert Penn Warren
1959 *Selected Poems 1928–58*, Stanley Kunitz
1960 *Heart's Needle*, W. D. Snodgrass
1961 *Times Three: Selected Verse From Three Decades*, Phyllis McGinley
1962 *Poems*, Alan Dugan
1963 *Pictures from Breughel*, William Carlos Williams
1964 *At the End of the Open Road*, Louis Simpson
1965 *77 Dream Songs*, John Berryman
1966 *Selected Poems (1930–1965)*, Richard Eberhart
1967 *Live or Die*, Anne Sexton
1968 *The Hard Hours*, Anthony Hecht
1969 *Of Being Numerous*, George Oppen
1970 *Untitled Subjects*, Richard Howard
1971 *The Carrier of Ladders*, William S. Merwin
1972 *Collected Poems*, James Wright
1973 *Up Country*, Maxine Winokur Kumin
1974 *The Dolphin*, Robert Lowell
1975 *Turtle Island*, Gary Snyder
1976 *Self-Portrait in a Convex Mirror*, John Ashbery
1977 *Divine Comedies*, James Merrill
1978 *Collected Poems*, Howard Nemerov
1979 *Now and Then: Poems 1976–1978*, Robert Penn Warren
1980 *Selected Poems*, Donald Justice
1981 *The Morning of the Poem*, James Schuyler
1982 *Collected Poems*, Sylvia Plath
1983 *Selected Poems*, Galway Kinnell
1984 *American Primitive*, Mary Oliver
1985 *Yin*, Carolyn Kizer
1986 *The Flying Change*, Henry Taylor
1987 *Thomas and Beulah*, Rita Dove
1988 *Partial Accounts: New and Selected Poems*, William Meredith
1989 *New and Collected Poems*, Richard Wilbur
1990 *The World Doesn't End*, Charles Simic
1991 *Near Changes*, Mona Van Duyn
1992 *Selected Poems*, James Tate
1993 *The Wild Iris*, Louise Glück

REPORTING

General Reporting (1917–52)
(Discontinued category)

1917 Herbert Bayard Swope (*New York World*)
1918 Harold A. Littledale (*New York Evening Post*)
1920 John J. Leary, Jr. (*New York World*)
1921 Louis Seibold (*New York World*)
1922 Kirke L. Simpson (Associated Press)
1923 Alva Johnston (*New York Times*)
1924 Magner White (*San Diego* [Calif.] *Sun*)
1925 James W. Mulroy and Alvin H. Goldstein (*Chicago Daily News*)
1926 William Burke Miller (*Louisville* [Ky.] *Courier-Journal*)
1927 John T. Rogers (*St. Louis* [Mo.] *Post-Dispatch*)
1929 Paul Y. Anderson (*St. Louis* [Mo.] *Post-Dispatch*)
1930 Russell D. Owen (*New York Times*); special award to W. O. Dapping (*Auburn* [N.Y.] *Citizen*)
1931 A. B. MacDonald (*Kansas City* [Mo.] *Star*)
1932 W. C. Richards, D. D. Martin, J. S. Pooler, F. D. Webb, J. N. W. Sloan (*Detroit Free Press*)
1933 Francis A. Jamieson (Associated Press)
1934 Royce Brier (*San Francisco Chronicle*)
1935 William H. Taylor (*New York Herald Tribune*)
1936 Lauren D. Lyman (*New York Times*)
1937 John J. O'Neill (*New York Herald Tribune*), William Leonard Laurence (*New York Times*), Howard W. Blakesl (Associated Press), Gobind Behari Lal (Universal Service), David Dietz (Scripps-Howard Newspaper Alliance)
1938 Raymond Sprigle (*Pittsburgh* [Pa.] *Post-Gazette*)
1939 Thomas Lunsford Stokes (Scripps-Howard Newspaper Alliance)
1940 S. Burton Heath (*New York World-Telegram*)
1941 Westbrook Pegler (*New York World-Telegram*)
1942 Stanton Delaplane (*San Francisco Chronicle*)
1943 George Weller (*Chicage Daily News*)
1944 Paul Schoenstein and associates (*New York Journal-American*)
1945 Jack S. McDowell (*San Francisco Call-Bulletin*)
1946 William Leonard Laurence (*New York Times*)
1947 Frederick Woltman (*New York World-Telegram*)
1948 George E. Goodwin (*Atlanta* [Ga.] *Journal*)
1949 Malcolm Johnson (*New York Sun*)
1950 Meyer Berger (*New York Times*)

1951 Edward S. Montgomery (*San Francisco Examiner*)
1952 George de Carvalho (*San Francisco Chronicle*)

Special Local Reporting (1953–84; no deadline)
(Discontinued category)
1953 Edward J. Mowery (*New York World-Telegram & Sun*)
1954 Alvin Scott McCoy (*Kansas City* [Mo.] *Star*)
1955 Roland Kenneth Towery (*Cuero* [Tex.] *Record*)
1956 Arthur Daley (*New York Times*)
1957 Wallace Turner and William Lambert (*Portland* [Oreg.] *Oregonian*)
1958 George Beveridge (*Washington* [D.C.] *Evening Star*)
1959 John Harold Brislin (*Scranton* [Pa.] *Tribune and Scrantonian*)
1960 Miriam Ottenberg (*Washington* [D.C.] *Evening Star*)
1961 Edgar May (*Buffalo* [N.Y.] *Evening News*)
1962 George Bliss (*Chicago Tribune*)
1963 Oscar O'Neal Griffin, Jr. (*Pecos* [Tex.] *Independent and Enterprise*)
1964 James V. Magee, Albert V. Gaudiosi, and Frederick A. Meyer (*Philadelphia Bulletin*)
1965 Gene Goltz (*Houston* [Tex.] *Post*)
1966 John A. Frasco (*Tampa* [Fla.] *Tribune*)
1967 Gene Miller (*Miami* [Fla.] *Herald*)
1968 J. Anthony Lukas (*New York Times*)
1969 Albert L. Delugach and Denny Walsh (*St. Louis* [Mo.] *Globe-Democrat*)
1970 Harold Eugene Martin (*Montgomery* [Ala.] *Journal*)
1971 William Hugh Jones (*Chicago Tribune*)
1972 Timothy Leland, Gerard M. O'Neill, Stephan A. Kurjian, and Ann DeSantis (*Boston Globe*)
1973 The Sun Newspapers, Omaha, Nebr.
1974 William Sherman (*New York Daily News*)
1975 *Indianapolis* (Ind.) *Star*
1976 *Chicago Tribune*
1977 Acel Moore and Wendell Rawls, Jr. (*Philadelphia Inquirer*)
1978 Anthony R. Dolan (*Stamford* [Conn.] *Advocate*)
1979 Gilbert M. Gaul and Elliot G. Jaspin (*Pottsville* [Pa.] *Republican*)
1980 Stephen A. Korkijian, Alexander B. Hawes, Jr., Nils Bruzelius, and Joan Vennochi (*Boston Globe*)
1981 Clark Hallas and Robert B. Lowe (*Arizona Daily Star*)
1982 Paul Henderson (*Seattle* [Wash.] *Times*)
1983 Loretta Tofani (*Washington Post*)
1984 *Boston Globe*

Investigative Reporting
1985 William K. Marimow (*Philadelphia Inquirer*) and Lucy Morgan and Jack Reed (*St. Petersburg* [Fla.] *Times*)
1986 Jeffrey A. Marx and Michael M. York (*Lexington* [Ky.] *Herald-Leader*)
1987 Daniel R. Biddle, H. G. Bissinger, and Fredric N. Tulky, (*Philadelphia Inquirer*) and John Woestendick (*Philadelphia Inquirer*)
1988 Dean Baquet, William C. Gaines, and Ann Marie Lipinski (*Chicago Tribune*)
1989 Bill Dedman (*Atlanta* [Ga.] *Journal & Constitution*)
1990 Lou Kilzer and Chris Ison (*Minneapolis-St. Paul* [Minn.] *Star Tribune*)
1991 Joseph T. Hallinan and Susan M. Headden (*Indianapolis Star*)
1992 Lorraine Adams and Dan Malone (*Dallas Morning News*)
1993 Jeff Brazil and Steve Berry (*Orlando* [Fla.] *Sentinel*)

General Local Reporting (1953–84; deadline)
(Discontinued category)
1953 *Providence* (R.I.) *Journal and Evening Bulletin*
1954 *Vicksburg* (Miss.) *Sunday Post-Herald*
1955 Mrs. Caro Brown (*Alice* [Tex.] *Daily Echo*)
1956 Lee Hills (*Detroit Free Press*)
1957 *Salt Lake City* (Utah) *Tribune*
1958 *Fargo* (N.D.) *Forum*
1959 Mary Lou Werner (*Washington* [D.C.] *Evening Star*)
1960 Jack Nelson (*Atlanta* [Ga.] *Constitution*)
1961 Sanche de Gramont (*New York Herald Tribune*)
1962 Robert D. Mullins (*Salt Lake City* [Utah] *Desert News*)
1963 Sylvan Fox, Anthony Shannon, and William Longgood (*New York World-Telegram & Sun*)
1964 Norman C. Miller (*Wall Street Journal*)
1965 Melvin H. Ruder (*Columbia Falls* [Mont.] *Hungry Horse News*)
1966 *Los Angeles Times* staff
1967 Robert V. Cox (*Chambersburg* [Pa.] *Public Opinion*)
1968 *Detroit Free Press*
1969 John Fetterman (*Louisville* [Ky.] *Times and Courier-Journal*)
1970 Thomas Fitzpatrick (*Chicago Sun-Times*)
1971 *Akron* (Ohio) *Beacon Journal*
1972 Richard Cooper and John Machacek (*Rochester* [N.Y.] *Times-Union*)
1973 *Chicago Tribune*
1974 Arthur M. Petacque and Hugh F. Hough (*Chicago Sun-Times*)
1975 *Xenia* (Ohio) *Daily Gazette*
1976 Gene Miller (*Miami* [Fla.] *Herald*)
1977 Margo Huston (*Milwaukee* [Wis.] *Journal*)
1978 Richard Whitt (*Louisville* [Ky.] *Courier-Journal*)
1979 *San Diego* (Calif.) *Evening Tribune*
1980 *Philadelphia Inquirer*
1981 *Longview* (Wash.) *Daily News*
1982 *Kansas City* (Mo.) *Star* and *Kansas City* (Mo.) *Times*
1983 *Fort Wayne* (Ind.) *News-Sentinel*
1984 *Newsday* (Garden City, N.Y.)

Explanatory Journalism
1985 Jon Franklin (*Baltimore* [Md.] *Sun*)
1986 *New York Times*
1987 Jeff Lyon and Peter Gormer (*Chicago Tribune*)
1988 Daniel Hertzberg and James B. Stewart (*Wall Street Journal*)
1989 David Hanners, William Snyder, and Karen Blessen (*Dallas* [Tex.] *Morning News*)
1990 Steve Coll and David A. Vise (*Washington Post*)
1991 Susan C. Faludi (*Wall Street Journal*)
1992 Robert S. Capers and Eric Lipton (*Hartford* [Conn.] *Courant*)
1993 Mike Toner (*Atlanta* [Ga.] *Journal-Constitution*)

Specialized Reporting (1985–90)
(Discontinued category)
1985 Randall Savage and Jackie Crosby (*Macon* [Ga.] *Telegraph and News*)
1986 Andrew Schneider and Mary Pat Flaherty (*Pittsburgh Press*)
1987 Alex S. Jones (*New York Times*)
1988 Walt Bogdanich (*Wall Street Journal*)
1989 Edward Humes (*Orange County* [Calif.] *Register*)
1990 Tamar Stieber (*Albuquerque* [N. Mex.] *Journal*)

General News Reporting (1985–90)
(Discontinued category)
1985 Thomas Turcol (*Virginian Pilot* and *Ledger-Star*)
1986 Edna Buchanan (*Miami* [Fla.] *Herald*)
1987 *Akron* (Ohio) *Beacon Journal*
1988 *Alabama Journal* and *Lawrence* (Mass.) *Eagle-Tribune*
1989 *Louisville* (Ky.) *Courier-Journal*
1990 *San Jose* (Calif.) *Mercury News*

Beat Reporting
1991 Natalie Angier (*New York Times*)
1992 Deborah Blum (*Sacramento* [Calif.] *Bee*)
1993 Paul Ingrassia and Joseph B. White (*Wall Street Journal*)

Spot News Reporting
1991 *Miami* (Fla.) *Herald*
1992 *New York Newsday*
1993 *Los Angeles Times* staff

General Correspondence (1929–47)
(Discontinued category)
1929 Paul Scott Mowrer (*Chicago Daily News*)
1930 Leland Stowe (*New York Herald Tribune*)
1931 H. R. Knickerbocker (*Philadelphia Public Ledger* and *New York Evening Post*)
1932 Walter Duranty (*New York Times*) and Charles G. Ross (*St. Louis* [Mo.] *Post-Dispatch*)
1933 Edgar Ansel Mowrer (*Chicago Daily News*)
1934 Frederick T. Birchall (*New York Times*)
1935 Arthur Krock (*New York Times*)
1936 Wilfred C. Barber (*Chicago Tribune*)
1937 Anne O'Hare McCormick (*New York Times*)
1938 Arthur Krock (*New York Times*)
1939 Louis P. Lochner (Associated Press)
1940 Otto D. Tolishus (*New York Times*)
1941 Group award for the public services and individual achievements of American news reporters in war zones
1942 Carlos P. Romulo (*Manila Philippines Herald*)
1943 Hanson W. Baldwin (*New York Times*)
1944 Ernest Taylor Pyle (Scripps-Howard Newspaper Alliance)
1945 Harold V. (Hal) Boyle (Associated Press)
1946 Arnaldo Cortesi (*New York Times*)
1947 Brooks Atkinson (*New York Times*)

National Reporting
1948 Bert Andrews (*New York Herald Tribune*) and Nat S. Finny (*Minneapolis* [Minn.] *Tribune*)
1949 Charles P. Trussel (*New York Times*)
1950 Edwin O. Guthman (*Seattle* [Wash.] *Times*)
1952 Anthony Leviero (*New York Times*)
1953 Don Whitehead (Associated Press)
1954 Richard Wilson (Cowles Newspapers)

1955 Anthony Lewis (*Washington* [D.C.] *Daily News*)
1956 Charles L. Bartlett (*Chattanooga* [Tenn.] *Times*)
1957 James B. Reston (*New York Times*)
1958 Relman Morin (Associated Press) and Clark Mollenhoff (*Des Moines* [Iowa] *Register & Tribune*)
1959 Howard Van Smith (*Miami* [Fla.] *News*)
1960 Vance Trimble (Scripps-Howard Newspaper Alliance)
1961 Edward R. Cony (*Wall Street Journal*)
1962 Nathan G. Caldwell and Gene S. Graham (*Nashville* [Tenn.] *Tennessean*)
1963 Anthony Lewis (*New York Times*)
1964 Merriman Smith (United Press International)
1965 Louis M. Kohlmeier (*Wall Street Journal*)
1966 Haynes Johnson (*Washington* [D.C.] *Evening Star*)
1967 Monroe W. Karmin and Stanley W. Penn (*Wall Street Journal*)
1968 Howard James (*Christian Science Monitor*) and Nathan K. Kotz (*Des Moines* [Iowa] *Register*)
1969 Robert Cahn (*Christian Science Monitor*)
1970 William J. Eaton (*Chicago Daily News*)
1971 Lucinda Franks and Thomas Powers (United Press International)
1972 Jack Anderson (United Features)
1973 Robert Boyd and Clark Hoyt (Knight Newspapers)
1974 James R. Polk (*Washington* [D.C.] *Star-News*)
1975 James B. Steele and Donald L. Bartlett (*Philadelphia Inquirer*)
1976 James Risser (*Des Moines* [Iowa] *Register*)
1977 Walter Mears (Associated Press)
1978 Gaylord Shaw (*Los Angeles Times*)
1979 James Risser (*Des Moines* [Iowa] *Register*)
1980 Charles Stafford and Bette Swenson Orsini (*St. Petersburg* [Fla.] *Times*)
1981 John M. Crewdson (*New York Times*)
1982 Rick Atkinson (*Kansas City* [Mo.] *Times*)
1983 *Boston Globe*
1984 John Noble Wilford (*New York Times*)
1985 Thomas J. Knudson (*Des Moines* [Iowa] *Register*)
1986 Craig Flournoy and George Rodrique (*Dallas Morning News*) and Arthur Howe (*Philadelphia Inquirer*)
1987 *Miami* (Fla.) *Herald* and *New York Times*
1988 Tim Weiner (*Philadelphia Inquirer*)
1989 Donald L. Barlett and James B. Steele (*Philadelphia Inquirer*)
1990 Ross Anderson, Bill Dietrich, Mary Ann Gwinn, and Eric Nalder (*Seattle* [Wash.] *Times*)
1991 Marjie Lundstrom and Rochelle Sharpe (*Gannett News Service*)
1992 Jeff Taylor and Mike McGraw (*Kansas City Star*)
1993 David Maraniss (*Washington* [D.C.] *Post*)

International Reporting
1948 Paul W. Ward (*Baltimore* [Md.] *Sun*)
1949 Price Day (*Baltimore* [Md.] *Sun*)
1950 Edmund Stevens (*Christian Science Monitor*)
1951 Keyes Beach and Fred Sparks (*Chicago Daily News*); Homer Bigart and Marguerite Higgins (*New York Herald Tribune*); Relman Morin and Don Whitehead (Associated Press)
1952 John M. Hightower (Associated Press)
1953 Austin Wehrwein (*Milwaukee* [Wis.] *Journal*)
1954 Jim G. Lucas (Scripps-Howard Newspaper Alliance)
1955 Harrison Salisbury (*New York Times*)
1956 William Randolph Hearst, Jr., Kingsbury Smith, and Frank Conniff (International News Service)
1957 Russell Jones (United Press)
1958 *New York Times*
1959 Joseph Martin and Philip Santora (*New York Daily News*)
1960 A. M. Rosenthal (*New York Times*)
1961 Lynn Heizerling (Associated Press)
1962 Walter Lippmann (*New York Herald Tribune* Syndicate)
1963 Hal Hendrix (*Miami* [Fla.] *News*)
1964 Malcolm W. Browne (Associated Press) and David Halberstam (*New York Times*)
1965 J. A. Livingston (*Philadelphia Bulletin*)
1966 Peter Arnett (Associated Press)
1967 R. John Hughes (*Christian Science Monitor*)
1968 Alfred Friendly (*Washington* [D.C.] *Post*)
1969 William Tuohy (*Los Angeles Times*)
1970 Seymour M. Hersh (Dispatch News Service)
1971 Jimmie Lee Hoagland (*Washington* [D.C.] *Post*)
1972 Peter R. Kann (*Wall Street Journal*)
1973 Max Frankel (*New York Times*)
1974 Hedrick Smith (*New York Times*)
1975 Ovie Carter and William Mullen (*Chicago Tribune*)
1976 Sydney H. Schanberg (*New York Times*)
1978 Henry Kamm (*New York Times*)
1979 Richard Ben Cramer (*Philadelphia Inquirer*)
1980 Joel Brinkley and Jay Mather (*Louisville* [Ky.] *Courier-Journal*)
1981 Shirley Christian (*Miami* [Fla.] *Herald*)
1982 John Darnton (*New York Times*)
1983 Thomas L. Friedman (*New York Times*) and Loren Jenkins (*Washington Post*)
1984 Karen Elliott House (*Wall Street Journal*)
1985 Josh Friedman, Dennis Bell, and Ozier Muhammad (*Newsday*)
1986 Lewis M. Simons, Pete Carey, and Katherine Ellison (*San Jose* [Calif.] *Mercury News*)
1987 Michael Parks (*Los Angeles Times*)
1988 Thomas L. Friedman (*New York Times*)
1989 Glenn Frankel (*Washington* [D.C.] *Post*) and Bill Keller (*New York Times*)
1990 Nicholas D. Kristof and Sheryl WuDunn (*New York Times*)
1991 Caryle Murphy (*Washington* [D.C.] *Post*) and Serge Schmemann (*New York Times*)
1992 Patrick J. Sloyan (*Newsday*)
1993 John F. Burns (*New York Times*) and Roy Gutman (*Newsday*)

Feature Writing
1979 Jon B. Franklin (*Baltimore* [Md.] *Evening Sun*)
1980 Madeleine Blais (*Miami Herald Tropic Magazine*)
1981 Teresa Carpenter (*Village Voice*, New York City)
1982 Saul Pett (Associated Press)
1983 Nan Robertson (*New York Times*)
1984 Peter Mark Rinearson (*Seattle* [Wash.] *Times*)
1985 Alice Steinbach (*Baltimore* [Md.] *Sun*)
1986 John Camp (*St. Paul* [Minn.] *Pioneer Press and Dispatch*)
1987 Steve Twomey (*Philadelphia Inquirer*)
1988 Jacqui Banaszynski (*St. Paul* [Minn.] *Pioneer Press and Dispatch*)
1989 David Zucchino (*Philadelphia Inquirer*)
1990 Dave Curtin (*Colorado Springs* [Colo.] *Gazette Telegraph*)
1991 Sheryl James (*St. Petersburg* [Fla.] *Times*)
1992 Howell Raines (*New York Times*)
1993 George Lardner, Jr. (*Washington* [D.C.] *Post*)

SPECIAL CITATIONS

1938 *Edmonton* (Alberta, Canada) *Journal*, a special bronze plaque for editorial leadership in defense of freedom of the press in the province of Alberta.
1941 *New York Times*, for the public educational value of its foreign news report.
1944 Richard Rodgers and Oscar Hammerstein II, for their musical *Oklahoma!* Byron Price, director of the Office of Censorship, for the creation and administration of the newspaper and radio codes. Mrs. William Allen White, for the interest and services of her husband during the past seven years as a member of the advisory board of the graduate school of journalism, Columbia University.
1945 The cartographers of the American press, for their war maps.
1947 (Pulitzer centennial year) Columbia University and the graduate school of journalism, for their efforts to maintain and advance the high standards governing the Pulitzer Prize awards. The *St. Louis Post-Dispatch*, for its unswerving adherence to the public and professional ideals of its founder and its leadership in the field of American journalism.
1948 Dr. Frank Fackenthal, for his interest and service.
1951 Cyrus L. Sulzberger (*New York Times*), for his exclusive interview with Archbishop Stepinac, in a Yugoslav prison.
1952 *Kansas City* (Mo.) *Star*, for coverage of 1951 floods; Max Kase (*New York Journal-American*), for exposures of bribery in college basketball.
1953 *New York Times*, for its 17-year publication of "News of the Week in Review," and Lester Markel, the founder.
1957 Kenneth Roberts, for his historical novels.
1958 Walter Lippmann (*New York Herald Tribune*), for "wisdom, perception and high sense of responsibility."
1960 Garrett Mattingly, for *The Armada*.
1961 Gannett Newspapers, for series "The Road to Integration."
1974 Roger Sessions, for his life's work in music.
1976 Scott Joplin, for contributions to American music. John Hohenberg, for administration of the Pulitzer Prizes and achievements as teacher and journalist.
1977 Alex Haley, for *Roots*.
1978 Richard Lee Strout (*Christian Science Monitor* and *New Republic*), for distinguished commentary. E. B. White, for literary work.
1982 Milton Babbitt, for "his life's work as a distinguished and seminal American composer."
1984 Theodore Seuss Geisel (Dr. Seuss), for his children's books.
1985 William Schuman, for "more than half a century of contribution to American music as composer and educational leader."
1987 Joseph Pulitzer Jr., for "extraordinary services to American journalism and letters during his 31 years as chairman of the Pulitzer Prize board and for his accomplishments as an editor and publisher."
1992 Art Spiegelman, for *Maus*.

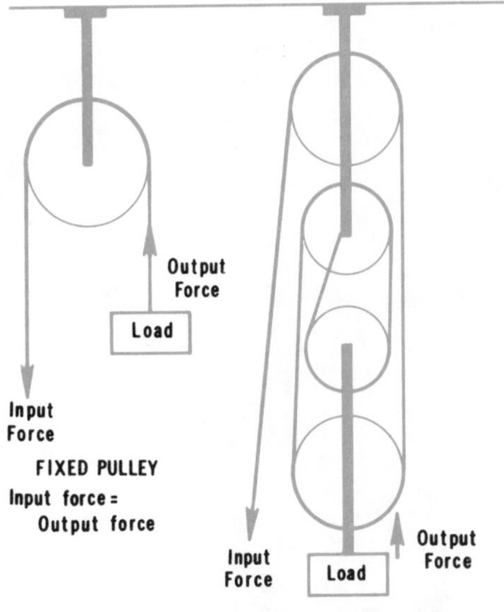

FIXED PULLEY
Input force = Output force

SYSTEM OF MOVABLE PULLEYS
Output force = Four times Input force
(Mechanical advantage equals four)

PULLEY, mechanical pulling or lifting device, consisting of a wheel, or sheave, mounted on an axis with a rope, or tackle, passing over the circumference. A pulley or hoisting apparatus is sometimes called block and tackle. Both the pulley and the wheel and axis can be viewed as simple machines that are special cases of the lever (q.v.). If the pulley is fixed, no mechanical advantage, or gain in transmission of force, occurs, and only the direction of the force applied through the rope is changed. A mechanical advantage can be gained, however, by a system of movable pulleys. Mathematically, the mechanical advantage is the ratio of output force divided by input force; ideally, it equals the number of rope strands supporting the movable load, excluding the strand on which the input force is applied. Friction reduces the actual mechanical advantage obtained and usually limits the number of pulleys employed to four.

PULLMAN, city, Whitman Co., SE Washington, on the South Fork of the Palouse R., near the Idaho border; inc. 1888. It is the seat of Washington State University (1890) and the commercial and transportation hub of a wheat-growing region. The community was settled in 1875. It is named for the American inventor George M. Pullman. Pop. (1980) 23,579; (1990) 23,478.

PULLMAN, George Mortimer (1831–97), American inventor, born in Brocton, N.Y. Originally trained as a cabinetmaker, he became a building contractor in Chicago in 1855. In 1863 he designed the first modern railroad sleeping car and patented his innovations—folding upper berths and seats that could extend into lower berths. In 1867 he organized the Pullman Palace Car Co., which manufactured sleeping cars, parlor cars, and dining cars. In 1880 he founded the town of Pullman, Ill., now part of Chicago, as a community for the workers of his company. The violent Pullman strike in 1894 occurred when the Pullman Palace Car Co. reduced wages without reducing rents in the company town.

PULLMAN STRIKE. *See* DEBS, EUGENE VICTOR; INJUNCTION; RAILROAD LABOR ORGANIZATIONS; TRADE UNIONS IN THE UNITED STATES; UNITED STATES OF AMERICA.

PULSAR. *See* STAR.

PULSE, in physiology, rhythmic expansion of the arteries resulting from passage of successive surges of blood, produced by continuing contractions of the heart. The arteries resemble elastic tubes, and at each contraction of the heart, 30 to 60 g (2 to 4 oz) of blood are forced into the already-filled vessels. The consequent distension passes along the arterial system at a rate of about 7 m (about 23 ft) a second until it reaches the capillaries, in which it is lost because of peripheral resistance to blood flow and lack of elasticity in the vessel walls.

The pulse may be felt wherever an artery passes over a solid structure, such as a bone or cartilage. The crest of the pulse wave represents the systolic pressure; the trough, the diastolic (*see* BLOOD PRESSURE). The rate of the pulse varies from 150 beats per minute in the embryo, to about 60 in the aged. Autosuggestion and certain training programs may alter the rate substantially (*see* BIOFEEDBACK; CONSCIOUSNESS, STATES OF; SPORTS MEDICINE). In disease, the pulse rate usually varies in direct ratio to the body temperature; this correspondence is so regular that an experienced physician can approximate the temperature of a patient from observation of the rate of the pulse. The pulse is commonly taken at the wrist, and changes in its rate, rhythm, and strength alert the specialist to existing or impending disease. A pulse may sometimes be observed in the large veins; it is usually twice as fast as the arterial pulse, and is caused by variations in pressure in the left auricle. *See* HEART.

PUMA, also cougar or mountain lion, *Felis* (or *Puma*) *concolor,* large member of the cat family (q.v.), Felidae. The puma is found from British Columbia to Patagonia. Its body can be 1.8 m (6 ft) long, exclusive of its long tail. The thick fur is yellowish-red above, lighter on the sides, and reddish-white on the belly; the muzzle, chin, throat, breast, and insides of the legs are whitish.

Puma, Felis concolor
Hugh Halliday–National Audubon Society

The head is relatively small, with a black spot above each eye. The female bears one to six young in a litter; the young have dark brown spots on the back, and the tail is ringed. Pumas hunt small animals, mainly at night. Because ranchers suspect them of killing cattle, the animals have been exterminated or are endangered in many areas.

For further information on this topic, see the Bibliography in volume 28, section 480.

PUMICE, igneous rock having a spongy or frothy texture, and composed largely of glass (q.v.). It is frequently made up of parallel fibers or threads, with intervening spaces to form a delicate structure. Pumice is produced by the expansion of the occluded, or internal, gases of lavas when they reach the surface of the earth (*see* LAVA). It is most abundantly developed in lavas of rhyolitic composition, because these are usually very viscous (*see* RHYOLITE).

PUMP, device used to raise, transfer, or compress liquids and gases. Four general classes of pumps for liquids are described below. In all of them, steps are taken to prevent cavitation, the formation of a vacuum, which would reduce the flow and damage the structure of the pump. Pumps used for gases and vapors are usually known as compressors (*see* AIR COMPRESSOR). The study of fluids in motion is called fluid dynamics (*see* FLUID MECHANICS).

Reciprocating Pumps. These consist of a piston moving back and forth in a cylinder with appropriate valves to regulate the flow of a liquid into and out of the cylinder. These pumps may be single or double acting. In the single acting pump, the pumping action may take place on only one side of the piston, as in the case of the common lift pump, in which the piston is moved up and down by hand. In the double acting pump, the pumping action may take place on both sides of the piston, as in the electricity or steam-driven boiler feed pump, in which water is supplied to a steam boiler under high pressure. These pumps can be single-stage or multistaged, that is, they may have one or more cylinders in series. *See* BOILER; STEAM; STEAM ENGINE.

Centrifugal Pumps. Also known as rotary pumps, these have a rotating impeller, or blade, that is immersed in the liquid, the rotation inducing an increase in pressure of the liquid by developing a centrifugal force. The impeller also gives the liquid a relatively high velocity that can be converted into pressure in a stationary part of the pump, known as the diffuser. In high-pressure pumps, a number of impellers may be used in series, and the diffusers following each impeller may contain guide vanes to reduce the liquid velocity gradually. For lower-pressure pumps, the diffuser is generally a spiral passage, known as a volute, with its cross-sectional area increasing gradually to reduce the velocity efficiently. The impeller must be surrounded by liquid when a centrifugal pump is started, that is, it must be primed. This can be done by placing a check-valve in the suction line, which holds the liquid in the pump when the impeller is not rotating. If this valve leaks, the pump may need to be primed by the introduction of liquid from an outside source such as the discharge reservoir. A centrifugal pump generally has a valve in the discharge line to control the flow and pressure.

For low flows and high pressures, the action of the impeller is largely radial as the centrifugal action governs the design. For higher flows and lower discharge pressures, the direction of the flow within the pump is more nearly parallel to the axis of the shaft, and the pump is said to have an axial flow. The impeller in this case acts as a propeller. The transition from one set of flow conditions to the other is gradual, and for intermediate conditions, the device is called a mixed-flow pump.

Jet Pumps. These depend on the high velocity of a relatively small stream of liquid or vapor to impart its energy into a larger flow of liquid. This is the principle used to inject water into a steam boiler, the vapor jet consisting of steam from the boiler. The steam is injected at a restricted section of the main flow, where, by Bernoulli's principle (q.v.), the pressure is reduced and the velocity increased. The steam is condensed in this section and the hot water mixture is then diffused to a low velocity and a pressure that can be higher than the boiler pressure, so that the water can be pumped into the boiler. Jet pumps of this type are simple in construction and are usually quite inefficient. Jet pumps have also been used to propel boats, particularly in shallow water where a conventional propeller might be damaged. *See* JET PROPULSION.

Other Pumps. A variety of positive-displacement pumps are also available, generally consisting of a rotating member with a number of lobes that move in a close-fitting casing. The liquid is trapped in the spaces between the lobes and then discharged into a region of higher pressure. A common device of this type is the gear pump, which consists of a pair of meshing gears. The lobes in this case are the gear teeth (*see* GEAR).

A simple but inefficient pump can also be con-

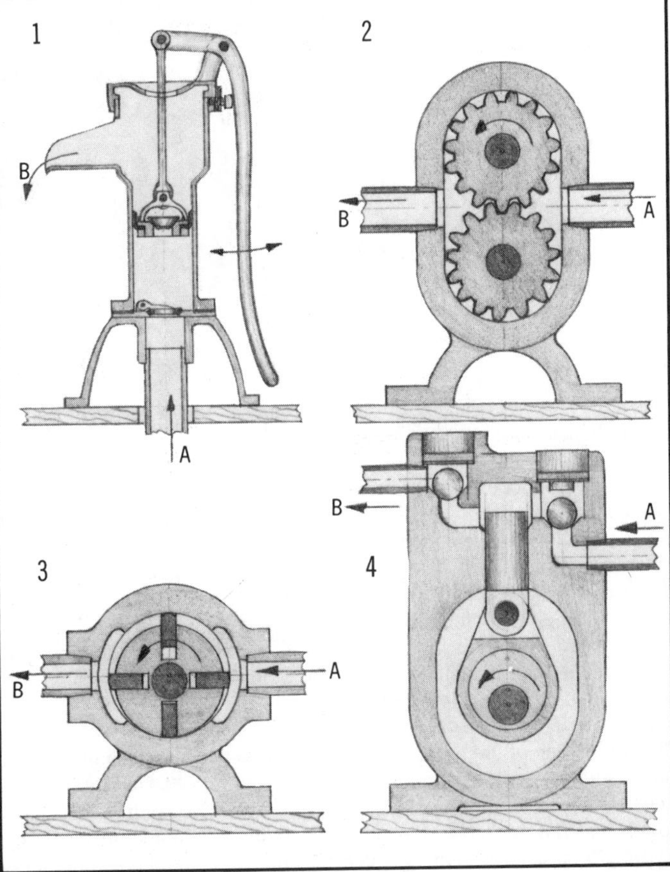

Types of pumps. (1) Hand suction or common lift; (2) Gear; (3) Vane; (4) Rotary-reciprocating. Arrows indicate direction of flow from suction "A" to discharge "B" when rotation is counterclockwise.

The earliest pumps built in ancient Persia were small, simple, pot-hung waterwheels that were driven, through a gear system, by a horizontal wheel turned by a human or an animal. In the more advanced system seen here, three wheels in sequence lift water to successively higher levels.

structed by having a screw turning in a casing and pushing the liquid along. A similar pump was first invented by the Greek geometrician and physicist Archimedes sometime after 300 BC.

In all these pumps, the liquid is discharged in a series of pulses and not continuously, so care must be taken to avoid resonant conditions in the discharge lines that could damage or destroy the installation. For reciprocating pumps, air chambers are frequently placed in the discharge line to reduce the magnitude of these pulsations and to make the flow more uniform. *See also* VACUUM; VACUUM TECHNOLOGY.

PUMPKIN, one of the common names for a genus, *Cucurbita,* of flowering plants that are characteristically spreading vines with showy yellow-orange flowers, large lobed leaves, and long twisting tendrils. The pumpkin genus is native to warmer parts of the New World and is an economically important member of the family Cucurbitaceae (*see* GOURD).

Pumpkins, squash, and some kinds of gourd are the fruits of four different species of this genus: *C. maxima, C. mixta, C. moschata,* and *C. pepo.* Summer squash, *C. pepo* var. *melopepo,* is eaten when the fruit is immature. Winter squash is derived from all four species and is eaten after the fruit has matured. Winter squash may be stored for winter consumption, hence the name. All four species also produce pumpkins, which are similar to winter squash; they are used mainly as pie filling and as jack-o'-lanterns.

PUNCTUATION, in written language, the use of standard marks to clarify meaning. Punctuation marks are also used to help convey the emphases and breathing pauses natural to speech, to indicate sentence structure, and to enhance readability. Punctuation varies from language to language and preferences for specific marks vary from writer to writer, but, within any given text, consistency is stylistically favored. The contemporary trend is toward a minimum of punctuation, with clarity as the main criterion for use. The most common punctuation marks of modern English usage are the following.

Period (.). Most sentences end with a period, which signals a strong pause. The mark is also used in decimals and after abbreviations that do not contain apostrophes.

Comma (,). The comma, a versatile and often misused punctuation mark, indicates a light pause and is chiefly utilized to separate a structural unit of a sentence. Commas appear most frequently to set off principal clauses, parenthetical material closely related to the main thought, direct quotations, forms of direct address, coordinate adjectives, and words or numbers that would otherwise be confusing. Current usage favors the insertion of a comma only where a pause is intended.

Semicolon (;). This mark represents a pause milder than a period but stronger than a comma. It is chiefly used between principal clauses and between components of a series, when the components are lengthy or already contain commas.

Colon (:). The colon most often stands between an introductory statement and an immediate amplification. It also follows the salutation of a formal letter and divides hours from minutes in statements of time.

Question Mark (?). With the exception of requests worded as queries, direct questions end with question marks; requests sometimes close with periods instead. In the body of a sentence a question mark between parentheses suggests doubt.

Exclamation Point (!). This mark ends a sentence expressing strong feeling, surprise, or incredulity.

Apostrophe ('). An apostrophe followed by the letter *s* at the end of a noun signifies possessive case. The mark followed by an *s* also pluralizes letters of the alphabet, figures, and words discussed as words. Within contracted words, apostrophes replace the eliminated letters.

Hyphen (-). Hyphens join many compound nouns, all compound adjectives, and, when they are spelled out, the elements of two-digit numbers and fractions. In word division (hyphenation) a partial word at the end of a line is followed by a hyphen and completed on the next line.

Dash (—). This mark usually stresses the materials that follow it. Dashes also emphasize parenthetical thoughts and convey sudden interruptions in thought.

Quotation Marks (" "). Direct quotations are preceded and followed by these marks. Slang and special-sense words and titles of short written works, such as poems, short stories, and songs, are also often set off by quotation marks.

Parentheses (( )). These marks enclose parenthetical matter of secondary importance.

Brackets ([ ]). Primarily used to enclose interpolated materials, brackets also set off parenthetical matter within passages already enclosed by parentheses.

Ellipsis (. . .). This mark stands for one or more omitted words; when the omission occurs at the end of a sentence, the ellipsis appears together with a period.

PUNIC WARS, name given to the three wars between Rome and Carthage in the 3d and 2d centuries BC. The adjective Punic (Lat. *Punicus*) is derived from Poeni, the name by which the Carthaginians, being of Phoenician descent, were known to the Romans.

First Punic War. The First Punic War (264–241 BC) was the outcome of growing political and economic rivalry between the two nations. It was initiated when a band of Campanian mercenary soldiers (Mamertines), besieged in the city of Messana (now Messina), in Sicily, requested aid from both Rome and Carthage against Hiero II, king of Syracuse. Carthage already controlled part of Sicily, and the Romans, responding to this request with the intention of driving the Carthaginians from the island, provoked a declaration of war. After building their first large navy, the Romans defeated a Carthaginian fleet off the Sicilian port of Mylae (*see* MYLAE, BATTLE OF) in 260 BC, but failed to capture Sicily. In 256 BC a Roman army under Roman general Marcus Atilius Regulus established a base in North Africa, but the following year the Carthaginians forced it to withdraw. For the next 13 years the war was fought in the area of Sicily. It ended with a major naval victory for the Romans in 241 BC. Sicily was then ceded to the Romans, who also seized the Carthaginian islands of Sardinia and Corsica in 237 BC.

Second Punic War. Hamilcar Barca, a distinguished Carthaginian general of the First Punic War, devoted the remainder of his life to building up Carthaginian power in Spain to compensate for the loss of Sicily. His son Hannibal became commander of the Carthaginian forces in this area in 221 BC, and in 219 BC he attacked and captured Saguntum, a Spanish city allied with Rome. This act brought on the Second Punic War (218–201 BC). In the spring of 218 BC

Hannibal swiftly marched a large army through Spain and Gaul and across the Alps to attack the Romans in Italy before they could complete their preparations for war. He crossed the dangerous mountains and secured a firm position in northern Italy. By 216 BC he had won two major victories, at Lake Trasimeno and the town of Cannae, and reached southern Italy. In spite of his requests, Hannibal received insufficient reinforcements and siege weapons from Carthage until 207 BC, when his brother Hasdrubal left Spain with an army to join him. Hasdrubal crossed the Alps, but in a battle at the Metaurus River, in northern Italy, he was killed and his troops defeated. Meanwhile, the Roman general Publius Cornelius Scipio Africanus, known as Scipio Africanus the Elder, had totally defeated the Carthaginians in Spain, and in 204 BC he landed an army in North Africa. The Carthaginians recalled Hannibal to Africa to defend them against Scipio. Leading an army of untrained recruits, he was decisively defeated by Scipio at the Battle of Zama in 202 BC. This battle marked the end of Carthage as a great power and the close of the Second Punic War. The Carthaginians were compelled to cede Spain and the islands of the Mediterranean still in their possession, relinquish their navy, and pay an indemnity to Rome.

Third Punic War. In the 2d century BC, however, Carthage continued to be commercially successful and, though only a minor power, a source of irritation to Rome. The Romans were further incited by the speeches of the censor Cato the Elder, who demanded *Delenda est Carthago* ("Carthage must be destroyed"). A minor Carthaginian breach of treaty gave the pretext for the Third Punic War (149–146 BC), in which the Romans, led by Scipio the Younger, captured the city of Carthage, razed it to the ground, and sold the surviving inhabitants into slavery.

For further information on this topic, see the Bibliography in volume 28, sections 887, 892.

PUNISHMENT, in modern criminal law, penalty inflicted by the state upon a person for committing a criminal offense.

In early societies punishment for a crime was left to the person wronged or to his or her kin, clan, or tribe. The punishments inflicted were characteristically cruel, and, by modern standards, out of proportion to the offense committed. Torture and capital punishment, prevalent early forms of punishment, evolved largely from old beliefs in vengeance. With the growing complexity of society and the centralization of governments, the right to punish was taken from the offended party and vested in the state.

Only at the end of the 18th century did significant call for improved criminal procedure arise. Punishment came to be thought of not only as express vindication but as a means of protecting the laws from abuse by individual members of the society. Deterrence and separation from society, rather than revenge, became the principal purposes of punishment, with the degree of penalty adjusted to reflect the nature of the crime. Ensuing reforms reduced the number of capital crimes, restricted corporal punishment, and virtually abolished mutilation, replacing most of these harsh measures with imprisonment. Emphasis began to be placed on rehabilitation for the good of society and the individual, rather than on punishment for its own sake.

The issue of punishment versus benign corrective treatment has persisted to this day. Arguments against punishment cite its essentially vindictive and peremptorily negative nature; its effects are viewed as ineffective and perhaps even destructive. Proponents of legal punishment, on the other hand, stress its value as a sobering deterrent to those criminally inclined and, in the case of imprisonment for its own sake, as a means for protecting society from chronic or dangerous lawbreakers. Criminal codes of the different states of the U.S. vary with regard to specific penalties that may be imposed for crimes.

For further information on this topic, see the Bibliography in volume 28, sections 301–3.

PUNJAB (Hindu, "five rivers"), historic region, NW portion of the subcontinent of India, now divided into the province of Punjab in Pakistan and the state of Punjab in India. The extreme NE part of the Punjab region lies in the Himalayan foothills, but most of the territory is a level plain sloping from an elevation of about 490 m (about 1600 ft) in the N to less than 61 m (200 ft) in the extreme SW. The region's name is derived from the five great rivers that traverse it: the Indus R, and its tributaries and the Jhelum, Chenab, Ravi, and Sutlej rivers. The chief cities of the Punjab include Amritsar (now in India), Lahore, Multan, Rawalpindi, and Sialkot (in Pakistan).

Most of the inhabitants are engaged in agriculture; the Punjab is the most important wheat-growing region of the subcontinent. The soil is very fertile, but much of it requires extensive irrigation. Punjabi industry is known for the products of native artisans, such as handloomed carpets, shawls, and rugs; work in gold, silver, brass, and copper; glazed tiles and pottery.

The climate of the plains is excessively hot and dry between April and August, with temperatures as high as 49° C (120° F). The rains of the monsoon season begin at the end of June. Win-

The entrance to the High Court Building in Chandigarh, capital of Punjab. The city was designed and built in the 1950s by an international team of architects. United Nations

ters are cool with some frosts. Annual rainfall ranges from about 915 mm (about 36 in) in the N to 102 mm (4 in) in the S.

In the Indian portion of the Punjab region about 65% of the population is Hindu, 30% Sikh, and 2% Muslim. In the Pakistani portion, about 97% is Muslim.

Punjab proper was annexed by Great Britain in 1849; for details on the early history of the Punjab, *see* SIKHS. Under the terms of the Indian independence Act of 1947, the Punjab was divided into the East Punjab province of the union of India and the West Punjab province of Pakistan. The area allotted to India was 96,809 sq km (37,378 sq mi), with a population of about 12,650,000, and the area given to Pakistan was 160,610 sq km (62,012 sq mi), with a population of about 18,800,000. The partition line followed the course of the Ravi and Sutlej rivers, allotting parts of Lahore, Rawalpindi, and Multan divisions to Pakistan and the remainder of the region to India.

In addition to Punjab proper, the Punjab region included 34 Indian, or Native, states, known as the Punjab States, with an area of 98,798 sq km (38,146 sq mi) and a population (1941) of 5,503,554. Following the partition, most Indian states joined the union of India.

Rioting and civil strife among Hindus, Muslims, and Sikhs began even before the 1947 partition, and in August, when the Punjabi partition was effected, open warfare erupted. The partition cut the Sikh community in half, and the Sikhs attempted to eliminate local Muslims, massacring many of them. As a result of the communal fighting, large numbers of Muslims, Hindus, and Sikhs abandoned their homes in the Punjab and immigrated to friendly territory.

The Pakistani portion of the Punjab region was amalgamated in 1955 into the province of West Pakistan; in 1970 it was reconstituted as Punjab province. In 1956 the Indian portion was merged with other provinces to form the present state of Punjab; for subsequent history, *see* PUNJAB (state of India).

PUNJAB, state, NW India, bordered on the N by Jammu and Kashmir State and Himachal Pradesh State, on the E by Uttar Pradesh State, on the S by Haryana State, on the S and SW by Rajasthan State, and on the W by Pakistan. Punjab State lies between the great systems of the Indus and Ganges rivers. Most of the state is an alluvial plain, irrigated by canals; the arid S border of the state edges on the Great Indian (or Thar) Desert. The Siwalik Hills rise sharply in the N of the state. Farming is the leading occupation; the major crops are wheat, maize, rice, pulses, sugarcane, and cotton. Among the livestock raised are buffalo and other cattle, sheep, goats, and poultry. The principal industries include the manufacture of textiles, sewing machines, sports goods, starch, fertilizers, bicycles, scientific instruments, electrical goods, and machine tools and the processing of sugar and pine oil.

The state of Punjab was formed on Nov. 1, 1956, by merging East Punjab States Union with Punjab and Patiala provinces of India (for earlier history of the area, *see* PUNJAB, historic region). Subsequently, the Sikhs in the new state demanded a Punjabi-speaking state. In 1966 most of Punjab was divided into Punjabi-speaking Punjab State and Hindi-speaking Haryana State. In 1985 an accord was reached with India to expand the boundaries of the Punjab State and make Chandigarh, formerly capital of both Punjab and Haryana states, the capital of Punjab only. Area, 50,376 sq km (19,450 sq mi); pop. (1981 prelim.) 16,669,755.

PUNTA ARENAS, city and port, S Chile, capital of Magallanes Region, on the Strait of Magellan. Punta Arenas is one of the southernmost cities in the world. An important trading center for the wool, hides, mutton, and timber produced in S Chile, the city has sawmills, tanneries, and facilities for processing frozen meat and canned fish. It is also the supply center for the oil industry on the nearby archipelago of Tierra del Fuego. Punta Arenas was founded in 1849 for the purpose of reinforcing Chilean claims of sovereignty over the Strait of Magellan. The city was a refueling station for shipping before the opening of the Panama Canal. In 1927 it was renamed Magallanes, but the original name was restored in 1938. Pop. (1987 est.) 111,700.

PUNTARENAS, city, W Costa Rica, capital of Puntarenas Province, on the Gulf of Nicoya (an arm of the Pacific Ocean). It is one of the country's major seaports; principal exports include bananas, coffee, and processed fish. The city is linked with San José by railroad and highway systems and is served by an international airport. Pop. (1984 prelim.) 29,224.

PUPPETS AND MARIONETTES, inanimate figures used in a theatrical performance to represent human beings, animals, or mythological personages; they vary in size and construction and may be operated by hand or with various other controls.

Types. The simplest puppet is the glove or mitten puppet, which fits over the hand of the puppeteer and is manipulated by the fingers. Rod or stick puppets are flat or three-dimensional figures manipulated by the puppeteer and one or more helpers, using rigid sticks or rods, from be-

The Muppets, created by Jim Henson, are among the most popular characters in the history of puppetry. Here, Henson poses with members of the Muppet family, including (at lower right) Miss Piggy and Kermit the frog.

low the stage surface. Typically, a single rod supports the head and neck, one or two additional rods control one or both arms, and the feet hang free. The marionette is operated by strings or wires from above, usually one to each of the hands and feet, one to the head, and another to the waist; additional strings may be added to achieve special movements. Marionettes and rod puppets are jointed so that individual sections may move independently. Ordinarily the puppet theater is a miniature one, resembling the booths at a fair or a miniature proscenium stage.

Puppet plays vary from simple scenes between two puppets, operated by a single puppeteer in a portable booth, to elaborate performances of opera and drama in a theater equipped with proportionately scaled scenery and furniture. The last-named performances require many figures, usually marionettes. Music is often an integral part of a puppet production. The dialogue may be provided by the operators, or a narrator may describe the action taking place. Recordings may also be used.

History. The history of puppets is long and complex. Puppets were known in ancient Egypt, in classical Greece, and in China. The rod puppets of Java and other parts of the East, for example, perform versions of folktales, appearing as shadows on a translucent sheet. The *bunraku,* or *jōruri,* theater of Japan uses puppets, or dolls, almost half life-size, manipulated by wires and levers worked by three black-clad people visible on stage. The puppets perform traditional heroic dramas or domestic tragedies while a narrator, accompanied by an orchestra, chants the story. Beginning in medieval times, European folk artists adapted hand puppets into national characters, such as the English Punch and Judy, the French Guignol, and the German Kasperle. These puppets play out traditional sketches featuring slapstick comedy, violent fights, and exaggerated incidents of domestic life. In the 18th and 19th centuries most of the forms of drama known to Western society were also performed by puppets or marionettes.

Today's puppets may be seen in nightclubs, in children's theaters, and on television. Similar animated figures may also appear as characters in films. Perhaps most familiar to American children are the hand puppets who appear on "Kukla,

Poster advertising the famous Punch and Judy puppet show. Bettmann Archive

Fran, and Ollie," "Sesame Street," "The Muppet Show," and other television shows. Among the most remarkable marionettes are those used to present Mozart operas in Salzburg, Austria. In New York City in the 1970s the marionettes of Bil Baird (1904–87) appeared in such stories as *Ali Baba and the Forty Thieves.*

For further information on this topic, see the Bibliography in volume 28, section 749.

PURANAS, Sanskrit writings about primordial times; part of the sacred literature of Hinduism. Tradition attributes the Puranas to Vyasa, a semilegendary *rishi,* or sage, purportedly the compiler also of the Veda and the epic poem *Mahabharata.* Scholars, however, regard the Puranas as having been compiled by many hands between the 4th and the 16th centuries AD.

In all, there are 18 great Puranas (many more subordinate works, and some modern ones, dealing with primordial times also are known as Puranas). All are written in verse, are represented as being divinely or supernaturally transmitted, and take the form of a dialogue between an interpreter and an inquirer. They vary in length from about 10,000 couplets each to more than 81,000 couplets; the 18 Puranas are said to contain, collectively, about 400,000 couplets. Each Purana is devoted largely to one of the three Hindu gods; each is also characteristically pantheistic, telling of other gods as well. Thus, six are devoted primarily to Brahma, six others to Siva, and the remaining six to Vishnu. On the whole, Vishnu is probably the most prominent.

According to tradition, each Purana is supposed to deal with five topics; this subject matter marks the Puranas as genuine and sets them all apart from other writings. The five distinguishing topics are the creation of the universe; the destruction and re-creation of the universe, including the history of humankind; the genealogy of the gods and holy sages; the reigns of the Manus; and the history of the lunar and solar dynasties. The Puranas date from a later time than the Veda and the epics and thus represent a different stage of Hinduism, in which the Vedic and epic concepts and legends concerning the Hindu pantheon gradually were transformed according to the sectarian tendencies of the masses.

PURCELL, Henry (1659–95), England's greatest native composer, who wrote with consummate skill music of virtually every kind known during the Restoration. His compositions combined elements of the French and Italian baroque and traditional English musical forms.

Born in Westminster (now London), Purcell was the son of a court musician and became a chorister in the Chapel Royal at the age of ten; when his voice broke, he was apprenticed to the keeper of the royal instruments and tuned the organ in Westminster Abbey. Purcell was appointed composer for the court violins in 1677 upon the death of Matthew Locke (1630–77). Three years later he succeeded John Blow (1649–1708) as abbey organist. He became organist at the Chapel Royal in 1682 and was appointed composer in ordinary to the King's Musick (1683), a major post, under Charles II; later he was harpsichord player to James II. Purcell also taught music to the aristocracy, wrote ceremonial odes and anthems for royal events, and composed for the stage, church, and home. He died in London on Nov. 21, 1695, and was buried under the organ in Westminster Abbey.

Purcell is most famous for his theatrical music. His only true opera is *Dido and Aeneas,* a masterpiece based on a tragedy by Nahum Tate (1652–1715) and first performed in about 1689. Other dramatic works, although called operas, are actually instrumental and vocal music written to accompany such plays as Thomas Betterton's *Dioclesian* (1690); John Dryden's *King Arthur* (1691); *The Fairy Queen* (1692), a masque adapted from Shakespeare's *Midsummer Night's Dream* (1692); and Dryden and Sir Robert Howard's *The Indian Queen* (1695; completed by Purcell's brother Daniel), which contains some of Purcell's most famous music. Purcell also wrote much fine sacred music, of which the anthem *My Heart Is Inditing* (1685), performed at the coronation of James II, is outstanding. His many songs and duets, both sacred and secular, are still highly regarded. His instrumental compositions include fantasias and sonatas, mostly for strings, and keyboard works.

PURDUE UNIVERSITY, state institution of higher learning, in Lafayette, Ind., with regional campuses in Fort Wayne, Hammond, Indianapolis, and Westville. Originally a land-grant college, Purdue was chartered in 1865 as the Indiana Agricultural College; the present name was adopted in 1869. The university includes schools of agriculture, consumer and family sciences, education, engineering, health science, liberal arts, management, nursing, pharmacy, science, social science,technology, and veterinary sciences, as well as a graduate school. Purdue confers the associate's, bachelor's, master's, doctoral and various professional degrees.

PURE FOOD AND DRUG ACTS, general designation for laws designed to ensure the safety, proper labeling, and purity of foods, drugs, vaccines, devices, and cosmetics. The most important such law in the U.S. is the Food, Drug, and Cosmetic Act of 1938, which is administered by the Food and Drug Administration (FDA) of the Department of Health and Human Services.

Foods, drugs, vaccines, medical devices, veterinary drugs, and cosmetics in interstate commerce must comply with the law, which protects both consumers and manufacturers. Factories where these products are prepared receive inspections covering sanitation, raw materials, adequate processing, and finished product. Penalties for violations include seizure of illegal goods, injunctions to restrain violative shipments, and criminal prosecution of those responsible for the violation, with fines up to $500,000, imprisonment up to 10 years, or both, for repeated offenses.

The first pure food and drug law was enacted in 1906 through the efforts of Harvey Washington Wiley and other crusaders who brought to public attention many abuses in the form of poor health practices and excessive prices. This law, as revised in 1938 and strengthened by subsequent amendments, gives consumers the greatest protection they have ever received from dangerous and impure foods and drugs; it requires labeling that will disclose the nature of the contents of the package when the buyer cannot see the product or judge its composition and value. It also provides safeguards against the introduction of untested new drugs.

A 1951 amendment required that drugs that cannot be used safely without medical supervision must be dispensed only upon prescription. The food additives amendment of 1958 required manufacturers to prove to the FDA the safety of additives before their use in foods. Color additive amendments in 1960 tightened requirements on colors used in foods, drugs, and cosmetics. Both banned the use in foods of substances that cause cancer in animals. Drug amendments passed in 1962 required manufacturers, for the first time, to prove to the FDA the effectiveness, as well as the safety, of drugs before they were marketed. Amendments in 1965 imposed strict controls on abused-drugs—depressants, stimulants, and hallucinogens. The Child Protection Act and the Fair Packaging and Labeling Act of 1966 gave additional protection to the consumer. The Medical Devices Act of 1976 amended the law by providing for controls over medical equipment.

PURGATORY, in Christian theology, state of purgation, in which, according to the Roman Catholic and Eastern churches, souls after death either are purified from venial sins or undergo the temporal punishment that, after the guilt of mortal sin has been remitted, still remains to be endured by the sinner. The ultimate happiness of their souls is supposed to be thus secured. On the existence of purgatory Greek and Latin churches are agreed; they also agree that it is a state of suffering. Although the Latins hold that this is by fire, the Greeks do not determine the manner of the suffering, but regard it as being caused by tribulation. The Council of Florence (1439) left this free for discussion.

The medieval doctrine and practice regarding purgatory were among the grounds for the protest of the Waldenses and were rejected by the Reformers. Protestants held that salvation had been achieved for humankind by Christ and was obtained by faith in Christ alone. A belief in an intermediate state and a period of education and probation on the other side of the grave has been held and taught in the Anglican church. The British religious leader John Henry Newman drew on the theology of purgatory for his poem "Dream of Gerontius," which the English composer Sir Edward Elgar set to music as an oratorio under the same title.

PURI, sometimes called Jagannath, town, E India, in Orissa State, on the Bay of Bengal. It is a seaport, resort, and market center. Its industries include handicrafts, fish curing, and rice milling. In the town is a 12th-century temple erected in honor of the Hindu god Vishnu, under his aspect as Juggernaut. Puri is the site of an annual festival attended by thousands of Hindu pilgrims in honor of Vishnu. Pop. (1981 prelim.) 101,089.

PURIM, one of the later Jewish festivals. Purim commemorates the deliverance of the Persian Jews from destruction in the reign of the Persian king Ahasuerus, or Xerxes I, as recorded in the Book of Esther. Held on the 14th and 15th days of the Jewish month of Adar (in the spring), it is celebrated by feasting and merriment, almsgiving, sending food to neighbors and friends, and chanting the text of Esther. It is perhaps the most joyous day of the Jewish year, with masquerades, plays, and drinking of wine even in the synagogue.

For further information on this topic, see the Bibliography in volume 28, sections 129, 344.

PURITANISM, a movement arising within the Church of England in the latter part of the 16th century, which sought to carry the reformation of that church beyond the point represented by the Elizabethan settlement (1559), an attempt to establish a middle course between Roman Catholicism and the ideas of the Protestant reformers (*see* CHURCH OF ENGLAND). It had a continuous life within the church until the Stuart Restoration (1660).

The term *Puritanism* is also used in a broader sense to refer to attitudes and values considered characteristic of the Puritans. Thus, the Separatists (q.v.) in the 16th century, the Quakers (*see* FRIENDS, SOCIETY OF) in the 17th century, and Noncomformists (q.v.) after the Restoration may be called Puritans, although they were no longer part of the established church. The founders of New England, for whom immigration to the New World was in fact if not in avowed intent withdrawal from the mother church, are also commonly called Puritans.

Finally, the word *puritanism* has often been used as a term of abuse in a way that does scant justice to historical Puritanism—for instance, when a rigid moralism, or the condemnation of innocent pleasure, or religious narrowness, is stigmatized as puritanical.

Even within the Church of England, a precise definition of Puritanism is elusive. The leading Puritan clergyman in Elizabeth's reign was Thomas Cartwright (1535–1603), who denied he was one. He is particularly remembered for his advocacy of presbyterian polity; but Puritanism cannot be identifed with presbyterianism (q.v.), because a major segment of the movement eventually adopted congregationalism (q.v.). A doctrinal distinction might be made between the Calvinistic theology of the Puritans and the Arminianism (q.v.) of Archbishop William Laud, their chief antagonist in the time of King Charles I, but in practice the line between Calvinist and Arminian was blurred. The essence of Puritanism is in the intensity of the Puritan's commitment to a morality, a form of worship, and a civil society strictly conforming to God's commandments.

In an anti-Puritan tract, A Glasse for the Times *(1641), the Puritans are attacked for their supposed aversion to the conventions of public worship.* The Granger Collection

Puritan theology is a version of Calvinism (q.v.). It asserts the basic sinfulness of humankind; but it also declares that by an eternal decree God has determined that some will be saved through the righteousness of Christ despite their sins. No one can be certain in this life what his or her eternal destiny will be. Nevertheless, the experience of conversion, in which the soul is touched by the Holy Spirit, so that the inward bias of the heart is turned from sinfulness to holiness, is at least some indication that one is of the elect.

The experience of conversion was therefore central to Puritan spirituality. Much of Puritan preaching was concerned with it: why not everyone will be converted; how conversion comes about—whether in a blinding flash as with St. Paul on the road to Damascus, or following well-defined stages of preparation; how one can distinguish the real thing from the counterfeit. Puritan spiritual life stressed self-discipline and introspection, through which one sought to determine whether particular spiritual strivings were genuine marks of sainthood. Although full assurance might never be attained, the conviction of having been chosen by God fortified the Puritans to contend with what they regarded as wantonness in society and faithfulness in the church, and to endure the hardships involved in trying to create a Christian commonwealth in the New World.

Puritanism was not static and unchanging. At first it simply stood for further reform of worship, but soon it began to attack episcopacy as unscriptural. At times the difference between the Puritans and the Anglicans seems to have been as much a matter of differing cultural values as of differing theological opinions, as when their Sabbatarianism (insistence on strict observance of the Sabbath) came into conflict with King James I's defense of sports and games on Sunday. Puritanism became a political as well as a religious movement when the parliamentary protest against Stuart despotism became entwined with the religious protest against Archbishop Laud's policy of enforced conformity (*see* ENGLISH REVOLUTION). Both in England during the Commonwealth (1649–60), and in 17th-century New England, Puritanism meant the direction and control of civil authority.

Nor was Puritanism a wholly cohesive movement. In the 1580s, the Separatists were bitterly condemned by other Puritans. When the Westminster Assembly (1643) sought to define doctrine and polity, the differences between Presbyterians and Independents (congregationalists) were manifest. In the turbulence of the 1640s, a number of small sects appeared, emphasizing that part of Puritan doctrine which acknowledges the work of the Holy Spirit in the soul of the believer to the neglect of that part which stands for social order and authority.

With the Stuart Restoration, many Puritans accepted the Book of Common Prayer (q.v.) and rule by bishops; others were forced into permanent nonconformity. In one sense, therefore, Puritanism failed. Its influence has persisted, however, entering into Methodism (q.v.) in the 18th century and evangelicalism (q.v.) in the 19th. Furthermore, in America, Puritan moralism and its sense of an elect people in covenant with God deeply affected the national character.

For further information on this topic, see the Bibliography in volume 28, section 96.

PURKINJE, Johannes Evangelista (1787–1869), Czech physiologist, who pioneered in the fields of histology (q.v.), embryology, pharmacology, and the workings of the eye, heart, and brain. Born in Libochovice and educated at the University of Prague, he became professor of physiology at the University of Breslau and later at the University of Prague. He invented the microtome, an instrument for slicing thin portions of tissue for microscopic examination. His histological discoveries include the sweat glands; the neurons, called Purkinje's cells, of the cerebellum; the muscular fibers, called Purkinje's fibers, in the tissue of the ventricles of the heart; and the nucleus of the human egg, called Purkinje's germinal vesicle. He also investigated the structure, function, and diseases of the eye; the effects of such drugs as opium; and identification by means of fingerprints.

PURPLE HEART, ORDER OF THE, oldest American decoration for military merit, originally established by George Washington in 1782. The original decoration, known as the Badge for Military Merit, consisted of a purple heart-shaped piece of silk, edged with a narrow binding of silver, and with the word *merit* stitched across the face in silver. The decoration was revived in 1932 as a heart-shaped medal with a center of purple enamel and a border and relief bust of Washington in gold color. On the reverse is the inscription "For Military Merit," with the decorated person's name engraved beneath.

The Purple Heart is awarded to members of the U.S. Armed Forces who have been killed or wounded in action against an enemy. It may also be awarded for maltreatment endured while a prisoner of war.

PURSLANE. *See* PORTULACA.

PURUS, river of South America, rising on the E slopes of the Andes Mts. in Peru. It is about 2980 km (about 1850 mi) long and winds generally NE across Brazil, passing through Acre State into Amazonas State, where, SW of Manaus, it becomes an important tributary of the Amazon R. The chief affluent of the Purus is the Acre R.

PUS, thick white or yellowish fluid, found at sites of bacterial infection (q.v.) of the body. Certain white blood cells, called phagocytes, migrate to the area of infection and engulf the invaders. They then kill the ingested bacteria by releasing toxic substances inside the cell. In the process the white blood cells also die, and these cells become constituents of pus. *See* ABSCESS; CARBUNCLE.

PUSAN (Jap. *Fusan* or *Husan*), city, SE South Korea, capital of South Kyŏngsang Province, on Korea Strait. Pusan is the second largest South Korean city and the principal seaport in the republic. Industrial establishments in the city include shipyards, railroad workshops, rubber factories, ironworks, textile mills, rice and salt refineries, and fisheries. The port has ferry service to the Japanese port of Shimonoseki. Pusan has several universities, among them Pusan National University (1946).

Pusan was invaded by the Japanese in 1592. The port was opened to Japanese trade in 1876 and to general foreign commerce in 1883. After 1910, when Korea became a Japanese protectorate, the city was the center of a flourishing trade with Japan. During the Korean War (1950–53), Pusan was a major port of entry and supply depot for UN forces. Pop. (1990 prelim.) 3,797,566.

PUSEY, Edward Bouverie (1800–82), British clergyman and theologian, a leader of the Oxford movement (q.v.).

Pusey was born near Oxford, England, on Aug. 22, 1800, and educated at Christ Church College, University of Oxford. In 1823 he was elected a fellow of Oriel College, Oxford, where he became affiliated with the British divine John Keble, the British religious leader John Henry Newman, and other members of the Oxford movement. Members of this group hoped to inspire greater devotion to the Church of England by stressing the church's catholic origins. In 1828 Pusey was ordained in the Church of England, appointed Regius Professor of Hebrew at Oxford, and made canon of Christ Church.

The Oxford movement began to publish *Tracts for the Times* in 1833, and Pusey contributed tracts on fasting and on baptism. When Newman left the Oxford movement in 1841, Pusey assumed leadership. In 1843 he delivered a sermon defending certain catholic beliefs, and he was suspended from preaching at the university for two years. In 1845 he aided in the formation of the first Anglican sisterhood. The following year his sermon "The Entire Absolution of the Penitent" established the Anglican practice of private confession. A later sermon, "The Rule of Faith," diminished the secessions to Roman Catholicism that his suspension had inspired. He died at Ascot Priory on Sept. 16, 1882. In addition to a number of brief theological treatises, Pusey published the scholarly *The Minor Prophets, with Commentary* (1860) and the three-part *Eirecon* (1865–70), an attempt to find a meeting ground for uniting the Roman Catholic church and the Church of England.

PUSEY, Nathan Marsh (1907–), American educator, born in Council Bluffs, Iowa, and educated at Harvard University. He served as a sophomore tutor at Lawrence College (now Lawrence University), Appleton, Wis., from 1935 to 1938, when he was appointed assistant professor of history and literature at Scripps College in Claremont, Calif. In 1940 he went to Wesleyan University in Middletown, Conn., where he taught classics for three years. Elected president of Lawrence College in 1944, Pusey became known as a brilliant administrator with strong convictions regarding the importance of the liberal arts in college education. He left Lawrence to succeed James Bryant Conant as president of Harvard University in 1953; he retired in 1971. Pusey is the author of *The Age of the Scholar* (1963) and *American Higher Education, 1945–1970* (1978).

PUSHKIN, Aleksandr Sergeyevich (1799–1837), Russian poet and author, who founded the literature of his language with epic and lyric poems, plays, novels, and short stories.

Pushkin was born June 6, 1799, in Moscow, into a noble family. He took particular pride in his great-grandfather Hannibal, a black general who served Peter the Great. Educated at the Imperial Lyceum at Tsarkoye Selo, Pushkin demonstrated an early poetic gift. In 1817 Pushkin was taken into the ministry of foreign affairs in Saint Petersburg; there he mingled in the social life of the capital and belonged to an underground revolutionary group. In 1820 his "Ode to Liberty" came to the attention of the authorities, and the young poet was exiled to the Caucasus; nonetheless, Pushkin continued to hold official posts.

That same year Pushkin published his *Ruslan and Ludmila,* a long romantic poem based on folklore, which earned him a reputation as one of Russia's most promising poetic talents. The influence of Lord Byron shows itself, along with Pushkin's own love of liberty, in his next major poems, *The Prisoner of the Caucasus* (1822), *The Fountain of Bakhchisarai* (1822), and *The Gypsies* (1823–24). He began his most famous work, *Eu-*

Aleksandr Pushkin

gene Onegin, in 1823; a Byronic love story with a realistic contemporary setting that has been described as the first of the great Russian novels (although in verse), it was not completed until 1831. Transferred to Odessa in 1823, he incurred the stern disapproval of a superior. He was dismissed from government service in 1824 and banished to his mother's estate near Pskov. There he wrote (1824–25) *Boris Godunov,* a Russian historical tragedy in the Shakespearean tradition, published six years later. In 1826 Czar Nicholas I, recognizing his enormous popularity, pardoned him. Pushkin continued to draw upon Russian history in two long poems, *Poltava* (1828) and *The Bronze Horseman* (1833), and in his novel of the Pugachev rebellion, *The Captain's Daughter* (1836). He also wrote short stories, the best known of which is "The Queen of Spades." Pushkin died Feb. 10, 1837, from wounds that he suffered in a duel which he had fought in St. Petersburg.

Pushkin provided a literary heritage for Russians, whose native language had hitherto been considered unfit for literature. He was also a versatile writer of great vigor and optimism who understood the many facets of the Russian character. His lyric poetry—said to be delightful to the Russian ear but untranslatable—and his simple, vivid prose were invaluable models for the writers who followed him.

PUSHTU *or* **PASHTO.** *See* INDO-IRANIAN LANGUAGES.

PUSSY WILLOW. *See* WILLOW.

PUTNAM, Israel (1718–90), American soldier, who fought in the French and Indian War and the American Revolution. Although always an energetic and inspiring leader, Putnam proved to be an indifferent military strategist when given high command late in life.

Born in Salem Village (now Danvers), Mass., on Jan 7, 1718, he moved to Pomfret, Conn., in 1740 and farmed there successfully. He was commissioned a lieutenant of Connecticut volunteers in 1756 and took part in actions at Ticonderoga, Montréal, and Havana, attaining the rank of lieutenant colonel by 1759. In 1764 he helped to relieve Chief Pontiac's siege of Detroit. A militant patriot, he reportedly left his plow in the field and went off to war when word of the battles of Lexington and Concord reached him. First a brigadier, then a major general, he helped to fortify Breed's Hill. He was in command of New York City until George Washington arrived in April 1776. At the Battle of Long Island he was forced to retreat. In 1777 he had to abandon Fort Montgomery and Fort Clinton in the Hudson highlands to the British. He commanded the American right wing on the Hudson until a stroke in December 1779 ended his service. He died in Pomfret on May 29, 1790.

Israel Putnam

PUTUMAYO, also Içá, river of South America. It rises in SW Colombia, in the Andes Mts., E of Pasto, and flows SE for about 1610 km (about 1000 mi). It forms a section of the boundary between Colombia and Ecuador and most of the Colombia-Peru border. In its lower course the Putumayo crosses into Brazil, where it is known as the Içá, and empties into the Amazon R. near Santo Antônio do Içá. The river is navigable during the rainy season for most of its length.

PUVIS DE CHAVANNES, Pierre Cécile (1824-98), French painter, born in Lyons. In Paris he studied briefly with the painters Eugène Delacroix and Thomas Couture (1815-79). In 1861 he exhibited *War* and *Peace,* two murals (Musée de Picardie, Amiens) that established his reputation as an artist. During the greater part of his career, he was occupied with important mural paintings for French public buildings. Puvis de Chavannes's easel paintings include *The Sacred Grove* (1887, Art Institute of Chicago) and *The Inspiring Muses Acclaiming Genius as Messenger of Light* (1894-98, Boston Public Library). Despite the growing emphasis on realism during his time, he favored allegorical themes, neoclassical style, and a subdued palette.

PU YI, Henry. *See* HSÜAN T'UNG.

PYGMALION, in Roman mythology, sculptor of Cyprus. Pygmalion hated women and resolved never to marry. He worked, however, for many months on a statue of a beautiful woman, and eventually fell madly in love with it. Disconsolate because the statue remained lifeless and could not respond to his caresses, Pygmalion prayed to Venus, goddess of love, to send him a maiden like his statue. Venus answered his prayer by endowing the statue with life. The maiden, whom Pygmalion called Galatea, returned his love and bore him a son, Paphos, from whom the city sacred to Venus received its name.

PYGMY, human subpopulation in which an average stature of less than 152 cm (60 in) is an inherited racial trait. Pygmy people were described by ancient Greek writers such as Homer and Herodotus. Today Pygmies are found in the tropical forests in central Africa and also in the Malay Peninsula (the Senang people), the Philippine Islands (the Aeta and other tribes), central New Guinea (several tribes), and the Andaman Islands of India. Nearly all groups live by hunting and gathering; most often, they speak the language of their neighbors.

African Pygmies—the most numerous Pygmy population, estimated variously at 150,000 to 300,000—are somewhat lighter complexioned than surrounding peoples and are believed to have lived in the Congo Valley before the arrival of other peoples. The best-known tribe, the Mbuti or Bambuti, are the shortest of all human groups, averaging about 130 cm (about 51 in) in height. Non-African Pygmy populations, often called Negritos, may also represent archaic populations. Blood typing and other studies indicate that the African, Asian, Oceanian, and Indian groups are genetically distinct from one another.

See also NEGRO; RACES, CLASSIFICATION OF.

PYLADES. *See* ELECTRA.

PYLE, Ernie, full name ERNEST TAYLOR PYLE (1900-45), American journalist, born near Dana, Ind. He attended the University of Indiana but left before graduating. He was a reporter, copy editor, and aviation editor until 1932, when he began to write a daily column for the Scripps-Howard and other newspapers as a roving reporter. His simple, warm, human style was widely popular, especially during World War II. In 1944 he was awarded a Pulitzer Prize in reporting, for his distinguished reports from the European battlefront. One year later, on the island of Ie Shima in the southwestern Pacific Ocean near Okinawa, he was killed by Japanese machine-gun fire. His columns, which eventually appeared in 200 newspapers, were published in book form as *Ernie Pyle in England* (1941), *Here Is Your War* (1943), and *Brave Men* (1944).

PYLE, Howard (1853-1911), American illustrator, teacher, and writer, born in Wilmington, Del. His stories and illustrations for *Harper's Weekly* and other periodicals established his reputation. From 1894 to 1900 he was director of illustration at the Drexel Institute of Technology, Philadelphia. In 1900 he established in Wilmington the Howard Pyle School of Art, where he conducted free courses in illustration. Pyle's work often deals with American history and medieval folklore; his illustrations feature a realistic style and a bold line.

PYLOS. *See* PÍLOS.

PYM, John (1583?-1643), English parliamentary leader, born in Brymore House, and educated at the University of Oxford. He was a Puritan leader, and served in every Parliament from 1614 until his death. He was prominent in the agitation that preceded the passage through Parliament (1628) of the Petition of Right, a list of grievances presented to King Charles I. He was also a major supporter of the so-called Grand Remonstrance of 1641, in which Parliament demanded governmental reforms. Pym was one of the five members of Parliament whom Charles attempted in vain to arrest in 1642. During the English Revolution, Pym was a member of the Committee of Safety and was responsible for the alliance that brought Scottish forces into England.

P'YŎNGYANG (Jap. *Heijo*), city, capital of North Korea, situated on the Taedong R., in the W section of the country, near the Yellow Sea. It is the principal commercial, manufacturing, administration, and cultural center of North Korea. Major products include metal and rubber items, textiles, processed food, machinery, building materials, armaments, and ceramics. The city is served by an international airport located in the vicinity.

Because it has periodically been devastated by war, P'yŏngyang has been rebuilt many times and is presently a well-planned modern city with beautiful parks and gardens and wide avenues lined with large apartment houses. It is the site of Kim Il Sung University (1946) and the affiliated Kim Hyong-chik Normal University, Kim Chaek Polytechnic Institute, and P'yŏngyang Medical Institute; the Academy of Sciences (1952); the Central Library; and the P'yŏngyang Theater. Points of interest include the remains of the ancient city walls, tombs from the 1st century BC, Buddhist temples, a great bronze statue of a horse of Korean legend, the Korean Central Historical Museum, and a fine arts museum.

Reputedly the oldest city in Korea, P'yŏngyang is said to have been established in 1122 BC. It later was the capital of the Koguryŏ dynasty from AD 427 to 668, when it was destroyed by invading Chinese forces. The Japanese held P'yŏngyang in 1592–93, and the Chinese captured and burned the city in 1627. A significant number of Western Christian missionaries settled here in the late 19th century. The Japanese occupied P'yŏngyang during 1910–45, calling it Heijo, and established numerous industries. In 1948 the city became the capital of North Korea. During the Korean War (1950–53), P'yŏngyang was occupied by UN forces in 1950 but was soon recaptured by Chinese and North Korean troops. The city was rebuilt after 1953 with Soviet and Chinese aid. Pop. (1984 est.) 2,639,400.

PYORRHEA, chronic disease that attacks the gums and bone surrounding and supporting the teeth. The disease begins with accumulation of tartar and debris from trapped particles of food beneath the gum margins. These accumulations cause inflammation of the gums. The bone around the roots of the teeth resorbs, the gums recede, and pockets of infection form in the affected surrounding tissues. This causes further destruction of the supporting bone and loosening of the teeth in their sockets. Eventually the teeth are lost. The most important cause of pyorrhea is poor dental hygiene; regular brushing of teeth and daily use of a dental floss will prevent the disease.

PYRAMID, in geometry, solid figure formed by connecting every point on or interior to a plane polygon to a single point not in the plane (see Fig. 1 and Fig. 2). A pyramid is thus a special case of a cone (q.v.) or of a polyhedron, a solid bounded by planes. The polygon (in Fig. 1, *ABC;* in Fig. 2, *DEFGH*) is the base of the pyramid, and the point *V* (or *W*) is the apex or vertex; the line segments, such as *VA* and *VB,* are the lateral edges of the pyramid, and the triangular sides, such as *VAB* and *VBC,* are the lateral faces. The altitude of a pyramid is the perpendicular distance from the vertex to the plane of the base.

A pyramid is called triangular, square, or hexagonal, according to whether its base is a triangle, a square, or a hexagon. A triangular pyramid, Fig. 1, is also called a tetrahedron; it is bounded by four triangles, any one of which may be considered the base.

A regular pyramid has a regular polygon as the base, with the vertex perpendicular to the base at its center; the slant height of a regular pyramid is the altitude (from the vertex) of any lateral face. A frustum of a pyramid is the solid between the base and a plane parallel to the base, as in Fig. 3. A truncated pyramid is the solid between the base and a plane cutting all lateral edges, as in Fig. 4.

The lateral area of a pyramid is the sum of the

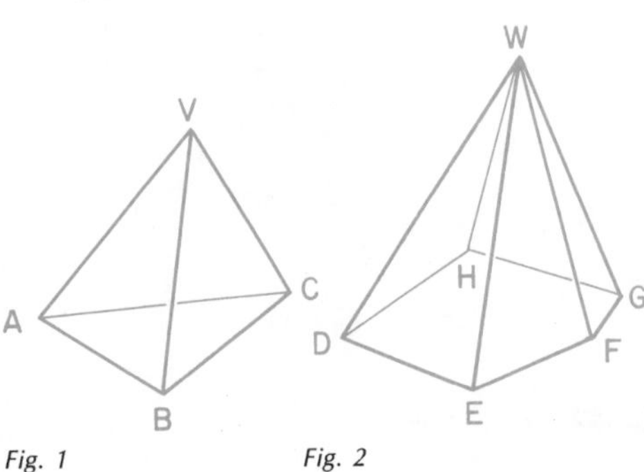

Fig. 1 *Fig. 2*

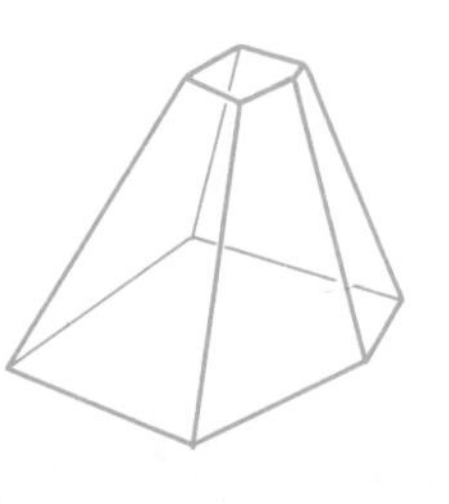
Fig. 3

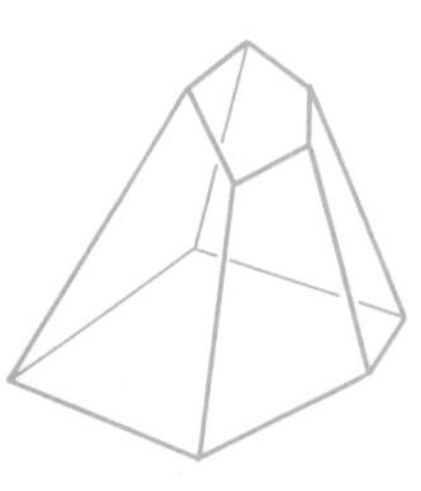
Fig. 4

areas of the lateral faces; in particular, the lateral area of a regular pyramid is $sp/2$, in which s is the slant height and p is the perimeter of the base. The volume of any pyramid is $hK/3$, in which h is the altitude of the pyramid and K is the area of the base. The volume of a pyramid is thus one-third of the volume of a prism that has the same base and altitude. J.Si.

For further information on this topic, see the Bibliography in volume 28, section 372.

PYRAMIDS, permanent structures built by the people of some ancient civilizations, found mainly in Egypt, Guatemala, Honduras, Mexico, and Peru. The Egyptian pyramids are pyramidal in form, with four triangular sides that meet at a point at the top; the New World pyramids are four-sided, flat-topped polyhedrons. Because both the Egyptian and the American structures are called pyramids, many people have erroneously assumed that the Egyptians influenced the rise of civilization in the New World.

The Egyptian pyramids were built from about 2700 BC to about 1000 BC; in the Americas, mound construction continued from 1200 BC until the Spanish conquest in AD 1519.

Egypt. The Egyptian pyramids differ from the American in their use as well as their shape. The Egyptian pyramids served as royal tombs; the American pyramids served as platforms for temples and palaces and are called temple mounds or platform mounds by archaeologists.

The outstanding group of pyramids in Egypt is at Giza, near Cairo. The largest, the Great Pyramid, was built as the tomb of the Pharaoh Khufu and is one of the Seven Wonders of the Ancient World. When built, the Great Pyramid measured 147 m (481 ft) high with a square base measuring 230 m (756 ft) on each side. The remains of about 70 pyramids may still be seen in Egypt and the Sudan. The prototype of the true pyramid in Egypt was the step pyramid, so called because its successive layers of stone suggest a series of enormous steps. The most famous and best preserved of the step pyramids is that at Saqqara, near Cairo, built about 2900 BC.

America. The New World pyramids were arranged around a ceremonial plaza. The earliest complex, built about 1200 BC, is at the Olmec site of La Venta in the state of Tabasco in southeastern Mexico. Presumably, the later ceremonial centers in central Mexico, the Mayan region of the Yucatán Peninsula, Guatemala, Honduras, and the Andean region of Peru were based on the Olmec plan. The largest temple mounds in the New World include the pyramid of Cholula outside Puebla, Mexico; the Pyramid of the Sun

The Second Pyramid and the Great Sphinx at Giza, Egypt. Although of colossal size, the pyramids were built to conform to a strict geometrical plan and carefully estimated slope.
American Export Lines

in Teotihuacán, near Mexico City; and the Huaca del Sol in Moche, Peru.

See also EGYPTIAN ART AND ARCHITECTURE; PRE-COLUMBIAN ART AND ARCHITECTURE.

For further information on this topic, see the Bibliography in volume 28, sections 645, 649.

PYRAMUS AND THISBE, two young lovers, in an ancient Babylonian story recounted in the *Metamorphoses* of the Roman poet Ovid. Their parents occupied adjacent houses, and the young people fell in love, but their parents forbade them to marry. The lovers held whispered conversations through a crack in the wall between their houses. Finally, they decided to meet at the tomb of Ninus, under a white mulberry tree. Arriving first, Thisbe saw a lion with jaws bloody from a recent kill. Fleeing, the maiden dropped her veil, which the lion tore in its bloody mouth. When Pyramus came, he saw the bloody veil and, believing Thisbe dead, plunged his sword in his side. His blood spurted upward, staining the white mulberries. Thisbe found him dying and stabbed herself. Ever since, the mulberry has been purple. Shakespeare included a travesty of the story in *A Midsummer Night's Dream.*

PYRENEES (Fr. *Pyrénées;* Span. *Pirineos*), mountain range, SW Europe, extending from the Bay of Biscay to the Mediterranean Sea and separating the Iberian Peninsula from the rest of Europe. Except in a few places, such as the area occupied by the tiny semiautonomous co-principality of Andorra, the boundary between France and Spain runs along the crest of the chain; approximately two-thirds of the mountains lie in Spain. The Pyrenees extend for about 435 km (about 270 mi) and cover roughly 55,374 sq km (roughly 21,380 sq mi); the maximum breadth of the system is about 129 km (about 80 mi).

The Pyrenees form a regular and continuous chain, divisible into W, central, and E sections. The W section, which runs from the Bay of Biscay to Somport Pass and merges into the Cantabrian Mountains of N Spain, has the lowest altitudes of the chain, with most of its peaks ranging between about 915 and 1220 m (about 3000 and 4000 ft) above sea level. The central Pyrenees extend to the Col de la Perche and contain the highest peaks of the system, including Pico de Aneto (3404 m/11,168 ft), the loftiest point in the chain; Monte Perdido (3355 m/11,007 ft); and Vignemale (3298 m/10,820 ft). The summits of the E Pyrenees, which extend to the Mediterranean, range between about 2135 and 2745 m (about 7000 and 9000 ft).

The Pyrenees, which are older than the Alps, were formed mainly during the Paleozoic and Mesozoic eras. The E half of the Pyrenees is composed mostly of granite and gneiss, whereas in the W half the lower slopes are made up of limestone and the peaks of granite. The Pyrenees are a climatic divide; the French slopes receive abundant precipitation, while the Spanish slopes have very little rainfall. Vegetation is most developed in the W, where the lower slopes are forested; in the E the mountains are almost entirely barren. The permanent snow line is at about 1829 m (6000 ft), and small glaciers are found in the high central section. Characteristic of the French Pyrenees, which are generally much steeper than the Spanish Pyrenees, are *gaves,* torrents that often drop from cliffs to form spectacular waterfalls.

The economy of the E Pyrenees is limited to Mediterranean-type agriculture, but in the W a number of manufacturing industries, powered by hydroelectricity generated by mountain streams, have been established. The only other industrial activity consists of mining—iron, lead, zinc, manganese, and coal are extracted—and marble quarrying. The few towns in the chain include Jaca and Ripoli in Spain and the famous pilgrimage center of Lourdes in France. The chain has many thermal and cold mineral springs, and well-known spas include Cauterets and Bagnères-de-Bigorre in France.

For further information on this topic, see the Bibliography in volume 28, section 867.

PYRENEES, PEACE OF THE, peace treaty between France and Spain, Nov. 7, 1659, that ended 24 years of warfare; it was signed on a neutral island in the Bidassoa River, near Hendaye, France. Spain ceded the region of Artois and parts of Flanders, Hainault, and Luxembourg; in the south, the cession of Roussillon made the Pyrenees the boundary between the two countries. The terms of the treaty also promised Marie Thérèse (1638–83), daughter of King Philip IV of Spain, in marriage to Louis XIV of France.

PYRITE, also iron pyrites or fool's gold, mineral composed of iron sulfide, FeS_2, the most common sulfide mineral. It crystallizes in the isometric system (*see* CRYSTAL) and frequently occurs as well-defined crystals as well as in massive formations. The mineral is brass yellow, is opaque, and has a metallic luster. The resemblance of pyrite to gold caused many prospectors to mistake it for gold, and it became known as fool's gold. It is distinguished from gold by its brittleness and by its hardness (q.v.), which ranges between 6 and 6.5; the sp.gr. is 4.95 to 5.1. Pyrite is a common mineral in sedimentary rocks and also occurs in igneous and metamorphic rocks. It is often associated with coal formations and sometimes occurs associated with gold or copper. Large deposits are found throughout the world; deposits in Spain and Portugal are particularly noteworthy. In the U.S. important deposits occur in Arizona, Colorado, New York, Pennsylvania, South Carolina, Tennessee, Utah, and Virginia. Pyrite is not mined as an iron ore, except in countries where iron-oxide ores are not available, because of the difficulty of removing the sulfur. It is used mainly in the commercial production of sulfuric acid (q.v.) and of copperas, or ferrous sulfate (*see* SULFUR).

Marcasite, a mineral of the same composition as pyrite, is called white iron pyrites. It is opaque, with a metallic luster, and is pale—bronze yellow or almost white when freshly fractured. The hardness is the same as that of pyrite. The specific gravity varies from 4.85 to 4.90. Marcasite is distinguished from pyrite by the difference in color, crystal habit, and by chemical tests. It is more easily decomposed than pyrite and is much less common in occurrence. Marcasite is used, to a much lesser extent than pyrite, in making sulfuric acid.

PYROMANIA, mental disorder in which fires are repeatedly deliberately set, without anger and not for monetary gain or other benefit, because the individual cannot resist the impulse to set fires. The individual experiences tension before setting the fire and pleasure, relief, or erotic gratification after setting the fire. Pyromania can often be treated by psychotherapy. The pyromaniac is legally considered an arsonist. *See* ARSON; MENTAL DISORDERS.

PYROXENES, group of silicate minerals that are closely related to each other in chemical composition and crystal form. The pyroxene minerals crystallize in the orthorhombic or monoclinic systems and all exhibit prismatic cleavage. Chemically they are silicates, containing calcium, magnesium, or iron, or alkali metals such as sodium and lithium. The group includes the minerals diopside, jadeite, augite, spodumene, and enstatite. The pyroxenes are closely related to the minerals of the amphibole group. The minerals of the latter group crystallize in the orthorhombic, monoclinic, and triclinic systems, but the crystals of the various species are similar in form. Chemically the amphiboles are silicates that contain the same groups of elements as the pyroxenes, but which also contain a hydroxyl (OH) group. Important amphiboles are hornblende (q.v.), anthophyllite, and tremolite.

PYRRHO (c. 360–c. 272 BC), ancient Greek philosopher, who introduced pure skepticism (q.v.) into Greek philosophy, founding the school known as Pyrrhonism, and who is thus considered the founder of philsophical skepticism. He was born in Elis and studied with the Greek philosopher Anaxarchus (fl. about 350 BC), a disciple of the Greek philosopher Democritus. Pyrrho accompanied Alexander the Great on his expedition to the East, and became acquainted with the teachings of the Persian magi (q.v.) and the Indian Brahmans (*see* BRAHMAN). Much of Pyrrho's long life was spent in seclusion. He did not put his doctrines into writing, and they are known chiefly from the works of his follower Timon of Phlius (fl. about 280 BC), a philosopher and writer of satires. Pyrrho taught that the real nature of things can never be truly comprehended, and hence objective knowledge is impossible to attain. He held that the correct attitude for the philosopher is imperturbability and complete suspension of judgment, and that in this attitude lies freedom from passion, calmness of mind, and tranquillity of soul, which constitute the highest human qualities.

PYRRHOTITE (Gr. *pyrrhos,* "flame-colored"), also magnetic pyrites, mineral possessing magnetic properties and composed of iron sulfide. It is a reddish-bronze opaque mineral having a metallic luster and crystallizing in the hexagonal system, usually in massive formation. The hardness varies from 3.5 to 4.5, and the specific gravity ranges between 4.58 and 4.64. pyrrhotite is a common constituent of igneous rocks and occurs associated with many other sulfides. Nickel minerals are often associated with pyrrhotite; nickeliferous pyrrhotite, for example, is a principal ore of nickel. Large quantities of the mineral are found in the Scandinavian countries, in Germany, and in Maine, Pennsylvania, and Tennessee in the U.S. The Canadian deposits discovered at Sudbury, Ont., are the most important nickeliferous deposits of pyrrhotite.

PYRRHUS (318?–272 BC), king of Epirus (307–272 BC), a district in ancient Greece. He succeeded to the throne in 307 BC, later lost it, but was restored as king in 295 BC. In the next ten years he increased his territories by the addition of the western parts of the neighboring kingdoms of Macedonia and Thessaly. He also helped to overthrow the Macedonian king Demetrius I Poliorcetes. Pyrrhus was driven out of his new territories, however, about 286 BC by his former ally Lysimachus, king of Thrace (c. 355–281 BC), who became king of all Macedonia.

In 281 BC the people of Tarentum (now Taranto), a Greek colony in southern Italy then at war with the Romans, requested the aid of Pyrrhus. Early in 280 BC he sailed for Tarentum with a force of 25,000 men and 20 elephants and in the same year defeated the Romans at Heraclea, in the Roman province of Lucania, but at great cost to his army; hence the expression Pyrrhic victory. In 279 BC Pyrrhus again defeated the Romans at excessive cost, at the Battle of Asculum, in the Roman province of Apulia.

Crossing over to Sicily, Pyrrhus aided the Sicilian Greeks in their struggle against the Carthaginians but aroused the ill will of the Greek people by his despotic attitude. He returned to Italy in 276 BC and the following year was defeated by the Romans under Manius Curius Dentatus (fl. 290–272 BC) in a great battle near Beneventum, in the Roman province of Samnium. Pyrrhus returned to Epirus with only one-third of his original force. In 273 BC, however, having attacked and defeated Antigonus II Gonatus, who had become king of Macedonia about 276 BC, he once more obtained possession of a large area of that country. In less than a year Pyrrhus was waging an unsuccessful war with the Spartans. He subsequently fled to Argos, where he was killed.

PYTHAGORAS (582?–500? BC), Greek philosopher and mathematician, whose doctrines strongly influenced Plato.

Born on the island of Sámos, Pythagoras was instructed in the teachings of the early Ionian philosophers Thales, Anaximander, and Anaximenes. He is said to have been driven from Sámos by his disgust for the tyranny of Polycrates (d. about 522 BC). About 530 BC he settled in Crotona, a Greek colony in southern Italy, where he founded a movement with religious, political, and philosophical aims, known as Pythagoreanism. The philosophy of Pythagoras is known only through the work of his disciples.

Pythagoras

Basic Doctrines. The Pythagoreans adhered to certain mysteries, similar in many respects to the Orphic mysteries (*see* MYSTERIES, ORPHISM). Obedience and silence, abstinence from food, simplicity in dress and possessions, and the habit of frequent self-examination were prescribed. The Pythagoreans believed in immortality and in the transmigration of souls. Pythagoras himself was said to have claimed that he had been Euphorbus, a warrior in the Trojan War, and that he had been permitted to bring into his earthly life the memory of all his previous existences.

Theory of Numbers. Among the extensive mathematical investigations carried on by the Pythagoreans were their studies of odd and even numbers and of prime and square numbers. From this arithmetical standpoint they cultivated the concept of number, which became for them the ultimate principle of all proportion, order, and harmony in the universe. Through such studies they established a scientific foundation for mathematics. In geometry the great discovery of the school was the hypotenuse theorem, or Pythagorean theorem, which states that the square of the hypotenuse of a right triangle is equal to the sum of the squares on the other two sides; Pythagorean numbers are numbers so related, for instance, 5, 4, and 3 ($5^2 = 4^2 + 3^2$).

Astronomy. The astronomy of the Pythagoreans marked an important advance in ancient scientific thought, for they were the first to consider the earth as a globe revolving with the other planets, including the sun, around a central fire. They explained the harmonious arrangement of things as that of bodies in a single, all-inclusive sphere of reality, moving according to a numerical scheme. Because the Pythagoreans thought that the heavenly bodies are separated from one another by intervals corresponding to the harmonic lengths of strings, they held that the movement of the spheres gives rise to a musical sound—the "harmony of the spheres."

PYTHAGOREAN THEOREM. *See* GEOMETRY; PYTHAGORAS.

PYTHIAS. *See* DAMON AND PHINTIAS.

PYTHON, in Greek mythology, great serpent, the son of Gaea, Mother Earth, produced from the slime left on the earth after the great flood. The monster lived in a cave near Delphi on Mount Parnassus and guarded the oracle there. The god Apollo slew the Python, claimed the oracle for himself, and was thereafter known as Pythian Apollo. The god was said to have established the Pythian Games to commemorate his victory.

PYTHON, any of 20 to 25 species of large, nonvenomous constrictor snakes, especially of the genus *Python,* which, with the related boas (*see*

A 5-m (16-ft), 91-kg (200-lb) Burmese python, Python molurus birittatus, *is displayed by keepers at the Bronx Zoo Reptile House. Pythons are gentle and sluggish when well fed.*
New York Zoological Society

BOA), comprise the family Boidae. Pythons inhabit tropical and subtropical regions of Africa, Asia, Australia, and the Pacific islands. They range from 1 to 10 m (3 to 33 ft) long and weigh as much as 140 kg (300 lb). Primitive snakes that retain vestiges of their lizard ancestry, they have plump, muscular bodies and two rudimentary hind limbs, conspicuous only in the male. The female lays 15 to 100 eggs, varying with size and species, and broods them until they hatch. Pythons are usually found near water, where they hide in foliage or hang from tree branches. They feed on small mammals by coiling around them and squeezing; the constriction suffocates, rather than crushes, the animals. Some large species can kill and swallow small pigs and goats. Only on rare occasions have they killed humans.

The reticulated python, *P. reticulatus,* of Southeast Asia is among the largest snakes, reaching a length of 10 m (33 ft). Other well-known pythons are the 7.5-m (25-ft) *P. molurus* of Asia, a favorite of snake handlers; the 6.5-m (23-ft) African rock python, *P. sebae;* and the 1.5-m (5-ft) ball, or royal, python, *P. regius,* of equatorial Africa, which curls into a ball and can be rolled on the ground.

For further information on this topic, see the Bibliography in volume 28, section 471.